85560

PLAIN
TALK

PLAIN TALK

*AN ANTHOLOGY
FROM THE LEADING
ANTI-COMMUNIST
MAGAZINE
OF THE 40s*

085560

**Edited by
ISAAC DON LEVINE**

ARLINGTON HOUSE·PUBLISHERS
NEW ROCHELLE, NEW YORK

Library of Congress Cataloging in Publication Data

Plain talk.

    1. World politics—1945-1955—Addresses, essays, lectures. 2. Communism—1945-
    —Addresses, essays, lectures. I. Levine, Isaac Don, 1892-
D843.P55   327′.09′045   76-3554
ISBN 0-87000-348-8

Manufactured in the United States of America

"Gulag"—Slavery, Inc.
The Documented Map of Forced Labor Camps in Soviet Russia
New Edition (1951) Prepared for the Free Trade Union Committee of the American
   Federation of Labor

To the Unknown Martyrs of Gulag

CONTENTS

BOOK 3

Collapse in China

BOOK 4

Global Spiderweb

BOOK 5

In the Land of Gulag

BOOK 6
From Churchill to Stalin

BOOK 7
On Freedom and Its Enemies

APPENDIX

INTRODUCTION

When Suzanne La Follette, a former associate editor of *Plain Talk*, learned of this project, she wrote me on July 27, 1975, from Palo Alto: "We have Solzhenitsyn sounding like an extended *Plain Talk* anthology." Beginning in 1946, when Moscow's aggressive empire-building was unmasked by Winston Churchill before the wide world, this compilation offers unique illumination of the benighted passage of the last 30 years. For only in the light of history—to employ a truism that needs to be repeated—can the confusing events of today assume their real shape and meaning.

There is a deeply significant parallel between the famous Iron Curtain address Churchill delivered at Fulton, Missouri, in March 1946, and the stirring message echoed across America by Aleksandr Solzhenitsyn in the summer of 1975. Both sounded alarms after periods of euphoria in the relations of the Soviet dictatorship with the free world. Churchill aroused a befuddled public from the One World illusions propagated by the peace-making confabulations at Teheran, Yalta, and Potsdam. Solzhenitsyn warned the American people that the détente—in quest of that still-elusive peace—celebrated at the Helsinki, Vladivostok, and Peking parleys was a snare and a delusion.

In a sense, these selections from the columns of *Plain Talk*, a little magazine that existed from 1946 to 1950, owe their reappearance to the publication of Solzhenitsyn's *The Gulag Archipelago,* for which they form a companion-volume. When the Russian masterpiece burst upon the literary horizon, there ensued a much-belated awakening of interest in a singular map named "Gulag-Slavery, Inc." that *Plain Talk* composed and disseminated in May 1947. The map, which is reproduced here, graphically depicted the locations of a myriad of penal camps dotting the vast land mass of the Soviet Union, and was documented with illustrations of official discharge "passports" issued to former Polish prisoners of war.

It was this map that played the role of matchmaker in the unusual mating of the great Russian novelist with the leadership of the American Federation of Labor. An international offshoot of the latter, the Free Trade Union Committee, ordered in 1951 from this writer a special edition of the map for distribution in foreign countries. Copies of that edition, translated into various languages, reached Russia. Solzhenitsyn referred to it in his memorable address of June 30 at the grand reception given for him in Washington by the

American Federation of Labor. "When liberal thinkers and wise men of the West, who had forgotten the meaning of the word liberty," he observed in his grateful acknowledgment, "were swearing that in the Soviet Union there were no concentration camps at all, the American Federation of Labor published in 1947 [an error in the date], a map of our concentration camps."

Although *Plain Talk* did the pioneering in exposing Gulag at a time when the major press organs of the country almost entirely ignored its existence, the magazine's concern went far beyond unveiling Soviet terror. As this collection demonstrates, *Plain Talk* was dedicated to the enlightenment of public opinion on all the insidious influences and deadly dangers threatening civilization from Communist ideology and imperialism. The reader will find the current crucial developments in Soviet-American relations mirrored in these selections, commencing with the first issue of October 1946.

It was three months earlier that three men in search of an editor drove up to our country home outside of Norwalk, Connecticut, for an afternoon conference on the lawn. One of the visitors was an old friend, Benjamin Mandel, who had known the Communist movement from the inside; he had even enrolled Whittaker Chambers in the Communist Party in 1925, but he early recovered from the Marxist virus. He spent the last years of his life as research director of the Senate Internal Security Subcommittee.

Mr. Mandel served as the guide to the mission. One of the protagonists was a Catholic priest of charming personality, a professor of sociology, the Rev. John F. Cronin, who was then an Assistant Director of the Department of Social Action of the National Catholic Welfare Conference in Washington. Years later, Father Cronin became Richard Nixon's close mentor on Communist affairs. On this occasion he served as mentor to Mr. Alfred Kohlberg, a New York merchant with business interests in China that had led him to discover some of the treacherous operations of the Communist underground. He was eager to finance—on a modest scale—to the limits of his moderate income, a publication devoted to combating the dark forces that were out to destroy our free society. Mr. Kohlberg's editorial contributions will be found in Book 3 of this volume, under the overall title "The Lie Marches On."

Our meeting, lasting many hours, marked the birth of *Plain Talk*. Mr. Kohlberg undertook to open a bank account of $25,000 for the project, to provide office quarters, free of rent, for the magazine in a building owned by him, and to carry on his payroll a staff of about five members. I offered my services free as a labor of love, and never was put on the *Plain Talk* payroll. This is reported here because of the rumors emanating from Communist sources that the real master of the publication was Mr. Kohlberg and that the editor was a mere puppet of his. The fact is that I was always in absolute control of the contents of *Plain Talk*.

Mr. Kohlberg was fond of quoting a statement made by me during our initial conference, to the effect that "one should not reveal more than 15 percent of the facts about the Communist conspiracy, as the American people would find the whole truth utterly unbelievable." That citation, which has appeared in print on several occasions, belongs to the record. I often rejected for publication revelations that I knew to be true, but which would have been contemptuously dismissed, for lack of convincing evidence, by the gullible press and public. And I made it a strict rule to avoid libelous epithets in the many searching exposes that we ran.

About a third of all the matter published in *Plain Talk* dealt with disclosures of Communist infiltration of the leadership of key labor unions. It is a standard practice of the Soviet strategy of aggrandizement to begin by capturing control of trade unions and thus build a base for a revolutionary seizure of power, particularly in a country where the Communist Party is a negligible minority. The course of the tragic developments in Portugal provides a model illustration of this tested Muscovite technique. To date I have not yet seen a step-by-step analysis of how the democratic revolution in Portugal was subverted by Communist-bossed labor unions, forced into a conspiratorial army straitjacket, and driven to the very edge of civil war. This is the kind of research *Plain Talk* would have undertaken were it in existence in 1975. In this anthology we have omitted nearly all the material, with the exception of the article on the Panama Canal, concerned with the struggles in the various unions against the Communist marauders. Those accounts become obsolete with the changed conditions in the country.

Why did *Plain Talk* go out of existence? It is a question many have asked. It had been launched as an experiment and its life of 44 months was prolonged through strenuous sacrifices and exertions. Ex-President Herbert C. Hoover tried for a while to put the magazine on a solid basis that would have enabled it to expand, but it was a half-hearted effort. The root of the problem was the lack of financial resources required to improve the publication with a new format and broader coverage under a competent business management.

In this volume the best of *Plain Talk* comes to life again. Every one of these selections testifies to the timeliness of their re-emergence in print now. This is, of course, due to the fact that the crisis heralded by Churchill in Fulton 30 years ago is still with us. For the conclusion of World War II was never sealed with a solemn pact. It ended only with an intermission. Witness the Helsinki Conference in July 1975, where the process of peacemaking continued with Russia's inch-by-inch attrition at the expense of the free world. It took but a few weeks for all to see that the Helsinki summit did not terminate the chronic crisis springing from World War II.

The complete war-guilt record of that catastrophe has not yet been revealed in the public prints, as a vital part of it lies buried in the Kremlin archives. The story of how Stalin deliberately triggered the outbreak of the war through his pact with Hitler that ushered in two years of the secret collaboration between Nazi Germany and Soviet Russia has never been brought home with force to the American people. Following Hitler's perfidious attack on his Communist partner, and the immediate embrace of Stalin by Churchill and Roosevelt, it was impossible in the United States to disturb the blissful alliance by any critical comments on Soviet policy. This observer retired into the storm cellar for three years, and only towards the end of 1944 was able to publish in an obscure quarterly magazine a report dissecting the anatomy of the Teheran Conference. It was followed, some months later, by an essay exposing the Yalta deals. These two essays, which anticipated Churchill's Iron Curtain speech by a couple of years, were soon reprinted without the author's knowledge in brochure form in Glasgow, Scotland; in Calcutta, India; and, after the war, in France. In the United States they are unknown, and are not even listed in the standard guides to journalistic literature. Together with a recent piece, "Détente and Reality," published in *Strategic Review* in 1974, the three articles are incorporated in an Appendix to this work. Both in spirit and historical material they are integrated with the body of *Plain Talk,* and provide a fitting frame for the mirror of the great crisis of our times.

Isaac Don Levine
August 22, 1975

BOOK 1

THE ROAD TO DÉTENTE

THE NEXT PEARL HARBOR

By ISAAC DON LEVINE

[*The present-day readers of this little essay, with which we introduced the first issue of* Plain Talk *to the public in October 1946, should turn to its companion piece in the same issue, "The Secret Battalion," by Harold J. Laski, Chairman of the British Labor Party. (See Book 4, page 167.) Penned by an authoritative Socialist spokesman of the Left, Laski's indictment of the Communist fifth column has never been surpassed in print since its publication.*]

TWO CATACLYSMIC weapons hold the fate of America and civilization in their grasp. Both are of unprecedented scope. The one destroys from without, the other from within. The one is capable of bringing sudden death to an entire segment of a great nation. The other slowly waters the bloodstream of a whole people. The one smashes matter, the other breaks the spirit. The two weapons are the atomic bomb and the fifth column.

At present the United States has the atomic bomb and Soviet Russia has the fifth column. It is the consensus of the topmost experts that she will shortly have the atomic bomb, too. Once totalitarian Russia is left in possession of both Apocalyptic weapons, it would be impossible to put up any effective defense against her aggression.

For the cardinal fact of our age is that there is no defense against atomic armaments. This is the conclusion of the special brain trust set up by the General Staff of the United States Army to find out if any military device could be projected against the atomic bomb. As disclosed by Joseph and Stewart Alsop in *The Saturday Evening Post,* the final verdict of our ablest professional soldiers, after long and careful study of an immense mass of secret data, was truly epoch-making:

"The only sure defense of this country is now the political defense."

The survival of America, according to our highest military experts, will therefore depend solely upon political safeguards. Which is another way of saying that American policy can no longer rest on strategic defenses, but must be based upon an international organization for the maintenance of peace, a world order

3

of good neighbors. But such an order can only exist where there is mutual confidence. In dealing with a major totalitarian regime, such confidence is impossible without insuring a minimum of basic liberties and human rights everywhere. Henceforth *America's only sure defense is world freedom.*

BUT STALIN has a world order all his own, and the advance guard of that order, the fifth column, wages ceaseless undercover warfare against the peace-loving fraternity of nations. While the atomic bomb is being kept in cold storage, the fifth column, the core of which in every country is the Communist Party, is operating at breakneck speed. . . .

The Soviet fifth column, superbly organized and led by an underground battalion of conspirators who are veterans in the game, has all along been acting on the assumption of the inevitability of such an armed conflict. We have the testimony of an unimpeachable witness, Herbert Morrison, who as Minister for Home Security in the Churchill cabinet was in an exceptional position to know the facts about the Communist fifth column. Speaking before the recent conference of the British Labor Party, Mr. Morrison declared that even during the war there had been "more than one case of espionage against the security of this country in which the Communists were involved."

By the time the atomic bomb project was launched, the Soviet fifth column had already achieved large-scale dimensions and strategic positions on this continent. As disclosed by the Royal Commission entrusted with the investigation of the Canadian Spy Ring, Uranium-235 had been stolen and smuggled out of the country by Communist fifth columnists.

The comprehensive report of the Canadian Royal Commission, perhaps the most revealing and least publicized document of the atomic age, affords a basis for calculating the extent and character of the fifth column in the United States. When all the factors are taken into consideration, such as population, military potential, proximity to Latin America and the unusual access to high places in Washington long enjoyed by the Communist Party, it is a moderate estimate that our Soviet fifth column now numbers between four and five thousand willful agents.

Far more shocking than the number of Stalin's agents is the fact that they command key positions. "Perhaps the most startling single aspect of the entire fifth column network," concludes the Canadian Royal Commission, "is the uncanny success with which the Soviet agents were able to find Canadians who were willing to betray their country and to supply to agents of a foreign power secret information to which they had access in the course of their work, despite oaths of allegiance, of office, and of secrecy which they had taken. Many of the Canadian public servants implicated in this espionage network were persons with an unusually high degree of education, and many were well regarded by those who worked with them in agencies and departments of the public service, as persons of marked ability and intelligence."

4

Stalin's fifth column in America is entrenched in all the policy-making branches of the Federal Government. It even infiltrated our departments of national defense. It controls many pivotal labor unions and critical industries, such as shipping and communications. The report of the Canadian Royal Commission and the evidence gathered by our own congressional inquiries show that legislators, journalists, scientists, educators, publishers, radio commentators, prominent figures of the stage and screen, public servants as well as businessmen are enrolled in the Soviet secret brigade.

It was through his fifth column, first forged in Moscow as a revolutionary weapon, that Stalin succeeded where Hitler had failed. With the aid of this weapon, Stalin was able to subvert our foreign policy and turn us into accomplices in restoring the totalitarian New Order which is now leveling its guns at us from all quarters.

THERE IS NO time to lose in forestalling another and greater Pearl Harbor. The elementary prerequisites of our national safety require the ruthless exposure and the elimination through democratic processes from our national life of the Soviet fifth column.

The next Pearl Harbor will not burst upon us in the Pacific. Nor will it break in the Atlantic. It is a safe prediction that it will explode on the home front. The loss of half of our fleet, such as we suffered on December 7, 1941, might appear as comparatively light damage in the next Pearl Harbor. For the Soviet fifth column is in position to strike a savage and paralyzing blow from within, prostrating the nation before the enemy unleashes its rain of atomic weapons. Unless we clean house at once, America will be dragged down, carrying civilization with her into the totalitarian abyss.

October 1946

A WORKABLE PLAN

FOR PEACE WITH RUSSIA

By ISAAC DON LEVINE

[If you substitute the name of Brezhnev for that of his master Stalin; of Kissinger for that of General Marshall; of President Ford for that of James F. Byrnes; and if "the Molotovs and Vishinskys" be replaced with "the Gromykos and Suslovs," the principles outlined in "A Workable Plan for Peace with Russia" remain as valid today as they were 30 years ago. As regards the treatment of China in the piece, it should be noted that even in 1946 it was known in limited circles that Stalin did not trust Mao's Communist leadership.]

OUR FAILURE TO DEVISE a working peace with Soviet Russia and to put it on a solid basis is now patent to all. What has not been brought home to the American people is that this failure primarily stems from the lack of a single global American foreign policy. . . .

So far, in our futile quests for a lasting peace, we have dealt with our major problem piecemeal. While Stalin plays his world game on one chessboard, the United States has been making moves in at least three disparate fields, Western Europe, Japan, and China, all of which are integral parts of Soviet strategy. . . .

Secretary Byrnes, who has devoted himself almost exclusively to Western Europe where he has been chasing the rainbows of world peace, began as an appeaser of the Kremlin and has developed into a critic of Soviet tactics. His so-called tough policy consists of administering rebukes which unfortunately are vitiated by futile pleas for cooperation. His policy of resorting to strong words while yielding one position after another could not but increase the Soviet appetite and encourage Soviet aggression.

General Marshall, it is no secret, has been his own Secretary of State in China, where he has been acting for a year as the President's special envoy. The failure of his mission, to bring the rebel Chinese Communists together with the government of China, has not been due to his shortcomings as a diplomat. His patience would do honor to a Talleyrand. But General Marshall went to China in 1945 to promote a policy which was formulated in 1943 as a means of buying Soviet cooperation in the war against Japan. Since then Stalin has shown his hand to the world. Yet General Marshall, shackled by a mission rendered obsolete long ago, has been struggling with an assignment originally designed by the pro-Soviet bloc in the State Department. . . .

General MacArthur's policy in Japan, which was openly sabotaged by the State Department in Washington, has yielded the highest return. Our position on the European continent has been largely frittered away. Our traditionally favorable position in China has been put in jeopardy. We have steadily lost face in both of these theatres. But our unimpaired control of Japan is the one trump card we still hold against Soviet imperialism. "Secretary of State" MacArthur has demonstrated how to deal with Russia most successfully by keeping the Soviet armed forces out of Japan, by confining Soviet diplomatic and fifth column activities to a minimum and, above all, by abstaining personally from participating in conferences with Stalin's emissaries and by holding as few such parleys as possible. General MacArthur has saved for the United States its strongest pawn in the game with the Kremlin, and in the very area which forms the Achilles heel of Russia.

A WORKABLE PLAN for a durable peace with the Soviet Union must be shaped with an eye to the weakest spot in Russia's strategic defenses.

Russia's face is in Europe. Her rear is in the Far East. Her population, her industries, her transportation, are predominantly in Europe. Her greatest strategic disability is the Pacific littoral which is precariously linked with the heart of the Soviet empire, and which is to Moscow what Manilla is to Washington.

That is why Russia has always been haunted by the fear of having to wage war simultaneously on two such far-flung and opposite fronts as the European and Pacific theatres. In modern times, the course of Russian diplomacy has been that of a pendulum swinging between the East and the West. Whenever Russia was threatened in Asia, she sought to secure her defenses in Europe, and whenever she was menaced in Europe, she endeavored to insure peace in her rear. The crucial fact about Russia's foreign policy is that she cannot and will not wage a major war on two fronts. . . .

In our relations with Russia, we have never stopped to appraise correctly her strategic weakness in relation to our own matchless power. America has never been haunted by the fear which dogs Soviet policy. In fact, we have just demonstrated our ability to conduct successfully two major wars against two titanic powers at two opposite poles at the same time. For no one can deny the magnitude of the American share in the struggle against Hitler's "fortress" in Europe. And inside the Kremlin there is no misconception as to the fact that America had almost singlehandedly brought the Japanese Empire down.

This key factor in the strategic alignment of the United States and Soviet Russia has been completely overlooked in all our quests for a workable understanding with Stalin's regime in our pursuit of world peace. Regardless of how it came to pass, we find ourselves in the same ring with Soviet Russia. . . . To send our fleet to the eastern Mediterranean, as we have done, may stave off temporarily Soviet aggression in the Dardanelles, but cannot provide a durable solution for that chronic trouble spot. . . .

But how can Soviet Russia be made to lift her iron curtains, withdraw her armed hordes, and call back home her fifth columns with its secret battalions of wreckers operating beyond her borders? The answer is not to be found in Europe, where our diplomats and molders of public opinion have vainly sought it. If you would make the bear that walks like a man behave in the West, prod him in his rear in the East.

IN THE FAR EAST, where Stalin lacks any base in Japan and has but an inadequate one in China, he is tremendously handicapped vis-à-vis the United States. Japan we dominate completely. The Central Government of China, the only one officially recognized by Moscow, is our traditional ally. The two great Asiatic powers on the Pacific, which are so situated as to overshadow completely the weak Russian rear, are our invaluable potential weapons in forging a durable peace in the world.

Stalin realizes his disadvantage in the Pacific, but America has so far muffed her position there. That is why Moscow has recently redoubled and intensified its efforts, both publicly and subversively, to drive a wedge between the United States and China and to set up a Communist bastion along our Far Eastern frontiers. The irony of it is that this is being promoted with the aid of our gullible diplomacy and of Stalin's stooges within our midst, who have been developing a frenzy of activity in favor of Communist China.

Yet it is not too late to devise a plan for a stable peace with Russia which would entail no undue sacrifices or risks. One might almost prescribe a step-by-step course of American action along the exposed Russian rear in the Far East which would quickly send the Russian bear in Europe back to his old lair. . . .

Let us launch a greatly expanded program for training a modern Chinese air force under the direction of General Chennault, now in the service of the Chinese government. Russia could not possibly raise objections to this step, for it was the Soviet government which had enabled the *Reichswehr* after the first World War to build secret war plants in Russia and to rearm Germany in preparation for the coming of Hitler. It is a procedure long sanctioned by international law. Our encouragement to private American citizens to develop a major Chinese air force would greatly discourage the Soviet appetite in Europe. And it would not be surprising if, at this stage, Stalin found it most propitious to announce the withdrawal of some of his forces from certain Western European areas.

. . . Washington could then demand the prompt Soviet fulfillment of all agreements in China by opening up the port of Dairen, by uncorking bottled-up northern Korea, and by restoring all of Manchuria to the Central Government. We might even invite Stalin to use his good offices with the rebel Chinese Communists to lay down their arms provided the United States secured from Chiang

Kai-shek guarantees that the insurgents would not be prosecuted and would be permitted to form a legal Communist Party as in all other countries. . . .

The prospect of having no foothold whatsoever in Japan is bound to have a seismic effect in the Kremlin and in all Soviet-controlled Europe. For Stalin would read into our course of action but one purpose: an American determination to attack Russia in the rear and to deprive her of her maritime provinces on the Pacific. This, in turn, would register at once in Soviet actions in the West. In his oriental wisdom, the wary Stalin would not take any more chances in "prodding with a sharp sickle"—in the sublime phrase of Churchill—the American Eagle.

It is the opinion of this writer that so long as we wielded our "big stick" in the Far East with prudence and calm it would not be long before the Red hordes voluntarily retreated from Western Europe, bartering along the way to be sure. The Molotovs and Vishinskys would change their voices and begin to coo like doves of peace. . . .

November 1946

THE FIRST YEAR OF THE TRUCE

By Isaac Don Levine

[*The following portentous note was struck not long after Winston Churchill put his imprint on the year of 1946 with his memorable address delivered at Fulton, Missouri, in which he warned that "from Stettin in the Baltic to Trieste in the Adriatic, an Iron Curtain has descended across the Continent." Thirty years later another prophet, Aleksandr Solzhenitsyn, the Nobel Prizewinner, deported from his native Russia, speaking in Washington, continued where Churchill left off. "Give up Korea and we will live quietly," Solzhenitsyn scornfully echoed the voices in the West that were still under the influence of the mirage of détente. "Give up Portugal, of course; give up Japan; give up Israel; give up Taiwan, the Philippines, Malaysia, Thailand." For three decades the free world has been losing ground to its enemies under the sham slogan of peace.*]

THE YEAR OF 1946 will go down in history as the first year of the truce following World War II.

It was to be a year consecrated to the making of a peace of justice, freedom, and honor. It opened with a journey to Moscow by Secretary of State Byrnes in quest of these high aims. It closed with a date for another trip to Moscow in pursuit of arrangements that would pass for peace.

For the plain truth is that, in the course of 1946, the grand peace degenerated into a shabby truce. Instead of building world peace upon solid foundations, we have entered into makeshift pacts based on compromise with tyranny.

Instead of attacking the problem of world peace with world vision as a single indivisible task, we have allowed the Soviet power to force us into making peace by attrition.

We have legalized Russia's illegal seizures during war. We have restricted the area of freedom on earth and correspondingly strengthened the forces of militarism and despotism. We have helped consolidate slavery in Western Europe over 120 million people who had been awaiting deliverance.

We have infused new blood into the Soviet dictatorship by putting an official seal on the sale of several of our gallant allies into bondage to Moscow. And by so doing we not only tightened its open grip upon all mankind, but we have also added strength to its secret Communist arm in our midst.

The greater the sway of Soviet Russia as a world power, the more insidious is the influence of its Communist conspirators within all free countries.

While sowing despair and creating want in the occupied lands through its puppet rulers, Moscow disseminates confusion and promotes social and moral disintegration in all other lands.

Its policies, international as well as domestic, in the field of diplomacy as well as in its underground activity, are predicated upon the proposition that the conflict between the Soviet system and those outside its orbit is irreconcilable.

Hence the Kremlin is engaged in evolving a temporary truce and imposing it upon America and the other nations. The files in Washington are bulging with evidence to that effect. But our peacemakers, continuing to dwell in their make-believe world, will not share these shocking facts with the common people. . . .

Yet somewhere in the hearts of the American people, and of men and women everywhere, the realization has grown during 1946 that peace, a real durable peace, is further away than ever. We have taken to a road laid upon the quicksands of compromise, a shaky and shifty road that may insure us a precarious armistice under the sham label of peace.

January 1947

MUST WE FIGHT RUSSIA?

By ISAAC DON LEVINE

[*In March 1947 President Truman, in his message to Congress, called for American military aid to Greece, where Stalin had unleashed powerful Red guerrilla forces designed to bring both Greece and Turkey into his satellite realm. The Truman Doctrine, as it was labeled, came in response to Great Britain's desperate pleas for American support against the armed Communist bands. But many Americans were puzzled why the United States took a firm stand against Communist aggression in Greece while it was openly courting the same aggressor in the Far East. One of the remedies suggested in this article called for a drastic shakeup of the clique of Soviet appeasers in the Department of State.*]

THE GREAT ACHIEVEMENT of President Truman's sudden and bold challenge to Soviet aggression in Greece and Turkey is that it has wrested the diplomatic initiative from Moscow for the first time in five years.

Ever since Harry Hopkins went to Russia to beg Stalin to accept unconditionally our lend-lease, Washington has been on the defensive in its relations with the Soviet Government. The humiliating repeated American invitations for personal meetings with Stalin, resulting in the President of the United States traveling as far as Teheran, near the Soviet border, to Yalta on Soviet territory, and then to Potsdam, in the Soviet zone, could not but encourage overbearing and unilateral conduct on the part of the Kremlin dictatorship. And the more we compromised, the more face we lost, the more offensive became Moscow's behavior in all directions and all fields.

When President Truman announced his new foreign policy, even the most astute commentators and observers expected a powerful countermove on the part of the Kremlin. The game of bluff which Stalin has played so steadily and unchallengingly had taken on the appearance of reality in the eyes of those who should have known better. But the Red bear had overplayed the part of an insolent and enraged character in the international circus, and a single cracking of the whip by Truman seems to have tamed him. All that Stalin could do in retaliation was to snub Secretary of State Marshall, and to receive in audience first Foreign Secretary Bidault and then Foreign Secretary Bevin.

In the meantime, Secretary Marshall, in Moscow, proposed that all the states at war with Germany should join in a general peace conference, and Under-Secretary Acheson, in Washington, proposed action in support of Korea, two moves which have served to retain the initiative in our hands. This temporary

11

advantage we must not barter away for a makeshift truce which would be sold to the people under the label of a durable peace.

If we can implement further the new Truman policy in ways which would effectively keep Stalin on the defensive everywhere and for all time—and we have the resources and the commanding positions to do so—then real and lasting peace could be secured in the world without bloodshed.

PRESIDENT TRUMAN HAS TAKEN the last step first in launching his policy designed to stop Soviet aggression, a policy for which public opinion had long since ripened. That the American people had become fed up on the insults and injuries heaped upon us by the Moscow rulers and by their undeviating sabotage of all efforts at world peace has been evident for many a moon. The Soviet chicanery in international relations and the Communist provocations on our domestic front were calculated to culminate sooner or later in a popular reaction. . . .

The so-called Truman doctrine, it is no longer a secret, was improvised at the last minute in response to the imminent Soviet threat to convert Greece into a puppet state through pressure from within and civil war fomented by camouflaged Soviet bands. With the fall of Greece, Turkey would unquestionably be in jeopardy and prove an easier prey to the Soviet squeeze. That, in turn, would put Italy next on the route of march of Soviet imperialism. The whole Mediterranean world, France, North Africa, and eventually Spain and Gibraltar, would one by one face the fate of Greece. Our top military and naval staffs, charged with the defense of the nation, could not with complacency view the Soviet demolition of the Mediterranean mosaic which had enabled us to strike fatal blows at Mussolini and Hitler. . . .

. . . The logical and most advantageous ground for the United States to checkmate Soviet aggression was and is the Far East. (This has been fully demonstrated in "A Workable Plan for Peace with Russia," published in *Plain Talk* for November 1946.)

However, we had maneuvered ourselves in China into a self-made trap. Under the impact of obsolescent policies originated at Yalta in wartime, when we sought Russia's aid against Japan, and under the influence of potent Communist propaganda, the United States delegated General Marshall to bring about a marriage between the Chinese Government and the Communist rebels in spite of the disastrous consequences which similar unions fostered by us had yielded in Poland and Yugoslavia. Blindly we had spent the entire critical year of 1946 denying to Chiang Kai-shek, who had fought Japan for seven years, the very aid which we now propose to give to Turkey! We had sold scrap iron and arms to Japan before Pearl Harbor, but we denied the same recognized international right to our ally, the Chinese Government. We had poured out billions in loans to Great Britain and France, but we refused to allow the im-

12

mense Chinese nation even the financial help which we are now offering to little Greece.

Finally, we had yielded to the Soviet and Communist agitation for the withdrawal of American troops from China. And we did so after General Marshall's assumption of the office of Secretary of State, without exacting a corresponding concession from the Soviet forces occupying large parts of Manchuria and keeping northern Korea sealed to us—both in violation of solemn agreements. . . .

In summary, by our incredible conduct in China we jammed our rudder and found it impossible to execute there a complete reversal of our course toward Russia. And yet it is in the Far East that we hold the trump cards. And it is there, where Moscow is weakest, that we can best implement our objective of inducing the Soviets to get out of all non-Russian areas in Europe and Asia and to retire to Russia's rightful and natural habitat. By stopping the Kremlin imperialism in Greece and in Turkey alone, we can obtain only a respite until Moscow turns on the heat in other areas, and she has at her disposal many pressure points around the globe, including Central and South America, which touch our interests and security.

. . . Having seized the initiative in the contest which Moscow had originated, we must follow it up with a series of right and left diplomatic "haymakers" applied to the Soviet Union's weakest spots. Only in this manner can Soviet arrogance be permanently squelched and the tide of Soviet aggression rolled back and brought to a dead stop. The following steps seem to be imperative for the implementation of President Truman's policy:

1. The publication of all the agreements, protocols, minutes and memoranda in the secret files of the White House relating to all the deals consummated or discussed between the President of the United States or his personal envoys and Marshal Stalin or his deputies. It has been customary to publish such records about a quarter of a century or so after the end of a war. In our atomic age we have already spanned that quarter of a century in the past two years. We are embarking upon a new course with a speed almost unprecedented in international relations. Although the State Department has made a start in the right direction by publishing a number of hitherto secret agreements, the full truth about all the commitments made at the Teheran, Yalta, Potsdam, Cairo, Quebec and Moscow Conferences (see "The Lie Marches On," page 130) still remains hidden from the American people. Yet without the truth we cannot have a sound diagnosis, which is essential to any cure. It will do America no good to have our government publish a collection of crucial documents on World War II in 1970, perhaps after World War III. The time is now. And such publication would consolidate the nation behind the so-called Truman doctrine.

2. Publication of all the documentary material in the possession of our gov-

ernment relating to the Stalin-Hitler Pact of August 1939, which ushered in the recent world war, and to the subsequent collaboration between Communist Russia and Nazi Germany until June 22, 1941. Out of respect for the sensibilities of the men in the Kremlin, all evidence on this subject had been kept out from the Nuremburg trial. . . .

3. A reparations bill should be presented to Moscow for the huge damages caused to the Allies during its twenty-two months of collaboration with Hitler. These would include (a) restitution for the invasion and sacking of Poland by the Red Army in September 1939; (b) compensation for all supplies furnished to Hitler and Mussolini by the Soviet Government during that period in the course of which we were already furnishing lend-lease to the Allies to aid in their desperate stand against the Axis; (c) compensation for losses suffered as a result of Tito's collaboration with the Nazis as in the proven case of the pact concluded by Josip Vinfan, his commander in Slovenia, with the German army; and (d) indemnity for the war guilt which Stalin shares with Hitler and for the worldwide sabotage by the Communist International of efforts to prosecute the war against the aggressors. The total of these various claims would make a sizable bill running into many billions of dollars, and would go a long way towards offsetting the fantastic figures of the Kremlin's claims of damages, figures which far exceed the total national wealth of the Soviet Union.

4. A drastic shakeup in the administration of our Far Eastern diplomacy, which must begin by the dismissal from the State Department of all the Soviet appeasers who have led the United States into a blind alley in the Asiatic theatre. The conduct of American affairs in the entire Pacific area should be entrusted to an outstanding personality with the rank of Deputy Secretary of State. There can be but one policy for the United States to follow in that vast zone, so vital to Russia, and which embraces Japan and China, a policy of countering the blows delivered to the Western world in all the countries dominated or ruled by Moscow. If Russia is to treat Finland, the Baltic countries, Poland, Czechoslovakia, Rumania, Albania, Bulgaria, Yugoslavia, Hungary, parts of Austria and Germany as her sphere of influence, from which Western economic and political and cultural influences are to be excluded, then what choice is there but to deal with her on a tit-for-tat basis? We must bind China to us by enabling her to regain Manchuria, to scotch swiftly her Communist rebellion, and by speeding her reconstruction and emergence as a world power. We must bind a democratic Japan to us with lasting ties, and begin by helping her expunge her Communist fifth column. And we must do the same for Korea. The price for our assistance can be plainly posted: Soviet Russia is to receive in all respects the same treatment in those countries which are our beneficiaries as she accords us and the rest of the non-Communist world in her puppet nations.

5. The compilation and publication by the United States Government of a complete record of all the rebuffs to our advances, all the acts of noncoopera-

tion, all the insults inflicted upon us, and of all the violations of agreements on the part of the Soviet Government since Pearl Harbor. This anthology might properly be put out under the title of "Uncle Sam—He Who Gets Slapped," and would make a volume which would once and for all prove to the Henry Wallaces and Claude Peppers and Joseph Davieses and Edgar Snows that everything they propose for our getting along with Russia has been tried over and over again. The patience, the generosity, the charity with which America's military and diplomatic representatives have sought to establish "an understanding" with the men in the Kremlin are utterly without precedent in relations between states. The American people would at last learn that Soviet Russia was never an ally, never more than an associated power, in the great conflict, and national opinion would be undivided in its support of the new policy.

MUST WE FIGHT RUSSIA? If Stalin capitulated in Iran in the face of a firm stand backed by Washington, he is sure to call off his adventure in Greece before a show of force. Those who make so much of Russian power in terms of her numerical superiority in soldiers overlook Russia's ravaged economy, her shattered industry and agriculture. Not until the Soviet Government begins to produce atomic bombs can Russian aggression be expected to assume any other form than of expansion by infiltration, intimidation, and through the blindness of other powers.

If it be the aim of the "Truman Doctrine" to administer a shot in the arm now to Greece, now to Turkey, tomorrow to Norway or to Italy, then the most we can achieve is an armed truce until the Kremlin has the A-bomb. We shall only have gained strategic positions the world over for the inevitable cataclysm.

Reason dictates but one aim of the new Truman policy: Russia must disgorge all she has gobbled up in Europe and in Asia that is not Russian, regardless of whether she exercises her control openly or through puppets and fifth columns. If the initiative which we have seized is exploited to the full and implemented by a series of bold diplomatic strokes designed to keep Stalin on the defensive, the Soviets can be made to retire from the Oder and the Danube across the Vistula.

Only then would the world breathe easily and be able to start on the road to reconstruction and peace. The Soviet dictatorship would suffer such immense loss of prestige both at home and abroad, that Communism would then be fighting for survival everywhere.

We do not have to fight Russia.

April 1947

Design for Stalin's Diplomatic Waterloo

By Isaac Don Levine

[*Against the myth that there was no middle course between a policy of appeasement and outright war with Soviet Russia,* Plain Talk *waged an unremitting campaign. Again and again, whenever an occasion presented itself, the editors proposed, in the interests of peace, constructive diplomatic measures grounded in a policy of superior power wielded without bluster and intimidation. The design here outlined was largely a response to the insolent and bullying behavior in the United Nations of Andrei Vishinsky, the Kremlin's Deputy Foreign Minister, who shocked American public opinion in 1947.*]

A CATARACT has been removed from the nation's vision by the crude surgeons of the Kremlin. Vishinsky's performance before the United Nations and Warsaw's dress rehearsal for the revival of the Comintern have at last opened the eyes of the country. It has finally become self-evident:

That there are two worlds fighting for survival on this earth, and that there never was one world in our time except as a mirage of propaganda;

That Stalin's Communism is firmly welded to the cause of world revolution, and that it never had renounced it for evolutionary socialism or democracy;

That Russian imperialism is as much a part of the Soviet order as German imperialism was part of National Socialism, and that there never was a chance of preserving peace in equal partnership with the Soviet Union;

That Soviet Russia was a fortuitous co-belligerent of ours in the war against Hitlerite aggression, and that it never was and never behaved as an ally of the Western world; and

That the United Nations is a grand forum for the crystallization of world opinion, and that it never has been regarded by Moscow as anything but a sounding board for its psychological warfare.

The time is gone for the application of mild measures to insure the avoidance of war. The steps that might have led, a year ago, to a settlement of the crisis in our relations with Moscow would be largely ineffectual today. Mouthing a "get tough" policy belongs to the antediluvian days of Germany's and Japan's collapse, and is bound to evoke smiles within the inner sanctum of the Kremlin at this late date.

Only a determined and well-calculated diplomatic offensive, backed by a display of superior force, can inflict a bloodless Waterloo on Stalin and dispel the threat of war. To be sure, there is nothing in the record of contemporary statesmanship to justify the expectation that the correct preventives will be applied at this time to avert another catastrophe. But the means are at our disposal to achieve just that, as they had been at the command of diplomats before the last two great wars. A bare outline of some of these means is contained in the following fourteen points:

Psychological Warfare

1. Slave Labor Inquiry. The Government of the United States should launch a formal move in the United Nations, under the proper provisions of the Charter, for an international inquiry into the slave labor system operated by the Soviet Government. The support of international labor is perhaps the most coveted weapon sought by the Kremlin for the arsenal of Communism. There are now available mountains of documentary evidence and thousands of eye-witnesses outside the Soviet Union to testify to the widespread network of forced labor camps throughout Russia. The precedents for international action against slavery have been established on many occasions in the League of Nations, with the consent of the Soviet Government. By convicting the Soviet regime in the court of public opinion of being the leading antilabor power in the world, we can demoralize its Communist International adherents everywhere, we can undermine to the point of destruction its fifth columns and reduce Stalin's military potential drastically. For to the Kremlin the loss of labor support is equivalent to the loss of many divisions in the field.

2. Free Elections. On the basis of the explicit pledges of the Soviet Government at Yalta for the holding of "free and unfettered elections" and under the provisions of the Charter of the United Nations, the United States should institute in the United Nations a move for the holding of new elections under U.N. supervision in all the countries of eastern and southeastern Europe. The elections held in Greece under the control of the great powers are a precedent for similar action in other countries dominated by Soviet forces. We have just proposed such supervised elections in Korea, in response to Molotov's initiative in calling for a withdrawal of American and Soviet troops from that country with the aim of turning it into another Soviet satellite. By seizing the initiative in urging free, supervised elections in all the Russian-dominated countries, the governments which have arisen since the war as a result of terror and Soviet intimidation could be barred from the United Nations.

3. The Test of Poland. The case of Poland formed a special and major part of the Yalta pact. We have repeatedly protested the Soviet Government's violation of the agreements relating to Polish independence and sovereignty. But we have done nothing about it. Yet Moscow's Polish puppet regime has given

17

us a precedent for action by its famous anti-Franco resolution which was passed by the General Assembly of the United Nations last December. With the substitution of the "Bierut-Communist Government of Poland" for the "Franco-Fascist Government of Spain" and of "Warsaw" for "Madrid," the United States could reintroduce that resolution declaring that the government of Poland had been usurped by elements who do not represent the Polish people, that it therefore be debarred from membership in international agencies until a new and acceptable government is formed in Poland, and that pending such a development, "all members of the United Nations immediately recall from Warsaw their ambassadors and ministers."

4. The Baltic States. The United States has never conceded the Soviet annexation of the three Baltic countries, Lithuania, Latvia and Estonia, and continues to extend diplomatic recognition to them. Our government is officially on record as condemning the "predatory activities" by which the "political independence and territorial integrity" of these countries were "deliberately annihilated." The depredations carried on in the Baltic lands since then by the Soviet conquerors alone justify an international inquiry on the grounds of humanity. But here is a case of transparent international aggression, in unequivocal violation of solemn agreements between Stalin himself and the three Baltic governments, which challenges everything the United Nations stands for. The Government of the United States should bring this case before the United Nations and, even allowing for certain legitimate claims to the Baltic littoral, insist on the peaceful adjustment of Moscow's relations with the three little countries in accord with its own covenants.

5. The Mystery of the Katyn Forest. The United Nations, upon our initiative, should open an international inquiry into the still-unsolved mystery of the 10,000 Polish officers, who had been taken prisoners by the Red Army, found slaughtered and buried in mass graves in the spring of 1943 in the vicinity of Smolensk. It will be recalled that the Polish Government in London appealed to the International Red Cross for an investigation, which Moscow used as a pretext for its rupture of diplomatic relations with that government. The Kremlin subsequently charged that the Germans, during their retreat, had murdered the prisoners. All the German documents and witnesses relating to the Katyn horror have been available since the end of the war, and there is no reason why the German culprits, if they were responsible for this added atrocity, should not be brought to trial. Yet the incriminating evidence has not been forthcoming, either from Moscow or from the Western governments. A proposal to probe this top criminal mystery of the war should be welcomed by the Soviet Government as a means of establishing its innocence.

6. Bill for Manchurian Loot. The looting of Manchuria by the Red Army through the removal of industrial installations valued at two billion dollars, according to Edwin W. Pauley, who was President Truman's special investigator on the spot, is cause for action by the United Nations. This crime was committed against an ally who had fought Japan for seven years, by Soviet Russia, a power which fought it for seven days. It was, in addition, an act grossly violating the secret Yalta pact by which we had purchased Stalin's unequivocal recognition of the Central Government of China. At a time when this government is in critical need of financial help, the least amends we can make for our shameful conduct at Yalta is to present a bill to Moscow for its Manchurian plunder, and submit it to the United Nations for international action.

7. *Outlawing the Communist Party in Japan.* So long as the Soviet masters of Northern Korea continue to bar all democratic non-Communist parties from their own zone of occupation, and employ this device to sabotage accord with the United States for the establishment of an independent Korea, there is no reason why we should continue to tolerate the Soviet-led Communist Party in Japan. Strict reciprocity is the surest basis for getting along with a totalitarian regime. The Communist Party in Japan is, of course, a Soviet fifth column. Japanese and Korean Communists have jointly formed military units which serve as auxiliaries to the Chinese and Russian Red Armies. By outlawing the Japanese Communists we would not only deliver a psychological blow to Soviet imperialism, but also render signal service to the democratic and pro-Western elements within Japan.

8. *Peace with Japan.* The proposal of former President Hoover to proceed with the conclusion of an immediate peace with Japan is one of the mightiest weapons in our diplomatic armory. At no point on the globe are we in a more favorable position to challenge Stalin's universal sabotage of peace than in Japan. As Great Britain, China, Australia, and the Netherlands, our principal allies in the Pacific, would join us in such a move, it could not be described as a separate peace. Moreover, since Soviet Russia only came in "for the kill" in the Pacific war, collecting her payment and trophies in advance by our grace, she has no claims to any rewards from peace with Japan. Such a diplomatic *coup* would also deal a death-blow to Communist propaganda that Russia had brought Japan to her knees, and would immensely enhance our prestige throughout Asia. Stalin, who helped Lenin conclude the separate peace at Brest-Litovsk when the Soviet Government deserted the Allies in the midst of World War I, could hardly have a case against us for making peace with Japan two and a half years after the cessation of hostilities.

9. *Diplomatic and Press Reciprocity.* The numerical strength of the personnel and the extent of facilities of our diplomatic, consular, commercial and press representatives in Soviet Russia should long ago have been regulated on the principle of complete reciprocity. The denial of Soviet visas to United States Senators was but a crowning step in a long series of restrictions and insults heaped upon American citizens in Russia with the sufferance of our government. There should be as many United States consulates in the Soviet Union as the latter has in our country. When an American consul, such as the one in Vladivostok, is compelled to live under floodlights at night and his movements are restricted at all times, the Soviet consul in San Francisco should be accorded exactly the same hospitality. The Kremlin's delusion that capitalist America is so eager for Soviet business that we will permit any number of its would-be customers to enter the United States should be ended once and for all by arranging an exchange on a quota-for-quota basis.

10. Voice of Russian Freedom. To counteract the Communist International Information Bureau just set up at Belgrade with the active cooperation of high Soviet officials, we should encourage the establishment of a Russian information center composed of all the democratic and liberal elements exiled by the Soviet dictatorship. Scattered throughout the Western world are many legitimate representatives of Russian democracy, including Alexander Kerensky, the head of the Provisional Government overthrown by the Bolshevist *coup,* and Victor Chernov, the head of the freely elected Constituent Assembly dispelled by Lenin and Trotsky with the help of Stalin. The voice of Russian freedom, stifled within Russia for thirty years, should sound the call of Russia's liberation as a challenge to the call of the Comintern for world dictatorship.

11. The Voice of Liberty. That should be the name and the function of the propaganda organization which we had set up as The Voice of America, and which has proved so ineffectual. In the face of "the increasing stream of abuse," in the phrase of Winston Churchill, which the Soviet Government has poured out through the radio in twenty-six languages since the end of the war, we proceeded on the bankrupt theory of appeasement, with the result that our "pollyanna" broadcasts were taken as a sign of weakness in the Kremlin. Its own mouthpieces became almost hysterical in their attacks upon the United States. What is long overdue is an effort to bring the ringing message of a free world to the oppressed peoples of the Soviet Union. The vast technical radio resources of the United States should be mobilized for a propaganda counterattack upon Stalin's totalitarianism with the aid of his many victims abroad who are our natural allies. Under such an onslaught the citadel of Communism would begin to crack from within, for uneasy lies the head of an usurper.

Display of Force

12. All-Out Aid to China. America's traditional ally in Asia, China, with its 400 million people, is potentially our strongest bulwark against Communist imperialism at the point where Soviet Russia is strategically weakest—in her Far

Eastern hinterland which lacks industry, means of communication, and is sparsely populated. To neglect this golden opportunity is nothing short of a crime to our national defense. The legitimate Central Government of China should receive the financial aid required for the country's reconstruction, so long as our funds are expended under American supervision. It should be permitted to purchase munitions and other military equipment needed to cope with and to crush the Communist rebel forces. It should be assisted in its efforts to regain all of Manchuria and other vital areas, in accordance with the Yalta pact of which Stalin is a signatory. And it should be enabled to develop a modern air force under the direction of American experts. With a reunited and strong China firmly on the side of the United States, all of Stalin's aggressive plans in Asia would be checkmated. Indeed, we would hold a Damocles sword over his head which might very well bring about a most conciliatory Soviet policy in Europe.

13. Immediate Peace with Austria. Mindful of the fact that Austria is the strategic pivot of southeastern Europe, we could cut Russia's Gordian knot in Europe by declaring a state of peace with Austria. The American people must realize that we never were at war with Austria, that Stalin had solemnly pledged at Teheran to restore Austrian independence, and that Moscow has consistently vetoed every attempt to re-establish an independent Austria. It goes without saying that such a move on our part, which might be interpreted as a challenge by the Red Army facing us on the Danube, could not be undertaken without first reinforcing our occupation units there. The announcement of the dispatch of a strong air force to our zone would insure our establishment and perpetuation of peace in Austria. And it would have a wholesome effect upon all the adjacent areas where Stalin's agents are spreading the germs of the next war.

14. American Foreign Legion. In view of the well-established fact that the Soviet Government has trained and equipped a so-called "Free German Army" of over 100,000 men, including a number of armored divisions, it is high time that we make effective use of hundreds of thousands of former soldiers. If Stalin can enroll former enemies in the Red Army, why can't we avail ourselves of the services of our former allies? There are 150,000 Polish veterans in Europe who fought our battles only to lose their country. There are 100,000 former Yugoslav soldiers in Western countries who, like the Poles, will not go back to live as slaves under Tito. There are other nationals of nations enchained by the Communist dictators. And there are several hundred thousand Russians who refuse to go back to serfdom and who are ready to give their lives for freedom.

The organization of a Foreign Legion in the American zone of Germany, officered and equipped and maintained by Americans, would offset the threat of Stalin's "Free German Army." At present Western Europe is haunted by fears that the Red Army could sweep through to the English Channel. A strong Foreign Legion would be a potent deterrent to any possible Soviet adventures and give us in Germany the power necessary to effect a general peace in Europe.

November 1947

UNMAKING THE SECRET PEACE

By ISAAC DON LEVINE

[*The end of 1947 marked a turning point in America's foreign policy, leading to the adoption of the Marshall Plan. For several years the Council of Foreign Ministers, representing the four major wartime Allies, had met in conferences to arrive at a lasting formula of peaceful coexistence with the Soviet Union. Secretary of State Marshall returned on April 28, 1947, from Moscow, where he had been attending a meeting of the Council, "shaken by the realization," in the words of George Kennan, "that the idea of approaching the solution of Europe's problems in collaboration with the Russians was a pipe dream." On December 15, 1947, after three weeks of wrangling in London, the Conference of the Council of Foreign Ministers "ended in total failure." This indictment of our conduct towards the Kremlin reflects the deep gloom that then enveloped the Western world.*]

IT IS DIFFICULT to resist the temptation to leaf through the New Year editorials of our great newspapers for 1944 and '45 and '46 and '47, on the threshold of another decisive year in the continuing twilight of civilization, marked by the breakdown of the London Peace Conference.

If you would explore the wilderness in which our mighty leaders of opinion and molders of policy have been wandering during these four years since the fatal Teheran Conference in December, 1943, go and consult their writings and statements on the eves of each New Year. You will either be nauseated by the pollyanna praises sung to the "peaceloving" Kremlin or you will be crushed by the blindness of our pathfinders who thrive on dispensing optimism to the millions.

Now that the harsh truth is beginning to dawn even on the most deluded among our mentors, it is more than ever necessary to tell the people the one fundamental truth which has been carefully hidden from them all these years,

22

and which is still wrapped in the foggy columns of our commentators and official spokesmen.

This truth is that we have not been engaged since V-J Day in the making of peace. *We have, in reality, been engaged in the unmaking of the secret peace framed, signed, and sealed at Teheran, Yalta, and Potsdam.*

This bitter truth must and will come out. The few who had the vision to see it and the courage to say it must get a hearing. The secret peace was made behind the backs of the peoples of the world, while men were still dying on the battlefields for its sake; it was made in an atmosphere filled with the propaganda fumes generated by the most massive and expensive propaganda machinery ever foisted upon a free world.

The secret peace, for which the Government of the United States must bear the major responsibility, cannot be matched in the long list of Carthaginian peace settlements in the history of man. Since the days of tribal chieftains, Parthian despots, Mongol invaders, and conquering Caesars, there has never been a peace as dishonorable, as treacherous, as irresponsible, as inhuman, and as short-sighted as the one negotiated by the little men with big names who crossed the Atlantic to meet the Moscow satraps and brought them ever-increasing offerings at the expense of humanity.

WE SOLD sovereign and intrepid Yugoslavia, after encouraging her resistance against the Nazi invaders, into the bondage of Soviet totalitarianism;

We agreed to the dismemberment of Poland, in the absence of her legally constituted representatives, when her sons were falling by the hundreds at Monte Cassino;

We then betrayed the legitimate Polish Government, with which we had solemnly fraternized, to the new Tartary;

We surrendered to Stalin's executioners Bulgaria and the democratic, anti-Fascist leaders of her people, after they had negotiated a provisional peace with us before the fall of Hitler;

We let down, similarly, the liberty-seeking forces in Rumania and Hungary, condemning them to servitude under ruthless foreign dictatorship;

We turned over to the mercies of that merciless power the three Baltic nations, Estonia, Latvia, and Lithuania, whose independence we had proudly and publicly vouchsafed during the war itself;

We gave Russia the city of Koenigsberg, which the Russian people had never claimed and do not wish;

We allowed the Red Army to occupy Prague, by the grace of diplomatic pressure and not because of military exigencies, so as to enable Moscow to hold a dagger at the vitals of Europe;

We nodded approval when the junta in the Kremlin dismembered and shackled the remainder of Finland;

We trampled upon the very soul of humanity when we consented to feed into the Soviet maw, by force if necessary, many hundreds of thousands of refugees and runaway Russians who, in their quest for freedom, had left or deserted the tyranny in their homeland;

We presented to Russia, gratis, the Kurile Islands, a vital link in the American defense system between the Aleutians and Japan;

We delivered, behind the back of our ally, China, control over two of her major strategic ports;

We encouraged the Chinese Communist satellites of Moscow to seize most of Manchuria, which contains more than one-half of the resources of all of China, and stood by when the Red Army had looted that province;

We betrayed the trust of the long-enslaved people of Korea by arbitrarily cutting their country in two and throwing the developed industrial north into the lap of the new enslaver.

And, in a supreme gesture of appeasement, we helped establish exclusive Soviet possession of eastern Germany as far as Berlin, arming Stalin with an ace weapon against us.

THE AMERICAN PEOPLE *were not* consulted in the perpetration of this none-too-complete catalogue of misdeeds that constitutes the framework of the secret peace we are now trying to dismantle. And many of those on our national scene who have had a hand in fashioning that monstrosity are continuing to befuddle the issue.

Already voices are being raised that the blame for the collapse of the London Conference, convoked to draft peace settlements for Germany and Austria, must be laid upon the instrument employed—the Council of Foreign Ministers. Already the misleaders of yesteryear are putting the emphasis on the procedure for the settlement of the differences, and not upon the differences themselves. We are asked to believe that the Council of Foreign Ministers could not solve the differences in public, but that the time-honored diplomatic means of private negotiations could produce an enduring peace. Nothing can be further from the truth.

The real issue is: How can we unmake the secret peace by which we have let an incendiary loose in the premises of civilization? The real and only question facing us is: How can we drive the marauder out of Europe and make him return to his own preserves?

It cannot be repeated too often that genuine peace will not be established until the area of freedom is restored. We must dissolve the chains we have forged in the secret peace, chains in which a dozen nations are now languishing. We must undo the crimes of Teheran, Yalta, and Potsdam. We must liberate those whom we have helped to fetter. And we must do more than render lip-service to the battle cries of justice and freedom before the light of a lasting peace will begin to glimmer on the horizon of a world in chaos.

January 1948

ON INDIRECT AGGRESSION

By Isaac Don Levine

[When, on March 11, 1948, Jan Masaryk, a friend of the United States who held the high post of Foreign Minister of Czechoslovakia, met sudden death in Prague, either by murder or suicide, the Western world was deeply shocked. It put the seal on the Soviet rape of the free Czech Republic. In the Defense Department in Washington there were apprehensions of all-out war with Russia in the near future. In preparation for the feared Soviet attack, President Truman urged Congress to adopt the Selective Service Act. Plain Talk never subscribed to the view that Stalin would risk launching an outright war against the United States and constantly warned against the Soviet strategy of indirect aggression.]

WILL THE enactment by Congress of Selective Service legislation and of universal military training, as urged by President Truman, make the position of the United States "unmistakably clear" to Moscow and compel it to give up its aggressive course?

So long as our foreign policy is not "unmistakably clear" both to the people and to the government of the United States, it is not likely that the stern warning sounded by the President at the joint session of Congress will have any lasting effect.

Stalin's junta may temporarily soften its attitude toward Finland by abstaining from the demand for virtual military control of that country. Stalin may restrain his hothead henchmen in Italy from following immediately the example of their comrades in Czechoslovakia. Such a decision on the part of the Politburo would be designed to lull us into another spell of false security.

Hitler tried this technique, and for a while it worked. But it is doubtful whether the Soviet steamroller can even be made to pause at this stage by such measures as the announced increase of American armed forces. It is a safe bet that this action had been discounted by Stalin and his general staff before embarking upon their adventures in Czechoslovakia, Finland, and Italy. These three fronts represent the center and the right and left flanks of a huge strategic arc calculated to embrace all of Western Europe in a Soviet vise.

Even the events in Czechoslovakia have not yet made "unmistakably clear" to the American public the full nature of indirect aggression. If you substitute the name of Henry A. Wallace for that of President Benes, it might be easier for every American to see what would happen to this nation if we followed the policy of fraternization with the Communists advocated by our own Benes from Iowa. For Czechoslovakia under Benes was a model of Soviet appeasement. There is not a trick in the bag of the Wallace camp which Benes did not employ. Ever since 1943 he wooed, he conciliated, he yielded, and he genuflected before the dictator in the Kremlin. But the more he accommodated the Red Bear, the greater grew the latter's appetite.

Such is the pattern of indirect aggression. It remains alien to the American public mind. We still adhere to the belief that Communists seek power only through the overthrow of government by force and violence. Just as Hitler used intimidation, espionage, propaganda, to undermine and seize Austria, so has Stalin in seizing Czechoslovakia. Both had their courtiers in their victims' citadels, waiting to lower the drawbridges and open the gates to the enemy.

HAVING UNCAGED, during the war years, the parent of all modern dictatorships, we proceeded to allow him to prey with impunity upon the flock of little nations which had looked to us for protection. For three years now we have fed the maw of the untamed Soviet tyranny, sacrificing one free country after another in the futile, amoral hope of sating the beast.

Can we stop the marauder now merely by elementary and belated acts of military preparedness? The dynamics of a victory-drunk military despotism on a rampage are such that only a display of superior force can halt it. After all, our possession of the A-bomb did not deter the men in the Kremlin from seeking conquest by indirect aggression.

Although Jefferson and Madison warned us a century and a half ago against usurpation from within, there is no clear national realization of the methods of modern usurpers. The lesson of Czechoslovakia should bring home to our lawmakers and leaders of public opinion that our first line of defense today is not on the open battlefield, but against the secret battalions of the fifth column.

The vanguard of the enemy is in our midst. In the press and in the colleges, in the churches and on the radio and in the theater, in the highest departments of the Federal government and in the councils of important labor unions, the agents of the Communist worldwide conspiracy are on the offensive, rallying around them gullible and innocent idealists. These quislings disintegrate our morale and confuse our foreign policy.

So LONG as the United States lacks an integrated global foreign policy, there is little reason to suppose that Stalin will mend his ways. So long as we undo with our left hand in the Far East what we are trying to build up with our right hand in Europe and the Near East, the camarilla in the Kremlin will not take us too seriously. So long as many of the Teheran-Yalta-Potsdam boys remain in the State Department service, Moscow will take it that we do not mean business.

First of all, let us make it unmistakably clear to the American people how the Soviet Government has responded during the last three years to every American advance. Let us open our diplomatic files to exhibit to the world the rebukes, the insults, and the injuries heaped upon the United States whenever our representatives sought Soviet cooperation and friendship.

This would create the requisite climate for an American foreign policy commanding respect from the cynical swashbucklers in Moscow. The next step short of war, which alone can effectively arrest the Communist tide in Europe, must be taken by us in the Pacific. Our trump cards against the Soviet power are there. We hold Japan and wield immense influence in China. We have not played these cards, partly because of fifth column sabotage.

Only by our actions in Tokyo and Nanking can we dispel the threats hanging over Finland and Italy and the rest of Europe. If we are not to be pushed out of Berlin, we must help Chiang Kai-shek in Manchuria. Only when our diplomacy takes the offensive in Japan and China will it become "unmistakably clear" to Stalin that the United States really intends to stop his aggression and remove the menace of a third world war from the horizon of mankind.

April 1948

OUR FIG-LEAF FOREIGN POLICY

By ISAAC DON LEVINE

[*Having taken two steps forward by the adoption of the Marshall Plan and the enactment of the draft, Secretary of State Marshall instructed General Walter Bedell Smith, U.S. Ambassador in Moscow, to take one step backward by calling on Foreign Minister Molotov to inform Stalin that "the door is always wide open for full discussions and the composing of our difficulties." This confidential "dovish" move quickly backfired with global repercussions. In violation of established diplomatic custom, and without notice to Washington, Molotov announced that the Kremlin had been invited to a high-level parley with the U.S. In London and Paris and other Allied quarters, there was dismay and an outburst of protests against American scheming to negotiate with Stalin behind their backs. On May 11 President Truman publicly reassured the world that there was no change in U.S. foreign policy. This was the origin of the essay on "Our Fig-Leaf Foreign Policy."*]

WHILE THE weary peoples of the earth are desperately seeking the road to peace, the two major political parties of the world's greatest power are floundering about without a foreign policy in this Presidential election year. That the bipartisan United States course in international relations has been erratic and compassless was demonstrated last month in a humiliating manner when Molotov stunned Washington by broadcasting Ambassador Walter Bedell Smith's confidential suggestions for a discussion of the differences between the two countries.

It is not the fiasco of the alleged bilateral peace parley, which was so adroitly exploited by Moscow for propaganda purposes, that proves the barrennesss of our diplomacy. Rivers of ink have been expended in the press on that aspect of the episode that startled the world. Nor is it of any lasting significance that Moscow pulled another of her Tartar tricks or that our diplomatists once more fumbled the ball and displayed gross ineptitude. For who, except the deluded, could doubt that, had Washington's initiative culminated in a private Russian-American conference, it would have inevitably ended in a fiasco even greater than those of Teheran, Yalta, and Potsdam?

What the American surprise move has revealed above all is that the helmsmen of our foreign policy are still suffering from one of the severest cases of myopia on record. As President Truman disclosed in his press conference, the advance made by Ambassador Smith had been discussed "from the first word to the yours truly" with the entire Cabinet. That Ambassador Smith, instead of delivering a verbal message, decided to buttress his statement by committing it to paper, was a *faux pas* of secondary importance. Of prime import is the wishful thinking which the message displayed, despite the stern lecture it contained upon the Soviet government's past misbehavior and the counsel to the Kremlin to mend its ways.

Birth of a Feeler

THE PLAIN truth is that we approached Moscow with an ambiguous invitation, not unlike the one with which the Soviet Ambassador, Merekalov, had approached the Nazi Foreign Office on April 17, 1939, and which is described by our own State Department in its official *Nazi-Soviet Relations* as the beginning of the "tentative efforts to improve German-Soviet relations." This may not have been the original conception in the minds of those who planned our latest move in Moscow. But, as finally amended by President Truman's various advisers, and as delivered to Molotov, it had all the earmarks of an appeasement feeler.

To be sure, we did not dot all the *i*'s. Yet we opened the door to a private and bilateral discussion. We did not inform France and Great Britain of our step, keeping them in the dark even after Molotov had delivered his reply to Smith's note. We must have had something to hide if we concealed it from London and Paris and from our own foreign envoys and representatives in the U.N. The Soviet government alone shared this secret with us for six days.

What was behind this fig-leaf diplomacy of ours? Secretary Marshall let the cat out of the bag on May 5, barely twenty-four hours after Ambassador Smith made his historic call on Molotov in Moscow. And those of us who can read between the lines, without having any inkling as to the strictly secret move under way just then, scented a familiar odor and realized that our foreign policy was still being conducted in the spirit of Yalta.

"A fundamental task of the United Nations and of our foreign policy is to dispel the misconceptions of the Soviet leaders," declared Secretary Marshall before the House Foreign Affairs Committee, in a hearing dealing with Congressional plans to amend the United Nations Charter in an attempt to insure peace. "It is a misconception to suppose that domination of the world by a single system is inevitable," added Secretary Marshall. "It is a misconception to suppose that differing systems cannot live side by side in peace. . . ."

How deep-seated is the streak of wishful thinking in our makeshift foreign policy was further exhibited by Secretary Marshall when he told the Congress that "once the European Recovery Program moved strongly forward and steps were taken to redress the present military 'disequilibrium' of the world, the United States might well obtain from the Russians concessions of the greatest value. . . ."

Here, in these statements by the official spokesman for the United States, we have summed up the three basic fallacies of the course which led to the abortive Smith-Molotov exchange, and which, if pursued, must lead to colossal disaster.

Incurable Fixation

THE FIRST and cardinal fallacy in Secretary Marshall's policy toward Moscow is the belief that it is possible by discussion, negotiation, or debate in international forums to dispel the Soviet misconceptions as to the capitalist world. This was the fatal error underlying Franklin Delano Roosevelt's "great design," which impelled him to seek a face-to-face encounter with Stalin and to go as far as Teheran and Yalta.

Whether we like it or not, it is high time that we all realize that the keystone of Soviet foreign policy is its unshakable belief that sooner or later war, a war to the death, is inevitable between the Communist and the non-Communist systems. Stalin, in all his actions, proceeds from this premise. The Kremlin may appease. It may even at times fear attack or encirclement. It may be genuinely anxious to make concessions, as it did to Hitler in 1939. But the Politburo never permits itself to deviate from the unalterable fixation that war is inevitable, and all our efforts to modify its neurosis have ended in failure.

The evidence of this is overwhelming in the Soviet government's own records written in the textbooks of the country, in the pronouncements of its recognized leaders, and in the Communist programs and instructions the world over. The dealings of the foreign powers with the Soviet government during the thirty years of its existence bear further voluminous testimony to this fixation. Indeed, the proof of it all has been cited again and again. But the myth persists in our midst that peace with Russia can be won by persuasion.

When Secretary Marshall declares that it is a misconception to suppose that domination of the world by a single system is inevitable, he unwittingly promotes Stalin's own cause. For Moscow, which believes that either Communism or capitalism must dominate the world, has consistently propagated the contrary idea among its opponents abroad. Moscow would have us believe that it is one of those "bourgeois prejudices"—just another capitalist misconception. Behind this effective smoke screen the Comintern made considerable headway in its day. And now, after all these years, Secretary Marshall is spreading it.

When Marshall proclaims it a misconception "to suppose that differing systems cannot live side by side in peace. . . . ," he literally echoes words used by Stalin himself in various interviews with journalists and visiting dignitaries since the end of the war. When the Soviet dictator, however, employs the expression "peace," he means "truce." Ever since Lenin, Soviet leaders have resorted to such assurances to lull the outside world into a false sense of security.

Stalin carried this old tune to new heights in his latest reply to Wallace's open letter. Measureless indeed must be the contempt in which the Kremlin satrap holds the leadership of the United States. Having felt our soft spots in Ambassador Smith's approach of May 4 and in Secretary Marshall's declaration of May 5, having further softened us with Molotov's haymaker, Stalin steps openly into our domestic political arena. He is gracious enough to accept the terms ghostwritten by his own stooges for his puppet, Henry Wallace!

Our Maginot Line

THE SECOND basic fallacy of our short-sighted policy to stop Communist aggression and Soviet imperialism is to be found in the belief that the effectuation of the European Recovery Program might result in important Soviet concessions to us. This view reflects the bipartisan delusion which is incorporated in the latest Marshall-Vandenberg plan, as expressed in the Senate resolution sponsored by Vandenberg. It is a scheme designed to help us turn the Western European union into an effective military organization against Soviet encroachment.

Instead of a formal alliance between the United States and the Western nations, Senator Vandenberg, with the backing of the State Department, would pave the way for the creation of an anti-Soviet Atlantic coalition by promoting regional associations under the U.N. Charter. It is assumed that Moscow does not see through this stratagem, that it is unaware of the existence of a permanent military committee of the Western European union, and that the United States is in a position to build up and to maintain a European army strong enough to clamp down the iron curtain on a line some eight hundred miles long.

It is a fallacy to suppose that pauperized Western Europe could afford a first-rate military establishment, even with the sinews of ERP behind it. But it is an even greater fallacy to imagine that our establishment of a Maginot Line to challenge the Soviet ramparts in the heart of Europe would result in Moscow's adoption of a policy of appeasement toward us.

A clue to what is in the mind of the Politburo on the subject may be had from the *London New Statesman and Nation,* which often reflects, albeit how innocently, a Soviet policy. Declaring that our military undertakings in Western Europe would frustrate the economic aims of the Recovery Program, the weekly added: "If the United States is determined to create a Maginot Line on the western side of the Iron Curtain, then the expendable forces required to man it will have to be provided by the United States, just as Rome once provided the legions to hold the limits of her empire."

Far from exacting concessions from the Kremlin by organizing Western Europe into an integrated military front, in a zone where the Soviet arms are strongest and the Communist hordes regimented into obedient underground legions and columns, this policy is sure to lead to further pressure by Moscow. The Vandenberg plan may very well have been a major factor in Molotov's unprecedented act of exposing to the world our confidential "peace feeler." As a counterstroke to our ambitious military projects, the resounding slap administered by Molotov raised Moscow's prestige with the masses and strengthened its claim to treat Western Europe as its special sphere of influence.

The Arms Race

THE THIRD basic fallacy inherent in our attitude toward Soviet imperialism is the supposition that our rearmament "might well obtain from the Russians concessions of the greatest value." This statement by Secretary Marshall is natural enough when it emanates from a general anxious, to use his words, "to redress the present military 'disequilibrium' of the world." It is disquieting when it is widely disseminated by political commentators and professional diplomats.

Since when has an insurance policy been a preventive of fire? Preparedness is insurance against such emergencies as Pearl Harbor. When an aggressor is prowling the world highways, it is foolhardy not to be armed and prepared for any eventuality. This is all that can be claimed for our catching up with the immense Soviet military establishment, including our plans for conscription and universal military training.

But preparedness is no preventive of war. Our awesome stockpile of atomic bombs did not deter Stalin from his adventures in Iran, the Balkans, on the Danube and the Adriatic, in Berlin, and on the Baltic. The cold war was initiated and prosecuted in the shadow of our A-bomb. All the experience of modern history goes to show that preparedness does not avert wars.

It is a grievous misconception and dangerous misinterpretation of the dictatorial mentality to raise hopes of coming "Russian concessions" when our military establishment matches that of the U.S.S.R. and its satellites. The contrary is to be expected, however disagreeable the prospect may be.

Instead of concessions, we should look forward to the Politburo's incitement of further infiltration of the free countries by means of fifth columns, a mode of warfare against which armed preparedness is helpless. Against our far-flung military bases, Soviet Russia maintains, in disguise, similar bases within the home confines of all non-Soviet nations.

Our rearmament is an imperative necessity, but don't let us blind ourselves to the truth. An armament race is sure to bring not conciliation but exacerbation of our relations with Moscow.

Our Ace in Asia

THE ZIGZAG course we have been pursuing in foreign relations has been nothing but an unsteady and shamefaced retreat by the monitors of Teheran, Yalta, and Potsdam. It is a course without an objective. Now and then, when its capriciousness becomes too evident, its foibles are hidden behind a fig leaf. The impotent United Nations, the half-baked Truman Doctrine and the extravagantly advertised Marshall Plan have served as such a foil.

At best, what passes for our foreign policy would freeze the uneasy truce between Soviet Russia and the Western world into a phony peace. In the preatomic age such a policy of drift was perhaps tolerable, although it had carried us into two successive world wars. With the atomic race darkening the horizon of civilization, any makeshift arrangement which would leave the Soviet power in possession of its vast loot would be a betrayal of humanity.

An effective foreign policy must have as its goal the disgorging by the imperialists of Moscow of the illicit trophies they had amassed through intimidation, infiltration, and outright aggression.

The foundation-stone of such a policy, as we have repeatedly pointed out, must be action—not where Russia is strongest but where she is weakest, not on her threshold but in her hinterland, in the Pacific and not in the Atlantic sphere.

By arming and equipping two hundred Chinese divisions to help the legitimate Central Government of Chiang Kai-shek, under American military supervision, to regain Manchuria, we would dispense with the need for universal military training or conscription.

The cost of such an operation would be a fraction of the financial burden to our taxpayers of the draft and U.M.T. Moreover, the Chinese people are eager to fight for Manchuria, which is their country. At present they are waging that fight against enormous odds, without adequate arms. And it is largely the fault of our diplomacy at Yalta that Moscow has been able to extend its influence over Manchuria and to establish bases in Chinese ports.

Stalin, along with Roosevelt and Churchill, recognized the Central Government of China. Stalin never questioned that government's title to Manchuria. Its redemption by the Chinese Republic would deprive Soviet Russia of the one great industrial bastion available to her in the Far East. For Manchuria in Communist hands is a mighty potential threat to the defenses of the United States in the Pacific.

At present we have the upper hand in the far Pacific. Five or ten years from now, with Manchuria a Soviet satellite, Russia will wield a club over the entire northern Pacific. Today the Far East, by virtue of our control of the intervening lanes of communication, is nearer to the United States than it is to Muscovy. Five or ten years from now, with the great resources of Manchuria developed, the situation may very well be reversed. Today Russia is in no position to face the possibility of a two-front war—in the West and in the East. A few years hence, she may have in Manchuria a war potential equal to that of all her western satellites between Trieste and Warsaw.

Elementary strategy dictates that in order to loosen the Soviet stranglehold on Europe it would be prudent to launch a diversion at a point some thousands of miles away from Russia's centers of population and industry, linked only by the precarious Siberian transportation line. Long before a modernized Chinese army was posed on the 1,100-mile frontier separating Manchuria from the Russian Far East, Moscow would offer those "concessions of the greatest value" which Secretary Marshall hopes to gain from his measures in Europe.

All that we have gained to date in the war of nerves is to enable Moscow to parade as the champion of a peace offensive. More than once we had wrested the initiative from Stalin's hands, as in the case of our Trieste move in the Italian elections, only to lose it through our fallacious diplomacy. The Smith-Marshall overtures to the Kremlin gave the Politburo the precious opportunity to put the United States on the defensive before the peace-starved masses of the Old World and the bewildered populace of our own country.

Now is the decisive political hour to formulate a truly constructive and workable American foreign policy. Such a policy must not be based upon wily secret diplomacy, nor upon discredited fallacies inspired by wishful thinking. It must be based upon a display of superior force, by injured China against her aggressor neighbor, as the only solid road to the liberation of Europe and to a firm peace.

June 1948

ACHESON'S OPPORTUNITY

By ISAAC DON LEVINE

[The prelude to the Korean War dates from March 1949, shortly after Dean Acheson became Secretary of State. That month the North Korean Communists initiated a series of probing armed attacks on South Korea that continued for over a year. Yet in Washington both the State Department and the Pentagon were so sure of South Korea's ability to overcome a Communist invasion from the north that in May the American Ambassador in Seoul was instructed to inform President Syngman Rhee of the order to withdraw from South Korea the United States troops—some 15,000 strong, still remaining there. Subsequently, on January 12, 1950, Secretary Acheson made his famous statement before the National Press Club that Korea lay outside the United States' defense perimeter in Asia. And on June 25 Stalin unleashed the great Communist offensive that caught Washington and the American military high command completely by surprise.]

THE NEW SECRETARY of State, Dean Acheson, is taking over the conduct of American foreign policy at its lowest point since Washington was burned by the British in the War of 1812.

In Europe, the United States is hanging on the ropes. For nearly a year now we have been clinging desperately to Berlin by means of the ephemeral airlift.

In the Pacific we are on the verge of a colossal disaster that would put China under Communist rule, destroy the fruits of our victory over Japan, and pave the way for the Soviet conquest of all of Asia.

How did we come to this calamitous pass three and a half years after the magnificent triumph of our arms in both the Atlantic and the Pacific theaters? Through our disregard of the basic principle underlying the balance of power in the atomic world:

An effective foreign policy must be global and indivisible.

Berlin and Shanghai, just as Iceland and Panama, are inseparable and interdependent parts of up-to-date diplomacy. Moscow has played its game on a single global chessboard. We have followed the habits of an obsolete age, dividing and disposing of our forces in separate compartments.

These habits may have worked for Roosevelt, Marshall, and the Joint Chiefs of Staff during the last war, when we concentrated on Europe as our first objective. They became obsolete with Hiroshima.

Hiroshima, like the closing chapter of every major war in history, ended on a revolutionary point in technology that presaged new modes of warfare for the future while discarding certain habits of diplomacy left over from the past.

Hiroshima unlocked before us history's last stretch of road. Beyond it there is no future. Both war and diplomacy face the ultimate in the released atom. Diplomacy, too, is on its last lap. Who can measure the responsibility that destiny has placed upon Mr. Acheson?

In 1946 and 1947 we made a series of diplomatic-strategic moves in the Near East, in Iran, Turkey, and Greece to protect our Atlantic lifeline in the Mediterranean. Toward the close of 1948 the Kremlin countered these moves in the Far East, with sweeping victories for its satellites in China, with the aim of jeopardizing our status in the Pacific.

How many people in the higher councils in Washington have grasped this simple truth? Mr. Acheson has the opportunity to demonstrate that the United States is capable of shaping and pursuing an effective foreign policy founded upon indivisible global strategy.

Such strategy must comprehend not only geographic but ideological forces. Not only is a base in Alaska interlaced with our security in Dakar, but Soviet and all totalitarian aggression in any area of the planet is inextricably linked with fifth column activities, with its propaganda and espionage, within our domestic premises.

Two years ago we wrote in connection with the Acheson-Lilienthal Report on Atomic Energy:

"Where does Mr. Acheson stand? Like Secretary of Commerce Averell Harriman, he has learned from bitter experience the true nature of the Soviet dictatorship and the impossibility of dealing with it on a give-and-take basis. But he has yet to acquire a real insight into the Soviet fifth column in our midst and in his own official environment in Washington."

This statement would appear to be as true today as it was two years ago. In his testimony before the Foreign Relations Committee of the Senate on his eligibility for the post of Secretary of State, Mr. Acheson showed how far he still is from comprehending Soviet machinations inside America. He took Alger Hiss, under Federal indictment for perjury in connection with the Whittaker Chambers espionage revelations, under his wing.

"Mr. Alger Hiss was an officer of the Department of State during most of the time that I served there," declared Mr. Acheson. "During that time he and I became friends and we remain friends." A tribute bound to give aid and comfort to the enemy within!

On the other hand, Mr. Acheson displayed an uncanny insight into the nature of the Soviet menace to peace and freedom. His statement on this phase of the modern world challenge surpasses anything uttered on the subject by any Secretary of State since Charles Evans Hughes. Acheson said:

"It is my view that Communism as a doctrine is economically fatal to a free country and to human rights and fundamental freedom. Communism as an aggressive factor in world conquest is fatal to independent governments and to free peoples."

How will Secretary Acheson implement this credo? How will he translate these sound views into sound foreign policy?

Already the signs are pointing to a Moscow stratagem of fresh appeasement designed to lull us into a false sense of security in Europe through some minor concessions while Communism gobbles up and consolidates its trophies in Asia.

Secretary Acheson's opportunity is clear: He can turn the tables on Moscow in China. Grave as the military situation of Chiang Kai-shek's Nationalist Government is, it is no more critical than that of Greece or of Iran when the United States stepped in and saved our defenses in the Near East.

February 1949

Retreat from San Francisco

By Isaac Don Levine

[*The formation of NATO—the North Atlantic Treaty Organization—in March 1949, was widely advertised as a deterrent to Soviet aggression. The events during the last twenty-seven years in Korea, Hungary, Indochina, the Middle East, Cuba and Czechoslovakia, show that the Kremlin incendiaries have pursued their special brand of warfare with more determination than ever. As the following essay points out, the chief merit of NATO has been to dissipate some of the exaggerated illusions about the United Nations as a peace-enforcing agency since its birth at San Francisco.*]

THE NORTH ATLANTIC Security Pact marks a milestone in the retreat from the magnificent self-delusion at San Francisco four years ago. The Grand Design fashioned for a believing world at Teheran and Yalta has now taken on the grim visage of a defensive military alliance. The edifice of world peace erected at San Francisco with such bewitching promise is being replaced by a dike against the swirling tide of aggression.

The Atlantic Pact is at best but a half-measure, even as Secretary Acheson himself averred in his public pronouncements when he launched it. This alone is progress. Yet the inadequacies of the Pact in furthering durable world peace are far greater than its sponsors grant.

Suppose the Atlantic Pact had been in existence in February 1948 when Moscow employed its Communist fifth column to engineer the putsch in Prague which resulted in the seizure of Czechoslovakia. What would have happened?

The Atlantic Pact provides only for consultations among the signatories in the case of an indirect attack. The members of the alliance would then have been confronted with this problem: Is the coup in Czechoslovakia a threat to peace? It is obvious that a neighbor of Czechoslovakia might very properly have regarded it as such whereas Canada, for instance, might have taken an opposite view.

The Atlantic Pact provides insurance only against armed attack. It does not provide any effective defense against indirect attack, i.e., conquest by infiltration and usurpation of power through fifth columns. Yet this is the paramount danger. Soviet imperialism has expanded by putsches and the incitement of civil war, so strikingly illustrated in the cases of Czechoslovakia and China. For Moscow has long since given up, in its worldwide campaign of aggrandizement, the doctrine of direct warfare in favor of covert warfare.

THE FOES of the North Atlantic Pact fall into two extreme camps. The Russia-first brigade merely echoes Moscow's propaganda, for the Kremlin had long ago discounted the instrument and is exploiting it as psychological warfare in inflaming passions against the United States as the chief protagonist of capitalism in the world.

The other camp consists of pre-atomic minds whose outcry is that the Pact scraps America's traditional policy of no foreign entanglements. The plain truth is that that policy has been scuttled again and again during the past decade. The new treaty recognizes America's manifest destiny in the age of air power which leaves no room for retreat on a shrunken globe. The Pact formalizes a state of affairs incorporated into the living body of this Republic by the secret agreements made at Yalta and by the promulgation of the Truman Doctrine.

The last vestiges of American isolationism were wiped out with the advent of atomic power. This is a harsh but inescapable fact. But even before America had unleashed the atom, we had conducted our international relations so as to entangle the country in a multiplicity of secret and open commitments. In the deepest sense, the Atlantic Pact is but the inevitable fruition of a foreign policy long in operation.

IT WOULD be folly, however, to pretend or to believe, as President Truman and Senator Vandenberg in their sponsorship of the Pact have naively indicated, that it would act as a war deterrent. It is widely maintained that the Pact would prevent acts of aggression by serving notice that an armed attack upon any signatory would be regarded by us as an attack upon the United States. The precedent cited for this is the belief that the Kaiser in 1914 and Hitler in 1939 would not have launched their adventures had Great Britain and the

United States unmistakably warned Germany that they would treat these as acts of war against them. That was probably true of the world then, but not now. In 1914 and in 1939 the system of the balance of power comprised many first-rate powers, some of which were not committed to a predictable course. The Kaiser did not figure on Britain's entry into the war when he backed the attack on Serbia in August 1914. Hitler did not figure on America's entry into the war when he decided to attack Poland in August 1939.

There can be no such miscalculation in a world which is divided into two, and only two, camps. The balance of power today is between two contestants, between Moscow and Washington. And Moscow has never displayed any doubts as to the position of the United States. The Berlin airlift, far surer than the Atlantic Pact, has served notice upon the Politburo of our determination to defend what remains of the Western world.

THE PACT does bring us nearer to the acute realities of the world crisis. It goes a long way toward dispelling the make-believe atmosphere still surrounding the United Nations. The crude Ernest Bevin, Britain's Foreign Secretary, let the cat out of the bag when he declared in the House of Commons, "just as the League of Nations did not fulfill its purposes, neither has the United Nations."

The North Atlantic Pact will supplant, not supplement, the U.N. Charter. The North Atlantic Council, to be set up as soon as the Pact is ratified, is bound to occupy the international stage held by the U.N. Security Council. The impotent rostrum of potent oratory will be replaced by a board handling the planet's explosive power in a businesslike manner.

The North Atlantic Pact can stop the march of Soviet imperialism and insure a lasting period of peace only if it is implemented by a positive policy in the Pacific. With our immense resources we can support for a measureable time the North Atlantic dike erected in the heart of Europe, but we shall only be forcing the Soviet floodwaters eastward, to spill toward the Indian Ocean and the China Sea. While we are damming up our front door against the onrush of Soviet imperialism we must also protect the rear of the house from the Communist torrents sweeping over Asia with mounting momentum.

April 1949

ACHESON'S WAY OUT

By ISAAC DON LEVINE

[*From the first issue, which featured an exposé on* The State Department Espionage Case—*the Amerasia affair—which made journalistic history from coast to coast (see Book 3, page 102), the Communist threat to China was in the forefront of the world news. "Acheson's Way Out" was written in the expectation that in May 1949 it was still not too late to avert the looming disaster in the Far East.*]

IT IS NOT yet too late for Secretary of State Acheson to inaugurate a constructive American policy in China, and to save the magnificent victory won by the United States in the Pacific less than four years ago from turning into "a tragedy for the whole Western world," in the apt phrase of *The New York Times.*

The situation of Soviet Russia at the time Hitler's mighty war machine was hammering at the gates of Moscow and Leningrad was far more precarious than that of Nationalist China today. Yet Harry Hopkins, as President Roosevelt's special envoy, rushed to Moscow to furnish Stalin an almost unlimited supply of lend-lease matériel. Hopkins was not deterred by the desertions to the enemy from the Red Army which were then taking place on a huge scale, by the corruption within the Soviet bureaucracy, which is more widespread than in China, and by the inefficiency and waste which are more prevalent in Russia than anywhere in the world. Furthermore, it is doubtful if Hitler's conquest of Russia in 1941 would have constituted as grave a peril to the security of the United States as Stalin's conquest of China, with its subsequent enslavement of all of Asia, would today.

Greece, two years ago, when Acheson, then Under-Secretary of State, promulgated the Truman Doctrine, was in far greater jeopardy than Nationalist China is at this writing. Yet the United States rushed a military mission and appropriated enormous funds to bolster tottering Greece from becoming a Communist satellite.

Both in Iran and Turkey, where the political regimes are akin to that of Nationalist China, the United States stepped in with military missions and with material aid to halt Soviet aggression.

IT WAS no accident that China, the pivot of American security in the Pacific and for a full century a keystone of United States diplomacy, is missing from the list of our postwar beneficiaries. This is the fruit of an insidious and assid-

39

uous effort by a school of pro-Soviet "experts" on the Far East who have infiltrated our State Department, boring from within our defenses in China. . . .

That at this late date Secretary of State Acheson should be a victim of this clique was hardly to be expected. To be sure, he inherited it from his predecessor, whose dismal failure in China still seems to shackle our policy there. . . . When Secretary Acheson, in his letter to Senator Connally, Chairman of the Foreign Relations Committee, fell for the billion-dollar hoax of American arms aid to China, he proved that he had swallowed a familiar Soviet line fed to him by his own staff.

Henry Wallace and Owen Lattimore and the *Daily Worker* and Agnes Smedley have for years been peddling the myth of many billions of dollars' worth of arms given by the United States to China since V-J Day. Secretary Acheson should have known better than to claim that we had furnished such postwar military aid to the tune of $1 billion. As Senators McCarran and Bridges showed, backed by cold figures, this aid totaled less than *one-fourth* of that amount.

During the same period the United States furnished to Soviet Russia and its European satellites, our sworn and avowed enemies today, aid to the tune of $1,453 billion! This figure has been kept from the American people, and is hardly ever to be encountered in the public prints.

It is clear that the southern half of China, still in the Nationalist hands, which also happens to be the rugged part of that great country, is a better return for our postwar investment there than our dismal harvest in Poland, Czechoslovakia, Hungary, Yugoslavia, Rumania, Bulgaria and Albania—not to speak of Russia.

A POSITIVE American policy in China should begin with action, not on the Yangtze, but on the Potomac. If Secretary Acheson would make a fresh start, this course is still open to him:

First, let us have an assistant secretary of state, of the caliber of Stanley K. Hornbeck, a veteran diplomatist, in charge of all Far Eastern affairs in the State Department. That should and would mean a clean sweep of the Teheran-Yalta-Potsdam boys, of the Stilwell set, and of the men involved in the infamous *Amerasia case* (theft of top secret documents in wartime). No sound policy can be built on rotten planks. Without a thorough housecleaning in all the bureaus concerned with our Pacific defenses, no constructive China policy is possible.

Second, let us have a first-rate ambassador in China. At present and for some years past we have had in China a caretaker left behind by Marshall—an unheard-of state of affairs on a vital and decisive front. A prerequisite to any positive policy in China is the replacement of the incumbent—"the ambassador nobody knows"—by an envoy everybody knows and trusts.

Third, let us dispatch a military mission to China, headed by a general of the stature of Mark Clark or Albert Wedemeyer, friendly to the cause of China's independence and whose very name would be a rallying standard for the people of China and a guarantee of great ability, integrity, and authority. Such an officer should be big enough to rise above the narrow West Point tradition, and be ready to enlist the cooperation of General Chennault, whose experience in Chinese aviation is indispensable.

Out of these three initial moves a constructive China policy is bound to grow. A loyal and competent staff in the State Department, an outstanding and experienced embassy in the field, and a brilliant military mission at the front, these three elements in their combined effort must of necessity dictate the steps and shape the course which would eventually redeem the independence of all of China and avert the disaster staring us in the face in the Pacific.

May 1949

SHANGHAI OVER BERLIN

By ISAAC DON LEVINE

[*Late in May 1949 the Council of Foreign Ministers met in Paris in an attempt to settle the differences over Germany through the partial withdrawals of the Allied and Soviet occupation forces to their respective home bases. Since then the issue has remained unresolved, but the fall of Shanghai to the Chinese Reds foreshadowed in 1949, as indicated in this piece, a development that became a real threat only in 1975, the danger of the Philippines being taken over by the Communist camp.*]

IT IS NOT the inspiring airlift which darkens the skies over Berlin. It is the long shadow of Shanghai which hangs over the eerie skeleton of the capital of the once-proud German Empire.

Between Berlin, released for a breathing spell from the iron grip of Moscow, and Asia's queen city of Shanghai sacrificed to the iron grip of the self-same Moscow, world catastrophe may well be in the making.

The shadow of Shanghai hovers over the Big Four as they meet in Paris to seek a settlement of the problem of Germany; it hangs over the Senate debate in Washington on the ratification of the Atlantic Pact; and it extends over the State Department's $1,450 billion program to arm the nations of Western Europe and the Near East.

We can patch up a peace in Germany. We can ratify the Atlantic Pact. We can equip and arm a score of divisions in Europe. But we cannot escape the long shadow of Shanghai, cast by the same monster we uncaged with such confident irresponsibility.

ARE WE ready to withdraw our troops from Germany, by prearranged stages, if necessary? This, above all, is what Moscow wants to know.

It is the heart of the problem facing the Paris conference. If we were as hardheaded as the Kremlin about it we would pose the issue in this form:

Is Moscow ready to withdraw its Red Army troops and fifth columns from Eastern Germany and all the satellite countries, by stages, if necessary?

For, as we wrote here in November 1946, "no lasting peace in the world is possible until the Soviet tide in Europe is rolled back beyond the Vistula." The events of the last three years should have demonstrated to all this elementary truth.

Moscow will make compromises on secondary issues such as the democratic Bonn constitution or the size of its share in the Ruhr production, so long as we leave unimpaired its bridgehead in Central Europe. Stalin knows from rich experience that he can always win against us in diplomatic warfare if only our armed forces can be induced to retire. In the shadow of Shanghai, he can afford to bide his time for the future Germany to coalesce and to ripen for his plucking.

LONG BEFORE Germany becomes a focus of the third World War, we venture to predict, the Philippines will be in danger, Australia will be in desperate need of help, Burma and India, and Indonesia will have been largely engulfed by the Soviet tide sweeping over Asia.

. . . Is it possible that statesmanship has been extinguished in America and that our diplomats will fiddle across the Atlantic while the enemy harvests half of humanity across the Pacific?

June 1949

SIN AND TREASON

By ISAAC DON LEVINE

[*This comment on a major piece contributed by Clare Boothe Luce to* Plain Talk
*(see Book 3, page 145), deals with a problem that is perhaps even more critical
today than it was in 1949. Can foreign policy be divorced from morality? Must
international trade be carried on without regard to human decency and ethical
values? The policies associated with Secretary of State Kissinger's declared
beliefs and the evangelical messages delivered to the world by Aleksandr
Solzhenitsyn have dramatized the underlying issue discussed in "Sin and
Treason."*]

CLARE BOOTHE LUCE, in her dissection of *The Mystery of Our China Policy*,
makes a noble attempt to get to the bottom of the baffling question of our age.
Why do they act that way? is the question which has been posed most frequently during the past twelve months of sensational disclosures.

Mrs. Luce uses China merely as a vehicle to probe a basic moral defect, and
makes a fresh contribution to an analysis of a condition bedeviling many minds.
She would have us believe that most of the trouble which we have been har-
vesting in China and elsewhere is the fruit not of treason but of sin, not of
conspiracy but of vanity.

It is an appealing theory. In a generation in which brother denounces brother, in which veritable chasms divide men of equal goodwill and patriotism, in
which vituperation has become the almost inseparable companion of argument,
it is good to have a voice such as that of Mrs. Luce raised in admonition to
this effect:

"Do not suspect your neighbor! Do not condemn those who are suspect!
Where you see espionage, it is but error. And where you apprehend treason, it
is in reality sin!"

But will this theory stand up in the hard light of inquiry? . . .

Now anyone who has studied totalitarian espionage recognizes that its chief
function is in being a weapon for the formulation of policy. Modern ideological
espionage differs from the old-fashioned military espionage in this respect. The
former is a vital element in setting a nation's course for war or peace, whereas
the latter is largely confined to aiding an enemy in operations when war is
already in progress.

This distinction is immense in scope. Totalitarian espionage may decide the
life of a nation, may help unleash a world war as it did in fashioning the
Hitler-Stalin Pact in 1939. Military espionage may contribute to the additional
destruction of human lives after the outbreak of hostilities.

Whether China is a victim of totalitarian espionage, of treason in our diplomatic services, is an enigma which history may not resolve for a long time. But there is at least sufficient evidence warranting scrutiny before judgment is passed in the charitable spirit of Mrs. Luce.

The *Amerasia* affair, otherwise known as "The State Department Espionage Case," involving the arrest of six officials and journalists in June 1945, in itself provides an acid test of the issue.

As compared with the so-called "pumpkin papers," nearly all of which have been published, the troves of top-secret files found in the offices of the obscure little magazine *Amerasia* and in the homes of its associates, numbering many hundreds of documents, must have furnished a complete mirror of our diplomacy in Asia.

And yet, not a single one of these documents has ever been published. It may very well be that the publication of the stolen *Amerasia* papers would explain most of the mysteries posed by Mrs. Luce and would show how we had come to adopt and follow our disastrous policy in China.

Did Stalin come to Teheran, Yalta, and Potsdam knowing in advance all the cards we held in our hands, familiar with all the moves planned on our diplomatic chessboard? If he did, and there is cogent evidence to that effect from American as well as foreign sources, then the matter cannot be dismissed with an emphasis merely on moral decay and human vanity.

WITHOUT moral decay, it goes without saying, there can be no ideological espionage. The generation of American intellectuals who went out, in the apt phrase of Mrs. Luce, "shopping for a faith," is part and parcel of a worldwide process. Joliot-Curie in France and Lord Haldane in Great Britain are brothers under the skin of their American counterparts. They really went shopping for power, to be sure, in the name of a Utopia to which they alone held the keys. And in the course of this quest, the means became the end. Everything becomes justified for the sake of reaching the end of the rainbow—falsification, oppression, denial of justice, terror, assassination, genocide, slavery, and of course, espionage and treason.

The soil of totalitarianism is this moral degeneration. It is a soil in which the briers of power choke off the blades of conscience. Both sin and treason thrive in it. They who in their pride maintain a vested interest in their past errors and they who are diabolically set upon attaining their ends go hand in hand. . . .

It is one thing to deplore the tragic failure of our wayward and spineless intellectuals who have lost the way to the truth and who lack the character to confess to their sins. It is not only charitable, but practical to help them "get out from under."

It is another thing to confuse these sinners with willful wreckers, with quislings, with men and women trained in espionage by a hostile power. And this is particularly grievous when so much about the Soviet fifth column in our midst remains wrapped in darkness.

For let us face the bitter fact that no truly competent, judicious, and comprehensive inquiry into the field by an unimpeachable and responsible body has ever been undertaken in this country. Neither the Administration nor the Committee on Un-American Activities has met these conditions. The first has been afraid of the skeletons in its closets, the second has undoubtedly indulged on many occasions in headline hunting and hasty verdicts. The various other investigations have produced their crops of sensations and cast shafts of light into the shadowy underground. When it is all added up, however, it is appalling to discover how little even our best minds are conversant with the nature and extent of the phenomenon.

However lurid the reality is, it is crucial that the sinners be not mistaken for conspirators, that the erring be not accused as traitors. Irresponsibility has not been confined to the camp of the totalitarians and their apologists. It has also afflicted the antitotalitarian camp. In both cases it breeds confusion. And confusion is water on the enemy's mill. If we cannot tread our way out of the present intellectual wilderness by seeking and following the discriminating line of truth and fair play which divides sin and treason, we can never reach the safe haven of freedom for all.

The mystery of our policy in China is wrapped in the riddle of our fifth column buried deep inside the enigma of the moral decay eating away at civilization.

July 1949

OUR FIRST LINE OF DEFENSE

By ISAAC DON LEVINE

[*The eleventh hour in the great crisis of American foreign policy in the Far East was striking when the pro-Soviet contingent inside the Department of State stabbed our ally, Chiang Kai-shek's Nationalist China, in the back. The stab was in the form of a report of 1,060 pages issued by Secretary Acheson. Its deadly character and aim are analyzed in the article "Our First Line of Defense."*]

WHEN SECRETARY of State Acheson declared before the Senate Foreign Relations and Armed Services Committees that America's "first line of defense is still in Europe," he exposed the chaos which underlies our foreign policy.

There was room for legitimate argument during the Second World War whether our first line of defense was in Europe or in Asia, in the Atlantic or in the Pacific.

Nazi Germany was a major menace to our security in Europe. Sabre-rattling Japan was an equally imminent threat to our defenses in Asia. Both continents had throughout history been the seats of numerous war-making powers. It was in keeping with tradition that after Pearl Harbor we had to decide where our first line of defense lay. Our strategists chose Europe.

No such choice confronts us in the cold war. The whole pattern of history has changed since 1945—and has indeed made such a choice obsolete. All the first-rate powers in Asia and in Europe have disappeared, all but one. And that one is both European and Asian. It faces America across the Atlantic and across the Pacific at once.

Now, a foreign policy which is not anchored in the primary strategic considerations of national defense rests upon a void. When such a policy is fashioned at a time like this to fit antediluvian conditions, with all of Asia in the throes of a quake and the British Empire agonized by a crisis, it borders on criminal negligence.

With the deluge of the Second World War behind us, our first line of defense is wherever the Communist power is. That should be the keystone of any foreign policy. But if we must deal with geographic concepts in relation to our defense, let us at least deal with postwar realities.

It is arguable whether the people of the United States would go to war should there be a Soviet seizure of power, on the order of the Czechoslovak coup, in Finland or in Norway. But most sober observers would agree that a Communist coup in the Philippines, resulting in the establishment in Manila of a Soviet regime, would drive the American people into a war of national defense.

AGAINST the background of the fatal flaw in Secretary Acheson's concept, his issuance of the White Paper on China acquires an ominousness far transcending the import of its massive documentary contents.

First and foremost is the question: Why the White Paper now? If all of Nationalist China had been overrun by Communist troops, if the Chinese Central Government had ceased to exist, if Nationalist armies of some 1.5 million men were no longer in the field, if Chiang Kai-shek were not rallying our priceless bastions, Korea and the Philippines, to a Pacific defense pact, the timing of Asia's diplomatic explosion could be justified.

But the position of Nationalist China at the beginning of August, on the eve of the release of the White Paper, was grave but not hopeless. It was not as critical as the position of France early in June 1940 when Mussolini delivered his infamous stab in the back.

"The hand that held the dagger has struck it into the back of its neighbor," President Roosevelt declared on that occasion in an address to the graduating class of the University of Virginia.

The position of Nationalist China today is not as critical as that of Japan early in August 1945, after Hiroshima, when Stalin struck at our prostrate enemy, the Mikado's empire, to garner for Moscow the trophies of a victory won with our blood.

In the history of American diplomacy there is no parallel for the Machiavellian actions of Mussolini and of Stalin. The China White Paper sets such a precedent for the first time. For what else does its publication at this stage signify but a stab in the back of a good neighbor and wartime ally?

It is known that China's ambassador in Washington, Dr. Wellington Koo, had called at the White House weeks before the White Paper was issued and posed the following questions, in effect, before President Truman:

"Why should the United States strike a finishing blow with its White Paper at the Nationalist forces while they are desperately struggling to hold the surging Communist armies? Was it the intent of the United States to speed the victory of the Communist elements? And was not the United States officially committed to a policy of containing and combatting Soviet aggression and Communist expansion throughout the world?"

It is known that President Truman was shocked at the ominous significance of the diplomatic weapon which was being forged in the State Department, under the supervision of Philip Jessup, by a sizable contingent of picked officials. His first reaction was, as usual, wholesome. He could not himself see any profit in our stepping on Nationalist China when it was down, although not down and out, and thereby hastening the triumph of Communist arms.

It was hardly reasonable to suppose that at the very moment when Secretary Acheson was pleading with Congress for another appropriation of many billions of dollars for the Marshall Plan, for an Atlantic defense pact, for an additional huge fund to rearm western Europe—all in the name of throttling Communist expansion—he would sponsor an act calculated to help unleash Communist power throughout Asia.

What did happen between the moment of President Truman's revulsion at the project and the day of the publication of the White Paper is still a mystery. It is not the first time, however, that major and crucial policy has been shaped in Washington by the lower echelons of entrenched bureaucracy, overriding the objections or misgivings of the highest authorities.

How and why President Truman came to yield to the Far Eastern "experts" in the State Department will undoubtedly make fascinating reading at some future date. But the step taken by Secretary Acheson has climaxed our unsavory record of Teheran, Yalta, and Potsdam with a leaf from the book of rapacious despots. There was far more justification for Stalin's last-minute attack on Japan and even more extenuation for Mussolini's stab in the back of France than there was for our using at this hour the dagger of the White Paper on sick China.

As a collection of historical documents, the China White Paper is more notable for its omissions than for its contents, filling the tome of 1,060 pages.

Its revelations were woefully short of sensational. Even the long-suppressed Wedemeyer report proved somewhat of a dud. The sensational feature of the White Paper was not in its disclosures, but in its impact. It was received by the country and the world as unmistakable notice that the United States had written Nationalist China off as lost.

It will take a good-sized book to fill in the glaring gaps in the White Paper and to set forth the black record in its entirety.

"This is a frank record," declared Secretary Acheson in his letter transmitting the White Paper to President Truman. "No available item has been omitted because it contains statements critical of our policy or might be the basis for future criticism."

Now let us glance at this frank record.

First, Owen Lattimore, dean of our pro-Soviet China school, whose books cultivated the theory of Chinese Communism as an indigenous and independent democratic movement, had been appointed by President Roosevelt to serve as adviser to Generalissimo Chiang Kai-shek during the war. In the 1,060 pages of the White Paper there is not a single reference to Owen Lattimore or to his important mission.

Second, Lauchlin Currie, one of President Roosevelt's executive secretaries, disclosed in Congressional testimony as having been strongly pro-Soviet, had been sent on two special missions to China. In the voluminous White Paper there is not a single reference to Mr. Currie or his missions.

Third, General Wedemeyer, following the Stilwell fiasco, was dispatched to China to save the military situation in a critical moment. He set up, in cooperation with Generalissimo Chiang Kai-shek, an organization which embraced, under the guidance of American military advisers, a great Chinese force. This smoothly working body was able to effect two major victories over Japanese arms at the height of the war, reversing the tide of Stilwell's days. In the White Paper, which castigates at every opportunity Chiang Kai-shek's noncooperation and the inefficiency and defeatism of the Chinese military, there is not a single reference to the successes of Wedemeyer's mission to the Kuomintang government.

Fourth, Wendell Willkie went as a special representative of President Roosevelt to China in 1942. The White Paper is noteworthy for its omission of Willkie's reports.

Fifth, Donald Nelson, who served as the American head of the War Production Board of China during the war, is another chief of a mission whose reports are absent from the White Paper.

These five items are picked at random from a potential long list of omissions which would require much research and verification. Here is a project for one of the numerous foundations or organizations devoted to the study of our foreign relations.

But will the Institute of Pacific Relations or the Foreign Policy Association or the Council on Foreign Relations, all more or less in the confidence of the State Department, sponsor such a study?

And is it accidental that most of the omissions noted deal with matters affecting Soviet interests in China? On the basis of past records, would it not be rational to suggest that there is a familiar pattern in the omissions in the White Paper?

It is manifest that Secretary Acheson has lost the historic opportunity, which was his six months ago upon assuming the office of Secretary of State, to salvage the bogged-down American foreign policy and to reforge it into a rounded and potent instrument for lasting peace.

The White Paper demonstrates that the ship of the State Department is still manned on its lower decks largely by the same crews which steered us into the treacherous waters of Teheran and Yalta and Potsdam. Regardless of the motives which inspire these craftsmen in diplomacy, they exercise tremendous influence over the staff on the captain's bridge. And Secretary Acheson has shown with the White Paper and with his pronunciamento on America's first line of defense that he is still a captive of disruptive or confused forces.

Almost simultaneously with the publication of the White Paper, Secretary Acheson announced the appointment of an advisory board headed by Dr. Jessup, chief architect of the White Paper, for the formulation of a new constructive policy in China. But how can the American people entrust such an assignment to the person who wielded the dagger which struck Nationalist China in the back?

The premises for a constructive foreign policy are not subject to discovery by any advisory board. They are time-tested and well-known. First, you must know your enemy and gauge the range of his operations. In the present instance, that range is global. Europe and Asia, the North and the South Poles, are all on America's first line of defense.

And second, there must be a will. When we turned over fifty destroyers to Great Britain no advisory board had to be created. There was a will first when we stopped Stalin's aggression in Iran and in Greece. When Berlin was on the point of being swallowed in the Soviet maw, a will gave birth to the airlift.

If we had the will, we could bring our Communist adversary down on the fields of Nationalist China, whose government is more dependent upon us now than ever before, and therefore more amenable to sound advice. We could enable the Chinese to fight for China, and incidentally for America, now rather than have our sons fight and die a decade later to redeem China and to defend America.

We must recognize that the world crisis is indivisible. The threatening economic collapse of Great Britain stems from a political source. The problem of redeeming Germany for the Western world harks back to the same source. The struggle for China as a means of pulverizing Asia springs from the same origin.

If we dared meet the gigantic challenge squarely, we would employ our vast resources to effect—and not by the sword—a fundamental remedy. The present policy of "normalization" of our relations with Moscow was inaugurated by Dr. Philip Jessup when he broached to Gromyko the question of lifting the Soviet blockade of Berlin. All the hopes that were raised in anticipation of the Four-Power conference over Germany have now been dashed to pieces. We had Soviet Russia hanging on the ropes with our airlift. Jessup's move resulted in putting the Soviets back in the same old ring.

At best our present course of "normalization" is calculated to achieve a stalemate, with Moscow in control of nearly half of Western Europe and most of Asia. Such a state of affairs condemns the world to chronic crises, to economic and political fits, and puts a fatal burden upon America.

Instead of re-arming a crippled western Europe, let us disarm the Red Army. This can be achieved at a fraction of the cost of the new arms program by encouraging, through inducements to resettlement, the mass desertion of soldiers and able-bodied men from the Soviet zones which would undermine the Soviet edifice from within.

Let us boldly pick up the banner of Asian liberation and independence. With Japan extinct as a sea power and in our camp, we can wield a weapon against the Soviets in China which would make the Kremlin aggressors run to cover in no time. General MacArthur, moved from Tokyo to Formosa or Chungking, could turn the Japanese weapon to most effective use.

The White Paper is a denial of the existence of a will to save Asia. The White Paper is at best a testimonial to spinelessness and a confession of guilty conduct in the past. It is not a promise of effective action. It is one more alarming token of a colossus adrift, of an America guided abroad by men who would buy precarious peace piecemeal with dollars and more dollars rather than steer the world toward a stable peace with vision, with initiative, with courage, with honor.

September 1949

ON THE ROAD TO CHAOS

By ISAAC DON LEVINE

[*From the fall of 1949, when the Soviets produced and exploded their first atomic bomb, to the summer of 1975, when Soviet nuclear submarines, capable of destroying totally all human habitation a'ong the Atlantic and Pacific coasts, have been lurking close to our shores, the United States has traveled a long, long way on the road to chaos.*]

IT TOOK President Truman's announcement that the Soviet dictatorship is in possession of atomic power to expose in all its nakedness the moral and intellectual poverty of the leadership of the Western World.

For something like a century Britain ruled the waves. It was not until the Kaiser's naval challenge to *Pax Britannica* that world war became inevitable.

The United States ruled the air waves for exactly four years. And the highly precarious *Pax Americana* has now been shattered by the Soviet atomic challenge.

In the glare of the President's bombshell, which burst upon the horizons of an already disordered world with immeasurably greater force than that of the atomic explosion over Hiroshima, the fatal flaws in our present conduct of human affairs stand out more blatantly than ever.

First, we are again invited to put our faith in the United Nations to control the A-bomb. It should now be obvious to all that the international organization which was powerless to stop the tiny puppet Albania, with its population of 1 million, from making war upon Greece, was born crippled at San Francisco. To Moscow the United Nations was never more than a forum for its propaganda and an arena for the waging of cold war. How long must we delude ourselves with hollow optimism?

Second, an agreement to outlaw the atomic bomb, as long as it is in the possession of an outlaw, is bound to remain either a chimera or a snare. The Soviet Government is an outlaw among governments. In a police state where terror rules and all channels of information are in an iron vise, it is inconceivable to have the control and inspection essential to the outlawing of the bomb. How long will it be before our gullible opinion-makers and clergymen realize that Modern Communism is not an idealistic crusade but a Satanic system?

Third, there is the fallacy of relying on the Soviet lack of transoceanic bombers to deliver the monstrous thing to our shores. The Soviet strategy of conquest is not predicated upon any such plan. The sheer possession of atomic power is a

51

source of immense prestige and a colossal whip of intimidation and terror in Soviet hands. With that whip Moscow, using the old artichoke method, would gobble up Western Europe, Asia, Africa, all the while singing lullabies of peace into our ears. After gathering a demoralized world under its own atomic umbrella, the Kremlin's strategy would have North America isolated and at its mercy.

We have reached and taken the last turn on the road of civilization. With pusillanimous helmsmen at the wheel, this may well become the road to chaos.

October 1949

TRUTH AND PEACE

By ISAAC DON LEVINE

[*The farewell issue of* Plain Talk *was going to press at the time President Truman announced the launching of broadcasting stations that would wage "a great campaign of truth" to counteract Soviet propaganda. It was welcome news that the United States would carry to hundreds of millions behind the Iron Curtain, through the Voice of America, Radio Free Europe, and, eventually, Radio Liberty, uncensored and undoctored reports on the state of the outside world. That was a much-needed remedy. But it was even more necessary to administer the "plain, simple, unvarnished truth" to the American people, who were befuddled by misleaders in the press, in the government and in the educational establishments, and were drugged with quack cures that, to this day, under the label of détente, afflict the national mind. In closing the last, the 44th, issue of* Plain Talk, *the editor penned its epitaph with this homily, which remained a cry in the wilderness throughout the ensuing 25 years: "Only those who live by the truth can help free the world with a campaign of truth."*]

PRESIDENT TRUMAN has announced the use of a new weapon in the cold war —the launching of "a great campaign of truth" against Soviet propaganda, "plain, simple, unvarnished truth." But he has not told us who is going to wield that weapon.

It has at last dawned upon our helmsmen in Washington that the Kremlin has garnered one victory after another, in Europe as well as in Asia, with the aid of poisonous propaganda. But does Washington realize that the Soviet vic-

52

tories in Europe as well as in Asia have been greatly facilitated by our own succumbing to the enemy's poison?

"They do not even know what we mean when we say 'democracy,' " President Truman declared in announcing his campaign to make millions "of uninformed or misinformed or unconvinced" people learn the truth about America and Russia.

But who first pinned the label of "democracy" upon the Communist tyranny? The tag which transformed the murderous Kremlin camarilla into a "freedom-loving" power was made in Washington. And how did this come to pass? Simply because we had ourselves swallowed the poisonous propaganda which we are now called upon to counteract in Europe and Asia.

And the effects of that poison on our own system are still very much in evidence. The "softening up" process has been going on for many years and the American mind has been befuddled and bedeviled so long that one may well pose the bald question:

Is American leadership sufficiently recovered from the Soviet poisoning to wage a campaign of unadulterated truth against that propaganda?

Returning from a ten-week survey of conditions in England, France, and Germany, your editor sees America as a doped giant awakening from a long spell of grogginess, trying to shake off the gremlins who have been drugging him. The air is filled with the painful sounds of a groping giant striving to recover the full possession of his mental faculties. When he does, the "plain, simple, unvarnished truth" will become manifest to all, and to Moscow first of all.

For nearly four years this publication has waged an unsparing and unflinching fight against Communist propaganda at home and abroad with "plain, simple, and unvarnished truth." It has been a solitary fight, treated with indifference by the powers-that-be in Washington.

Today President Truman speaks the language with which we launched our crusade four years ago. Today Secretary Acheson strikes keynotes which must sound very familiar to our old readers. The truths which we have proclaimed since October 1946 are being introduced to the American people as a newly discovered weapon to victory in the cold war.

Truth is a mighty weapon—in the right hands. The lie is a mighty weapon, too, as Stalin has demonstrated. If we are to lead the nation out of its perilous pass with a campaign of truth, let us not delude ourselves into thinking that we can do so with Truth, Inc., with a vastly expanded and bureaucratized machine of counterpropaganda.

Only those who live by truth can help free the world with a campaign of truth.

May 1950

BOOK 2

UNDER THE ATOMIC CLOUD

THE PREVENTION OF
ATOMIC WAR

By BERTRAND RUSSELL

[*From the beginning of the atomic age, for over 30 years now, all mankind has been living under the sign of Hiroshima. Fear has infected the world, and consciously or subconsciously the dread of the atom has guided the behavior of men and nations everywhere. Few have been the voices of reason heard in the Western world. Despite his irrational behavior during the last years, when he was in his nineties and a captive of a coterie of fanatical America-haters, Bertrand Russell proved himself a major prophet of the century. The son of Viscount Amberley, born in 1872 to the title of the Earl of Russell, he was already renowned as a philosopher and mathematician when he became an active pacifist during World War I. After visiting Soviet Russia as a member of a British Labor Delegation, he published in 1920 his* Practice and Theory of Bolshevism *in which he excoriated the Soviet despotism as "Asiatic Communism." In 1923 he authored* The A.B.C. of Atoms. *In 1946 he wrote the present article, "The Prevention of Atomic War," which made the rounds of several magazines of national circulation that rejected it for publication. It finally appeared in print in* Polemic, *an obscure British periodical. The editor of* Plain Talk, *who enjoyed Russell's friendship since 1924, did not agree with all the points made in the essay, but was glad to publish it on this side of the Atlantic in February 1947. It stands as an admirable introduction to this selection of reprints on nuclear arms and warfare.*]

THE ATOMIC BOMB has set a problem to mankind which must be solved if any tolerable existence is to be possible for the human race. The problem is that of abolishing large-scale war, not at some distant future date, but quickly, before there has been time for another vast conflict to break out.

If the next great war were to occur within the next two or three years, it would probably lead to a quick victory for the United States and its allies, since no other Power would have atomic bombs. But if there is no war in the near future, there will have been time for Russia to manufacture atomic bombs—and not only Russia, but many other nations, great and small.

It must be assumed that bombs will soon become much cheaper and much more destructive than those dropped on the Japanese. In addition to bombs there is the possibility of spraying large regions with radioactive substances which will exterminate all life in their neighborhood. Given a little carelessness, life on this planet may be made impossible. . . .

It is entirely clear that there is only one way in which great wars can be permanently prevented, and that is the establishment of an international government with a monopoly of serious armed force. When I speak of an international government, I mean one that really governs, not an amiable façade like the League of Nations, or a pretentious sham like the United Nations under its present constitution. An international government, if it is to be able to preserve peace, must have the only atomic bombs, the only plant for producing them, the only air force, the only battleships, and, generally, whatever is necessary to make it irresistible. Its atomic staff, its air squadrons, the crews of its battleships, and its infantry regiments must each severally be composed of men of many different nations; there must be no possibility of the development of national feeling in any unit larger than a company. Every member of the international armed force should be carefully trained in loyalty to the international government. . . .

There is one other method by which, in theory, the peace of the world could be secured, and that is the supremacy of one nation or of one closely allied group of nations. By this method Rome secured the peace of the Mediterranean area for several centuries. America at the moment, if it were bellicose and imperialistic, could compel the rest of the world to disarm, and establish a world-wide monopoly of American armed forces. But the country has no wish for such enterprises, and in a few years the opportunity will be gone.

In the near future, a world war, however terrible, would probably end in American victory without the destruction of civilization in the Western hemisphere, and American victory would no doubt lead to a world government under the hegemony of the United States—a result which, for my part, I should welcome with enthusiasm.

But if, as seems more likely, there is no world war until Russia has an adequate supply of atomic bombs, plans for world peace will have to reckon with Russia and America as roughly equal Powers, and an international government, if it is to be established before the outbreak of an utterly disastrous war, will have to be created by agreement rather than by force.

Short of actual force, however, the government of the United States, with the support of Great Britain and a number of other Powers, could do a great deal towards the creation of an international government. An alliance could be formed, consisting in the first place of all North and South America, the British Commonwealth, France, Belgium, Holland, Scandinavia, and Spain (after dealing with Franco). This alliance should proclaim certain international purposes, and declare its willingness to be joined by any Power that subscribed to those purposes. . . . Every possible effort should be made to induce Russia to become a member of the alliance. In this way international government might grow up gradually.

THERE IS, HOWEVER, a strong body of opinion which favors a different course. Instead of trying to create a strong organization which would at first not include Russia, those who favor this opinion prefer a weak organization, the United Nations, of which Russia is already a member. If this is to be anything more than a weak evasion of the problem, it must be supplemented by a vigorous attempt to alter the constitution of the United Nations.

At present, there is machinery for preventing Finland from attacking Russia, but none for preventing Russia from attacking Finland. There is, in fact, nothing to hinder a Great Power from waging aggressive war, whether against another Great Power or against a small defenseless neighbor. The only wars prevented by the organization of the United Nations are those that are not at all likely to occur.

If the United Nations Organization is to serve any useful purpose, three successive reforms are necessary. First, the veto of the Great Powers must be abolished, and majorities must be declared competent to decide on all questions that come before the organization; second, the contingents of the various Powers to the armed forces of the organization must be increased until they become stronger than any national armed forces; third, the contingents, instead of remaining national blocks, must be distributed so that no considerable unit retains any national feeling or national cohesion. When all these things have been done, but not before, the United Nations Organization may become a means of averting great wars.

All this may seem Utopian, and perhaps it is. Politicians and diplomats are trained in evasion and ambiguity; most of them will prefer to offer a sham which can be obtained with little effort rather than an effective measure that is sure to encounter strenuous opposition, but they will dress up the sham so skillfully that many people will be deceived. Those to whom the survival of mankind is more important than victory in the next election must strive to enlighten the public while there is still time, and perhaps we can succeed.

The men of science, to whom politics is an alien art, find themselves suddenly faced with great responsibilities which they do not know how to fulfill. By their discoveries they have put immense powers, for good or evil, into the hands of ordinary men who have not the training required for a rapid change in age-old mental habits. The political world is complex, and understanding nuclei is no help in understanding diplomacy. But the same intelligence which enabled physicists to understand nuclei will enable them to understand politics, provided they realize that the problems are complex and that slapdash solutions will not work.

Although people speak of the "Big Three" or the "Big Five," there are in fact two Powers, the United States and the U.S.S.R., which far surpass all others in strength. Other Powers are, some of them, satellites of the one, some of the other, some hesitantly neutral. All other important Powers, including Great Britain, are, I think, prepared to acquiesce in the limitations of national sovereignty that are called for by the atomic bomb. This is not owing to any superior wisdom, but because their national sovereignty is already at the mercy of the Big Two. (E.g., the British have to submit to Bretton Woods and the Chinese, unless vigorously supported by America, to the loss of Port Arthur and the South Manchurian Railway.) The problem of establishing an international authority is therefore a problem of which the solution rests with America and Russia.

Russia, since it is a dictatorship in which public opinion has no free means of expression, can only be dealt with on the governmental level. Stalin and Molotov, or their successors, will have to be persuaded that it is to the national interest of Russia to permit the creation of an effective international government.

I do not think the necessary persuasion can be effected except by governments, especially the government of the United States. Nor do I think that the persuasion can be effected by arguments of principle. The only possible way, in my opinion, is by a mixture of cajolery and threat, making it plain to the Soviet authorities that refusal will entail disaster, while acceptance will not.

Persuasion in the United States, where there is freedom of propaganda, is a different matter. If things do not go as we might wish, the fault is usually not with the politicians, though they get the blame; the fault is with public opinion, to which the politicians, as democrats, quite legitimately give way. What is needed is an immense campaign of public education.

The average American voter, very naturally, is annoyed by the way in which the follies of Europe and Asia compel America to go to war; in his emotions he is an isolationist, even when hard facts have convinced his reason that isolationism is no longer practicable. He wishes the Atlantic were still as wide as in Washington's day, and is apt to forget the arguments against isolationism whenever business is prosperous.

To MEET THIS DIFFICULTY it is necessary to bring home, not only to administrators or Congressmen, but to the average American citizen, the dangers to which, within a few years, America will be exposed, and the impossibility of warding off the dangers except by a partial surrender of sovereignty. The first reaction of nine people out of ten will be to urge that America should have more bombs than any one else, so that an attack by any other nation would be obviously folly. The fallacy in this point of view must be made plain to all and sundry.

It must be pointed out that America has already been involved in two world wars as a direct result of the fear of being involved: both in 1914 and in 1939 Germany would not have gone to war if America had pronounced in advance against neutrality. It must be made clear that the same thing would inevitably happen again: a war between Russia and China, or between Russia and Great

Britain, would be sure to involve the United States. Next, the utter disaster of an atomic war must be made clear, and it must be demonstrated that there is no defense against a surprise attack.

Finally it must be proved that there is no hope in Kellogg Pacts, declarations of universal good will, alliances, or paper prohibitions of the use of atomic bombs. All this must be set forth in speech and in writing throughout the length and breadth of the land, by men having no motive except public spirit and the hope that the world in which they have lived may still exist in their children's time. . . .

The policy most likely to lead to peace is not one of unadulterated pacificism. A complete pacifist might say: "Peace with Russia can always be preserved by yielding to every Russian demand." This is the policy of appeasement, pursued, with disastrous results, by the British and French Governments in the years before the war that is now ended.

I myself supported this policy on pacifist grounds, but I now hold that I was mistaken. Such a policy encourages continually greater demands on the part of the Power to be appeased, until at last some demand is made which is felt to be intolerable, and the whole trend is suddenly reversed. It is not by giving the appearance of cowardice or unworthy submission that the peace of the world can be secured.

In dealing with the Soviet Government, what is most needed is *definiteness*. The American and British Governments should state what issues they consider vital, and on other issues they should allow Russia a free hand. Within this framework they should be as conciliatory as possible. They should make it clear that genuine international cooperation is what they most desire. But although peace should be their goal, they should not let it appear that they are for peace at any price. At a certain stage, when their plans for an international government are ripe, they should offer them to the world, and enlist the greatest possible amount of support; I think they should offer them through the medium of the United Nations.

If Russia acquiesced willingly, all would be well. If not, it would be necessary to bring pressure to bear, even to the extent of risking war, for in that case it is pretty certain that Russia would agree. If Russia does not agree to join in forming an international government, there will be war sooner or later; it is therefore wise to use any degree of pressure that may be necessary. But pressure should not be applied until every possible conciliatory approach has been tried and has failed. I have little doubt that such a policy, vigorously pursued, would in the end secure Russian acquiescence.

The issue is the most momentous with which mankind has ever been faced. If it is not solved, war will exterminate the civilized portion of mankind, except for such remnants as may have been engaged in exploring the Antarctic continent or investigating the theology of Tibetan Lamas. These will be too few to reestablish civilized communities.

If mankind, in the course of a millenium or two, slowly climbs back to its present intellectual level, it is to be presumed that it will again inflict a similar catastrophe upon itself. If any of the things that we value are to survive, the problem must be solved. How it can be solved is clear; the difficulty is to persuade the human race to acquiesce in its own survival. I cannot believe that this task is impossible.

February 1947

Our Atomic UNRRA

By Isaac Don Levine

[*The world-shaking issue of atomic power that Bertrand Russell described as "the most momentous with which mankind has ever been faced," was frivolously dropped into the lap of a gullible freshman Senator from Connecticut, Brien McMahon, in 1945, a few months after his election to the upper chamber of Congress. For the next two years, McMahon, as Chairman of the Senate's Special Committee on Atomic Energy, was a principal figure in a campaign for an atomic policy based on the belief, to cite McMahon's later confession, "that Russia and the world should get the secrets of atomic energy in time." Another protagonist of that campaign was David E. Lilienthal, whose nomination to head the United States Atomic Energy Commission was a subject of bitter national controversy for months. There arose the alarming prospect that Washington would turn over to the United Nations the control of atomic power, tantamount to a giveaway to Stalin of America's unique and exclusive weapon. This is the background of the report on "Our Atomic UNRRA" (the latter standing for the U.N. Relief and Rehabilitation Administration—which dispensed free aid to many nations). The fruit of weeks of investigation, this article was widely disseminated and, coupled with Bertrand Russell's stern warnings against the appeasement of the Kremlin, helped arrest the burgeoning spirit of détente aggressively promoted by the influential community of conscience-stricken scientists who had fathered the A-bomb.*]

BEHIND THE RISE of the most powerful commission in the history of the United States, the Lilienthal Atomic Energy Commission, is the still-untold story of our puzzling atomic policy. It is a story with many features of a vast conspiracy woven of the triple webs of atomic espionage, atomic propaganda and atomic diplomacy.

As the five civilian members of the Atomic Energy Commission, appointed by

President Truman under strange circumstances in the confusion of the last days preceding the recent election, face confirmation at the hands of the United States Senate, many questions press for answers. And although some of the pieces necessary to solve the riddle why we set out to establish a kind of atomic UNRRA are not yet available, enough has become known to make a shocking pattern.

When did we first promise the Soviet Government to put the atomic bomb under international control? This is where the mystery begins. Did it occur at Potsdam, in July 1945, three weeks before Hiroshima, when President Truman told Stalin of our magic secret weapon?

If so, was it intended by international control to turn over the atomic discovery to the United Nations Security Council under the existing power of veto, which would allow an aggressor to escape punishment? This enigma was also the crux of the conflict between the Bernard Baruch and Henry Wallace schools of atomic politics.

And was Bernard Baruch's sudden and demonstrative resignation as America's atomic representative to the United Nations caused by his fear that the newly created Commission under David E. Lilienthal, an adherent of the Wallace school, might, by easy stages, turn over the atomic power to Soviet Russia?

Topping these is the crucial question: Who will protect the bomb now? Is the world's mightiest weapon, upon which depends the security of the nation and of free civilization, safe in the hands of a purely civilian body dominated by political innocents?

How did it happen that President Truman had failed to consult either Bernard Baruch or Secretary of State Byrnes in his selection of the five members of the Atomic Energy Commission?

Is it true that Under Secretary Dean Acheson picked the members of the Commission behind the backs of Byrnes and Baruch, the same Mr. Acheson who, with Lilienthal, had sponsored the State Department's Report on the International Control of Atomic Energy which by-passed the issue of the veto and of penalties?

What significance are we to attach to the fact that the majority of the five members of the Lilienthal Commission may be described as Wallace liberals, who might be inclined out of lofty humanitarian motives to let Stalin have atomic power as well as the nullifying power of the veto, i.e., without effective safeguards?

Unequivocal answers to all of these questions would enable the people of the United States to formulate a sober atomic policy in accord with the best interests of our national defense. It must be a policy which would eliminate any possibility of the weapon of world mastery falling into the hands of a tyranny capable of enslaving all humanity.

THREE WEEKS BEFORE the A-bomb burst upon the world with all its incalculable

63

force, President Truman went to Potsdam in the belief that he was bearing with him the secret of the ages. This was the beginning of our incredible adventure in atomic diplomacy. Stalin was to be taken by surprise and in an overwhelmed condition be led meekly into the family circle.

It can now be told that when the President broke the great news to Stalin, the Soviet dictator hardly batted an eye. He received the intelligence in such a casual manner, displaying so little interest in the subject, that both the President and Secretary Byrnes were discomfited and decided Stalin simply did not appreciate the immensity of the atomic discovery. To this day there are personages in Washington who are convinced that Stalin had no previous knowledge of the A-bomb and regarded it as just Yankee big talk.

President Truman, on the other hand, did not know then that for more than two years Soviet espionage had been dogging the steps of our atomic projects, that at least 100 scientific workers in the atomic laboratories and plants in the United States and Canada had during that period conveyed information to Soviet agents, that samples of Uranium-235 had been smuggled to Russia, and that Stalin probably knew more about our atomic achievements than the newly installed President of the United States.

From this moment on, Stalin had the initiative at Potsdam. He seized an opportunity later to reproach the United States and Great Britain for violating wartime agreement which provided for an exchange by the Allies of information on weapons. When Stalin wanted to know why Washington had withheld from Soviet Russia the secret atomic weapon, our spokesmen did not counter by a blunt recital of the numerous Soviet failures during the war to share with the Western Allies the facts and means vital to the conduct of military operations. Instead a vague offer was made to put the atomic bomb under the international control of the United Nations, which was tantamount to giving the A-bomb to Stalin. It must be remembered that Truman and Byrnes had gone to Potsdam—and not Stalin to Washington—after the abject surrenders at Teheran and Yalta, a journey which by its very nature could only spell further appeasement.

This was implemented by the formal declaration of November 15, 1945, by President Truman, Prime Ministers Clement Attlee and Mackenzie King of Great Britain and Canada, in which the A-bomb was offered to the United Nations after "appropriate controls" were set up. Stalin has interpreted it to mean that such controls would be devised under the Charter of the United Nations, without abolishing the right of veto.

Six weeks later came the Moscow Conference. It was on December 27, 1945, that the Moscow agreement was announced under the terms of which Secretary Byrnes had committed the United States to the establishment of a United Nations Commission for Atomic Energy Control. In the months which had elapsed since Potsdam, several other highly significant developments had occurred, all seemingly unrelated to the unquenchable Soviet curiosity about the atomic discovery.

First came the publication by our War Department of the now-famous Smyth report, which assembled in one neat volume the widely scattered labors of many years and countries, giving away something like 97 percent of atomic knowledge. Since Great Britain and Canada shared it with us anyway, was the publication intended for the only other major nation that did not have it, Soviet Russia?

Strangely enough, there soon came an announcement by a group of atomic scientists that the United States had "no enduring monopoly" on the A-bomb. It was followed by Senator McMahon's advocacy of civilian control of atomic energy, later translated into the law through the creation of the Atomic Energy Commission. Senator McMahon has since confessed that he had been motivated by the belief "that Russia and the world should get the secrets of atomic energy in time." The campaign centering around the McMahon Bill was echoed by the inexplicable rise of national committees of atomic scientists, run by professional propagandists, who proceeded to agitate public opinion in the direction of Soviet interests.

To cap it all, came the Molotov warning of November 7, 1945, which was true to the well-established practice of the professional thieves who are the first to raise the cry, "Stop thief!" Molotov warned the western powers against "atomic diplomacy," a warning designed to bludgeon our leadership into a policy of submission to Moscow.

THE CIRCUMSTANCES surrounding the appearance of David E. Lilienthal, of TVA fame, in the atomic picture, and the behind-the-scenes influence which led to the State Department's creation of its own Atomic Committee under the chairmanship of Dean Acheson, may very well merit investigation by the Senate before it confirms the newly established Atomic Energy Commission.

The Acheson committee served merely as a front. All the work was done by a board of consultants under Mr. Lilienthal. This board consisted of five members and a secretary, Mr. Carroll L. Wilson, but actually there was a seventh member, a former aide to Mr. Lilienthal at TVA who was now serving as legislative assistant to Under Secretary Acheson in the State Department. His name was Herbert S. Marks.

Although officially it was a board of five, Mr. Marks left for posterity an unforgettable account of its deliberations under the Arabian Nights title of "Seven Men on a Problem." Fittingly enough, this account appeared in *The New Yorker* of August 17, 1946, filling sixteen columns and describing in detail the labors of the seven superplanners over a period of two months. From this uninhibited interview it is clear that Mr. Marks, if the reporter is to be believed, had a major share in formulating the Acheson-Lilienthal Report which laid the foundation for American atomic policy.

The essential feature of this basic plan, released as a State Department document on March 28, 1946, was its total omission of any punitive provisions for violators of our priceless atomic power. It proposed an international atomic corporation on the assumption that the whole planet was as free, as open, as peace-loving, and as devoted to civil rights and to democratic processes as the United States, Canada, Switzerland, or Sweden. At best, the plan, fashioned under the hammering of ideological crusaders, was Utopian. A less charitable view might raise the question as to the way the State Department proposals dovetailed with the drive behind the McMahon Bill for purely civilian control of atomic energy and the equally powerful drive on the atomic propaganda front to share the colossal power with Soviet Russia.

No wonder that Henry A. Wallace, our arch-Utopian, told a meeting of the Political Action Committee at New York City on April 12, 1946, that President Roosevelt would have approved and supported the Acheson-Lilienthal proposals on atomic energy.

The appointment of Bernard M. Baruch, however, as United States representative on the United Nations Atomic Commission, led to unforeseen consequences. No doubt the revelations of the vast Soviet espionage ring in Canada, as reported by the Royal Commission, had their effect upon Mr. Baruch and his associates. When the latter group had finished with the Acheson-Lilienthal plan and had it drastically revised for submission to the United Nations in June 1946, the American proposal had a set of teeth in it. Not that, in the view of this writer, there can be any effective set of teeth put into any paper agreement with the Soviet Government. But the Baruch committee made the utmost of an inherently bad situation.

What was this situation? For some unaccountable reason America was hell bent upon sharing the atomic weapon with the Soviet dictatorship, and at the very time when Moscow was violating treaties, raping independent countries, launching aggressive moves in various strategic zones, and heaping insult and injury upon the United States. By the time Mr. Baruch took up his assignment, we had committed ourselves to international control of atomic energy, and to its civilian control at home. We had developed a guilt complex under the corrupting influence of insidious Soviet propaganda. We were clearly determined to share the atomic discovery, regardless of the patent fact that no moral or political or purely selfish basis for such sharing existed.

The Baruch plan proposed an international treaty as a prerequisite for the setting up of the Atomic Development Authority which, according to the Acheson-Lilienthal draft, was to be built on UNRRA lines. It provides that the United States is to develop and install atomic power plants for civilian use throughout the world, including Soviet Russia. The Baruch plan provided for various safeguards, the major one of which was the abolition of the veto power in matters relating to atomic energy by the signatories of the atomic treaty, i.e., by the recipients of our atomic gift.

IT IS NO LONGER a secret that the Baruch plan met with terrific opposition. Only part of the story has been given to the American people. Thus it became known only in September that Wallace had addressed a long and confidential letter to President Truman on July 23, in which he assailed the Baruch proposals and distorted them so as to argue in favor of the Soviet view of the issue. But it was not generally known that Under Secretary Acheson spearheaded the inside forces against the Baruch plan. "I state categorically—and the truth can only be provided by Congressional investigation," declared George E. Sokolsky in his syndicated column after the resignation of Baruch, "that Dean Acheson never personally approved of Baruch's rejection of the veto."

The unsolicited and secret Wallace advice to President Truman was strangely followed one day later, on July 24, by the summary rejection by Soviet representative Gromyko of the Baruch proposals "either as a whole or in separate parts." A Congressional inquiry might profitably look into the real authorship of the pretentious communication from the then-Secretary of Commerce to the President.

President Truman himself never faced the issue raised by his representative to the United Nations Atomic Energy Commission and never gave him his unqualified support. The election campaign was on, and the pro-Soviet forces were most active. While Baruch was pressing his fight for the acceptance of his plan, the Acheson-Lilienthal group was organizing behind the scenes to take over the coming Atomic Energy Commission. Even before the adoption of the McMahon Bill, Clare Boothe Luce, who, incidentally, voted for it, had declared on July 17 in the House, that David Lilienthal was "according to rumor slated to be one of the five Atomic Commissioners."

The conflict between Baruch and Wallace burst into the open after the release on September 17 by the latter of his secret letter to the President. It will be recalled that Mr. Baruch requested a retraction of various misrepresentations made by Mr. Wallace, that such a retraction was promised but never delivered.

Towards the end of September at a conference in Chicago of the CIO Political Action Committee; the Independent Citizens Committee of the Arts, Sciences and Professions; and the National Citizens Political Action Committee, this pro-Soviet bloc joined the fray on the side of Mr. Wallace. The Chicago meeting adopted a platform in which the Baruch plan was assailed on the basis of the misrepresentations which Mr. Wallace had originally submitted to the President.

While the Baruch-Wallace controversy was holding the stage, the Atomic Energy Commission was being formed without benefit of publicity. It has been established that President Truman did ask Mr. Baruch, in the course of two calls made by the latter at the White House, to suggest his candidates to head the Atomic Energy Commission. One of these conferences took place in the presence of Secretary Byrnes. Mr. Baruch proposed President Karl Compton of the Massachusetts Institute of Technology or President James B. Conant of Harvard. These nominees refused to take the post.

About this time a large American concern which had manufactured precision machinery used in the making of the A-bomb, received an order from the
Soviet Purchasing Commission for approximately $1.5 million worth of equip-
ment, accompanied by specifications and blueprints which could only have
been stolen in the United States or Canada. This shocking revelation is known
to have been brought to the attention of Mr. Baruch and his associates. It is no
longer a secret that Mr. Baruch used his influence to stop the execution of this
order, which made him the special target of the Soviet diplomats as well as
the pro-Soviet elements in our midst.

Late in October the make-up of the new Atomic Energy Commission became
known to a source who had it directly from the White House. The information
was conveyed to Bernard Baruch, who could not believe it. The President had
not consulted him about any of his selections. Secretary Byrnes was too pre-
occupied with the meeting of the Council of Foreign Ministers to keep in
touch with the matter.

On the morning of October 28, at the height of the pre-election excitement,
The Boston Post published an exclusive story by its Washington correspondent,
Robert L. Norton, announcing President Truman's selection of Lilienthal as
chairman of the Atomic Energy Commission and correctly naming the other
members, with one exception.

"None of the members of the commission are well-known national figures,"
reported Mr. Norton. "Whether or not these appointments would be approved
by the Senate is problematical. It is stated here that Bernard M. Baruch, who
is responsible for the American plan for control of the atomic bomb, was not
consulted on the appointments."

Secretary Byrnes was informed that morning of the composition of the Commission. At first he would not believe it, as he, too, had not been consulted by
the President. Yet his own Under Secretary, Dean Acheson, was the architect
of this Commission.

When assured of the authenticity of the information, Secretary Byrnes called
the White House for an appointment to see the President. The conference was
set for the noon hour that day. At eleven o'clock President Truman received
the press and announced to the country his appointments to the Atomic Commission.

Secretary Byrnes did not call on the President that noon.

So well prepared was Mr. Lilienthal for his new duties, which he was to
assume only on January 1, 1947, that, on the day following his appointment, he
announced from Washington that the Atomic Energy Commission would take
over the Army's atomic project. And as his first step, Mr. Lilienthal named a
temporary staff which included Herbert S. Marks, Acheson's assistant, and
Carroll L. Wilson, both of whom had served on the original Acheson-Lilienthal
board.

Simultaneously Mr. Lilienthal came out in a public address with strong and well-taken criticisms of the Baruch plan, arguing that an international treaty would not provide the needed security. He went on to contend with considerable force that inspection as a sole safeguard would be quite unworkable. And then, strangely enough, Mr. Lilienthal went back to his original visionary scheme of a world corporation under an international authority composed of "the elite of the scientific world." That such a class would also be the elite of political innocents, ideally misfitted to cope with totalitarian chicanery, Mr. Lilienthal omitted to state.

WHETHER IT WAS DUE to the American refusal to fulfill the Soviet order for atomic instruments or to the outcome of the November election or to the victory of the Acheson-Lilienthal combine resulting in a commission which was believed to favor sharing the atomic secrets with Russia, there followed, late in November, an apparent about-face on the part of the Kremlin. Mr. Molotov unexpectedly came out for international "inspection" and made one of his famous equivocal statements on the veto which was hailed by our gullible commentators as a reversal of the Soviet policy of the previous July.

In the meantime, the United Nations Atomic Commission, which had before it the Baruch plan, was to finish its tenure on December 31 and to be reconstituted on the rotation system in 1947. Mr. Baruch pressed for action in the face of dogged Soviet resistance, which he finally achieved on December 30. His plan, with Russia abstaining, was finally reported out to the Security Council. This really terminated Mr. Baruch's ambassadorship to the United Nations, unless President Truman had offered to reappoint him as deputy on atomic affairs to serve with Mr. Warren Austin, United States delegate on the Security Council.

President Truman made no such offer. Mr. Baruch then called the President. The conversation which ensued would make a gem in the story of our atomic politics. Mr. Baruch informed the President of his strange status, indicating that the question of disarmament was scheduled for early discussion before the Security Council. The President listened and said nothing. Mr. Baruch then asked what the President wanted him to do, pointing out that he had no intention of passing out of the atomic picture quietly. Still the President made no response. When Mr. Baruch declared that he would have to make his resignation public and wanted to know what to do about it, the President replied that he, Baruch, knew best what to do. On January 4, Mr. Baruch presented his resignation at the White House. As was generally reported, the President was in, but he did not receive his atomic envoy. Baruch then handed in his resignation to Secretary Byrnes.

ON JANUARY 1, 1947, the fabulous two-billion-dollar atomic empire, extending over eighteen states, including a number of great plants with a total personnel of 43,700, was transferred from the War Department to the civilian Atomic Energy Commission. A new chapter in the most revolutionary discovery

69

in history was about to open, a chapter which promised to lead to an atomic crisis.

Had Henry Wallace been President of the United States, the character of the Atomic Energy Commission, with one possible exception, could hardly have been any different. In fact, this is revealed by the reception given to the Truman appointments by *The New Republic* in the very issue in which Henry A. Wallace announced, as editor-elect, that he wanted *The New Republic* "to be a window on the future . . . always in terms of action."

Anticipating this assignment of serving as a "window on the future," the editors of our leading organ of innocent confusion hailed the Truman appointments as a triumph. "The men whom Truman chose, in a moment of good judgment, guarantee that the victory is solid and complete," crowed Wallace's associates. No doubt as to the completeness of the victory, but whose victory? And as to Truman's "good judgment," how strange that the real architect of the Commission, Dean Acheson, received no credit at all for the feat.

Regarding the appointment of David E. Lilienthal as chairman of the Atomic Commission, *The New Republic* could find no other words than to say, "the only possible adjective applicable to this choice is 'perfect.' " It went on to add that "for the other two members, Sumner Pike and William W. Waymack, the drama critics' word 'adequate' is woefully insufficient." About the one scientist on the Commission, Dr. Robert E. Bacher, the mouthpiece which Wallace elected to make his own went out of the way to "praise God" for "the integrity of his social philosophy." It should be stated in all fairness that it also bestowed its blessings upon the one conservative member of the Commission, Rear Admiral Lewis L. Strauss.

In its exultation, *The New Republic,* true to its tradition of gullibility in international affairs, pointed to the inner nub of the whole matter. "By an intelligent policy for making scientific information available," it wrote, "the Commission . . . can make known to scientists of other nations those basic facts which, once understood, lead with the inevitability of a geometric proposition to one conclusion, the one which Acheson and Lilienthal were constrained to reach seven months ago."

The Acheson-Lilienthal conclusion, as given in the State Department Report, dealt with the disclosure of information as an essential of international action. It proposed the division of "our secret information into three categories" and their release by easy stages.

"When the plan is in full operation there will no longer be secrets about atomic energy," are the concluding words of the Acheson-Lilienthal Report. "We believe that this is the firmest basis of security; for in the long term there can be no international control and no international cooperation which does not presuppose international community of knowledge."

The plan, it cannot be too strongly emphasized, provided no punishment for violators of the peace, for no abolition or modification of the veto power. If

Moscow had secretly devised and prepared a plan for making the United States set up an atomic UNRRA, with the idea of foisting it upon a gullible America through its innumerable "fronts," it could hardly have differed in this respect from the Acheson-Lilienthal plan.

Now who are the men entrusted with the secret of the atomic bomb and with our development of atomic energy the world over? Are they mostly persons representing the Baruch school standing for the abolition of the veto, i.e. for penalties, in international control of atomic power? Or are they largely of the school believing that Stalin's dictatorship is a new kind of democracy, and that we should share with it the almost unlimited riches of atomic energy?

Although Dean Acheson has no official connection with the Atomic Energy Commission, he remains one of the spiritual parents of our atomic UNRRA. Moreover, as Under Secretary he will be in charge of international atomic relations. Where does Mr. Acheson stand? Like Secretary of Commerce Averell Harriman, he has learned from bitter experience the true nature of the Soviet dictatorship and the impossibility of dealing with it on a give-and-take basis. But he has yet to acquire a real insight into the Soviet fifth column in our midst and in his own official environment in Washington.

David E. Lilienthal, the chairman of the Atomic Commission, who has been called by Harold Ickes "the busiest propagandist the United States has ever produced," is a man whose loyalty to this country could not be questioned and whose ability as an executive is widely and justly recognized. Yet Mr. Lilienthal has a record as an "innocent" in the worldwide jungles of Soviet policies which has been matched by many eminent leaders, such as that of the late Neville Chamberlain in the diplomatic jungle of Ribbentrop and Hitler, and that of the astute Churchill himself in the dark Tito-Stalin woods.

The record shows, and an entire volume of Hearings Before the Special Committee on Un-American Activities, as well as more recent testimony corroborates it, that right under the nose of Director Lilienthal of the TVA widespread Communist activities had been carried on for years. Mr. Lilienthal himself was sufficiently innocent to act as sponsor and speaker for the Southern Conference for Human Welfare, known as a Communist front. His daughter Nancy, an employee of the Department of Labor and a member of the United Public Workers, a Communist-dominated union, only recently displayed her strong pro-Soviet attitude. At the beginning of December 1946, at a meeting of her local, a proposal had been made to endorse the resolution of the Atlantic City CIO convention condemning Communism. The fight against the endorsement was led, with success, by Nancy Lilienthal. It may be that Nancy's outlook had been conditioned not by her father, but by her mother. For Mrs. Lilienthal is reliably reported to have belonged, in the middle thirties, to several "front" organizations.

Mr. William Wesley Waymack, who had acquired distinction as the editor of the *Des Moines Register and Tribune,* is one of those liberals who represent a cross between the late Wendell Willkie and Henry A. Wallace. He is a natural believer in the goodness of man, even the men in the Kremlin. It was the owner of his paper, Mike Cowles, who accompanied Willkie on his one-world voyage, originally designed as Soviet propaganda, to promote Stalin's campaign for a second front, and whose magazine sponsored Elliott Roosevelt's more recent flight into Stalin's dizzying political stratosphere. Mr. Waymack's incurable innocence in matters pertaining to Moscow is typical. He joined organizations, such as the Russian War Relief, the Committee for Medical Aid to Russia, the Institute of Pacific Relations, and that strange outfit fathered by Louis Dolivet first under the name of Free World and lately as Americans United for World Organization.

Mr. Sumner Pike, ecstatically described by Jerome Frank in *The New Republic* as a Republican businessman who is a good poker player possessing infinite charm, and who had served as an assistant to Harry Hopkins after making a fortune in Wall Street, is a man without a record on Soviet issues, although he has made his pilgrimage to Soviet Russia. Perhaps this is what *The New Republic* had in mind when it said of Messrs. Waymack and Pike that they are "precisely the types with precisely the backgrounds for a job of such overwhelming importance," and that would also go for the "social philosophy" of the young Dr. Robert E. Bacher, who as a physicist ranks among the foremost in the United States.

DOMINATED BY INNOCENTS of the Wallace stripe, the Atomic Energy Commission is bound to attract a personnel raised in the same pseudo-liberal school of thought on international questions. One of the key men in the new Commission is Herbert S. Marks, who had been attached to the Acheson-Lilienthal board. Mr. Marks, a native of Pennsylvania and honor graduate from Harvard, had served for five years as counsel to the TVA under Lilienthal.

While in the State Department, Mr. Marks is known to have held "liberal" views on the subject of Soviet Russia, similar to the ones which his chief, Dean Acheson, tried to promulgate at first in our foreign relations. No one has ever impugned the loyalty or patriotism of Mr. Marks, but one witness before the Un-American Activities Committee did link him with alleged pro-Communist activities. The witness was Mrs. Muriel S. Williams, of Chattanooga, Tennessee, a clerk in the TVA and a self-admitted member of the Communist Party. Mrs. Williams testified on July 6, 1940, in the course of an interrogation on various persons identified with pro-Communist activities, as follows:

Mr. Barker: And Herbert Marks, you know Herbert Marks?

Mrs. Williams: Yes.

Mr. Barker: And you attended meetings with Herbert Marks?

Mrs. Williams: Well, you see when you say this meeting business—yes.

Mr. Marks has also been a member of the National Lawyers Guild, which is controlled by Communists and from which Adolph A. Berle, Jr., Robert Jackson, Ferdinand Pecora, and other eminent jurists had resigned in protest.

Three days after the Atomic Commission began to function, a general advisory committee of scientists was set up. In his absence, J. R. Oppenheimer was elected to be chairman of this group. Now Dr. Oppenheimer is recognized as one of the discoverers of atomic power and builders of the A-bomb. He had served as one of the members of the board of consultants in the preparation of the Acheson-Lilienthal Report.

Politically, Dr. Oppenheimer is an innocent of innocents. As far back as April 1940 he had joined a Communist front committee which defended New York City public school teachers charged with Communist activities. He was a member of the American Committee for the Protection of Foreign-Born, one of the most notorious "fronts." He was reported to be a subscriber to *People's World*, the California counterpart of the *Daily Worker*, an official Communist publication.

THE REPORT OF THE CANADIAN Royal Commission, which lifted a corner of the curtain hiding the enormous network of Soviet atomic espionage, should be made compulsory reading for all atomic scientists, from Albert Einstein to the student in physics or chemistry. It reveals the incredible political naïveté of our best scientific minds. It also shows a frightening moral degeneracy among idealists fallen under the spell of totalitarian propaganda.

That our own atomic scientists, including some identified with the Lilienthal Commission, have been either victims of or innocent participants in the pro-Soviet atomic propaganda campaign waged in this country is beyond dispute. The role played by such propaganda in the shaping of our blundering atomic policy may properly be the subject of a separate investigation. It is part of that overall design which would surrender to the world's leading despotism the key to global domination.

The American people have a right to know the stark truth about the politics of the atom. They have a right to demand of Congress that it turn the searchlight upon the influences which shaped our atomic behavior. The dark links between the Canadian spy ring and its American partners must be exposed. The pro-Soviet propaganda brigade must be investigated. Above all, the American people should get an answer to the two-billion-dollar question:

What is to prevent the Soviet Government and its puppets from expelling our inspectors and technicians—under the UNRRA precedents already set by Tito —after we have developed and installed atomic energy plants in their countries?

February 1947

73

WHO ARE THE A-BOMB SPIES?

By HOWARD RUSHMORE

[*When President Truman told Stalin at the Potsdam Conference in July 1945 of the unprecedented secret weapon which the United States had developed, the Soviet leader, to the surprise of all those present, dismissed the matter with a shrug of the shoulders. Truman did not know that a network of Stalin's spies, beginning with Dr. Klaus Fuchs and Professor Clarence Hiskey, had been on the inside of the hush-hush Manhattan Project that was charged with the making of the A-bomb. While influential public figures were openly advocating sharing our atomic secrets with the Kremlin, its underground sources were supplying Stalin with invaluable stolen data. Plain Talk was aware of the awesome dimensions of Soviet espionage (see Book 4, GLOBAL SPIDERWEB). In January 1948, more than two years before Professor Hiskey of the Brooklyn Polytechnic Institute was indicted in the District of Columbia for contempt of Congress, Howard Rushmore, a former member of the staff of the Communist Daily Worker, wrote this revealing vignette in which the main character is introduced by his initials. As for the other figure, the Canadian-born Arthur Adams who in 1946 slipped away from FBI agents that had him under surveillance, the White House would not authorize his arrest. The reason given by the State Department, as disclosed by Oliver Pilat in his book The Atom Spies was "that working up a national spy fever would not contribute to pending efforts on the part of the United States to reach a decent postwar understanding with the Russians." Those efforts were still pending in 1975.*]

A PROFESSOR of a private technical school in Brooklyn gathers his papers together, takes a subway to meet his wife who runs a small dress shop a few blocks away.

In the swanky area of Manhattan's Madison Avenue, a neat looking blonde puts the diamonds away in her jewelry store and closes up for the evening. Nearby, a vice-president of an important electrical manufacturing company is still at work.

Over on plushy West End Avenue, a well-to-do doctor gives a patient advice on stomach ulcers. At Pennsylvania Station, the daughter of a Wall Street millionaire arrives from Washington for a weekend rest from her Federal job.

Under ordinary circumstances, this would be a cross-section of life in America—of people at work, at play, average people in our democratic society.

However, these persons, unmolested in the daily pursuit of liberty and happiness, are members of the most dangerous spy ring in the history of the United States.

For three years they helped Stalin's ace agent attempt to steal the secret of our atom bomb. In some measure they succeeded.

The professor, working for the Chicago division of the atomic project, was discovered by the FBI giving secret data, in 1943, to a Russian undercover agent going under the name of Arthur Adams.

In the FBI files in Washington are complete records of the professor's activity in this line. This professor, whose initials are C. H., was never arrested.

His wife, M. H., used her dress shop as a "mail drop" for her husband and more than 100 other persons for two years. She was the recipient of atomic data from Oak Ridge and Los Alamos. Her telephone was tapped, her mail intercepted, her actions photographed by security agents during the war years.

M. H. relayed the atomic data to the owner of the Madison Avenue jewelry store, a woman who was the only foreign-born contact on Adams' list of confederates. She, in turn, would visit Adams at the Peter Cooper Hotel, 39th Street and Lexington Avenue.

This store owner would bring to the Soviet agent the various atomic data sent to the "mail drop" of M. H., which was in Brooklyn.

Adams would then pass the precious data to the Soviet Embassy via two methods. One was through the electric company's vice-president, whose last name begins with B. The other was through the daughter of the millionaire, whose initials are J. H.

The millionaire's daughter would take some of the documents stolen from Los Alamos, Chicago, and Oak Ridge in her overnight bag on her return trips to Washington.

The material then went by courier direct to the Soviet Embassy.

The business executive, whose firm made radar equipment for the Army and Navy during the war, would take atomic data in his briefcase and give it to a Russian official who used his Amtorg connections to visit the electrical company and pick up the contents of the briefcase.

On West End Avenue, the wealthy doctor would send code messages to Soviet Russia, giving details of Adams' progress.

THIS ISN'T cloak-and-dagger mystery stuff. These are facts, obtained by investigators who worked for two years trailing, photographing, and tapping telephone calls of Adams and his confederates.

There are many other members of this spy ring, none of whom, at this writing, has been arrested.

It is now common knowledge in inner press circles that J. Edgar Hoover, who used more than 200 of his best agents to track down the facts, pleaded with the White House and the State Department to allow the arrest of members of the most dangerous spy ring in America's history.

Not even Adams was molested. While he served Stalin's cause here and had accounts in twelve New York banks ranging into six figures, the Soviet spy was "employed" at a Fifth Avenue Communist record shop at the salary of $75 a week. The initials of this concern, which provided Adams with a cover, are K. R.

No one knows where Adams is now. What is known is that he and his ring did obtain invaluable atomic data. What is known is that dozens of American citizens involved in espionage and guilty of treason, have never been arrested.

In Brooklyn, the professor teaches his science class. . . . In Manhattan, the business executive figures up his income tax. . . .

January 1948

BULLITT'S WARNING

By WILLIAM C. BULLITT in *The Great Globe Itself* (1946)

[*William Christian Bullitt, whose mission to Moscow in 1919 as President Wilson's special envoy made history, perceived early the Soviet role in the nuclear age and sounded this prophetic warning in 1946. Having served as the first United States ambassador to the Soviet Union, Bullitt acquired an unequaled understanding of the nature of the Communist dictatorship in the Kremlin. That is evidenced in his book, a forgotten classic, from which these lines were cited in* Plain Talk *in April 1948. Bullitt had regarded as disastrous the policy of appeasement leading to Teheran and Yalta that his patron, President Franklin Delano Roosevelt, had pursued. It ended with F.D.R.'s rudely breaking all relations with Bullitt, severing a friendship of many years. Bullitt died on February 15, 1967, in Paris, where he had served as United States ambassador to France for five years.*]

THE SOVIET UNION remains a totalitarian dictatorship, controlled by men who, of their own volition, by their own will, deliberately and consciously, have chosen to declare themselves the enemies of all peoples who live in freedom. Those men will not recoil from using the atomic bomb for reasons of humanity. If they had it now, and we did not have it, they would be using it now to impose their dictatorship on all the world. They will recoil from using it only for fear of overwhelming retaliation. There will be no true peace on earth, but only an armistice, so long as that privileged and persecuting caste controls the peoples of the Soviet Union. . . . We can build up such moral and physical force against them by uniting the democracies of the world that, when they succeed in manufacturing the atomic bomb, they will not dare to use it, because they will fear to use it. But until the peoples of the Soviet Union control their own government and live like ourselves in freedom and democracy, they will not be permitted by their masters to live with us in peace as fellow citizens of a united world.

WE KNOW that we can get peace only by the extension throughout the earth of the area of democracy, freedom, and human decency. If our government, in the name of seeking peace, continues to let that area be conquered, it will prepare for us not peace, but a desperate war against overwhelming forces of Communist-driven slaves.

MUST IT BE WAR?

By GEORGE HAMILTON COMBS

[*With some slight updating, the debate between George Hamilton Combs and H. R. Knickerbocker, published in 1948, goes on to this day among thinking citizens throughout the United States. Mr. Combs, for years a prominent radio news analyst, a native of Kansas City, a former Democratic Congressman, took the view that the conflict with the Soviet power was irreconcilable because "the driving force of Communism" came "from the deep springs of Russian nationalism."*]

ON A HOT NIGHT late this summer eight men, each expert in some field of foreign affairs, were attending a New York dinner party. The conversation skittered up and down the scale of world affairs and finally slid around to Russia, where it stayed. After an hour of desultory talk, the host took an informal poll of his guests as to whether they expected war with Soviet Union, and if so, in how long a time.

One man believed there was a good chance of avoiding war. Seven thought war inevitable.

Of those who feared war could not be averted, two thought it fairly remote —that is, six or eight years away. The others expected it sooner. The median guess was three years, or about the time the U.S.S.R. is expected to go into heavy production of the atom bomb.

Now these speculations are not intrinsically important, even if the opinions were informed, reasoned conclusions drawn from careful study of the world situation. The importance of the estimates derives chiefly from the fact that they mirror American opinion. A large preponderance of American thought accepts, if it is not reconciled to, the ineluctable nature of the threat. We as a nation think war is coming. We even fix the date—roughly about 1952. If we are young enough, we keep our uniforms in mothballs. We are not sanguine about living long lives.

But here is the dismaying paradox: expecting war, we are willing to let it be fought on the other fellow's timetable. Bowing to the virtual certainty of war, we will not face the logical challenge of our own beliefs.

Sentimentally, we reject the duty of preparing to wage war *at that moment best calculated to serve our national interest.* Fascinated and paralyzed by so hideous a prospect, we refuse to think in terms of how and when and on whose terms that war should be prosecuted.

Deep in our hearts most of us feel about like this: Soviet Russia is intent upon either world conquest or its equivalent, Communist world revolution. We cannot allow this—hence war must come. Russia is not prepared for war now. She is still exhausted from the last struggle and she does not yet possess the ultimate weapons. Therefore, she will wait until she can be fairly sure of winning . . . and we fairly sure of losing.

Q.E.D.?

But since we are incorrigible romantics, we shy away from the duty of capping our deduction with its dread conclusion. Every tug of humanitarianism and every pull of decency hauls us away from a simple mental operation. We are reluctant to formulate even a *contingent* decision: to act at that time when the dangers of delay counterbalance the diminishing chances of peace. Of this prudence we will have none. Not even coldly calculated tables of probability will sway us from our determination to be the victim of aggression, a form of political masochism which, however noble, may also be fatal to our very existence.

BUT, YOU SAY, I don't accept the basic premise of war's inevitability. How then can I be driven to concurrence in a conclusion I find remarkably distasteful? Space is too limited to permit of elaboration of already familiar arguments, but a summary might be useful.

First, the doctrine of inevitability is implicit in the structure of the Lenin-Stalin philosophy. World revolution is the keystone of Communist dogma. Interlarded in every Lenin instruction and every Stalin homily to the Communists are references to the winning of world power by force and violence.

Wrote Lenin: "We live not only in a state but in a system of states, and the existence of the Soviet Republic next to a number of imperialist (capitalist) states for a long time is unthinkable. In the end, either the one or the other will have the better of it. . . . Until that end comes, a series of most terrible conflicts between the Soviet Republic and the bourgeois states is inevitable. This means that the . . . proletariat, if it wants and will rule, must prove this also by its military organization."

In short, all Soviet policy is based upon the belief that war must come. Any policy so conditioned will look solely to the selection of the most propitious moment to join the issue.

Moreover, there is internal evidence that Russia believes the climax is imminent. Only a few months ago she banished to the outer darkness one of her foremost economists, who had the hardihood to warn that American capitalism was not necessarily on its last legs at this particular moment. The Kremlin has counted on American economic collapse as the signal for its assertion of Communist hegemony in Europe and Asia. Soviet Russia must also be mindful of the stern admonition of Lenin that the bourgeois countries would go to war as a sort of last despairing gasp of capitalism. So, whether in the belief that her historic moment has dawned or that she must forestall the last bloody spasmodic lunge of capitalism, she proceeds, or seems to proceed, on the dogma of war's certainty . . . and has made her dispositions accordingly.

SECONDLY, we may well examine the record of the last few years for evidences of her plan to deal with the world unilaterally. Without dredging up contemporary history, we can safely generalize that almost no step she has taken is consistent with a program of international amity. On the contrary, every such step has been consonant only with the objective of foisting Soviet control on both Europe and Asia, a program we could no more view with equanimity, as the diplomats say, than we could accept Nazi hegemony in the Old World.

It can lead only to surrender—or to war. For the only hope of stopping Soviet imperialism in Europe is to administer it such a crushing nonmilitary defeat as will drive the Kremlin to war before the full dimensions of the disaster have had time to materialize, or the results to harden into permanent Soviet catastrophe.

By this standard, the German problem becomes insoluble. No matter what expedient adjustments may be made of the Berlin blockade, the interests of the two forces in Germany are so diametrically opposed that neither can afford to yield any large measure of position or policy.

Similarly, if the Marshall Plan is given time to work, the moment of supreme opportunity—the hour of Europe's chaos—will have passed for Stalin. There is no risk too great, no adventure too bold, if it will dissipate the chances of Western economic recovery. True, there is here a delicate matter of timing. The Marshall Plan must be defeated, but it would be better if overt hostilities did not explode until the Soviets are ready for war. Within the context of a two- or three-year struggle, twin objectives must be reached: the frustration of democratic recovery and the readying of the Soviet Union for battle.

Recently Edwin James, writing in *The New York Times* from Paris, pointed out that the Western Powers have underestimated Moscow's plans and that we err gravely if we think the leaders are bluffing in their European expansionism. Reflecting the nearly unanimous view of European diplomats that war is unavoidable, Mr. James however points out that some Soviet leaders quite sincerely believe that the United States has long planned war against the U.S.S.R.

While this might seem to pass the burden of persuasion to us, the Soviet attitude is far too intransigent to yield to polite reassurances from Washington. In the basic Communist dogma of "capitalism's last death-rattle," the idea of inevitable war is so deeply imbedded that it cannot be erased by either democratic word or deed. If the demobilization of the American Army, the mothballing of the American Navy, and the dismantling of the American Air Force did not convince the Communists of our good faith, there is little hope that hearty words of friendship will accomplish it. But one suspects some psychological rooting of this fear. It probably is the articulation of Communism's own avowed aim of world revolution and of Lenin's blunt assertion that the two worlds could not coexist. It is easy to translate this into a morbid fixation about the sinister purposes of one's enemy, for such we have certainly become in the Soviet lexicon.

Within three years' time, or less, Soviet Russia will have vastly improved her strategic position and patched up most of her war industries. She will doubtless be manufacturing the atomic bomb and turning out more German Snorkel-type submarines, against which we have developed no defense. Our control of the seas will be materially menaced. Using B-29s as models and the engineering brains of her captive German scientists, she will be making fleets of strategic bombers. Her experimentation in germ warfare will have made even more substantial progress.

On the political front, she will have infiltrated the Middle East and perhaps much of Africa. Her agents in southeastern Asia will have turned everything from India to Burma into a steaming cauldron of hate and conflict. Her Chinese allies will have vanquished the Chiang Kai-shek government and local Communists will have seized southern Korea. She will have developed bases from which to launch an attack upon Alaska, now almost indefensible. She may, if her disturbances upset the operation of the Marshall Plan, have reduced France and Italy to impotence, if she has not in fact brought them to satellite positions. She will undoubtedly seek to swallow Scandinavia in two or three easy gulps and use these northern outposts as additional bases from which to wage transpolar war against America's industrial north.

Any economic recession in the United States—and one may well be expected even if it is not of fatal proportions—would provide fertile ground for enfeebling agitation here. South America would be further infiltrated as a base of operations against the Panama Canal—even now in an exposed position.

So long as Russia thinks war certain to come, she will not entertain any sincere program for cooperation or friendship with the "imperialistic" powers, the principal one of which she has designated as the United States. At best we shall be offered delays and superficial plans of accord to mask her real purposes.

Nor is the Soviet timetable of revolution projected into the remote future. At the time of the Russian Revolution, the Bolsheviks were genuinely surprised that the rest of the world did not join in the uprising for which they had pointed the way. The architects of Communism expected their triumph in Russia to communicate itself to the workers of all Western Europe. And now that Communism is riding around in the husky vehicle of an historic Russian nationalism, the Kremlin is impatient of delays. It will hardly hold its blows until the balance of the world is cushioned against their impact. It will scarcely sit by impotently and watch its chances of immediate success evaporating in the heat of a rejuvenated Western industrial society.

In short, the danger of a *laissez-faire* attitude on the part of Uncle Sam is that his abhorrence of war may lead him into a period he fondly believes is watchful waiting, but which, in reality, is more waiting than watching. During that interval, his putative enemy may be merrily cooking the witches' brew of his utter destruction.

Now it is one of the political facts of life that America will not wage an aggressive war. That may be high-minded and noble; it may also be fatuous and unrealistic, but there it is, as apparent as measles. We must not be the one to strike the first blow, runs the touching folk-belief. No matter that in this age of nuclear fragmentation, the first blow may also be the last one: we must still stand up and take the first haymaker. Otherwise the war isn't legal. Give the highwayman at least one clear shot at you before you call the gendarmes or try to kick him in the groin.

But this American attitude is so firmly fixed in our tradition and prejudices that we might as well recognize it as one of the great immutable laws of political life.

WHAT THEN may we do to shield ourselves?

It is doubtful that the program here advanced will be adequate but it will at least suffice to precipitate the issue and to give us an outside chance of fighting the war on our own terms or under conditions which we had some part in creating.

First, we should demand the immediate execution of an acceptable peace treaty calling for the retirement of the Red Army to the borders of Russia, appending a time-condition both for the signing of the treaty and the Russian withdrawal.

Second, we should demand the immediate disbanding of the Cominform-Comintern—fomenting world revolution—and the cessation of the activities of the American section of the Communist Party. (It was a pledge to do this latter thing that induced President Roosevelt to extend diplomatic recognition.)

Third, we should call for the immediate return of all lend-lease property still owing to us from Russia.

Fourth, we should ask for substantial assurances of nonaggression against the Scandinavian countries, and the complete abstention of the Kremlin from any activity in Palestine and the Middle East.

Fifth, there should be full and immediate international inspection and control of atomic energy.

Sixth, we should notify the Kremlin that we shall expect the immediate abandonment of aid to the Chinese Communists, as well as a pledge that it will cease its instigation and arming of Korean Communists and that it will afford us and China full treaty privileges in the ceded ports of northern China.

If the Soviet Union accepts these conditions—wonderful! There will be no war. But, to indulge in the flattest understatement of the year, the demands will probably be rejected. We should therefore be prepared to take countervailing steps, which might be:

The immediate withdrawal of diplomatic recognition from the U.S.S.R. and satellites.

An offer of asylum to all Red Army soldiers in Germany and Austria who wish to escape from Soviet tyranny.

A brisk propaganda campaign aimed at the Russian people, assuring them that these punitive steps were not being taken against them but against the Communist hierarchy.

The full use of American economic power to isolate Soviet Russia from any form of world trade.

The closing of the Panama and Suez Canals to Soviet shipping and a warning that all Soviet vessels touching American ports are liable to confiscation for unpaid lend-lease balances.

Immediate air force aid to Chiang Kai-shek.

The working out of an accommodation with Franco, who, detestable though he is, still controls the Southern Pyrenees and ingress into the Mediterranean, which American and other Western armies would probably have to use both as bastion and jumping-off place for future attacks.

The developing of air bases in Africa, which would probably be the cockpit of a war between the East and West.

The immediate improvement of the highway to Alaska and the surveying of the route for railroad building.

The conclusion of a hard-and fast military alliance not only with Western Europe and Scandinavia but with Greece, Turkey, Iran, Iraq, Israel, Egypt, and the other Middle Eastern countries, each country to afford the United States full right to air bases and naval facilities.

It may be argued that these steps would be tantamount to a declaration of war. The realist would insist that they merely anticipate the measures we must surely take under any circumstances within the next two or three years . . . when Russia has the atom bomb.

Not a shot would be fired, but adequate defensive measures would have been undertaken and Uncle Sam would have assured himself that if a war is to be fought against the Soviets it will not be on their terms and in their time, but on his terms and in his time. We may tremble about taking a decisive step but we are beginning dimly to recognize that we can't equate delay with security or reconcile hope with realism. We know that Russian Communism, harnessed to the stout collar of Russian nationalism, is far more inimical to the United States than the threat of Nazi conquest was.

Haters of war will ask, quite properly but quite irrelevantly, how we expect to win a war with Soviet Russia and whether we will try to occupy that vast country. To this the only reply is that no one knows, but that the question is not relevant to this discussion, which assumes that war is inevitable and that America's duty is plainly to put itself into such a position that it will not lose the war when it comes. The problems thus raised would be no easier of solution if the Kremlin initiated a war in its own time and under circumstances it thought auspicious.

Many sincere people protest quakingly, "What good is all this going to do? You can't stop Communism with bullets, or 'you can't shoot an idea.'" This also is irrelevant, if we predicate our reasoning on the idea that war is unavoidable. It will not be a matter of choice for us whether we want to try to stop Communism with bullets. Indeed, the question will be put the other way; the Soviets may be asking, can the proletariat crush democracy with bombs? And all the time, they'll be trying to find out empirically.

Aside from its irrelevance, the question is vexing for another reason. It is puerile. Of course you can't shoot an idea, but you can shoot the man who disseminates the idea at gunpoint.

A further fact is that we are not concerned with the spectre of a Socialist Europe, just as we are not alarmed by Britain's Socialist government. We are afraid of a *Sovietized* Europe and Asia, with the driving force of Communism coming from the deep springs of Russian nationalism. Without that direction, Communism might well be just another floundering ideology. It is this realization that binds the Communists of other countries so tightly to the Soviet Republic.

No one in his right mind wants war with the Soviet Union—or for that matter, with Timbuctoo. We would never have considered going to war against the Soviets as a protest against their own internal tyrannies or their adherence to Communistic doctrine. That is supremely their own business. When they so propagate those doctrines by word and sword that they endanger the freedom of the world and our own security and weal, it becomes a matter of lively concern to the United States. And when the Kremlin gives clear evidence that it intends continuing upon a course hurtful to American interest, we can have no qualms about putting ourselves in the best possible position to resist its bold designs.

We might have thought Communist dogma was mellowing, but when Moscow, insistent upon its doctrine that only environment fixes character and attributes, forced the genes to follow the party line, we realized that there was only a diminishing chance of persuading the men in the Kremlin that rationality—and its fruit of peace—are possible. If they controvert biology, they will surely reject political reason and sanity.

So repellent is the idea of war that the mere outlining of these dangers and the steps suggested to combat them has given this writer real pain. But there is little virtue in seeking a sentimental solution of a problem posed by ruthless men in the pursuit of a fanatical ideology. If we feel that atavistic sense of grave danger, our humanitarianism will but betray us if it relies upon adventitious escape or solution. Should Stalin die, the fires of the revolutionary spirit may very possibly mount rather than diminish. A new resurgence of Red Army influence in the Kremlin would bring war sooner. A recrudescence of party spirit would intensify the flames and multiply the dangers.

What we can see as danger, we must resist as evil.

October 1948

It Need Not Be War

By H. R. KNICKERBOCKER

[*H. R. Knickerbocker, a native of Texas, a distinguished foreign correspondent who was awarded a 1939 Pulitzer Prize for his reportage on the European scene, urged patience upon the United States in its tug-of-war with Communist Russia. He proceeded from the premise that nowhere in the doctrine of Lenin and Stalin was there a suggestion that the Soviet world "should make its own preventive war." Knickerbocker's conclusion is as timely as ever: "Russia believes time works for her. We believe time works for us."*]

IT NEED NOT be war. If we have the will to wait, we may see the menace dissolve, for the Soviet system contains the seed of its own destruction. That seed is under-production.

Russian production is not only far behind that of the United States, but it is losing ground in relation to us. This deficiency in the Soviet system will persist as long as the system lasts. It has nothing to do with the damage caused by the war. It dooms the Soviet Empire to permanent inferiority in the ability to make offensive war.

The argument for making a preventive war against Russia is that she will attack us when she believes she can win; that she will eventually believe she can win because she is growing stronger than we economically, politically, and militarily. She is growing stronger economically because the total production of the Soviet Union is overtaking and will outstrip the production of the free world. She is growing stronger politically because her conquest of territory since 1939 has added to her control 12 nations and 120 million people in Europe, and some 75 million subjects in important areas of the Far East; while her efforts to undermine the capitalist world from within continue and are threateningly successful. She is growing stronger militarily because she already possesses land forces too numerous for us to match, a formidable submarine navy, and air force capable of checkmating ours; and within a few years will have the atom bomb.

In a word, we should fight Russia while we still have a chance because her capacity to make war is growing faster than ours.

But none of these claims is true.

Russia is not gaining on America economically. The Soviet system requires about four men to do the work of one in the Western world. Under the Soviet system, in 1940, 198 million people turned out a gross national product of 30 billion dollars. In the same year, 148 million people in America turned out a gross national product of 100 billion dollars. Each Russian produced about $150 worth; each American about $688 worth.

The Soviets required 1,600,000 bookkeepers to keep accounts on their 30 billion dollar business. The United States required 800,000 bookkeepers to keep accounts on their 100 billion dollar business. The Soviets had one bookkeeper for every $1,800 worth of product. The United States had one bookkeeper for every $12,000 worth of product. The Soviets required 2 million political policemen to keep watch and punish the population. The United States required none.

A significant part of Soviet energy goes into keeping books and keeping watch. When to that is added the terror, the fear of responsibility, and the difficulty of planning intelligently for 198 million people, the sum is failure to produce more than one-fourth as much as a free economy. More important, the growth of Soviet economy is slower than the growth of free Western economy. This is the key to the future. It is given us by the Russian planners themselves.

WE HAVE the key from the Soviet record of physical production. Though the Kremlin shrank from no statistical distortion to help its aims, though it liquidated planners who failed to cooperate, to keep a straight record of physical production was indispensable for its own private guidance. For the public, the Kremlin economists translated the physical record into a system of ruble prices and came up with an index of total Soviet production which has made war seem inevitable.

The index made it appear that Soviet total production, 100 in 1913, reached that level again in 1928, and at the end of the first Five Year Plan in 1934 became 336, and at the end of the second Five Year Plan in 1938 became 635, and under the third Five Year Plan became 852 in 1940, the last year before the war.

The United States only doubled its production from 1913 to 1938. The Soviet index showed Russia had increased its production by six times in the same period.

This persuaded the Russian people that they were going ahead three times faster than the United States. Soon others believed it too. In 1928 the non-Soviet world refused to take the first Five Year Plan seriously. Skepticism lessened as American engineers and correspondents reported on Russian construction. When it was finally realized that the Five Year Plan was a reality, suddenly all its claims began to be entertained as worth serious consideration. First-class non-Soviet economists accepted the Soviet index of production. The League of Nations used it as a point of reference. Governments based their calculations on it.

The public could be forgiven for being influenced by it. Today, with all the recent American awakening to the Kremlin's intentions, our judgment of Soviet power is unconsciously based upon the Soviet index of production. But that index is as deceiving as the mirrors in carnivals which make the figure grotesquely short or tall.

To correct the distortion was like the work of a bank examiner untangling "cooked" ledgers. To conceal their private record of physical production the Russians frequently published percentages of quantities sometimes known, sometimes unknown to outsiders. Diligent "bourgeois" economists, pursuing a percentage here, linking it with a percentage there, finding clues in Russian speeches and obscure Soviet journals, finally traced enough basic data to make a reliable table of total Russian physical production. This was then valued in scientifically weighted international units which made a new, true index.

It showed Russian national income in billions of international unit dollars as 19.47 in 1913; 19.67 in 1928; 20.29 in 1934 and 30.38 in 1938. American national income in 1913 was 33 and in 1938 it was 64, in billions of 1935–39 dollars; to continue the record, it was 107 in 1942 and 118 in 1946.

Thus, after passing through the worst depression in history, American industrial production in 1938 was double that of 1913. The Russians during two Five Year Plans toiled and hungered, shivered and deprived themselves of all but a brutally low subsistence to achieve an increase of a bare 50 percent of their prerevolutionary production. The truth was one-twelfth of the Soviet claim, 50 instead of 600 percent.

The progressive hardships exacted by the system from the Russian people are indicated by the basic Soviet statistics showing that an American worker's

86

house of four or five rooms would have been occupied in Russia by 14 people in 1928, 17 people in 1934, 20 people in 1938 and 30 people today.

Economically, time works against the Kremlin.

POLITICALLY, the limit of Russian advance in Europe has probably been reached with the Sovietization of those states which the war brought under Moscow's control. This process matured with the Communist seizure of the government of Czechoslovakia.

Two consequences of Sovietization appear. First, a precipitate decline of industrial and agricultural production in the states taken over by the Russians. Second, the development of internal resistance to the Russian regime by the local Communist parties, as in Yugoslavia and Poland. The theoretical addition of war potential to Russia's strength has been diminished in the satellite states by so much that it is a question whether they represent a true increase of power or not. They certainly do not balance the loss the Kremlin sustained in its hopes of Communist conquest of France and Italy.

Russian territorial expansion in Europe and the Middle East has been definitely checked in Iran, Turkey, Greece, Trieste, Italy, France, and Germany. In all these places Moscow recoiled for fear of World War III.

The advance of the Communist idea has ceased. It is retreating. Its best chance for winning in a fair election was in Italy. It failed. Its best chance for winning in a civil war was in France. The Communists avoided the contest. Its once tolerant Socialist friends in Britain have become violent opponents.

Throughout the continent, the popular view of the Soviet Union has changed. It took three years of experience with Soviet power to weaken the faith of the masses that Moscow meant well by them. This faith has not been dispelled, but it is weaker and is growing still weaker. In perspective, this gradual acquaintance of the world with the true character and practices of the Stalinist state may be assessed as the decisive factor in the history of these times.

In Germany, though the Red Army maintains its grip on its sector, the Russian position has weakened. The airlift has won not only the sympathy of the German people but their confidence that the West will win. Germany has disproved the contention that Communism always profits by bad economic conditions. The Germans who are suffering the most are the most opposed to Communism. They are the Germans in the Russian zone.

It may be that Stalin is deliberately using Berlin to divert our attention from Asia where Communism is making spectacular inroads into the defenseless societies of states formerly protected by Western power. But there seems reason to hope that America's coming administration will put means at the disposal of these societies to defend themselves. Aside from that, the balance of power in the Far East can hardly be said to have tipped against us if we can with some confidence count now upon Japan to be an ally against Soviet Russia.

COMMUNIST undermining of the Western world from within is becoming less and less effective. In this country an awakened public has driven the Communist fifth column back to the hard core of the professional party, with a fringe of fellow-travelers which diminishes steadily as the connection between native Communism and Russia, and the reactionary egotistic character of the Soviet Union becomes clearer. Communist trade union leaders have lost strong point after strong point, and whereas a year or two ago they controlled important sectors of American labor, they cling now with difficulty to a few scattered posts.

In the Western intellectual world, the deserters from the Soviet cause document a great revolt. Arthur Koestler, André Gide, André Malraux, Ignazio Silone, lead an army of protest against the betrayer of their hopes. How many Russian intellectuals would join them if they could?

Not a single well-known man in art or science has gone over to the Soviet side since the end of the war. Communism lacks recruits, even among the youth. The universities and colleges happily still nourish idealists, but those deceived by the Soviet myth no longer monopolize the field. On the campus Koestler has replaced John Reed. Youth has begun to identify Communism with reaction. Worse, it is old hat.

MILITARILY the power of the Russian state has declined in relation to the Allies and will decline still more as Allied defense plans mature. Russia enjoyed the best military ratio to the Allies in the period from 1945 to 1947 when the Americans and the British demobilized while the Soviet army reorganized.

Now, for the first time, the United States at peace is preparing for war. We are assembling a powerful army. The Navy is confident it can handle the Russian Schnorkels; the Air Force is sure of its supremacy; an ever-increasing number of atom bombs is ready, and industry is rehearsing for conversion. Though we are not mobilized we are more ready for war than we ever have been in peacetime.

Great Britain, which only a short time ago was deploring our refusal to appease Russia, is rearming as she did after Hitler's march into Prague. She has ordered one hundred warships out of reserve. She has stopped demobilization and called for half a million recruits. A new generation of RAF combat pilots are climbing into new jet planes.

The Western Union of Britain, France, Belgium, the Netherlands, and Luxembourg is organizing a military general staff to direct the defense against the Red Army. It is probable we will join the Western Union. No longer is the continent resigned to being overrun by the Soviet Army. The hope and plan are now to hold the Russians on the line of the Rhine until Allied destruction by air of the Russian heart and head loosens the clutch of the Soviet fist.

We are repeatedly told that the Russians will have a workable atomic bomb by 1952. It seems to be taken for granted that they will immediately use it.

But mere possession of the bomb will not give Moscow the superiority she needs to encourage her to make war. If she has the bomb by 1952 the United States will still have had ten years more experience, and the stockpile of ten years to use in the initial atomic battles.

The contention that the United States could be knocked out by a surprise atomic attack is not reasonable. World War III would be between two continents, each so large that a single blow, even with atomic bombs, could not result in victory. If we today attacked Russia with atomic bombs it would take many more blows than one to knock her out.

But we do not need to knock her out. We need fear her attack only if we relax the effort which now convinces her she cannot win. Stalin may suffer from defective information, the occupational disease of tyrants. He could only stumble into war by mistaking the mood and power of the United States. In principle it is impossible for Soviet Russia to go to war over an incident. In 1939 Stalin's Red Army fought two major battles against the Japanese in Manchuria but there was no war. The local forces fought it out and nothing was said to the outside world. Stalin doubtless would like to have a confidential war with us in Berlin today, but he knows we would not keep that secret, and he believes he can afford to wait. He believes in Lenin.

LENIN's prediction that war is inevitable between the Soviet and capitalistic worlds was based on his belief that the Soviet world would overtake and outstrip the capitalist world. If the capitalist world recognized it was losing the race, it would attack the Soviet Union. If the capitalist world failed to recognize its danger in time, the Soviet Union would attack. But Lenin's prophecy took no account of the possibility that the capitalist world might be winning the race so plainly that it neither felt it necessary to attack nor to fear successful attack.

Nowhere in the doctrine of Lenin or Stalin is to be found a suggestion that the Soviet world, facing a growing enemy, should make its own preventive war. They never admitted the thought that the capitalist enemy could improve; it must always be in decline. The Kremlin put this doctrine inexorably into practice when it watched and even abetted the growth of the German and Japanese power.

It betrays a short acquaintance with Moscow to believe the Kremlin has become more fanatical. Moscow's decree that genetics must obey Marx is no more fanatical than her insistence from the beginning that physics and trigonometry must follow the party line. Fundamental Bolshevik doctrine is the same in 1948 as in 1918. Fresh discovery of Moscow's fanaticism and initial realization of the Kremlin's will to aggress shock many people into the hasty conclusion that, as the bandits obviously want to get into Fort Knox, they will certainly try to storm it. We all know how wicked the bandits are; they have been wicked a long time. What we need to know now is how strong they are.

The Kremlin is in no hurry. It thinks it absurd to hurry history. If Europe recovers, that will disappoint the Politburo; but it is the queerest misreading of Bolshevik doctrine to think that they would risk the treasure of Soviet power to check an upcurve in the doomed capitalist economy.

Lenin did not intend his prophecy to be a directive for Soviet suicide. Stalin is more cautious than Lenin. He waited fourteen years after he ousted Trotsky from power before he felt safe enough to kill him. Stalin wants to destroy the capitalist world. But he wants to be safe. He will wait until the odds are on his side.

Russia believes time works for her. We believe time works for us. Time dictates that we wait, for the odds on our side will become even greater. Let us see who is right. Prudence does not dictate that we make war now.

November 1948

WHO'LL DROP THE NEXT ATOM BOMB?

By GEORGE FIELDING ELIOT

[*George Fielding Eliot, a native of Brooklyn who achieved national fame as an expert on military affairs and international relations, both as an author and radio analyst, took a view very close to that of Bertrand Russell. Writing late in 1949, after the Soviet Union shocked the world by exploding its first experimental atomic bomb, Eliot proposed that the United States serve an ultimatum on Stalin to place Soviet atomic production "under the control of the World Atomic Authority, as provided in the majority report of the United Nations Commission on Atomic Energy." It goes without saying that Eliot's proposal and warning fell on deaf ears both in Washington and in the rest of the country.*]

IT'S ALMOST an article of faith with Americans that this country will never start a war. Our whole national security system has been based on the idea that we will never be the aggressor. For years this idea has been brought in whenever an American statesman or an American general has made a speech touching on national defense. We will never attack anybody. If war starts, somebody else strikes the first blow. Not us.

Pearl Harbor didn't change that basic line of thought. We were attacked. We thereupon pulled up our pants and beat the tar out of the fellow who attacked us. That's the American way of doing things. I've heard capable, well-informed Americans say just that with a kind of naïve pride.

And now the Soviet Union has exploded its first experimental atomic bomb and, having thus proven the worth of its atomic procedures so far, is busily going ahead with the manufacture of a stockpile of atomic bombs.

So—we sit on our hands and wait for an atomic Pearl Harbor?

But just a minute—let's adjust our sense of proportion. Pearl Harbor, after all, was a distant island outpost, not a part of our home territory. The fleet that was based there was a principal target of the attackers. From the Japanese point of view the fleet was the most important target they could reach with a surprise attack. It was not the fault of the Jap planners, but just our own astonishing good luck, that the most important ships of the fleet (the aircraft carriers) were at sea when the blow fell.

Any future enemy, armed with atomic weapons, who plans an atomic surprise attack against the United States, will reason just as the Japs reasoned: what is the most important damage I can do with my first blow, to reap the full advantage of surprise? He will reason, as the Japs reasoned, that his major objective is to gain time, to prevent the mobilization of the vast power of America against him while he proceeds to overrun his neighbors. Our seaport cities and our air bases, through which that power must flow if it is to be sent overseas; our industrial centers, which generate that power; and our national capital, from which the use of that power is directed, will be obvious targets. If not all of these can be attacked at once, then the most important ones (i.e., those most valuable to us) will be selected.

If such an attempt is made, and is even partially successful, no one will be inclined to speak of Pearl Harbor in the same breath thereafter.

But, it may be said, we have no such enemy, plotting our destruction. Oh, yes, we have. Let's clear up that point before we go any further.

The present rulers of the Soviet Union are our deadly and implacable enemies, committed to the destruction of our free institutions, to the destruction of freedom itself as we understand it. They will never feel safe until they have enslaved the entire world. Don't take my word for this. I can quote you far better authority—Lenin and Stalin.

ONE OF the major signposts which will mark, to Stalin's mind, the coming of the crisis will be acquisition by the Soviet Union of a store of atomic bombs and long-range airplanes. He will then be in possession of weapons with which he can truly contribute to "the further disintegration of imperialism"—by which he means, of course, the United States and the free nations of Western Europe.

Now that signpost is actually in sight. It's right there, just down the road a piece.

So it's hardly surprising that the six-power atomic discussion group at Lake Success has just presented another report of deadlock—five powers against one, five powers who want real and effective atomic safeguards, the Soviet Union stubbornly refusing to go along.

Can it be that the Soviet Union does not really want atomic safeguards? And that what the Soviet Union really wants is to develop atomic weapons for its own use? They will be most effective if used by surprise, in a sudden blow at an enemy's vitals. The gentlemen in the Kremlin may feel convinced that the American people will never use atomic power against Russia or any one else in that fashion. They know that they themselves will be only too ready to do so when their preparations have been completed. So a surprise weapon is more valuable to them than to us.

At any rate, they have exploded an atomic bomb; we may be quite sure that they are making more, and meanwhile they are showing no change whatever in their stubborn refusal to talk about effective international controls. So what do we do now?

We have, of course, a little time in which to make up our minds. One experimental bomb is not a whole stockpile, and there will be no Soviet surprise attack until they not only have a stockpile they think is adequate to knock us silly with the first blow, but the means of delivering the bombs to American targets. These means may include a long-range air force (which is being developed but isn't strong enough yet) or they may include guided missiles fired from submarines, such as we're experimenting with in the current Pacific maneuvers. The Soviet Navy has the submarines, but if the guided missiles are still experimental with us they're probably no further advanced with the Russians. So, as I said, we have a little time to think,—maybe a year, maybe even two.

OUR FIRST inclination will be to wait, to hope for miracles (such as sudden Soviet agreement to a worldwide atomic control system with teeth in it), and to go on saying: "Anyway, the Kremlin doesn't really want war—and if they do, let them strike the first blow."

But will we go on thinking and saying this?

We are now entering a period of the greatest strain and anxiety. We shall be confronted with a long series of demands and pressures, one after the other, like the Hitlerian procession: Rhineland-Austria-Sudetenland-Czechoslovakia-Danzig. As each Soviet demand is pressed, there will be behind it the spoken or unspoken threat of atomic war. As we face each of them, the cry will go up that the Dardanelles, or Greece, or Soviet control of the Ruhr, or this or that, "isn't worth a war." (Remember how we used to hear the wail: "Will you fight for Danzig?") But this time our fears will be more than just the fears of a terrible war in which our young men must die on foreign soil and our normal happy course of life be interrupted. They will be fears for our homes, our cities, our dear ones; fears lest we shall bring death and destruction to millions of American men, women, and children right here in our own homeland; fears, in the last basic analysis, for our own lives.

In this process, the Kremlin may acquire piecemeal a number of vital strategic positions, and will thus grow stronger and stronger until as last we shall have to fight, at a grave disadvantage and against a foe who will have used every moment of time thus gained in building more and more atomic bombs.

Yet if we have not thought our problem through in advance, we are quite likely to temporize, to wait, to waste time in futile argument, to hope for the best while not preparing for the worst—until the Kremlin is ready to throw down the atomic gauntlet of final challenge.

But it is very certain that this intensification of the strain of the cold war, the rising fear that knowledge of Soviet atomic progress will engender in every American heart, may have another result. At each stage of the mounting crisis, some voices will be heard crying: "Let's act now! Let's put an end to this menace while we can still do so without fear of serious atomic reprisal!"

As the strain grows, these voices will grow louder and more insistent, and willy-nilly, more of us will listen to them with the ears of our hearts, however repulsive they may be to the ears of our minds.

For the time being, remember, we continue to be the exclusive possessor of the only atomic-bomb stockpile in the world. We have a long-range air force. We have bases under our own control, or the control of our allies, in many parts of the world. We have aircraft carriers, which are mobile air bases which can be sent anywhere there is water enough to float them.

We are—and shall continue to be for some months—in a military position to say to the Soviet rulers:

"See here. We've been pleading with you for years to join with us in placing atomic production under safeguarded international control, so that no one can ever again use it as a means of destruction. You've consistently refused to do this. Now we know that you have made your first atomic bomb, and are producing others. We consider our safety as a people endangered by this fact. We do not propose to wait until you can confront us with a lot of aggressive demands, with an atomic war of mutual annihilation as the alternative to yielding. We demand of you that you place your atomic production under the control of the World Atomic Authority, as provided in the majority report of the United Nations Commission on Atomic Energy, here and now.

"If you agree, we are prepared to do the same. There is nothing to debate about details; they have all been threshed out through weary years of argument. You have 48 hours in which to make up your minds. If we do not receive a favorable reply from you within that time, followed immediately by arrangements for the admission of agents of the World Atomic Authority to your territory, we shall be compelled to use the atomic weapons in our possession for the immediate destruction of your atomic plants and installations."

You RECOIL in horror from the suggestion that any American government should ever thus speak for the American people, but remember, you haven't faced up to the grim new facts of life as yet. You've read the headlines, maybe you've even read a few paragraphs of the story under the headlines, but you haven't had time to absorb the full meaning of what has happened. And of course you—like all of us—are nursing the silly hope that maybe the bad men will go away and not bother us after all. Anyway, we have a year—lots can happen in a year. How's your golf game?

Right now is the time to begin our thinking about the coming atomic crisis while we can do it calmly and reasonably. For not only must we make up our minds and steel our hearts, if we are going to act effectively in self-preservation when we have to, but we must make some very material and essential preparations. Of course we'll have to continue making atomic bombs, and building up the military power which will enable us to deliver them where and when necessity may require. We'll also have to speed up our help to our friends in Western Europe to put themselves in a reasonable state of defense so that it won't be easy, as it would be now, for the Soviet Union to reply to our ultimatum with a threat to overrun and massacre the French, the Dutch, the Norwegians, and our other European allies and associates.

But beyond all this, we and our allies will have to establish the World Atomic Authority, and have it ready and functioning by the time the zero hour comes. It would be better to do this under the mandate of a majority decision of the General Assembly of the United Nations. The Soviet Union won't agree, probably, but most of the rest of the world will be happy to agree. Perhaps we shouldn't take the risk of actually putting our atomic plants under the control of the World Atomic Authority until the Soviet Union has been induced or compelled to do likewise. But the World Atomic Authority must be established as a going concern, with the sanction of world majority support, so that it can be ready when it is needed. This will take time, even to set up a skeleton organization and planning staff.

Otherwise, at the crucial moment, the Soviet Union may stall us off, and gain invaluable weeks or months, by saying: "All right, let's set up our World Atomic Authority and we'll see how it works." Infinite delay could be produced in the process. We'd look foolish issuing a 48-hour ultimatum that would take 48 weeks to put into effect. Remember, it has already taken the Atomic Energy Commission of the United Nations more than three years just to work out the basic principles of how such an authority can operate. And setting it up will take time, too.

But the major preparation must be in our own minds and hearts. This will be the hardest part of the task, yet the price of failing to see clearly and think clearly may well be destruction or slavery.

The men who make our foreign and our military policies see and think clearly enough. They may have guessed wrong—indeed they did guess wrong—as to the exact timing of the Soviet atomic explosion, but they've known all along it was coming.

Then why, you well may ask, are they soft-pedalling it now? Why does Secretary of Defense Johnson warn reporters not to "overplay" it? (How in Heaven's name *could* they overplay it?) Why has every official statement since the announcement of "an atomic explosion" in the Soviet Union fairly dripped with soothing syrup?

One reason for the official playdown is the desire to get through this session of the United Nations General Assembly without throwing away any chance, however slight, of reaching an atomic agreement with the Soviet Union. Nobody really believes such a chance exists, but at least it's desirable not to take any bellicose stand, to be able to say honestly that we tried our best.

But there's another more fundamental reason for the official attitude. It's simply that the top-flight policy-makers don't believe the public is ready to accept the stark, savage truth. They're afraid that as the dreadful alternative becomes clear, there will be increased pressure, backed by moralizers and do-gooders, to accept some kind of atomic agreement which won't have real teeth in it, anything so that folks can go comfortably back to sleep again, soothed by the illusion of security. There are already signs of this kind of thinking; there are already evidences of a desire to avoid the terrible responsibility of having to decide one way or the other.

The constant emphasis of Soviet propaganda on "warmongering" is, of course, the reverse of the shield. The men in the Kremlin realize well enough what is coming. *They* know we'll have to face the fact of a Soviet atomic stockpile some day. They want to guard themselves as well as they can against any American reaction which might upset all their plans and comfort them with the alternative of giving up their atomic supported scheme of conquest or having their installations destroyed by our atomic bombs. So they hammer away at the "warmongers" theme. They try to instill in us a sense of guilt, a distrust of our own statesmen and military people, and of our allies. They try to picture us to the rest of the world as a military colossus, arming that we may dominate others. That's why they always call us "imperialists." They hope that when their A-day comes, we'll be restrained by conscientious objections from getting really tough about it.

We ought to be spending quite a lot of time discussing this situation, thinking about it, searching our consciences and exercising our minds.

The decision we must make when that time comes should not be the result of panic, or of growing strain which has at last become unbearable. It should be the result of thoughtful, even prayerful consideration by all of us; it should have the support of thorough preparation, and of an undivided national will.

And let us not waste the unforgiving hours and days in the cherishing of futile hopes. The enemy will remain the enemy. There can be no change as long as the present Soviet chiefs remain in power, as long as Soviet policy is governed by the ideas so ominously laid down by Stalin.

A long succession of megalomaniacs have postured and strutted across the stage of recent history—the Kaiser, Mussolini, Hitler, the Japanese warlords. None of them could keep his big mouth shut and concert his plans in secret. They all had to boast of what they meant to do to us. We laughed at them all—until it was too late.

Now we are warned again—and this time by one who is acquiring the means to strike us to the heart. We had better believe him this time—or it will really be too late.

December 1949

SOVIET EMPIRE

By LEOPOLD SCHWARZSCHILD

[*In introducing Leopold Schwarzschild to the readers of* Plain Talk, *the editor described him as follows: "Founder and editor in Berlin in 1920 of the independent review,* Das Tagebuch, *which he revived in Paris after the rise of Hitler" and as author of* World in Trance *which attracted international attention when "Winston Churchill sent copies to members of his Cabinet and to the Prime Ministers of the Dominions as a course in contemporary diplomacy." Broken in spirit by the global advance of Communist imperalism, Schwarzschild came to a tragic end in 1953.*]

THE TRIBULATIONS awaiting us in the new half-century now beginning cannot be fathomed. But we can take inventory of our precarious position in the upset world balance of power.

One hundred and fifty million Americans are now confronted with a unified mass of 750 million peoples. It is the biggest human machine that has ever existed in history. As regards manpower, which, if properly organized and equipped is still the main ingredient of power, we have been dwarfed. As for area, the territory of this bloc is five times larger than ours.

The one superiority America still enjoys, its industrial potential, is impaired by the incorporation into the Soviet Empire of quite a number of hitherto foreign industrial zones. Mere quantitative and qualitative inferiorities in industrial capacity, moreover, can be compensated for to a large extent by sacrificing more blood. And even in wartime much of our industrial potency will remain mortgaged for nonmilitary necessities considered the absolute minimum here, and totally unknown over there.

Allies of the first magnitude with which to plug the gap of our own deficiencies are no longer to be found, because none exist. Even the addition of the nations participating in the Atlantic Pact brings the total population up to no more than 331 million as against 750. But the Atlantic alliance is, moreover, a thing of many glaring weaknesses and uncertainties. The French Army, for instance, is likely to include in its ranks some 30 percent Communists. A glance at the map of the Atlantic bloc reveals a hodgepodge of widely scattered, disconnected entities which would not easily be able to help each other. Without a miracle in the hour of trial, the Atlantic patchwork will fall far short of its face value.

None of the items constituting this inventory is unknown. Yet few have so far realized what their sum total amounts to. This nation is still all but unaware of the jeopardy into which it has been precipitated from the very summits of power within less than five years. The men who led it on this disastrous road are still leading it, and naturally they do their level best to prevent the people from grasping the real state of things.

U-Boats Ahead

IF IT IS true that the Soviets already have from 360 to 460 of the German-designed Schnorkel submarines, and will have 750 at the end of 1951, then we have been dealt another stunning blow. From the point of view of the immediate future, these vessels might hold more menace than the atom bomb.

Let us recall that the Germans started World War II with no more than 30 ocean-going U-boats. Subsequently, it is true, they built nearly a thousand. But as the methods of hunting them down were well developed from the outset, they were sunk almost as fast as they were commissioned, and no more than 100 were ever in service at the same time. Yet even so small a number came within an ace of carrying the day for Hitler. The submarine peril, Churchill tells us in his memoirs, "was the only thing which ever really frightened me during the war."

No further gauge is required to measure the peril of 750 submarines operating simultaneously—and, above all, submarines of a type against which no promising method of either defense or attack has so far been devised. Carrying men and matériel across the oceans would seem to become flatly impossible in the face of so tremendous a force.

February 1950

BOOK 3

COLLAPSE IN CHINA

An American Policy for China

By Henry P. Van Dusen

[*The abortive diplomacy of the United States vis-à-vis the expanding Communist empire since World War II can be fully appraised only when America's disastrous course in the Far East and Southeast Asia is retraced. The humiliating defeats suffered by the United States in Vietnam and Cambodia were foreseen and forecast by various contributors to* Plain Talk. *One of the earliest alarms sounded in its columns came from a noncontroversial authoritative source, Dr. Henry P. Van Dusen, President of the Union Theological Seminary in New York. His warning was issued upon his return from a visit to China in the summer of 1946, where he conferred at length with General George C. Marshall, then President Truman's special envoy, and with many Chinese leaders. Seeking to forestall "a titanic duel" between Soviet Russia and the United States, Van Dusen penned this trenchant piece four years before the outbreak of the Korean War, which occurred some fifteen years before our sanguinary entrapment in Indochina.*]

WHAT SHOULD BE the policy of the United States toward China in this hour of grave crisis? There is a characteristically paradoxical but pregnant saying of Chesterton: The only important thing about knowing the truth is to know the really important truths. Certainly in an issue as momentous as this, the one essential is to lay our minds firmly upon the few really important truths. These basic truths may be set forth in a series of propositions leading to the answer to our question.

1. The controlling objective of American foreign policy must be to forestall a war which looms not merely as a possibility but as a probability.

2. If World War III comes, however it may start, it will become in essence a titanic duel between Soviet Russia with her satellites, on the one hand, and the United States, the British Commonwealth, and their Western European and American associates, on the other.

3. If World War III comes, it may well break out, not in Europe or the Near East, but in Eastern Asia where Russia and America face one another along a common frontier. Wherever it begins, it is likely to involve the United States

101

most vitally along that frontier. However it originates, the issue of World War III may be determined in Eastern Asia.

4. China in Communist hands would be the most probable, one may almost say certain, prelude to World War III.

5. Therefore, what transpires in China in the immediate future is of more direct and vital consequence to the security of the United States than what occurs almost anywhere else in the world. When Japan attacked China in 1937, President Roosevelt sought to arouse his nation to the significance of the event by proposing the creation of a "quarantine" around the aggressor. His proposal was generally rejected by the American people; it took Pearl Harbor and all that followed to drive home upon them the truth of his warning. As the European War broke, President Roosevelt declared that the Rhine constituted America's strategic frontier. He was derided as a warmonger; it took the sacrifice of thousands of lives and billions in wealth to prove to the people that he was right. Today, for those who are willing to face realities unafraid, one thing is clear: America's most important strategic frontier is not on the Rhine or the Elbe or at the Dardanelles. It is on the border-line of Soviet-American confrontation in Northern China.

6. Consequently, the United States *must* lend every practicable support to the constituted Government of China.

November 1946

THE STATE DEPARTMENT ESPIONAGE CASE

By EMMANUEL S. LARSEN

[*The country was shaken in June 1945 by the bombshell announcement of the arrest of six persons, including several State Department officials, under the provisions of the Espionage Act. The action followed a raid on the offices of an obscure publication,* Amerasia, *where the F.B.I. discovered some 1700 filched government documents, including 540 classified papers dealing with military and diplomatic matters. For several years, in Congress, in the press, and in the courts, the* Amerasia *affair, as it became known, was a source of news.* Plain Talk *made its debut with a journalistic "scoop" that attracted national attention: an inside account, "The State Department Espionage Case," by Emmanuel Sigurd Larsen, one of the arrested officials. Born in 1897 in San Rafael, Cali-*

BEHIND THE now-famous State Department Espionage Case, involving the arrest of six persons of whom I was one, an arrest which shocked the nation on June 7, 1945, is the story of a highly-organized campaign to switch American policy in the Far East from its long-tested course to the Soviet line. It is a story which has never been told before in full. Many sensational though little-explained developments, such as the General Stilwell Affair, the resignation of Undersecretary Joseph C. Grew and Ambassador Patrick Hurley and the emergence of a pro-Soviet bloc in the Far Eastern Division of the State Department, are interlaced with the Case of the Six, as the episode became known.

I have devoted many months to a plodding investigation of the case in which I became entangled, primarily to rehabilitate my reputation and to establish my complete innocence. I have collaborated with Congressman George Dondero of Michigan, who sponsored the creation of the House Committee which is about to undertake an inquiry into all the circumstances of the disposition of the State Department Espionage Case, and have offered my fullest cooperation to the chairman of that committee, Congressman Samuel Hobbs. In the course of my own explorations, I have uncovered sufficient material to convince me that further probing into the matter might assume proportions even more far-reaching than those of the Pearl Harbor Investigation.

It is the mysterious whitewash of the chief actors of the Espionage Case which the Congress has directed the Hobbs Committee to investigate. But from behind that whitewash there emerges the pattern of a major operation performed upon Uncle Sam without his being conscious of it. That operation vitally affects our main ramparts in the Pacific. In consequence of this operation General Marshall was sent on a foredoomed mission to China designed to promote Soviet expansion on our Asiatic frontier. It was a mission which could not but come to grief and which may yet bring untold sorrow to the American people.

How did it happen that the United States began to turn in 1944 upon its loyal ally, the Chiang Kai-shek Government, which had for seven years fought Japan, and to assume the sponsorship of the rebel Communist regime which collaborated with the Japanese during the period of the Stalin-Hitler Pact?

How did it come to pass that Washington since 1944 has been seeking to foist Communist members upon the sole recognized and legitimate government of China, a maneuver equivalent to an attempt by a powerful China to introduce Earl Browder and William Z. Foster into key positions in the United States government?

How did it transpire that our top-ranking military leader, General Marshall, should have promoted an agreement in China under which American officers would be training and equipping rebel Chinese Communist units at the very time when they were ambushing our marines and when Communists the world over were waging a war of nerves upon the United States?

Whose was the hand which forced the sensational resignation of Undersecretary of State Joseph C. Grew and his replacement by Dean Acheson? And was the same hand responsible for driving Ambassador Patrick Hurley into a blind alley and retirement?

The answers to all of these questions came to me as I unraveled the main threads of the tangled State Department Espionage Case. But many more questions still remain to be solved.

ON JUNE 7, 1945, while a tense nation was entering upon the climax of the war with Japan, and exactly five weeks before the atomic bomb was dropped upon Hiroshima, our country was shaken by an announcement from Washington: the FBI had the previous night arrested on charges of violating the Espionage Act two State Department officials, one Naval Intelligence officer and three New York journalists.

I was arrested in my home in Washington the evening of June 6, after a hard day's work in the State Department where I was employed as a research expert in Chinese affairs. When two FBI agents knocked at the door of our modest apartment as I sat down to dinner with my wife Thelma and our little daughter Linda, I could not believe it and thought it was some sort of a joke when they informed me that I was under arrest.

The search of my home lasted late into the night, and it provided the saddest hours of our lives. After a grueling interrogation, I was brought, still in a state of utter bewilderment, to the office of the United States Commissioner.

There I found myself sitting next to John Stewart Service, a leading figure in the pro-Soviet group in the China Section of the State Department, and to Lieut. Andrew Roth, liaison officer between the Office of Naval Intelligence and the State Department, whom I also knew as an adherent of pro-Soviet policies. Both of them were arrested separately the same night in Washington.

In New York that night of June 6 three other arrests were made simultaneously. Philip Jacob Jaffe, publisher and editor of the obscure magazine *Amerasia,* specializing in Far Eastern affairs, was picked up after a raid on his offices. At the same time Kate Louise Mitchell, co-editor of *Amerasia,* a companion and intimate collaborator of Jaffe's for years, was put under arrest. Another colleague of Jaffe, the journalist Mark Julius Gayn, a contributor on the Far East to *Amerasia* and leading national magazines, was also taken into custody in New York.

The search in the offices of *Amerasia* yielded a trove of more than 100 files containing, according to Congressman Dondero, top secret and highly confidential papers stolen from the State Department, War Department, Navy Department, Office of Strategic Services, Office of Postal and Telegraph Censorship, and the OWI at a time when we were at war with both Germany and Japan. Mr. Dondero described some of these documents before the House of Representatives on April 18th last as follows:

"First. One document marked 'secret' and obviously originating in the Navy Department dealt with the schedule and the targets for the bombing of Japan. This particular document was known to be in the possession of Philip Jaffe during the early spring of 1945 and before the program had been effected. That information in the hands of our enemies could have cost us many precious American lives.

"Second. Another document, marked 'top secret' and likewise originating in the Navy Department, dealt with the disposition of the Japanese fleet subsequent to the major naval battle of October 1944, and gave the location and class of each Japanese warship.

"Third. Another document, stolen from the Office of Postal and Telegraph Censorship, was a secret report on the Far East and so stamped as to leave no doubt in anybody's mind that the mere possession of it by an unauthorized person was a clear violation of the Espionage Act.

"Fourth. Another document was stolen from the Office of Military Intelligence and consisted of 22 pages containing information obtained from Japanese prisoners of war. When our military officials question prisoners of war, it is for the purpose of getting secret military information of the enemy's plans.

"Fifth. Another stolen document, particularly illuminating, and of present great importance to our policy in China, was a lengthy detailed report showing complete disposition of the units in the army of Chiang Kai-shek, where located, how placed, under whose command, naming the units, division by division, and showing their military strength. It is easy to visualize the consequences of this information in the hands of the Communist forces in China, then and now."

As disclosed by Congressman Dondero, one of the documents was "of such exceptional military importance and so closely guarded in its limited transmission that it was delivered personally into the hands of the Chief of the Office of Naval Intelligence." Many of the confidential papers bore this imprint:

This document contains information affecting the national defense of the United States within the meaning of the Espionage Act, 50, United States Code 31-32, as amended. Its transmission or the revelation of its contents in any manner to an unauthorized person is prohibited by law.

In the offices of *Amerasia,* which boasted a total circulation of 1700, the government agents found a large photocopying department, the operation of which, according to Congressman Dondero, could not possibly have been an essential part of the business of such a limited publication. "This department," stated Mr. Dondero, "was working through the night, in the small hours of morning, and even on Sundays." Where these photostats went and how far they traveled is one of the several pivotal mysteries awaiting solution in the whole case.

Probably not one informed American in 20,000 had ever heard of *Amerasia.* But those of us who had to do with research or policy-making in the field of our international relations in Asia were well aware of the potent influence this almost unknown publication exercised upon the conduct of American foreign policy.

The magazine first came to my attention during my employment as an analyst in Chinese affairs in the Office of Naval Intelligence, where I had served for about nine years from October 1935, to September 1944. After having spent nearly twenty-five years of my life in China, where my father was a university instructor and where I grew up and mastered Chinese like a native, I returned to the United States. Before entering the government service, I did postgraduate work at the University of Chicago and later at Columbia University on a Rockefeller scholarship.

It was during the war, while working in the Office of Naval Intelligence as a civilian, that circumstances led me unsuspectingly to my fateful meeting with Philip Jaffe, the dominant figure in the Espionage Case.

One of the officers I had met in the Far Eastern branch of the Naval Intelligence was a brilliant young man, Andrew Roth, who had been commissioned a junior lieutenant after completing a special course in the Japanese language. My friendship with Roth, who was a youth of 26, never became intimate. We frequently lunched together. Occasionally we met in the evening for a potluck dinner and a good argument.

Roth knew my special hobby, as did many of my associates and acquaintances. Ever since 1923 I had been collecting patiently from every conceivable source biographical data on Chinese personalities, military and political, and my file of several thousand cards contained off-the-record material about the careers of the chief figures in the great drama of modern China.

ONE day Roth came to my desk in the Navy Department around noon time and asked me whether I had had my lunch. As I was free, I accepted his invitation to join him for a snack. While we walked up Pennsylvania Avenue, Roth asked me whether I knew Philip Jaffe, the publisher and editor of *Amerasia*. My answer being in the negative, he remarked that Jaffe was a friend of his and that he was interested in the biographies of Chinese leaders, so that the two of us should have a lot in common.

Roth suggested that I get together with Jaffe who was in a position to trade information with me about personalities. When asked how I could meet Jaffe, he smilingly imformed me that Jaffe was in Washington that day, that he, Roth, was just then on his way to meet him for luncheon, and that he would be glad to take me along and introduce me.

We walked over to the Statler Hotel and met Jaffe in the lobby. First we had a cocktail in his room and then we had lunch in the restaurant. We discussed the conditions under which we could exchange information about Chinese leaders. Jaffe said that he visited Washington about once a month and that he would ask me on these visits for certain biographical material. If I didn't have it ready on my cards, I would prepare it for him and he would pick it up on his next trip. In return, he would supply me with information about the individuals I was studying. I was quite happy to have this new source of information, especially since I expected to get data on the Communist figures in China, a little-known field.

Most of the Chinese experts in the Office of Naval Intelligence were satisfied with the superficial and generally negligible official biographies, whereas what I sought for my collection was the "dirt" about a man's career, the unpublished facts about his past and the real reasons for his switching from one faction to another. I had a hard time explaining to my superiors the importance of collecting such data about China, which was governed not so much by ideologies as by personalities.

It was not until after my arrest a year later, when I went over in my mind again and again the various conversations I had had with Roth, that I began to question the seeming coincidence of my meeting with Jaffe. I asked myself why Roth, who had been so interested in bringing us together for the exchange of information, never once inquired afterwards about my relations with Jaffe. It now occurred to me that Roth's avoidance of the subject was not quite normal. And ever since I have been pestered by the thought: "Had not that casual meeting with Jaffe, which brought so much distress to me, been carefully prearranged?"

After meeting Jaffe, I naturally began to follow *Amerasia* with increased interest. Often I was surprised to discover how closely the situation in Asia as presented in Jaffe's magazine corresponded to that given by our naval and military attaches and by the State Department's field representatives in China.

In June 1944 *Amerasia* came out with a sharp attack on Undersecretary Grew, who was opposed to the proposed bombing of Emperor Hirohito's palace and who was reputed to favor the retention of the monarchy after the defeat of Japan as a stabilizing element in the Far East. This view of Mr. Grew's, which General MacArthur later put into effect, was a challenge to the pro-Soviet group in the China Section, whose objective was internal revolution in Japan.

Never having been identified with any Communist organization or "front," I did not suspect anything untoward in the attack upon Mr. Grew. I did notice, however, that Roth had taken a deep interest in Jaffe's criticism of the Undersecretary. Roth told me that he was working on a book in which he would arraign Grew's policies.

I ascribed the anti-Grew campaign to the differences between the Grew school in the State Department which favored a stable Japan as the keystone of American postwar policy in the Pacific and the school which favored a strong China as our best security in Asia.

When Jaffe came to Washington on his next trip, he invited me and my wife to dinner at a Chinese restaurant. In the course of our conversation he told me that he was worried by a report that Undersecretary Grew had been angered by the attack in *Amerasia.* It was obvious that the report had come to him from an inside source in the State Department.

At the same time Vice-President Henry A. Wallace was dispatched on a mission to China, the main purpose of which was to induce Chiang Kai-shek to form a united front with the Communist insurgents. The mission followed upon the outbreak of the so-called Kazak Incident in the early part of 1944 in which Soviet Russia was involved.

The American public was not allowed to know the facts reported by American observers in China, namely, that Moscow had come to the aid of the Chinese Communists in the remote Sinkiang province by engineering an uprising there. This was two years before the Iran Incident. It was done to divert Nationalist troops from the Communist areas. Five full divisions were sent by Chiang Kai-shek into Sinkiang, thus weakening the front against the Japanese and opening the gates of the northwestern Shensi and Kansu provinces to the Communists.

Even before Wallace returned from the Far East, Moscow, which was not at war with Japan, launched a propaganda drive against the recognized government of China. On July 18 the mouthpiece of the Kremlin, *War and the Working Class,* published a warning to Chungking to end its conflict with the Communist forces.

This was the opening gun in a smear campaign which soon was reflected in the so-called liberal press in the United States. Our veteran ally Chiang Kai-shek was denounced as a Fascist. Correspondents and commentators who had never raised their voices against the dictatorship in Russia now echoed the Soviet-inspired vituperation of the Kuomintang regime as a dangerous dictatorship.

The question as to whether Soviet Russia would enter the war against Japan was uppermost in Allied councils in those days. China's foreign minister, T. V. Soong, told our Ambassador Gauss that he was convinced that Russia would attack Japan when Germany was defeated, but would do so for the sole purpose of sovietizing the Far East. Soong warned that America's headaches would commence only then. It was a warning which Washington completely disregarded.

On September 1, 1944, I was transferred from the Naval Intelligence to the State Department, where I was attached to the planning and research unit entrusted with the drafting of basic postwar policy toward China, Japan, Korea, Siam, and other Far Eastern zones. I discovered, to my amazement, that the State Department had no clearcut general policy, but was run by cliques which pursued their own preconceived aims and were often in violent conflict.

The pro-Soviet group in the China Section, whose views were reflected by *Amerasia,* and whose members were in touch with Jaffe and Roth, formed a particularly compact clique. Secretary Ludden of the American Embassy in Chungking was a leading figure in the group. So was John Davies, a native of Chengtu, who acted as State Department attaché with our military observers in China.

He seemed to believe and report almost anything in the way of information against the Kuomintang and Chiang Kai-shek, swallowing whole and relaying nearly everything that the Communists gave him. Mr. Davies held the view that the Chinese Communists were a breed apart from the Soviet elements and had no intention of aligning themselves with Soviet Russia.

John Stewart Service, a junior colleague and friend of Mr. Davies, who was stationed as a field representative in China and acted as political adviser to General Stilwell, tried hard to convince Washington that the rebel Communists were pursuing a policy of avoiding civil war. I remember that Ambassador Gauss did not quite subscribe to this theory. I also recall that in an attempt to discredit Ambassador Gauss's analysis of the Communist-Kuomintang conflict, Mr. John Carter Vincent, chief of the China Section, suggested that it was the failure of the Kuomintang to back the reforms championed by the Communists that was largely responsible for the difficulties in China.

Playing the part of a lone wolf, although 100 percent in accord with the pro-Soviet China Group, was John W. Emmerson, who served as political adviser to Admiral Chester Nimitz in both Chinese and Japanese affairs.

I remember how our Consul in Kweilin had interviewed General Li Chi-shen on the subject of the Democratic League, which was represented in official dispatches as a liberal organization, and how he waxed hot in his report in an effort to impress Washington with all the abuses heaped by General Li upon the Chungking Government. It appeared strange to me that a United States official should have been so receptive to violent criticism of the government to which he was accredited. At no time did any of these field representatives report upon the Communists who had helped create the Democratic League and who manipulated it as a leftist "front."

The encouragement extended to the Chinese Communists by many of our officials there and by some of the writers whom they were inspiring was such that the Reds in China declared they would sit back and wait for stronger United States pressure upon Chiang Kai-shek. This pressure did not fail to be forthcoming.

In the early fall of 1944 Donald M. Nelson and General Patrick Hurley were dispatched to China as the President's special envoys to inform Chiang Kai-shek of American disappointment over his failure to form a united front with the Communists. The two envoys requested the Generalissimo to reorganize his Cabinet and to place an American general in command of the Chinese armies. It was understood that General Stilwell would be the American commander.

Chiang Kai-shek was at first inclined to make some compromise for the sake of Allied unity, but not at the expense of Chinese sovereignty. President Roosevelt exerted his own direct pressure on the Generalissimo to back up his envoy's demands.

Then came the Stilwell incident. John S. Service, Stilwell's political adviser, accompanied a highly secret military commission to Communist headquarters at Yenan. Upon the return of this mission, old "Vinegar" Joe demanded that Chiang Kai-shek permit him to equip and arm some 500,000 Chinese Communists and put them in the field alongside the Nationalist armies against the Japanese. Chiang Kai-shek saw in this American proposal a Soviet plot to build up the very rebel forces which had been waging civil war against his government. He requested the recall of General Stilwell.

The day before President Roosevelt announced that Stilwell had been relieved of his command, on October 30, 1944, John S. Service submitted his report No. 40 to the State Department. As disclosed months later by General Hurley in his testimony before the Senate Foreign Relations Committee, that report was "a general statement of how to let fall the government I was sent over there to sustain. The report was circulated among the Communists I was trying to harmonize with the Chiang Kai-shek government."

During these and the ensuing months Philip Jaffe and Kate Mitchell made numerous trips from New York to Washington. Mr. Jaffe would call me and collect whatever biographical data on Chinese personalities I had, but I found it increasingly strange that he would not reciprocate with the promised biographical information on the Communist figures that I needed.

THE Espionage Case itself had its origin with the appearance in the December 1944 issue of *Amerasia* of an article containing unadulterated passages from an extremely confidential report to the Office of Strategic Services. Two employees of the OSS were struck by the passages which they had read in the original and became curious as to how the information turned up in the columns of *Amerasia*. A preliminary investigation conducted by OSS disclosed that various other secret documents were in possession of Jaffe, Kate Mitchell, and Mark Gayn, all of *Amerasia*.

The FBI then took charge of the affair. As established by Congressman Dondero, the government agents spent several months on the case. In the course of their quest, it was found that John S. Service was in communication from China with Mr. Jaffe. The substance of some of Service's confidential messages to the State Department reached the offices of *Amerasia* in New York before they arrived in Washington. Among the papers found in possession of Mr. Jaffe was Document No. 58, one of Mr. Service's secret reports, entitled "Generalissimo Chiang Kai-shek—Decline of his Prestige and Criticism of and Opposition to his Leadership."

In the course of the FBI investigation *Amerasia* was revealed as the center of a constellation of Communist zealots and their satellite fellow-travellers. The ramifications of *Amerasia* reached far beyond those of a modest academic publication. It appeared, for instance, that Owen Lattimore, consultant to OWI and to the State Department on Far Eastern affairs, was formerly an editor of *Amerasia*. Another former editor was Frederick Vanderbilt Field, a columnist for *The Daily Worker* and secretary of the American Council of the Institute of Pacific Relations, with which Kate Mitchell had been affiliated in various capacities since 1933.

The publisher of *Amerasia* was a prosperous manufacturer of greeting cards who had a rather unusual record for a well-to-do businessman. Mr. Philip Jacob Jaffe, naturalized in 1923, had served as contributing editor of *Labor Defender,* monthly magazine of the International Labor Defense, a Communist organization, in 1933. From 1934 to 1936 he had been a member of the editorial board of *China Today,* publication of the pro-Soviet American Friends of the Chinese People, under his admitted alias of J. W. Phillips. Under that name he presided in 1933 over a banquet at which Earl Browder was a speaker. He had lectured at the Jefferson School of Social Science, an avowed Communist Party institution. In addition to several other pro-Soviet organizations, he was a member of the Board of Directors of the National Council of American-Soviet Friendship. *The New York Times* described him on June 7, 1945 (subsequent to his arrest), as "an active supporter of pro-Communist and pro-Soviet movements for a number of years."

What *The New York Times* did not know and what I could not possibly know, but what was established during the investigation, according to the information gathered by Congressman Dondero, was the following: that Jaffe is known to have visited Earl Browder's apartment several times in the spring of 1945; that he dined on more than one occasion at the Soviet consulate in New York; that when the Chinese Communist delegate, Tung Pi-wu, while in the United States in April 1945 to attend the San Francisco Conference, visited New York, he met Earl Browder one day in Jaffe's apartment; that Jaffe had been a liberal contributor to pro-Soviet causes and funds; and that at one time Jaffe had in his possession a message sent by Ambassador Hurley to his wife, advising her not to rent their home on Chesapeake Bay for the summer, inasmuch as he expected to return to the United States before the end of the summer.

How this strictly personal message fell into Jaffe's hands was never ascertained. But Congressional sources did establish the remarkable fact that Mr. Jaffe once reserved two tables at a hotel banquet held to launch a pro-Communist China front in the name of "The fifth floor, 35 East 12th Street," the national headquarters of the American Communist Party.

Kate L. Mitchell, co-editor of *Amerasia,* was a Buffalo heiress whose income from a trust fund has been estimated to run as high as $15,000 a year. Born in 1908, a graduate of Bryn Mawr, widely traveled and a student of Asiatic problems, Miss Mitchell was so close to Jaffe that she had in her possession keys to all the files in the office of *Amerasia.* When John Stewart Service returned from China, Miss Mitchell gave a party at which he was present. He had previously attended a special press conference held by the Institute of Pacific Relations in which he supported the position of the Chinese Communists.

Lieutenant Andrew Roth, a rising *Amerasia* star and protegé of Jaffe's, is a native New Yorker who had attended City College. Mr. Dondero disclosed that Roth had been placed in his key post of liaison officer between Naval Intelligence and the State Department "despite a totally unfavorable report resulting from an investigation by the Office of Naval Intelligence itself when he first applied for his commission."

Mark J. Gayn, a native of Manchuria, whose articles in leading magazines were based upon confidential documents supplied by Jaffe, was frequently consulted by the latter after his Washington trips, particularly in Japanese affairs. On at least one occasion John S. Service was known to have visited Gayn in his apartment. I had never met Gayn and was barely acquainted with Service.

OF MANY of these vital facts I was ignorant before my arrest. The political background of Jaffe and Miss Mitchell and their confreres was completely foreign to me. I knew Jaffe and his group as the editor of a magazine which had almost semiofficial standing among the left-wingers in the State Department. In spite of the fact that I was gathering biographical material on Chinese leaders for Mr. Jaffe, I did not go along with the *Amerasia* circle in questions of our policy in the Far East.

In the spring of 1945, when it was generally believed that our next step in the war would be an invasion of China, the problem of Manchuria came up for discussion and analysis in the State Department. In the event of our seizure of Manchuria, were we to hand it over eventually to any local Chinese faction, even the Communists? Mr. Robert Feary, a well-meaning former official of our Embassy in Japan, who drew his knowledge of China largely from the field dispatches of the pro-Soviet school, proposed that we turn over Manchuria to the Chinese Communists if Chiang Kai-shek's troops were not there to take it over immediately.

The proposal struck me as outrageous, since President Roosevelt had promised Chiang Kai-shek at the Cairo Conference that Manchuria would revert to his nation, by which we unmistakably meant the properly constituted government of China. I launched the initial protest against this and was able to bring about the defeat of the plan.

Shortly after this meeting on Manchurian policy, I was warned by a young foreign service officer of Scandinavian extraction in a friendly way that I would soon get into trouble if I opposed the anti-Kuomintang group in the China Section. Soon afterwards I ran into Lieutenant Roth in the street, and he told me that John Carter Vincent, head of the China Section, suspected me of being "too close to the Chiang Kai-shek crowd." I resented the remark, since I had but purely social relations with the Chinese Embassy in Washington. I wondered afterwards whether Roth had used a fabricated story merely to test me.

Late in May, I was surprised to find Andrew Roth in my apartment when I returned home from the office. He was in an extremely nervous state. He told me that he and his wife had intended to drop in upon us that evening, that she had gone shopping, and that in the meanwhile he had received some upsetting news which he was anxious to convey to her. It appeared that he had been ordered to go to Honolulu and that he was making preparations to leave when suddenly his orders were canceled. He evinced so much uneasiness and seemed so reluctant to talk about the matter that I was somewhat baffled.

When his charming wife Renee arrived about an hour or so later, happy and smiling, she was dumbfounded and put out by the bad news. I tried to comfort her by saying that the Navy probably would have a better job for her husband, but she brushed my remark aside in a peeved manner that indicated anxiety and fear.

Is it possible that both Roth and his wife were already aware that they were being shadowed and investigated, but said nothing about it to me? I myself felt perfectly at ease, for I had not the faintest notion that I was standing on the brink of disaster.

IT WAS JUST about this time that Mark Gayn, who had made his plans the previous year, prepared to go abroad as a foreign correspondent for the *Chicago Sun*. He suddenly called upon George Taylor, in charge of the Far Eastern Section at the OWI in Washington, and asked him to authorize the decontrol of some confidential government documents which Gayn claimed to have used for current articles.

Mr. Taylor issued a letter decontrolling certain papers. This letter Mr. Gayn presented at the New York office of the OWI, and is alleged to have persuaded the person in charge of the files there to interpret Mr. Taylor's authorization so broadly as to cover all the documents Gayn had in his possession.

My arrest in the evening of June 6 came to me like a bolt from the blue. The FBI agents found in my apartment three to four thousand cards of my collection of data on Chinese personalities, and half a dozen folders of reports and memoranda dealing with political and geographic problems in Asia. Some of these were confidential papers I had taken home to study. None of the documents was of a military character which would affect national security. It was a common practice in Washington among overworked government employees to take home confidential papers to work on.

When word of our arrests had spread through Washington, there was general burning of official papers, taken home innocently or otherwise, all over the Capital.

The strange course which the Espionage Case took from the moment of our arrests became evident to me that night, even when I was led into the office of the United States Commissioner for arraignment. On June 6 Andrew Roth was still a uniformed lieutenant in the service of the United States Navy. That night, as I beheld him a fellow-prisoner, I was surprised to find him wearing civilian clothes. Upon inquiry I learned that literally overnight Lieutenant Roth had been mustered out of the service. It was not until later that it had dawned on me how grave it might have been for Roth to face charges under the Espionage Act in wartime while still an officer in the Naval Intelligence.

When Kate Mitchell was arrested in New York that night she had in her possession, according to Congressman Dondero, a highly confidential military document entitled "Plan of Battle Operations for Soldiers." It was a paper of such importance that army officers were subject to courtmartial if they lost their copies. Also in the possession of Miss Mitchell were found documents from the OSS and the Office of Naval Intelligence. These were part of the huge files of top secret material gathered by Jaffe.

Mark Gayn, who had made use at various times of *Amerasia* files, had more than 200 secret documents in his apartment at the time of his arrest. Mr. Gayn was the only one of the *Amerasia* group to admit, on the night of his arrest, in a signed statement, that he had been found in possession of confidential government papers.

Mr. Jaffe, either before the arrest or upon his release on bail, is known to have used the authorization to decontrol certain papers issued to Gayn by the OWI in some inexplicable manner so as to claim exemption for all the documents found in his own possession.

ON JUNE 8, the day after the arrests, Mr. Joseph C. Grew, then Acting Secretary of State, announced to the country that "a comprehensive security program is to be continued unrelentingly in order to stop completely the illegal and disloyal conveyance of confidential and other secret information to unauthorized persons."

Philip Jaffe, speaking for himself and Miss Mitchell the following day, upon their release on bail, countered with a statement to the press: "The Red-baiting character of this case is scandalous and often libelous."

114

Mark Gayn raised the cry of the freedom of the press, which certain so-called liberal publications took up so as to eclipse in the public mind the charges under the Espionage Act. Popular radio commentators echoed the cry.

Undersecretary Grew became a target for a campaign of vilification as chief culprit in the case. The former Lieutenant Andrew Roth wrote a series of articles in a New York evening paper and published a book in which he attacked Grew as the father of a dangerous State Department policy in the Far East and as the main prop of the throne in Japan, which was represented as being in the way of a "democratic" transformation in that country.

While public attention was largely focused upon extraneous issues, the Espionage Case itself was following a special course behind the scenes. It appeared that Kate Mitchell had an influential uncle in Buffalo, a reputable attorney by the name of James M. Mitchell, former president of the New York State Bar Association. Mr. Mitchell was a member of a very influential law firm in Buffalo, Kenefick, Cooke, Mitchell, Bass & Letchworth. The New York City correspondents of that law firm include the most redoubtable Colonel Joseph M. Hartfield, extremely well known and extremely influential in government circles in Washington. Colonel Hartfield, who is regarded by some as one of the most powerful political lawyers in the country, made at least four trips to Washington, where he called on top officials of the Department of Justice in the matter.

At the same time Congressman Emanuel Celler of New York interested himself in the defense of the New York figures involved in the case. To what extent he exerted his influence has never been determined. It was perhaps only a coincidence that his law partner, Mr. Arthur Sheinberg, appeared as Jaffe's New York attorney when his case was called before the Criminal Division No. 1 of the District Court of the District of Columbia.

My own attorney was Arthur J. Hilland, whose first demand on me was that I tell him the truth and nothing but the truth. As I had nothing to conceal, my principal worry was my wife's difficulty in raising the $10,000 bail, for we were people of most modest means.

The grand jury heard first the testimony of Service, Gayn, and Miss Mitchell. At the end of June it was announced that new evidence would be presented by the Justice Department and additional persons would be charged with espionage.

The grand jury proceedings are, of course, secret. But it has been reported to me that John Service had accused me of furnishing Jaffe with documents found in his possession, which was a complete and vicious fabrication. According to Congressman Dondero, for some unaccountable reasons the government attorneys presented to the grand jury only a part of the evidence in their possession.

On August 10 came the sensational announcement that the grand jury had dropped the indictments against Service, Gayn, and Miss Mitchell. The clearing of these three was the signal for a renewed campaign against Undersecretary Grew in the press. Within the State Department, it was generally known Dean Acheson headed the anti-Grew faction.

The evening of August 13, J. Raymond Walsh, research director of CIO-PAC, outspoken Soviet partisan, made over the radio a strong plea for the defendants in the Espionage Case. Of John Service he said: "His arrest brought some exceedingly powerful people within the government to his defense. Again one can easily infer that those who began this affair wished they hadn't. . . ."

A substantial fund for the defense of Mr. Service had been raised with the help of Mortimer Graves, Secretary of The American Council of Learned Societies. No one of the pro-Soviet group bothered about my defense.

On August 14 Assistant Secretary of State Dean Acheson tendered his resignation to Secretary Byrnes. For a moment it looked as if Mr. Grew had won out. But that same day, August 14, the newly installed Secretary Byrnes addressed a letter to John Service, congratulating him on the "happy termination" of his ordeal and reinstating him to active duty "for important work in connection with Far Eastern affairs." At the same time, Undersecretary Grew wrote to Service a more formal letter expressing his pleasure at being returned to duty and praising his enviable record.

IT WAS ABOUT this time that Joseph E. Davies, of *Mission to Moscow* fame, was alleged to have declared that Acheson made Grew's resignation from the service a condition of his returning to the State Department.

Two days later Undersecretary Grew, after a lifetime in the diplomatic service, resigned and President Truman announced that Dean Acheson would take over the post of Undersecretary of State.

On September 29 the news that Jaffe had changed his plea from "not guilty" to that of "guilty" of the unauthorized possession of government documents and was fined $2500 hit me like a bombshell. It appeared that by some strange coincidence Jaffe's case had been called before Justice Proctor of the District Court on a Saturday morning. Robert Hitchcock, of Buffalo, had presented the case for the Department of Justice. The court asked for a brief statement of the government's case, which Mr. Hitchcock promised to do in "less than five minutes."

The FBI has the authority to make arrests only upon the presentation of adequate evidence, but it has nothing to do with the court's disposal of such evidence.

"I have heretofore charged and reiterate now," declared Congressman Dondero on the floor of the House, "that the Court before whom these cases were brought was not fully informed of the facts. A summary of the court proceedings had been furnished to me, which shows no evidence or exhibit obtained by the Federal Bureau of Investigation presented to the court. Jaffe's counsel told the court that Jaffe had no intention of harming the government, and United States Attorney Hitchcock told the court there was no element of disloyalty in connection with the case."

My own situation was growing more deplorable and my financial circumstances more straitened. I had been put "on leave without-pay" status pending the outcome of the case. I had no means to cover the expenses of my defense. For weeks I had lain awake nights hoping for a speedy trial, expecting an acquittal.

I now resolved to go to New York to look up Mr. Jaffe. I telephoned the office of *Amerasia* and he somewhat reluctantly agreed to see me. I told him of my financial plight and he agreed to defray the costs of my defense as well as to pay the fine which might be imposed upon me. At this time, in October, the only two of the Case of Six left on the calendar, were those of myself and of Andrew Roth.

To run ahead of the story, my own case came up on November 2. Upon insistent advice, I decided not to contest it as I had planned, and pleaded *nolo contendere*. The court imposed a fine of five hundred dollars, which was paid by Mr. Jaffe's representative. He also paid all other expenses in my case, which ran to an additional three thousand dollars. As for Andrew Roth, the indictment against him was dismissed in February 1946 for insufficient evidence.

During my conference with Mr. Jaffe in October, he dropped a remark which one could never forget.

"Well, we've suffered a lot," he said, "but, anyhow, we got Grew out."

Ambassador Hurley was next to go. The road was clear for the pro-Soviet China bloc to take over the Far Eastern Division of the State Department. The policy which General Stilwell attempted to force down the throat of our ally Chiang Kai-shek as a means of defeating Japan was entrusted to General Marshall *after* Japan's defeat by America and *after* the rape of Manchuria by Soviet forces.—EDITOR'S NOTE.

October 1946

IPR—THE REAL CHINA LOBBY

By SHEPPARD MARLEY

[*The Institute of Pacific Relations was the spearhead of the Communist propaganda campaign in the United States promoting Soviet interests in the Far East. Many prominent American businessmen in their political innocence lent their names to the Institute, which was one of the major factors in the eventual rise of Red China. To expose its insidious influence,* Plain Talk *assigned a highly qualified researcher who, under the assumed name of Sheppard Marley, contributed an exposé of the IPR published in two installments in December 1946 and January 1947. The real identity of the author cannot be disclosed without his permission even now. Suffice it to add that he has achieved distinction as a professor in one of the Ivy League universities.*]

I

SOME TIME AGO the Institute of Pacific Relations placed the following notice in
the "Personals" column of the *Saturday Review of Literature*:

> Long on curiosity—short on time? IPR popular pamphlets make you a scintil-
> lating conversationalist on the Far East. You can deftly discuss everything from
> Australian slang to the problems of China and the Philippines. Send for a list
> of Institute of Pacific Relations pamphlets today. Box 939-K.

If a reader of this semi-intellectual lonely-hearts column had made a slight
error in the box number and written to 938-K instead of the IPR's 939-K, he
would have received an answer from the gentleman who inserted the following
notice in the same issue: "Will lady in a quiet castle seek spiritual relaxation
through exchange of correspondence with a highly learned gentleman?"

What the IPR copywriter deftly neglected to mention in this prospectus designed for the busy dilettante was that the publications of the Institute of Pacific Relations are likely to make the deft conversationalist sound similar to a
Daily Worker editorial, though on a much more genteel level. For the IPR is
still another of the respectable monied organizations into which fellow-travelers
have infiltrated and have developed workers in their own image. The peculiar
conjuncture of social conditions and psychological ailments which has resulted
in the dissemination of Stalinist propaganda by groups supported mainly with
capitalist money is a problem for the academicians. Here we merely offer
another case study.

The Institute of Pacific Relations came into being in July 1925 in Honolulu, at
an international conference of which the chief engineer was Mr. Edward C.
Carter, the present executive vice-chairman of the American Council of the
Institute of Pacific Relations and apparently its most influential officer. The intricate nature of the administrative setup of the Institute makes it ideal for
control by a few well-placed persons. Small wonder then that many of its leading and most prolific writers are dependable fellow-travelers who faithfully
follow the tortuous path Stalin sets—even if they have to slow down around the
sharp turns of Soviet policy.

The Institute's activity seldom reaches any large section of the public directly,
and few persons know that it exists. It is doubtful if one out of 1,000 of the
parents of boys who fought their way across the Pacific, from Guadalcanal to
Okinawa, has ever heard of this organization. Yet in government circles, including those where America's high policy in the Pacific is determined, the influence of the Institute of Pacific Relations has been enormous and is apparently
growing.

During the recent war, the Institute supplied many agencies with experts on
the Far East. Four IPR staff members worked for the China section of the
UNRRA. Three others did research for MacArthur's headquarters on Japanese

reconstruction. William L. Holland was the head of the O.W.I. in China. Owen Lattimore was President Roosevelt's gift to Chiang Kai-shek for a time and President Truman's special adviser to MacArthur as well as Far Eastern head of O.W.I. The IPR supplied lesser lights to the O.W.I., O.S.S., and the State Department. Not all of these workers who joined government agencies were Communists or fellow-travelers. The IPR, however, frequently provided research specialists who were interested mainly in the furthering of Stalin's aims in the Far East.

Many IPR trustees reached positions of considerable importance. In 1941 Lauchlin Currie was President Roosevelt's special emissary to China. William C. Johnstone worked on a special assignment for the State Department. George E. Taylor was director of the O.W.I.'s Far Eastern section and later in the State Department's Office of International Information and Cultural Affairs. Benjamin Kizer, a Spokane lawyer, headed the UNRRA in China.

The Institute's aid to the government was not limited to supplying experts of varying degrees, for the government bought 750,000 IPR pamphlets for soldiers in the Pacific and Asiatic theaters. Schools, too, have been influenced by IPR publications, especially the series published jointly with the Webster Company of St. Louis, designed for a fourteen-year-old reading level. In three and a half years this series sold over a million copies.

Another way in which the IPR influences public opinion is through the newspapers and periodical press. As the IPR itself does not tire of saying, no one seems to know anything about the Far East. The harried editorial writer is immeasurably pleased, then, when he sees on his desk a neat publicity release and a copy of an article on some aspect of Chinese politics which he can now proceed to discuss as deftly as though he had read the IPR's notice in the *Saturday Review of Literature.*

LIKE MOST ASSOCIATIONS into which the Communists and fellow-travelers have moved, the IPR reveals certain inconsistencies and peculiarities of policy that can be explained only by the ideological affiliations of its most important figures.

Operating more cleverly in IPR than in most groups they have entered, the Communists and their friends have been able to keep the reputation of this outfit pretty clean. But evidence of their work is easily noted when one takes the IPR material in bulk and breaks it down into two types: the controversial and non-controversial. What has buffaloed most readers of IPR books, pamphlets, and periodicals is that so much of the stuff is of a very scholarly nature, not at all on subjects that arouse the emotions any more readily than do articles on Chinese pottery. Yet in the last decade or so, at least two out of every three articles in IPR's two journals [*Pacific Affairs,* quarterly, and *Far Eastern Survey,* biweekly] on such hot subjects as Chinese politics, the Soviet Union, and the general political situation in the Far East with respect to those two countries and the United States, have been written by such staunch defenders of Stalin as T. A. Bisson,

Owen Lattimore, Harriet Moore, Laurence Salisbury, and others not too numerous to mention in due time.

It may be claimed that by selecting excerpts and quoting "out of context" any writer can be shown to believe almost anything. This is frequently true. Yet the weight of the evidence that links the IPR to the Communist line is too great to pass off with such platitudes. The writings of the fellow-travelers and outright Communists in IPR publications constitute only a small part of the total IPR material—but they constitute its most vital part and they deal with the subjects that are most significant for American foreign policy, international relations and public education.

The IPR's chief method of disclaiming responsibility for what appears under its sponsorship is to include a statement in its publications that the views expressed are those of the writers, not of the IPR or any of its component units. But no one is ever fooled by such disavowals, not even IPR people. Owen Lattimore, who edited the IPR quarterly, *Pacific Affairs,* from 1934 to 1941, wrote in a report of the IPR secretariat in 1936: "The fact that there is a printed notice in each number (of *Pacific Affairs*) specifically declaring that each contributor is personally responsible for his own statements of opinion and that neither the national councils nor the Institute as a whole can be held responsible, has meant little."

The IPR has often protested that it does not select its writers according to their political beliefs, but because of their scholarship and research ability. One wonders, nevertheless, whether the bulk of the IPR publications would yield an impression any different from the one it does now if it were *not* being used as a front for Communist propaganda. It could hardly do better work for Stalin even if it had been set up by his agents.

THE INSTITUTE OF PACIFIC RELATIONS is composed of ten member bodies from each of the following countries: Australia, Canada, China, France, Netherlands-Netherlands Indies, New Zealand, the Philippines, the United Kingdom, the Soviet Union, and the United States. The Pacific Council, nominally the ruling body, has one representative from each of these National Councils. With the members of the Pacific Council scattered over thousands of miles, there is little centralized control. Actually the American Council is the main unit, and the one most familiar to Americans as well as the one most afflicted with the disease of Stalinist apologetics. Like the parent organization, the American Council is itself a nightmare of administrative complexity. In recent years there has been no meeting of the membership, which now is just below 2,000.

Genuine power in the American Council of the IPR is vested in the Executive Committee of the Board of Trustees. Of the eight members of this ruling group, the four most vocal are Communists and fellow travelers. This is what the broad and respectable front of IPR conceals. The big four are Edward C.

Carter, Frederick Vanderbilt Field, Harriet L. Moore, and Owen Lattimore. All four, with the recent exception of Field, who has joined the Communist Party, move exclusively on the higher levels of gentility in American academic and political life.

Edward C. Carter, the leading light in the IPR, is not the intellectual type. He has written rather infrequently, but his affiliations are nevertheless enlightening. For many years he was on the Board of Directors of the American-Russian Institute, which publishes a quarterly dedicated to the scholarly adulation of all that takes place in Stalin's Russia. He has contributed to *Soviet Russia Today,* a less esoteric market for pro-Soviet articles. In 1938 he signed a statement, published in that magazine, defending the Moscow mock trials. During most of the war years he was a member of the Board of Directors of Russian War Relief.

The case of Frederick Vanderbilt Field is more obvious. Now a member of the Communist Party, Field is the *Daily Worker's* special expert on the Far East, and an associate editor of the Communist weekly, *New Masses.*

Harriet L. Moore has the usual Communist front connections. She was secretary of the Russian War Relief and a member of the Board of Directors of the American-Russian Institute, whose publications she edits. She has also been on the editorial board of *Amerasia,* long a tooter of Stalin's horn among those interested in Far Eastern affairs. This is the magazine which figured as the focal point in the State Department Espionage Case, as reported by E. S. Larsen, in *Plain Talk* for October.

Of the four chief policy-makers of IPR, Owen Lattimore is the best known and most respected in academic circles. He is now director of the Walter Hines Page School of International Relations at Johns Hopkins University. He too has served his stint on the editorial board of *Amerasia,* and has defended the Moscow purge trials.

Through his editorship of the quarterly, *Pacific Affairs,* from 1934 to 1941, Owen Lattimore was able to exert considerable influence in IPR. When he took it over, *Pacific Affairs* was dull, unknown, and devoted mainly to research and statements apparently carefully pruned to remove the slightest trace of a positive point of view about anything more controversial than the depth of the Sulu Sea. As fascism spread and the threat of war increased, Lattimore published articles that took a forthright stand; but in general he followed the Popular Front line then in vogue. *Pacific Affairs* contained contributions generally favorable to Soviet Russia, against America's neutrality policy, and in praise of the Chinese Communists.

IS THE IPR A PRESSURE GROUP or a research outfit? The letter from Owen Latimore to Edward C. Carter (on page 123), a remarkable document in several respects, should settle this question once and for all, although the stream of

121

highly opinionated writing emanating from the IPR for years furnishes a clear enough answer. Three characteristics stand out in a study of the IPR publications:

First, there is not to be found in its literature any fundamental criticism of the Soviet Union, either of its internal regime or its foreign policy.

Second, there has been abundant and vigorous criticism of the Chinese government and, especially in recent years, equally strong and prominent espousal of the cause of the Chinese Communists.

Third, there was until Pearl Harbor relatively little criticism on the part of the IPR of Japan's internal regime or its foreign policy.

Indeed, in the light of the accompanying letter from Mr. Lattimore to Mr. Carter and of the additional pieces of evidence as to the IPR's ties with the Japanese imperialists, there is room for a Congressional inquiry into this still dark field. In a subsequent article we shall deal with the first two aspects of the IPR's activity, namely, its pro-Soviet and anti-Chiang Kai-shek stands. Here we shall confine ourselves to five salient features of the strange marriage between the IPR and the Japanese war lords:

1. Owen Lattimore wrote his letter on May 18, 1938, less than ten months after Japan launched its undeclared war on China and but a few weeks after Hitler's annexation of Austria, events which were regarded in Moscow as the beginnings of World War II. In this missive Mr. Lattimore proposed the dismemberment of China and a settlement with Japan on the basis of "what China is and what Japan is, as of 1939, rather than what either country was as of 1936." The occasion for this communication was a memorandum by a Chinese pro-Communist, Chen Han-seng, who had outlined a study of Chinese foreign policy to cover the period of 1931–39. Mr. Carter, upon the receipt of the extraordinary letter, is on record in a memorandum dated May 20, 1938, addressed to Miriam Farley of the IPR, as follows: "This morning I have received Owen Lattimore's comment with which of course I agree." All that remains to be added on this point is that neither Mr. Lattimore nor Mr. Carter made clear the purpose of the proposed settlement: Was it intended to help Japan retain the vast areas in North China gained by her aggression or to enable the Chinese Communists to extend their domains as they did in 1945?

2. Lattimore's suggestion, with which Mr. Carter agreed, contemplated direct action by the IPR in the political field, something which it has been at pains to deny frequently. As recently as October 24, 1946, Mr. Carter wrote to a critic of his organization: "The IPR is not an action group and I can assure you it has never set up an action group of any nature whatever." It is obvious from Lattimore's letter that "in pressing for terms of settlement" the IPR certainly qualified as a pressure group, which is hardly distinguishable from an "action group."

Is it possible that Mr. Carter, finding himself on the horns of a dilemma, really

Mr. Edward C. Carter
129 East 52nd Street
New York City

Dear Carter:

I have just been reading with great interest Chen Han-seng's memorandum of 27 April attached to your letter of 9 May. As I shall be going with Fred* to a regional conference at Seattle at the end of this week and so shall have to miss Holland when he passes through, I am replying directly.

As usual, Chen Han-seng has picked out the really crucial points. The IPR stands to maintain and increase its reputation by presenting the constructive possibilities of a Far Eastern settlement. All reactionary estimates of "what is China" will be based on pre-war China and will exclude changes occurring in the course of the war. In pressing for terms of settlement, the IPR is in a better position than any other agency to gage the character and extent of changes occurring during the war; it could and should establish what China is and what Japan is, as of 1939, rather than what either country was as of 1936.

Of course in order to establish the "is" of 1939, the taking off point must be the "was" up to 1937; but the "was" should be only the taking off point and the major emphasis should be consistently applied to the processes of change in 1937 and 1938 and the levels attained and further trends indicated as of 1939.

Yours very sincerely,
(*signed*) OWEN LATTIMORE

---

*Probably Frederick Vanderbilt Field, millionaire Communist. *Ed.*

had meant to endorse the idea of turning over half of China to the Communists and not to the Japanese? For this is what he wrote on October 24th, 1946:

"One of your most fantastically inaccurate statements is the accusation that Mr. Owen Lattimore, back in 1938 and 1939, advocated peace in China by turning over half of China to the Japanese. Mr. Lattimore was far ahead of the vast majority of Americans in recognizing the nature and danger of Japanese aggression—years before our government and people were fully alive to its menace."

3. In 1936 a Japanese scientific expedition was permitted by the United States to cruise freely in the waters along the Alaska coast, where it took soundings. Around the same time the Japanese tried to establish fisheries rights in the same areas. In both of these ventures, it has been charged by Miller

Freeman, Pacific coast publisher and former Navy Intelligence officer, that the Japanese were aided by the chairman of the American Council of the IPR at the time, who was also a member of a special advisory committee on trade and commerce in the Department of State.

4. Upton Close, writer and radio commentator, made the following signed statement: "A few days prior to the Pearl Harbor disaster, Mr. Trammel (of the National Broadcasting Company) received a letter from E. C. Carter, head of the Institute of Pacific Relations, demanding that I be dropped from the air because I was 'anti-Japanese.'"

5. The Japan Council of the IPR served the interests of aggression. A dispatch of December 7, 1945, by Frank Kelley, then in Tokyo as correspondent for the New York *Herald Tribune,* describes how in Japan the IPR was used as a front for imperialist purposes. Prince Fumimaro Konoye, who was Premier of Japan during much of the crucial period between the renewed war on China in 1937 and the attack upon Pearl Harbor four and a half years later, took a deep interest in his country's IPR chapter. He put his personal, trusted aides into the key posts in the Japanese IPR, which was supported largely with funds contributed by the very industrialists who helped the militarists plan and carry out wars of aggression throughout the Pacific area. It was Konoye who had ordered the preparation of a report explaining Japan's need for expansion because of "population pressure." This report was read to the IPR international conference of 1936, which was held in Yosemite National Park, in California.

The chief secretary of the Japan Council of IPR, according to Mr. Kelley in the *Herald Tribune,* was Tomohiko Ushiba, Konoye's private secretary. Through Ushiba, Prince Konoye kept in touch with Edward C. Carter, then chief of the IPR's "international secretariat," so that he could "keep watch on American State Department policies." Far Eastern experts, such as abound in the IPR, must surely have known that Prince Konoye was among the leading exponents of Japanese aggression for many years before Pearl Harbor. Yet there is no evidence that the Institute ever took any steps to prevent its use as a front for the dissemination of propaganda in the United States and for the gathering of inside political and military information about this country.

Unlike the pink pills served by Dr. Carter when treating Russia or China, these five points bearing upon the relations between the IPR and the imperialists of Japan cannot be sugar-coated. The responsible directors of the IPR, which is in the nature of a higher educational institution, owe it to the public to probe fully into its baffling ties with the Mikado's servants. Considering the semiofficial status which the IPR has acquired in the policy-making branches of the Federal Government, the Congress owes it to the country to investigate the history of the organization, its obscure foreign links, its unduly complex administrative setup, and its alliances with pro-Soviet and pro-Communist elements both at home and abroad.

In August 1945 the *Daily Worker* printed a letter signed by twenty-one persons protesting United States policy in China, attacking the Chinese government, and defending the Chinese Communists. Among the signers were the following frequent contributors to the publications of the Institute of Pacific Relations: Frederick Vanderbilt Field, T. A. Bisson, Laurence E. Salisbury, and Nym Wales, who is the wife of Edgar Snow.

Late in 1945 the New York State Committee of the Communist Party planned a "Campaign of Struggle Against the United States Imperialist Intervention in China." Included in the instructions to the faithful was a statement urging "concentration during this campaign on the sale and distribution" of a number of pamphlets and books by such well-known objective students of public affairs as J. Stalin and Gunther Stein, whose *The Challenge of Red China* made the honor roll. A few months after the distribution of these instructions, the American Council of the IPR sent out a circular advertising Stein's book which it had not even sponsored.

IPR contributors abound in the Committee for a Democratic Far Eastern Policy, which might more properly be called the Committee for a Stalinist Far Eastern Policy. Field and Nym Wales are on the Committee's Board of Directors. Among its thirteen "consultants," the following eight have written for the IPR: Bisson, Salisbury, Stein, Israel Epstein, Kumar Goshal, Maxwell Stewart, Kate Mitchell, and Philip Jaffe, both of the latter leading figures in the *Amerasia* espionage case described by E. S. Larsen in the October issue of *Plain Talk*.

It is not surprising, therefore, that IPR publications have been filled with the contributions of such other friends and champions of Soviet Russia as Anna Louise Strong, Michael Greenberg, Michael Lindsay, Abraham Chapman, Evans F. Carlson, Edgar Snow, and William Mandel.

As for the tie between the eminently respectable IPR and *Amerasia,* there is ample room for further investigation. It is an established fact that when the IPR had its headquarters at 129 East 52nd Street, New York City, the offices of *Amerasia* were then in an adjoining building; so intimate was the relationship between them that an opening had been made in the walls for a special doorway to connect the two. It has not been established, however, whether at that time *Amerasia* had already been filching top secret documents in Washington. Nor has it been ascertained whether the large photocopying department which, according to Congressman Dondero, was working "through the night, in the small hours of the morning and even on Sundays" photostating the stolen papers, had already been installed in the offices of *Amerasia.*

Just as ample are the grounds for further investigation into the conduct of the head of the IPR, Edward C. Carter, in his capacity as chairman of the committee in charge of allocations of the United China Relief, which had disbursed $900,000 through Madame Sun Yat-sen without a public accounting on her part.

In this connection, a memorandum prepared in September 1942 for the American Council of the Institute of Pacific Relations by Robert Barnett, who went to China for the United China Relief and who is now with the Korean Division of the Department of State, is of moment. The memorandum, entitled "The Outlook in Free China," was marked *Confidential: not for circulation or quotation.* In it, Mr. Barnett reported objectively on a series of interviews he had had with various Chinese leaders, including General Chou En-lai, representative in Chungking of the Chinese Communist party. The interview took place on April 22, 1942, during one of the blackest periods of the war for the Allies, when the Chinese Communists made common cause with Generalissimo Chiang Kai-shek against the Japanese.

When asked by Mr. Barnett how American friends could most effectively provide relief for the Border Regions in China under Communist control, Chou En-lai replied:

"So far as relief to Border Regions is concerned, for example, the only channel is through Madame Chiang Kai-shek who is genuinely interested in relief work in every area of China. She has recently helped the Chinese Communists. . . . To channelize assistance through Madame Sun Yet-sen alone excites immediate opposition, although small sums of money may occasionally find their way through. Foreigners wishing to help the Communists should work with Madame Chiang, Madame Sun, and Madame Kung, acting jointly under Madame Chiang's name."

Despite this injunction from the recognized leader of the Chinese Communists, who were then wholeheartedly cooperating with the Kuomintang, Mr. Carter and his associates transmitted the $900,000 worth of American relief exclusively to Madame Sun Yat-sen. The contributors of this aid have never been able to learn why the American officials of the United China Relief displayed more pro-Communist zeal than the Communist leader nor what happened to the funds and supplies collected in the United States.

THE LITERARY ASPECT of the IPR affords a definite clue to its character: it has never been guilty of criticizing the conduct of the Soviet government in any fundamental respect. Not so clear has been the administrative setup of the organization, which has puzzled even some of its ranking members. But most of the time the doubts raised about the forces behind the IPR are quickly resolved through the personality of its guiding spirit, Edward C. Carter. Dr. Carter may serve pink pills. But his own diet is strictly beyond reproach. Leading a literary caravan of Communists and fellow-travelers, he has managed himself to retain the conservative label and the reputation of an independent and impartial policy-maker.

Yet among the articles and books that have appeared under the IPR imprint have been such opinionated products as those of Frederick V. Field. Because of his acknowledged membership in the Communist party, it is sufficient to observe that nothing Mr. Field has written for the IPR has ever deviated from the party line in any important respect, and he has written on the most controversial political issues. It is pertinent, however, to cite an example of the coordination of views between the Communist press and IPR publications.

In the summer of 1943 it became evident that the Stalinists no longer thought it necessary to maintain the favorable attitude toward the government of Chiang Kai-shek that had developed out of the war against Japan. In discussing "The Crisis in China" in the *New Masses* of August 24, 1943, Field reviewed the current crop of articles against the Chinese government, noting especially the contributions by a certain missionary, Creighton Lacy; by a writer in the official Soviet publication *War and the Working Class*; and by T. A. Bisson, Y. Y. Hsu, and Lawrence K. Rosinger. The last three were frequent contributors to IPR publications.

The article by Bisson to which Field referred appeared in the IPR's biweekly, *Far Eastern Survey,* for July 14, 1943. It marked the beginning of the turn in sentiment expressed by many other IPR writers on the Kuomintang Communist issue in China. Bisson came up with this analysis of the internal situation: "A year or more before Pearl Harbor, therefore, two Chinas had definitely emerged. . . . One is generally called Kuomintang China; the other is called Communist China." These were misnomers, he added, for the two Chinas could be more accurately called "feudal" China and "democratic" China.

Now by a strange coincidence Field carried out the same line of argument in the *New Masses* of July 13, 1943. Mr. Bisson had served his stint on the editorial board of *Amerasia* and contributed to *Soviet Russia Today.* In August 1939, the very month of the Stalin-Hitler pact, Bisson was one of the signers of the memorable "letter of the 400" which whitewashed Soviet policy.

There was nothing new about this whitewashing of Soviet deeds and misdeeds on the part of IPR associates. In 1938 Owen Lattimore, one of the main pillars of the organization, printed in *Pacific Affairs* a discussion of the Moscow purge "trials" by the well-known fellow-traveler, Mary Van Kleeck, in which she accepted Moscow's official version without question. William Henry Chamberlin, in a letter in the following issue, disputed this interpretation, pointing out some inconsistencies in the "trials" and the lack of objective evidence against the defendants. To this letter Lattimore added his own views, supporting the conduct of the mock trails which he regarded as evidence of democracy in the Soviet Union. The purge tribunals were, according to him, "a triumph for democracy."

Mr. Lattimore, who had in 1937 condemned the Japanese aggression upon China, could never bring himself to view the Soviet Union's attacks upon Finland and Poland as aggression. In the last issue of *Pacific Affairs* edited by him, and which appeared before the German invasion of Russia, Lattimore claimed that since the causes of the war were not "only the wrongs done to Britain by Germany," merely settling these matters would not be settling the main issues. "The prime wrongs," he continued, "were those that were done to China, Ethiopia, Spain, Czechoslovakia, and Albania—not by Japan and Italy and Germany alone, but by Britain and France and the United States as well."

Because the omission of Russia from the list of culprits was conspicuous, Lattimore added a footnote: "I have not here dealt with Poland, Finland, the Baltic and Balkan and Scandinavian countries, and so forth, because what they have suffered has been the result, not the cause, of war." This remarkable statement, besides whitewashing the Soviet Union, was Lattimore's own timid contribution to the Communist party's and fellow-travelers' campaign, spearheaded by the American Peace Mobilization, to stop aid to Britain and to show the futility of fighting Hitler during his pact with Stalin. . . .

FREDERICK VANDERBILT FIELD, the "millionaire Communist," who serves as secretary of the American Council of the Institute of Pacific Relations is in one capacity the closest link between this organization and the Communist party. In one of his other capacities he links the IPR with that citadel of the Republican party, the *New York Herald Tribune*, whose foreign editor, Joseph Barnes, is his lifelong comrade-in-arms. . . .

The Field-Barnes team was part of the original brain trust of the IPR. Mr. Barnes will be remembered as the literary companion of Wendell Willkie on his tour of Soviet Russia and as one of the chiefs of the OWI who had been dismissed by Elmer Davis with the approval of President Roosevelt on account of his alleged pro-Soviet attitude.

Mr. Barnes and Mr. Field formed a friendship at Harvard University more than twenty years ago. Barnes first went to the Soviet Union in the summer of 1928 and returned to it in 1931, when he entered the employ of the Soviet branch of the IPR as a research specialist. Upon his return to the United States he became intimately associated with Field in a tourist enterprise which specialized in arranging study tours of the Soviet Union. At the same time both were active in the IPR.

Mr. Barnes then married on November 1, 1936, Elizabeth Brown Field, who in the elections of that year registered as a Communist in New York City. In an article in the *Atlantic Monthly* for January 1937, entitled "The American Dream," Mr. Barnes eulogized Earl Browder, William Z. Foster, and the other American Communist leaders as the "spiritual inheritors of the Founding Fathers."

To be sure, nothing as explicit may be found in the writings of the other brain trusters in the official publications of the IPR. There its leading experts have endeavored, particularly in recent years, to present Communists as reformers and liberals. Thus in 1944, after the Soviet line toward Chiang Kai-shek had changed, the new editor of the *Far Eastern Review,* Mr. Laurence E.

Salisbury, joined his colleague Bisson in denying that the Chinese Communists were Communists. "The term can be used correctly only in quotation marks," wrote Mr. Salisbury.

The question when a Communist is a "Communist" or just a Communist is one to which IPR writers have given plenty of thought. Following the formal dissolution of the Communist International, there was a worldwide propaganda campaign to divorce in the public mind all foreign Communist elements, whether in the Balkans or in China, from any connection with Moscow. Maxwell S. Stewart, a veteran upholder of Soviet policies, wrote in his IPR pamphlet on "War-Time China" published in 1944, that Chinese Communists are like no other Communists the world over, for they attract many "progressive and patriotic Chinese who know little of the doctrines of Karl Marx or Stalin and care less."

This familiar song describing Communists as democrats and "agrarians" could not but confuse and befuddle public opinion. But the experts in the IPR know only too well that the entire leadership of the Chinese Communist movement is avowedly Marxian, and just as avowedly loyal to Lenin and Stalin. They know more. They know the unbroken and massive record of intimate relations since 1921 between Moscow and the Chinese Communist party. And they know that the regime of the latter in the provinces controlled by Yenan is as totalitarian as Stalin's own in Russia proper.

MANY PROMINENT CITIZENS who have lent their prestige and financial support to the IPR are still convinced that it is an impartial research group only. Such is the case of W. W. Waymack, editor of the *Des Moines Register and Tribune,* who in a formal statement asserted that if one wished, one could also prove from its writings "that the IPR is anti-Communist." Mr. Waymack would indeed be hard put to it to adduce any such proof. A comprehensive examination of the literary output of the IPR shows that, like the official Communist press, it has never been guilty of such oversights in regard to the Soviet government.

This feature of the Institute's activity should be investigated by its patrons, just as its interlocking organizational set-up deserves thorough scrutiny. The outside affiliations, public and private, of IPR leaders and writers can also bear investigation. It will be found that the net effect of the IPR literature, especially that of the American Council, has been the defense of Stalin's tyranny at home and of his aggression abroad.

December 1946

THE LIE MARCHES ON

By ALFRED KOHLBERG

[*There were two China lobbies. One was the cabal inside the State Department that influenced and guided General Stilwell and General Marshall, with
the aid of the Institute of Pacific Relations and leading organs of the press;
this dark force, which was largely responsible for the loss of mainland China
to Communism, has to this day remained unknown to the American people.
And then there was the China Lobby that has become a fixture of the history
of our times, a figment of Red and misguided liberals' propaganda, which
centered around a single patriotic citizen, Alfred Kohlberg, an importer of
linens from China, who occupied an inconspicuous showroom on the street
floor of 37th Street, New York. Here Mr. Kohlberg, an ordinary well-to-do
merchant, like thousands of others in his district, presided over a China Policy
Association that he had organized. Its circulars became familiar to hundreds of
newspaper editors because of Mr. Kohlberg's homespun outpourings, which
he had multigraphed in the basement of his shop. Every now and then Mr.
Kohlberg would convoke an after-dinner meeting of his committee, attended
by a score or more of anti-Communist citizens, which would pass a resolution
that rarely made the columns of important newspapers. This was the dimen-
sion of the so-called China Lobby which has been perpetuated in the mythology
of our times. As publisher of* Plain Talk, *Mr. Kohlberg would now and then
send over to the office by messenger an exhortative manuscript, which the
editor would subject to ruthless treatment and send back for the author's
approval. I cannot recall an occasion when Mr. Kohlberg protested against my
surgery. But there was much substance in his contributions. The following
condensation of several of Mr. Kohlberg's pieces, (April and May 1947; December 1948; January 1949; and April 1950) will merit the attention of future
historians as a log of America's tragic role in China. It will be noted that Mr.
Kohlberg's last warning against Soviet Russia's coming push toward the Dardanelles Straits and Indochina came two months before Stalin's puppets struck
in Korea.*]

I

ON MARCH 18 LAST, Molotov tossed a missile into the Moscow Conference
on the German peace treaty and rattled a number of skeletons in the White
House with echoes resounding around the world. Molotov disclosed a top secret
agreement made at Yalta by the Big Three, and in doing so forced the State
Department in Washington and the Foreign Office in London to release for the
first time a number of other secret pacts. If governments knew shame, March 18,
the date on which a Soviet commissar divulged to the American people some-

thing which their highest elected representatives had concealed from them, would be a day of national mourning. A week later the State Department hurriedly issued for publication various agreements and clauses, including those previously suppressed, adopted at the Teheran, Yalta, and Potsdam conferences. "State Department officials said," reported *The New York Times,* "that the texts made public today included every word and piece of punctuation that the Chiefs of State signed at the three historic meetings."

Less than two and a half years had passed since President Franklin D. Roosevelt, two weeks before the national elections which resulted in his being chosen for a fourth term, declared in his memorable speech before the Foreign Policy Association in New York on October 21, 1944:

> After my return from Teheran, I stated officially that no secret commitments had been made. The issue then is between my veracity and the continuing assertions of those who have no responsibility in the foreign field.

A little more than three months later President Roosevelt went to the Yalta Conference, which may very well go down in history as the real and decisive peace conference of World War II. Upon his return, the President addressed an historic Joint Session of Congress on March 2, 1945, in the course of which he solemnly declared:

> Quite naturally, this conference concerned itself only with the European war and with the political problems of Europe, and not with the Pacific war.

The chorus of approval which hailed the announced decisions of Yalta, as embodied in a round-up by the Associated Press of nationwide comment, makes weird reading after Molotov's diplomatic cocktail. Our great newspapers and opinion-makers were simply jubilant. "A milestone on the road to victory and peace . . . bringing Russia, Britain and the United States closer together," was the general view of the Yalta Conference.

It was not long after Yalta that numerous leaks in the secret deals made there began to appear, challenging the official assurances given to the American people. But it was not until exactly one year later that Secretary of State Byrnes was forced to make public the text of a secret pact which completely belied the President's declaration to the Congress that Yalta "concerned itself only with the European war." The unprecedented sellout of China, in her absence and behind her back, which was formally signed on February 11, 1945 by Stalin, Roosevelt, and Churchill, was made public the following February. Although Byrnes had been present during most of the Yalta Conference, he announced that he had not known of this top secret agreement until seven months afterwards, September 2, 1945, weeks *after* he had assumed the office of Secretary of State.

This is not the place to analyze the enormity of the crime committed towards our tested ally, China, for the sake of our adventurous courtship of the dubious

Soviet power which had been a partner of the treacherous Hitler. Nor is this the occasion to question Secretary Byrnes' almost inexplicable ignorance of a major instrument of war and peace as he departed with President Truman for Potsdam to confer with the Russian and British Chiefs of State.

As to the veracity of President Roosevelt on the subject of the secret commitments made at Teheran, the challenge had not been made openly until the publication of the book *Defeat In Victory* by the former Polish Ambassador to the United States, Jan Ciechanowski. It was the same Molotov who challenged Roosevelt's veracity, in the presence of Stalin, Churchill, Eden, and Ambassador Harriman, in the course of the conference with Premier Mikolajczyk of Poland. But it has been known in informed circles since October 1944 that grave commitments with respect to Poland were made at Teheran.

EVIDENCE IS NOT LACKING that the skeletons in the White House archives are still there, and that the State Department has released only such agreements as have been on file in its safes. We know from published and unpublished diplomatic sources close to President Roosevelt that he had kept certain state pacts under lock and key as part of his personal diplomacy, and that he shared these topmost secrets only to a limited degree even with his most important ambassadors.

Not all the secret agreements were formal papers signed by the Big Three. Some were in the form of protocols, of verbal understandings. Others were in the form of memoranda embodying assurances of support of claims tantamount to commitments; and still others were in the form of notes and minutes of conversations between ambassadors and foreign ministers which proved decisive milestones in the development of our fatal foreign policy.

Among the skeletons in the White House which cry for release, and which the American people should force into the open without any further delay, unless we want to let Molotov do it first, are the following:

The Curzon Line Agreement. Hitherto unpublished and undoubtedly still reposing in a White House cabinet is President Roosevelt's commitment made to Stalin at Teheran in November 1943 to turn over to Soviet Russia about 40 percent of Poland's territory without consulting or even informing the recognized and legitimate government of our Polish ally.

It was on October 13, 1944, that Molotov sprang his big surprise when he reminded the obdurate Premier Mikolajczyk, who resisted all efforts to make him accept the partition of his country, that President Roosevelt had agreed to the Curzon Line as Poland's eastern frontier. Incidentally, this was substantially the same line which Hitler had conceded to Stalin under the pact of August 1939. Molotov had turned to Churchill and Harriman, in Stalin's presence, and challenged them to deny his assertion. Churchill and Harriman remained silent. Mikolajczyk then compelled Harriman to transmit to President Roosevelt in Washington an urgent plea for the verification of Molotov's claim. It was a claim which seemed unbelievable not long after assurances from President Roosevelt to the contrary.

Eight days later the President made his statement before the Foreign Policy Association in New York that he had made no secret commitments at Teheran! Yet Mikolajczyk never received a clear-cut answer to his inquiry. And the American people are still to have a look at the record of the secret deal consummated at Teheran on the dismemberment of Poland. The lie marches on . . .

The Deal on the Soviet's Three Votes in the UN. Originally suppressed in the official declarations on the Yalta Conference, it was only a matter of weeks before the sensational news had leaked out that we had agreed to give the Soviet Union three votes in the Assembly of the United Nations. Here was a secret pact which had nothing to do with military operations. It will be recalled that Secretary of State Stettinius has not been informed of this arrangement, and was in a predicament when questioned by a host of newsmen.

On March 29, 1945, the White House, after confirming the fact of the secret deal, told the country that "the American representatives stated that if the United Nations Organization agreed to let the Soviet republics have three votes, the United States would ask for three votes also."

Now, at San Francisco, Molotov asked for and got the additional votes pledged at Yalta. But the United States did not apply for its part of the alleged bargain, and was satisfied with but a single vote.

Somewhere in the White House files there must be ample documentary material bearing upon the suspicious and questionable circumstances of this transaction.

The Agreement on Repatriation of Soviet Nationals. One of the most shocking secret pacts was our deal at Yalta to turn over to the Soviet authorities all fugitive Soviet nationals or citizens of countries under Soviet control, including war prisoners in the United States who refused to return to Soviet Russia.

Under this inhuman arrangement we sent to their deaths hundreds of thousands of men, in contravention of the Geneva Convention.

The full story of this sinister piece of diplomacy has never been told. Suffice it to say that Secretary of War Stimson and the War Department had fought tooth and nail against the Soviet proposals for weeks before the Yalta Conference. While the President was already in the Crimea, our military chiefs had finally worked out a formula to meet Stalin's demand to conduct with our aid a worldwide purge of his political opponents. That formula was cabled to President Roosevelt at Yalta, but arrived after the commitment had been made to Stalin. Where are all the papers on the subject and all the gruesome details of our partnership in terror?

The Partition of Korea. Where are the facts on this deal? There is reason to believe that at Yalta, where 300 Americans were present and 16,000 Soviet bottles of liquor were consumed, we did not have a single representative thoroughly familiar with the geography of the Far East. When the Soviet delegates made the demand for control of Korea, one of the U.S. "experts" spotted a line on the map bisecting that unhappy country. It looked like a "natural" to him, something like a Korean Curzon Line, and was there and then accepted as the dividing line to forestall any argument. It will be recalled that Korea had been promised her independence under the terms of the Cairo Declaration.

Almost immediately after the decision had been made, another American discovered that the "natural" line was the 38th parallel of latitude. Of course the Russians knew it all along. For nearly all the Korean industry was north of the 38th parallel, and was in their zone. Furthermore, the line cut across Korea in a manner which gave us a tip of the peninsula to which we had no access by land.

Spheres of Influence. The allegation that at Teheran and Yalta negotiations were conducted providing for a division of the world into Soviet and non-Soviet spheres of influence has been made frequently in high diplomatic quarters. Whether such agreements were signed or not, it is authoritatively believed that Russia's expansion in Europe as far west as the Stettin-Trieste line, with the exception of Greece and European Turkey, was part of a deal; that in return for Stalin's recognition—on paper—of Chiang Kai-shek's Central Government of China, we consented to Moscow's staking out a special sphere of influence embracing large non-Russian areas in Asia; and that at Potsdam the secret deal of Yalta involving China was implemented in writing by the representatives of the Big Three.

PRESIDENT TRUMAN DECLARED last year that all the secret agreements concluded by Roosevelt had been made public. Then came Molotov's recent revelation and the subsequent disclosure by the State Department of a batch of secret pacts. We know that not all of these have been given out. Not until the White House skeletons are unearthed and our secret diplomacy exposed in full, can we hope to develop a foreign policy built on the rock of truth. Until then—the lie marches on . . .

II

WHY IS IT THAT what is good enough for Greece and Turkey, two countries in which we never had a primary interest, is not good enough for China, our ally against Japan long before Pearl Harbor?

The answer to the question will be found by probing into the case of John Carter Vincent, director of the office of Far Eastern Affairs, and chief figure in the pro-Soviet China clique in the State Department. A scrutiny of his record should provide the key to the major puzzle of America's foreign policy today.

Our nation has been maneuvered into a course directly opposite to that which was ours in the critical days preceding Pearl Harbor. It was on November 26, 1941, that Secretary of State Cordell Hull handed his historic note to Ambassador Nomura in which was laid down our irreducible minimum basis for peace with Japan. The most important point in Secretary Hull's note read:

"The Government of the United States and the Government of Japan will not support—militarily, politically, economically—any Government or regime in China other than the National Government of the Republic of China with capital temporarily at Chungking."

Eleven days later Japan went to war with us because of her refusal to accept our terms. For the last three years, we have officially taken the position of *not* supporting the National Government of China.

This has been made crystal clear upon the promulgation of the Truman Doctrine. We have offered loans to Greece and Turkey while we deny a long-earmarked loan to China. We have proposed to furnish military aid to Greece and Turkey while belaboring China for lacking parliamentary government. And we have undertaken to fight Communism in the Eastern Mediterranean while we have been consistently seeking to foist it upon China.

These differences are too striking to escape general notice. But what remains to be established is how it all came to be. Whose hand reversed our foreign policy in the most vital area of our national defense?

If you would know how it happened that America's traditional policy of the Open Door in China had been scrapped in favor of Soviet appeasement, look at the record of John Carter Vincent who, according to the *Washington Daily News,* has been "putting a *For Communists Only* sign on the Open Door."

Probably few Americans are even familiar with the name of John Carter Vincent, who has been described authoritatively as being, to all practical purposes, "Secretary of State for China." . . .

IT WAS NOT VERY LONG before President Truman's proposal to loan $400 million to Greece and Turkey had been advanced that John Carter Vincent made a formal address before the National Foreign Trade Council and enunciated his own doctrine in these startling words: "I believe it is unsound to invest private or public capital in countries where . . . a government is wasting its substance on excessive armament, where the threat or fact of civil war exists, where tendencies toward government monopolization exclude American business, or where undemocratic concepts of government are controlling."

Here was a policy which does fit the case of the Soviet Union. But Mr. Vincent would never apply it to Communist Russia. It is a policy which might very well be interpreted as fitting Greece and Turkey. But Mr. Vincent was speaking of China. And what he had in mind, as the Scripps-Howard newspapers pointed out editorially, was the Chinese Government's "wasting its substance on excessive armament." Against whom? Against Communist rebels and not a foreign foe. Which is the reason why Mr. Vincent has opposed the granting of the

$500 million credit earmarked for China unless Chiang Kai-shek forms a coalition with the Communists.

There was really nothing new about Mr. Vincent's promotion of the Communist cause in the Far East. It came into the open early in September 1946, when General MacArthur issued a warning against the danger of Communism in Japan. On September 4, 1946, the *New York Herald Tribune* quoted Vincent as charging MacArthur with launching an anti-Soviet campaign in violation of State Department directives, which have never been disclosed, to use Japan for "building a bridge of friendship to the Soviet Union." . . .

Without specifically mentioning John Carter Vincent, the *Washington Daily News* expressed prevailing opinion when it declared:

> The incident again points the finger at Moscow apologists in the State Department who are working to defeat American policy wherever there is a clash of interests between the United States and the Soviet Union. Until the Department is purged of such influences none of our missions overseas will be protected against such attacks. If the Department fails to clean its own house, the problem is one demanding the attention of Congress.

Even more shocking than the public slap at MacArthur was Mr. Vincent's official conduct in the Dairen Incident last December. An American naval vessel was summarily ordered out of the Chinese port of Dairen by the commander of the Soviet occupation forces. This was a flagrant violation by Soviet authorities of the Yalta Pact and of all international customs. Moreover, the Sino-Soviet Pact of 1945 had clearly provided that Dairen be turned over to the Chinese as soon as it "ceased to be a zone of active hostilities."

Mr. Vincent, director of our Far Eastern Affairs did not hesitate to authorize a spokesman to inform the public that the Russians were acting within their rights. That alone should have sufficed, in other days, to have a subordinate like Mr. Vincent dropped from the diplomatic service or demoted to the rank of clerk in a New Zealand consulate. . . .

. . . The decision of the State Department to withdraw our troops from China had been preceded by a worldwide Communist campaign, from Moscow to Shanghai to New York, waged during 1946. And that in turn had been presaged by a significant pronouncement made by William Z. Foster before the National Committee of the Communist Party on November 18, 1945, a pronouncement which Mr. John Carter Vincent may or may not have found necessary to read. For those who would explore the devious ways of American policy in the Far East, Foster's declaration, as reported in the *Daily Worker* for December 2, 1945, is worth recalling:

> On the international scale, the key task, as emphasized in Comrade Dennis's report, is to stop American intervention in China . . . The war in China is the key of all problems on the international front and it is here, above all else, where we have to deal the hardest blow to reaction . . . On the question of China, which is

our key concentration, as Comrade Dennis pointed out, we want to hold 500 meetings all over the country to mobilize all the forces of the people that we can reach to put a stop to the intervention in China. Our Party must use every ounce of its strength and skill and organizational ability to make these 500 meetings a success.

Within a week after the announcement of the withdrawal of our armed detachments from China, Mr. Vincent attained the high-water mark of his singular career in an address at Cornell University on January 21, 1947. He deprecated the view that it would be "advantageous for our defense to throw our weight or influence on the side of the *status quo*" in China.

What a neat diplomatic way of saying the preservation of the National Government of China, the cornerstone of our policy which led to Pearl Harbor, was no longer our concern! . . .

As reported in the *New York Times*, Mr. Vincent was out to encourage "progressive" elements in China. Some Americans might have remembered that these "progressives" were ambushing United States Marines in their peaceful pursuits at that very time.

. . . Early in 1941, Mr. Vincent took up the post of Consul at Shanghai, becoming a few months later, under Ambassador Clarence Gauss, counselor of the Embassy at Chungking. . . . While in Chungking in August 1941, Mr. Vincent came in close contact with Owen Lattimore, one of the best-informed Americans on the far places of China, who had been sent by President Roosevelt to act as political adviser to Chiang Kai-shek. Mr. Lattimore will be remembered as the leading propagandist of the doctrine that the Chinese Communists are not real Communists but true democrats who are merely innocuous reformers. This was, of course, before the Chinese Communist leaders began to denounce America as "an imperialist enemy worse than the Japanese."

There is no record that John Carter Vincent or any other State Department officials of the Lattimore school had ever taken the trouble to become familiar with the massive evidence of the unbroken relations between the Chinese Communist Party with the Communist International, or of the repeated professions by the Chinese Communist leaders of their 100 percent loyalty to the line of Marxism-Leninism-Stalinism. . . .

It was not long afterwards that Lieutenant Andrew Roth, of the Naval Intelligence, who was attached to Vincent's section and who was arrested and charged with espionage in the *Amerasia* affair, dropped a significant remark to his colleague, E. S. Larsen. "I ran into Lieutenant Roth on the street," Larsen narrates, "and he told me that John Carter Vincent, head of the China section, suspected me of being 'too close to the Chiang Kai-shek crowd.' "

Actually the boys of the Lattimore school had changed their tune about Chiang Kai-shek in the summer of 1943, following Moscow's turnabout in the spring of that year. During the first two years of the conflict between Stalin and Hitler, the Communist line towards Chiang Kai-shek was one of apparent conciliation. Then suddenly the National Government which had fought valiantly all alone Russia's and America's enemy, Japan, for nearly six years, became a target of denunciation as a "feudal" and "reactionary" regime.

At that time students of Chinese affairs were puzzled by the Communist switch. Did not Russia still want to use China to keep Japan from attacking Siberia?

Only in 1946 was the key to this puzzle found. It came out at the Nuremberg trial. Evidence was offered, but ruled out, that Hitler had proposed a separate peace to Stalin in the spring of 1943, after Stalingrad. Stalin received the proposal favorably and stated his terms, but the terms were too stiff for Hitler and negotiations broke down. News of these negotiations leaked to the Japs, and Stalin felt sure that they would no longer attack him to bolster a German ally already willing to quit. Russia needed China no more, so her legions of open and secret propagandists were put to work to weaken the National Government and to plan postwar chaos and the Communist seizure of power.

These same methods were used on our European allies, Poland and Yugoslavia. That they did not work as well in China was due to Chiang Kai-shek's firm stand and not to our State Department which followed the Soviet line even more closely in the Far East than in Eastern Europe.

The turning point in American Far Eastern policy came with the memorable mission of Henry A. Wallace to China in the summer of 1944. His guides and advisers on the trip were Owen Lattimore, John Carter Vincent, and John Hazard who had been prepared for his role by five years of study in the Soviet Union. Vice President Wallace, who had not yet been scrapped by the Democratic Convention, made his report, which remains secret to this day. It is, however, known that the high point of Wallace's "study" was that *the government of Chiang Kai-shek would collapse within 90 days.* That was in July 1944.

A hint of the authorship of the Wallace state paper may be found in an article in the April 1, 1947, issue of *World Report,* in which private sources in the Far Eastern Office of the State Department (believed none other than John Carter Vincent himself) are quoted as expecting "the fall of Chiang and his government." Among recommendations made by Wallace to President Roosevelt were the proposal that the United States back Mao Tse-tung, leader of the Chinese Communists, as the "Tito" of China, and the plan that we arm the Chinese Communists, a policy later taken up by General Stilwell under the influence of pro-Soviet advisers.

It was on the issue of arming the Communists that the conflict between Ambassador Hurley and the Vincent clique developed. One of Vincent's comrades, John S. Service, who figured unenviably in the State Department Espionage Case, who acted as Stilwell's political mentor, submitted, in October 1944, a report to Washington which cut the ground from under Ambassador Hurley. That report, Hurley later testified before the Senate Foreign Relations Committee, was "a general statement of how to let fall the government I was sent over there to sustain. The report was circulated among the Communists I was trying to harmonize with the Chiang Kai-shek government."

Some months later, while Ambassador Hurley was in Washington on official business, Vincent's career men back in China utilized the occasion to undermine Hurley's policy. On February 28, 1945, they sent a message to Washington in which they "specifically recommended that we furnish Lend-Lease arms and equipment to the belligerent Communist armed party in China."

This sabotage by the staff allied with Vincent finally caused Ambassador Hurley to offer his resignation in November 1945. Secretary Byrnes persuaded him to remain on certain conditions. These were embodied in a set of instructions which were dictated to a stenographer in the presence of Byrnes. When Hurley returned the following morning to receive the signed instructions, he found that important points had been deleted. He tried to see the Secretary and was told that he was out. Proceeding to the office of the Far Eastern division, he learned that the changes had been made by John Carter Vincent. He then resigned.

THE MYSTERIOUS AMERICAN policy in China, which has made many a Senator and Congressman wonder why the Truman Doctrine of stemming Communism is not being applied in the Far East, is largely the handiwork of the pro-Soviet bloc headed by John Carter Vincent. He and his associates helped shape the shameful secret Yalta deal by which we had delivered a loyal and tested ally, the National Government of China, without its knowledge, to Stalin's new imperialism. This Red "cell," as the Scripp-Howard press had editorially characterized it, has been "found fronting for the Soviet viewpoint on every issue. . . . The Department's Far Eastern Division is notoriously leftist in its views, and its operations distort the American position in all areas under its direction." . . .

III

As THIS is written Manchuria has fallen; the line of the Great Wall of China has been breached; Tsinan-fu, capital of Shantung Province, is in Communist hands; and it is reported that 1,000,000 troops are now engaged in battle for Suchow on whose fate Shanghai and Nanking depend. Our correspondents and columnists join in declaring that if Chiang Kai-shek is defeated at Suchow, the entire Yangtze Valley, with its 200 million people, will lie open to the Communists.

If it be true that the National Government of China faces imminent defeat it would represent the ultimate triumph of American foreign policy in that vast and populous country. Our policy-makers would have preferred that China be handed over to the Communists without the great battles now being fought.

These battles reveal only too clearly the lies which form the basis of our China policy— that the Chinese Communists are not real Communists, but just "liberals," "progressives," "democrats" and "agrarian reformers."

Certain of our policy-makers fear that these battles may scare us into action in support of Chiang Kai-shek before it is really too late. That we had a policy-making group in the State Department which would have preferred the peaceful conquest of China by the Communists is evidenced by the President's official statements of December 15, 1945, and December 18, 1946, in which he called on Chiang Kai-shek to accept the Communists into key posts in the government, while allowing retention of their own armies. Had Chiang agreed, the aim of Communist seizure of China would have been accomplished more speedily, with less death and destruction, and without leaving any possibility of American intervention. In that case, the pattern would have been the same as was followed by the "coalition" governments of Yugoslavia, Poland, and Czechoslovakia, all of which were taken over "peacefully" without the intervention of the Soviet Army.

But Chiang Kai-shek refused to fall for the alternating pressures of General Marshall and of the blandishments of Ambassador Stuart. General Marshall's part seems best explained by his intense personal dislike for Chiang Kai-shek, which came to a head when Chiang, in September 1944, refused to accede to the Stilwell-Marshall-Roosevelt ultimatum demanding the turning over of both civilian and military control to General Stilwell, as reported in Stilwell's *Diary*. Marshall's dislike of Chiang made it easy for him to swallow the directives of the State Department pro-Soviet clique prepared for him when he left for China in 1945.

So profound was Marshall's confusion that thirteen months later, when he left China to return to Washington as Secretary of State, after innumerable experiences with the treacherous Communist "hatchet-man" and chief negotiator, Chou En-lai, he could report to the world that there were "liberals" . . . "a splendid group of men" in the Chinese Communist Party, although he added that they "as yet lack the political power to exercise a controlling influence." Privately, he named Chou En-lai as the leader of this group of Communist "liberals." In a radio speech immediately after Marshall's statement, Chou, the "liberal," stated: "The essence of the policy of American imperialism is to colonize China." . . .

FOR NEARLY a century the United States has had two main planks in its foreign policy. The first, of course, was the Monroe Doctrine. The second was the Open Door Policy in China. Both have been upheld by changing administrations, sometimes feebly, at other times even at the risk of war.

No change in this traditional policy had occurred in the White House even as late as 1943, when, at Cairo, Roosevelt, Churchill, and Chiang Kai-shek pledged the restoration to the Republic of China of "all the territories Japan has stolen from the Chinese, such as Manchuria, Formosa, and the Pescadores."

One week later, Roosevelt met Stalin at Teheran. Shortly afterwards the President dispatched General Stilwell to Chungking to tell Chiang Kai-shek that the promises of supplies made at Cairo had been canceled under Stalin's pressure. Nevertheless, Roosevelt still adhered to the policy of backing Chiang Kai-shek and Nationalist China when the war in Europe had ended.

By this time, the pro-Soviet claque in the United States was in full cry against China. The Institute of Pacific Relations violated its rule against taking sides and put out a special release to the press (July 14) castigating Chiang's government as reactionary, feudal, and corrupt and presenting the Communists as democratic reformers. . . .

. . . A large part of the arms shipped to China under lend-lease before V-J Day and more than half the ammunition were destroyed by the American Army before delivery to the Chinese. A $500 million loan earmarked for China was canceled, UNRRA supplies were in considerable part diverted to the Chinese Communists and much of what did not reach the Communists was deliberately destroyed. Not a single firearm, from revolver to cannon, has been permitted to be shipped to the Chinese Government since V-J day.

Now that the administrators of the Wallace-Marshall policy see triumph at hand, after three years of preventing aid to Chiang Kai-shek, they tell us it is too late. It is rumored that our Washington policy-makers have instructed Ambassador Stuart to make Chiang Kai-shek an offer—to fly him and his family to safety in the United States, if he decides to flee. There could be no better design to destroy the remaining morale of anti-Communist China. This has been assured through a "leak" of this report to the press, even before Chiang Kai-shek had time to reject indignantly this insulting offer, so as to arouse fear in the people of China that their Generalissimo would desert them. . . .

In Eastern Europe, in the Soviet Union, in Northern Korea, Manchuria, and North China, more than 500 million people now live, work, starve, and suffer under the Dictatorship of the Proletariat in the Kremlin. If China falls, all Southeast Asia, already torn by Communist-led rebellions, will follow quickly. If this happens, the total population enslaved by Moscow will be approximately 1160 millions, more than half the people of the world. When will America wake up?

IV

The Washington grapevine has been buzzing with a rumor that Soviet Ambassador Panyushkin had served notice upon President Truman or, according to some, upon Secretary Marshall, that "further aid to the Nationalist Government of China would be considered an unfriendly act."

We have no way of ascertaining how much truth there is in the report, but the Homeric American tragedy being enacted across the Pacific is a fitting illustration to the insiders' talk in Washington.

The redoubtable Panyushkin measures up to the role, for he is the only surviving Soviet ex-Ambassador to China, no mean achievement for a Kremlin diplomat. Without exception, all his predecessors as envoys to China have fallen under Stalin's axe upon their recall home.

The promotion of the surviving Panyushkin to the supreme assignment of doing a little pushing around of the Tarzan-like Uncle Sam could not have been a mere accident on the part of the wily set in the Politburo. . . .

On one point there can be no division of opinion: our course in China is in the best tradition of Teheran, Yalta, and Potsdam, a course originally charted for us by Stalin and Molotov and the Panyushkins.

REMEMBER TITO? We had for years tried to force Chiang Kai-shek into a Titoesque mold through the lofty stratagem of a coalition government. We succeeded in Yugoslavia, but Nationalist China resisted our pressure.

Remember Mikolajczyk? Falling in line with the dictates of the Kremlin, he had carried out a coalition policy in Poland which seemed to us to suit ideally the generalissimo of another valiant ally of ours. Unlike our Polish protegé, the head of the Republic of China continued to balk at our suasions and proddings.

Remember Czechoslovakia and Rumania and Bulgaria and Hungary? We backed the magic motto of coalition government, coined for us by the avowed and secret dupes of Moscow. The Iron Curtain has enfolded and garroted our friends—the friends of democracy and freedom—in all those countries. That has not prevented us from pursuing the same old will-of-the-wisp in China, where our ramparts are a matter of life or death to American security in the Pacific.

These ramparts have been crumbling under the propaganda drills of those who have been telling us that "you can do business with the Chinese Communists." (It worked with Hitler, it is still working somewhat sluggishly with Stalin, why not with Mao Tse-tung?)

It is a familiar song: the Chinese Communists need us—for $5 billion we can secure their friendship. It was only yesterday that "good old Joe's" friendship was to be had for $10 billion.

THE THEME of this song burst upon the front pages of our press when Paul G. Hoffman, head of the ECA, reversed himself after a three-day visit in Shanghai and announced that the United States would continue aid to China if the Communists or a coalition government should overthrow Chiang Kai-shek.

Who can measure at this date, in billions of dollars or millions of lives, the full value to Stalin and his Panyushkins of this stab in the back delivered by our traveling envoy to our ally against Japan?

The American correspondents in China recorded the Hoffman venture into the realm of higher diplomacy as a devastating "psychological blow" to the government of the Republic of China, the same government which we had solemnly sworn to uphold at Cairo and Teheran and Yalta—in the treaties designed for public consumption only.

In the secret agreements, designed to be kept from "the forgotten man," we had delivered anti-Communist China into the clutches of Communist imperialism, an undertaking which could not be consummated without getting Chiang Kai-shek's head into the noose of a coalition government. Secretary Marshall failed in his mission to mate the Nationalist tigers with the Red vipers. Paul Hoffman has carried on the fatal errand of his illustrious master with a sublime sense of irresponsibility. . . .

Must all our ramparts in Asia crumble into dust before the eyes of America can be opened? Is it our destiny to fight for our life with our back only against Canada or Mexico as bulwarks in the race for the survival of civilization?

V

THE VICTORY of communism in Continental China and its advance into Burma, Indochina, and Malaya has changed the entire strategic situation in the Pacific to the great advantage of the Soviet Union. . . .

What do these developments mean in terms of American defense in the Pacific?

They mean, first, that the outer defenses of our West Coast now run from Alaska through the Aleutians—by-passing the Kurile Islands which were secretly handed to Stalin at Yalta—to Japan, Okinawa, and Guam. . . .

Our Pacific coast cities, from Seattle to San Diego, lie within two to six hours flying time from the Alaskan airfields; which means that they would be open to attack by medium-range bombers, of which the Soviets are believed to have several thousand. . . .

There have been promises of better defenses for Alaska and the Pacific Northwest. But to prepare an adequate defense system will take years. Since this country, as a democracy, will not strike first, and since Russia will probably not strike until it has consolidated its enormous conquests, both East and West, we may yet have a few years of uneasy peace. A wise Administration would use that time not only to strengthen our Pacific coast defenses, but to carry out a far more fundamental plan.

At Washington, on January 1, 1942, the Soviet Government signed the Atlantic Charter. At Potsdam, in July 1945, it adhered to the terms of the Declaration of Cairo. Had Stalin been forced to respect those agreements, the Soviets would now be within their 1939 borders with 180 million people, instead of sprawling from the Elbe and the Adriatic to the South China Sea and headed toward the Straits and Indonesia.

Our strategic objective should be a return to the basis of those agreements.

If we can accomplish that, the danger of war will be removed. And therein lies the great importance of Formosa.

On Formosa and Hainan Islands are 500,000 Chinese Nationalist troops. Those on Hainan are mostly evacuated forces rather badly armed. Quick action, but only quick action, could save them. Those on Formosa are in good shape, full of fight, with six divisions equipped with American arms. Another 75,000 not so well equipped, stand on the Chusan and Kinmen Islands, just a few miles off the China coast (Kinmen only four miles). They have defeated, killed, or captured, or driven into the sea the Communist troops sent against them in two assaults. In Continental China there are still pockets of Nationalist resistance, some large, some small.

IN 1949 Congress voted $75 million for arms for "the general area of China." It is still untouched. The President put it in the hands of the State Department. If President Truman would transfer this from the State Department—which has announced that it has no plan and whose roving ambassador, Philip Jessup, policymaker for Asia, recently announced that Communism "is not a danger which need cause consternation"—to the Department of Defense, the Red tide could be reversed. . . .

A re-won non-Communist China would flank the Soviet Far East and its Trans-Siberian railroad for 2,000 miles, making that area strategically untenable. Here, then, lies the long road to peace and to real security for our Pacific coast.

What are the chances of success?

They lie in the will to succeed and in the competence of the American commander, who should be the Commanding General U.S.A.F.F.E. (U.S. Armed Forces, Far East), Douglas MacArthur. This man, who said "I shall return," and who did return, seems the logical choice to lead the first move toward redemption of the pledges of the Atlantic Charter and the Declarations of Washington, Moscow, and Cairo; toward the objectives for which 350,000 young Americans died in the far corners of the earth.

Only when America's pledges have been made good, when the world may again trust us and we may trust ourselves, when Soviet Russia is forced back within its borders, its satellite tyrannies and fifth columns destroyed, can we hope to live at peace in a free world.

I, April 1947; II, May 1947;
III, December 1948; IV, January 1949; V, April 1950

THE MYSTERY OF OUR

CHINA POLICY

By CLARE BOOTHE LUCE

[Clare Boothe Luce was in a state of religious exaltation when she wrote this essay, "The Mystery of Our China Policy," later reissued as a pamphlet. Mrs. Luce, whose interpretation of the sources of our debacle in China did not quite fit the facts as brought out in these pages, treated the forces responsible for the developments across the Pacific with large-hearted Christian benevolence. In his editorial comment, "Sin and Treason," see page 43, the editor of Plain Talk, dissected Mrs. Luce's diagnosis as untenable. Mrs. Luce, who started off Plain Talk by subscribing to it for 100 of her influential friends and acquaintances, had no illusion about Communist terror, but like so many figures of the American elite could not bring herself to believe that the Western intelligentsia had been inoculated with the cancer of treason.]

THE AMERICAN people are confronted today with the mystery of American policy in China since V-J Day.

Back in October 1939, Winston Churchill said that Soviet Russia was "a riddle wrapped in a mystery inside an enigma." The strategy and goal of the Soviets were never a secret to Churchill. The strategy was world revolution. The goal was world domination. His puzzlement at that time—it was during the Communazi Pact—concerned Russia's tactics. Did they call for Russian neutrality in the war, or Russian entrance on the side of her partner, Adolf Hitler?

But the mystery that confronts us in studying American policy in China since V-J Day *does* raise the question of goals. The announced goal of our government is to contain Communist expansion in all areas vital to our security. Certainly a free China, a China friendly to the United States, a China opposed to Communism, is the very cornerstone of that goal in the Pacific.

But a fact confronts us, difficult to dispose of as the *corpus delicti*: the tactics and means employed to date by our State Department do not seem to have been designed to accomplish that very end! Our Far East policy has led step by step toward the collapse of a free China, and the erection of a vast Soviet empire in the Pacific.

The best way to set about solving a mystery is to eliminate false theories. You do not always find the true one. But you do, paradoxically, get a better idea of what a mystery is—certainly of its magnitude and significance—when you see quite clearly what it is *not*.

Let's examine the theories most often offered in the press and on Capitol Hill to explain our enigmatic China policy.

First Theory

AN UNFRIENDLY and uninformed American public opinion has made it impossible to count on public cooperation with any forceful policy against the Chinese Communists.

True or false? False.

Americans are interested in the Orient. Hundreds of thousands of Americans fought there for four years. Many died there. All of them learned about the strategic importance of China the hard way—in a global war. They have not forgotten the lesson. During the war, the leftist and Communist press loudly deplored the fact that millions of Americans seemed more interested in the Orient than in Europe. Even the President had trouble keeping America's mind on Europe first, until the second front opened.

At no time during the past four years has the State Department tried to use existing friendly opinions as leverage for further aid to a free China. At no time has it tried to create public opinions behind a firm and vigorous policy in the Orient.

Why? We are faced with a mystery.

Second Theory

CHINA IS falling to the Communists because the members of the Far East division in the State Department are ignorant of Russian aims and America's interests in the Orient.

True or false? False.

America's Far East policy took definite shape even before Elihu Root's "Open Door" policy gave it a popular name. Abraham Lincoln, in the middle of a desperate civil war, took note that the great imperial powers of his day were set to make one last imperialistic grab—to dismember China. China was then an absolute monarchy. But it was not unfriendly to the U.S.A. And it was free from domination by any of the great powers. Lincoln sent a Massachusetts Congressman, Anson Burlingame, as an envoy to China to protest. Our nation then had no great navies, no fleets of giant bombers, no atom bomb. It had a State Department, however, that knew that our security in the Pacific called for a free China. It had the eloquence of Burlingame, and the moral prestige of Lincoln. China was not dismembered. Where there was the will, there was the way.

The policies of Theodore Roosevelt and Elihu Root, at the time of the Boxer Rebellion Indemnity and the Russo-Japanese War; of Herbert Hoover and Henry Stimson, when the Japanese invaded Manchuria; of Mr. Roosevelt and

Mr. Hull before Pearl Harbor when the Japanese threatened to close the Burma Road, were all policies based on the permanent importance to our security of friendship with China and her freedom from the influence or domination of any major power unfriendly to us.

The State Department has abandoned this *historic* policy. It has done this when it must know that doing so can only help one other power: the Soviet Union. Indeed, it may, at long last, help to bring true Russia's ancient dream of a vast Asiatic empire, extending from Manila to Teheran.

Why? We are faced with a mystery.

Third Theory

THE AVERAGE man in the street may be interested in China, but military and political experts have advised the State Department to "let Chiang's China down easily."

True or false? False.

The *Congressional Record* bulges with dispassionate editorials and closely reasoned articles by able and distinguished Americans in behalf of free China. It bristles with speeches full of facts and figures made by members of both parties. There is, in the government files, voluminous testimony made by many military and diplomatic experts before the House and Senate Foreign Relations Committees. They nearly all warn the State Department of the dangers of abandoning the historic policy of previous Presidents. Only Henry Wallace seems to approve highly of the conduct of affairs in China. Indeed there are few—almost no—expressions in support of the State Department position, except those written by Communists or fellow-travelers. The whole time I was in the Congress I heard only three speeches made in favor of State Department China policy. These were made by Vito Marcantonio and a west coast Congressman called Hugh DeLacey. DeLacey was defeated in 1946 on account of his rabidly pro-Moscow affiliations.

The State Department has consistently turned a deaf ear to the advice of many experts, to all, indeed, who are adherents of our historic Pacific policy. It has even suppressed reports from government officials—like the now-famous suppressed report of General Wedemeyer, which offered suggestions as to how our errors in China might be redeemed.

Why? We are faced with a mystery.

Fourth Theory

THE STATE DEPARTMENT thinks that the Chinese Communists are not Communists, like the Russian Marxists, but "agrarian reformists."

True or false? False.

The Chinese Communists themselves have always insisted that they were bona-fide Communists, all Moscow-minded, and many Moscow-trained. They have never made a secret of their Soviet orthodoxy. Their recent statements expressing open hatred for the U.S.A. and devotion to Soviet Russia leave no doubt as to their orthodox Red views and loyalties. "Agrarian reform" is their platform promise. Communism is their party principle.

The use of the term "agrarian reformists" was dictated by the American Communist party line to confuse the public. It could not have confused the Far East division in the State Department. Nevertheless, the State Department made no effort to correct this opinion in the mind of the public, or when it was voiced on Capitol Hill.

Why? We are faced with a mystery.

Fifth Theory

THE KUOMINTANG Government of Generalissimo Chiang Kai-shek is full of corruption, and the State Department is loath to aid a corrupt government. True or false?

No sincere friend of China will deny the charge of corruption in that unhappy, ravaged country. Drought and starvation, floods and bombings and massacres; total war has rolled back and forth over China for ten years. Corruption is most especially a product of war's tyrannies and tribulations. Corruption has not been unknown in American politics, even in days of peace and prosperity. The European black marketeer in his black Rolls Royce is a familiar figure today on the lush, unbombed French Riviera.

Nevertheless, the smear word "corruption" has been trumpeted by the Communists throughout America as the real reason we must not aid China. It has also found its whispered way via the government grapevines to the Congressional cloakrooms.

Let us admit that corruption exists and reforms are needed. Still, are the questions of another nation's domestic struggles with internal corruption and reform the primarily relevant ones in our international diplomacy? And if by chance they *are* the revelant ones, by what ethical standards does our State Department find financial corruption—or black marketeering—more reprehensible than the persecution, torture, and murder of individuals and groups for their political beliefs?

Corruption is *not* the policy of the Kuomintang. Free Chinese deplore it as much as you or I do. But murder—mass murder—genocide—*is* an official principle of Communists. It is practiced by them, in and out of season, with no apology or compunction.

The primary function of our State Department is not to pass final judgment on the morals of other countries. It is to secure, through all proper diplomatic means short of war, the safety of our own country.

Here is the relevant question about Chiang's China: Is it friendly? There has never been any doubt, even in the State Department, that the Kuomintang Government was anti-Soviet and pro-American.

The State Department has never publicly corrected the Communist party-line story that moral indignation over corruption in Chinese politics has largely motivated it in withholding effective aid from China.

Why? We are faced with a mystery.

Sixth Theory

INFORMATION from the Orient received in Washington has been deliberately angled or falsified by Soviet agents there. Our consulates, our embassies, our foreign agents gathering the news on which action has been taken have been receiving poisoned reports.

True of false?

In some instances this may be true. But as a full explanation of why the Far East division has furthered Communism in the Pacific, it is insufficient. No doubt here and there an American official has been duped by some wily Red into sending home slanted dope. But we must steadfastly refuse to believe in the gullibility of all our civil servants in the field and at home. If our State Department, over a period of four or five years, cannot distinguish truths from falsehoods, doctored reports from straight ones, news from enemy propaganda —then Hitler and Stalin are right: our democracy is finished. It can no longer protect itself.

One fact destroys this theory, and all theories of State Department incompetence and ignorance concerning Soviet methods. The State Department has shown intelligence, force and vision in fighting the cold war against Soviet expansion in Europe.

It has failed to do so in the Orient. Why? We are faced with a mystery.

Seventh Theory

IT WAS "too late" to extend effective aid to Free China and "too much" was needed to make aid effective.

True or false? Absolutely false.

When was it too late? One year ago? Two years ago? Three years ago? Or was it and is it always "too late" just *today?*

Those who are interested in what we could have done in the past, and still can do to save China from Communism, should read the testimony of General Chennault before the Senate Foreign Relations Committee, May 3.

It is foolish to deny that effective aid now will be more painful and costly than it would have been when it was first called for. It will always seem to cost too much to fight a cold war. But it would actually cost everything we've got to fight a hot one, in which we'd find a billion and a half Orientals lined up on Russia's side against us.

No people's resources are unlimited. They must be used prudently even in extremities. But we must always be willing to tap the limit of our resources in our own defense.

We cannot defeat worldwide Communist aggression on a budget. We cannot even win a two-by-four war against a handful of guerrillas on a budget, as we are now finding out in Greece. A budgeted war is a lost war. If our desire to contain the Communists in Asia or Europe is conditioned by how much it will cost—we are defeated now.

The State Department has never come out openly to defend the "too late" or "too expensive" theories. The defense of these, like the "corruption" and "agrarian reform" theories, has been publicly made by our home-grown Communists and Wallaceites.

The State Department has used all the forces of publicity at its command to create public opinion for vast sums for free Europe. But it has maintained silence on raising even a fraction of that aid for a free China.

Why? We are still faced with a mystery.

There remains one theory so often mentioned in the press we cannot fail to note it here. This theory holds that our government has long been honeycombed by Communists and their bonded fellow-travelers. American Communists have penetrated, in depth and height, into the State Department. They have been operating deliberately, and as daringly as they can, for a decade or more to bring about a Soviet world.

They are, this theory holds, the most normal and presentable of men, indeed typical-looking Americans. Most of them entered government service young, because that's when Communism first caught their passionate and youthful imaginations. They have grown up in the Department. There they are notable only for their modest demeanor and their dislike of publicity—always a quality that endears one bureaucrat to others less modest. They have earned the loyalty of all their other colleagues by their capacity to work long hard hours. They even take stuffed briefcases home with them at night. They will always do some higher-up's reports—his homework, so to speak—for him, without asking any credit. They are full of advice and help on wearisome details—particularly those concerning Russia. So long as they could, the theory goes, these infiltrated traitors duped their colleagues about Soviet postwar intentions in Europe. Operating in the background, they were responsible for the tragic blunders at Teheran and Yalta and Potsdam. Then events began to speak—or rather shriek—for themselves in Middle Europe, in Poland, in Berlin. They were ordered to let up pressure on the Western front, and to try to "settle" for the Soviet domination of Asia.

True or false? You and I believe this unhappy theory is false. It is, of course, not possible to *prove* that it is false. But because it is repugnant to our sense of patriotism, and the respect in which we hold our fellow Americans, we just don't *want* to believe it.

THE PARTISANS of this lurid theory which holds that we have spies and traitors in our government—just as they do in the governments of Asia and Europe —claim it may soon be proved by a startling new development from the Big Four Conference. They claim that Stalin will make an offer to concede some of our requests on Germany in exchange for our recognition of the Communist regime in China. They insist that these same Moscow-minded Americans will tell Dean Acheson to accept it. Why? Because it is too late in Asia! Because it would cost too much! Because Chiang's China is corrupt! Because the Commies are really giving the people needed reforms! Because Chinese Communists will be more like Tito than real Communists! Because their information from the Orient shows that the Russians have been "stopped" there, and are sending little or no aid to the Chinese Communist leaders now! Because only the same old China fans will criticize such a deal! Because the American people are interested primarily in getting peace in Europe!

I, for one, do not believe this will happen. Mr. Acheson has plainly said he will not buy "a flea-bitten dog" in Europe. I am certain he will not buy all the fleas, without any dog at all, in Asia.

And that ends all the popular and false theories generally presented to explain our China policy.

We are still left with the mystery of why we have a policy which serves today, as it has for four long years, the interests of the Kremlin, and greatly disserves those of our own country.

YOU PROBABLY think I have some theory. You are right. But it is not a new theory. The only thing original about it is its name: it is called Original Sin.

The Christian believes that pride is the root of Original Sin. Pride prevents man from choosing intelligently between good and evil. And pride prevents him, when he knows he has done wrong or made a mistake, from "owning up" to it.

Is it possible that human pride is at the bottom of most of the troubles in our State Department?

We know that the tragic failure of our times has been the failure of many of America's so-called "intellectuals" to grasp the economic, political, and spiritual consequences of the Soviet ideology. This failure to grasp abstract ideas, and to make deductions from them, has made these American "intellectuals" unworthy of the honor and respect they ought to enjoy in a country that has been called to world leadership. But their failure was the failure of a whole postwar generation of intellectuals.

Too many of our bright young people who emerged from college in the early thirties to go to office or government or bureau or editorial desk had no deep-rooted convictions or reasoned philosophy of their own. They had not been educated to use their minds on abstractions; that is to say, to *reason*. Naturally, they could not reason well enough to follow the tortuous, ingenious, false but rational dialectics of Communism. The trouble with what most of them *thought*, was that they didn't. These young, good-willed, energetic young men often found their way into places in our government, on our radios, and in our newspapers. There they bought Russia on a rising market. They bought it because subconsciously they were shopping for a faith. They bought it because it was fashionable in Washington, in the early New Deal days, to be a little leftist. They bought it because Soviet solutions to our industrial problems promised a quick, cheap, easy way to justice, which did away with the need to deal with Original Sin in rich or poor. They bought it because Soviet solutions for the European and Asiatic masses promised a cheap, easy way to world peace. They bought it because they believed in Russian promises. In short, they bought it because they had warm hearts, but not sound heads. And in word, law, and act they reflected the philosophy they had bought.

Unhappily, they could not dump this philosophy so easily on a falling market! They could not "get out from under." In various government bureaus, these men, now growing older—and sadder—and wiser—had come to have a *vested interest in their errors.* To confess them, in all *humility,* not only galled their pride: worse, it might cost them their livelihood, their jobs, the respect of the community.

The State Department officials had their own vested interests, and their original errors at Teheran and Yalta are indeed incalculable.

A Christian says his *mea culpa, mea maxima culpa* in the secrecy of the confessional and gets absolution from his priest. But the politician, columnist, bureaucrat, military figure who says *mea culpa* even to his colleagues, is likely to get the razz and the boot! The sacrifice of pride and post was too great a price for most of them to pay for a clear conscience and a clean balance sheet!

REMEMBER, these men were not Communists. In most cases they were not even consciously fellow-travelers. But they were easily "worked on" by Communists and fellow-travelers. Communists and fellow-travelers massaged their egos with "favorable publicity."

All men yearn for flattery, approbation; they all yearn to be told they are noble at heart, that they keep the people's interests first and foremost. Now anyone with the smallest knowledge of governmental or bureaucratic life knows that public servants get very little from either the public or their colleagues but abuse; even in highest offices they are not spared. The Communists long ago learned the Achilles heel of many public servants: the desire for an occasional kind word for services rendered. They persuaded these men, whenever they took action favorable to the U.S.S.R., that they were acting with extraordinary intellect, tremendous heart, magnificent vision.

We have an admirable example of where this satanic technique of constantly poured-on flattery led one liberal of the thirties: it led Henry Wallace into the complete captivity of American Communists. And remember, although he is to all *practical* purposes a Communist tool, he can say with complete honesty that he is an American and not a Communist party member. If this could happen to Henry Wallace—a man of wide political experience, of good background and education—a man who had been Vice-President of the United States, can we not assume that it has happened to some younger, less experienced men in obscure posts in our government?

I suggest then that the frightening inability, or prideful unwillingness of some members of government to free themselves from the continuing consequences of their first intellectual puppy love raptures for Communism, or to do without diabolic flattery they got from the Communist-inspired left-wing press, is largely to blame for our China policy today.

One should never dig a hole without filling it. But after all, is not the theory of Original Sin the most reasonable and charitable we can give for the failure of our government to aid China?

July 1949

TUG-OF-WAR IN KOREA

By ROBERT T. OLIVER

[*The American collapse in Indochina was instantly followed by temblors in Korea and the Philippines. The threat of a second Korean War in 1975 focused a still timely searchlight on Professor Robert T. Oliver's warning in May 1947, three years before the first Korean War burst upon a heedless United States. "The crucial test of Russian-American ability to solve their difficulties peacefully," he predicted then, "will come in Korea. And it is coming very soon." Professor Oliver had spent the summer of 1946 in Korea, and his report provided testimony as to the Soviet technique of indirect aggression and the suicidal American policy of appeasement by supporting coalitions with Communist fifth columns. During the past 30 years the balance of power in Asia has shifted fundamentally, what with the rivalry between Moscow and Peking, but the myopia afflicting American diplomacy remains incurable. Regardless of the status of North Korea, whether it be a satellite of Russia or of Mao's China,*

153

the United States would face a deadly dilemma, not unlike the one in Vietnam, should the Red Koreans descend upon South Korea and upon the considerable American forces stationed there.]

KOREA IS THE COUNTRY in the middle. The two most powerful nations of the world have ripped that country in two, in a secret agreement the nature of which they still refuse to divulge, and politically and economically Korea is rapidly bleeding to death. Korea is the chief testing spot in the Far East— perhaps in the whole world—of the new Truman Doctrine of supporting native democratic regimes against Communist infiltration and destruction. The crucial test of Russian-American ability to solve their difficulties peacefully will come in Korea. And it is coming very soon.

A Russian army is ruling north Korea, down to the 38th parallel, under the ruthless but efficient pattern of a totalitarian dictatorship. An American army in south Korea is sincerely but clumsily attempting to force an American pattern upon a people schooled in a 4,000-year-old tradition of self-rule. Both Russians and Americans are confronted by a stubborn nationalism and insistence upon absolute independence that is so strong the Japanese could not destroy it in a full generation of the most cruel and crafty tyranny.

A newspaperman just back from a three-day stopover in Seoul, capital of Korea, snorted when I asked him what he thought of the "Irish of the Orient." "Huh!" he grunted, "The Irish at least know who they're fighting, but the Koreans aren't on anybody's side."

My newspaper friend went to Korea with a very simple pattern in his mind. He saw Korea as a battleground where Russia and the United States are warily eyeing one another like two dogs who will either back away or leap at one another's throat. To him Korea is simply an adventitious *locus* on which the Russian-American drama of conflict is rapidly drawing toward its climax. So far as his thinking went, it was correct. But he failed to understand that, for Koreans, this conflict, however vital, is secondary to their main determination— which is that their ancient independence must and shall be restored. The Koreans are, indeed, upon somebody's side: their own.

THE SOVIET-AMERICAN RIVALRY in Korea is dictated by the strategic location of that 86,000-square mile peninsula. Korea is in the heart of the vital strategic triangle of North Asia. When Japan controlled that peninsula, it was used both as a continental base and as a corridor of conquest by which to accomplish the seizure of Manchuria and the attack on China. In Russian control, Korea would be the key to complete domination of all Asia north of Hong Kong. If the United States possessed permanent military bases in Korea, we should have a loaded rifle pointed at Russia's doorway into the Pacific.

Aside from its military significance, Korea is a rich economic prize. It possesses sufficient gold, silver, zinc, lead, copper, iron, tungsten, graphite, kaolin, coal, and hydroelectric power resources to permit the development of large-scale industry. It raises an exportable surplus of rice, and in fisheries exports it was at one time third among the nations of the world. Of even more importance to Russia, Korea has 16 excellent all-weather ports.

The interests of all Pacific powers, and the stability and peace of Asia, demand that Korea shall be completely independent. This is why a promise of independence was made at Cairo and reaffirmed at Potsdam. But when the great powers met at Moscow in December 1945, the best they could devise was a plan for a five-year trusteeship over Korea to be administered jointly by the United States, Russia, China, and Great Britain.

Despite all the persuasion and intimidation directed against them, all Koreans except Communists have refused to accept the trusteeship plan. In a survey made last March in the county of Kim Chun Pukto, where 23,343 families were queried, 1.9 percent favored trusteeship, and 92.3 percent opposed it, with the rest not registering an opinion. Yet Russian-American negotiations for reuniting Korea and setting up an all-Korea government have broken down because the Russians insist that only Koreans who favor trusteeship could be admitted to such a government!

Korean opposition to trusteeship stresses that (1) it is not independence, such as they have been promised; (2) it is an insult to a highly cultivated people who ruled themselves for forty centuries; and (3) it could not possibly work, because the Russians (and perhaps other powers, too) would constantly intrigue for special advantages and cause such confusion that it would have to be extended until one or another great power could gain permanent control.

Korean nationalists demand that since Russia and the United States cannot solve their differences over Korea, both should withdraw and let the problem be decided by the United Nations. This is precisely the point made by Secretary Marshall in his blunt statement on the Korean problem delivered to the Russians on April 11. Marshall proposed an immediate reconvening of the joint Russian-American conference to settle the Korean impasse, with the proviso that, if the conference does not succeed, the United Nations be invited to assume jurisdiction. On April 16 the Chinese government demanded that Korea immediately be granted its complete independence, and asked that if this is not done the problem should be resubmitted to a four-power conference of the United States, Russia, China, and Great Britain. It seems that every interested power is now agreed on at least two points: (1) that the Korean situation as it now exists is an international scandal; and (2) that it must be promptly and justly solved.

RUSSIAN RULE IN NORTH KOREA commenced with an orgy of looting, raping, and terrorism. Then it settled down to a pattern already made familiar in eastern Europe. A single political party, the North Korean Labor Party, was recognized. Freedom of speech, of press, of religion, and of assembly were strictly denied. Koreans in the Russian zone were forbidden to listen to radio programs from outside. No Korean is permitted to travel outside his own *goon* (township) without Soviet identification papers. A barrage of pro-Communist propaganda has been showered upon the 10 million Koreans who live north of the 38th parallel, heavily spiced with descriptions of American blunders in south Korea.

All land owned by the Japanese and all large landholdings of Koreans were taken over by the Soviet forces, and "redistributed" to farmers who would yield to Communist domination. Korean "collaborators" were punished by having their property seized, by being imprisoned, or by being executed. A "collaborator" in the Russian dictionary is any Korean who owned property beyond his immediate needs, and any who continued to prefer independence to cooperation with the Soviet regime.

Last November an "election" was held in north Korea, in which the people were herded to the polls to vote on the single slate of candidates nominated by the North Korea Labor Party. The method of voting was to place a white box on one table and a black box on another, with armed guards stationed between. The voters approached the boxes and dropped a pellet in the white box to support the slate, or in the black box to oppose it. By this method a vote of 99.2 percent was registered for the candidates. The Russians cite this as "proof" that north Korea now has the most democratic government on earth, chosen overwhelmingly by the people themselves!

At the time of the defeat of Japan, Korea had no Communist problem for it had no Communist population. Russians brought back into north Korea some 300,000 Korean Communists from Siberia and Manchuria. They have permitted the escape of over 800,000 irreconcilables who have entered the American zone as refugees. And they have drafted all Korean men in their zone who are between the ages of 17 and 25 into a Communist-trained and -dominated army. General John R. Hodge, commander of American forces in south Korea, estimates the potential size of this impressed army at 500,000. As he says, there is no conceivable reason for it except to threaten the conquest of all Korea.

COMMUNIST PARTY MEMBERSHIP in south Korea is estimated by its own leaders at only 20,000 in a population of twenty million. It is well organized and well financed. . . .

The American Military Government has insisted upon free speech and upon complete recognition of the Communists as a domestic political party. This has persisted despite repeated statements from General Hodge's headquarters of indisputable evidence that the south Korean Communists are operating directly upon orders from Moscow.

When the Americans landed in south Korea, they found a Communist organization already established. Financed by the Russians and actively aided by the Japanese during the weeks preceding American entry, this organization appeared to be much more extensive than it was. Since the American aim was one of close cooperation with Russia, hopefully based on the expectation of an early and amicable agreement for joint withdrawal, our Military Government sought to force upon the Korean nationalists a policy of coalition with the leftist leaders. To implement this aim, a "Coalition Committee" was established as the only Korean group with which the American authorities would deal.

But Korean nationalists, led by astute, American-educated, lifelong patriot Dr. Syngman Rhee, refused to enter into any such coalition. As Dr. Rhee has repeatedly pointed out, coalition with agents of a foreign government is only another way of surrendering Korean independence. Dr. Rhee made a triumphal tour of south Korea in the spring of 1946, rallying the people to a solid anti-Communist program. As a result, the so-called "Coalition Committee" actually represented only the leftist parties, and was co-chairmaned by Kimm Kiusic and Lyuh Woon Heung, both of whom were branded as fellow-travelers by Korean nationalists.

In November 1946 the American Military Government took a step toward "self-government" for south Korea by permitting the election of 45 members for an Interim Legislature. Forty-three of the elected members were nationalists, and two were Communists. Then, in consultation with the Coalition Committee, General Hodge appointed an additional 45 members—only one of whom represented Dr. Rhee's nationalist party, and 28 of whom were leftists tinged with fellow-traveler sympathies.

Immediately after this demonstration of "democracy," Dr. Rhee left for the United States to seek, on the top policy level, a change of American practices in Korea. . . .

Our rule of south Korea has also been seriously handicapped by the division of the country into two zones. The minerals, hydroelectric power, coal, and, consequently, the heavy industry are almost all in the Russian zone. The best rice lands are in the south. The lifeblood of Korea has always flowed north and south. Yet the "iron curtain" is so impenetrable that eleven weeks of negotiation were required to secure even a once-a-week exchange of mail across the 38th parallel. The coal that used to heat south Korean homes has been sent to Siberia. The industrial products upon which south Korea depends have been shut out. Even families that were separated by the sudden swoop of the Russians down to the dividing line have been unable to reunite, or (in many cases) even to establish communication. . . .

BEYOND ANY DISPUTE, from the points of view of the United States, world peace, and justice to the Korean people, the Korean situation has been very badly handled. Men of good will within the United States government are as eager as anyone to rectify it. But no clear and acceptable program has yet emerged. Responsibility is still so divided and confused among the State, War, and Treasury departments that progress toward a solution is almost impossible. Only President Truman himself has authority sufficient to cut the Gordian knot, and thus far he has not done so. . . .

May 1947

ARE THE PHILIPPINES NEXT?

By BRUNO KROKER

[*In the face of the menacing anti-American rumblings in the Philippines, would Washington still adhere to Secretary of State Acheson's declaration that "an attack on the Philippines could not and would not be tolerated by the United States"? This question comes to the fore in the report of Bruno Kroker, who devoted most of his observations to the widespread activities of the Huk Communist guerrillas then ravaging the country. But Mr. Kroker, a German who had spent 14 years in the Far East, mostly in China, also cast his perceptive eye upon the key American bastion in the Pacific, and raised an issue fraught with awesome consequences.*]

CAN THE United States hold the defensive perimeter of the Pacific, as Secretary of State Acheson has vowed to do, if the Philippine Islands succumb to an *attack from within*?

There are numerous danger signals of a coming internal explosion in the Philippines which may lead to the establishment of a Soviet republic there. During my recent stay in the Islands I saw the familiar Communist pattern of Trojan Horse tactics developing in a manner similar to that which operated in Nationalist China and in Czechoslovakia.

In the Far East, from which I recently arrived after a sojourn of fourteen years, keen observers are wondering if the Philippines are next on the agenda of Moscow, and are asking what the United States would do in the event of a Communist coup in Manila.

The statement of Secretary Acheson before the National Press Club on January 12 last, left no doubt as to Washington's attitude in case of an attack on the Philippines by a foreign power. "The essential parts of the defensive perimeter of the Pacific must and will be held," Mr. Acheson declared, continuing: "The defensive perimeter runs from the Ryukyus to the Philippine Islands . . . an attack on the Philippines could not and would not be tolerated by the United States. But I hasten to add that no one perceives the imminence of any such attack."

No responsible person doubts that the United States will honor Secretary Acheson's pledge to defend the Philippines in case of attack from without. But what will Washington do if the internal strife in the Philippines, fomented and exacerbated by agents of the Cominform, bursts into a general conflagration?

Under a seemingly normal surface the Philippines are a tinder box of unrest which has increased in tension as the United States military and naval establishments have been reduced during 1949. The Philippine Archipelago of some 7,000 islands, having a coastline longer than that of the Atlantic and Pacific shores of the United States combined, is virtually unprotected today, and forms the most vulnerable spot in the defensive perimeter of the United States in the Pacific.

Luzon, most prosperous and vital of the islands, is little more distant from Formosa (or about 600 miles) than the latter is from Amoy and the South China coast, now under Communist control. . . . The Red tidal wave which has swept over China is now washing at America's defensive perimeter in the Pacific. Its impact upon the Philippines has far from reached a climax. The Filipino republic is a seething cauldron which may boil over after the fall of Formosa, and present to the people of the United States the most pressing issue which has yet confronted them since the end of World War II.

February 1950

SMOG IN THE COLD WAR

By EDNA LONIGAN

[In this essay, "Smog in the Cold War," the anatomy of the political climate in the United States created by the Soviet propaganda is laid bare. Edna Lonigan's article, written in 1949, makes a fitting summation of the forces that produced the American debacle in the Far East and that were operative in the recent fiasco suffered by the United States in Southeast Asia. Miss Lonigan, a Barnard College graduate, started as a teacher of economics and rose to become a special aide to the Secretary of the Treasury. After studying government controls in totalitarian Germany and Russia, she turned into a militant libertarian and was associated editorially with Plain Talk during its existence.]

A FEW WEEKS ago Americans were shocked to read in their morning papers that in peaceful Pennsylvania towns people had been killed in their own homes by a dense fog in which particles of poisonous chemicals were invisibly mixed, a kind of poison gas. Soon physicians, city officials, and industrial chemists were mobilized to locate the source of the poison, and the smog was dispersed.

We do not yet realize that the American people are smothered in a deep political fog, through which deadly particles of poisoned opinion enter our minds undetected. But the political smog is not accidental. It is synthetically produced by experts in dissimulation.

By their skill in producing poisonous political fog, the Soviet leaders have succeeded in their intention of diverting us from our proper interests in foreign affairs, and in making our government a catspaw for their foreign policy. We shall discuss the making of political smog in connection with China, but we will see that it is equally applicable to other areas of our foreign and our domestic affairs.

The attitude of the American people is one of active friendliness toward China. But our government is permitting the Chinese nation to be dismembered when that dismemberment is contrary both to loyalty to a valiant ally and regard for our own self-interest. The American people have no effect on foreign policy because the cloud of smog hides from them what is actually happening in China, and what our government is doing about it.

We all know Soviet aims in China, but they are worth reviewing briefly in terms of the two-front strategy.

AFTER THE 1917 REVOLUTION, Bolshevism set out to embrace Western Europe and reach the Atlantic. There were fierce struggles in Poland, Hungary, the Balkans, Italy, and Germany, but the Iron Curtain was shoved back far to the East.

It was because Russia was blocked in Western Europe that she turned to China. She sent her best men to the Far East. They helped Chiang Kai-shek with political and military "advice," which he gladly accepted. She set up schools in Moscow for the training of Chinese and other Orientals in revolutionary strategy, and we are gathering the fruits of that planting in the revolutions that are brewing in every country in Asia.

The reason Chiang Kai-shek is "a Fascist, a supporter of monopoly capitalism, a protector of landlordism, an exploiter of the poor, a powerful dictator, and a total failure who cannot hold his country together"—all according to Communist propaganda—is because in 1927 he broke abruptly with Moscow, which was interested in the spread of Soviet power. Since the Communists were ruthless and cruel and had deeply penetrated into every phase of the public life of China, he used methods that were ruthless and cruel to prevent them from betraying his country. Without approving all his methods, we should be much better able to understand Chiang's desperate remedies than we were in 1927.

We have here described this pattern in detail because it has been repeated so clearly in 1945–1949.

After V-E Day the Russians moved into Western Europe as fast and as far as they could go. The Communists were stopped again, on a line going north and south through Central Europe, much nearer the Atlantic. They had consumed the nations of Eastern Europe. And they were stopped only after our active intervention.

As soon as the "west front" was stabilized, they turned to China. They have

160

had long experience in exploiting Asiatic nations. They have a trained corps of leaders and the nucleus of a "party" in every country in Asia. Once again China is the battleground, and Chiang is the head of the forces which are battling to hold the Communists on the eastern front until we see that the war in Asia is an integral part of the cold war in the West.

The Soviet advance into Western Europe and their advance in the East through China are inseparable. They are planned as one campaign. Russia is today waging a two-front offensive, in which every move on the Western front (in Europe) is related to every move on the Eastern front (in China)—and both are directed against us.

What would be the simplest way for the Russians to neutralize our influence on one of the fronts? The answer is political smog. The strategy is to throw up a political fog, and in that fog to plant poisonous particles which will effectively render us unwilling to continue the struggle.

THE FIRST WARNING of the new strategy came in the midst of the campaign against Germany.

In 1943 a rash of statements suddenly appeared in the papers criticizing the Chinese Government for refusing to allow its students in America to choose what courses they wished. This outburst obviously included more than met the eye. First, most Chinese students here were men of draft age, who had been released by their country to do work of value in the war. They were no more a problem in academic freedom than were the "ninety-day wonders" who filled our campuses in this country. In any honest discussion of the regimentation of students, obviously Russia would have been criticized most severely because it had long ago abandoned the idea that students had individual rights in the choice of an education. In the third place, the outcry came from a group of people and places which made a remarkably clear pattern.

The criticisms of the Chinese Government have come from the same people, the same agencies, and the same places which were always most active in voicing the Communist party line. There is also a pattern in timing, in the speed with which protests move from one point to another. The timing is a little too good, a little too quick, to be natural.

To anyone who had been studying Soviet propaganda techniques it was obvious that the Soviet Government had turned its whole apparatus in America to the task of vilifying the government of China, in order to split us off from giving them any aid when Russia closed in for the kill.

In the cold war of propaganda and poison gas, this was the declaration of war. It was clear notice that the coalition was over. Russia knew that Hitler's defeat was just a matter of months, and she was embarked on the next campaign. She was preparing to split the alliance, as a means ultimately of knifing the United States.

161

The attack on Chinese educational policy was a trifle. It was a dress rehearsal, a trial run. It was designed to see whether the plans were working, whether the pieces fitted. Then the real attack began.

THE METHOD was very simple. The confusion was produced by a subtle and brilliant cross-play between disloyal officials in our government and Communist writers organized and directed to echo the propaganda line. Whenever pro-Soviet officials in our government took a line that favored Russia, obedient writers were assigned the task of building up their reputations, of echoing their ideas, of bringing out "evidence" that the situation was lost in China. Whenever people who knew our foreign policy analyzed the books or articles or news dispatches, and said that they were not correct, the Soviet supporters brought forth their government officials, and said, "It must be true. The United States Government says so."

The trick was to hide the fact that the written and printed statements were an artificial product, the "unity" carefully stage managed; that the governmental pronouncements were part of the same show, and that they all came from the same source. Most Americans would not be suspicious. Those who were would be so busy explaining that they could not convert the others.

We have recently heard the details of how Communist agents found their way into high places in government, where they were assigned the task of confusing our government's policy and the statements that officials made to the public. We need not develop that here. Less is known about the way in which the same thing was done in the writing field, and how the two methods interlocked to increase the confusion.

The method in the writing field was to plan, far in advance, the publication of a series of books on China, which were to come out about six months or so apart. On the surface the books were very different. One would be a quick survey by a reporter on wartime life in Chungking. The next might be a careful technical study of the geography and ethnology of the Mongolian border. Then would come a novel about wartime life in China, followed by reports of a trip into Yenan, or a study of landlordism or of agrarian "reforms." Next might come a biography of an American officer in the Army or the Marines.

These books—so different on the surface—had one thing in common. They were the fog, designed to obscure what was happening in China by a curtain realistically depicting what *might* have happened. But planted within that fog were the particles of poison. In each work, in reportage or drama or scientific facts, carefully planted at just the right intervals, were the symbols—Chiang, the dictator; Chiang, the defender of landlordism; the slanting reference to "feudalism"; the moral revulsion against corruption; the wicked Chinese officials, making money out of the sufferings of the poor. "Feudal" landlords grinding the faces of the workers, dishonest officials, nepotism, were all there. On the other hand there were always a few shining symbols. All was well in Yenan, where a new "democracy" was rising, invisible to the naked eye, but clear to those whose hearts were pure. Here were elections, division of farms among the peasants, lessons in reading, all the marks of "progress."

THIS WAS ALL as realistic as anything Belasco ever did. And as strictly theater. The technique of verisimilitude in detail was the same, neat references to "facts," quotations from "authorities," footnotes, local color, everything synthetic that could be made to look like the real thing.

To make the effect even stronger, the pro-Communists, through their influence in book reviewing, often have it so arranged that books which transmit the smog are reviewed—by other experts in smog. Books which give straight facts are reviewed—as you can guess—by the same experts in smog. Some book clubs have also been very useful in giving wide distribution to books which carried the hidden particles of poisonous propaganda.

On the radio, the propaganda network always manages to have questions of China policy debated by two opposing groups—those who use open argument, and those who use the symbolism and suggestion of political smog. The radio networks have been persuaded that, in the interests of impartiality (!) they must give the experts in smog half of all the time available for discussion of China. Needless to say, the people whose reputation is constantly being built up soon acquire the name of "experts," who must of course be invited on subsequent programs.

The technique has dozens of other advantages. For example, a slanted book comes out. People with experience rush to answer it, which takes time. At just about the time the critics are ready with a rebuttal of a book on agricultural conditions in West China, the Kremlin propagandists are ready with a new book on the latest gossip in Nanking. Which does the public read? You can guess.

This device performs the double function of keeping serious students of our foreign policy busy answering dead books, while keeping the public entertained by a stream of new and lively ones.

THE COMMUNISTS were helped by their long period of preparation. They had of course started long before they were ready for public activity to send their people into China as correspondents, usually of the most conservative papers. They put their people into government jobs where they could be sent to China to "study conditions." Then they sent the people they had placed in academic jobs on missions to China to report on whether government officials really understood the weighty Chinese problem. Strange to say, they usually found that officials sympathetic to the propaganda line did understand the grave problems of China. The others were clearly inadequate to deal with such deep questions.

So effective have the Communists been in sending their people into good jobs in the China field, that more and more "experts" today are of the Communist persuasion. We are now at the point where anyone who claims to be an expert on China must have his political credentials carefully examined.

The Communists got into the Army radio broadcasting. They got into our State Department agencies in China, into UNRRA, and then into the Marshall Plan agencies, as Alfred Kohlberg showed in a statement before the Senate Appropriations Committee.

Communist sympathizers in Washington and in our staffs in China converted General Stilwell to the theory of Chinese corruption. When they could not convert General Hurley, they used their propaganda network in this country to besmirch his reputation. They kept General Wedemeyer from being made Ambassador to China. They wrote the instructions which General Marshall carried to China, and which called upon Chiang to set up a *united front,* like the Communist fronts in Poland and Czechoslovakia. If we were to interfere at all in the internal affairs of China, which are really none of our business, we should have stood for a two-party system, as in the United States, not a one-party system, as in Russia. We had no more right to demand that China bring Communists into her government than China would have to demand that we keep the Communists who have crept into our State Department. Finally, the insulting terms in which the instructions of General Marshall were worded were carefully designed to destroy any good-will we might have left when the meaning of the message was made clear.

Every one of these policies was supported by a continuing repetition, à la Goebbels, of the themes on which the Communist propaganda campaign rested, carefully planted in the books coming out periodically under Communist planning and direction.

There is one more stone to make the arch complete. Every suggestion was planted in the mind of the public when it was off guard, through indirect suggestion, not open statement, by symbols which appealed to the subconscious, where we react emotionally, not critically. This technique is explained in *Mein Kampf.*

February 1949

BOOK 4

GLOBAL SPIDERWEB

THE SECRET BATTALION

By Harold J. Laski

[*This authoritative analysis of the Communist fifth column by Professor Harold J. Laski has not been surpassed in print since its original publication. He wrote it when he was Chairman of the British Labour Party, at the time the Communists sought to disrupt it from within and then capture it. A Leftist Socialist, Laski was a brilliant but unstable and unpredictable intellectual. The appearance of this essay signed by Laski—a darling of the equally maladjusted "liberals" in the United States—was designed to open their starry eyes to the realities of the Soviet system.*]

A CENTURY and a half of action and discussion have gone to the elaboration of the central Communist technique. A massive body of evidence has been accumulated in its support, above all the evidence built upon the experience of Russia, and the habits of states, especially the Nazi and Fascists states, in the twenty years between the two wars. We must look at this body of doctrine as it influences the behavior of its exponents while they are working towards the seizure of power in a capitalist society.

In the first phase, they are half an agitation and half a conspiracy. It is difficult to exaggerate the tribute that Communists deserve for the courage and devotion and tireless energy they bring to their work of agitation; they have all the zeal of passionate crusaders. But the conspirational side of their work, above all because of the philosophy in which it is imbedded, creates habits of a different order. They are working against a ruthless enemy in an unseen war which sooner or later will seek their destruction in open battle.

They must therefore destroy the very parties with which they seek alliance in order to command their resources for their own ends. To do this, they must declare that they are at one with them, loyal to their principles, ready to accept their rules, prepared to serve under their leaders. But since none of these declarations are true, they must also, at the same time, deny these principles, maneuver round the rules, and do all in their power both to discredit the leaders they agree to serve and, if possible, secure their places when they are discredited.

They act like a secret battalion of paratroopers within the brigade whose discipline they have accepted. They meet secretly to propose their own line of action; they have one set of rules to regulate their conduct to one another, and a different set of rules to be observed towards those not in the battalion. Organized as a conspiracy, their major desire is not to select the best possible leadership in ability and character for the end socialism desires; it is to get those upon whom they can count for uncritical and devoted obedience to their orders into the key positions of a movement or party they enter to use for their own purposes. The contradiction between the open profession and the secret purpose makes them willing to sacrifice all regard for truth and straight dealing in social relations to the conquest of that vanguard they need for the future. They require from their own members the complete and unquestioning sacrifice of their consciences to the decisions their inner leadership makes.

This outlook legitimizes the strange alliances, the curious twists and turns of policy, the angry invective, the dual morality, by which Communism is known so widely. Since the dialectic of history makes the outline of the future obvious in the large, even if the path to the future be obscure, the Communist, in acting on behalf of the future, justifies in his own eyes conduct which in others he roundly, even passionately, condemns. He develops an elaborate and tortuous casuistry which permits him to make agreements, to accept obligations, which he can break whenever his service to that future of which he alone has the key, appears to demand it.

That appears beyond dispute as soon as one examines the working of the dictatorship of the proletariat and the revolutionary terror it has thus far involved. No one can honestly doubt that this dictatorship of the proletariat means the dictatorship of the Party over the proletariat; and no one can doubt that the vital power of the Communist Party in Russia is centralized in a small body of men who determine the policies it is to follow. That is why there is no writ of *Habeas Corpus* in the Soviet Union. That is also why the psychology of the great treason trials resembles, to an outsider, nothing so much as a nightmare come to real life from a novel of Dostoievski. That is why, even after a quarter of a century, Russia remains so isolated from the Western world that a large part of the normal interchange between scholars and scientists is still frowned upon by the authorities.

In Germany there were moments when the Communists cooperated, before 1933, with the forces of Nazism, as in the well-known case of the Berlin transport strike. In Britain they supported the government in its resistance to Hitler from September 3rd to October 7th, 1939; from October 7th, 1939, until June 22, 1941, they preached incessantly that this was an imperialist war and insisted on a negotiated peace, even holding a "People's Convention" in 1941 for this purpose in the hope of splitting both the Labour Party and the trade unions; though when Germany attacked Russia on June 22nd, 1941, they immediately devoted all their energy to proving that the "imperialist" war had become a war for freedom and democracy.

168

I accept as a fact beyond dispute the devotion of Communists to their party. But in light of experience I am bound to suggest that devotion so absolute develops in those who are moved by it a power within themselves to make simple truth and plain honesty things of secondary importance to be sacrificed by a coercive casuistry whenever Communists, by so doing, believe they can serve their party. After all, we have seen history falsified, documents forged, men and women, even when they were leaders, slandered and broken by these means.

It is a natural mode of behavior in a party that conceives itself as a beleaguered army fighting a relentless enemy in a hostile territory. It makes conspiracy endemic in such a party, it makes success the sole criterion of methods, and thereby it justifies for itself as a party means that it is prompt to condemn in others when others employ them. It makes victory so overwhelmingly important that the ends for which the victory has been won may become unattainable through the means employed. For historically, means cannot be separated from ends; they enter into them and transform their nature.

It is notable that whenever the unity sought by Communists has been accepted by other parties, it is the Communist Party alone which has benefitted by that unity. It is notable that, as in France and Norway and Czechoslovakia, even a common front which maintains a separate party life and organization, has proved an unhappy and bitter experience. And it has always been the case because the casuistry of Communism permits to its members a moral laxity which becomes an obligation if the Central Committee of the Communist Party decides so to define it. The result is a corruption, both of the mind and of the heart, which is alike contemptuous of reason and careless of truth. For the moment, the Communist Party must disguise itself as "an ordinary democratic Party." Any Communists who are troubled by the duality of this outlook, as Dimitrov told the Bulgarian Communist Party, "are either not Marxists or they are provocateurs."

Obviously the assumption is that one aim can be announced and another aim practiced. Obviously the aim to be practiced is to enter social democratic parties to discredit their leaders and to capture their organization from within. When they are stabbed in the back and out of the way, the field is set for the final battle between capitalism and Communism. In this way, the Communists want to capture the working-class forces wherever possible so that where, as in Great Britain, they wield the state-power, they are part of the outer defenses of Russia; or where, as in the United States, they are not yet a government, they can at least serve as an organized barrier against anti-Russian action.

The real purpose inherent in the strategy which Communists everywhere are ultimately determined to employ is the organization of catastrophe. It assumes the inevitability of violent revolution; therefrom it assumes that democracy, with its reliance on constitutional methods, is no more than a temporary phase between the forcible seizure of power by the bourgeoisie and the forcible seizure of power by the proletariat. It therefore works, quite deliberately, towards the one-party state. It denies the right of opposition, the rule of law, freedom of speech or association, the duty of the individual citizen to put his own conscience before his party's orders.

October 1946

THE INSIDE STORY OF

THE MARZANI CASE

By J. ANTHONY PANUCH
Former Deputy Assistant Secretary of State

[*This is a unique documentary report that makes an exciting true-detective story. Coupled with the saga of the Amerasia case (Book 3, page 102) and the account of the Hiss-Chambers affair (Book 4, page 197), "The Marzani Case" shows the almost insuperable difficulties in the way of uncovering and bringing to justice Soviet collaborators infiltrated in key government positions. The author of this remarkable exposé, J. Anthony Panuch, was a distinguished lawyer, a dedicated patriot, who served as Deputy Assistant Secretary of State. His report dramatizes the crucial issues facing the American people today: Is suspicion of disloyalty on the part of a Federal employe sufficient ground for his dismissal? Does the burden of proof rest on the suspect who should establish his innocence, or on the Federal Government that should establish his guilt? Is it a privilege or is it an inalienable right to be a civil servant? Marzani fought a great legal battle but was convicted and served a term in a Federal penitentiary.*]

THE INSIDE STORY of the Marzani case can now be told. It provides a revealing insight into the problems confronting government administrators in coping with the menace of Communist infiltration, without wholesale violations of civil liberties and rudimentary standards of American decency and fair play.

The story begins in October of 1945 when Secretary of State James F. Byrnes appointed me Deputy Assistant Secretary of State for Administration and at the same time designated me as coordinator of the merger with the Department of State of such war agencies as the Office of War Information (OWI), Foreign Economic Administration (FEA), and several others. This vast merger, involving close to 25,000 Federal employees, also funds and properties of these war agencies, had to be accomplished in less than ninety days—by January 1, 1946.

It was an homeric task. One of the principal jobs was the "screening" of the war agency personnel thus transferred to the Department of State, in order to determine their suitability for employment in the highly confidential work of the Department. For this purpose the Department maintained a corps of trained investigators, under the experienced direction of Chief Special Agent Thomas F. Fitch.

Moreover, when Secretary Byrnes took office he found himself plagued with organizational difficulties in the investigative set-up of the Department, inherited from the preceding regime. One of these was a jurisdictional conflict between the office of Chief Special Agent Fitch and a newly established three-man "security-office" under the energetic Bob Bannerman. The confusion resulting from this bit of bureaucratic politics did not help the Department's problem of screening the large numbers of transferee personnel.

The screening job became virtually desperate when the sudden and unexpected merger of 1946 literally dumped thousands of new employees on the Department. Carl Marzani was one of those thus transferred to the Department of State as a member of the Presentation Division of the OSS.

I MET Marzani early in November of 1946. At that time Col. Carter Burgess, formerly aide to Lt. Gen. Bedell Smith and wartime secretary of SHAEF, was Executive Officer to Mr. Donald Russell, Assistant Secretary of State for Administration and myself. Col. Burgess was working closely with me on a plan for the reorganization of the State Department's antiquated communications system. In this work we were being assisted by Maj. Gen. Otto Nelson, formerly Assistant to Gen. McNarney, Deputy Chief of Staff to Gen. Marshall.

As we wrestled with our complex task all of us agreed that what we urgently needed was a graphic presentation of the reorganization plan in operation. Accordingly we welcomed General Nelson's proposal that the Presentation Division, newly acquired by transfer from OSS, be assigned to take on the graphic display job. The General went on to explain that one of the best men in the Division and one who had worked with him in the War Department and in Italy would "do a job" for us. His name, Marzani. He phoned Marzani and asked him to come over.

In about a half-hour Marzani arrived. He was still wearing his sergeant's uniform with the patch and insignia of the Mediterranean Theater. He was of medium size, compactly built, with a sallow complexion and an unusual pair of hazel-brown eyes. His motions and mannerisms were quick and nervous, his facial expressions mobile. He spoke expressively, a sort of New Yorkese with an overlay of foreign accent. His response to our difficulties was swift and intelligent.. He not only grasped and correctly appraised the complexities of the problem with which we were confronted, but came up quickly with his idea of how it could best be translated into graphic form. "Roughs," he said, "would be in our hands in a week." And they were. Gen. Nelson, Col. Burgess, and I were delighted with the concept of the proposed display.

In those hectic reorganization days of the winter of 1945–46 the "front office" was pleased with the work of the Presentation Division. We called on this Division whenever it was required to illustrate some complex problem of organization. In all of this work Marzani was the "spark plug." We were grateful to Gen. Nelson for "discovering" him.

But in April of 1946 the long arm of security began to cast its shadow over Marzani. Early that month Bob Bannerman presented me with a batch of files variously stamped "confidential," "secret," and "top secret." These, he explained, were the first concrete results of the Security Office's checks on some of the personnel taken over from the war agencies under the merger. I thumbed through the "top secret" folders and came to one captioned "Carl Aldo Marzani." Automatically I turned to the covering report and its concluding paragraph, which read: "The Security Committee considers Marzani a grave security risk and recommends termination of his services in the Department."

I could scarcely believe my eyes. This was incredible. I turned to Bannerman and said: "Bob, are you crazy? Marzani has handled some of the hottest stuff in the OSS and in the War Department. Col. Burgess and Gen. Nelson both knew him and they would laugh at anyone who said Marzani was a security risk."

Bannerman's reply was, "That may be, but read the whole report."

I did, with an increasing sense of unreality. Carl Aldo Marzani . . . alias . . . Tony Whales . . . member of the Communist Party . . . in New York in 1941 . . . signed petition for the election of Earl Browder as Congressman on the Communist Party ticket . . . wife a member of the Communist Party, name Edith Charles . . . Activities in the American Negro Congress . . . Campaigned against conscription . . . urged revolution . . .

I had read enough. "How good is the proof on this? Has Tom Fitch got the witnesses?" I asked Bannerman. His reply was that Fitch had not prepared the report, but that its substance was all derived from confidential files of various governmental investigative agencies and considered by him to be reliable. I asked him for his recommendation. It was his opinion that we should terminate Marzani's connection with the Department. I pointed out to him that, under civil service regulations to terminate, i.e., to "fire," Marzani we would have to prefer charges. And in this case the charge would have to be that, since Marzani was a member of the Communist Party, there was a presumption against his loyalty to the Government of the United States which would require his separation from its service.

It is one thing, I explained, to prefer charges of disloyalty against a Federal employee with civil service standing, an entirely different matter to prove them before the Commission's loyalty board. Particularly in a case like Marzani's, where his record of war service had been glowingly praised by high officers of the supersecret OSS and the War Department. Then, too, Marzani being a veteran of World War II had, under the Veterans Preference Act, certain rights of appeal to the Civil Service Commission from any adverse determination of the Department with respect to his employment. This was a case where one had to be *sure*.

While the report was devastating, I was troubled by the fact that it seemed to be based largely on hearsay. I questioned Bannerman more closely. Who had prepared the report? He said Morse Allen, his assistant. I pointed out that Allen certainly could not testify to the charges of his personal knowledge—which Bannerman admitted. I then asked Bannerman whether he himself had gone below the surface of any of the confidential reports from the investigative agencies—had talked to any "flesh and blood" witness with respect to the charges. He admitted that he had not; but reiterated that the reports emanated from so-called confidential informants whose identity the investigative agencies supplying the information would under no circumstances disclose.

Patiently I pointed out to Bannerman that in this case the Department was in an unenviable dilemma. Here we had in our hands derogatory information with respect to the loyalty of a State Department employee, one who had access to key information—yet we were not in a position to prefer and sustain charges of disloyalty against him. Somewhat less patiently I explained to Bannerman that our investigative staff, which was costing the taxpayers over $400,000 a year, ought to be able to prove or disprove charges as serious as these by digging up the witnesses; that we should not be forced to rely exclusively on reports of other agencies—who would not disclose the sources of their information.

Bannerman, after some further discussion, agreed this was so. He suggested, however, that possibly Marzani might resign of his own accord if a proper approach was made. This seemed like an excellent idea. Accordingly I told Bannerman to set up a meeting for us with Col. Fearing (Marzani's immediate superior) to discuss the matter. This was held some time late in April and was attended by Fearing, Bannerman, and myself. We all agreed that if Marzani were "fired" he would fight, and that on the present record we would not be able to sustain the charges. After weighing all the factors it was agreed that Fearing should ask Marzani to resign. Against the possibility of his not resigning when requested, I told Bannerman to coordinate with Fitch and leave no stone unturned in their joint efforts to locate any reputable witnesses who could and would personally testify in support of the charges against Marzani.

A FEW WEEKS later the phone in my office rang. It was Col. Fearing, reporting that Marzani had refused to resign. I asked the Colonel for details on what had happened. Fearing replied, "Nothing much. Our talk was short and to the point. He said to me, 'Why should I resign, what's the reason?' I said, 'Security considerations.' He said, 'That's the bunk—I'll take it up with Russell.' "

"So you have him in your lap now!" laughed Fearing and hung up.

And Marzani was indeed in my lap if he appealed to Don Russell (Assistant Secretary of State for Administration). The matter in that eventuality would be turned over to me for my recommendations with respect to the action to be taken by the Secretary of State, since I was in charge of overall security administration under Mr. Russell.

Perspiration rolled down the inside of my starched collar as I laid down the receiver. Could I talk Marzani into resigning? Suppose I could not? In the state of the available evidence we would be "in a box." For if Marzani was in fact a subversive, he would be alerted, and further development of evidence with respect to his activities would be difficult if not impossible. He could and would immediately and effectively "cover up." Since there was no tangible evidence of his Communist affiliations and activities it would be difficult to make a case against Marzani which would stand up even in the Department, to say nothing of an appeal to the Civil Service Commission or the courts. Hearsay was not enough. Secretary Byrnes, as former Associate Justice of the Supreme Court of the United States, would hardly be one to authorize dismissal of an employee on the serious charge of disloyalty unless such a charge was supported by clear and substantial evidence. We were a long way from evidence of that kind.

To make the situation more complicated, there seemed to be no other ground on which we could get rid of Marzani. He certainly was not incompetent or insubordinate, addicted to intoxicants, or notoriously immoral.

I did not have very long to wait. During the last week in May Marzani called my office for an appointment to discuss his "personal status" in the Department.

Marzani came in a little before 10 o'clock on June 1. In the informal way of the State Department we were on a first name basis. I called him "Carl" and he called me "Joe." We sat down in the two deep chairs by the fireplace. I lit a cigar; he, a cigarette. Watching him, I wondered what his "fade in" would be. He was neatly dressed in a tan gabardine suit with a light green shirt and a tie of darker green. He seemed entirely at his ease. Except for a pink flush on his cheek bones—which might have been attributable to the heat of a Washington June—and a glitter in his eyes, he showed no evidence of tension or emotion. After a few preliminary amenities he came right to the point. He said:

"Joe, Fearing asked for my resignation on security grounds. Did you know about it?"

I said, "Yes, Carl, I did."

"Did you authorize him to do it?"

I told him I had. There was a silence. I wondered what was coming next. I had not long to wait. "What are the charges?" His voice, usually husky and not unpleasant, now had a metallic ring, and his brown eyes seemed to have turned a bleak gray. "I'm entitled to know what the charges against me are."

"You certainly are, Carl," I conceded, "and they're serious." I then listed them, watching him carefully for his reaction. As I reached the end of my recital I thought I detected a look of relief pass over his face. When I had concluded, he said "Is that all?" His comeback to my amazed "Good Lord, isn't that enough!" furnished another surprise. He was almost casual. "Joe, all of that is old stuff; there's nothing to any of it." Before I could even reply that such grave charges could not be laughed off with a bare denial, he let me have it.

"How often do I have to prove that these charges are the bunk?" he shouted. "It's the same old stuff that they pulled on me in OSS back in 1943 and it was exploded then as completely phoney!" He shook his finger at me and asked, "How do you think I could have been rated eligible for a job in OSS, if any of this stuff was true?"

He had me there. But here was a chance to get educated. So I asked him "Well, Carl, how *did* you get rated eligible for OSS with these charges on the books?"

He paused to light a cigarette; inhaled deeply and settled back in his chair. He said:

"I'll tell you. Back in 1943 I was in the OSS—just getting started, when the Civil Service Commission rated me ineligible. I went to my bosses, Ed Mason and Emil Despres, and told them what had happened. They went to Gen. Donovan and told him the story; he said he would call up the Commission. I nosed around on my own and found out what some of the charges against me were. When I knew what the score was, I decided to fight it out. I demanded a hearing before the Civil Service Commission's Loyalty Board."

If what Marzani said was true, this was a bold maneuver. He went on:

"I had a formal hearing before the Commission's Loyalty Board on the charges which had been made against me." Pointing his finger at me—speaking slowly—he said, *"Joe, these were the very same charges which you've listed this morning."*

He paused to let this sink in and continued.

"Well, at the hearing before the Loyalty Board I introduced a complete history of my life in documented form. I myself testified under oath. I called witnesses, people who knew me all my life, people under whom I worked in and out of Government, and *they* all testified under oath. There is a complete transcript of the record of the hearing in the confidential files of the Civil Service Commission. On that record, which incidentally you should look over in case you're interested, I was entirely cleared of disloyalty charges by the Civil Service Commission and rated eligible for service with OSS."

I was flabbergasted. For if what Marzani said was true, I could imagine the cries of "double jeopardy" that would have been raised, to the embarrassment of the Secretary of State and the Department, if we had attempted to "fire" Marzani in 1946 on the very same *disloyalty charges which the Civil Service Commission had dismissed in 1943.*

I pulled myself together and said, "Well, Carl, if what you say is true it certainly puts a different light on the matter. I'll have to read the Civil Service Commission's records and we will talk again." With this the conference got off to a discussion of Marzani's experiences in OSS, his prior history, education, and travels.

That two-hour conference was one I knew would be vivid in my memory for a long time to come.

EARLY ON Monday of the next week I got busy. I wanted to know and know fast whether our security people had seen the Civil Service Commission's record of the Marzani hearing, and, if so, why no mention had been made of it in the security report on Marzani which had been submitted to me by Bannerman. My cross-examination of Bannerman and his aides disclosed that they had not seen the record. Enraged and disgusted, I immediately requisitioned it and read it with the greatest care. There was no question about it— the hearing by the Civil Service Commission's Loyalty Board in 1943 *did involve the very same charges which our security people had made against Marzani.* After the hearing, the Commission *had* rated Marzani eligible for employment in the OSS. Marzani's amazing story was true.

Despite this, there was something in the whole setup that did not ring true. The basic testimony in the hearing was Marzani's own, plus "character" witnesses testifying in his behalf. Strangely enough, the Commission had introduced no evidence to support the charges against Marzani.

However, the failure of the Security Office in the Marzani case had shaken my confidence in the operation of the Department's personnel investigation setup. I immediately launched a thoroughgoing examination which disclosed an extremely disturbing situation. While the Chief Special Agent, Tom Fitch, was charged with the duty of investigating State Department employees for security and fitness—a function for which Congress had appropriated funds at a rate of $400,000 a year—Fitch's operation was being thwarted by the activities of the newly established "Security Office." The end product was intrigue— working at cross purposes—with resulting chaos and irresponsibility.

The investigation also showed that the Security Office had arranged things in such fashion that the Department's Chief Special Agent was excluded from liaison with the FBI; that the Security Committee (a supposedly impartial body whose sole function was to *evaluate* evidence produced by the Department's investigators and security officers in respect of personnel) was operating under the chairmanship of Bob Bannerman and was composed for the most part of members of his own staff. We thus had a situation where investigators sat in judgment on the quality of the evidence which they had gathered—acting not only as investigators but as prosecutors, court and jury—a "kangaroo court." Finally, I found that *the "Security Committee" had excluded from its membership* the State Department's outstanding expert on Communist doctrine and subversive techniques of infiltration!

Upon Secretary Byrnes' return from the Paris Conference in July of 1946, and with his approval, we overhauled our entire personnel security operation. The job of investigation of personnel was firmly placed under Tom Fitch, the Chief Special Agent. Bannerman was requested to confine himself to the coordination of Fitch's reports, with such information as might be available at FBI, ONI, G2, etc. To bolster up the Department's sagging communications and physical security operation I personally appealed to Gen. Carter Clarke, then Deputy Chief of Staff, G2, to give us his best security officer. He recommended Col. Stanley Goodrich, who was immediately employed and placed in charge of our physical and communications security system—working directly out of my office. The "kangaroo court" Security Committee was scrapped, to be replaced by a *group of high officials of the Department whose sole duty was to evaluate the evidence developed by the investigators,* and make recommendations to the Assistant Secretary for Administration. This time the group *included* the Department's top expert on Communists and Communist techniques. Mr. Samuel Klaus, a lawyer experienced in the detection and control of subversive activities as a member of the staff of the General Counsel of the Treasury Department, was designated counsel to the new security group. *To shield this group from improper pressures in security matters its identity was kept secret. Its membership was designated by secret written order of the Secretary of State.* Its counsel was appointed by similar order.

By the end of July 1946 I was confident that the blueprints of the new security setup in the Department of State were as good as experience and skill could contrive. But we had to get the organization out of the blueprint stage and into operations.

Throughout the first six months of the year members of Congress had been demanding a purge of alleged subversives in the Department. Indeed, late in June of 1946 the Appropriations Committee of the Senate tacked the so-called McCarran rider to the Department's appropriation bill for the fiscal year 1947. This rider, which had been prepared by me at the request of Senators McCarran and Bridges, gave the Secretary of State the power to dismiss any employee of the Department without regard to Civil Service rules or regulations if, in the Secretary's discretion, such action was warranted in the interests of the government. Both Senator McCarran, Chairman of the Committee, and Senator Bridges, the then ranking Republican member (now chairman) told me in no uncertain terms that they expected the Department to use the power thus granted. Since Secretary Byrnes' policy was that even under the rider he would not dismiss an employee for reasons of disloyalty unless there was some substantial evidence of such disloyalty, it was up to the new security organization to do a job of getting the evidence.

As SECURITY COUNSEL, Klaus and Chief Special Agent Fitch started the tremendous job of reinvestigating several hundred selected security cases. I did not hear much about Marzani—although his case was high on the priority list—until September of 1946. Early that month Klaus came to me and requested permission for Agent Fitch to send a strong task force to undertake a thorough combing of the secret records of the New York City Police Department. I gave the mission my hearty approval and asked to be kept fully and currently informed of progress.

Our first real "pay dirt" in this effort came late in October. Sam Klaus reported to me that our investigators had found some interesting data on "Tony Whales" in the secret records of the New York Police Department's Anti-Subversive Squad, a unit organized by Mayor LaGuardia for the sole purpose of infiltrating Communist activities in New York during the war. A few days later Klaus reported that these records appeared to bear out the charges involving Marzani's Communist activities.

We were on a warm trail at long last! Our men went into high gear. Klaus and Fitch had their staff analyze and follow through on the reports. Their author, a college-bred Negro detective, Archer Drew—later to become the star witness against Marzani—confirmed the story of the records in minute detail. Finally, under close questioning, he described Tony Whales. The description checked remarkably with that of Carl Marzani. I directed that we obtain immediate and unequivocal identification of Marzani as Whales.

Klaus obtained three separate photographs of Marzani and inserted each in a panel of other pictures of people with somewhat similar cast of features. These were taken from Washington to New York and Archer Drew was asked whether Tony Whales appeared in any of the panels. *Each time he unerringly and instantly identified Marzani as Tony Whales!*

At this point, and for the first time in the case, the efforts of Klaus and Fitch had produced a "flesh and blood" witness who could and would testify as to Marzani's Communist affiliations and activities. For the first time we had positive proof that Marzani had lied about his Communist affiliations to the FBI in 1942, to the Civil Service Commission in 1943, and to the Department of State in 1946. In the case of the FBI and the Civil Service Commission, where his statements had been given under oath, he had committed perjury. Unfortunately a criminal proceeding was barred by the Federal Statute of Limitations, which requires action to be started within two years of the commission of the crime.

The best remaining basis for criminal action against Marzani appeared to be his willful concealment of his Communist membership, affiliations, and activities in connection with his employment in the State Department. However, the

Federal statute on this type of fraud had never been tested in court in a loyalty case and there was some doubt among the Department's lawyers as to whether criminal prosecution would be successful. Klaus and I concluded, however, that this was a case in which the statute clearly applied.

We also felt that if prosecution in the Marzani case was successful, it would immeasurably help in the solution of the problem of subversives in the Federal Government. It has been my experience that subversives find it not too difficult to remain in the service of the government through the simple expedient of concealing their real affiliations and sympathies. They correctly discount the chance of detection as improbable—involving usually an "induced" resignation. Even in the event of dismissal it was not too difficult to find another "billet." *But* if such misrepresentation or concealment involved a real danger of criminal prosecution and a definite possibility of a term in the Federal Penitentiary, Klaus and I felt that there would be an exodus of Commies, fellow-travelers and other subversives from the Federal Service.

THE FIRST STEP was to obtain the Secretary's authority for Marzani's dismissal and his approval of our reference of the matter to the Department of Justice. This had to await the Secretary's return to the Department after the completion of the work of the Council of Foreign Ministers. In the meantime, we were feverishly developing evidence of Marzani's Communistic activities in New York.

Despite our utmost efforts to prevent Marzani from becoming aware of these activities, he managed to get word, through his Communist contacts in New York, that something was "cooking." He called on me on November 15 to tell me that he was "tired" of being persecuted and that he had decided to resign from the department and enter private business. It was apparent to me that Marzani knew he would be fired and that he probably would be prosecuted for his fraud in concealing his Communist connections. It was smart strategy for him to "resign" before dismissal and indictment.

I listened noncommittally. It was too late for Marzani to resign. His case was even then—out of my hands—on its way to the Security Committee and then to Mr. Russell and finally to Mr. Byrnes for action. When he left I immediately issued orders that his resignation was not to be accepted. So far as the Department of State was concerned, Marzani could not be permitted to resign. The Department was in possession of evidence indicating that he had committed a crime. Accordingly, it was obvious that he had to be dismissed under the McCarran rider *in the best interests of the government.* After that, his case had to be referred to the Department of Justice.

On December 20, shortly after the Secretary's return from New York, I was authorized to sign Marzani's notice of dismissal under the McCarran rider. This was sent to him by registered mail the same day. Shortly thereafter Sam Klaus was authorized by Mr. Russell to present the matter to Attorney-General

Tom Clark. Immediately after his conference with Klaus the Attorney-General ordered presentation of the matter to the next Grand Jury and the case was assigned for preparation to John R. Kelley, Jr., Special Assistant to the Attorney-General.

AT THE OUTSET Kelley was somewhat dubious of the chances of obtaining an indictment, much less a conviction, in the case. As he saw it, the law of the case depended on the untested fraud statute. Furthermore, there were really only two key witnesses to sustain the case—Archer Drew, the New York City Police detective, and myself. In a critical case of "first impression" such as this, involving all sorts of political dynamite, any prosecutor likes to have an abundance of evidence and plenty of good witnesses. Kelley was no exception. It was Sam Klaus, working in close cooperation with Kelley, who slowly but surely overcame the latter's doubts. Klaus brought Drew down from New York and after one conference with the detective, Kelley knew he had a potential star witness. He decided to proceed full steam ahead.

The Grand Jury was impaneled and after hearing Detective Drew, myself, and others, promptly handed down an indictment on eleven counts against Marzani. As the slow but inexorable process of Federal justice began to catch up with Marzani, the Communist Party high command began to take an interest in the case. They knew that a conviction in this case would mark the beginning of the end of their subversive operations in the government.

During the period that the case was awaiting trial Marzani was kept under strict surveillance. He was in constant communication with key Communists throughout the country. While he was represented by Washington counsel, we knew that the real strategy of his defense was being developed by the party's brain trust in New York. Finally, early in May the case was reached for trial and "all the chips were down." Failure to obtain a conviction was certain to send the President's $25 million Employee Loyalty Program floundering on the rocks of administrative uncertainty.

The opening court skirmish turned on the selection of the jury. The counsel for the defense repeatedly excused the "solid citizen" type of prospective juror. The jury, as finally impaneled, included nine Negroes. We knew that Marzani intended to stress his activities in the American Negro Congress as benevolent rather than subversive. While the prosecution felt that Marzani did not have a chance of acquittal on the evidence that would be produced against him at the trial, there was always a possibility of a "hung" jury. For it takes just one juror to bring about a disagreement and a new trial.

Marzani and his counsel were obviously elated. They evidently felt that the possibility of a disagreement was excellent. They literally exuded confidence as the trial began. From my own experience in the trial of many cases in the courts of New York, I shared somewhat the prosecution's fears with respect to the outcome.

The trial opened sleepily. The Government prosecutor, Mr. Kelley, was the soul of caution. He leaned backwards in his efforts to introduce nothing in evidence that would give rise to the slightest possibility of error. It was sound strategy to undertry the case. If the government attempted to bear down, Marzani would undoubtedly raise the cry of "Persecution."

On about the fourth day of the trial I was called as the Government's first chief witness. The substance of my direct testimony was brief. First, my official position in the Department of State, its scope, my responsibilities in the field of security, my relationships with Marzani, the time that I first learned of any derogatory information about him involving his loyalty. Then Prosecutor Kelley came to the heart of the case—my conversation with Marzani on June 1, 1946. The climax came when I told the story of the Department's development of the real evidence of Marzani's Communist relationships and activities, in October-November of 1946, and his prompt dismissal under the McCarran rider in December.

As the defense attorney rose to cross-examine, I wondered, sitting in the witness chair, what his tactics would be. For obviously it was vitally necessary for the defense to overcome the effect of my testimony. After a few ineffective efforts to shake my recollection (a preliminary cross-examination routine) the defense attorney got down to business. First he repeatedly brought out that there had been no one present at the June 1 conference except Marzani and myself. *Then he produced a paper prepared by Marzani which purported to set forth what was said by him and by me at the conference of June 1—all in direct quotes.*

As the defense counsel read to me, statement by statement, what I allegedly had said and what Marzani claimed *he* had said, I began to grasp the pattern of the defense strategy.

If the jury believed Marzani's version of the crucial conversation of June 1, it followed that he and I *had never discussed the question of his loyalty or his Communist activities and affiliations.* We *had* discussed, according to him, the folly of the Department's "anti-Soviet" policy and agreed that it was bad. We—according to Marzani—deplored J. Edgar Hoover's "witch-hunting" and that of certain members of Congress. We allegedly had agreed that the real security risks in the Department were the so-called "liberals" who "blabbed out State Department secrets at cocktail parties and to newspaper columnists." The first thing to be noticed about this anticipatory cross-examination was that it followed the Communist party-line—to attack a firm foreign policy as anti-Soviet; to smear J. Edgar Hoover and members of Congress as witch-hunters; to divert suspicion to liberals as the real subversives. Marzani was putting on a show for the comrades.

But he was also laying the foundation of his defense, in which he hoped the sole issue would be his word against mine. If the jury believed his story that we did not discuss his Communist Party affiliations and operations on June 1, then Marzani did *not* lie about them to me in my capacity as an official of the Department of State, and an acquittal was likely to follow. If he as much as convinced *one* juror, there would be a disagreement and a new trial. This could go on *ad infinitum* until the Department of Justice eventually *nolle-prossed* the case out of sheer weariness and frustration.

MY HUNCH on the strategy of the defense proved quite accurate. As the case progressed, Marzani's plan to confuse the issues in the mind of the jury became more and more apparent, always coupled with the tacit insinuation that he was being framed by the Government to provide a Roman holiday for the witch-hunters in the Republican Congress. The "pitch" was having real effect on the jury and even on the press correspondents.

Fortunately Prosecutor Kelley had some aces of his own to play. Marzani, of course, knew that the key witness to his communistic activities was detective Archer Drew. But what he did not know was that through the unremitting efforts of Sam Klaus and Tom Fitch the prosecution had on tap two former members of the Communist Party who—prior to their expulsion—had known Marzani as a Communist and who were prepared to identify him as Tony Whales. Kelley decided to put these two witnesses on the stand before he climaxed his case with Archer Drew.

This brilliant handling of the case paid dividends. Marzani was shaken to be identified in open court by two former members of the Communist Party. And he could attack this testimony only by arguing that a Communist can never be believed even under oath—a line with extremely dangerous implications to his own case. By this time the case had reached its high point of suspense. The jury was alert. The newspapermen who, up to this time, had been taking a restrained view of the testimony, were now taking copious notes. Prosecutor Kelley, now fully warmed up to his work, unfolded his climax carefully.

First he introduced the testimony of Lt. Gallagher, a distinguished-looking veteran of the New York Police force. Gallagher testified how in 1940, under orders from Mayor LaGuardia, he had set up an "undercover" operation for the sole purpose of penetrating the Communist organization in New York City. A most important part of the mission of this group, he explained, was the detection of subversive operations among the Negro groups in New York. For this assignment a Negro detective was required. After careful study of all available candidates, Gallagher testified, Archer Drew was selected for this delicate and vital job.

With this introduction, Archer Drew took the stand. He identified his official reports on Marzani's activities which, four years ago, he had filed in Police Headquarters. Under careful questioning he then launched into a description of his undercover operations. He told the story of how he joined the party and was given the party name of "Bill Easley"; how "Tony Whales" and he became friends; how he visited Tony and his wife "Edith Charles" at their apartment. He recounted how Tony told him of his boyhood struggles, of his fight to get an education, of his entry into Williams College, of his studies in England and his trip around the world. Drew painted a vivid picture of the close relationship existing between himself and Tony Whales; of their frequent discussion of the objectives of the Communist Party and the best methods of their achievement.

At the conclusion of this testimony, Prosecutor Kelley asked Drew to say whether Tony Whales was in the courtroom. Unhesitatingly Drew pointed to Marzani and cried: "That's Tony—that's Tony Whales."

The effect of Drew's identification of Marzani as Tony Whales was electrifying to the jury. Even the most laconic of the press correspondents were writing feverishly; some were rushing out of the courtroom to flash the news to catch the late edition of the Washington afternoon papers. Marzani, his sallow face an ashen gray, was whispering excitedly to his lawyer who was shaking his head doubtfully.

After the defense's cross-examination of Archer Drew—which merely tightened the noose about Marzani—the Government rested its case.

The trial dragged on for several more days, through a procession of character witnesses, climaxed by Marzani's hysterical testimony in his own behalf, which was riddled by Prosecutor Kelley's cross-examination. But for all practical purposes, Marzani's fate was settled when Drew pointed him out.

After both sides rested and the lawyers summed up, Judge Keech instructed the jury in a charge which was a model of fairness. The jury retired; elected a foreman; returned with a conviction of Marzani on all eleven counts. "School was out" for Carl Aldo Marzani.

WITH MARZANI'S CONVICTION a *fait accompli*, I was off on a long-delayed mission to Germany. On the airliner I opened the current issue of *Newsweek* and was somewhat surprised to see a picture of Marzani leading off the feature article. I had been close to the Marzani case for so long that I had become numb to its significance as a matter of public interest. To me, aside from its element of counterespionage, the case represented a difficult technical problem in the arduous but unspectacular business of developing a basic criminal sanction on which the government could build an effective counterinfiltration program.

As I read the arresting caption under Marzani's picture, "His conviction gave the government hope," I could not help wondering whether the average reader would realize the tremendous amount of planning, professional skill, and sheer tenacity on the part of all concerned which had been required to convict Marzani the hard way—in open court and before a jury virtually of his own choosing.

October 1947

THE RED SPY NET

By Thomas M. Johnson

[*Thomas M. Johnson, veteran newspaperman and war correspondent and a member of the Military Intelligence Reserve Society, in this contribution to* Plain Talk *furnished a general outline of "The Red Spy Net" as then known only to insiders in Washington. Mr. Johnson had co-authored, with Will Irwin, a book,* What You Should Know about Spies and Saboteurs, *issued in 1943.*]

THE WORLD'S MOST FORMIDABLE intelligence service, the largest and most threatening in the history of espionage, is penetrating and victimizing this country on a scale undreamed by the average American. By every means, open and concealed, Soviet spies are taking advantage of our trustfulness to milk us of every fact, method or discovery whose acquisition can help the U.S.S.R. in its rivalry with us. . . .

The Russians are using against us every trick they were caught using in Canada, but on a far greater scale. Here, as there, they laid the foundations during the war, when as "Allies" they were allowed to send to both countries large military and industrial missions. In the United States some 3,300 Russians, including many experts posing as underlings, swarmed over the country, visiting factories, laboratories, testing grounds. They asked questions, took notes, were denied little save the atomic secret at which other and more secret Russian agents were already nibbling.

Not only were all members of these missions trained and ordered to make reports; some were master spies who, under cover of their authorized work, gathered military, naval, technical, and diplomatic intelligence. Over them all is the MVD, the political police formerly known as the NKVD. The various networks consist of numerous groups or "cells" whose members seldom know one another as spies. In Canada during the war these networks totaled ten; here, perhaps 50. In each large city there was at least one network; in Detroit, Chicago, Los Angeles, New York, more than one; in Washington perhaps ten. In the capital their military intelligence alone had five cryptographers as compared with one in Ottawa. . . .

Today the leaders of the Russian espionage apparatus are frequently changed to confuse our authorities and give more Russians experience in America. Some agents are ostensibly Soviet government representatives; others come with forged American passports and provided with a false name and life story.

Acting independently of the regular networks is a special group of ace operatives, who ignore the local "apparatus" and execute extraordinary missions, including assassination and kidnapping. They work under the supreme direction of the Chief of the Interior Department, Laurenti Beria, member of the all-powerful Politburo, who reports to Stalin personally. The preparation in the United States of the assassination of Trotsky in Mexico City; the mysterious and still unexplained disappearance from her hotel in West 57th Street of Juliet Stuart Poyntz, American Communist firebrand believed to have been in the Soviet service; the still unsolved murder of Carlo Tresca, anti-Communist labor editor, in New York; and the "suicide" by a dum-dum bullet of General Walter Krivitsky, former Soviet intelligence officer, in a Washington hotel room, are all believed to have been the work of this special group of operatives.

THE HAPPIEST hunting ground for Communist spies is Washington, where there are many secrets and too little secrecy. The United Public Workers of America, a CIO union with a pro-Communist record, has thousands of members in the State, War, Navy, and other government departments, and many have access to files and documents. It has lately organized Panama Canal Zone workers.

A small group of fellow-travelers nearly got approval for a proposal that all our defenses—fortifications, airfields, naval bases—should be photographed and mapped and the results "made available to Congress" and everyone else, including the "apparatus." This unprecedented enterprise of auto-espionage was to have been financed with a million American dollars. It was detected only because an alert intelligence officer remembered having seen its sponsors included on a suspect list.

Much confidential information about our foreign policy moves, including many secret papers, has reached Communist circles. Fellow-travelers within the State Department have sometimes influenced even the making of our foreign policy.

In Russia, American diplomats are spied upon by the MVD. If they study Russian, the teachers are usually MVD agents. So are the embassy servants. So many listening devices had been discovered in our Moscow embassy, including one in a wall next to the desk where the Ambassador dictated his secret cables, that before the recent conference General Marshall ordered a special check. It revealed nothing. But the British found in their embassy six microphones of a new type almost undetectable. . . .

Amtorg, which represents the U.S.S.R. in dealing with American business, has also led in another large-scale legal intelligence operation: the acquisition by Russia of a description of virtually every industrial, chemical, and military discovery or appliance ever patented in the United States. Our archaic laws direct the Patent Office to sell abstracts descriptive of all patents to all bidders at ten to 25 cents each. The Russians order them by the thousands; one single order was for 60,000. They now have abstracts describing airplanes, parachutes, bomb sights, range finders, tanks, methods of making explosives, and many other industrial techniques.

In addition, they have demanded and received from us all German patents, including military developments, which we seized from 1941 through 1944. From a recent listing of 1,500 to 2,000 such items, they ordered 1,000.

The Russians give us little or nothing in return. They reveal about 50 Russian patents a year, but that is all. To our inquiries about German patents, they make scant reply or none. Russia holds the shipyards where, at the war's end the Germans were building fast new submarines which we still do not know how best to counter. Russia also holds the German experts who know these submarines' secrets. But she will tell us nothing, and meets inquiries with scowling suspicion.

June 1947

STALIN'S HAND IN THE PANAMA CANAL

By RALPH DE TOLEDANO

[The looming crisis over the future control of the Panama Canal makes it especially timely to reprint now "Stalin's Hand in the Panama Canal." The seeds of Soviet imperialism were planted around the jugular vein of the United States decades ago, just as they were lodged deep in the soil of many strategic lands all over the globe, from Poland to Cuba. Yet if anyone had suggested in 1946 that Cuba, a rampart of the Monroe Doctrine, would within a few years become a military outpost of Muscovite colonialism, the idea would have been regarded as the ravings of a lunatic. Today, when the anatomy of the Kremlin's underground fifth column in Portugal is fully exposed, the evidence presented by Ralph de Toledano in this article takes on an ominous color. The author had seen service in the Caribbean during World War II and had for years been a student of Falangist and Communist activities in Latin America. He is now a well-known syndicated columnist.]

WHEN THE United Public Workers, whose flagrant pro-Soviet record is unsurpassed among the labor unions of America, suddenly launched a whirlwind drive last July to organize the government employes in the Panama Canal Zone, the question arose before the men in charge of our national defense:

"Is Stalin's hand in it?"

186

The Soviet government, even as those of Germany and Japan in their days, has long taken an unhealthy interest in the "Big Ditch"—the keystone of the American defense system. As far back as 1933 the world was treated to the sensational exposure of an international espionage ring which showed Stalin's hand deep in the military establishment of the Panama Canal.

Now the leadership of the United Public Workers has demonstrated its un-swerving loyalty to the Soviet system on numerous occasions, as our examina-tion of the record will reveal. This is the union whose constitution favors the right of Federal employes to strike, a provision denounced by President Truman last June when he warned that if it ever happened the Government would cease to exist.

Why did the United Public Workers suddenly descend upon the faraway Canal Zone in its organizing activities when there are so many richer fields to cultivate right here at home? This question became a veritable challenge when it was announced officially by the CIO last September that 17,000 United States employes in the Canal Zone had been brought under the banner of the United Public Workers, forming in one swoop the largest local in that union.

As there is no private industry in the Canal Zone, the entire working force in our key defense area is claimed as being under the jurisdiction of the United Public Workers. This includes such diverse groups as teachers, hotel and restau-rant workers, locomotive engineers, nurses, doctors, power plant workers, truck drivers, painters, machinists, street cleaners, sales girls, bookkeepers.

No wonder that top government officials have expressed their anxiety over this development as a possible threat to the security of the country in the event of war.

If Stalin has in the Canal Zone, too, his "secret battalion" for "the organiza-tion of catastrophe"—as described by none other than Harold J. Laski—then he would be in a position to strike a deadly blow of sabotage at the jugular vein of our system of defense. Through such an operation he could paralyze our navy and immobilize a whole fleet of aircraft carriers in a moment of crisis.

PANAMA BEGAN TO WITNESS unusual Communist activity in July 1931, during our great depression. It was two years after Stalin had declared before the special American Commission of the Communist International that "when a revolutionary crisis develops in America, that will be the beginning of the end of world capitalism as a whole."

That month, I am reliably informed, a raid on a three-story building in West 16th Street, Panama City, disclosed an underground Communist press. Many arrests followed. Leaflets and other papers taken in the raids showed that the Communist Party of Panama described itself as a section of the Communist International.

The following year a certain mysterious Russian, Ivan Krassin, was arrested in Panama. It then appeared that Moscow had access to incoming and outgoing telegrams at Panama through an employe of the All America Cables & Radio Corporation.

In October 1932 a postal clerk in the Canal Zone opened a "dead letter" which had been returned to Cristobal because it had not been claimed at its destination.

The contents of the letter included two secret military documents, a summary memorandum on the anti-aircraft practice of the artillery in the Canal Zone and the text of the so-called White Plan described by the sender as "a complete plan for the subjection of Panama in the case of revolution!" The White Plan was regarded by our military authorities as a vital secret plan for the defense of the Canal Zone.

While the investigation into the matter was going on, Colonel C. G. Bunker, in command of Fort Sherman in the Canal Zone, discovered that confidential documents were missing from his files. This was in the spring of 1933.

There followed the arrest on espionage charges of Corporal Robert Osman, Headquarters Battery, First Coast Artillery, stationed at Fort Sherman. He was found to have had connections in New York City and admitted receiving money from a certain Communist whom he knew as Harry Duryea.

From Panama the threads ran to New York City. Osman was found in possession of a photograph of a Russian girl who went under the name of Frema Karry, of 6801 Bay Parkway, Brooklyn. Miss "Karry" who then vanished without trace, had written to Osman boasting of "being a cog in the machine" of the Communist movement. The "dead letter" had been addressed to a Mr. Herman Meyers of 1859 East 9th Street, Brooklyn. It proved impossible to locate or identify Mr. Meyers. The mysterious Harry Duryea gave a mailing address in care of Dr. Joseph Stenbuck, of 444 Park Avenue, New York City, but the mention of Duryea's name there elicited no information.

There were many other threads running from "Big Ditch" to New York. Among the papers seized in the Panama City raids there had been a letter from one Arnold Reid, representative in Panama of the Colonial Committee of the Young Communist League of America. He wrote: "Immediately communicate with B. Small, 3451 Giles Place, Bronx." The correspondent in the Bronx was alleged in official reports to be a Communist Party member.

The Osman case attracted national attention. He was courtmartialed, found guilty, and sentenced to twenty years at hard labor. One day in September 1933, a middle-aged couple called on Louis Waldman, New York labor attorney, with an introduction from a prominent labor leader. They were the parents of Corporal Robert Osman. They pleaded with him to take over the defense of their son. After inquiring into the matter, he agreed to do so and went down to Panama to appeal the case, which eventually ended in an acquittal of Osman.

Throughout his investigations, the identity of Harry Duryea remained a major mystery. On March 21, 1934, *The New York Times* carried the following dispatch from Paris:

A world-wide spy ring with a recruiting center in New York and formed to deal in military secrets of the United States and other countries, was said by the authorities to have been revealed by a Mr. and Mrs. Robert Gordon Switz.

On May 8, 1934, en route to Panama, in the lobby of the Hotel National in Havana, Mr. Waldman picked up the March 26th issue of *Time*. As he leafed through it, his attention was caught by a photograph. Acting on a hunch, he tore out the page and took it with him.

"When I saw Osman, I took this photograph from my pocket," writes Waldman in the chapter "Espionage in the Caribbean" of his autobiography, *Labor Lawyer*. "I cut it out so as to expose the face, head, and shoulders of the photograph. The picture showed the long, narrow head of a young man with a small, ungenerous, dissipated mouth, cynical, pulled up to one side almost to the point of distortion; the nose was long and thin with a slight malformation at the bridge; and even in the black and white photograph the shading of the full and wavy hair suggested that it might be blond.

"Laying the picture before Osman, and watching him narrowly, I asked: 'Robert, tell me the truth, do you know who this man is?'

"Without a moment's hesitation the young corporal replied: 'Sure, I do. That's my friend, Harry Duryea!'"

THE SWITZES had been arrested by the French police on December 18, 1933, and found in possession of a collection of baffling documents. Held incommunicado for several months, the Switzes maintained their innocence until confronted with their thumbprints discovered on a package of film brought from Switzerland which contained a key to a secret code for espionage communications. The Switzes then confessed and admitted meeting agents of an international spy ring in Berlin in July 1933.

Photographs of Robert Gordon Switz in the press led to his identification by Osman as Harry Duryea, his Communist patron. The investigation disclosed that Switz had registered at a hotel in Colon, Panama, on May 26, 1932, and on March 27, 1933, the latter date coinciding with the time when Colonel Bunker discovered the disappearance of secret documents.

As a result of the confessions by the Switzes, a number of persons, including some high French officers, received long prison sentences. When General Walter Krivitsky, erstwhile chief of the Soviet secret service in Western Europe, who was found shot under mysterious circumstances in Washington in February 1940, was asked about Switz and a certain "Alfred Tilden" mentioned in the press, he replied:

"Switz? Yes, I knew him. And this 'Alfred'—I knew *him* well. . . . He was Soviet espionage chief in the United States in the early thirties."

Such is the background of Stalin's interest in the Panama Canal.

ONE WEEK after the birth of the United Public Workers there was a May

Day parade in Panama City. Three thousand participated in the march, thousands watched. The marchers demanded the establishment of diplomatic relations between Panama and the Soviet Union. They carried banners calling upon the masses "to break the chains of capitalism" and denouncing "Anglo-American imperialism."

The following day, on May 2, "Operation Panama," as it was labeled in the pro-Communist press, was formally launched. "A spectacular organizing drive in the Panama Canal Zone has brought 17,000 U.S. Government employes who work for the Panama Canal into the ranks of the CIO Public Workers," announced *The CIO News* on September 2, 1946.

In a poor country such as Panama, the comrades have been able to begin publication of a kind of naïve *New Masses*, 76 pages thick with a two-color glossy cover, devoted to attacks on "el imperialismo yanqui" and to the glorification of the Soviet wonderland which is not imperialist "because it is a socialist state and therefore has no need to exploit weak countries."

In the first issue of *ACLA*, an editorial titled "The Soviet Union, Defender of Latin America," takes up the question of espionage. The editors state that "while the American embassies are nests of spies . . . the diplomatic centers of the Soviet Union are agencies for peace and aid . . . which assure the stability and development of our economy."

The editors of *ACLA* forgot to tell the people of Panama of the recent revelations of Soviet machinations in the northern neighbor of the United States, Canada, where the Soviet Embassy was exposed by its own trusted official to be a nest of vast hemispheric espionage.

THE PANAMA CANAL has long been regarded by our leading military authorities as the key to our Atlantic and Pacific defenses, as well as the central pivot of our security in Latin America. For this reason, the Government of the Canal Zone, with its complex administration, is semimilitary in character and has been placed in the hands of the United States Army. Its employes are, in the civilian field, as vital to our defenses as the civilian employes of our War Department, for they have access to secret technical and military information of the highest value. Who controls these employes is a matter of major concern to the nation, transcending any questions of the rights of labor unions in the ordinary sense.

November 1946

STALIN'S BLUEPRINT FOR A

SOVIET BLACK BELT IN THE U.S.A.

By GEORGE S. SCHUYLER

[George S. Schuyler, the country's leading black columnist, who gained national recognition as the author of Black No More and Slaves Today, has been a tireless champion of justice for his race and an uncompromising foe of Communism and Fascism. In this report on "Stalin's Blueprint for a Soviet Black Belt in the U.S.A.," Schuyler turned a spotlight on a virtually unknown phase of the Kremlin's subversive operations, foreshadowing the numerous plots masterminded by Moscow in the resurgent and strife-ridden African continent.]

THE CREATION of a Negro Republic, to be carved out of the former Confederate States through bloody rebellion of the "black proletarians and peasantry," is again the order of the day on the Communist world front.

This fantastic plan has been the cornerstone of Moscow's policy for American Negroes since the Third International, at its October 1928 meeting, handed down a ukase to the American branch of the world conspiracy:

"The main Communist slogan must be: *The right of self-determination for the Negro in the Black Belt.*"

More explicit were resolutions of the Communist International of 1930, which declared that the Negro population of the Black Belt could win this right "only through successful revolutionary struggle for power against the American bourgeoisie, through wresting the Negro's right of self-determination from American imperialism; thus the slogan of self-determination is a real slogan of national rebellion."

Nothing could be plainer as a blueprint for trouble. The country is to be wracked with civil war, and in the resultant confusion the Communists are to seize power and destroy democracy as they did in Russia. The American Negro problem will be solved—by the extermination of the Negroes, a typically sanguinary Communist solution.

The talk of a separate Negro state was soft-pedaled in the late 1930s, when Communism became "Twentieth Century Americanism" and assumed a conciliatory pose. Taken up again in the period of Stalin-Hitler friendship, the plan was hurriedly shelved after the Nazis invaded Russia; the inflaming of racial sores did not fit into the Communist win-the-war program.

Now the plans for Negro nationhood have been officially revived, as part of the renewed ultrarevolutionary line originally laid down by Stalin himself for colonial peoples everywhere except in Soviet colonies. It must be remembered that Joseph Stalin began his Soviet career under Lenin as Commissar of Nationalities and is touchy on this subject. He will tolerate no exceptions to the rules of procedure prescribed for all "colonial peoples." Comrades, black or white, who dare suggest that colored Americans are in a rather different situation than the people of India, the Philippines, or the Ukraine, find themselves quickly expelled as deviationists and tools of imperialism.

No wonder that in its December 1946 "Resolution on the Question of Negro Rights and Self-Determination," the Communist Party went back to its erstwhile insanity by "recognizing the struggle for equal rights as a movement toward full nationhood . . . in the Black Belt areas where they are in the majority."

As described in detail by William Z. Foster, U.S. Communist Party head, and his Negro yes-men, the Black Belt Republic would be an "independent nation" on the Soviet autonomous model. It would deal with other nations—and "particularly the United States"—as a sovereign equal.

Confiscation of the property of white landowners and capitalists for the benefit of Negro farmers would be an essential part of the Black Belt program, according to the resurrected resolutions of the Comintern. And it is obvious that the private property of Negroes would not be spared while that of whites was being confiscated.

A map of the republic of the future, widely circulated in the past, has, since the end of the war, been restored to respectability in Communist propaganda literature aimed at the Negro. Embracing counties with a preponderantly Negro population, the republic runs a zigzag course from the top of Virginia deep into Texas. In the process a number of areas with preponderantly white population are cut off from direct contact with the rest of the country; whether these isolated regions would be given corridors to the U.S. mainland, the map does not indicate.

The geography of the plan was dealt with in *The Negroes in a Soviet America,* a pamphlet published in 1935 and again in favor. The authors, a Communist hack, James S. Allen, and a colored member of the Red Brain Trust and one-time candidate for Vice-President, James W. Ford, explain:

"The actual extent of this new republic would in all probability be approximately the present area in which Negroes constitute the majority of the population; in other words, it would be approximately the present plantation area. It would be certain to include such cities as Richmond and Norfolk, Va.; Columbia and Charleston, S.C.; Atlanta, Savannah, and Macon, Ga.; Montgomery, Ala.; New Orleans and Shreveport, La.; Little Rock, Ark.; and Memphis, Tenn. In the actual determination of the boundaries of the new republic, other industrial cities may be included.

"This would mean," they continue, "that the Negro people in the Black Belt will have the right to choose for themselves between federation and separation from the United States as a whole. . . . In stating our position on this question, we are guided not only by the theoretical principles of the Communist Party, but by the actual experience of the Russian Revolution."

The self-determination program shows that the Kremlin can be far from "realistic" or practical in its expansionist plans. Not one American Negro out of a hundred thousand regards the plan as anything but the sheerest lunacy. A segregated state or reservation is the one "solution" of their problem most repugnant to the majority of American Negroes. Moreover, an "Ethiopian state" is the very bugaboo which the Ku Klux Klan have taught the majority of white Southerners to fear most.

The plan deserves attention, nevertheless, for what it reveals of the Communist attitude toward the Negro—a reckless readiness to sacrifice Negro lives without limit in promoting the Stalinist dream of power in America. And the Negro Republic scheme is at once the symbol and the instrument of a broader conspiracy to use American Negroes as pawns in the Kremlin game.

Early in its career the American Communist Party began to cultivate the loyalty and friendship of the Negroes. The color problem has been the weakest link in American democracy, and the Reds sought to exploit it to the fullest. Being underprivileged and humiliated, the Negroes were expected to be easily corralled expendables in Moscow's bid for power.

The activation of the enterprise waited for 1930, after Stalin had consolidated his dictatorial power at home. Since then young Negroes have been sent to Moscow for training as agitators and wreckers; futile campaigns and drives calculated to sharpen race feelings have been launched; no trick has been missed in inflaming Southern white apprehensions and prejudice.

The Communists have persistently exploited Negro misery. They have sought to confuse every public issue by insisting cynically on immediate solutions of centuries-old problems. They have intrigued without let-up, and sometimes successfully, to undermine or to capture Negro organizations. . . .

While the Communist conspiracy has fallen flat as far as the Negro masses are concerned, it has been notably successful among Negro professionals and so-called intellectuals. . . .

In May 1940 even the eminent Dr. W. E. B. Du Bois, who had long been the target of Communist attack, surrendered and became a contributing editor of the Communist *New Masses*. On November 30, 1946, the principal Negro papers carried a statement by Dr. Robert V. Weaver, an official of the American Council on Race Relations, in praise of the Soviet Union. These were merely symptomatic of the spreading contagion among Negro intellectuals.

Having hooked such eminent Negroes, the Communists do not despair of finally "capturing" the rest of the race. Even these well-known voices, however, will scarcely be enough to woo the average Negro into the Red fold. They may not be too literate, but they know a Red light when they see it. Totalitarian systems, even with Russian dressing, are too reminiscent of slavery to fascinate the Negro.

If they ever expect their conspiracy to bear fruit, Moscow's agents here will have to come up with something more rational than the Negro Republic. But nobody can say they have not tried.

June 1947

INSIDE THE COMINTERN

By VICTOR SERGE

[Although the Communist International was forma'ly dissolved by Stalin during World War II, the vast inside machinery of the organization remained intact and in service under different labels. Victor Serge, who had for years been identified with the Comintern "apparat," unveiled in this piece some of its key functions, including the fact that nearly all the leaders of Communist parties abroad "were also part of the Soviet espionage." Serge, the son of a famous Russian revo'utionist, was born in Belgium, was imprisoned in Spain, and reached Russia in January 1919, where he served on the Executive Committee of the Comintern. As a Trotskyist, he was expelled from the Soviet Union in 1936 and settled in Mexico. He was the author of numerous historical works and several novels dealing with the contemporary revolutionary movement.]

IT WAS OBVIOUS, on May 15, 1943, when the dissolution of the Communist International was announced by the Praesidium of its Executive Committee, that this could only be a maneuver unless a tremendous political change took place within the Soviet Union itself. Today this view has been demonstrated completely.

The dissolution of the Comintern was published over the signatures of Dimitrov, Ercoli (alias Togliatti), Florin, Gottwald, Kolarov, Koeplennig, Kuusiinen, Manuilsky, Marty, Pieck, Zhdanov, Thorez—with the approval of Dolores Ibarruri (La Pasionaria), Lehtinen, Pauker, and Rakosi. With the exception of Lehtinen and Florin, all the signers of the document are today functioning as heads of Communist parties in Europe, whose every act is directed and coordinated by the Political Bureau [Politburo] of the Communist party in Soviet Russia. Many of them are key members of European governments.

The decision to dissolve the Comintern was furthermore couched in deliberately vague terms: "to dissolve the Communist International as the directing

194

body of the international workers' movement and to free the sections of the C.I. from the obligations derived from the statutes and resolutions of the International." This equivocal statement reveals two points:

1. That the "dissolved" Comintern "as the directing body of the International workers' movement" could and did continue to exist as something else, for example as a center for documentation, study, and political activity, as an instrument of the Soviet government and the Soviet Communist party—in reality, the same organism.

2. That the statutes and resolutions of the Comintern congresses—which had not met for a long time—had never been anything more than outdated rhetoric.

I took part in the transformation of the Comintern from an aggregation of revolutionary parties sympathetic to the Russian revolution (1919–23) into a "single centralized party" (1924–27) which ruled out all dissident thinking or local autonomy on the part of the various national units. After 1927 the Comintern became a wing of the Soviet government machine, an annex of its Foreign Office through the totalitarian Politburo of the Russian Communist party. Party discipline was maintained by the firing squads.

More and more, the Comintern agents, sent out on missions from Moscow to the Communist parties of other countries, became absolute dictators, laying down the law set by the Politburo. More and more, they became part of the espionage and counter-espionage systems of the U.S.S.R. These services were set up in two independent departments: military intelligence and secret police (GPU, then NKVD, now MVD). The secret police picked out the Comintern agents and had iron control of their actions. Sometimes Comintern agents were also used in the military intelligence services of the Red Army.

I know it to be a fact that, with but three exceptions, all the leaders of Communist parties between 1927 and 1930 were also part of the Soviet espionage, working directly under the GPU-NKVD. As soon as a Communist working in an arsenal, a shipyard, or a strategic area showed any "possibilities" for the required "idealism," he would be taken over by special agents who would integrate him in their network.

THE CENTRAL BUREAUS of the Comintern in Moscow, located in a vast building opposite the Kremlin, guarded by the GPU, became a sort of worldwide intelligence center such as exists in no other country in the world. The central apparatus of the Comintern was subdivided into regional bureaus for the Latin countries, Central Europe, Scandinavia, the Middle East, the Far East, North America, Latin America, etc. These subdivisions varied with the needs of the moment. Each of these bureaus is, in turn, subdivided by countries. Economists, sociologists, political analysts examine with microscopic care the literature, press, secret intelligence, and other pertinent information stemming from the country of their specialization. They study the political configuration of these countries, and on the basis of their forecasts, the activities of Soviet agents throughout the world are outlined. This digested information and the elaborate plans worked out are finally submitted to the Politburo, passing through the hands of the party secretariat.

The financial service of the Comintern, and it must not be confused with its official treasury which is theoretically fed by contributions from member parties, pays out with Politburo authorizations the sums necessary to carry out its secret activities. If secretly subsidized publishing houses are to be set up, a movement financed, a "bourgeois" or reactionary paper "influenced," sympathizers or functionaries paid off, it is handled by a secret commission—which has always been secret even to most of the Comintern leaders. This commission is appointed by the Politburo and is run by high functionaries of the GPU-NKVD.

The ten years since the bloody purges of 1936–37 liquidated the Comintern's former staffs have witnessed the formation of a new highly qualified personnel in this organization. A colossal set of archives has been accumulated and kept strictly up to date. No government anywhere has at its disposal as complete and documented an archive *on its own country!* Filed with the Comintern are the dossiers of sympathizers, active Communists, agents, subagents, anti-Communists, intellectuals, politicians, businessmen—all the material showing their usefulness to the Soviet Union, their corruptibility, their value in the struggle against the world. Two years after the "dissolution" of the Comintern, dossiers of the heads of the Canadian Communist party, removed by Igor Gouzenko from the files of the Soviet Embassy in Ottawa, included notations such as "Sam Carr, alias Frank, member of the Labor Progressive Party, see detailed biography at the Center, Comintern."

There has never been any question of "dissolving" or "liquidating" this remarkable inner organization. It has become an integral part of the Soviet state mechanism. And it would be stupid to doubt that these Comintern bureaus continue to gather their intelligence data, to stuff their dossiers, to supply their agents. If the Politburo were to decide to "reconstitute" the Comintern, under its old name or a fancy new one, officially or unofficially, it could do so with the scrawl of a pen—complete to the last dossier and the last pay voucher.

February 1947

THE HISS-CHAMBERS CASE

By ISAAC DON LEVINE

[*Eight months before the Chambers-Hiss affair made front-page news across the nation, the editor of* Plain Talk, *in the issue of December 1947, alerted the public to the forthcoming revelation of a great spy ring in the U.S.A. Without naming Alger Hiss, the editor described him as "one who had played a leading role at Yalta and in organizing the United Nations," and who "delivered confidential papers to Communist agents who microfilmed them for dispatch to Moscow." The article forecast the early outbreak of a "major political quake," which occurred the following August. It reached a climax four months later when Chambers produced the celebrated "pumpkin papers." During this exciting period, the editor, who had been closely following the affair from its inception, reported his experiences in a series of articles that are here reproduced exactly as originally printed. There is one item in the account that calls for correction: the British code clerk named King, exposed by Krivitsky as a Soviet spy, was not executed in the Tower of London as first reported; he was given a ten-year team in prison. The six related installments included in this chapter originally appeared as "Stalin's Spy Ring" in December 1947; "The Inside Story of Our Soviet Underworld" in September, October, and November 1948; "Sequel to Chambers' Story" in January 1949; and "Ten Years Too Late" in February 1950.*]

I

THE COMING sensational case involving a great Soviet spy ring in the United States, as a result of a grand jury investigation which has been going on in New York for several months, is merely a continuation of the famous Canadian inquiry into Communist espionage. When Prime Minister Mackenzie King visited President Truman in October 1945 to acquaint him with the shocking revelations made by Igor Gouzenko, the Soviet Embassy code clerk, he was instrumental in starting the FBI machinery to ferret out evidence of the Soviet underground networks on the North American continent.

It became clear to President Truman, after Mackenzie King's visit, that the Canadian case, in which a score of Soviet officials and Communist Party stalwarts figured, was but a small section of a vast secret beehive operating from the Panama Canal to Alaska. Several compartments of this have been probed by the grand jury, sending shivers through the entire hierarchy of the American Communist Party, and portending something like a major political 'quake upon the publication of the facts uncovered. These will show that:

Several of the topmost officials of the Communist Party in this country were acting as agents of Stalin's secret service, engaged in recruiting spies and filching state documents;

The intricate espionage organization in which more than one hundred scientists and clerical workers were engaged, since the beginning of 1943, in gathering secret information about our atomic development, leading to the transmission of uranium-235 to Russia, was under the direct supervision of avowed Communist Party leaders.

The secret plans and blueprints of our B-36 Superfortress, long before its launching and going into action, had mysteriously and unaccountably found their way to the Treasury Department and into the hands of a ranking official there, whose function was in the field of international finance, and that they later passed into the hands of Soviet agents;

Several of the highest officers of the old National Labor Relations Board were clandestine members of the Communist Party and formed a secret spy "centre" in Washington;

Certain high and trusted officials in the State Department, including one who had played a leading role at Yalta and in organizing the United Nations, delivered confidential papers to Communist agents who microfilmed them for dispatch to Moscow;

Certain leading lights in the councils of the CIO and the PCA were deeply involved in espionage and other illicit activities;

One of the ghostwriters for a prominent United States Southern senator of pronounced pro-Soviet sentiments was an underground operative of the network;

Various disguised quarters were used by the ring in Washington, New York, and elsewhere—such as a violin studio, a jewelry shop in a fashionable district, and a documentary film establishment—for the purposes of transacting espionage business, transmitting microfilmed information, and receiving funds from couriers.

II

THE SHOCK to which the country was treated only last month, when Whittaker Chambers, a senior editor of *Time* magazine, and Elizabeth T. Bentley, Vassar graduate, revealed some of the inside operations of Soviet espionage in Washington, was a nine-year-old tale to this writer.

When Mr. Chambers disclosed to the world that the facts in his possession had been called to the attention of President Roosevelt's secretary, the late Marvin H. McIntyre, and that they were later detailed to Adolf A. Berle, Jr., then Assistant Secretary of State and White House confidant, he broke the seal of official secrecy hiding some exciting pages of current history.

My intimate contact with that fantastic and almost incredible global political underworld of which Chambers and Bentley had been denizens in the United

States began some eight months before the outbreak of World War II. It all started in January 1939 with my collaboration with General Walter Krivitsky, former Chief of the Soviet Secret Service in Western Europe who two years later was found dead in a Washington hotel under mysterious circumstances, with a dum-dum bullet in his head.

The wide world, which was shaken by Krivitsky's revelations, had never been told that he had been invited by the British Government to come to London for consultations in Soviet espionage matters and that his still-unexplained violent end followed his return from England.

The publication in the spring of 1939 by *The Saturday Evening Post* of Krivitsky's sensational articles, in which he foretold the Stalin-Hitler pact, gave the key to the baffling purge of the Red Army generals, and divulged the kidnapping and counterfeiting rings operated by the Soviet Government, brought Whittaker Chambers to me. Through a mutual friend, now one of the editors of an important monthly magazine, Chambers sought me out with his story some time in May. He had been tremendously impressed by Krivitsky's exposures. Chambers behaved like a man full of fears and suspicions. And no wonder, for he was leading the life of a hunted animal—hunted by Soviet underworld killers operating freely in the great metropolis.

I would not have believed it possible a few months earlier, before I met Krivitsky, that such things could be on this continent. But I had had some startling experiences in the meantime.

In the first week of March, a few days before the appearance on the newsstands of the issue of *The Saturday Evening Post* containing the first of Krivitsky's series of articles, he had a luncheon date in a Times Square cafeteria with Mr. S., the labor editor of a foreign-language newspaper. During lunch they discovered that they were being watched by two men at a nearby table. Suddenly Krivitsky turned deathly pale. He recognized in one of his eavesdropping neighbors a certain Comrade Bassoff, an OGPU agent he had known well in Moscow.

As Krivitsky and S. made for the cashier and the exit, they were accosted by the other two. Bassoff spoke up: "Hello, Walter." Krivitsky returned the acknowledgement. Bassoff then indicated that he knew of Krivitsky's break with the Soviet service, and suggested that they betake themselves somewhere for a heart to heart talk. While Krivitsky parried the invitation, he and S. found themselves at the corner of 43rd Street and Broadway, followed by Bassoff and his unidentified mate.

The New York Times Annex Building, which houses the editorial offices of that newspaper, lay a couple of hundred feet away on 43rd Street. The labor reporter of *The New York Times,* Joseph Shaplen, was a friend of Mr. S. and had met Krivitsky. There lay safety. Above all, Krivitsky thought, Bassoff and his colleague must not trail him to his most secret quarters. Krivitsky and S. made for the third floor, the city room, followed by Bassoff who kept up some pleasant chatter about various comrades. Bassoff's companion remained behind. Krivitsky was sure that he would stand watch outside.

Mr. Shaplen was out. Krivitsky and S. said they would wait for him. Marooned in the waiting room of America's greatest newspaper, within a few feet of an oblivious city editor, was the ex-Chief of Soviet Intelligence in Western Europe, and one of Stalin's ace bloodhounds hot on his trail. As the news from all over the globe was pouring in behind the thin partition, the staff of editors and reporters never suspected that on the bench outside, within their grasp, sat the man with the world's biggest story of the year—in circumstances which alone would have made a national sensation.

THE HUNTER and the quarry, Bassoff and Krivitsky, stayed in the waiting room and chatted for half an hour while S. was trying frantically to telephone a few friends to come to the rescue. I was not at home. Benjamin Stolberg, the well-known writer on labor, was reached. He got in touch with Suzanne La Follette. Both of these acquaintances of Krivitsky's and friends of Mr. Shaplen responded to the call and rushed to the *Times*.

Bassoff departed and Mr. Shaplen returned to his office to find himself involved in a melodramatic situation. Krivitsky was sure that Bassoff and his accomplice would trail him if he left for his clandestine home. The siege in the *Times* waiting room continued all afternoon while methods of escape were under discussion. Mr. Shaplen finally reached me and I hastened to the scene. After a council of war it was decided to wait until the approach of the theater hour when the entire block would be cleared of traffic. I left to fetch my car.

Toward eight o'clock my wife and I drove over to West 43rd Street. I asked one of the mounted policemen on duty if he would let me park for not more than five minutes to pick up some people from the *Times* offices. He was agreeable. Before entering the building, however, I looked for the two men, Bassoff and his colleague, whose description Krivitsky had furnished me. I spotted one figure loafing in a recess of the *Times* Annex Building, not far from the main entrance. I briskly buttonholed him and authoritatively asked him what he was about. This took him off his guard, he mumbled something, and moved away. From my subsequent description Krivitsky was positive that I had spotted Bassoff's companion.

Within a matter of minutes I took Krivitsky and some of the group down, hustled them into my car and made off through the deserted block toward 8th Avenue. It was impossible for any pursuers to pick up our trail, as there was not a taxicab in sight.

Footnote: At the time, *The Saturday Evening Post* made reference to this episode without identifying *The New York Times*—to protect Mr. Shaplen, who has since passed away.

THAT WHITTAKER Chambers, a native son of America, could live in a state of terror in the land of the free, sleeping with a rifle at his side, behind drawn curtains, to guard his wife and two children from Soviet vengeance, did not seem incredible to me after my experiences with Krivitsky. Yet I knew that even among veteran journalists and high government officials the painful truth would be disbelieved and at best taken with many grains of salt. I became conscious of a chasm dividing people of my own circle and beliefs, who would not comprehend the realities I was dealing with.

Little by little Chambers gained confidence in me. He finally agreed to my proposal to bring him together with Krivitsky. By now I was aware from my intimate conversations with each that tying the two men together were many threads of the international Soviet network. Agents operating under different aliases and on various forged passports, commuting between Moscow and New York and a score of other capitals, peopled the shadowy world common to both men, one a veteran of the Comintern and Soviet military intelligence services, the other a gifted intellectual of Long Island origin, who had embraced Communism in his youth. It was like bringing together the North and South Poles.

For some hours I assisted in breaking the ice and getting conversation started. As the evening progressed, my education and my amazement grew apace. One secret OGPU mission after another in the United States was exhumed in my presence, and each of the two men contributed identifying details. Passing before me was a gallery of rogues who moved about in certain central areas of Manhattan. Outstanding among them was a man by the name of "Oscar"—the first mention of whom galvanized both.

Now, "Oscar" had been an intimate protegé of Krivitsky's in Moscow. Chambers did not know his real name, which was Markin, but he knew his case only too well. "Oscar" had died after a severe beating by three men in a New York speakeasy in 1932. Moscow had never believed that "Oscar's" death was anything but the result of a political plot. Krivitsky had been in on the various investigations which the Moscow headquarters of the Soviet Secret Service conducted into "Oscar's" violent death. And Chambers had been in touch with people who quietly arranged for "Oscar's" medical death certificate and for his unobtrusive burial by L. L., another Soviet agent.

The case of "Oscar" was remarkable because he had been something of a *Wunderkind* in the Soviet underworld. Molotov himself had received him upon his return from an inspection trip to the United States and accepted his recommendations to reorganize the Soviet espionage services here by putting the Comintern and Communist Party networks under military intelligence direction. "Oscar" was sent back to the United States by Molotov to carry out this reorganization which had caused bitter feuds among the Communist underground agents in this country. His sudden death under strange circumstances came soon afterwards. No wonder Moscow did not believe the official version of his death.

I retired after midnight while Krivitsky and Chambers were still exploring the ramifications of the "Oscar" mystery. When I awoke in the morning the light was still on in the front room, and the two men were still talking, exchanging details, filling in gaps, and rounding out the pattern of a vast subterranean domain familiar to only the two of them.

Before Whittaker Chambers had unfolded the full canvas of Soviet espionage in high quarters in Washington, Krivitsky had confided in me, under circumstances which permitted of no doubt, some appalling information. He knew of at least two full-fledged Soviet spies in the inner sanctums of the British Government. One was a code clerk in the secretariat of the Cabinet. Krivitsky gave me his name. The other was in a similar post with the Committee of Imperial Defence. Krivitsky did not know his real name, but knew his background and could describe his appearance. It had taken Stalin perhaps three years of manipulation, according to Krivitsky, at a cost of $200,000, to plant his man under the most respectable auspices in the top secret office of the British Cabinet.

The two Soviet spies did not know of each other's existence. The Kremlin was not only in receipt of all the vital secrets of an agonized world under the threat of Hitler's aggression, but was in a position to check one agent against the other. The thought that Hitler, with whom Stalin was then secretly negotiating, might have access to all this was indeed terrifying. And so was the realization that Stalin had similar plants in Washington in places as high as the White House.

III

"The war is here!"

Walter Krivitsky flung these words at me nearly a week before the outbreak of World War II when I drove out to his hiding place, a little cottage near Carmel, New York. It was shortly after the astounding news of August 23, 1939, of Ribbentrop's visit to Moscow and the conclusion of the Stalin-Hitler pact.

Krivitsky was in a state of terrific excitement. He had been the first to give to an incredulous world, with my collaboration, the inside story of the Soviet-Nazi negotiations in an article in *The Saturday Evening Post* entitled "Stalin Appeases Hitler." When it appeared in the early spring of that year, many "experts" shook their heads skeptically. Later, Wesley Stout, then editor of the *Post,* observed to me (to run ahead of my story), in connection with the Communist campaign to discredit Krivitsky's revelations:

"It took two great world powers to get together to vindicate Krivitsky's story."

Even now there are those who are confused over the meaning of the Stalin-Hitler deal. In the last week of August 1939, many informed people were bewildered by the bombshell from the Kremlin.

I went out to see Krivitsky to talk over the mounting international crisis. In view of the new Stalin-Hitler partnership, I was especially anxious over some of the shocking disclosures which had been made to me by Krivitsky and Whittaker Chambers. To Krivitsky this partnership allowed of no misinterpretation. As soon as it was announced, he took it as tantamount to a declaration of war. He dismissed with impatience all the other explanations and theories advanced in the press as to the significance of the pact. As far as he was concerned, Stalin had fired on August 23 the first gun of another world war.

THE TWO code clerks in the highest offices of the British Government, whose employment in Stalin's secret service had been disclosed to me earlier by Krivitsky, were very much on my mind. I saw two deadly pipelines running from the British supreme command, via Moscow, to Hitler's headquarters. It was a paralyzing thought. I endeavored to ferret out every bit of identifying information in the possession of Krivitsky about the two agents, particularly the one whose name he did not know. I learned that this second agent was of Scottish origin, with an artistic background.

I also recalled to Krivitsky the startling item which had cropped out during his first all-night meeting with Whittaker Chambers, involving a major on the general staff of the U.S. Army, a graduate of West Point. It appeared that this officer, who was given to excessive drinking, had been maneuvered into becoming a paid spy of the Soviet military intelligence. His premature death was regarded as a blow by the chiefs of the Soviet underworld. I tried to find out from Krivitsky if the Kremlin had, to his knowledge, any other agents in our national defense departments.

Krivitsky was sure that there were many underground channels running from Washington to Moscow. He told me that when William C. Bullitt, first American Ambassador to the U.S.S.R. following our recognition of the Soviet Government in 1933, arrived in Moscow with a carefully picked staff, at least one member on that staff was a Soviet agent.

The thought that an American official of good breeding and education in the exclusive foreign service could be a secret Communist agent in a United States Embassy abroad was truly shocking to me. All that Krivitsky knew was that at the Moscow headquarters of the Soviet secret police they were aware of everything that went on within the Embassy, including the contents of the major communications between Washington and Ambassador Bullitt. Krivitsky did not know the name of the informer, but he did know that he was an American official.

I was haunted by the fear that much of the crucial confidential information which reached Washington from London and Paris would be siphoned to the Kremlin and thence to Hitler's command in Berlin by his Soviet partner.

Within a day or two of my talk with Krivitsky I sought out Whittaker Chambers, who now held an editorial job on *Time* magazine, and who had become very friendly with the former Chief of Soviet Military Intelligence in Western Europe. Mr. Chambers, too, was in a state of great agitation over the Stalin-Hitler pact. He felt that something had to be done about it. I urged upon him the need to make all his information available to the proper authorities in Washington. He realized his grave responsibility, and agreed to reveal everything privately to President Roosevelt if I could arrange an unobtrusive visit for him to the White House.

For the first time Chambers, who had been keeping his living quarters a deep secret, jotted down for me his Long Island telephone number on a *Time* office memo blank. It was understood that I would communicate with him from Washington.

MY CALL on Marvin H. McIntyre, secretary to President Roosevelt, did not produce the anticipated result. McIntyre was most friendly and sympathetic, but he did not think that this was a matter to take up directly with the President, over the heads of the men entrusted with such affairs. He asked me if I knew Adolf A. Berle, Jr., then Assistant Secretary of State and confidential adviser to the President, and told me that he was the man to see.

I called on Mr. Berle, whom I knew well, and explained my errand to him. It was not advisable, I pointed out, for Chambers to meet with him at the State Department. Mr. Berle then suggested that I bring Chambers to his home for dinner, on Saturday evening, September 2. The Berles were occupying Woodley House, the historic estate in the residential heart of Washington belonging to ex-Secretary of War Henry L. Stimson.

In the meantime the war came. On September 1 Hitler launched his attack on Poland. I communicated with Chambers, who was somewhat disappointed that I had been unable to take him to the President, but who readily accepted Berle's invitation to a private dinner. As one of the leading members of Roosevelt's brain trust, Berle was known to have the ear of the President.

Chambers flew down to Washington on Saturday afternoon, September 2. It was the day of the great suspense. The world's No. 1 question was whether Great Britain would live up to her solemn pledge to defend Poland and declare war on Germany. When Chambers joined me at the Hay-Adams House where I was staying, I soon perceived that under the impact of Hitler's wanton aggression he would talk freely of his underground experiences to Mr. Berle.

After dinner, when Mrs. Berle had retired, the three of us took up for the first time the subject of the conference. It was a very warm evening. The scene of the conversation and the startling autobiographical story unfolded by Chambers was the study, then the lawn under a magnificent old tree, and then the study again when Berle began to make notes.

It was my understanding that this information would be conveyed by Berle direct to the President and that Chambers would suffer no ill consequences from his revelations. It would have been unseemly on my part to jot down there and then the names of the government officials and of Communist agents involved in the Soviet underground rings described by Chambers. Most of these came to me as news. I endeavored, however, to memorize as many as possible.

THE GENERAL picture drawn by Chambers that night was of two Soviet undercover "centers" or rings which, to his first-hand knowledge, had operated in Washington for years. One concerned itself with the control of labor and with patronage for Communists in the Federal service; the other with political and military affairs. Both groups were gathering and supplying confidential data to Moscow.

We learned that the business of filching from State Department and other secret government files had been well organized by the Communist "apparatus," that most of the time important papers would be microfilmed and replaced before they had been missed, and that the material would be delivered to Soviet couriers, operating under aliases, for transmission to Russia.

It was clear that Chambers knew his way about official Washington like a veteran in the Federal employ, and he showed unusual familiarity with the inside of the State Department. He named six of its officials as having knowingly furnished confidential data to Soviet undercover agents. Mr. Berle and I were shocked by the list, which included the Hiss brothers, then in inconspicuous positions.

As a result of questioning by Berle, it was explained by Chambers that the great majority of the government employees collaborating with the Communist rings were doing so out of idealistic, and not mercenary, motives. Their loyalty to the Soviet Union took precedence over their oath of office, accounting for their disloyalty to the United States. At that time this was still a novel doctrine even to such a well-informed public figure as Berle. Subsequently, seven years later, the Canadian Royal Commission, investigating the famous espionage case in which officials of trust had acted as agents of the Soviet Government, made much of this point. That idealists and fanatics can and have served as spies has since become a commonplace.

When Chambers cited as an illustration of this phenomenon the case of a deputy to a Cabinet officer, a certain assistant secretary of an important department, who was collaborating with Soviet agencies and sharing with them confidential matters of national policy, Mr. Berle exclaimed:

"But I know X X very well, and I can't believe it!"

I, too, was shaken by the argument which followed. Chambers tried to impress upon us the nature of totalitarian espionage, that Moscow would prize information about pending government policies and decisions more highly than routine military blueprints. The contents of a telephone conversation, for instance, between President Roosevelt and our ambassador in Paris or London would be worth more to Stalin than the design of some new ordnance. The name of the deputy Cabinet officer, however, remained engraved in my memory.

Upon my return after midnight to the Hay-Adams House, where I took leave of Whittaker Chambers, I jotted down on a sheet of hotel stationery most of the names that had been revealed during the evening. I could not recall, for example, the first name of Donald Hiss, and in my list of State Department officials the Hiss brothers are recorded as follows: ". . . Hiss. Alger Hiss." Similarly, the name of Lauchlin Currie, with which I was not familiar then, was written down by me as "Lockwood Curry."

The name of Nathan Gregory Silvermaster, described by the House Un-American Activities Committee as "heading an espionage ring of government employes" and as having maintained in subsequent years an association with Dr. Edward U. Condon, Wallace-appointed head of the Bureau of Standards engaged in atomic research, was also unfamiliar to me.

My memorandum includes these notes: "Nathan Silbermeister, alias Gregory Masters, Greg. Silvermaster, Nathan Silvermaster—personal statistician to President in Agr. Dept." As I now peruse this memorandum, it is patent that I was scouring my memory for the various names which had suggested themselves to me in connection with Silvermaster's identity.

In the Soviet labor-patronage ring, it had been disclosed by Chambers that night, the key figures were several Communist advisers to John L. Lewis in the top councils of the CIO. This was still the period when Mr. Lewis, who knew Communist treachery well, was cynically building his labor empire with Stalin's tools. In turn, these tools were using John L. Lewis to establish their underground network to exercise a stranglehold upon American defense and industry. The secretary of a small but vital CIO union was, it appeared, a secret member of the Communist Party, exploiting the office for the purpose of planting or recruiting Soviet agents.

The president of this union was a friend of mine. I was then expecting immediate repercussions from the Chambers-Berle meeting. I was convinced that the matter would go to the President and that a clean sweep would follow after a full investigation, resulting in a national sensation. I felt it my duty to warn my friend of the CIO union of the impending inquiry which might expose a whole brigade of spies in his organization, and compromise him.

We made a luncheon date. To escape attention, we drove out to a small restaurant near Arlington, Virginia, overlooking the valley of the Potomac. There I told him of my suspicions in connection with his union and of my expectations that the White House would move soon, now that the war was on and that Stalin had aligned himself with Hitler. He confirmed my information about the secretary of his union. He had, it seemed, for some time shared my worst suspicions.

We were lunching in the garden of the restaurant which was quite empty. A few tables away two men were sitting, engrossed in conversation. Suddenly my companion expressed his astonishment when he recognized the two men.

One of them was Lawrence Todd, veteran Washington correspondent for Tass, the official Soviet news agency. I, too, recognized him. Lunching with Todd was the deputy to the Cabinet officer who had been named by Chambers to Berle a few days earlier!

My friend knew this high government official well. He thought it advisable for us to change our positions so that we would not be observed by the other couple, as Todd knew me. We speculated over the motives which had led an assistant secretary to make a date under such circumstances with the representative of the Communist regime then affiliated with the war-waging Nazis. (In the National Press Club in Washington the Tass and *Daily Worker* correspondents became untouchables upon the conclusion of the Stalin-Hitler pact.)

While awaiting developments from the Chambers disclosures, I was oppressed by the information which Krivitsky had imparted to me about the two trusted officials in the innermost councils of the British Government who were acting as agents for the Kremlin. I was determined to bring the matter to the attention of the highest British authority in this country.

IV

WHILE Hilter and Stalin were jointly feasting on the bones of Poland, the thought of the two Soviet spies within the highest offices of the British Government became unbearable to me. I felt that I must impart the information to Lord Lothian, then British Ambassador to the United States. In this I was supported by a ranking official of the State Department whom I had consulted in the matter. Upon learning of the facts which General Krivitsky had confided to me, the official offered to arrange for a suitable introduction to Lord Lothian.

The British Ambassador, who had started his career as secretary to Lloyd George during World War I, was familiar with the revelations of Krivitsky in *The Saturday Evening Post,* and was curious to learn something about the man who had played a leading role in Soviet counterespionage in Western Europe. He betrayed a certain skepticism when I gave him the reason for my visit. He could hardly bring himself to believe that Moscow had one man in the code room of the British Cabinet and another in the Committee of Imperial Defence. In the case of the latter, I indicated something of the background and professional training of the agent, as Krivitsky had described him, but made it clear that I did not know his name.

All I could tell Lord Lothian was that I had cause to have implicit confidence in Krivitsky, that he had conveyed the precious information to me before the outbreak of the war without any thought of its being passed on, and that it would be easy to check whether a man going under the name given me by Krivitsky was on the staff of the British Cabinet.

"And what is his name?" Lord Lothian inquired with a slight smile.

"King," I replied. "That's his last name and that is all I know. Now, Your

Excellency, you should be able to find out if there is a Mr. King in the code room of the British Cabinet."

I left the British Embassy on Massachusetts Avenue in Washington not knowing whether anything would come of my strange call, yet it was as if a load had fallen off my shoulders. There was no doubt in my mind that the British intelligence service would know how to handle the matter with the utmost discretion, and establish the facts.

A COUPLE of weeks later, in October 1939, I received a long distance call from Washington. It was the British Embassy and the secretary to Lord Lothian inquired when I would next be in Washington. It appeared that there was some urgency behind the call and I set an early date for my next trip to the capital.

This time Lord Lothian was eager to see me. Word had arrived confirming the unbelievable. There *was* a code clerk named King on the staff of the British Cabinet! And he had been kept under observation long enough to establish that he was a Soviet agent, vindicating Krivitsky's report.

It was made clear to me that while King was in custody and under investigation, the British Government was most anxious to get on the trail of the second Soviet spy Krivitsky had described. Whereupon Ambassador Lothian introduced me to Mr. Victor Mallet, counsellor at the Embassy and later British wartime envoy to Sweden.

Mr. Mallet disclosed to me that his government in London was deeply interested in securing Krivitsky's cooperation in ferreting out the Soviet espionage agents in Britain who, in view of the Stalin-Hitler pact, could be regarded as Nazi collaborators. Would Krivitsky accept an invitation to undertake a secret mission to England? Mr. Mallet asked me this question and many others about him. He consulted with me as to the best way of enlisting Krivitsky's help.

I impressed upon the Embassy counsellor that any financial inducement which the British Government might wish to offer Krivitsky would only antagonize him and insure his rejection of the proposal. I had to explain at length that Krivitsky's service in the Soviet military intelligence had been motivated by ideological, and not mercenary, considerations, that his ambition was to serve the Allies in their fight against Hitler and in this manner redeem himself for his past services to Stalin, now Hitler's ally.

Ideological espionage was still a fairly new phenomenon in those days, and Mr. Mallet was obviously surprised at the type depicted by me. He was interested in the psychological factors in Krivitsky's makeup. Having convinced himself that not money but prestige was the key to getting Krivitsky's assistance, Mr. Mallet discussed with me the best approach to the man.

I SUGGESTED that Louis Waldman, the New York labor lawyer who was handling Krivitsky's residence status with the United States immigration authorities, would be the right person to broach the matter to his client. At the same time I indicated that Mr. Waldman, a Socialist, was a personal friend of Herbert Morrison, the British labor leader whom I had met in his home. Since Morrison was then a member of the War Cabinet, Krivitsky would be more inclined to undertake the mission under auspices which would assure him sympathetic treatment and the fullest protection. For Morrison, like Waldman, was and is a Socialist of strong anti-Communist views, the camp toward which Krivitsky leaned most.

This was especially important, I emphasized, because Krivitsky had once surreptitiously visited England while in the Soviet secret service. I only knew the bare fact of that trip, and had no idea under what identity he had entered and left the country. But I felt that this would worry Krivitsky and that he would seek the utmost safeguards before entrusting himself to the police authorities of Great Britain.

During the ensuing weeks, while the arrangements were being made through Mr. Waldman for Krivitsky's secret journey to England, I kept in touch with developments. The case against King was closed before Krivitsky left this country in December 1939 for England via Canada where his family took up residence during his absence.

Word reached me that King had been tried, convicted of treason, and executed in the Tower of London. A garbled account of this hitherto unrevealed episode was published by Randolph Churchill, son of Winston Churchill, nearly six years later. Randolph Churchill cited this case as evidence of the perils of Soviet infiltration in the ruling spheres of the Western nations.

SOME MONTHS later, in the spring of 1940, a brief dispatch from abroad in the American press, quoting an official Moscow organ, conveyed to the initiated the information that a major Soviet underground ring had been broken up in England. To me this meant that Krivitsky had been of considerable service to the Allied cause on his mission, and I wondered whether the Kremlin had gotten wind of his presence in England.

The elimination from key positions of two such assets to the Kremlin as its pair of priceless agents within the British Government must have rocked the Politburo. Although the Communists everywhere had been instructed to open a smear campaign in left-wing publications against Krivitsky, which had achieved considerable success in the United States among fuzzy-minded liberals, the master minds in Moscow knew too well Krivitsky's real record and his signal achievements while heading the Soviet counterespionage in Western Europe.

They knew that Krivitsky had received the rank of "Komdiv"—commander of a division—then equivalent to a brigadier general in the Red Army, because of a feat in espionage he had pulled off right under Mussolini's nose. It was an assignment that had taken him two years to carry out, involving the highly secret blueprints of a war vessel designed by Marconi. And Moscow also knew that Krivitsky had been able to organize within Nazi Germany, from his secret headquarters in Holland, an underground unit of death-defying men operating almost within reach of Hitler's Chancellery.

With these facts in mind, it was natural for me to conclude that the Politburo's suspicion would fall upon Krivitsky in consequence of the collapse of the British apparatus. I feared that the long arm of Stalin's vengeance would reach out after him. Krivitsky himself, after rejoining his family in Canada where he remained until October 1940, seemed to have shrugged off such fears.

He and his family re-entered the United States from Canada with the intention of settling here and becoming American citizens.

On MONDAY morning, February 10, 1941, in Washington, D.C., at the Bellevue Hotel near the Union Station, a man by the name of Walter Poref was found by the police in an unconscious condition from a gunshot wound. He never regained consciousness and was pronounced dead within an hour and a half. The late afternoon papers carried the sensational news, "Krivitsky, Foe of Stalin, Slain." He had assumed the name of Poref.

During the fourteen weeks in the United States following his return from abroad, my own subsequent investigation revealed, Krivitsky had established contacts in literary circles which were permeated by left-wingers. That he became extremely incautious in his daily rounds is evidenced by the fact that he cultivated at least one person who was secretly a Communist Party member. Of course, Krivitsky never suspected such an affiliation in the environment in which he had met this person.

Yet he should have known better, just as Trotsky should have known better than to admit into his domestic entourage in Mexico his future assassin. Krivitsky was trained enough to know that Stalin and his vendetta machine could never forget nor forgive a high secret service operative for delivering to the capitalist enemy such valuable weapons as the two agents inside the British Government. To the Kremlin, retribution was essential as an object lesson to other shaky operatives who might be tempted to emulate the Krivitskys.

"In my opinion General Walter Krivitsky did not commit suicide," Louis Waldman, his attorney, announced as he hurried to Washington to inquire into the mysterious death.

"The shot that killed Krivitsky had penetrated the right temple with the result that his brains had been blown out, and a gaping and horrible wound was left. The coroner described this as a *blast wound*. A sizable portion of his head had been badly mutilated," records Mr. Waldman in his autobiographical *Labor Lawyer* (Dutton & Co.), continuing:

"Although the police had virtually closed the case, this tragedy, I felt, was not as simple as it appeared to a routine police mind. I had asked the police a number of questions and had discovered an amazing catalogue of omissions. Room number 532, where the General's body had been discovered, had been released at two o'clock that very afternoon even before I had been informed of my client's death. . . . The room had been cleaned and all traces of the tragedy removed. . . .

"The bullet which had killed Krivitsky had not been recovered from a wall of the room which it had entered, nor was it ever taken out, as far as I know. The gun which the police claimed had killed Krivitsky had not been found in either hand of the dead man, but was at his left side on the bed. His right hand, slightly bent, lay across his chest. A bullet had been fired from the revolver, but was it the same bullet which had killed him? The police had not troubled to take fingerprints from the gun, despite the fact that it had been only partly covered with blood. . . . Under these unusual circumstances, I found it impossible to accept the police 'verdict' of suicide."

In my mind, the mystery of Krivitsky's death has always been linked with his mission to London. Louis Waldman, who made the arrangements for that mission, reports: "As a result of Krivitsky's special trip to England a few months earlier, a serious disruption of fifth column activities had resulted. Again in January 1941, the British were seeking to have the General return to London. This second visit might have proven even more harmful to Soviet espionage than the first."

V

IF WHITTAKER CHAMBERS had chosen to keep silent, the shocking truth about the Soviet espionage ring in the State Department would still remain a deep secret from the American people.

This is the key to the prime issue raised by the Chambers revelations. If, in 1938, when there was no Soviet-American rivalry, Moscow's underground machine was pumping out of the offices of the Secretary of State highly confidential papers at the rate of some 30 a week, then what is the extent of Soviet espionage in Washington in 1948?

During these ten years, the United States and the Soviet Union were partners in the war against Nazi Germany. We courted the rulers in the Kremlin, we cultivated certain ideological bonds with them, and surely that must have produced a large crop of ideological traitors.

How long will it take for us to be abreast of the new recruits in Moscow's underground network and its present-day operations, when we have hardly caught up with the disclosures of 1938? Must we wait until 1958 to get the evidence from the future emulator of Chambers?

If Whittaker Chambers had not commenced some five years ago to talk in journalistic circles about his amazing experiences as an underground Communist, our government and our press would in all probability have maintained their attitude of indifference and disbelief toward any reports of widespread Soviet espionage.

If Whittaker Chambers had not volunteered his information in his appearance before the House Committee on Un-American Activities early last August —an appearance which came in consequence of his talking—the country would perhaps never have learned the details of the sordid epic unfolded day after day in the daily press.

My own painful experiences in trying to break through with the truth since 1939 only serve to underscore the signal service rendered, of his own free will, to America and to humanity by Whittaker Chambers.

When I first found myself in possession of the appalling facts, I was sure that I could storm the citadels of political and journalistic power, and help smash the subterranean empire of treason in the capital. It took me about six months, from September 1939 to March 1940, to spend myself in fruitless assaults upon the blindness or naïveté or apathy or irresponsibility or helplessness of those whom I approached with the Chambers story.

But as I look back to my first involvement in the affair, I can recall ten specific instances, over a period of seven years, of my efforts to reveal the truth. I outlined the salient features of the story to ten public figures. To only the first two did I disclose the name of Whittaker Chambers. These ten were:

Marvin H. McIntyre, secretary to President Roosevelt. At the end of August 1939, after the signing of the Stalin-Hitler pact, I called on Mr. McIntyre at the White House and asked him to arrange for a private audience with President Roosevelt for Whittaker Chambers, a former Soviet agent in Washington, who had some astounding information of the veracity of which I was utterly convinced. I indicated to Mr. McIntyre the nature of the disclosures in all its gravity. He referred me to Mr. Berle, then Assistant Secretary of State in charge of Intelligence.

Adolf A. Berle, Jr. At a private dinner in his home on September 2, to which I brought Whittaker Chambers, Mr. Berle listened to Mr. Chambers' description of two underground Soviet rings operating in Washington. The startling information included names of many Federal officials who had supplied top secret documents to Chambers for transmission to Moscow. Six of those named were State Department employees, including Alger Hiss, his brother, and one Wadleigh. It was Chambers' and my understanding that the information would be conveyed by Mr. Berle to the President and that Chambers would not be punished for his service.

Loy Henderson, then chief of the Russian section in the State Department and now U.S. Ambassador to India. To Mr. Henderson, a close friend, who had served in our Embassy in Moscow and who was deeply concerned over Soviet infiltration, I confided much of what had been divulged at Mr. Berle's home. I was worried lest important papers relating to our Russian policy, then in Mr. Henderson's jurisdiction, would find their way to the Kremlin. I took it for granted that Mr. Henderson would put the security officers of the State Department on the alert.

Adelaide Neall, lifetime assistant to the late George Horace Lorimer and then a senior editor on *The Saturday Evening Post.* In the course of several visits to Philadelphia, I kept Miss Neall in touch with developments, expecting a national sensation as a result of government action on Chambers' revelations. I had hoped to do a series of articles for the *Post* reviewing the story in all its frightening ramifications.

Senator Warren R. Austin, now U.S. chief representative at the U.N. Having formed a close friendship with Senator Austin of Vermont on a tour of the Near East in 1936, I went to him in the early months of 1940 with a fairly comprehensive account of the Soviet underworld in Washington. It seemed to me then, and I made no secret of it, that the information on Communist espionage, if presented under his authoritative auspices to the American people, might justly earn for him the nomination of the Republican Party for the Presidency and enable him to clean house in Washington. Senator Austin did not react to my disclosures as I had hoped.

Martin Dies, then chairman of the Un-American Activities Committee. After virtually giving up hope of Executive action on the Chambers disclosures, I submitted to Martin Dies in a private conference in March 1940 sufficient facts to convince him of the need for an intensive probe. We agreed that it would take a staff of 12 ace investigators to secure the evidence on Communist espionage in Washington, an assignment for which the Committee lacked the necessary funds. Shortly after our conference Chairman Dies issued a public statement through the Associated Press to the effect that he had uncovered a "lead" on far-flung Soviet secret police operations in the United States and that he would hear testimony soon from "the head of the OGPU" in this country. The hearing was, of course, never held.

William C. Bullitt, former U.S. Ambassador to Soviet Russia and to France. At a breakfast conference with Mr. Bullitt at his Anchorage Hotel apartment I related the main points of the Chambers-Krivitsky revelations. A confidant and favorite of President Roosevelt at that time, Mr. Bullitt, who had known me since 1918, was sufficiently stirred to indicate that he would take the matter to the White House at the first opportunity. I had informed him of my conversations with Mr. Berle and my conferences with Loy Henderson who had served under Bullitt in Moscow.

Walter Winchell, columnist and frequent White House guest. A year and a half after my first efforts to bring into the open the Chambers story, in March 1941, I called on Walter Winchell at the Roney Plaza Hotel in Miami. In the course of a long talk dealing with subversive activities, when he informed me of having President Roosevelt's ear, I acquainted Mr. Winchell with much of the information furnished by Chambers and told him that at least six Soviet agents were known to have operated within the State Department alone. Mr. Winchell, greatly shaken, indicated that he would take the matter to the highest quarters. In his broadcast of December 12 last he announced that he had carried the story to President Roosevelt.

Governor Thomas E. Dewey. In the early summer of 1944, a couple of weeks before the Republican convention, I was invited to a private luncheon with Governor Dewey in his apartment at the Roosevelt Hotel in New York City. I sketched for the Governor the underground Communist spider-web in the Federal service, with special emphasis on the operations of the Soviet unit in the State Department as described by Chambers. I urged upon Dewey the vital need for informing the American people during the campaign of the shocking state of affairs inside Washington. Governor Dewey pledged vigorous action, if elected, in clearing out the nests of treason from official Washington.

Henry R. Luce, publisher of *Time, Life,* and *Fortune.* The late Raymond Leslie Buell, formerly the head of the Foreign Policy Association, arranged early in 1946 for my meeting Mr. Luce at lunch at the St. Regis Hotel. Without once mentioning or otherwise identifying his employee, Whittaker Chambers, I described to the powerful publisher the underground Soviet apparatus in the State Department which had been exposed to the authorities by a former Communist agent who was an editor of a national magazine. Mr. Luce obviously had no idea that the editor in question was on his own staff! It is only fair to add that my disclosure to Mr. Luce was intended merely as an illustration for his benefit of the vast scope of Soviet espionage in the United States.

IF WE are ever to get to the bottom of the traitorous and multicelled underworld planted within our free and carefree government, we must recognize the patriotic motives which led Whittaker Chambers to make amends for his past sins by offering to his government and his country incontrovertible proof of Soviet espionage.

It is not generally known that Mr. Chambers began to atone for his past long before his recent disclosures. He cooperated some seven years ago with the Rapp-Coudert Committee in New York in ferreting out subversive Communists among the teachers in our public schools. During the war he cooperated unreservedly with naval intelligence officers in their efforts to identify secret Communist agents in the armed services.

214

Above all, the American people should be grateful to Chambers for preserving the microfilms and the other documentary evidence of the deadly germs in the bloodstream of our nation. *Chambers could have destroyed all the evidence and been the better off for it.* His possible error of judgment in not bringing forth the precious evidence earlier is inconsequential as compared with the enormity of the error committed by those who refused to heed his warnings.

Punishment on any technical ground or severe censure by the press of the course of action pursued by Whittaker Chambers would be punishing the American people by discouraging any further disclosures. The great challenge of the Chambers-Hiss affair is how to unearth and expose the entire subterranean labyrinth installed within America by Soviet technicians.

The government of Canada knew how to meet this challenge. It rewarded the Soviet code clerk, Igor Gouzenko, who came forward with a batch of documents showing widespread Communist espionage, by conferring upon him Canadian citizenship and other emoluments.

If the government of the United States recognized the service rendered by Whittaker Chambers to our national defense, it would encourage many an underground Soviet agent on the point of deserting the Communist fold to come out into the open. Only in this manner can we catch up with Stalin's secret brigade operating *now* in our midst, and keep pace with Moscow's operations in the cold war.

VI

HAD THERE been an immediate investigation of the Whittaker Chambers revelations when this writer took him to Assistant Secretary of State Adolf A. Berle, Jr., in 1939, at the outbreak of World War II, incalculable injury to America and world peace might have been averted.

The verdict of the jury in the Alger Hiss perjury trial must not be permitted to distort our view of the historical meaning of the case, and to permit the widespread misconception that Mr. Chambers had been gunning for Mr. Hiss to prevail.

The record of the facts laid before Mr. Berle in my presence by Chambers and recently retrieved from secret government files, proves beyond any doubt that Chambers, without individual bias or favor, presented a case against an espionage ring of some twenty members in the Federal service.

It was the knowledge of the presence of a secret battalion of Soviet agents in the highest policy-making bodies of the government which drove me to seek action through the White House and which impelled me to *induce* Whittaker Chambers to tell his story.

Throughout the ensuing years, beginning with 1943, as the records of government interrogators of Mr. Chambers show, Mr. Hiss had never been singled out either by Chambers or by this writer for special attention.

Had Washington acted to purge itself ten years ago of Stalin's fifth column
—and the dereliction was not only on the part of the Executive but also of the
Congressional branch—it would have unquestionably affected the course of
history.

Unless Hiss takes the one course still open to him, waives the statute of limitations and demands a trial on the merits of the case—on charges of espionage—
the present verdict must stand as a monument to the folly of a confused
generation.

December 1947–February 1950

SUMMATION TO THE JURY

People of the United States vs Alger Hiss

By THOMAS F. MURPHY

Assistant U.S. Attorney

[*There has been a revival of interest in the Hiss-Chambers case following the
downfall of President Nixon. Several leading publishers have contracted for
books on the affair and a prestigious magazine,* Commentary, *devoted 15 pages
to a minute study of the evidence, "Was Alger Hiss Guilty?" (August 1975) by
Professor of Trial Techniques at Cornell Law School, Irving Younger. This lends
the character of an historic landmark to the summation of the case delivered
to the jury on July 7, 1949, by Government Prosecutor Thomas F. Murphy.
Regarding it as a classical document among the records of celebrated trials,*
Plain Talk *published the highlights of the text. The first trial of Hiss, in which
Murphy was pitted against the histrionic Lloyd Paul Stryker, ended with a
hung jury. The second trial closed in January 1950 with the conviction of Hiss
for perjury and a five-year prison sentence.*]

IT IS hard sometimes to distinguish between reason and emotion, but I think
when you get to the juryroom and you sit down, not disturbed by lawyers or
judges, and argue this with yourselves and ask your neighbor and your fellow
juror what is the reason for this, or what is the reason for that, you will find that
there are some facts here that are uncontradicted. Let us see what they are.

There is no doubt that Mr. Chambers had in his possession copies of original State Department documents. That fact is uncontradicted.

We have shown you here, and there are three witnesses for you—the type-writer, the original State Department documents, and the documents in this case—three solid witnesses.

What is the first undisputed fact? Mr. Chambers had in his possession, and they are now in this courtroom, documents which are undoubtedly copies, in some cases verbatim copies, of original, secret, confidential State Department documents.

What is the next uncontradicted fact? The documents themselves are all dated in the first three months of 1938. No dispute about that.

The next is that they were all copies, of course; except the handwritten documents, but the typewritten documents were all copied, except No. 10, on the Hiss typewriter.

I say that is uncontradicted. Mr. Chambers had these documents, admittedly copied from State Department documents, dated the first three months in 1938 and on the Hiss typewriter.

Now, the Judge will charge you that the United States Supreme Court, not too many years ago, in 1945, has laid down the rule that in federal courts per-jury is proved by two ways: One, by two witnesses, or, by one witness and cor-roborating evidence. We fit into the second class: one witness and corroborating evidence. The witness is Mr. Chambers, and he told you in no uncertain terms that, pursuant to an arrangement, these documents, these very documents were given to him by that defendant when Chambers was a functionary of the Com-munist Party. What is the corroboration? The corroboration, aside from every-thing else, is the typewritten documents themselves, admitted, uncontradicted, typed on this typewriter, the Hiss typewriter.

Let me give you a real homely example of corroboration: Let us suppose that one of your children was apprehended by you in the kitchen with jam on his face and you asked him whether he was in the pantry and had some jam and he said, "No." Admittedly you did not see him. Now, what does your normal, everyday intelligence tell you happened? It tells you that the boy was lying. Why? Why, there is the jam on his face. It does not prove that he put it in his mouth, but there it is and we are only mortals, and we don't have to take a stomach pump and empty the boy's stomach out to prove he lied. We have the jam on his face. That is what we have here.

Emotional Factors

WHAT ARE some of the emotional factors that you are going to be confronted with? We are human beings and we have emotions.

Now one emotional factor is that this defendant is a clean-cut, handsome, intelligent, American-born male of some 44 years. That is an emotional factor.

Mr. Chambers is short and fat and he had bad teeth. Those are emotional facts. Mrs. Chambers is plain and severe. Mrs. Hiss is demure and attractive, and intelligent to boot. Very intelligent. But those are emotional facts.

Now, Mr. Stryker said that he was going to call as a witness for this defendant the shade of Oliver Wendell Holmes. He was going to call the ghost of that revered Justice and have that ghost testify from that chair on behalf of this defendant. And I said to myself, "Well, if he is going to call the shade of Justice Holmes, there are a couple of shades that I would like to call here." One man's name was Judas Iscariot and the other's Major General Benedict Arnold.

Let us see how they stack up, one against the other. Well, he did not call the shade, but he did call 15 character witnesses from all walks of life, two from our highest court.

That is something that you want to think about, whether two judges from the United States Supreme Court could with propriety come into this courtroom.

They, of course, didn't know anything about the facts in this case. They didn't tell you anything about the guilt or innocence of this man. They testified in substance to his good reputation, the reputation for truthfulness and loyalty.

Now, reputation is considered by the defense important. They brought 15 people, and oddly enough, the one man—the one man who was a neighbor, the one man who was in the house, in and out of the house at 30th Street, Volta Place, Geoffrey May, do you remember him?—the one man who was there time and time again—they didn't ask him.

But let me dwell just a minute on reputation. I daresay that Judas Iscariot had a fairly good reputation. He was one of the Twelve. He was next to God, and we know what he did.

Major General Benedict Arnold came from a fine family. He was one of the first to go into the Revolutionary War, captured Fort Ticonderoga, was made a colonel. He led the siege against Quebec, got wounded, was made a brigadier general. When the Revolutionary troops were in possession of Philadelphia, Benedict Arnold was the man in charge, and he was court-martialed. Some money found its way into his pocket. And he testified in that court-martial:

"Before you, gentlemen and soldiers, I, as a gentleman and a soldier, tell you that I am innocent of this charge."

At that very time he had been dealing eight months with the British, eight months. He was trying to get $10,000. But he told his superior officers, "I tell you gentlemen and soldiers, I am innocent."

And what happened? He was made a major general and sold out West Point. He wasn't caught. But if he had been caught, don't you think he could have called George Washington as a reputation witness?

Those 15 witnesses have nothing to do with the facts in this case. Those are the facts, those three witnesses there, the typewriter, the original State Department documents, and the evidence in this case, right there.

Now Mr. Stryker first told you, in his opening, to beware of Whittaker Chambers. He said he was a moral leper, a thief. . . . And who is Whittaker Chambers? Why, he is the bosom pal of this defendant. He is the man that this defendant gave a Ford to, the man that he gave his apartment to, this moral leper. He said he met him in the latter part of 1934, perhaps early in '35, and took him to New York.

This was the man the defendant often associated himself with, this man now described as a moral leper.

What is the defendant? If Mr. Stryker calls Mr. Chambers a moral leper, what is the defendant Hiss? What is the name for an employee of this government who takes government papers and gives them to a Communist espionage agent?

Alger Hiss was a traitor, a traitor to this country, another Benedict Arnold, another Judas Iscariot, another Judge Manton. Right in this building twelve jurors like yourselves tried a man from a high place, from the United States Circuit Court of Appeals, higher in level than Judge Kaufman here, a United States Circuit Court Judge [Manton].

Someone said that roses that fester stink worse than weeds. And a brilliant man like this man, who betrays his trust, stinks. Inside of that smiling face that heart is black and cancerous. He is a traitor.

BECAUSE he was living with a woman not his wife, before he was married, he [Stryker] tells you that Chambers has no respect for womankind. You saw Mr. Chambers on the stand and you saw his wife, the mother of his children. Does a man who is married to one woman for 18 years, who is the father of her two children, have no regard for womankind?

You heard Mrs. Chambers say, when she was being belabored by Mr. Stryker, "He is a great man." That is what she thought of her husband. "He is a great man." That is courage.

Now another statement Mr. Stryker made in his opening is about Mr. Adolf A. Berle, [former] Assistant Secretary of State. Mr. Stryker told us, "Now we have Mr. Berle's sworn testimony to this event which was at the time of the Hitler-Stalin Pact, I think, about September, 1939, and Mr. Berle under oath says that he did not even say that he, Hiss, was a Communist."

Mr. Berle was not called by Mr. Stryker, and I suggest to you that the reason is obvious and that is Mr. Berle would have said, "Oh, yes, Mr. Chambers told me in 1939 when I was the Intelligence officer for Mr. Roosevelt that Hiss was a Communist—1939."

The Motive

NOW THIS trial has been in progress since May 31st. I don't know how many witnesses have been produced by the government and the defense, and not once have I been able to find out what the defendant charges here was the motive of Chambers. What was his motive? What was the motive of the senior editor of *Time*—getting $30,000 a year—to come forward with these papers?

Well, this morning I heard something about a political campaign. Mr. Stryker did not say in so many words that that was the motive. He skirted around that a little bit. Let us see now, what was the senior editor of *Time* going to get as a result of injecting himself in a political campaign? I assume we will have to agree that he was not going to get a $30,000 job in the government. It goes without saying that the assistant district attorneys don't get that. Judge Kaufman gets $15,000. Do you know what members of the Cabinet get? Do you know what people in charge of different agencies get? Nothing like $30,000. What was he going to get if his side won, and what was his side? Could it be some political advantage? There is no testimony that the man ever concerned himself with politics after 1938. He was intensely interested in politics prior to 1938. He was interested in Communist politics, with his friend Alger Hiss.

No motive has been proved. No motive has ever been suggested on the witness stand here. Mr. Chambers would not have come forward now with these documents unless it was true—that motive was not touched upon—truth. Mr. Chambers desired the truth.

How did Mr. Stryker know all about the initmate life of the Chambers'? Do you think it was the result of some very, very mysterious investigation that he and his colleagues conducted? Do you think that he had some pipeline down, down deep that brought up all this information—that he discovered it? Wasn't it obvious to you, as I told you in my opening, that there was not a blessed thing that the defense did not know before this trial commenced? They had examined Mr. and Mrs. Chambers under oath in Baltimore for some 1,300 pages. That examination commenced, I think, in the early part of November 1948 and concluded in the latter part of March 1949. How many lawyers appearing in the United States would love the opportunity of cross-examining, without restriction, without objection, the government witness before the trial?

Not only did they have all of that information which Mr. Chambers said he did not refuse to answer, but they had the testimony of the House Committee in printed form. They had copies of the Hisses' own statements, that they had made to the grand jury, and armed with all of that they came into court and tried to impress you with the fact that all of this information was obtained by virtue of their own industry, secretly. Not only did they have all that, but they had these very documents. They also had the standards of four typewritten letters that the expert used as a standard of comparison. They knew everything. They even had the typewriter.

Armed with all that, and armed with it in black and white, this defense was conceived to avoid the facts.

Do you remember how shocked Mr. Stryker was when Mr. Chambers told about the $400 loan, and he said, "That's the first time you testified to that." I told him it was the first time that he, Mr. Stryker, heard it, the one thing they hadn't heard before.

And what did they do with it? They fumbled; they dropped the ball on that one.

Inside the Hiss Homes

WHERE IS his [Chambers'] testimony corroborated? In what respect do we know as rational beings that he told the truth? In what respect do we know that Hiss lied?

You determine where the lie is in this case by examining and placing side by side the testimony of the Hisses and the Chambers'. One that struck me as being very cogent was the description of the houses, the inside layout of the rooms. Bear in mind, the Hisses say that neither of the Chambers' were in 30th Street or Volta Place. We have a description from Mr. Chambers and from Mrs. Chambers concerning the inside of the house. Mrs. Chambers, in describing Volta Place, said:

"The Volta Street house was a walled-in garden house. The walls were wide. You entered through a gate, went up several steps, turned to the left on a stoned-in porch and entered the living room. The living room and dining room occupied that floor, with a stairway to the right leading to the bedroom. The third, that is the attic, was Timmie's quarters. The first room upstairs was a small room in which leading off the stairway, I believe, was no doorway or enclosure, before you get into that little room where the box piano was.

"The next room beyond that was a bedroom occupied by Mr. and Mrs. Hiss, which contained—which has a flowered chintz bedspread which I recall Mrs. Hiss bought at a sale at Hutzler's, because I too was looking at this article."

Now what did Mrs. Hiss do to contradict that? You may recall the difficulty I had with Mrs. Hiss. My recollection is that it took about ten minutes to find out which was the front of the house. We couldn't quite agree as to where the front door was. There was no dispute that the dining room and living room were on the ground floor. Nothing was said about upstairs.

In connection with 30th Street, Mrs. Chambers testified:

"The 30th Street house, I believe, was a little white house, one of three party houses, that is, with party walls. There were two iron rails as you came onto about two or three steps entering immediately into a pink living room lined on either side with books. To the left in the rear of the house was a stairway that went down into a dining room—did I say the living room was pink? The walls were very thin, and as they were party walls you could hear the noises of the neighbors and we were particularly careful to speak low.

"Downstairs the dining room was green. As I say, the picture that I gave to Priscilla was on the far wall as you come down the stairway. In the lower lefthand center of the wall—to the left of the center I will say—there was a settee, one of those spindle-backed porch settees, in the far part of the living room. Upstairs—no, I never was upstairs. I don't know."

Now, Mrs. Hiss contradicted that by saying the house was yellow and not white, that there were seven or eight steps and not two or three, and that the living room was green and not pink.

Is it possible in the nature of things for two people to describe two houses in such detail and not to have been there? Is it humanly possible? Consider that when you ask yourself who is lying.

The August Session

NEXT WE come, on the issue of credibility, to the Commodore Hotel. This was an executive session. It was the opportunity that Mr. Hiss was crying for. He wanted to see who it was that made these accusations against him.

You recall his testimony that on August 3rd of last year he received innumerable phone calls saying that Mr. Chambers had testified in Congress that he was a Communist and he straightway sent the telegram demanding to be heard under oath, and he was given that opportunity on August 5th.

He told the members of Congress that the name Whittaker Chambers meant nothing to him. He read in the papers that morning that Mr. Chambers had given some details of his, Mr. Hiss's, personal life. He didn't say what the details were, just that there was some sort of a leak, and he started to think. Bear in mind, he hadn't done any thinking prior to that, but he started to think who could that person be? And he wrote the name George Crosley. He wrote the name of a man that he said he hadn't seen since 1936; he wrote the name of a man whose articles he had never seen written or published.

And he went down to Congress with it and told them that perhaps they were referring to a man named George Crosley, a free lance writer that he knew back in '34–'35, referring to a man that he sublet his apartment to for the summer months; in order to clinch the deal, he threw in a Ford, just sort of threw it in. "That must be the fellow, George Crosley, and here it is, I have written it down, I think I drove him to New York; he once borrowed a couple of bucks; I didn't bother much with him; in fact, he stayed at our house at one time, on P Street. He was going to move in, and the van didn't show up, so we put him up as goodhearted people do sometimes to tenants, fed him. That must be the fellow, George Crosley."

But he wanted to see him. Up at the Commodore Hotel in executive session, he was given the opportunity of a confrontation. You remember how that went along? He first asked Chambers whether or not his voice—or I think he asked one of the Congressmen—whether the pitch of his voice after he talked a little bit was not a little different than when he testified before, a little less resonant, I think he said.

He had him talk. In fact, he had him read something. Then he asked whether the witness couldn't open his mouth so he could look at his teeth. I don't suppose he ever saw the man with his mouth closed, but he wanted to see the teeth. This man that he knew, this Crosley, had bad teeth.

Well, Chambers opened his mouth and he looked in, and having looked, he then wanted to know the dentist's name. See, that would be important. He also wanted to know when the dental work was done. That would help him recognize his man.

He heard him talk. The pitch was a little high. He didn't say, "Yes, that is the man." Then he asked, "Did you sublease an apartment from me on 29th Street?" Chambers said no, he didn't. He then said, "Did you occupy an apartment of mine on 29th Street?" "Yes, I did." "Well," he said, "how do you explain that apparent inconsistency to say you did not sublease it and nevertheless you say you occupied it?" And as I remember the answer it was, "You and I, Alger, were Communists together." And then he [Hiss] says, "I now recognize him from what he has just said. I am convinced that this is George Crosley." Not from the teeth, not from the pitch of the voice, not from his jowls, hair, size, stature, not from any visual inspection. That subleasing was what did it. That is the confrontation. That is what actually happened, and not what he said on that stand when testifying for Mr. Stryker. He said, "I recognized him without hesitation."

He knew who Whittaker Chambers was. Whittaker Chambers was his pal from the old underground days. Whittaker Chambers, his friend from 1935 to 1938. He knew him as Carl, but don't you think, in the years that went by, [he knew] what happened to Whittaker Chambers? Don't you think he read *Time* magazine? Don't you think he watched the masthead year after year and he saw that name in there?

The Automobile

Now ABOUT the car: Let us assume that he could not honestly remember what year it was that he gave the car away. There is no doubt in your mind that you would remember to whom you gave it. We don't give automobiles away frequently. He said he only gave one away. You would remember to whom you gave it and the circumstances of the giving for many, many years.

He first testified that the giving of the car was to clinch the rental agreement, a rental agreement in the year 1935 when things were a little tough. No written lease, nothing like that, just an oral agreement, no rent in advance. This Harvard man, a brilliant law student, then a lawyer, practicing law with the Nye Committee, permitted a man whom he did not know too well, did not know where he worked, did not know where he could reach him, permitted him to become a subtenant of his without a written lease, without demanding the money in advance, and then, to clinch the bargain in 1935, gave him a Ford.

Later on he said he gave him "the use" of the Ford. That is Mr. Hiss's forte.

He is able to distinguish, to combine truth with half-truth, a little bit to color it, a little bit more to testify, and then, if placed in a corner, to rely upon the truthful part, and you have to be pretty good to do that, and he is pretty good.

Now, he said he gave the car in 1936. That is, he completely divested himself of the car in 1936, in the summer, because he promised to give it to him in April of the year before. It was a promise made and a promise fulfilled. Of course he guy gypped him a little bit in between, beat him out of the rent, touched him for $30 or so, a complete moocher, but he made a promise, and, by God, when the man said, "Where is the car?" "Here it is." And he gave him the car.

But what does the assignment of title say? The assignment of title, which was introduced in evidence here, says, "For value received the undersigned hereby sells, assigns and transfers unto Cherner Motor Company, 1781 Florida Avenue, N.W., the motor vehicle described on the reverse side of this certificate, and the undersigned hereby warrants the title" and so forth, and the signature of the assignor, "Alger Hiss." "Sworn to July 23, 1936. W. Marvin Smith, Notary Public." As a matter of fact, I think Mr. Hiss testified that he wrote in the name "Cherner Motor Company" himself.

That is what he said under oath on July 23, 1936. That is what he said he did with that Ford automobile. He assigned, transferred, and sold that car to Cherner Motor Company, and Judge Kaufman would not let me prove what happened after that.

The Rugs

ONE THING more to add to the list of things that will help you decide who lied. Mr. Chambers testified that he bought four Oriental rugs with money he received from Bykov. He had his friend, Professor Meyer Schapiro from Columbia, buy them for him.

First of all, the man who testified first, Mr. Touloukian, the rug man, said he sold four Oriental rugs, approximately 9x12, for eight hundred and some odd dollars. It was paid for with the check of the professor, together with $276.71 in cash, making a total of $876.71, and then delivered, and here it is in evidence, delivered on December 29, 1936, to Dr. Schapiro, 279 West 4th Street, and receipted by Mrs. Schapiro December 29, 1936. There is the check of Dr. Schapiro.

Dr. Schapiro says that he sent them at Chambers' request to somebody in Washington whose first name started with the word Sol. Chambers testified that he gave one of these rugs to Alger Hiss in the city of Washington and told him that it was a gift from the Russian people in gratitude, and Mr. Hiss says he did get a rug, it is about 9x12, he did get it from Chambers. He still has it, but he has no idea why he gave it to him.

There are the facts that cannot be controverted. There is nothing you can do about those dates. They are on the exhibits. They are going to stay there and they are going to follow Alger Hiss to his grave.

The Typewriter

NOW THE typewriter: Before we discuss that typewriter keep in mind, if you will, the uncontradicted evidence of Mr. Russell, the man from the typewriter concern. He testified that Mr. Hiss's Wall Street law firm, Debevoise, Plimpton & McLean, through Mr. Rosenwald, rented a Woodstock typewriter on February 24, 1949, and returned it May 24, 1949, three months after, a typewriter just like Defendant's Exhibit S. This Wall Street law firm hired and had possession of a Woodstock typewriter like that.

Now on November 17, 1948, when Mr. Chambers offered in evidence in Baltimore handwritten and typewritten documents, it must have become obvious to the lawyers present that a typewriter, or a typewriter specimen, was immediately going to become important because if, as Mr. Chambers testified, these documents were typed by the Hisses in 1938, that was the jam on the boy's face. So it became very, very important to find (1) the typewriter itself or (2) specimens from that typewriter so as to prove the authenticity of Mr. Chambers' statement.

This [Hiss] was a man of high places, who was then president of the Carnegie Endowment for World Peace. What could he do? He only had two choices, he could call up the chairman and say, "Well, you got me at last," or deny it. He had no other choice. He had to get in there and get in there first. So what did he do with this typewriter?

He knew and he testified on the stand on cross-examination that the obtaining of standards of comparison was the first order of business as far as the government was concerned. He wanted to help. He wanted to help this government of yours and mine. He wanted to track down and nail this horrible story of treason and corrupt dealing by a paid employee of the United States—a confidant of our late President. Yes, sir, he wanted to help. So what did he do? He made a special trip, he said, and came down to Baltimore so he could be examined by some FBI agents. He told them that they had an old typewriter, yes they had it, but they disposed of it in 1938 to a second-hand dealer in Georgetown.

That was to help the FBI find the typewriter. They thereby eliminated all the other cities in the United States and said, "Georgetown, Washington, D.C., that is the place to start." So they looked and they looked and they could not find it. But they did find specimens. They did find letters written by the Hisses on that typewriter, and their expert looked at them, just as a ballistics expert looks at a bullet, and said, "Yes, those documents except the one we know as No. 10, were all written on the same typewriter that these specimens were written on." It brought us a little closer to Alger Hiss.

Now in looking for this typewriter, the FBI also had some other help from the Hisses. You can see how that first help saved the government a lot of money and time, but he wanted to help. That was the only thing he wanted to do in December, was to help the FBI.

Mrs. Hiss told the grand jury that their maid, Claudi Catlett, was dead. You can see how that would help. You could just eliminate her from the list of people to see.

But they found it [the typewriter]. How? They went to the same sources that we did. The FBI agents saw the Catlett boys at the end of January 1949, and they denied knowing anything about a Hiss typewriter. That is what they told the FBI. But what did they tell the Hisses? That little Catlett boy said he went to Donald Hiss the day after and said the FBI agents were around inquiring about a typewriter, and then things started to buzz.

We find Mr. Rosenwald, a fellow classmate [of Hiss], out in Detroit in the end of January. And then we know the story, how through the smaller of the Catlett boys the typewriter was traced through his family, through the sister, and finally into Mr. Lockey's hands, and then Mr. Lockey sold it to Mr. McLean, and the receipt says April 19, 1949, for $15.00. So you can see how this helped.

Now the Hisses knew that the typewriter formed a connecting link between Chambers and them. They knew that from the period from May or June 1937 until his defection in April of 1938 that that typewriter was going all the time, and if there ever was going to be a charge against the Hisses, that would be the immutable witness forever against them. So what did they do? Did they sell it? Of course not. If they sold it, there would always be a record as it passed from one person to another. They got rid of it by giving it to the Catletts. They figured, "Well, here are a couple of boys, uneducated; they don't type. It will fall into disuse and get banged around. It will never be traceable back to us again."

Until [Hiss] was indicted he never once mentioned it to his lawyers. Of course, he never told the grand jury either, but he did tell one of the Catlett boys. He said, "If the FBI ever come looking for a typewriter, don't telephone me, but tell my brother Donald." In other words, he could let it sit. If the agents did not find the Catletts, all well and good.

Now what did Perry Catlett say in his own statement in May 1949? He says he got it [the typewriter] during a moving. He does not remember whether it was before or after or during, which is, I think, an honest way of recalling what the facts are. What he does remember, however, was that he took it to the northwest corner of Connecticut and K Streets, to see whether he could have it fixed.

Now it turns out upon investigation that that is probably correct, but unfortunately for the defense the Woodstock people did not come there until September 15, 1938. Now let us assume that the boy was in error when he told the agent that he went to the northwest corner of Connecticut and K, as the defense intimated possibly it could have been the other Woodstock shop down the block, on K Street. Well, we checked that, and you heard the witness say that the shop did not come into existence until May, 1938. Take your choice. But those are the facts that you cannot change. September and May, 1938.

Now the boy Raymond said that when the FBI agent was there to see him, he called up his real estate agent to find out when they moved to P Street, and he found out they moved there on January 17, 1938. That date is important, too, because both Catlett boys said that after the Hisses gave them the typewriter, they took it to P Street. Let us assume that they got the typewriter about January 1, 1938.

Who typed these documents? The Catletts, from the evidence here, did not know Mr. Chambers. They said that they could not type. Are we supposed to visualize Chambers coming around to the Catlett house at night and typing these documents himself?

I submit that two things must be clear; one, that the typewriter was in the possession of the Hiss family until at least Mr. Chambers' defection, until he left the party; and two, that the Catletts had the typewriter for some time after that.

Now let us go to another element of corroboration: if Mr. Chambers was the cunning, unscrupulous, conniving liar Mr. Stryker would have you believe, he certainly missed the bill on the Peterboro trip. If he did not, in truth and in fact, go to Peterboro with the Hisses, why would he mention the day? Why would he mention the name of the hotel? Why would he mention the owner's name? God, if that isn't going in with your chin out. The reason is that it is true.

Exactly $400

NOW ANOTHER item, the $400. You know the story. Mr. Chambers says that Hiss gave him $400 and he used that to help pay for that car. The car was bought by his wife from the Schmidt Motor Company in November 1937. He used it in his break from the party.

Now if his statement was untrue, there, of course, could not be any $400 withdrawal from the bank. But if his statement was true and there was an exact $400 withdrawal, he, too, is psychic. He did not have the bank account. He did not say $350, he did not say $500, or $425, but an even $400. What did they do with it? Mrs. Hiss said she bought all of these items for her Volta Place house. I too am going to ask the ladies on the jury, is that the way you do it when you have a checking account and a charge account, and you have not moved in? Do you take the $400 out in one lump? Do you go around and buy curtains and items for the house to be delivered later and pay for them in cash? If you are going to have them delivered later you might as well pay by check. Is that $400 explanation reasonable to you or is it just another lie, another peg upon which you can tell which side credibility lies?

The Government's Exhibit 17 is the one that hurt. That is the one that scored. That is a pretty good typing job. And what did she say in there? She said she was going to the university in order that she might take courses at Mercy Hospital. That is what Mrs. Chambers testified that Mrs. Hiss talked of, "taking courses."

Now why did it hurt? Because she too must have been psychic to know about that plan, or else, if she was not psychic, she was chumming with Mrs. Hiss, and I submit that is how she knew it.

Let me speak now about the lawsuit. He [Hiss] had to bring the lawsuit. In self-defense he had to bring the lawsuit. And they spent an awful lot of time examining Mr. Chambers. Mr. Chambers had rights in that lawsuit. Did he examine Mr. Hiss? Did he examine Mrs. Hiss? No, of course not. He has a defense in that lawsuit. The defense of truth. He took him at his dare. Why? Because he is a man of courage, because he is telling the truth.

Mr. Dulles' Testimony

Now John Foster Dulles. Mr. Stryker didn't know what the contradiction was. You remember he asked Judge Kaufman to help? You remember he said, "I don't understand. Would the Judge or maybe somebody tell me? I don't quite see the point." Well, it was right there. He put the lie in this man's mouth on three separate occasions. That is what he [Hiss] does; a little bit of the truth and a little bit of a lie. He told Mr. Dulles and he told us on the stand that he was the one who brought up the question of resignation. Mr. Dulles said that he saw him, and that he told him, Mr. Dulles, that he satisfied the FBI in 1948. Can you imagine satisfying them, getting a certificate of clearance, "O.K., FBI?"

You heard what the witness said here. When they had the dinner of the trustees of the Carnegie Endowment, he was asked, "Didn't you tell the House Un-American Committee that you checked, personally checked with Justice Byrnes, that you contacted him directly?" And then it comes out that Mr. Acheson did it.

Now these documents. Let me look at those. Give me Number 1. May 28th. Moscow. This was a summary, to tell his boss of important matters like trade agreements. He knew it was in his handwriting when I introduced the document. He recognized his handwriting, when he saw that I had proof of the document. The document, ladies and gentlemen, is a copy verbatim, and that is a summary on an important trade agreement matter.

And one thing more, notice the way it is creased. That is a paper that was thrown in a wastepaper basket! With those creases? You know how that got out of the office?

Look at all of them, look at every one of them. Wastepaper basket, my eye! Look at the crease in that. Look at the phrasing there. There is the summary on the top, "30 Potez-63, latest French type, a lighter bomber-pursuit." And then to make it clear for the photographer, it is all written out. That would have been enough to tell Mr. Sayre about it, a man interested in trade agreements, about some French bomber-pursuit planes.

And finally, one thing more, Dr. Binger. I objected to a doctor being allowed to sit within the rail of this courtroom. I thought it was unfair. I thought his testimony was incompetent in any event, but Judge Kaufman thought otherwise. How would you like to sit on that chair and have some psychiatrist look at you for seven days? Did you see any change in Mr. Chambers? He was telling the truth, and that is why he did not fear him, or any other of the settings and props that have been going around in this case.

And again, finally, you are the second jury to hear this story. The grand jury heard the same story. The grand jury heard this traitor and Mr. Chambers, and that grand jury indicted Hiss. It indicted Hiss because he lied. He lied to them, and I submit he lied to you. The grand jury said that he lied twice on December 15. And as a representative of 130 million people of this country, I ask you to concur in that charge of the grand jury. I ask you as a representative of the United States Government to come back and put the lie in that man's face.

August 1949

School for Treason

By John Chamberlain

[*Soon after the conviction of Alger Hiss, John Chamberlain faced the question: Why do intellectuals fall for totalitarian ideology? Many good people could not bring themselves to believe that a well-educated and well-provided person like Alger Hiss would join the Communist camp. The press did not spotlight the activities as Soviet spies of Dr. Allan Nunn May and Dr. Raymond Boyer, who figured in the revelations of the Canadian Royal Commission. Nor were the psychological portraits of Kim Philby, Donald Maclean, Guy Burgess, and Klaus Fuchs, to cite but a few, unmasked to public view. In this essay written for* Plain Talk, *Chamberlain attacked the big question with penetrating insight. Having gained a national reputation in his youth as a brilliant book reviewer for* The New York Times, *he has in recent years won recognition as one of the country's foremost libertarian journalists.*]

IT WAS the day after the Alger Hiss verdict. I had run into an old friend on the train, a history professor from an Ivy League university who had worked in Washington during the war. "You know," he said, alluding to his Washington experience, "if I had been asked to hand on any important information to Alger Hiss, who was my superior in the wartime chain of command, I'd have done so without hesitation. That's what staggers me. It's hard to believe that anyone as high in the government could have betrayed the country."

In exhibiting this strong will-to-disbelieve in the matter of the Hiss jury verdict, my friend was not acting as an aberrant individual. He was simply acting as an American. Americans don't like to think badly of people. It is an endearing characteristic.

Historians and journalists, however, cannot be judged by the endearing qualities of their souls. They are the "clerks" in whose hands we place the determination of truth, no matter how harsh it is. If they can't be relied upon to get to the bottom of things no matter whom it hurts, then we are indeed bereft of the moral clarification necessary to leadership.

The fact remains that the journalists who have commented most widely on the Hiss case have shown an almost universal tendency to run away from the evidence. The Baltimore *Sun,* for example, didn't want to believe the Hiss verdict because Alger Hiss was a "Baltimorean of such distinguished attainments and of such high promise that, however indirectly, the self-esteem of the community is somehow affected by his downfall." Marquis Childs, the columnist, didn't want to believe it because, as he said, "it is a reminder of a time that many would prefer to forget . . . a time when doubt and mistrust had eaten deeply into the American faith in America." *The Christian Science Monitor* didn't want to believe it because it couldn't reconcile the evidence the jury accepted with "Mr. Hiss's record of apparent devotion to his country." The Washington *Post* didn't want to believe it because it was a belated vindication of the House Un-American Activities Committee.

With such commentary spread out on the breakfast tables of middle-class America, it is small wonder that people are confused about the inroads which Communist infiltration tactics have made. "How," asks a businessman who has read the editorials, "how could a man of Mr. Hiss's background and education become a Communist?" To convince this man of the possibility, I found I had to go back a long way. Going back involved bringing up a lot of things about that time which Marquis Childs has said "many would prefer to forget." It involved, in particular, bringing up what might be called the inner history of New York City opinion-making, which has such an effect on book and magazine publishing in general. The businessman was interested. But he wanted concrete cases.

Well, what is a concrete case when you are referring to an almost impalpable pressure? Communists don't go around showing their party cards. Nevertheless, their work is as obvious to the initiated as the track of a mole across a well-tended lawn. You don't have to see the mole to know where he has been. . . .

This sort of pressure, organized in a hundred ways varying from subtle to crude, got its effects at the source of opinion-making. Readers in publishing houses, badgered by the fellow-traveling element, exercised birth control on manuscripts. Timid editors gave collectivist books to collectivist reviewers. The idea-atmosphere of New York, poisoned at the source, infected the colleges. It certainly infected a segment of New Deal Washington. It did not follow that all Communists became traitors. But they were *prepared by their ideology to become such if necessary.*

JUST WHAT effect did the idea-atmosphere have on Alger Hiss? One can only guess at that. But the point I wanted to make for my businessman friend was that many people in exactly Mr. Hiss's circumstances were "had" by the Communist manipulation of New York City opinion-making enterprises. . . . My friend the businessman was still mystified by the fact that middle-class intellectuals, graduates of good American universities, could have fallen for the collectivist line.

But why? why? persisted the businessman. The answer may possibly be found in the works of Freud which deal with the revolt of the sons against the fathers; or it may be found in the books of Europeans about the "circulation of the élite" and the "declassed intellectual." The psychopathology of the phenomenon needs further study, but the fact remains. And nobody should be surprised by the law school graduate of genteel background who becomes a Communist. The real surprise is that an occasional proletarian becomes a Communist.

I labor these points in connection with the Hiss verdict because they should be ABC to a journalist of Marquis Childs' understanding and sophistication. . . . Why, then, should he be surprised by the verdict in the Hiss case? Why should he be so fearful of talking about it?

Again, it comes down to that endearing characteristic of Americans. They are willing to believe that infiltration and intellectual double-dealing leading to treason are part of the pattern of European politics. But they hate to admit that "it can happen here." One can love them for feeling that way about their own country. But "it has happened here," and anyone who cut his intellectual eye teeth in New York opinion-making circles in the 1930's knows all about it. It is time that everybody else knew about it, too.

April 1950

BOOK 5

IN THE LAND OF GULAG

"Gulag"—Slavery, Inc.

By Isaac Don Levine

[The term "Gulag" was introduced into the vocabularies of every major nationality on earth by Aleksandr Solzhenitsyn with the publication, early in 1973, of his celebrated Gulag Archipelago. *Twenty-six years before its linguistic debut,* Plain Talk, *in its issue of May 1947, ran this account by its editor under the caption " 'Gulag'—Slavery Inc." Accompanying it was an even more significant item, a unique map that documented and illustrated the meaning of "Archipelago" in relation to "Gulag." All over the map, all the way from Finland to Kamchatka, hundreds of small and large circles depicted, as if they were that many islands, individual concentration camps as well as scores of sprawling constellations of prison labor colonies. The concrete data for the compilation of the map came from Soviet official identity papers issued to Polish prisoners, who called them passports, upon their discharge from the penal camps late in 1941. General W. Anders was then taken out of jail by Stalin and permitted to organize the Polish Army that achieved glory in the Battle of Monte Cassino. Fourteen thousand of these original "passports," bearing Soviet seals and signatures, repose in the archives of the Hoover Institution at Stanford University.]*

GULAG—THE SOVIET SLAVE LABOR TRUST—is an abbreviation of *Glavnoye Upravlenye Lagerei*, or Office of Penal Labor Camps, a department of the MVD, the Ministry of the Interior (formerly known as the NKVD—Russian equivalent of the Gestapo).

There are over 14 million forced laborers in GULAG, scattered through scores of penal colonies, each a Devil's Island at its worst, living in unspeakable wretchedness, on the edge of death by starvation and disease, and slaving twelve hours a day under arbitrary taskmasters.

The existence of this state monopoly in expendable human flesh has been known for many years and recognized as a chief source of revenue for the Communist regime. As far back as 1930, the U.S. Treasury clamped an embargo on Soviet pulpwood and matches as products of "forced labor." But for the first time, *incontrovertible proof* of the GULAG system and its vast ramifications has been brought out of Russia.

235

The dotted circles represent forced labor colonies, each a sprawling area comprisi
constellation of concentration camps under a separate administration.

- Reproduced here in black-and-white, and cut to one-third of its size, is the centerp
  of the PLAIN TALK DOCU-MAP and photographs of emaciated GULAG children.
- The original is in color, measures 17x22 inches, is printed on special paper,
  includes documentary evidence in the form of photostats of prisoners' identity pa

SLAVE CAMPS IN U.S.S.R.

ADMINISTRATIVE AREAS

ringed dots denote individual concentration camps operated by municipalities under
ontrol of local NKVD authorities.

e Docu-Map, with its complete explanatory text, is one of the most remarkable com-
lations of our day, and affords a graphic insight into what has been until now the
ost carefully guarded secret of current life in Soviet Russia.

During the period of the Stalin-Hitler Pact, about 1.6 million Poles—men, women and children—were deported by the Soviet authorities to GULAG colonies in the Farth North and in Siberia. On August 12, 1941, as a result of the Polish-Soviet Agreement, an amnesty was granted to the Polish internees in Russia. 114,000 of these released Poles eventually reached Iran, forming the backbone of the Polish Army which fought gloriously in Italy.

Nearly 14,000 affidavits, plus other documentary evidence and crude maps made by ex-inmates of Soviet prisons and concentration camps, served as the basis of this Docu-Map. All of these came from the liberated inmates, many of whom supplemented their affidavits with detailed statements of their experiences as Soviet captives.

ON THE BASIS OF THE MASS of documentary evidence gathered from the amnestied deportees, it has been established that the average mortality rate in GULAG exceeds 12 percent a year. In other words, every eight years its total population perishes. It is, of course being constantly replenished, so that Slavery, Inc. is never short of manpower—Russia's cheapest commodity.

GULAG's human reservoir is a cross-section of Soviet society. It ranges from recalcitrant peasants and workers to Red Army generals in disgrace, and includes the intellectual classes and the industrial bureaucracy. Grimly ironic is the fact that GULAG has been the final home for thousands of Communist expatriates who took refuge in the land of their dreams only to end up in slave labor columns.

Since the end of the war, some two million Japanese war prisoners, about one million German war prisoners, and not less than two million repatriated Russian war prisoners, treated as deserters with whom they are lumped, have been added to GULAG's rolls. Most of the Japanese prisoners are engaged in a great project, secretly building railroads through northeastern Siberia, not indicated in the Docu-Map.

The boundaries of the slave labor regions have been drawn here with a view to understatement. All the territory controlled by GULAG, if consolidated, would make a submerged empire exceeding in area the boundaries of Western Europe.

THE FOLLOWING LIST DETAILS the types of industries operated by GULAG—the Penal Labor Trust of the Soviet Government. Although complete on the basis of available documentary evidence, the forty-odd colonies shown here do not exhaust all the geographic divisions of GULAG known to exist in the Soviet Union today.

- **Sorokski**—Light metal mines; construction of railways, tunnels, canals, electric works, and airfields; brickworks; quarries, timber camps, and fisheries.
- **Severo-Nickel,** south of Murmansk: aluminum, nickel, copper, lead, and

zinc mines. **Belomor-Baltiski,** construction and maintenance of the White Sea-Baltic Canal.

● **Solovki, Onega, Kargopol, Sev-Dvina, Kuloyski, Vytegra, Ust-Vym, Unzha**—Timber and paper industry; railway and canal construction; quarries and brickworks; farming; settlement building; construction of airfields; road making.

● **Northern Railway Camps**—Construction and maintenance of railroad from Dvina River to the Arctic.

● **Volgastroy, Ukhta, Pechora, Vorkutstroy, Vyatka**—Construction and maintenance of the Volga-Baltic Canal; power stations and railways; petroleum, cement, and pig iron works; coal and asphalt mines; heavy water (A-bomb) project; road building; timber and farming; brickworks and quarries; construction of airfields.

● **Ussolski, Bezymyanski-Samara, Osobstroy, Temnikovski, Yuj-Kavkaz**—War industries; construction of underground airfields and fortifications; dyke and road building; women's labor camps; manufacture of wood products; timber and farming; quarries and brickworks; railway construction.

● **Ivdel, Sverdlovsk and Northern Urals, Narym, Tobolsk, Norylsk, Camps of Complete Isolation**—Iron, coal, and precious metal mines; airplane factories; airfield construction; metallurgical industry; railway and road construction; timber and farming; quarries and brickworks.

● **Karaganda, Sibirski (including Tomasin), Krasnoyarski, Uj-Sibirski**—Coal, iron, and light metal mines; construction of factories and settlements; textile industries and tanneries; distilleries; quarries and brickworks; farming and timber; railway and road construction.

● **Yakutsk, Sev-Vostochni (Magadan-Kolyma), Chukotski, Kamchatka**—Gold, platinum, and lead mines; road and airfield construction; timber industry; quarries; fisheries and canneries.

● **Burenski, Dalne-Vostochni, Nijni-Amur, Sakhalin**—Harbor works; railway and road construction; fortifications and airfields; military installations.

● **Novaya Zemlya**—Coal mines and fisheries in the most isolated area in Soviet Russia, an island in the Arctic Circle.

A NUMBER OF NEW PROJECTS are known to have been launched by GULAG since the end of the war. These are being carried on with prison labor in newly established penal colonies, the locations of which have not been verified by documentary evidence from Soviet sources. For this reason we have omitted them from the Docu-Map. It usually takes some years to authenticate the existence of a slave labor area behind the triple iron curtain shielding GULAG operations.

I Dwelt with Death

By Andrey A. Stotski

Translated by Ann Su Cardwell

[*As a condensation of the encyclopedic revelations of life under the Soviet regime, this soul-stirring account is unrivaled. It offers a microcosmic insight into the hell of Gulag by one of its first survivors to reach England after the war, Andrey A. Stotski, a graduate of the School of Foreign Commerce at the University of Lwow. He was seized there by the Russian NKVD in March 1940 after the Soviet-Nazi partition of Poland and shipped off to a penal camp on the remote Arctic island of Novaya Zemlya, almost in the vicinity of the North Pole. His narrative, translated by Ann Su Cardwell, was serialized in* Plain Talk *in four issues, from May to August 1949, and left a powerful impression upon its readers.*]

I

THE DAY IS AT ITS CLOSE. A silence that is maddening reigns in my cell and in the corridor. I wait, certain that six armed guards and their officer will appear for me, as they have appeared for others. Each rifle will have one bullet—for me. I am unable to think of anything except death. I try to pray, but I cannot. The words of my prayers are confused, for all I can think of is that death is near.

The door creaks on its hinges, then opens wide, and armed soldiers enter. Following them is a tall slender young fellow—their commander. I know what they are—the execution squad. The young chap orders me out into the corridor. No, I need not take my belongings. I look around the dark little stone cell for the last time and am moved by a queer feeling that I am leaving a place grown dear to me. I am glad that I wear long trousers, so that the disgraceful trembling of my legs escapes notice. The squad separates into two sets of threes, and with me between them we pass into the corridor. The strong electric light blinds me. We reach the door leading outside and get into a van, before which stands Biekman, who had been the prosecutor in my case. Is it possible that he has come to bid me good bye?

He came towards me, his eyes unnaturally bright.

"This is your last chance to save yourself," he began. "Only tell us where your associates are hiding, give us their names and everything will be all right for you. You know where those men are."

"You also know," I replied. "At least so you said at the beginning of your examination of me."

"You're no fool"—and his voice was sharp. "You know we don't know. If we did we wouldn't have asked you."

"Well, if their life and liberty depends upon me," I answered, "they will continue to be free. And that is my final word on that subject."

Biekman made an angry grimace and growled:

"You devil! I'd like to shoot you like a dog!"

"And what else do you propose to do, since you are taking me to execution?"

"None of your funny business! You know where you're going."

"How would I know? I've spent the entire time in my cell. Then the execution squad comes for me—and certainly not just to take me out for a stroll."

"But you wrote that request for clemency to Stalin?" Biekman's voice registered surprise.

"No. I didn't write a request and I didn't sign the one prepared and brought to me."

"Impossible! Look here." And he took from his pocket a sheet of paper I recognized. In the dotted lines was all the data that had been taken down during my examination. Underneath was what was supposed to be my signature, in clumsy script bearing no resemblance to mine.

"Citizen Biekman," I said, "you are well acquainted with my signature. Tell me, is this in any respect like it?"

"N-no. But I thought your hand probably was shaky. I don't understand what this means . . ."

"Well, I do. If a citizen of Poland signs a document of this kind, by that act he acknowledges the justice of the sentence passed on him, so he accepts Soviet citizenship, and legalizes the 'plebiscite' carried out on our territories. Now you ought to understand why I wouldn't sign such a request, and why somebody falsified my signature. You know it wasn't done to save me."

Biekman stood and stared at me. Suddenly he appeared to have an idea. He looked at me with an air of understanding, though he spoke jeeringly.

"You are a clever fellow, Andrey Adolfovich. A patriot—a Polish patriot . . ."

Then he lowered his voice and leaning towards me, so that he was almost speaking into my ear:

"Andrey Adolfovich, remember that I never struck you, that I never wished you harm . . ."

"Yes—but your men took me and beat me."

"You know what the NKVD orders are. And if I hadn't executed them, I myself would have been stood against a wall."

"Better not talk too much, citizen. You might bring on trouble for yourself," I ventured.

"I'm not afraid of talking to a Pole. You didn't betray your friends. You won't betray me." And he looked me straight in the eye.

"I'll tell you something, Biekman, later. If you really are a man, grant this favor. Give me your word that tomorrow you will take me to your room—if I'm alive tomorrow."

"You will be, and I'll take you to my room at 4 tomorrow afternoon. We'll talk as long as you like. Goodbye."

During this conversation the "squad" had stood at a respectful distance. It is not allowed to listen to a prosecutor's talk with prisoners.

Again I was back within my four stone walls. The sound of the closing door made me aware that I was alone. I lay down on the bunk and my body began to tremble like so much jelly. Tears streamed down my face. I was alive! I touched my body in various places and each time it responded to my touch. My nervous system was functioning. I looked about the cell and could see. I sniffed, and my nostrils recognized the mouldy cellar air. I was alive!

When I endeavored to think of my family, their faces swam before my eyes like strange moving pictures. My wife had the figure of my mother. My mother was dressed in the youthful garments of my wife, the face was not that of my mother, yet somehow I knew this was my mother.

And I tried to pray, to return thanks that my life had been spared. But what a strange prayer. A hundred times I repeated but the one word God, and nothing more. I could not find another word. I comforted myself with the feeling that God understands. And finally I knew what I wanted to say:

"I thank Thee, God."

BIEKMAN KEPT HIS WORD, and sent for me that afternoon. We climbed the stairs, familiar to me from my visits to the "examiner," and entered the familiar room. On those occasions I had never experienced fear. But today my legs were unsteady, for I felt that here was a meeting where I, the pupil, would represent the West, while my teacher would represent the East. He had probably given his life to the study of his materialistic dialectics, of which I knew nothing at all. My only weapon was Soviet practice today in Poland.

Biekman received me exceedingly politely. On the table were cigaerttes and candy. For me, my host said. I sat down opposite him and lighted a cigarette, thinking I hadn't smoked for a long time.

It was I who spoke first.

"Have you finished your investigation of me?"

Biekman nodded.

"How am I to understand this conversation? Is it to be a free discussion on the part of each of us or will you attempt to convince me without giving me a chance to defend my position?"

"We'll begin," he answered, "with your telling me about your life before the war, about your cities and villages, and your industries and trade. About the life of the peasants and the working people, and your schools and your recreation. Then I'll give you an account of the same things in the Soviet Union."

So I began. I told him all I knew, not hiding the blemishes and faults. It was so easy to do when it was a matter of comparison. Toward the end of my "presentation" I talked about Polish laws and institutions protecting the peasants and working class. Biekman listened intently. I gave statistics showing the average worker's pay in comparison with prices of articles of everyday necessity. I told him what percent of the average worker's pay went for food, for shelter, for clothing, for entertainment.

"That's not true!" he interrupted.

I stiffened, and asked him whether he intended to believe me or not, for if he did not, there was no use in going on. We might as well return to the status of judge and prisoner.

Confused, Biekman explained:

"They told us quite different things, Andrey Adolfovich. They said that poverty was universal in Poland, and that there was a terrible gulf between the bourgeoisie and the proletariat."

I continued with illustrations from other spheres of Polish life, and it was evident that what I said was making an impression, though my listener kept shaking his head and repeating:

"Impossible! Impossible."

A soldier came in with a tray, on which to my surprise I saw two covers, one of which Biekman placed before me, politely inviting me to eat. The sight of good food, so long outside my ken, made me realize how removed I had been from civilization. I looked at my miserable clothes. I was ragged, dirty, lousy, and unshaven. My host, noticing my embarrassment, suggested that I might like to wash. The pleasure I had in washing in a real wash basin and using real toilet soap! God, what pleasure! And when I sat down to eat, there was a plate in front of me, in my left hand I had a fork and in my right an authentic table knife. No one who has not sat in a Soviet prison can understand the joy of using these simple things.

After the meal, which was excellent, Biekman began to tell me about the Soviet Union. Manifestly he was endeavoring to be objective, speaking carefully and using no propaganda slogans. He admitted that there is poverty in his country but tried to minimize it and excuse it. Of Moscow only did he talk enthusiastically, describing its beautiful subway and luxurious public buildings. He spoke at length of Soviet industry, its development and Americanization, said the government was making great efforts to improve agriculture, but that not all the peasants are persuaded of the value of common ownership. Of course, there are imperfections in the country's economic system. The worker on a collective farm suffers hunger, no matter how much he produces. And this makes him unwilling to work. Neither is the working man satisfied, for prices make what he needs beyond his reach. But these things, Biekman argued, are not important. The only thing that matters is the moral side of this gigantic performance. The goal is the happiness and welfare of future generations, and to reach that goal it is necessary to destroy more than one good past achievement. Likewise, people who stand in the way must be destroyed.

I asked him about the development of Communism as he foresaw it, whether it was an experiment that would be confined to the Soviet Union or whether it was to take in the entire world.

"Naturally, it must conquer the world," he replied. "All of it, with no exceptions. Two reasons. First, because only the whole world can be an autarchy. Second, any country that remains outside would be a menace to the entire Union."

I pretended astonishment.

"How can that be? Let us suppose that South Africa is the only state outside the Soviet Union. How could a weak state like that be a menace to the powerful U.S.S.R.?"

"Militarily it couldn't. But I have in mind the moral propaganda strength of such a country."

"Therefore, in your opinion, the so-called capitalist countries do possess a certain moral power?"

"Of course. That strength lies in liberty, in the freedom of political thinking and religion, in every man's freedom to think and believe what he pleases."

"Then on what do you base your belief that the Soviet form of government will achieve full happiness for man sooner than the normal, freely developing capitalistic forms of government?"

"On my deep faith in it," was his answer.

Thus the conversation continued, politely but frankly, until Biekman admitted:

"I don't know which of us is right. Time will tell."

I thanked him and rose.

"You have greatly helped your Polish friends," remarked Biekman. "Now I know that I am not dealing with personal enemies, nor with bandits and thieves, but with the inhabitants of another planet."

"You are right. You also are from another planet, yet only a weak boundary line separates, or rather, did separate us."

"No, Andrey Adolfovich. You should not have corrected yourself. That boundary continues to separate us."

THE NEXT MORNING strange wardens roused me. I was to pack my things and go with them. "Pack" meant put on my coat, put my few valuables—a piece of soap I had managed to steal, a bit of string and five cigarettes which the generous Biekman had given me—in my pocket, and take my extra shirt and my towel in my hand.

I was conducted to a prison van waiting in the dark little inside courtyard. The doors were slammed and locked, the car moved off quickly. After a ride of some fifteen minutes the van stopped. Ordered out, we prisoners jumped to the ground and gazed curiously at each other. A very fat officer approached our little group.

"What transport is this?" he asked our guard.

"A transport of men from Prison No. 39 whose death sentences have been commuted," obediently answered the guard.

The officer curled his lip contemptuously, ordered us to stand in line and began to look us over. Certain of us he ordered to show our hands and flex our muscles. Judging from his expression he was not much pleased. After he had examined the last prisoner in line, he stepped off to one side, lighted a cigarette and uttered one word:

"Carrion!"

We were in Prison No. 4, on Jachowicz Street in Lwow. It was much better equipped than our previous abode. We read that our cell had been designed to hold 9 persons. Not bad, we remarked, after we had counted and found we were 81—only 9 times the maximum when it was Polish.

The cell was well supplied with barred and screened windows, and was light. There were no bunks. We worked out a sleeping plan by dividing the group into 4 and lying down in 4 ranks on spaces marked off by string.

The worst feature of life in this prison was that we had no word from our families. Not until the end of October 1940 were we given small pieces of paper, loaned ends of pencils—the length of each accurately noted, so that we could not cut off a bit and hide it—and permitted to write. I wrote to my wife, of whom I had rejoiced to get news from a recently arrived prisoner, a policeman, who had protected and befriended her on one occasion while she waited in a bread line. The policeman also wrote, sending his card to my wife's address. We were allowed to say that we were well or not well, to give a word of greeting, and to ask for underwear, tobacco, sugar, and onions. Nothing else. Reluctantly I wrote the word "money" under one of the words in my message, hoping it would thus escape the eye of the prison authorities.

Ten days later my policeman friend and I got our first packages. Everything we had asked for was there, and in addition my wife sent me 50 roubles. On one of the rouble notes, written in script so small it attracted no attention, was a message from my beloved, telling me not to despair, that she was well, working, earning a living, and "to be of good courage and wait."

Despite our isolation we got some news from outside—through messages and from newly arrived prisoners. We learned of the heroic defense of Britain and of how it beat off the air attacks. We hoped for and actually awaited the sound of planes and the bursting of bombs over our prison—a sound that would be the harbinger of our own and our country's liberation. But the Bolsheviks were as sure of themselves, as deep in their idyll with Hitler as ever.

A year passed. Another 13th of March (1941), the anniversary of my arrest, was with us. The morning sun was melting the icicles on the iron bars of our prison windows. We sat as usual, variously occupying ourselves with—nothing, when the door was opened and one of the wardens stepped into the cell. In his hand he held a sheet of paper. He called for attention, lifted the paper and read off five names, among them mine. When he had finished, he ordered:

"Get your things together!"

The door opened again and we were ordered into the corridor. There were 43 of us now, strangers to each other, in the dark cell to which we were assigned.

The head warden, accompanied by his assistant, several NKD men in uniform, and a civilian entered. No longer were we in doubt about what was going to happen. We were to learn our sentences. Would there be a trial?

"No, there won't be a trial," said an elderly individual. "They'll just hand out sentences. They call it *Osoboye Sovieshchanie* (Special Board)."

We were ranged in a line in front of a little door opposite the one by which we had entered. Very soon the door opened, an overseer appeared, and ordered the first man in the line to come in. In a few minutes this prisoner reappeared, a pink card clutched in his hand. He passed along the line, his face more ashen than usual, whispering:

"Eight years—eight years—eight years."

Others went in and came out with pink, blue or green cards. A blue card meant 5 years, a green 3. At last it was my turn. I went in. Behind the desk sat that little civilian who had been with the warden—the prosecutor. In appearance he was young and his face was intelligent. A score or more of the cards lay in front of him. On a corner of the desk lay a big ugly *nagan* (revolver). He looked at me and asked curtly.

"Your surname, given name, and your father's name?"

"Andrey Adolfovich Stotski."

"Your sentence—8 years DTL."

My card was neither pink, blue, nor green, but brown. I did not understand why this exceptional treatment, so I asked the prosecutor.

"All the other cards," he answered, "indicate sentences to ITL (Correctional Labor Camp), but you go to one of the DTL—Distant Hard Labor Camps."

And he rose from his chair and from a paper in his hand read me my sentence:

"You have been sentenced, Andrey Adolfovich Stotski, to 8 years in a distant hard labor camp. You are thus given the opportunity to wipe out your crimes by your labor and by living according to Soviet laws. You are privileged to write to your family once each month. You may also have a visit from some member of your family once a month. In your first letter you may list what you need and may then receive such articles. But all metal objects and all things having to do with a religious cult are forbidden. Try to provide yourself with warm underwear and clothing. That is all I have to say."

I was one of four who had got brown cards, the others being Adamczyk, a bank clerk from Bialystok, and two Ukrainians. All of us had been beaten dur-

246

ing our investigations those first months in prison, all of us had refused to give information. All of us had been condemned to die and later reprieved.

ADAMCZYK CAME AND SAT DOWN near me. He was exceedingly depressed and for a few minutes we sat in silence.

"I wanted to ask you," he began—"Do you know how to write?"

"Of course," I replied in some surprise. "Did you take me for an illiterate?"

"You know well enough what I mean. You have told us interesting tales. Can you write as well?"

"I've never tried."

"Then promise me you will write the story of all we've lived through. I can't, for I am convinced I'll never live to get out of this hell."

"You idiot!" I endeavored to brace him up. "That's no mood in which to face the test. Head up! You must keep two objectives in mind—to live through it and to return."

"I have nobody to return to. My wife and two children were killed in church by a Soviet bomb. My 80-year old mother was deported to Siberia—a 'capitalist parasite.' My sister, a teacher in Sopockinie, was raped by several scores of Bolsheviks, one after another, and went stark mad. Her husband, who attempted to protect her, was bound and compelled helplessly to look on, then had his body ripped open by Soviet bayonets. I have nobody to return to."

I had no reply. Under such conditions I would not want to return either. I could not. And I was suddenly stricken with terror, remembering that I, too, had a wife and mother and sister. All I could say was that in me he had a friend who would like henceforth to be his brother.

At this moment two groups of guards came in, one our regular prison guards, the other consisting of some 20 Mongolians armed from head to foot. Two desks were carried in and two chairs, and the officer with each group sat down. We were lined up along the wall, and ordered to stand quietly. Our group of prison guards began to search us.

While this was in progress, but before my turn for examination had come, the "package" warden came in.

"Stotski, a package from your wife," he said to me in a low voice. He took me to a side room, with nothing in sight but a great stuffed sack in a corner.

"There's your package," he said.

On closer view I recognized it as a big sack we had used for various purposes at home. It now contained what was for one in my circumstances a veritable fortune. There were suits of underwear, sweaters and gloves, sugar and fats. What vast effort, ingenuity, and money my wife and mother must have expended to obtain all these things so necessary to me!

"Your wife is a beautiful woman, very beautiful," the warden casually remarked. His speech froze every muscle in my body. Had she been too beautiful?

"No need to worry," he assured me. "You care a great deal for her?"

"A very great deal."

"Then I'll tell you something else. Tomorrow afternoon you will see her. She's to come at 3 o'clock."

I went through my examination. When all of us had been transferred to the other side of the cell, the commander of the convoy guards called out:

"Get the trucks ready for 4 o'clock. Two will hold the lot. I'll be back here at two-thirty."

All the officials and guards went out, leaving us prisoners alone. Nobody felt like talking.

The next day I was elated that I was to see my wife, yet at the same time distressed that she should see me in such a wretched state. I was dirty, unkempt, unshaven, ragged. Quickly I changed my tattered old pants for a fresh pair from the bag, and put on one of the sweaters. Adamczyk, no less excited than I, made a comb of his fingers and tried to put my hair in order. One of the prisoners had a basin and had got some water, in which he permitted me to wash my face and hands. I dampened my hair and slicked it down.

Adamczyk took me to a spot under the grated window where it was a little brighter and looking me over critically declared I didn't look bad at all, in fact I made a fine appearance. I knew very well that he was lying but I wanted so to believe him. I was dripping with perspiration so excited was I, and talked constantly like one in a fever.

ADAMCZYK COACHED me on what I was to say. That of course I was strong and well, that we would be able to write to each other, that they would soon free me, since I was innocent. I was not to mention our deportation. I was to be composed, smiling, unworried, confident that my family would be safe and that the future would be better for all of us. Word for word I repeated it all after him like a lesson difficult to learn because it is not understood. My head was in a whirl, my thinking chaotic. I was to see my wife after a year of absolute isolation, knowing too that during the next eight years I would neither see her nor hear from her nor anything about her.

The commanders and the guards returned, which meant that it was the hour of two-thirty and that in half an hour . . .

The door creaked, and I knew before it opened and the "package" warden appeared that my wife had come. I jumped to my feet without waiting an order. The warden spoke to the men at the desk, they nodded, one of them looked at me and said:

"Your wife is here to see you."

"Yes," said his companion, "but you have been examined and transferred. Your papers have been given to the convoy commander. You will have to see him . . ."

I turned to the convoy commander, who stood looking at me with his laughing, slant black eyes.

"The sight of your wife would give you pleasure? Of course it would—Then you shall not see her."

As calmly as I could I said:

"According to Soviet law that is my right."

"All of you here are outside the law. The law is for people like me."

Again as quietly as I could I said:

"But that law was made especially for prisoners. The prosecutor read it to each of us."

"You are talking nonsense," he snapped. "Anyhow, if what you say were so, it would concern only persons in prison. You are part of a transport. And you know what the transport regulations are? During transport a prisoner has no rights. Any guard may shoot him if he likes, and I won't punish him. On the contrary, I'll praise him."

I moved slowly back to my place, helpless, hopeless, suddenly an old man.

ABOUT 7 O'COCK WE WERE herded into the square about which the prison was built and with our belongings loaded into the two trucks waiting there. We sat cross-legged in rows on the floor, our heads level with the sides of the car. Our things were thrown in after us, landing on heads or backs or knees. There was not the faintest chance of escape, no possibility even of changing position. The truck's sides bristled with guards. We passed through the streets of Lwow— streets absolutely empty. We were taken to the freight station.

The guards jumped down from the sides of the truck. We heard the baying of dogs—and knew what that meant. We climbed out, each clinging desperately to his belongings. Shouting and yelling, the guards got us in ranks of fours, facing a train that in length surpassed any our imagination had pictured, for there was no end to it, neither front nor rear, as far as we could see. All the cars were box cars and from the roof of each protruded a long stovepipe.

We shivered with cold. We waited—and waited, for what, of course, we did not know. After a while we heard the mingled clamor of people's voices and dogs' baying, and cautiously looking around saw that another transport of human freight had arrived. They were drawn up in fours just as we were, in groups of forty each. A throng of Bolsheviks moved about among us. Some led dogs on long leashes, others carried drawn revolvers. There was considerable commotion and from the group of prisoners standing next us we learned that a bold fellow had dared to light a cigarette and that a dog which had been set on him, had obediently done its work.

The prisoner lay moaning, torn and bleeding on the ground. By this time it was too dark to see well, so we could not tell how seriously the fellow had suffered, but two steps away stood a huge snarling dog. Then a startling thing happened. The injured man rose and threw himself upon the beast, the poor crazed human hanging upon the throat of the powerful animal. The guards at once became highly interested spectators, for the moment forgetting their duty to keep watch on us. They urged on first the dog and then the man and for a brief time the issue did seem doubtful. The prisoner was literally fighting with teeth and claws, for such his bloody hands had become. The dog was weakening. We prisoners, witnessing the gruesome battle in which our representative was vanquishing our opponent, were as if hypnotized. But our triumph was short-lived. The dog's master thought the time had come to intervene. A shot rang out, and the man fell.

II

WE WERE ORDERED to move to the train. Our car reminded us of an old cracked pot. When our eyes became accustomed to the darkness of the interior, we saw a tiny iron stove at either end of the car, and tiers of shelves made of rough, fresh lumber. Behind the stove was a long, narrow metal drain with sharp edges. It has been installed, as a guard later explained, out of respect for "culture," that we might not have to "go into a corner."

It was terribly cold in the car, and there was not a lump of coal nor a piece of wood with which to make a fire. During the two days and nights the train stood in the Lwow yards, we were given nothing to eat or drink. This was a regular Soviet procedure, intended to break all spirit of opposition in the prisoners.

Then began our ten-days' journey into the unknown. Our food consisted of salt herring, sometimes with a sort of gruel. The fish tasted like gall. We scooped up one handful of water a day from a wooden bucket that was set inside the car for a quarter of an hour.

Out of 43 of us, seven belonged to a class called in Poland "intelligentsia," that is, the professional and upper middle class. Twenty-five were peasant farmers and artisans; they were much more hostile toward the Bolsheviks than were the intelligentsia. The third group consisted of eight Communists, who had been active party workers in prewar Poland. These were the most abject of all, for they were shut off from the Bolsheviks by the wall of the law, and from the rest of us by polite but icy indifference.

On the fifth day several of us developed cases of frostbite. The peasants tore down some of the boards from the shelf-bunks. Somebody dug up matches, and a fire was made. In the delightful warmth we took off our clothes and began that most humiliating of all occupations—searching for lice. Suddenly the train stopped in an open field. As quickly as we could we smothered the fire, but it was too late. The Bolsheviks must have noticed smoke issuing from the stove-pipe vent. The door slid along the grooves, and up stepped several armed Mongolians.

"What were you burning in the stove?"

"Boards from the shelves."

The leader ordered us outside, just as we were—stripped to our underwear.

There we were stood in two rows and commanded to fall face down in the snow. Meanwhile the dogs had been unleashed. We knew that if we moved the dogs would tear us to pieces.

They kept us in this position in the snow for almost a whole hour. One or two tried to make a concealed movement, and had their throats and the backs of the necks torn by the dogs. At the end of the hour the leader of the convoy guard ordered us to get up. Five lay still, too nearly frozen to heed him. The rest of us were ordered to carry them into the car.

Closing the door, the leader said: "Now I guess you'll be warmer."

We went to work to revive our comrades, but were successful with only two. Three had frozen to death. We placed the frozen human clods on the cracks between the boards of the floor, and thus, by protecting us from the cold drafts, even after death our companions helped us.

Next morning the train stopped on the barren steppe. The corpses were thrown out upon the snow, and at the same time we noticed bodies being flung from other cars.

That evening a Ukrainian boy had an attack of hysteria, laughing and crying in turn, and calling for his mother. We asked him how old he was.

"Fifteen."

"Why were you sentenced?"

"Treason," he said proudly.

The Bolshevik commissar had asked him in school if he loved the Soviet Union. He had replied that he could not, since his innocent sister and brother had been arrested and his sister had "died" during the investigation. His own arrest followed, then his sentence as a traitor.

That night the train pulled into a great city station. We were ordered out of the car, packed into trucks, and driven through the deserted streets. The truck halted before the great barred gates of what looked like a former palace. Above the gate, on an ostentatious plaster scroll, was a crude inscription in cyrillic letters: The Kharkov Prison for Transients. We were in the capital of the Ukraine.

Our cell was certainly not meant to hold more than ten persons. More than 130 had been packed into it. The "toilets" were merely drains in the floor above which to squat, man close against man. Animals would have been ashamed. The writing on the walls read like a hotel register. It was curious that under each Polish name was written an officer's rank. I remember seeing the names of Lieutenant Gorski, Captain Gustaw Zawadski, Lieutenant Nowosad and Major Stepien. In very small script under some of the names was "sl. st." or "regular army." Army men should not have been in a civilian prison.

One day something that two years before might have been called pickled fish but was now a putrid mass, was pushed through the doors. Conflicting instincts warred in me. One urged me to eat, no matter what the food. The other warned against poisoning myself. But the first won. I swallowed the rotting food.

In the evening I was paying for my folly with bloody dysentery. I became so weak that I could not get to one of the drains and I lay in the mess of blood and water excreta. Then I heard Serge, a good-natured Cossack prisoner, shouting and kicking the door with all his might. He told the entire cell of my trouble, and soon all were shouting for help. It got results. A frightened woman in a white hospital coat appeared.

I soon found myself in the prison hospital. They gave me a hot bath. I got out of the tub red as a lobster, but clean!

Next morning the nurse took me to see the prison doctor. His Russian was worse than mine; he must be from one of the smaller republics—perhaps Georgia—I thought. To his inquiry I replied that I felt better, but not stronger. In fact, I felt as if I were slowly disintegrating.

"Why?"

I decided to tell him my whole story. And when I had concluded, he spoke—in Polish!

"To whom do you think you are talking?" he asked. "To a prisoner like yourself. I am a Pole. My name is Pancer. I'll do everything I can to help you, but it won't be much. However, I'll try to keep you in the hospital as long as I'm doctor here. Your 'nurse' is a Pole, and when you're sure you're not overheard, you may speak Polish. There are two Poles among the patients we have here."

A handclasp, a long, understanding look, and I crept back to my bed and slept like a rock.

NOT ONLY THE Polish doctor, but all the Soviet doctors, orderlies, and nurses were devoted, diligent, and kind. They gave us hospital diet.

Here in the hospital, I became acquainted with young people from the Soviet intelligentsia. Most of the patients belonged to that class.

One Russian patient, who had killed her husband and child, was the only person there who had been sentenced for what would have been a crime in other countries. I had quite a conversation with this unusually attractive, even "sweet-faced" woman, during which I learned that she did not at all repent her crime, committed six years before she was sent to prison. She had done the murders in a pact with her lover, an official of the Ukrainian Republic. Only when the lover grew tired of her because she had become pregnant, did he have her arrested and sentenced.

"If I hadn't been such a fool, if I'd known better how to hold him, and hadn't got the idea that having a baby would be fine, I'd still be free," Vera concluded with conviction.

In the corner of my ward lay three youths arrested at the Aviation School in Moscow. They had been in training as aviators and commanders. One foolish step—some unconcealed dissatisfaction about unfair grades they had received—

and all three were under arrest. A whole array of charges read to them—then sentences of eight years at hard labor.

I went over to talk with them, introducing myself as a Pole. "Does imprisonment mean the end of your careers?" I asked.

"Not at all. Soviet prisons are a kind of school. They have this great advantage over bourgeois prisons—a prison sentence carries no stigma. Freed prisoners go back to their former lives and are just as much Soviet citizens as anybody else. There is no such thing as a 'mark of shame.' A Soviet Army officer returns to his former rank."

"And the NKVD forgets about them?" I asked.

"No, we can't say they do. For reasons of security they can't."

Our conversation ended with the three young men as certain that the Soviet Union was the most progressive country in the world as they had been when we began.

On April 10 there was considerable commotion in the hospital. A medical commission was making the rounds, reading the temperature charts, looking for able-bodied prisoners. I saw the nurse, with soundless lips, utter the one word "transport." I asked Dr. Prancer to find out the destination for me.

In an hour or so he came in hurriedly and beckoned to me to go into his office. There he told me that the transport was to consist largely of Poles, that there would be no Russian criminals in the lot, and that they were to go to the west of the Urals. The next transports were assigned to the gold mines in the Kolyma area.

I thought it would be better for me to go with the first lot. Dr. Pancer agreed. He would have liked to have me stay on, but his own tenure was uncertain. There was one obstacle to my going. My sentence was for hard labor, and this was designated as light and moderately hard. Dr. Pancer suggested that he put my name in as a volunteer. Perhaps that way I could get in.

The next morning I joined my companions in the prison courtyard. By this time we were so accustomed to being loaded into trucks and onto freight cars, that we went through it automatically, paying scant attention to the shouted orders. Our car was relatively comfortable. There were a bucket of coal and scraps of wood beside the little iron stove. We were a congenial group—22 of us were Poles; 12 were boys in their late teens who were refugees from Carpathian Ruthenia; for seasoning we had one Russian, a thief by profession.

As the first week of our journey neared its end, those in charge informed us that we were to be taken to a bathhouse. We could not believe it until each of us was given a microscopic piece of soap, which smelled to heaven of dried herring.

Accompanied by guards and dogs, we left the car, taking with us, as ordered, all our possessions. All about us was an endless plain covered with unsmirched snow. One of the convoy commanders gave us marching directions, and we set off like a herd of animals with the guards behind us as drivers. After a long hour of stumbling through deep snow, we were halted, and one by one were half-pushed inside a typical Soviet prison. We were driven into the cells, and there the worst disillusionment of all awaited us. Water at least four inches deep covered the cement floor.

In silence we stood waiting, holding our poor rags, while the cold water seeped into our old shoes and chilled us to the bone. One of the Carpatho-Ruthenians endured it as long as he could, then wildly pounded on the stout door and threw his body against it. No sound came from the other side. We yelled like a crowd of demons.

A long while passed and then a Bolshevik appeared, chewing and bringing the odor of smoked sausage and garlic—to us the most enchanting fragrance in the world. "What's this about?" he growled.

One of our more restrained members, a former lawyer, Dr. Roszacki, explained that he was sure the authorities did not know that the floor was covered with water, that we had understood we were to wait for a bath, and that the "citizen commander" should put us in another cell. The Bolshevik, attemping to preserve an official tone, informed us that we were *standing* in the bath. The water was not heated because we had arrived unexpectedly. Besides, for such scoundrels as we, warm water was unnecessary. We must know, too, that lice do not like cold water. They die in it, and a few of us might die too, but nobody would weep over that.

In that "bathhouse" we spent five endlessly long days. Not all of us came out of it alive. Corpses had to be removed from all the cells, five from ours— Captain Dzierzynski of Warsaw; a man named Treszka, from Lwow; Dr. Cybulski, from Grodno; and two young Carpatho-Ruthenians.

AGAIN WE WERE on the road, this time going north. Sixteen days after we had departed from Kharkov, we left the car to begin our forced labor in Kozva, a distribution center.

Kozva is situated on a steep slope above the Pechora River. It belonged to the Vorkut group of mining and colonizing labor camps known in Russian as *Vorkut-stroy*. Near us were the railroad-building and timber-floating camps of the Pechora River. South of these stretched the camps of the forced laborers who were building a railroad to the north, hence their name, *Sievzheldorlag*, composed of the first syllable of four Russian words, meaning Northern Railway Camps.

What does a forced labor camp look like? The high palisades are topped with multiple strands of barbed wire. A prisoner who succeeded in escaping would be some 500 miles from human habitation. But every precaution is taken to prevent escape, for many a prisoner would choose death from hunger in the wilderness to hopeless years of slave existence at a subhuman level. At each of the four corners of the camp rise towers, 45 to 50 feet high, capped with a small guardroom, where an armed soldier with a marksman's rating is always on the alert. Outside the palisades are the barracks and tents where the guards and the free employees live. Inside, the prisoners live in barracks that are only half above ground—more like animals' dens than dwellings of men.

The few poor articles still possessed by the prisoners who were once inhabitants of a "bourgeois" country, had immense value here in the far north. With such articles a prisoner could buy food, *machorka* (a kind of coarse tobacco) and work more acceptable to him.

Through barter of this kind I was able to get an assignment to easier labor. I had held on to an old navy-blue serge suit, an object of wonder to all my Russian fellow-prisoners. A report of this extraordinary apparel reached the ears of the director of the health personnnel, Dr. Kalayev; and so one evening he summoned me. He began with a friendly question about how I was feeling and whether or not I found my work too heavy for me. I parried the question, since I did not yet know what he had in mind. It appeared that I owned a nice suit, and he, Kalayev, was director of a division. The conclusion was, plainly, the suit for him, something in exchange for me. Of course I agreed. Kalayev asked me if I had ever had anything to do with medicine. I lied boldly that I had had three years of medical training. I presume Kalayev knew it was a lie, but he gave no sign, and addressing me as his "dear young colleague" told me that on the morrow I would be temporarily released from physical work on the grounds of illness, and that then we would have time to talk over matters more definitely.

Early the next day I was in Dr. Kalayev's office. He said he had to use me as an assistant, for the medical staff was very small. But he was not speaking the truth; a whole brigade of doctors and hospital orderlies were being kept at hard labor. Among these were two professors from the Moscow Academy of Medicine—Alexander Pavlovich Protopopov and Nicholas Ivanovich Griaznov. There was a Russian emigrant from Esthonia, Dr. Semuchin, who, during that country's independence, had been physician to President Kallio. There were two young Latvian doctors from Riga, Dahle and Felstein, a dentist from Helsinki, Dr. Vaalamainen, and scores of Russian, Lithuanian and Latvian hospital attendants. All of these were kept at felling trees. Guards jeeringly called them "tree surgeons."

That afternoon I made the acquaintance of two other doctors who had been working for some time in the health section. One was a young Russian enthusiast named Neiman, who was continually longing for the days of the democratic Kerensky. The other was Zavadil, a Czech who, ten years before had come to this "land of his dreams."

A new hospital was under construction; I was to become its doctor's assistant and business manager. The doctor would probably be Protopopov. In the meantime, a clinic was opened under the direction of the young Latvian, Dr. Felstein, and I went to him every evening to learn when to give a patient aspirin and when quinine, to distinguish between injections into veins and muscles and under the skin, and to recognize malaria by the thickened, hardened spleen.

There was a queer little fellow called Kozlov in the permanent personnel's kitchen. He had been a sailor in Czarist times and one of the earliest revolutionaries. He had risen to be chief of the Cheka in Omsk. Then it had become the GPU but "the same devil," Kozlov said. Bad luck came, he was caught in the theft of a large sum of money, and sentenced to 15 years in prison, eight of which he had served.

I remarked that the verdict seemed just, since he had committed a crime.

"Oh, you child, you child! They didn't send me to prison because I stole, but because another fellow higher up meant to steal it, and I beat him to it."

As an "expert on justice," Kozlov acquainted me with the Soviet judiciary system. There were, he said, three kinds of courts in the U.S.S.R. The most advertised and most spurious were the revolutionary tribunals, in which the judges were members of the working class. Before such a court met, the chief of the NKVD of that district discreetly visited these "representatives of the working class," plainly told them what punishment they were to demand and what they were finally to agree upon. Just let any "free representative of the working people" try not to follow instructions! He would himself soon be under arrest.

The other two courts were, he said, at least less hypocritical. Both were NKVD courts—one a tribunal, the other "on the spot."

Protopopov came in. Kozlov shut up like a clam—not because he did not like Protopopov, but because the kind of thing we were discussing was never the subject of conversation among three people. It is more difficult to deny things when there are three. I bade Kozlov good day, and left with my future chief.

Protopopov let me in on a great secret. In an abandoned dugout he had discovered some old, frozen potatoes. Though they were unfit for food, he knew how to convert them into vodka. We had only to find somebody who could rig up a secret still. Maybe one could make a good thing of it . . .

I avoided answering by going back to the subject of Soviet courts which I been discussing with Kozlov. The doctor did not reply at once, and when he did, he began to talk as if he were delivering a lecture from his professor's chair. His young friend—that is, I—must first learn the official view of Soviet justice. In capitalistic countries, punishment was meted out immediately after the offender was judged guilty. In the U.S.S.R. this was not the case. Frequently a criminal went unpunished. The NKVD occupied itself only with collecting all the evidence of a crime, and for that reason maintained enormous files. If, a few years after committing a crime, the offender became "inconvenient," he was then arrested and sentenced, even though the offense had occurred far in the past. Thus the NKVD is not an institution to preserve the social order but a spy system with ramifications everywhere. It is a common saying, and a true one, that "the NKVD knows everything."

The NKVD did not use its information as such information would be used in the West. The chief factor in any arrest was political—meaning that the arrested one was for some reason undesirable to the regime. Conditions of life in the U.S.S.R. are such that a person cannot live without breaking the law. Prices are so incredibly high and wages so low that people must steal or die. The NKVD knows this; it is aware of the theft and bribes, but up to a certain point remains blind. The one and all-powerful party's political line penetrates into every corner of life, so that even the most ardent Communist can be at the same time both a criminal and a Soviet prophet. Kozlov was willing to assert that everyone in the U.S.S.R. was guilty of some crime, but unconscious of it. Hence the universal fear of the NKVD and the attitude of servility toward it that could only be described as completely Byzantine.

The incident that resulted in Protopopov's arrest and sentence was simple and typical. Politically, his record had been spotless. He had even been a member of the political board, the *Aktiv*, of his academy. He had never made any criticisms, had attended the meetings and applauded when told to do so. But he could not live on his salary. It cost a lot to support a wife and children, especially in Moscow. So sometimes he took home a bit of butter from the hospital, sometimes sold alcohol and ether. All the other professors did the same thing. The purchasers were more than once the same NKVD officials who later became his judges.

Then a young lecturer, Rudzutak, appeared at the Academy of Medicine— able, ambitious, and the brother of the Commissar of Industry. Unfortunately for Protopopov, his specialty was the same as that of the newcomer, who wanted very much to become a professor in the Moscow Academy. The ambition was attained quickly. Protopopov was simply summoned to the NKVD, shown the record of his offenses, and informed of his sentence to eight years' labor.

"Had I not been a pediatrician, but a surgeon, I might still be a free man," concluded Protopopov sadly.

I MET MANY PRISONERS who had completed their terms years before, but were still in prison with no expectation of ever being released. I asked them why they did not write protests to the authorities.

"As if we hadn't! But it was only a waste of paper."

About 60 percent of the Soviet prisoners I met had been charged with theft, to which poverty had forced them. When I asked them why they had not made it clear to the authorities that their wages were insufficient, they explained that it was far better to go to prison as a thief than as a saboteur of government policy, since the latter charge would put them in camps far distant and much worse. Protests are equivalent to a hostile attitude toward the government—the one crime that brings sentence immediately upon discovery.

One of the other doctors, Griaznov, was the victim of such a charge. He had been a modest, unpretentious professor in the Moscow Academy. This is the story:

"I learned that in the *Univermag* (department store) there were men's shoes, and as my own were in tatters, I went to buy a pair. They asked me who I was and I presented my professor's identification card. Then they asked me if I did not know that the academy had its own store, to which I replied 'of course,' but that that store had only toothpaste and matches.

"Then the salesman stiffened and said that even if he had shoes he wouldn't sell to me or to any rotten intelligentsia. But he had no men's shoes in stock. He could let me have a pair of ladies' ballroom slippers . . . And I turned away saying, under my breath, that in all Moscow one couldn't find a pair of shoes. . . ."

The next day Griaznov was under arrest. Behind closed doors the presiding officer accused him of spreading false reports of a shoe shortage in Moscow. His guilt was all the greater because as a professor he was in touch with representatives of the foreign bourgeoisie. No use in denying that, for the NKVD knew all about it. And besides, it was not true about the shoes. The store was well supplied with all sorts, including women's ballroom slippers. Griaznov protested that there were no men's shoes, and was told that the NKVD had that very day made an inspection of the store and had found quantities of men's shoes. Sentence was passed, and Griaznov began the long journey north. He now had abundant time to consider why a certain salesman in the *Univermag* did not like the intelligentsia.

Another fellow who interested me was the raven-haired Cossack, Bondarev. He was a professional soldier, a cavalry lieutenant. A certain Ukrainian official had fallen in love with his wife, and proposed that the couple get a divorce. They refused to part, for they loved each other. The official had a brother-in-law in the NKVD who agreed to "take care of" Bondarev.

So the Cossack was arrested; but he put up a stout fight and his commandant gave him a good reputation. At his trial they began to put him through an examination on Marxist theory, and Bondarev, fearing they would catch him on some point, replied that as a soldier devoted to his profession he had no time for politics, that the political commissar in the army took care of that for him. As a result, the verdict was very severe—a soldier of the Red Army must know the political line and the fundamentals of the Soviet faith. The presiding officer at this tribunal was the brother-in-law of the "comrade commissar" who had fallen in love with the Cossack's beautiful wife.

Nearly all the prisoners in the camp told similar stories. It was with real pleasure that I met a fellow who was said to have murdered his wife and two children. Of us all, he was the one "right man in the right place."

But there was one more prisoner I cannot forget. Comrade Braun, an elderly Jew with the face of a fanatic, had led an interesting life. The idea that revolution is the only method of doing away with social and economic differences had been firmly fixed in his mind forty years before, when he was a student in his native Leipzig. He joined a group who thought as he did, and rapidly rose to a position that gave him the acquaintance of Lenin, Rosa Luxemburg, Radek, Litvinov, Zinoviev, and Kamenev. He traveled widely, published illegal propaganda, reveled in danger.

To Russia, chosen as the first land for the realization of his beloved plans, he came in 1915. Soon he was deep in revolutionary activities. The revolution broke, crowning the life work of many, but not of Braun, who, now that the destructive period was past, concentrated on constructive work. Proudly he declared that he had never sent a person to prison or to death. For he had conceived his mission to be apostolic—to convert, to convince that it was worthwhile to devote one's life to such a splendid cause.

As long as Lenin lived things went well. It was easy to blame all shortcomings on the fact that it was just the beginning of the new life. After Lenin's death came disillusionment and bitterness. Braun saw Bolshevik blunders, thefts, and corruption which exceeded those of Czarist days. He saw that the crimes of the Cheka were worse than the bloody excesses of the Czar's Okhrana. Although he himself lived very humbly, he saw the luxury with which Soviet commissars surrounded themselves. Aroused, Braun went to Stalin himself. What the conversation was like he did not tell me, but the expression that came over his face at the mention of the visit was full of hatred. He fell silent for a while, then half-whispered, as if to himself: "I hate evil people, consciously evil people."

He was arrested.

And now this Old Bolshevik would answer only with curses when I asked him about the building of a Socialist state. How fine it would be, I thought, if Braun could return to Europe with me. But I knew he would never return.

PROTOPOPOV HAD GIVEN me no peace. He was continually talking to me about his plan to make vodka out of the frozen potatoes, and I found myself seeking a chemist for him. The man chosen was a Finnish citizen, but he had known many lands in the process of eluding government authorities. Deported from the United States, he had not been quite sure which of the European countries to honor with his presence. In the end he had decided upon the Soviet Union, with his arrest the logical result. Believing such a statement would help him to a real career here, he had informed the surprised Bolsheviks that for twenty years he had been carrying on Communist work abroad. It got him instead an immediate hard labor sentence in the far north on the ground that as a Western Communist he was a Trotskyist.

He welcomed our proposal, and when our "hospital" was ready for occupancy, he became our first patient. Protopopov diagnosed his illness as one requiring long walks in the fresh air and this gave Kashtan—we may call him that—freedom of action. Proceeding with great caution, he began little by little to carry pieces of old pipe, a bucket, and a teakettle to an abandoned dugout. When he had got all of it there, he assembled the distilling apparatus, and muddy-gray liquid began to drip from the pipe. In due time the triumphant Kashtan was able to fill four quart bottles.

At that point Protopopov took over. From the drug supplies he brought a vial of mint drops for flavoring. We began to drink. The stuff had little to remind us of vodka. Yet it was vodka, as we knew when our heads swam.

My role in the affair was that of salesman; of course, not for money but through barter. I told the cooks in the "better" kitchen about my treasure which, of course, had come from the medical supplies in my care. Soon I had NKVD patrons. They had *machorka*, sugar, fats, political favors to exchange.

One afternoon I waited impatiently in the reception office while Dr. Protopopov took his daily "walk," for I had had to receive a new patient. The fellow was yelling at the top of his voice, but I had not the faintest idea of what was the matter with him. After a much longer walk than customary, Protopopov entered in a fine humor. I noticed that he seemed suddenly to have grown stout, and that he was looking about furtively. Indicating by a nod that I was to follow, he went into his own part of the tent building. There he took off his coat and I saw the reason for his increased girth—a huge slab of meat, tied flat around his middle.

That night was devoted entirely to leg of reindeer. Kashtan came in, bringing a bucket of vodka. Reindeer soup was simmering and giving off a delicious odor. Steak was sizzling on a piece of tin that served as a frying pan. The three of us sat down to our meal and ate as if we had never before seen food. The vodka was of much better quality; Kashtan explained that he had put it through the apparatus three times and he was sure the Soviet state distilleries themselves would not be ashamed of it.

"It's easy to see that you fellows are new to this country," sighed Protopopov. "Just as we are enjoying a real feast, you have to bring up the State!"

OUR HOSPITAL DEVELOPED nicely. Protopopov was tireless in his efforts to find the really ill and exhausted in the camp. Far be it from me to make a saint of him. I didn't like this sly glutton, forever thinking of lies and underhand dealing, but I realized that these traits had been acquired through the life he had been compelled to live. Once, at a Health Section meeting, I heard him speak with emotion of the need for "Soviet competition in labor, according to the sacred orders of the brilliant commander of the peoples." A little while afterward, in his own room, I heard him laugh at his speech and calculate the advantages it might bring.

Yet when I recall how he labored with the sick, how willingly he got up any time of the night to attend a patient, I cannot but admire the man.

On May 11, Protopopov, Kashtan, and I were summoned to the local NKVD investigation office. We knew at once what was in the wind, and while Protopopov and I were indifferent, Kashtan trembled like an aspen leaf.

Protopopov was called first, and to my surprise he took all the blame. Yes he had distilled vodka, for he needed it for medicinal purposes. He was asked if its sales to other prisoners were also necessary for medical reasons. To this he had no ready answer. My conversation with the commissar was much shorter. As there was no sense in denial, I admitted to my share.

The Bolsheviks could not afford to lose the services of a doctor like Protopopov, so he was sent to a more remote camp. As for me, they recalled that my sentence had specified a "distant hard labor camp," and no "spa" like this.

Early the following day, May 12, 1951, Protopopov was one of a group of prisoners started to the coal mines near Abdorsk. In the afternoon two guards conducted me to a landing pier, where we waited three hours until a great throng of prisoners, all swarthy-faced Mongols, came down the mountain on foot.

The prisoners were emaciated and in rags. To my surprise, I saw a former cell-mate, Adamczyk, and three other Polish citizens. Five of us among 1,400 natives. All we could learn of our destination from the jeering guards was: "You're going where the seal scratches itself and the white bear combs its fur."

III

We waited, standing motionless and silent on the icy pier. Perhaps, I thought, it would be warmer on the boat. It was inhumanly cold in this godless country; even the sky was a terrible cold-blue.

The men around me all wore ragged gray or black padded prison garb, and their legs and feet were wrapped in rags. A little way off I discovered a curious group—the figures shorter and somewhat stouter, the faces framed in long hair hanging below their caps. Women! I shared my discovery with Adamczyk, who answered in an indifferent voice:

"Yes, there are about 200 of them. Unfortunate creatures. You have no conception of what happened to them during the journey here. . . . Maybe they wanted it that way. Nine-tenths of them are either professional or amateur prostitutes. The rest are too old."

After that we again became part of the great silence.

Suddenly that silence was shattered by a woman's hysterical laughter. As if it had been a signal, all the prisoners began to yell, and our meaningless noises were a better symbol of our hate than curses would have been.

The noise was splashed, as it were, by a few swift staccato sounds—shots from guards' guns. A body near us crumpled, writhed, then lay still. The yelling became wilder, and again the shots splashed. Now the crowd just whispered. Somebody near, speaking Russian, asked in guarded tones:

"Is there a God, or not?"

How much longer we waited before black smoke was discernible up the river I do not know. The little steamer, its paddle wheel working industriously, was towing a barge. NKVD men in charge of the transport called to the prisoners to fasten the barge to the pier and lay the planks. The ropes cast ashore grew taut. The barge drew nearer. Men who were just remnants of flesh and bone struggled and, oddly enough, accomplished their task. One of the men began vomiting blood and was contorted with pain. Death throes soon took him, and his troubles were over. Others fell from time to time, but they never let go the rope.

Finally the barge awaited its load of prisoners. Cursing at us, the guards ordered us to line up. In ten different formations they ranged us, twenty times they counted us.

We crossed the gangplank and went down into the very bottom of the barge. The normal ceiling height in the hold, a little over eight feet, had seemed excessive for prisoners. Moreover, with that height, two barges would have been required for 1,400 prisoners. So they had put in a second floor, making the ceiling less than four feet; and they put 700 on each floor. It was impossible to stand or to lie down. Squatting or sitting in a cramped position—that was the choice. After an hour of waiting, we heard the bottom of the barge scrape the river bed, and then we were moving out.

There were five of us Poles who kept together. We began to talk about our country and our past, but this proved too painful. So we speculated about our future. According to rumor we were on our way to Novaya Zemlya, to the coal mines, where the work would be very hard, perhaps killing. Would it be possible to rescue ourselves in any human and decent fashion from that hell? Adamczyk, while certain that some of the Polish deportees would leave the U.S.S.R. alive, was pessimistic about his own fate, remarking that he probably would become an integral part of the accursed steppe or tundra or *taiga*.

The only light we had in the lower part of the barge came from the opening in the top that served as an entrance and through cracks in the plank which made our ceiling and the floor of the "deck" above. We could distinguish only the persons very close to us.

The sanitary conditions grew revolting. In a corner stood the familiar ugly *parasha*, to which everybody in time made his way . . . in time, for the queue was always long, there being just one *parasha* for 700 men. The result was what one would expect—the floor was like that of a stable.

From another group came the announcement that one of their number had died. There was no reply from the guards, but in a few minutes down came ropes with huge hooks attached, followed by curt instructions from above to fasten the hooks to the corpse. No matter if they went into the flesh. Dead men don't feel. What had, a brief hour ago, been a living being was hauled up and soon after we heard the dull splash as it hit the water.

Voices here and there began to shout for "bread," for "soup," for "something to eat." Soon, on those same hooks that had clutched the dead man, came buckets of soup and bread tied in bundles. We divided the bread with pieces of iron serving us as knives—though possession of such was strictly forbidden—as accurately as if we had used a druggist's scales. Woe betide the man who tried to get a larger portion than was his right. The soup was quite a different matter. There were 14 ten-quart buckets, one for every 50 prisoners, which meant one small cup of soup per man. But we had no cups. There seemed to be two possible solutions. One was that we should lap up the soup like dogs, two men at a time. But in that case the quantity could not be controlled. The second, and approved, was that we should each cup one hand and, ten at a time, dip into the bucket together, until the contents were exhausted.

A woman's hysterical half-whimper, half-laughter reached our ears. What could be happening? We were promptly enlightened by the conversation in our vicinity, and Adamczyk and I looked at each other speechless. He cursed and ground his teeth.

The oath gave each of us some relief, but it could not help the unfortunate women, who indeed no longer defended their "honor," having quite forgotten the meaning of that word, but who did crave a little rest, a little mercy.

THUS PASSED THE DAYS and nights for us below in the barge, though we scarcely knew day from night, for we received our food at any hour it pleased the cooks and the guard to give it to us. One might wake up from sleep and find his pillow—his neighbor—strangely cold, which meant that he had died. And instead of being sorrowful, one might instead feel grateful, because now there would be more room for oneself.

The deaths were so frequent by this time that the guards left the hooks within our reach, so that all we had to do was fasten them into the body and jerk the ropes hard. Among the last victims was one from our number—one of the White Ruthenians. From our memories of a life that was now an eternity away, we recalled the prayers for the dead and commended to God this soul who had surely gone to Him. How we envied this man whose troubles were now over. And yet none of us could bring our will to the point of suicide. No, death would have to come when God pleased.

Some days after the death of our friend, the barge was towed to a landing, a ladder was let down through the hole in the center, and we were ordered to climb out. Our muscles, cramped and stiffened by those weeks of unnatural position and lack of use, made the climb painful, but our eagerness to see daylight and stretch our limbs drove us to action. Yet when we did get out, the strong sunlight, plus the dazzling reflection from the expanse of snow-covered tundra, made us for the moment helplessly blind. When we could look at each other, we saw a ragged, filthy, unshaven crowd, with unkempt, vermin-infested hair, and hands covered with sores.

On shore were a few warehouses and barracks, a sort of port. In the distance were other barracks huddled together within a palisaded square, with the usual towers at the corner. Another labor camp. After we had all got ashore they counted us, for the first time in three weeks. We were just about half as many as had left Kozva. Lined up in ranks of four, we were led off to the barracks in the port, which we learned was called Niarion-Mor in the speech of the Komi natives. It consisted of one pier where the water was deep enough for sea-going boats to come in. And at this pier the boat which would take us to Novaya Zemlya would tie up.

We discovered a well in the camp and with all haste set to washing ourselves, as if we feared somebody would come up and drive us away. Afterwards we went into the barracks and lay down on the bunks, to revel in the comfort of stretching out numbed and cramped muscles. The bunks were only boards, but we asked nothing better. Behind the barracks were long, deep latrines, where one could go when he liked and remain as long as he liked. No luxurious hotel accommodations had ever made so favorable an impression upon us as did these primitive conveniences. Man's happiness is relative. What gave us joy and set us to laughing and joking after our bitter experiences would have driven a man suddenly transported from Western life to madness or suicide.

Our food was fantastically plentiful. Each of us received a dish full of cooked cereal, a piece of boiled fish, and a hunk of bread. We ate greedily, dared to ask for a second helping, and to our surprise got it. The secret of our full feeding was learned later from one of the cooks. The port authorities had been informed that two barges with 2,800 prisoners would arrive. Allowing for 800 deaths en route, the cooks were ordered to prepare a meal for 2,000. When we arrived with less than 1,000, we got all that had been made ready.

Next morning the big steamer that was to take us to Novaya Zemlya came in, the now familiar red flag at its mast. On its prow shone in great gold letters *Ordjonikidze*. The following day the *politruk* (political commissar) of the ship gave us information regarding deck regulations for prisoners. First, under no consideration were we to enter into conversation with a member of the crew. All questions were to be addressed to our guards, or in the last resort, to him. We were forbidden to sing, to shout, or even to speak aloud. We were limited to whispering. From time to time we would be taken on deck in groups of 50, under guard, and there we could walk that part of the deck indicated by white paint.

Twenty days we were on the *Ordjonikidze*, infinitely better days than those spent in the barge. We had an abundance of space and time to sleep, and we slept night and day.

One day during a walk on deck somebody got access to the *politruk's* things and robbed him. The Russian who had committed the theft had successfully hidden everything except a belt, which seemed to him so like ordinary belts that he saw no need of hiding it. But he had neglected to note the *politruk's* initials clumsily scratched on the buckle. The game was up. The unlucky fellow was grabbed by guards and tossed overboard into the icy water, where he floundered for a half hour or so before merciful death took him.

This manner of dealing with one of their number had a tremendous effect upon his comrades. When they returned below deck the place was filled with a murmur like that of a swarm of angry bees. Knives that hitherto had been carefully kept from sight came out menacingly. Mutiny was in the air, when a group of guards appeared in the doorway, and emptied their revolvers into the crowd. After that there was no more muttering, only a sound like a dog's whining came from one corner, and soon that was stilled.

On June 21 we again caught sight of land and saw that we were very slowly approaching it. The next morning early we were in the port. Several hours were spent waiting, during which time a hoarse voice came from the loudspeaker on a tall mast near the water's edge. By straining our ears to hear we made out occasional words—"aviation"—"aviators"—"Kiev"—"Odessa"—"Germans."

Our hearts beat violently. Adamczyk and I stood as if frozen, but burning with the same thought, with hope, groundless as that might seem.

The loudspeaker suddenly fell silent. But it was disconnected too late. This was the morning of June 22. The German army had crossed the Soviet frontier at many points. German aviators at the same time had begun bombing Soviet cities. A new war had burst into flames, which would bring death to many, but for us hope of return to life.

THERE WERE 727 of us, including the women, who had survived out of the 1,400 when the count was made after landing on Novaya Zemlya and the march to the mines was begun. Alongside the prisoner column walked guards and unleashed dogs, well-trained animals that attacked no prisoner as long as he did not leave the ranks. We were hurried along at an inhuman pace, and orders to move "faster! faster!" kept coming. We did not then understand the reason for the haste.

The first prisoner dropped before we had gone a mile. He was ahead of me in the line, so I could see what was happening. It was a Russian, barefooted, his feet raw lumps of flesh. A guard walked up to the prostrate figure, put his pistol to the prisoner's head, and shouted:

"Get up!"

Either there was no reply or it was so low we could not hear. The guard leaned over and searched the fellow's pockets. Finding nothing, he again put his pistol to the prisoner's head and fired. Blood and brains oozed out to mingle with the tundra's mud.

While this was going on we had unconsciously slackened our pace and now, just as unconsciously, we stepped out more quickly, as if in flight from something. One of the Russian prisoners remarked aloud and almost insolently:

"Don't be scared. You have a few days yet before the Germans can get here."

At once the line was halted and the humorist was sought, without success, however, until a Latvian, unquestionably out of fright, pointed out the culprit. The operation we had witnessed only a little while before was repeated—a revolver against a man's head, a splitskull—and we were on the way again. A minute later a cry of pain broke from the Latvian as he crumpled to the ground with blood spurting from his back. The Russian prisoner had been avenged by one of his comrades.

At the end of two hours we had our first rest. Exhausted, we dropped and lay as if dead in the mud or snow. To rouse us and get us on the road once more, the guards shouted and struck us on the back with their rifles. Indifferently we looked on while the guards attempted to "persuade" the weaker ones to get to their feet. The result was the same in each case—a pistol shot—and the diminished line moved on. The surviving women were loaded on the sleds, and thus we proceeded until evening.

About eight o'clock we reached a huge empty barracks, intended for the use of prisoner groups on the way to the mines. Two guards came out to meet us and direct us inside, where we lay down close together on the hard earthern floor. All of us were too exhausted to desire more than warmth and rest, and to get warmth we curled up and packed together as closely as possible.

The guards brought food—hard, dry bread, a little "marmalade," onion and dried fish. I wanted to eat and yet I did not want to, for my throat and stomach were giving me pain.

In the morning a number of the prisoners either could not or would not get up, as always happened after a rest. Others were past waking. One of the two local guards appeared and announced that those who were really unable to go further might wait for the next transport.

Emboldened by the frightful loss we had suffered and our exhausted condition, I asked:

"Don't you realize that unless we are given a long rest not half of us will finish the trip?"

The reply was made with characteristic Soviet bluntness. They knew that not more than a third would live to finish. They had radioed to the mines that in five days they could expect 200 people out of the 727 who were en route.

"Do you think that those who get there will be good for any kind of work in the mines?" I ventured.

And again a straight answer:

"You need not be able to work. Your main qualification is that you can die."

Leaving some 50 of our number in the barracks, we moved on. Before we were well away, the sound of pistol shots, at deliberately measured brief intervals, reached us. The evening of that second day the last of our White Ruthenian friends began vomiting blood, dropped out of the line, and sat down.

"Kill me, you —"

Thus with a curse on his blood-and-foam-flecked lips a naturally religious man passed out of life, the guard's revolver at the back of his head.

On the evening of the fifth day we saw ahead of us guard towers, barracks, and a mountain of coal, and we knew we were reaching our destination. We entered through a gate above which was the sign: "Stakhanov Labor Camp—Bichovnik."

MORE OF US had survived than expected, 422 instead of 200. After the count we were led to a great empty barracks and ordered to go to bed. There would be nothing to eat—we were too late.

The next morning we had the indescribable delight of visiting the bath-house, which was in a dugout, and of having a bath while our clothing was being disinfected. Then, clad in hospital orderlies' aprons, we went to the doctor's office and were registered—all except one who fell to the floor during his bath and never got up again.

Every one of us was a fit candidate for the little hospital. But since it had only 24 beds and ten were occupied, the doctor and his orderly were faced with a real problem. Dr. Pimenov, a Soviet citizen, solved it as best he could, taking in 28 of our group by putting two in a bed. On the basis of my "previous medical experience," I volunteered for service in bandaging. Adamczyk laughed at me, saying I was crazy, and he went off to the barracks to sleep while I had to work.

But the next day showed the wisdom of my course. All the members of our group, with the exception of those exempted by the doctor, were ordered into the mines. I was to be used four more days to help in bandaging. Pimenov gave me pills and vitamins to build me up and clear my blood, and I saved some to give Adamczyk.,

Late that evening I returned to our barracks, but the brigade to which Adamczyk belonged had not come in. Not finding him there, I went back to the clinic, hoping to have a talk with Pimenov. What I wanted was news about the war.

Yes, he admitted very cautiously, as if he were not quite sure of me, the Germans were advancing very rapidly. Then he wanted to know about my sentence. He was not interested in the fact that I had received the death sentence and had been reprieved. Every prisoner here was in that category. But what was my offense? Proudly I told him, revolutionary activities, in reality the fact that I was a Pole and therefore considered a Soviet enemy. Pimenov sighed as if with relief, and the conversation continued. Everybody in the camp, he said, was building up hope on the German invasion. Not that the Germans would reach Novaya Zemlya. But if they took Leningrad, and then Archangelsk —we would be free. God in heaven! How strange that word "free" sounded, he said. Yet that might happen before winter. He added that about 85 percent of the prisoners die each winter.

When I went back to the barracks Adamczyk was there eating supper, and after he had finished I asked him how things had gone.

"We have a week without fixed quotas while we learn. Then we must get out seven and a half tons of coal per person a day, 15 tons for two working as a team. Old miners say that's physically impossible. We can get out only half that amount, but we can deceive them about the balance. Twelve hours of work with a half-hour break for food. Miners' food, especially for those who make the quota, is even good."

A Russian prisoner, in the bunk on the other side of me, broke in. He was an old-timer at Bichovnik, having arrived the preceding fall, and had been one of the few to come through the winter. We learned that there were forty-odd mines in this vicinity, each with its own camp of approximately 500 prisoners. Our camp, Bichovnik, No. 37, was the only one with more and was the base of supplies for all the rest. The mine supervisor was an old man "from Czarist days," an engineer with an unpronounceable name. Certainly he was not a Russian.

The day before I was to go to the mines, Pimenov asked me if I would not like to have my "illness" extended. I was tempted, but thanked him and refused, requesting him to put Adamczyk, who was hardly able to drag one foot after another, on the sick list for a few days.

The next morning I was assigned to Boboyan's brigade. Boboyan, a common thief, had been sentenced for having criminal intentions toward the whole Soviet Union! With an air of distinction and seriousness worthy of a better enterprise, he received me as a member of his brigade, telling me that if I so desired I might be a *borelschchyk*. Since I did not know the meaning of that magic word, Boboyan explained that it designated a miner operating a pneumatic drill. That almost took my breath away. Pneumatic drills in this out-of-the-world place! Impossible.

An hour later I was standing in a sloping gallery, a pneumatic drill in my hands, while Boboyan gave me instructions regarding its use. The first day's work did not leave me excessively tired. At its close the NKVD made inspection and I was a little ashamed that I had not noticed their presence and had worked with all the ardor of a beginner.

Boboyan reasoned that the fellow who measured the output was certain to be one who could be tricked. And in this he was justified. The brigade worked in parallel sections along the gallery. In 12 hours two men were supposed to dig 15 tons of coal, four men 30 tons. The output of each two men was separated by wooden stakes from the output of the team on the opposite side of the gallery. Naturally no one could produce the quota demanded. So what happened? The controller walked along one side of the corridor and calculated the number of cubic feet, and hence the ton production, by measuring the distance from the wall to the stakes. When he passed, the stakes were quietly shifted away from the opposite wall and on his return to check production on that side, the quotas were in order. Nothing could have been easier, and in a very short time we had made records as Stakhanovites.

The general belief among the prisoners was that the fantastic Stakhanovite records throughout Russia were rigged in the same fashion. Bribery, beginning

268

with the controllers in the mines, who bribe the regional controllers, who in turn bribe the commissars of their Soviet republics, who in turn bribe the higher officials of the Soviet Union.

Only one field of production, according to Boboyan, was free from this practice of falsifying production figures. That was war industry, where propaganda played no part, where everything was shrouded in secrecy and production was played down instead of exaggerated.

The quality of the prisoner's food depended upon the quality and quantity of his work. Men who did not produce their quota went to the "first kettle." This was starvation diet. The "second" was for the "hundred percenters" and beginners, like myself, and was normal Soviet prison fare. The other kettles contained increasingly better food, the best being that of the "administration" cauldron, which was almost equal to the food of free citizens.

When the line before the "second kettle" had moved along so that my turn came, I handed my two pans through the little window. Into one the cook dished a little hot soup and a spoonful of cereal. In my second pan I got a little hot water, in which I could soak my hoarded bread. It was not tasty, but I had long since learned to disregard taste and eat everything I could get hold of.

Our gallery entrance was some 1500 meters (something under a mile) distant from the camp. The tundra we walked over was gray and soft as the finest carpet, but the gray was patched with snow and away behind the camp glistened a glacier, resplendent in the rays of the morning sun. Take any direction across the tundra and you would come to the sea, where the coasts were as lonely and undisturbed as they had been for the past 5,000 years.

The descent into the mine was by way of a cage on an incline leading to a depth of more than 1,300 feet. Mechanics were installing a steam engine which was to replace human muscles, but at this time the coal was brought up and let down its shaft by the hand labor of a prisoner brigade.

Work went on without a break, one 12-hour shift taking over the tools from the other going off. How long could men stand such a life, without even one day's rest? The official statistics said not longer than a year. Even those most clever at deceiving had to do a certain amount of work, and just a little was murderous in the Arctic climate and under those conditions. Sometimes we stole a brief rest or a little sleep, leaving a man on watch at the entrance of our cut, for there were frequent visits from coal officials and NKVD men. The discovery of "planned sabotage" is the beginning of many a career. And in the mines, a higher position meant better food, which was a great incentive indeed.

After working hours we returned to our barracks to begin again the monotonous round. In the winter season, which began in August, the dark night skies became a backdrop for the unearthly brilliance of the northern lights. When snow lay deep on the tundra, white-trousered rabbits flashed by, and we heard the mournful call of the white partridge. The white bears, however, were very cautious and only when the fearful blizzard of the north began to blow did they come up to the camp confines in search of food. Then we heard their melancholy howling, heard them bark like dogs and whimper like infants.

ON THE MORNING of July 14 I found Adamczyk dead in his bunk. Now I felt alone, utterly alone. Probably, I thought, I would soon follow him. Was death the beginning of a new life? The day before, I had been talking with Dr. Pimenov and he had told me Adamczyk's case was hopeless, since he had no will to live because he had lost all his family.

"Be prepared for his death," Pimenov had said. "They will throw him into a pit and cover him with quicklime. But if you want to bury him, ask leave of your brigadier. You can get a tool and a sled from the storehouse—and bury him somewhere yourself. My Chrabry will make you a little metal plate with whatever you want to say on it. Chrabry knows the Latin alphabet."

And now that death had come, I followed this advice, and in addition pulled two little pieces of board out of one of the barracks. That night snow fell and, for some reason which I could not explain, I was glad. Somehow it seemed more fitting that my countryman should go in a wintry season. Next morning I got permission to go outside the camp limits. I put Adamczyk's body on the little sled, and having chosen my spot, set to work. The frozen earth was like iron and the pick would only break off little lumps, though I drove with all my might. When I paused out of breath, it suddenly occurred to me that there would be nobody to dig a grave for me—that I would be the last. And therefor I *must* live, there was no other course. Foolish, you say? Perhaps, but not to one in my situation.

I had been digging for six hours, but still the hole was not deep enough to enclose the body, though Adamczyk was a small man. I kept at the digging, occasionally glancing at the calm face of my dead comrade. A great envy took possession of me, that he should enjoy such peace and rest while I must struggle and toil on this cursed island.

Not until evening was the hole ready. Even then I discovered it was still a little short and I would have to bend the corpse to get it in—macabre work. But in that inhuman cold the stiffened figure would not bend, and I was forced to lay it across the sled and break it. My teeth chattered, and not merely from the cold. But at last Adamczyk was in the grave and, utterly exhausted, I threw the clods in upon him, heaping the brown mass into a clumsy mound. At the head I set a rude cross made of the two little boards fastened together with wire. The next day I would fix to it the metal strip Chrabry was making.

All was finished and now I could go. No, I had forgotten the prayer.

"Forgive me, friend," I murmured. "That was inexcusable. I simply forogt. Perhaps because you need no prayer—you who are now in heaven."

I did not know what the priest says at the grave. So I just said Our Father and the Hail Mary . . . and knelt and meditated.

Suddenly, although I heard nothing, I was conscious of somebody standing behind me.

IV

I LOOKED AROUND and saw the old miner, the tall old engineer with the unpronounceable name. He stood with hands folded on his breast as if in prayer, and gave me a kindly glance from under his bushy brows. In a chanting voice Polish words came:

"Grant him, Father, eternal rest."

Like an echo I answered:

"And may the eternal light guide him for ages and ages. Amen."

I was grateful to the engineer for bringing to my mind the words of the proper prayer. At the same time I was ashamed, and looked at him questioningly. Though all this was a mystery to me, I was not surprised. I was no longer capable of surprise. The questions he asked were both an answer and a further mystery.

"You are a Pole?"

"Yes," I replied.

"And he—?"

"Yes."

"Then let us pray for our fellow countryman," and his words sounded like a command.

After the prayer we sang *godzinki,* in low-pitched voices. The old engineer's voice was hoarse yet musical, but I was continually off key. At the close my companion remarked:

"As a musician you couldn't get a kopeck."

"Not even a grosh," I corrected him.

"I beg your pardon. Not a grosh," he agreed, taken aback that he had used the Russian "kopeck" instead of the Polish "grosh."

At the camp gate we separated, he going to the barracks of the authorities and I to my own.

The next day I learned that I had been transferred to another labor brigade, whose brigadier was Samonov, a colonel in the Czar's army, who had spent all the years of the Bolshevik regime in prison or labor camps. Samonov explained that my transfer had been the result of intervention by the "comrade overseer." I was now assigned to work above ground, which was generally regarded as much lighter labor than that in the mines. The "comrade overseer" must be none other than the old engineer who had helped me with the funeral services.

"Cruelty Has a Human Heart"

THE BRIGADE I now joined heaped the coal in mounds alongside a line where a railway track connecting with the port was to be laid. Nora, a dog half airedale, half shepherd, stood guard over us. Her eyes were dark and beautiful, her blond coat fluffy, her body neat and muscular, her ears properly "on the alert," and her tail a curly decoration.

Yet none of us liked her. She treated her caretakers with what, from a human being, would be described as haughty disdain. Us prisoners she appeared to consider creatures of a lower order.

"A woman is not known until she opens her mouth," Samonov remarked. And that was certainly true of Nora. When her mouth was closed, she was a beautiful dog. When it was opened, displaying the widespread jaws set with their sharp white fangs, she was a terrible animal, a satan in a dog's hide.

There were just two words that Nora took any interest in—*Gani, dierzhi!* (Pursue, hold!). When the chain was removed she would spend some time sniffing the tracks of the man she was to get, then, with legs stiff as pokers, take a few steps, and all of a sudden dash off in the chase.

Such occasions were rare indeed here on Novaya Zemlya, where escape was hopeless. Yet I did witness one attempt made by a member of my own brigade the third day of my association with it. Why the attempt was made we never knew, for no man in his senses would think of such a thing.

The fellow looked normal except for his eyes, which were continually moving, never resting on anything for a moment. And then we saw his lips covered with foam, saw him break away and run as fast as he could go. He was a poor Russian thief, the "offspring of the broom and the canal," as the priceless Samonov remarked. His wasted body was only theoretically protected from the biting Arctic cold. A shirt much too large for him hung outside his pants, to cover the holes in the latter garment, of which he was extremely proud. For they were not the usual padded pants of the prisoners, but real pants, which some ten years before must have been worn by a foreign diplomat or a Moscow dandy. He wore no socks, only an old pair of galoshes, through which his toes peeked.

In such a costume Sasha the thief dashed for his liberty. If it was a flight, it was well characterized by Samonov:

"He was not fleeing from them (the NKVD); his soul was making its escape from the body."

Several prisoners near him started to run after him to bring him back, but were prevented from doing so by the guards, who stood still and permitted the hapless man to flee across the icy-cold limitless expanse of snow.

Then one of the guards brought out a small sled, to which were harnessed seven jumping and snapping cousins of Nora. Sasha kept running as fast as he could go, stumbling from time to time because of his clumsy galoshes, plunging face downward into the snow, scrambling to his feet and hurrying on again.

The dog team, with a well-known guard who was their master seated in the sled, set off with a yelp. In one hand the driver held a whip and the reins, in the other Nora's leash. The race lasted a gruellingly long time, the sled moving in almost leisurely fashion over the snow. In the meantime a bugle call brought all the other brigades of the night shift to join us. The incident was to be used as a lesson, it appeared.

The fleeing man fell and this time did not rise. A minute later the pursuing guard in the sled bent over the prostrate figure and did something which we could not make out. Then he cracked his whip over the backs of the dogs, and the sled, making a wide arc, approached us in a cloud of snow dust. Nora, loosed from the leash, leaped along beside it. When they drew nearer we saw that, tied to the strong rope attached to Nora, was the unfortunate fugitive. His body dragging through the snow, was responsible for the clouds of snow dust. We looked at the snow under our feet. It was sharp and icy, glittering and hard as diamonds. And Sasha was approaching us face down. The whole group was now in front of us. Nora sat down on her haunches, watching closely to see what would happen next.

Vanya, the guard, got off the sled and walked up to the quivering body on the snow. With his foot he turned it face upward. The clothes of which Sasha had been so proud were no more. Just the sleeves of the shirt clung to him, remnants of the pants clung to the leather belt. The galoshes had disappeared altogether. The face, breast, and thighs of Sasha had ceased to be members of a human body and had become one bloody mass.

"It reminds me of the chopped meat for Tartar cutlets, in the long-ago Czarist days, except it has no onions," murmured Samonov to himself.

The "chopped meat" was still alive, every bleeding muscle aquiver, and a strange sound issued from its mouth. Nora's master was not satisfied. Unfastening the heavy whip from his belt he began to beat Sasha, who had been reduced to such a condition that he felt nothing. Realizing this, the guard stopped and, looking around, was reminded of Nora's presence. Over his face spread the ghost of a smile as he leaned over and whispered something to the dog.

Nora rose and slowly and cautiously approached the wretch on the ground, while all of us held our breath. The beast sniffed all around him and then opened wide her terrible mouth, and with her long, rough tongue began to lick Sasha's bleeding body. Finally she lay down by the remains of the man, pushing up close to him as if to protect him from the cold.

Vanya cursed and went off without a word. Somebody among the prisoners began to sob. Nora pushed still closer to what had once been a man.

Sasha, of course, died. But Nora stayed by his side. And after that she was a wholly different Nora. When the guards were not around, she crept to us and in dog fashion begged to be petted. But this lasted only three days; then we found her kennel empty. We could not imagine what had happened. Later, in access of good humor, Vanya, her guard, told us:

"She was no longer of any use to us. The fool softened and forgot her business. So we ground her up for croquettes. They are good made of dog meat."

THAT EVENING my new acquaintance, the engineer, summoned me to him. Long shall I remember that August 1, 1941, when the air was filled with snow driven by the howling *purga,* the terrible wind whose fury no one can understand who has not experienced it.

The engineer sat before a small plain table covered with papers. As I entered he looked up at me, and I saw that his eyes were filled with tears. He threw out an abrupt question.

"You know?"

When I replied that I knew nothing he rose and began to speak slowly and solemnly.

"Yesterday the Polish Government signed an accord with the Soviet Union. By this agreement all Polish citizens will be let out of prisons and labor camps and on Russian territory a Polish army will be organized under its own commanders."

I was speechless for a minute. Then I said.

"They are to let us all go?"

"Yes, absolutely all Polish citizens."

"I can't believe it! It must be a rumor."

"It is the truth, announced both from Moscow and London. The agreement with Poland followed a British-Soviet accord."

For a few minutes the overseer sat thinking, then began to shuffle the papers on the table, as if looking for something. Finally he picked up one and handed it to me.

"And here you have a nice little surprise, something personal," he said. "You have been appointed my assistant, to work in mine No. 37. You won't fit into this situation long, but we don't know how long you'll have to wait for a return transport."

I was taken completely by surprise. "I, the overseer's assistant? But I haven't the slightest conception of that work!"

"That doesn't matter. The important thing is that I find it noted in this document that you are an engineer."

"But I am not! They 'christened' me an engineer-economist in Russian, which in Polish means simply—merchant!"

"Don't be a fool, man! No training is needed for this job. You won't have the least occasion to use technical knowledge. You'll simply watch over the work in the mine, shout at the men and urge them to work."

"Then there is all the more reason why I shouldn't take it."

The old man looked at me angrily.

"Lord, what unheard-of idiocy! You will urge the men on only when the NKVD are around. The rest of the time you will live on friendly terms with your fellow-prisoners. They will understand, I assure you."

I agreed to try. The old engineer expressed his satisfatcion and told me to come over the next morning with my things.

"But," he said, "remember that in the presence of others we must talk only of unimportant matters and in Russian."

As I left him I said that we would return to freedom and to Poland together.

"I have no one to whom to return," he replied sorrowfully. "My family all died here. I am one of *their* citizens."

IN FULL BLAST the *purga* was upon us, howling and driving clouds of snow dust out of the north down on the camp. To make matters worse, the cold became more intense and the brigade went to work bundled in all their own rags and all of those of their sleeping comrades of the other shift. The camp commander gave prisoners working outside the barracks padded cotton masks that covered the face, leaving openings only for the eyes. The health office got orders to give us vaseline with which we were to smear our faces. From the camp exit to the entrance of the mine, a distance of roughly 500 meters, a heavy hempen rope was stretched. This guiding line was to prevent our going astray in the blinding blizzard and to aid us in keeping on our feet.

Occasionally there was a break in the gloom of the darkened tundra and through it streamed rays of sunlight—bleak, cold, ghastly sunlight. Old-timers who were well acquainted with such weather assured us that this was not so bad. The *purga* would continue, they said, for two weeks, then cease for a week, only to begin afresh and last without a break for five weeks. And this second one, they assured us, was felt by everything alive, even by creatures so superbly prepared for winter as the polar bears. The preceding year a prisoner named Kola Riabev had found a she-bear and three cubs frozen to death within twenty meters of the camp. The only creature that can be secure against a *purga* is a human being, who lives in a strong, compactly built, well-heated cabin or else deep down in the earth. Both of these possibilities were open to us. The only trouble was that stretch between camp and mine. Down in the corridors and galleries there was not even an echo of the storm. The only noise was that of the picks and the cranes.

I felt very strange in my new role as assistant to the overseer. I now lived in a little room in the barracks with the old overseer, and at his request spent the evening telling him about life in Poland. He listened eagerly, as if he feared to lose a word. Sometimes he wept. Despite our close association I did not yet know his name, for the purely Russian "Ivan Ivanov" by which he was known could only be a pseudonym. One evening I made so bold as to ask him. His was a White Ruthenian name, he said, the same as that of one of our great Polish historical figures, and "Ivan Ivanov" was only a translation of the Polish "Jan, son of Jan."

On one of those August nights when the *purga* was still howling, we were roused from sleep by the shaking and pounding of the door. I opened it and, along with the freezing cold, in came two bundled men. One took off his padded mask and we recognized Boboyan, his face drawn with fear. He shouted to the old overseer, who still lay in his bunk.

"Ivan Ivanov! The 7th gallery has collapsed and buried eight of my people! There was a crack somewhere, and gas is pouring in. Come!"

The engineer was out of bed with the first words. He dressed with lightning-quick movements, and I marveled at his apparent youthfulness. He was ready before I was.

"Come!" he said to me.

We found all the men of the night shift collected at the entrance to the mine. A murmur of hope rose as the old engineer approached. Here was somebody who would save the men, they said. We all forgot that we were prisoners, that our lives were of no particular value, that we did not know the trapped men, that Boboyan's brigade was generally disliked. The important thing was that we were human beings and down there were other human beings who might perish.

The engineer quickly got what information was to be had, started toward the collapsed gallery, but was warned of the danger of gas. His response was to say to me:

"Give me your lamp, Andrey Adolfovich, and come with me."

I took my little safety lamp and followed my chief. The entrance to the gallery did not permit us to walk erect. We advanced a few steps; the old engineer cautiously lowered the lamp to the ground and, when it did not go out, took a few steps more. Each time there was the least change of floor level he made the test with the lamp. Finally the light went out and he sent me back to relight it and to bring another. When I returned we fastened the lamps high on our chests and pushed forward.

"We'll keep on as long as one lamp burns," he said.

When we were only a few feet from the cave-in the engineer's lamp went out. He took my lamp and, holding it on a level with his chin, moved on with me at his heels. A little further, and he told me to stay where I was. Beneath my feet I could feel one of the support beams, which meant that the surface where I was standing was at least 20 centimeters (about eight inches), above the floor level. My companion advanced to the mass blocking the passage, examined it and turned back quickly. The uncertain flickering of the lamp told me why— gas.

On the way back to the exit the engineer was silent. As we reached it he said simply,

"Andrey, you must try to save them. I'll assign men to help you."

I replied that of course I would undertake it, but my manner must have betrayed my surprise, for he said:

"You wonder why I am not doing it myself? I'm too short. The gas has already risen too high. Those who go in must be as tall as or taller than you. You will advance with a rope, one end of which we shall hold here. If need be, we will drag you out."

He chose his men, tied a rope around the middle of each of us, and gave each man a pick. With our lamps fastened to our necks we started down again.

I do not know how long we worked at the heap of fallen coal blocking our path before we heard faint sounds from the other side. Before long we had an opening large enough to make communication possible and learned that four of the eight men were still alive. Two had been crushed by the cave-in, two suffocated by gas. The survivors could not help us, as they were on high supports at some distance from the opening we had made. After five hours further digging we had a tunnel wide enough for a man to crawl through. I slid in and began throwing lumps of coal into the hole in front of me, in an attempt to form a sort of bridge across which the marooned men could make their way to the opening; but I soon was convinced of the futility of that procedure. I went back to the engineer for instructions, telling my companions to remain where they were.

Somehow I managed to get out and explain the situation, but I heard none of the instructions I had come for. I had fainted.

When I regained consciousness I was in a clean white hospital bed, with Dr. Pimenov and Chrabry bending over me. Behind them stood a third person in a white hospital apron. A woman! And a beautiful woman at that!

My mind went back at once to the accident, and I began asking questions. In answer Pimenov pointed to the four beds near me. That was sufficient. I knew the four rescued men were in them.

The next time I woke I felt much stronger. Pimenov was sitting beside me, and this time he replied to my questioning. I had been in the hospital, he told me, for three days, during which time I had been either unconscious or asleep. I asked him how long the rescue work had taken, and he said 27 hours.

"How many hours did I work with my team?"

"Seventeen. All the night through until eight o'clock the next evening."

That afternoon the little hospital was in a frenzy of cleaning and being put in order, and later in the day the chief of this network of camps paid us a visit. This was the first opportunity I had had to get a look at the lord of life and death on Novaya Zemlya. He was a corpulent fellow, probably in his middle fifties, with a manner by no means fear-inspiring, and a smile that was even friendly. Was it a holiday expression, I wondered? I had seen three of his deputies on earlier occasions. The director of Department 3, Obiediev, was a specialist in mass executions for "sabotaging the war effort." He was responsible for the execution of the Latvians, Dr. Sejnas, Kaups, Kulmans and Zanezis; the Estonians, Piroo, Grosfield, Simpovnen; the Finnish engineer, Kivilein; the Lithuanians, Zankieviczius and Dr. Strinkas; and the hospital orderly, Vaniszviaitis. With his own hand he had shot an Englishman, James Stuart Lowbridge, who had been in the camp. The second of this pleasant trio was the director of camp defense, Grotis. Among human trash there are few to equal him. The last of the three was the political commissar of the camp guards, Feigenbaum—quiet, but a cruel fanatic of the worst type.

Yet today all four wore a friendly air. They smiled at each of us prisoner-patients and, I am ashamed to confess it, especially at me. The chief smiled most graciously of all. Dr. Pimenov politely indicated who were the rescued and who the rescuers.,

The upshot of the visit, so far as I was concerned, was the information given me of the Soviet-Polish agreement. The sudden announcement of my freedom left me both stunned and unbelieving. The nurse told me afterward that I had turned white as paper and lain absolutely still. Only when the chief inquired what I meant to do with my liberty did I reply—that I would go to join the Polish Army. As he left I heard him tell Pimenov that I must be able to travel in three days, as a transport of invalids designated for the "investigation" headquarters would be leaving Novaya Zemlya on August 17th.

How could I believe what they promised when I knew that they went straight from the hospital to the camp prison, where six miners were being held as responsible for the cave-in, and saw them executed as "criminal saboteurs," "Trotskyists," "Hitler spies"? And when four of these unfortunates were not instantly killed, the chief and the director of Department 3 finished them off themselves? This information came from the nurse that very evening.

EARLY ON THE morning of the 17th the death camp was agog with the legal departure of some of its inhabitants. Naturally I was the main object of attention, for I was soon to be a free man. Prisoner after prisoner came to me and gave me scraps of paper with the names of his family, or, when no paper was available, whispered the names of persons and cities. I tried to impress them all on my memory, and promised each man to pass on word of him if opportunity came.

One request was unforgettable, for there was no mention of names or places, only a message. It came from Vanya Kandalov, who pulled me off to one side and made quite a speech.

"I have nobody to send word to," he began. "If any of my family is alive, I am dead to them. The name I'm known by here is false. You'll soon be out of this great forced labor camp called the Soviet Union. And when you get to Western Europe I want you to hunt up the local Communists and warn them never, under any circumstances, to come to this hell. And if they won't heed that, at least they must leave their wives and children at home. I didn't. Tell them furthermore that the most rotten, most corrupt Western government is heaven compared with the Soviet. You will do what I ask?"

I replied that I would, but that people would not believe me.

"And when you meet André Gide," he added, "tell him I learned too late that everything he wrote about the U.S.S.R. was true, and that the truth I have learned from experience is ten times worse than what he wrote."

Shortly after noon we 36 fortunates were lined up and each was given three kilos of bread, two ounces of sugar and two dried fish. The first 17 kilometers (about ten miles) were to be made on foot; the rest of the journey to the port, 110 kilometers (approximately 70 miles), on the little railroad that had just been completed. I was the only physically able man in the group. The rest were sick or crippled who could hardly keep on their feet. The wonderful news that they were to leave Novaya Zemlya gave them strength to do what would otherwise have been impossible for them.

We boarded a steamer the next morning, bound for liberty! Strange, but vivid as are all the details of my life preceding that event, I can recall nothing of our departure except a feeling of exaltation—the almost incredible fact that I, a Pole, was returning from Novaya Zemlya to the living world. We stood on deck and took a last look at that forbidding land.

On the seventh day we sighted the continent and on the morning of the eighth we felt solid ground beneath our feet. We were not directed to the transients' barracks in the port (at the mouth of the Pechora), but marched a little way up the river to what in our eyes was one of the wonders of the world—a real railroad track, on which stood a puffing engine and five cars. But we were not pleased to see our old guard replaced by another group composed of silent, gloomy-faced, slant-eyed Mongols.

Up to this time we had not the least idea of our destination. Now one of the guards told us that the railroad connected the port of Niarion-Mor, at the mouth of the Pechora, with the river port at the confluence of the rivers Asa and Pechora; that the "investigation camp" was located there, and that there I would receive papers and go out a free man. It was not a long line, something like 300 kilometers (over 185 miles), but being new, with 20 temporary bridges and various other slowing-up features, normal speed could not be attempted.

At the "investigation camp" each of us received a bundle of 14 pounds of bread, one pound of margarine, 40 cigarettes and two packages of *machorka* (coarse tobacco). Each of us also received 150 rubles in cash. Thus equipped, we were to travel something like 625 miles on the river before we would reach a railroad line. A barge awaited us in the port and would leave when the load was complete, probably in the next day or two.

A large party of Polish women was brought on board before we sailed. Meeting them, though they were strangers, was like meeting, at long last, members of our own families. They had come from the Vorkutsk Camp for Women, some 35 miles away. That evening a third group of prisoners arrived, and our contingent was complete. We built a fire on deck, and chattered and sang and laughed like little children.

On September 21 began that gypsy trek, by barge and train, that was to take us across more than 2,000 miles of Soviet territory and bring us, on October 19, to the city where the Polish Army headquarters had been established and where our rehabilitation as human beings began. It was not long before we left Russia for Iran and the battlefields of North Africa and Italy.

May–August, 1949

Journey to Magadan

By T. L.

Translated by Ann Su Cardwell

[Like Andrey Stotski, the author of "Journey to Magadan" was a native of Lwow where she achieved distinction as a radio script writer. A woman of singular courage, Madame T. L. came out of the Gulag inferno to join the Polish Army formed by General Anders. Her Soviet penal "passport" is among the thousands stored at Stanford University. We reprint here only fragments of her complete story as it appeared in Plain Talk. *They are sufficient to reveal the truth about the appalling ordeal to which millions of innocent human beings have been subjected under the Soviet regime.]*

I

THE PEAL OF THE DOORBELL brought me bolt upright and wide awake. The only people in Lwow who rang doorbells violently in the middle of the night during January 1940 were the Soviet secret police, the NKVD. The loud sound of the doorbell, then, almost paralyzed me with fear, but immediately I regained control. In the pitch darkness I reached for my light switch and saw by my watch, as I drew on my slippers, that it lacked a few minutes of three o'clock. While I was tying the belt of my bathrobe, Kasia, my housekeeper and maid-of-all-work, came in from her room and together we went to the door.

Neither of us had any doubt as to who was there. Since the autumn of 1939 the NKVD had arrested and deported and executed, but in the first week in January 1940 they had begun arrests and deportations on a wholesale scale. Trains loaded with Polish men, women, and children were passing through Lwow on their way no one knew where, and the martyrdom of these people was something we knew but were powerless to mitigate.

Kasia and I had not spoken a word. She opened the door and I faced my callers. There were half a dozen, all in NKVD uniform and well armed. The officer announced that they had come to search the apartment, and they proceeded to do this. In other circumstances, their unfamiliarity with such modest possessions as mine would have been amusing. They were searching for evidence of hostility to the Soviet Union; and what odd bits they collected! A photograph of my mother holding a kitten; an English picture—"Oho! English! well, well, interesting"—a picture of an American cowboy that my little boy had cut out of an advertisement. The cowboy held a pistol in each hand. "Where are those pistols?" they demanded. "Give them up!". . .

The search finished, they ordered me to come along with them. I asked for permission to put on some clothes, as the night was bitter cold and snow was deep in the streets. They could see that I was in my nightgown, bathrobe, and slippers.

"Come as you are. Get along!" and they began pushing me to the door. But Kasia broke away from the man holding her, threw herself in front of the door, and declared that she would not let them take me in that manner, saying, "Officer, you must be a human being as well as an official."

Much to my surprise, he yielded and stood with watch in hand to count the five minutes he granted me. The soldiers watched me while I quickly dressed. Then I ran into the adjoining room where my little son lay, wide awake but huddled under the covers with tight-shut eyes. I had barely time to whisper a few words to him and say goodbye before the soldiers ordered me to go. . . .

I was in a small cell crowded with other women. In the days of free Poland this cell had held one person, its measurements being about 3 feet by 9. Now it was furnished with four wooden shelves, or bunks, one above another, a little table on which was a bucket of water, and a night-soil bucket, called a *parasha.* Seven women were on the bunks. In a few moments the door opened and another was pushed in, making nine in all. . . .

Talking and thinking were the only occupations possible on the crowded bunks, and during the first six weeks I could sleep only in snatches, so that I had the nights for thought as well. My thinking got nowhere. My companions tried to console each other and me by saying, "Have patience, this cannot be forever, a time will come." But I remembered too well the speech made by the Red Army major who took charge of the Lwow radio station; he had said,

"The Soviet Union is like a ship. The waves oppose it, the winds oppose it, but it sails on. Nothing will stop it. It is invincible. And if any of you here imagine that there will ever again be a Poland, let me tell you that such a thing is not even to be dreamed of. What the Soviet Union once clutches, it never lets go." . . .

Each morning each prisoner received a quarter of claylike bread, the day's ration, and a cup of "tea." This was water slightly colored and flavored by some herb or grain, not tea; its virtue was that it was hot, and sweetened with the prisoner's daily portion of sugar, less than a teaspoonful. At noon the cell door again opened a little way and through the aperture we extended little crockery bowls to get a diminutive helping of cereal. Sometimes this was flavored with dried herbs; as a rule it was cereal, salt, and water, nothing more. There was no trace of fat in it and never any meat. In the evening we received the same dole.

Once during the five months that I spent in that cell, we were given a real treat, a quantity of onions which we treasured and made last for a long time.

We had no plates, knives, or forks, only the little bowl and a wooden spoon apiece. I took my spoon with me from prison to prison and now it is a souvenir of those incredible years.

Soviet prison rules provide that prisoners be taken into the open air daily for ten to twenty minutes but, as everyone who has lived under the authority of the USSR knows, regulations and practice are quite different things. It was six weeks from the morning I entered that cell before I again saw daylight. Then my head swam and my eyes were blinded by it. Even so, I was more fortunate than many prisoners whom I met later. One woman with a small child had been kept six months in a dusky cell before she was allowed in the prison yard. . . .

IN JUNE WE WERE transferred to another section of the prison, in which common criminals were confined. This was a large cell, already overcrowded with more than 130 prisoners, for the most part thieves, prostitutes, even women guilty of murder. Some of these were little less than frightening, especially those who had a vicious hatred for all educated or propertied people. Mingled with these were innocent girls of fourteen or fifteen, against whom there were no charges at all. The hygienic and sanitary conditions can be judged from the fact that with us were women far gone with syphilis and that only two *parasha* were provided.

As punishment for any infraction of rules, we were all deprived of water. Once we had no water for twenty-four hours and salt fish was the midday meal. In this cell, too, we underwent most rigorous inspection; women with long hair were ordered to unbraid it, and an NKVD man explored the inside of our mouths with his finger. . . .

At first it was almost unbearable to see people tortured, to hear the screams and groans. But something happens to a person in such circumstances, if he survives it. One day it seemed as if something inside me broke, and thereafter I was numb to what went on. Had I not been, I could not have lived through the three months in Zamarstynow and come out sane. . . .

Every few days one would be taken from our cell and not return, but immediately another was put in. So many of these were young Polish and Ukrainian girls—eighteen, nineteen, twenty years old. They came with hair torn out by the roots, fingers broken, toes crushed, teeth knocked out or broken, jaws fractured. From their condition we knew what judge had questioned them, for each NKVD official had his own method. . . .

Soviet regulations forbid the imprisonment of persons not yet thirteen. Yet I saw boys in Zamarstynow who were eleven years old; I talked with them and they told me their age. Their cell was no lighter than ours, being on the basement level, but they did receive better food and more humane treatment. Only one of the 11-year-olds had been beaten. The boys who were 14 and 15 were beaten brutally, and the 16-year-old was put to the torture. Yet he lived, for I met him later in Russia.

THERE WERE ATTACKS and insults so gross that calm could not be maintained. One day one of the men guards ordered me to strip. Suddenly losing control of myself, I picked up the heavy ski shoes that I had put on when I was arrested and hurled them at his head, one after the other. He was utterly unprepared. One heel struck him under the eye, the other on the nose, and in my fury I jumped at him, yelling in his face that I would have him before the superintendent, the judge, and all the other officials I could think of. I knew the rules, I knew that no guard had a right to order women to strip before him for daily "review."

And nothing happened to me because of this incredible action. It seemed that I knew how to fight. Where had I learned that it is no use for a woman to use her fists, that her weapons are her shoes? . . .

II

. . . AFTER A YEAR and four months of imprisonment I had become used to sudden orders, but still I was unprepared for hearing my sentence: eight years at hard labor. The verdict, based on article 54, section 2-11 of the penal code of the Soviet Ukrainian Republic, dealing with participation in armed uprising and membership in a counterrevolutionary organization, had been pronounced without trial. There could be no appeal. . . .

Irka, a twenty-year-old Ukrainian girl and I were marched, one day towards the end of May, by guards with fixed bayonets across the petal-strewn Sobieski orchard along the road to the station. The guards were impatient, roughly urging us on. Irka, weakened by imprisonment and bad treatment, collapsed. A peasant cart came along. Our escorts halted it and put us in it. One of the men, noticed that I carried my fur coat rolled into a bundle, remarked:

"It will be a good thing to wrap her in when we bury her."

"A waste of fur," laughed his companion.

At the station I saw a boy of about twelve standing with a group of men. He was fighting to keep from crying. From the other side of the tall board fence separating his party from the station platform came a woman's voice, calling:

"My son, my son! Give me back my son!"

"We'll give you the devil, you bitch, not your son," an NKVD man answered with a laugh.

Irka and I, with six others, were put into a fourth-class Soviet passenger car equipped for the use of the NKVD. It had four tiers of bunks, each shelf intended for two persons. So scant was the space between these that only in the lowest one could the occupant take a sitting position. Persons on the other three tiers were compelled to lie down. Bars, like an animal's cage, separated these tiers from the narrow corridor that ran the length of the car. The only window—and that barred—was in the corridor. Thus I began my journey out of Poland. . . .

Not until we reached Kharkov was I ordered to leave the car. In the temporary cell to which I was taken, the walls were closely covered with the names of thousands of Poles who had passed that way. To find a place where I could put my own name and address I had to stand on the shoulders of two other prisoners. On the 12th of June, 14 of us women prisoners were taken out and started off again. . . .

There were four Ukrainian women from the vicinity of Stalingrad. All of them were sentenced for participation in religious activities. One of them had already served a ten-year term. Within two months after her release she was re-arrested on the charge of organizing prayer meetings. Natasha, an old Russian peasant grandmother, had been taken because she had permitted marriage and christening ceremonies to be performed secretly in her home. And lastly there was Rosa, a Polish Jewess who had been given a prison sentence for helping the family of a Polish political prisoner. While in a Kiev prison she gave birth to a daughter, Genia, now eight months old.

AGAIN THERE WERE days of travel under a broiling sun, maddening thirst, gnawing hunger and from dusk to daylight torment from bedbugs. We tried to protect the baby by putting her into a hammock made of a diaper slung between the tiers of shelves, but to no avail. The vermin swarmed over the infant and left her bleeding. If we chanced to have a guard who was human, he would buy bread and milk at the various stations with money little Genia's mother gave him. But the guards were not always so agreeable. Once two whole days passed when the baby had nothing but water with a bit of sugar in it—the sugar being a lump one of the prisoners had saved like so much gold. Only when it was evident that the baby was seriously ill and the mother screamed so that the men prisoners in the car ahead began to make trouble, did our guard promise to get a doctor at the next station.

And then he talked about the kindness of the NKVD in getting a doctor for a child on a journey. But he did not speak of the case of Lieut. Pieczonka, who had died from thirst while his companions had implored the guards to give him water. . . .

WE WERE TAKEN ACROSS the southern Siberian steppe to Novosibirsk and there unloaded, like so many heads of cattle, with heavily armed men guarding us and fierce dogs ready to attack slow-moving prisoners. In the blazing heat and the stifling dust we were hurried away to one of the Novosibirsk prisons, No. 2, as I recall. . . .

Five days of this and again, this time in company with men prisoners, we were taken to the station on foot. We were given bread and salt herrings as food for the journey. Baby Genia slept in her mother's arms. . . .

Once again we were loaded into the bedbug-ridden prison cars, and very soon the terrible days of travel were resumed, days of torture from thirst and with nothing to eat but bread. We lost count completely of the days, so much was each of them like its predecessor. Grass-covered steppe aglow with crimson wild tulips and iris, a stream or lake, a little birch forest—thus the scene repeated itself endlessly, with the heat of the sun steadily increasing in intensity, broiling us captives, with never a drop of liquid and our only food moldy bread, in the suffocating atmosphere of the inhumanly crowded convict car. But our escort had plenty of food and drink. Right behind our car was their traveling kitchen, from which the wind brought tantalizing odors and whiffs of delicious dishes. . . .

THE BREAD HAD GIVEN OUT, and we no longer had anything to eat. Our bodies were beginning to bloat, our arms were swollen, our legs were like so much wood from lack of ability to move about. . . .

IT WAS NIGHT when our train pulled into the Vladivostok station. The city, in the midst of a blackout test, was shrouded in darkness. The station loomed huge in the night, but we prisoners were not taken inside it. We were herded in the open the whole night through, while the rain came down in torrents. Our chief concern was to keep little Genia, Rosa's baby, from being drenched. Only at daybreak did it occur to the guards to move us a little farther up the railroad yards that we might stand under the shelter of a bridge.

At last we were again on a train. Though the car was not a prison car, men and women were not separated, and we were each permitted to visit the toilet at one end of the car once during the trip. A vulgar old Bolshevik sat in front of the door to the toilet and gave each person entering, man or woman, a blow on the back. When he slapped me, I yelled at him and threatened to have him reported and arrested. This worked like magic.

The "lager," or forced labor camp, to which we were taken was a place of horrors. It contained both men and women prisoners, their quarters separated by a barbed wire fence. There were 230 women here at this time, and we were crowded in one barracks that swarmed with lice and bedbugs. Only those prisoners who worked received food. And since there was far from enough work for all, prostitution flourished. . . .

One morning both men and women prisoners were marched down to the seashore, where all day long waiting boats were loaded with human freight. For the first time we realized how many Poles there had been in the men's camp. Why these sudden orders or whither we would be taken we did not know, but a whispered message from the men had informed us that a Polish-Soviet understanding of some sort had been reached. We were, we felt sure, already free and what was going on here certainly aroused our suspicion of dirty work somewhere.

Some time after noon we women were taken to the wharf. Of the 130 of us, only 5 were Poles, one was a Ukrainian from Lwow, several were Russian political prisoners, and all the rest were Soviet women criminals known as *shalman.* This is a term impossible to translate into a Western language, for civilization knows no such class. The women *shalman* are a group of utterly abandoned women, given to all kinds of crimes and the pursuit of pleasures of the lowest order where every art and every wickedness of the devil become flesh. Here was material for the vilest pornography, debauchery of the most extreme degree, and sadistic cruelty. Such was the company with whom ten or a dozen of us respectable women were being sent off. . . .

The women were placed in quarters directly below the flat deck, where the entire space had been divided into sections of bunk length, with three tiers of bunks built in. By the time I got in every bunk was occupied, and the *shalman* were cursing and shoving each other about. I backed into a corner and put my sack with my coat on it between my feet, resigned to spend the night thus. Soon I could feel the motion of the boat and knew that we were again on our restless journeying from one Soviet camp to another.

From beyond the partitions came the sound of an accordion and of soldiers singing. And then I felt my good Polish kerchief slipping off my head. I grabbed for the hand that was pulling it and as I did so, other thieving claws began to tear off my woolen sweater. It was clear that the *shalman* were taking advantage of my blindness in the darkness and of the noise made by the soldiers' singing to help themselves. My desperate situation made me frantic and I fought back with a strength that only despair and fury could give to so weakened a body. But I could not hold out and in short order somebody gave me a blow in the face that knocked me flat. My head struck the door, which opened at that instant and there stood the captain. The light from a lamp fell upon me bleeding, and on my torn clothes. But the thieves got nothing.

The second time I was attacked I again refused to give in, for I knew that anybody who once permitted herself to be terrorized was lost. I was threatened with knives and with having my eyes gouged out if I went to the official in charge for help. But I would not be frightened and brought the official in, although he came unwillingly. Nobody liked to get into conflict with the *shalman*. By the time he arrived, however, I had succeeded in getting back most of my things. From that moment I had always to be on guard and watch for traps. Once I came near tripping and going overboard headlong. More than once I was almost pushed down the stairs on the way to or from the toilet. I had to take care lest a lurch of the barge should fling me upon an outstretched knife. I had to look sharp or my food disappeared from under my eyes. The *shalman* always referred to me as "the political prisoner," "the bourgeoise," "the Polish lady."

Once I said to one of these women:

"You are young and pretty, but you have as much malice in you as the devil himself."

"How can I be different?" she replied. "I live in hell, the devil is my brother." . . .

One row followed another on this Dantesque voyage. Perhaps the worst occurred when one of the Russian men prisoners in a card game staked the bread allotment of that day for his group—and lost. A riot ensued, in which knives were used, with frightful results. I looked across and saw the floor slippery with blood and brains.

On sunny days sections of the deck floor that formed the ceiling of our quarters were raised. The sun and fresh air came in, and so did the men prisoners. The participants in the orgies that followed were so devoid of a sense of shame that no one was so much as asked to look in the other direction. The Bolshevik moral code was satisfied by the NKVD men flashing lights into the corners at night to make sure that no man was hidden in our quarters.

Our course now turned eastward. We passed through the strait north of the Japanese island of Hokkaido, within rifle shot of that island's shores, and then out into the open sea.

III

FOR SEVEN DAYS we sailed on the open sea and then we entered port in the Bay of Nagayevo. The men and women were put in separate groups and led on foot to the regional capital Magadan, many miles inland. The camp there was situated at the foot of a mountain and was enclosed both by barbed wire and rocky slopes. . . . .

It was in the fish-packing industry that we prisoners were to be used. The overseer, a young fellow, had himself been a prisoner and all working under him were prisoners. Men and women had their meals in a common hall, but were housed in separate barracks.

I was assigned to work in the salting room with a woman known as Marusia. This was terribly hard, heavy work, for together we had to pack 6,600 of the big, many-pound salmon in the course of an eleven-hour day. At noon work was stopped for an hour, and prisoners who had attained the quota for the past 12 hours (that morning and the preceding afternoon) received the full daily portion of bread, about a pound and three-quarters. With the bread, part of which we had to save for breakfast and supper or go breadless, we had porridge and a piece of fish fried in seal blubber. For the morning and evening meals a stew of fish heads was served us.

"Stakhanovites," or those who exceeded the work quotas, were rewarded with an extra half pound of bread and *bliny*, Russian pancakes, in addition to their day's ration. Those who completed only 50 percent of the quota received a fraction over a pound of bread, and reduced portion of porridge, fish and stew. Prisoners who could not turn in even 50 percent of the work quota got three-quarters of a pound of bread and a plate of soup at noon—nothing more. . . .

FOR FOUR DAYS I worked in the salting room. At the end of that time I lay on the boards of my bunk so full of pain I could not keep back the tears. My hands were so cramped they were useless, and in addition they were raw from continual immersion in salt handling icy fish. I made a plea to be transferred to another kind of labor, and was assigned to cleaning fish. The change brought no relief, for here I had to clean 1700 fish daily, and my arms simply refused to obey my will.

Through the intervention of the camp doctor, herself a prisoner, I was shifted to lighter work. This time I was set to packing herrings, 220 pounds to the barrel, 13 barrels a day the quota. But I never made the quota. My only ambition was to do enough work to entitle me to sufficient food on which to live, and by reaching 50 percent of the standard I could get along.

One day the prisoners who were Polish citizens went to the manager and said: "We know that you have no right to force us to do hard labor. We know that an agreement has been reached between the Soviet and Polish governments."

"What agreement are you talking about? I've never heard anything about an agreement. Somebody's been telling you fairy tales. Get back to your work!" . . .

I made some interesting acquaintances at this camp. One was a worker in the bath house. He was a taciturn man, by the name of Berman, a Jew with a long black beard, who stood out by his more cultivated speech. Once I ventured to ask him in German who he was.

"*Ein Mensch* (a human being)," was his laconic reply.

Later on he confessed to me that he was an Englishman, that he had been born in London, that somewhere in England—but he would not say where—he had a home and family, and that he was a journalist.

"Can I help you, when I get out?" I asked.

"To what purpose?" he asked in a lifeless tone. "Nothing can help me. They have all forgotten about me. And if they did remember—nothing could be done."

At the end of 24 days I was moved again, thanks to the recommendations of another kind-hearted woman doctor. I was put on board a barge to be towed by a boat. Hala Storozuk, another Polish prisoner who had been taken very ill and was told by the doctor that she needed an operation for appendicitis, was also on board and a number of Russian women prisoners. Where were we being taken this time?

"To a sanitarium," the authorities replied with a knowing smile. . . .

In the morning we were rounded up again, Hala and I in the lead, the *shalman* behind us, three guards and a dog at one side, and started off on foot on a 22 mile march. Hala's side was giving her much pain and she reminded the authorities of their promise to send her to a hospital. They just laughed and told us to get on. We reminded them that we had read the news of the amnesty granted us in the Soviet-Polish agreement of July 1941. We might as well have saved our breath.

After six miles walking I gave out altogether and had to stop. My feet were blistered, raw and bleeding. The coarse heavy shoes I wore rubbed the skin off and from the sores thus opened pus and blood were seeping into the shoes. But the guards dragged me to my feet and threatened to set the dog on me.

I tried to walk but neither Hala, who could scarcely stand on her feet, nor I was able to stay in the front. A soldier came up and gave Hala a heavy blow in the back that knocked her over. That act infuriated me and I shouted at him:

"Where are our rights? You have signed the pact with us and yet you treat us like the worst of convicts!" I kept yelling and cursing him.

"We are Polish women, and for that blow you shall go to prison!"

"What?" he answered, "you're Polish women and boast of it?" And set the dog on me, as he drew his revolver.

I knew that I must not let the dog knock me over for, according to Soviet law, if a dog brings a prisoner to the ground, it is assumed that the prisoner has been in flight and the guard is permitted to shoot. I instinctively braced myself, feet wide apart to meet the shock, and as the dog lunged at me rammed my padded prison jacket into his huge red mouth. This brought the beast to a sudden halt and left the guard stupefied. The soldier in command of our party ran back to see what was happening. He stopped a cart that was passing, and ordered me to proceed to Talon in it. But poor Hala was left to go on foot.

. . . I WAS RESTING on a log when suddenly Katia, one of two *shalman* I avoided as I would the devil, stealthily approached. She was small and wiry, supposedly 23 years old, but no one would have thought her less than fifty. Her face was so pock-marked that it resembled a sieve, and two little black eyes, bright with cunning, did not add to her attractiveness.

I gripped my bucket, thankful that it was iron, as Katia faced me in this lonely little clearing. But Katia took no notice. Instead, she looked around guardedly, put her finger to her lips, and leaned towards me.

"Listen, you Polish lady, now that we are alone, tell me—" she hesitated, looking around to see that we were really alone. "I saw you, and I know you pray. Tell me, is there a God?"

My grip relaxed on the bucket.

"There is."

"How do you know?"

"Because I pray every day and God does take care of me. And you know that I shall be free very soon."

"I've heard that but I don't believe it. Who would ever be allowed to leave this place? But listen, and remember, not a word to anybody," and here she pulled a knife out of a pocket. "I prayed once, too, that God would let me get out of here. And nothing happened. There is no God."

"And why did you think that God would listen to you when you are so wicked?" I asked her.

"Tell me," she began again. "Tell me, what is it like in your country? . . . Is life in your country different from ours here? Is it true that people can really enjoy life there?"

"It is true, Katiushka," and I described to her what life was like in Poland.

"You see," she sighed wearily when I stopped speaking, "I, too, would so like to have enjoyed life—to enjoy life!"

IV

"You are going to Magadan—to be 'liberated,' " the director spoke sharply.

Strength flowed back into me. The barracks was suddenly changed into a place of beauty. And then—I began vomiting. The good news was too much for me.

I was taken to Balagonnoy on a truck loaded with sacks of cabbages. Here I was sent to the barracks which was the best of all—the one reserved for mothers and infants. I asked for permission to visit the doctor as the stiffened bandages were becoming more and more painful. The doctor shook his head as he unwound the old bandages and put on fresh ones, apologizing because he had nothing but calico.

"The war—," he explained.

"Of course," I agreed. The Soviet Union was now in its fourth month of war. . . .

The camp director came in to see me and told me that the papers declaring me free might come any day, but that until they arrived he would have to treat me as a prisoner. But nobody paid any attention to me and I went about the camp as I pleased.

In the camp dining hall I sat opposite two women whose features and bearing set them apart from the others. They were good-looking Jewesses, obviously from the upper social strata of Western civilization. They were conversing in German. Curious to learn their story, I ventured to make some comment.

"You speak German? You are a foreigner? What a pleasure to meet someone from the world outside!" they greeted me.

The women were eager and pathetically happy to talk with someone who knew Berlin and Vienna, music and books. They told me that they came from Berlin; one was the wife of an engineer, the other of a lawyer. When the Nazis began to persecute the Jews, these men had fled with their wives to the Soviet Union. Misfortune came to them almost at once. All were arrested, accused of being German spies. The wives, separated from their husbands, had been sent to labor camps. They never learned what happened to their husbands, though five years had passed since their parting.

"You are going to be free? Lucky lady. Nobody will take note of us. We are people without a country," said Irma, the younger of the two, and suddenly rose from the table, adding:

290

"I must go and feed my baby."

She looked at me curiously.

"If you still hold to European standards of morality, you are shocked, I'm sure," she said. "Well, what was I to do? I held out as long as I could. I simply cannot, cannot, cannot—" and her voice rose almost to a despairing wail.

"Do you realize what it means to be sentenced to hard labor for life? Even for 15 years? For such a prisoner there is no hope of release, none. And, besides, I am not strong enough for such labor. A child saves a woman from it for a certain length of time. And to think I had my own beautiful home, that I had a family. And now—never can I. . . . Can you understand what that means?"

Her companion listened to this emotional outpouring with her lips curled in a cynical smile. "I have had three," she said, "and left them in other camps. I prefer having a baby every year to hard labor. I've got to look around now for the father of a fourth since the third has been taken from me. My only stipulations are that he shall not be too old or too odorous. I have never grown accustomed to the smells and never shall."

. . . LATE AT NIGHT I was deposited in one of the town prisons. I was given nothing to eat, just taken to a dilapidated barracks. By the glimmer of the lantern in the jailer's hand, I saw wooden platform beds around the wall. I hastily sought a place on one of these communal bunks for myself. As I lay down I touched another body and instinctively drew away.

"Have no fear—I'm clean." The voice was beautiful, the tone disarmingly friendly, the language spoken that of a cultured Russian.

And this is how began one of the strangest nights I ever spent in a Soviet prison. My bedfellow talked the whole night through, telling me her story. She had been the first wife of a Soviet Ambassador to Great Britain and, in the ten years she had now spent in Soviet labor camps, this was the first time she had been thrown in with someone to whom she could unburden herself. . . .

A thin, sallow-faced, shrewish-featured woman came in and speaking in a fluent, parrot-like manner, she informed me that there would be an official ceremony setting me free, that I would be put on a steamer, be supplied with new clothes, that I would travel first class on the train, that I would be provided with both food and money for the train trip, and finally that I would be going to the Polish Army.

I listened like one in a daze. . . .

One evening the camp director surprised me by inviting me to visit the camp theater with her. Considering the conditions under which the entertainment was presented, I have never seen anything better. In quality it was comparable to what I once saw at the Casino de Paris. But why should it not have been good? Here was the prima donna of the Kiev Opera, Vengerova, who possessed a magnificent voice; here were the ballerinas of the Moscow Opera,

Gamilton and Tartakovskaya; here was Gertz, a good pianist, and Tarasova, a wonderful dramatic actress, and a fine stage director. They were not visiting artists, they were prisoners.

Artists were treated better than the average prisoner, though they were not excused from hard labor. I saw a young woman who had won the Moscow beauty prize, Vera Popova, scrubbing floors. All prisoners of this type were "politicals." Somewhere somebody had said something . . . sometime had thoughtlessly regretted something. . . . And nothing more was needed to earn the speaker a ten- or fifteen-year sentence. . . .

October was almost gone when a guard arrived to take me to a photographer. There I learned that I was free, actually FREE. I fainted. When I recovered I returned to camp, a free woman, unattended by a soldier. But no steamer was arriving for some days, so I was still to live in the camp. . . .

I was still waiting for the steamer when the anniversary of the October Revolution came around. It was the custom of prison officials to carry out a thorough inspection before every holiday, on which occasion practically everything a prisoner had been able to accumulate was taken from her.

When the searching party at last appeared, all the prisoners were awakened. But I lay quite still and gave no sign that I was awake. As they drew near me, I could tell that the guard was in the lead.

"Hey there! Get up!"

I showed no sign of being awake.

"Auntie, show your basket."

Still I "slept."

Again he demanded that I show my basket. Opening my eyes, I said:

"I have no basket and if I had I wouldn't show it to you."

"The devil! Is she drunk?" he asked, turning to the overseer. "Then show whatever you've got!"

"A bag."

"Hand it over!"

"I won't. I will not allow you to search my things. Go on to bed. Good night."

"Are you a lunatic? Hand over that bag!"

"No, for I am a free woman."

"Free! And in a forced labor camp? Such 'free women' as you are searched like others in the barracks." And with a guffaw he caught hold of my feet to pull me out of bed.

"Have you permission from the prosecutor to make the search?" I asked.

"I have. And since you are a free woman, where's your passport?"

"Here it is." And I pushed the paper toward him. He jumped back as if it had burned him, straightened up stiffly, and saluted.

"I did not know—" he stammered.

"It is all in order," I said calmly. "Now show me your permit from the prosecutor."

"No—well, I haven't it with me. I left it in the office."

"Yes? Then you have no permit. And you are acting in the name of the prosecutor? You are exceeding your authority, aren't you? And do you know that you can be imprisoned for that? Tomorrow I shall make a report to the prosecutor himself, who happens to be a special friend of mine."

The barracks went wild.

TWO DAYS LATER I was called to the office and handed 315 rubles, a quilted jacket, felt boots, a blanket well sprinkled with holes, and a kerchief for my head. At the port I joined 32 Polish men on our journey to Polish Army head-quarters—long, weary weeks of hunger before we finally reached our destination in European Russia and our ultimate liberation. I did not taste real freedom until we crossed the border into Iran.

THE MYSTERY OF KATYN

By EUGENE LYONS

[One of the foremost journalists of our time, Eugene Lyons has, since the publication in 1937 of his Assignment in Utopia—now recognized as a classic in its field—conducted an unremitting crusade against the Soviet regime of slavery and terror. In numerous books and innumerable articles, and as editor of the old American Mercury and as senior editor of the Reader's Digest, Mr. Lyons has made major contributions to the defense of freedom in the world. In "The Mystery of Katyn," he unmasked the real perpetrators of one of the monumental crimes of the century. He concluded his exposé by urging a full and impartial inquiry into the Katyn massacre. Three years later, in 1952, a Congressional Committee carried out his injunction and in a voluminous and documented report completely backed his findings. Ten years later, in 1962, the University of Notre Dame Press brought out Death in the Forest, a study by J. K. Zawodny, who marshaled all the available evidence of the monstrous slaughter.]

ONE OF the most hideous atrocities of the last war—the cold-blooded murder of some 14,500 Polish prisoners of war, about 8,500 of them army officers—made headlines in the final two years of the conflict. The ghastly memory of this slaughter was briefly revived at the Nuremberg trial, where it figured in the indictment of the German war criminals. Since then it has been blanketed in silence.

This, of course, is entirely satisfactory to the murderers. They are eager that it be written off as "an unsolved mystery" and forgotten. But it is not satisfactory to the Polish people. And it should not be satisfactory to democratic world opinion: the crime is a challenge both to our conscience and to our political common sense.

The available evidence of guilt is largely circumstantial. But it is overwhelming. Though the subject is appalingly grim, unraveling the "mystery" is a fascinating process. It should appeal alike to connoisseurs of crime stories and students of totalitarian techniques. A powerful dictatorship, with unlimited perjury, forgery, and propaganda at its command, has tried desperately to cover up its bloody tracks—and failed. It has left an extraordinary number of damning clues.

WHEN the Red Army, by agreement with Hitler, invaded Poland in September 1939, it carried off a quarter of a million prisoners. Three former convents in Western Russia—at Kozielsk, Starobielsk and Oshtakov—were turned into special detention camps for the more valuable prisoners. Of their aggregate population of some 15,000, over 8,500 were officers, the rest being cadets, guards, gendarmes, frontier guards, etc.

Until April 1940 these prisoners corresponded with friends and relatives in Poland. But early that month the camps began to be broken up and their evacuation was completed by the second week in May. Though led to believe that they were going home, the prisoners in fact were put on trains for Russian destinations, in contingents of a few hundred at a time.

One group, totaling 448 and drawn from all three camps, was collected at a small camp at Pavlishchev Bor. In June these selected men—apparently told off for future interrogation or for other reasons—were moved to Griazovets, near Vologda. They continued in touch with the outer world; mail addressed to them at the original camps was forwarded to the new one.

But the rest, about 14,500, were never heard from again. Their mail to the old camps was returned to senders marked *Retour — parti.* More than nine years have passed, but not one of them has returned or given any sign of life.

Only this much was ascertained by Polish authorities through the handful of survivors at Griazovets and other sources: the Starobielsk prisoners were detrained at Kharkov, those from Oshtakov at Viazma, *those from Kozielsk at the village station of Gnezdevo, near Smolensk.* At each of these terminals the Poles were packed into autobuses in batches of 30 or more and hauled off to their mysterious fate. Having delivered their human freight, the vehicles returned for more until the job was completed.

Polish Soldiers Liberated

IN JUNE 1941 Hitler smashed the pact of friendship with Stalin by invading the Soviet Union. The Polish Government in London instantly declared its readiness to join forces with Russia against the common Nazi foe. A formal alliance between the two nations followed in August.

In accordance with its terms, there began the formation of a Polish Army on Soviet territory from prisoners amnestied by Stalin's order. General Anders emerged from his long ordeal of torture in an NKVD prison to head this force. He counted confidently on the thousands of officers in Soviet detention, among them 14 generals, for his command personnel.

From all corners of the Soviet land liberated Poles—sick, fevered, emaciated, in rags—flowed to the Polish training camp at Buzuluk. Among them were several hundred officers from Griazovets, some others from NKVD prisons. But not a single one of the 14,500 others turned up.

Weeks passed, then months, without a sign of life from the great bulk of prisoners evacuated from those three convents. The alerted underground in Poland reported that evidently not one of them had returned home or had communicated with his family.

Anxious, then desperate, inquiries were directed to the Soviet authorities through military and diplomatic channels. A Polish commission set up inside Russia for continuous investigation labored tirelessly but to no avail. A vague hope that the missing thousands might be in the Arctic areas, cut off by winter, faded out when spring came, then summer.

At the Russian end the Poles met only embarrassed and confused evasions. At first Soviet officials took the line that all the men had been released in April and May of 1940. Since none of them had reached Poland, however, this patent falsehood was soon dropped. Thereafter everyone, from the Soviet Ambassador in London to Stalin in the Kremlin, settled on an exasperating formula: the men had been duly amnestied but their whereabouts was unknown.

Stalin "Looks Into" the Case

THREE TIMES the problem was pressed upon Stalin personally. In November 14, 1941, in the presence of Molotov, he assured Polish Ambassador Kot that he "will look into the matter." Then and there he strode to a telephone and had himself put through, presumably to NKVD headquarters. He demanded the facts about the missing Poles.

A few minutes later the call was returned. Stalin listened gravely in silence, then put back the receiver without a word. For the rest of the interview he did not again allude to the subject. Had he been given an answer he could not share with his Polish guests? Or had it all been a piece of theater to confuse the issue?

Six weeks later, on December 3, the Polish Premier, General Sikorski, accompanied by General Anders, was conferring with the Soviet dictator. Informed that not one of the missing thousands had as yet put in an appearance, Stalin said quietly: "This is impossible. They have escaped."

"Where could they escape to?" Anders asked.

"Well . . ." Stalin shrugged, "to Manchuria."

He then promised that "special instructions will be issued to the executive authorities." Further, he expressed the opinion that the officers "certainly have been amnestied but have not yet arrived."

The third occasion was a Kremlin conference between Stalin and General Anders on March 18, 1942. His government and his army, the general explained, were deeply alarmed by the disappearance of such a large number of their countrymen.

"I have already given orders that they be freed," Stalin replied with a touch of impatience. "I do not know where they are. Why should we keep them? Maybe they were in camps in the territories which have been taken by the Germans and dispersed."

This was the first time that the theory of capture by the Germans was injected, and merely as a vague guess. The guess would be suddenly promoted to a definite claim—*after the discovery and identification of thousands of corpses.*

The Grisly Discovery

IN RETROSPECT, perhaps the gravest mistake the Poles made in those anguished years of waiting and searching was that they did not take the world into their confidence. Because the mystery implied possible foul play by the Soviet ally, and also because they still hoped the men were alive somewhere, they chose to keep a despairing silence.

Had the Allied peoples known about the strange disappearance of 14,500 prisoners, they would have grasped the horrifying significance of the German announcement on April 13, 1943. Coming out of a clear sky, the gruesome sensation was for the most part dismissed as another Goebbels propaganda trick.

The Germans announced that in a forsaken area of pine woods and juniper shrubs called Katyn Forest, near Smolensk, they had discovered "mass graves" of "about 10,000 Polish officers." On account of a peculiarity of the soil, the corpses were still fairly well preserved. All of them, according to the announcement, had been killed in April and early May, 1940, by revolver shots in the back of the head—almost an official method of execution by Stalin's police.

The date of the massacre was obviously the most vital element in the macabre equation; it would determine whether the Smolensk area was in Russian or in German hands when the crime was committed. It was fixed, according to the Germans, by thousands of newspapers, letters, diaries found on the bodies and in the graves.

In seven of the graves, not one of these documents bore a date later than April 22, 1940. Diaries stopped abruptly at that point, sometimes with a scrawled entry about the journey from Kozielsk to Gnezdevo in foul wintry weather. In an eighth grave the latest date indicated was May 11, 1940. From carved crosses, cigarette cases, and other keepsakes in their pockets—and from the names of hundreds who could be identified—it was clear that *all the victims had been brought from the same place: the camp at Kozielsk.*

The Germans therefore charged flatly that the men had been murdered by their Russian captors in April and May 1940.

The Soviet retort, after a few days' silence, was a countercharge of "lies, fabrications, hideous frame-up." The Russian version, as elaborated in further statements, was approximately as follows:

The Polish prisoners of war from all three convents were transferred in April and May of 1940 to three camps, 25 to 54 kilometers west of Smolensk, to work on railroad repairs, and in the summer of 1941 fell to the German invaders. A few months later they were murdered and buried in Katyn Forest. But in early 1943, with the loss of that territory to the Russians imminent, the Germans decided to throw the blame for the crime on the Soviets. Accordingly they dug up their victims, removed all papers bearing dates later than May 1940, added corpses with "touched-up documents" and in April staged their bogus discovery.

In London the Poles were well aware of the cynical, lying Nazi propaganda techniques. They knew that no species of ghoulishness was beyond the Goebbels imagination. But in this instance the German story was too plausible—it fitted too well into what little was already known—to be brushed off lightly.

The Belated Soviet Report

THE GRISLY burial place was *only two miles from the Gnezdevo station where the Kozielsk prisoners had been detrained.* The alleged dates of the massacre coincided with the weeks when the prisoners had been suddenly engulfed in silence. It seemed remarkable, moreover, that the Russians should now offer such a detailed and explicit story, though they had been unable to supply any information before the bodies were discovered.

If the last known whereabouts of the missing men had been west of Smolensk, if they had been captured by the German invaders, why hadn't the Poles been apprised of these simple facts? Soviet-Polish relations were then entirely cordial. Stalin, Molotov, Vishinsky, the NKVD chiefs, the Soviet Embassy in London, all of whom had at various times asserted they had no information whatever, might have said, "Unfortunately your officers were taken by the enemy." That would have cleared the Kremlin and ended the insistent questioning.

Normal Soviet procedure was to evacuate prisoners in the path of the advancing Germans. In cases where the evacuation could not be carried out in time, prisoners were "liquidated" to keep them out of the enemy's hands. It is hardly credible that the most valuable body of prisoners in Soviet custody, the flower of the Polish officers' corps, would have been left as a prize to the invaders. Had their abandonment been unavoidable, certainly such a serious loss would have been promptly and fully reported to the higher authorities.

Failure to inform the Poles during the years before the bodies were exhumed threw doubt, to put it mildly, on the belated Soviet account. In any event, the Poles would have been less than human, and derelict in their duty, if they had not acted to get at the truth of the story. The families and friends of the thousands of missing officers would not have brooked inaction.

First the Sikorski Government dispatched underground units to the scene of the ghastly discovery. They confirmed the exhumation, the identity of the victims, the availability of the extensive documentary materials. But they placed the number of corpses at about 4,000. Evidently the Germans, knowing how many Poles were missing, used the higher and more sensational figure; indeed, they searched the surrounding woods and marshlands diligently for additional graves.

(The Russians, incidentally, have followed the Nazi lead in adhering to the larger estimates—no doubt because the actual number of Katyn corpses, 4,253, leaves over 10,000 still to be accounted for.)

Then the Polish Government proposed that a neutral commission under auspices of the International Red Cross undertake an impartial investigation. The Germans immediately agreed. The Soviets not only rejected the proposal in anger but made it the pretext for breaking off diplomatic relations.

In August 1943 Berlin made public a detailed report by a European Medical Commission composed of scientists drawn from thirteen countries—Nazi-held countries, except for a Swiss professor. Its findings supported fully the initial German announcement.

A few months later the Red Army retrieved the Smolensk area. A commission made up entirely of Soviet scientists—without even a representative of the Polish stooge group, the Lublin Committee—again exhumed the bodies at Katyn Forest. Its report, in January 1944, reiterated the original Soviet version: The "11,000 Polish officers" (the estimate was raised) were killed by the Germans in August and September 1941; more than a year later the bodies were dug up and the documents "edited" in preparation for the sham discovery of April 1943.

One revealing episode in connection with this report must be recounted at once. A group of foreign correspondents was brought to the scene from Moscow to see the corpses and interview the Soviet investigators. Scores of local witnesses whose testimony was exhibited had all repeated the August and September dates; so had the scientists. But American newsmen asked a simple question that threw their hosts completely off balance. If the men had been massacred in August, why were they wearing overcoats, woolen socks and underwear, heavy scarves, fur gloves, and other winter clothes?

The only answer they got was that the Smolensk climate was unpredictable and that August 1941 had been a wintry month. This was a crude lie improvised in panic. Meteorological data and inquiries among former residents of that region have left no margin for doubt that it had been normal summer weather.

In its published form, under the title *Truth About Katyn*, the Soviet report conveniently gave the alleged dates of execution as "from September to December." But the testimony of about 100 witnesses, in the same document, apparently could not be altered and it still referred only to August and September.

Interment of the victims in soil that tended to mummify the corpses and preserve documents was the murderers' most serious blunder. They did not foresee the likelihood of a future exhumation. Failure to choose a date which would explain the winter apparel was a blunder of another order—an example of how even the most experienced liars may be hoisted by their own petard.

Which Date Is Credible?

THUS two totalitarian states, both of which were perfectly capable of mass murder, accused one another of the Katyn Forest holocaust.

The readiness of Berlin to permit the International Red Cross or some other neutral body to examine the facts, the furious refusal of Moscow to countenance such a thing, cannot be ignored in appraising what lawyers call "'consciousness of guilt." But beyond that there is a long array of direct and indirect proofs all pointing in the same direction. I shall limit myself to those that seem to me most striking. This or that piece of evidence or logical deduction may be open to argument, but their aggregate weight seems to be conclusive.

Only two sets of dates have been advanced. *Either the Poles were murdered in April-May 1940, in which case the Russians are guilty, or in August-September 1941, in which case the Germans are guilty.*

Which set is more credible?

The heavy winter clothing virtually rules out August, when the mean temperature in the Smolensk region is 65 degrees. It is entirely consistent with April, when the mean temperature is 40 degrees. In summer weather the prisoners might have carried their winter garments with them in bundles, but they would scarcely have worn woolen underwear, sweaters and greatcoats.

Moreover, as the European Medical Commission pointed out, no insects or traces of insects were found on any of the bodies or in the graves. In that marshy forest area, teeming with summer insects, this points to a cold-weather burial.

Another circumstance is worth mentioning. One of the mass graves—No. 5 in the record—was in ground lower than the rest and closest to the marshy part of the area. Upon being excavated underground water welled up. This grave could not have been dug to its depth in warm temperature; it must have been made in winter or early spring when the ground was frozen.

By way of camouflage, young spruce trees had been planted on the graves. Microscopic analysis by experts of the European Commission established that they were five years old and had been transplanted when two years old. The three-year interval corresponds to the time between April-May 1940 and the discovery of the corpses in 1943.

Now consider the Soviet hypothesis of a German frame-up. Suppose the Germans had murdered their Polish captives in August-September 1941, and subsequently manipulated the evidence to shift the blame on the Russians. Why, in that case, did they select April-May 1940 as the time of the crime rather than some date closer to the actual murder date?

Obviously the earlier the date selected, the more difficult would be the job of "doctoring" the documents; evidences of a longer interval would have to be obliterated. It meant that more telltale diaries or pages from diaries, more newspapers and correspondence, had to be eliminated. The earlier the date selected, the greater was the danger that *postdated* letters, papers, etc., might be found on the corpses, no matter how thorough the screening of more than 4,000 bodies.

In short, the Germans would have been prompted by practical considerations to designate the latest possible date, rather than April-May 1940, which was the earliest possible. Even from the political standpoint, it would have been more convenient to "postpone" the crime instead of fixing it at a time when the Hitler-Stalin pact of friendship was still in its honeymoon.

There was an even more compelling reason for the authors of such a frame-up to use the latest possible date in their charges. According to the Soviet version, the 14,500 prisoners had been working on public highways in a populated region for about fourteen months before their capture and sixteen months before their murder. The later the date alleged, the less risk that they would be given the lie by people who had seen any of the victims alive *after* that date.

The frame-up theory does not stand up in the light of common sense in other respects.

Though relatively well preserved, the bodies were virtually mummified—flesh, clothes and contents of pockets were usually welded together. The removal of objects from pockets required fine scalpel work in slitting cloth and extracting papers without damaging them. The Soviet story asks us to believe that the Germans, early in 1943, seventeen or eighteen months after the original burial, removed every scrap of paper from 4,000 corpses; separated those of the "wrong" dates; and then *replaced the rest* in the mummified pockets without leaving traces of the elaborate operation!

The normal mind rejects this picture as technically preposterous. Some incriminating letters, cards, or bits of newsprint would have escaped the most painstaking revision. Diaries with entries later than May 1940 might have been removed and destroyed. But how does it happen that the diaries found in the graves end abruptly with April 1940 entries? Why would so many prisoners have chosen to stop keeping their private record at about the same time? In none of the diaries is there any indication of torn-out pages.

With reference to the thousands of newspapers and scraps of newspaper, the supposition of a frame-up is especially far-fetched. Hundreds of scraps had been used to wrap small personal belongings found in pockets. The Germans would have been obliged not only to find thousands of old Soviet papers of the proper dates to "plant" on the corpses. They would have had to unwrap those objects—and rewrap them in older scraps of the proper date! The whole procedure is not believable; that it could have been carried out without a few revealing slip-ups, without some exhumed object being found wrapped in post-dated paper, is too great a strain on credulity.

Soviet Murder Methods Used

I HAVE already mentioned the method of execution, the familiar Soviet pistol shot at the base of the skull. The Germans in their notorious mass murders used machineguns and gas chambers. But perhaps they deliberately imitated the Soviet techniques in order to shift the blame?

That would assume a plan to pin guilt on the Russians at the time of the massacre. The Soviet version itself, however, asserts clearly that the frame-up was decided upon *long after the commission of the crime.* It is hardly likely that the Germans, in their hour of mounting victory, had foreseen defeat and exposure; that in 1941 they would have taken precautions to hide their tracks in 1943.

The same illogic is implicit in a number of other physical facts. For instance, about 250 victims had their hands tied behind their backs, and in some cases their greatcoats tied over their heads. (These no doubt were prisoners who offered resistance.) The rope used for binding them was indisputably of Russian manufacture. The method of tying it—an ingenious knot which tightened the more the victim struggled—was one that is almost standard in Soviet police practice. Also, many bodies showed bayonet wounds on their thighs and backs; without exception they were of the radial, four-blade pattern inflicted *only by Russian bayonets.*

We can scarcely credit the claim that German killers in 1941 went to such lengths to divert suspicion to the Russians in years to come. It is a claim ruled out by another curious fact:

The bullets were of a German make, from the factories of Genschow & Co. This must have seemed so damaging to the Germans that they were careful not to mention it in their first announcements. Later it was established that the Genschow firm had produced arms and munitions almost exclusively for export to Russia and the Baltic countries.

But if the Germans had used a Soviet method of execution, Russian rope and bayonets, to conceal their crime, would they have been so careless and stupid as to use German pistols and bullets? They had plenty of captured Soviet arms. Thus the German origin of the bullets argues strongly against the whole frame-up theory. The Soviet report, as a matter of fact, did not claim the bullets as evidence against the Germans.

Strange Coincidences

MOSCOW'S story presents another challenge to common sense. All the missing men, it states, had been in the Smolensk district in camps (exact location, curiously enough, not given) for fourteen months before the outbreak of the Russo-German war. Why had their mail been returned to senders, though mail to prisoners in other areas was being delivered? Even assuming that a tight censorship had for some undisclosed reason been imposed only on these 14,500, it seems too much to believe that not one of them, working on the roads, had failed to smuggle out a message to some friend or relative.

Those camps, if they existed, raise a further problem. They were located, according to the claim, between 25 and 54 kilometers west of Smolensk. Why, then, were the Kozielsk prisoners detained at Gnezdevo, which is only 13 kilometers west of Smolensk? There are stations at frequent intervals on that railroad.

At Gnezdevo, it will be recalled, the Poles were taken away in small batches by an autobus, which then returned for more. According to entries in diaries, these vehicles returned *at intervals of about half an hour.* That would be about right if the destination were Katyn Forest, two miles away. It would be impossible if the destination were 12 to 41 kilometers away.

The Soviet report said at one point: "The presence of Polish prisoners of war in the autumn of 1941 in Smolensk district is also confirmed by the fact that the Germans made numerous round-ups of those war prisoners who had escaped from the camps." In that case, it is surpassingly strange that not one of the missing 14,500 had made good his escape, or at least established contact with his friends or family.

Incidentally, a few weeks after the German invasion of Russia the Soviet Ambassador in London, Mr. Maisky, gave the Polish Government an accounting of the Polish prisoners in his country. Sir Alexander Cadogan of the British Foreign Office was present. Although Mr. Maisky mentioned many smaller groups, he did not say a word about the alleged three camps in the Smolensk area—camps that supposedly held the flower of the Polish Army. The "oversight" argues against the existence of any such camps.

A clinching refutation of the Soviet account, finally, is to be found in the circumstance that only *prisoners from Kozielsk*—and roughly *all* the prisoners from Kozielsk—were buried in Katyn Forest. Had the inmates of all three officers' camps fallen into German hands, they would inevitably have been mixed up. The Germans could have had no practical reason and no possibility for keeping together the 4,253 men who happened to have been in the same camp a year before.

More than that, from information provided by the Griazovets survivors we know that certain officers were evacuated from Kozielsk in the same convoy and placed together in the same autobus at Gnezdevo. Then they were identified side by side or close together in the same Katyn Forest grave. This is quite natural if they were taken directly from the station to their death. It is wholly inexplicable if they had remained alive for eighteen months and passed through the reshufflings of new camps, road work, the chaos of capture by the

Germans. For men accidentally in the same convoy in April 1940 to appear side by side in the same grave in August 1941 would be a coincidence close to miraculous.

Testimony of Mikolajczyk

THE VERDICT is inescapable. *The 4,253 Poles unearthed from common graves at Katyn Forest were murdered by Stalin's NKVD.*

Where are the prisoners of Starobielsk and Oshtakov? By analogy we must assume that their mass graves are somewhere near Kharkov and Viazma respectively. The very fact that the Kremlin persists in lumping all these prisoners together, and in placing the Katyn total at ten or eleven thousand, betrays an anxiety to divert inquiry from the victims not yet located or exhumed.

Upon his return to Soviet-dominated Poland in June 1945, former Prime Minister Mikolajczyk reports, he was approached by General Prosecutor Sawicki with the proposal that a public inquiry be staged to "acquit the Russians" of the Katyn blood-bath. "Katyn stays in the heart of the Polish people," Sawicki said. "We should have a comprehensive hearing." He wished to know what Mikolajczyk was prepared to testify.

"Only what I know," Mikolajczyk replied, and proceeded to outline such facts as he had gathered while a member of his Government in London exile. The Prosecutor left in undisguised disgust. Later, together with Minister of Justice Swiatkowski, he flew to Moscow to confer about the project. There has been no hearing.

That the postwar Warsaw regime did undertake an unpublicized investigation of its own has become known only recently. A prominent Krakow lawyer, Roman Martini, was put in charge. Apparently the Communist rulers erred in choosing an honest man. Martini's report not only flatly accused Soviet Russia of the crime but named some of the NKVD officers in command of the grim job. This we know through a colleague of Martini who escaped to Sweden and published the whole tale in the Stockholm *Dagens Nyheter* of February 13, 1948.

Several days after he had delivered his report and returned to Krakow, Roman Martini was assassinated by two young Communists, according to the Stockholm account. The killers were arrested but quickly "escaped" from the Krakow penitentiary.

Two pieces of intelligence that seem to fit into the jigsaw puzzle deserve mention. The first involves "General" Zygmunt Berling, a Pole who early cast his lot with the Soviets. In the late spring of 1940 he was among a group of "cooperative" Polish officers meeting with Soviet military and police officials, including the head of the NKVD, Lavrenti Beria, and his deputy, Merkulov. The subject under discussion was formation of a Polish unit to serve with the Red Army.

At one point Berling asked permission to interview certain high-ranking Polish military men, with a view to enlarging his staff. Beria's reply was cryptic. Neither Berling nor the others—from whom we have the story—could fathom its horror until three years later, when the mass graves were uncovered.

"Unfortunately," Beria said, *"these men are no longer available. A mistake was made."*

The use of the word "mistake" is curious. But it begins to make sense when related to the second matter: a story recently spread in London and credited to a member of the Soviet Embassy there. We have no way of knowing, of course, whether it is wholly or even partly true.

According to this account, Stalin was asked by the Red Army what disposition he wished to make of its fat catch of Polish officers. Stalin thereupon took a piece of his personal stationery and wrote on it one word: *Liquidate!* It is a word of many meanings, and perhaps the dictator did not mean physical extermination. But the Red Army chose the most gruesome interpretation and turned the bloody task over to specialists in such matters, the NKVD.

At the War Crimes Trial

THE COURTROOM at Nuremberg where German war criminals were being tried was filled with the ghosts of the murdered Poles. Their presence plagued the Soviet representatives among the Allied judges and prosecutors.

To have ignored one of the most publicized war crimes would have come too close to an admission of guilt. The Soviets therefore wrote into the indictment the charge that "In September 1941, 11,000 Polish officers who were prisoners of war were killed in the Katyn Forest near Smolensk."

The world was thus presented with an ironic spectacle: criminals prosecuting others for their own crime. They saw to it, however, that the proceedings remained firmly under their own control. Even the Polish satellite regime was not allowed to intrude. Warsaw had submitted a voluminous list of charges against the Germans but the crime that was "in the heart of the Polish people" was not included. That was reserved for Russian handling, solo.

The Katyn affair was dealt with gingerly at Nuremberg on July 1-3, 1946. The star Soviet witness was Professor Markov, a Bulgarian member of the 13-nation European Medical Commission which had attested the German accusation in 1943. Markov, of course, declared that the Commission had faked its report under German duress. The court was not apprised that this Markov had been arrested by the Soviet occupation forces in Bulgaria and that, like all subjects behind the iron curtain, he was not exactly a free agent.

More important, the court was not informed that other members of that European Commission, living in liberated countries, were available for questioning *but were not called.* We know today that they would have refuted Markov's statements and confirmed their original verdict of Soviet guilt.

One of these men is Prof. F. Naville of the University of Geneva. In a signed article in the Swiss press he has declared that the Commission's report had been reached through free and unhampered inquiry. In a letter to a New York journalist, Julius Epstein, he wrote on June 28, 1948:

"Neither the German Government nor any other government exercised any pressure upon me in my researches concerning Katyn. . . . I have not changed my opinion and continue to believe what I signed in the protocol of April 1943, at Smolensk. . . . I am a physician and do not concern myself with the political aspects of the affair."

Another member of the Commission, Prof. V. M. Palmieri of the University of Naples, wrote to Mr. Epstein on July 16, 1948:

"I was not subjected to any pressure on the part of the German Government before or during our investigation."

The Soviet prosecutors limited themselves to the one witness whom they controlled and were careful not to summon any colleague of his who could testify freely. Nevertheless, *the Nuremberg judgment failed to mention the Katyn charge.* It was in the indictment—but not in the verdict. Rarely had silence spoken so eloquently. Though crimes involving a few dozen victims were dealt with in detail, this terrifying massacre of thousands was passed over without a single word. *Even the Soviet minority judgment does not mention Katyn.*

Indirectly, therefore, Nuremberg has exonerated the Germans of this crime, and this is tantamount to a verdict of guilty against the Soviet Government. The Kremlin stands convicted of the gruesome deed.

The aura of uncertainty around this fact, the prevailing idea that Katyn is an "unsolved mystery," is a product of the former appeasement policy with relation to the Soviet Union. Whatever the reasons of expediency for the conspiracy of silence during the war, they are no longer valid. There is not an excuse in morals or policy for continuing to shield Moscow against condemnation by world public opinion.

The British Government knows the facts as intimately as the Poles do. From the outset all documents and information on the case was transmitted to them. The British kept silent and urged the Poles to do the same on grounds of wartime morale. Those grounds no longer exist. Much of the physical evidence in the case, captured from the Germans, is believed to be in the hands of the American Government. Again there is not a shadow of justification for not releasing them for competent study.

A full, open, impartial scientific appraisal of the appalling atrocity is in order. It is the least the Allies owe to the Polish people—and to the 14,500 victims. An uninhibited exposure of all the terrifying facts would be politically valuable, moreover, in proving to all mankind the real character of the dictatorship which is today conducting a cold war against freedom.

October 1949

DEATH ROW

By NICHOLAY DIDENKO

[*To those who will question the credibility of this hair-raising report we can give only one effective answer: Had anyone reported to the world before the war that Hitler had gas chambers and crematoria in operation to put millions of human beings to death, few would have given credence to it.*

Nicholay Didenko, the author of this fragment from a forthcoming auto-biographical book, exists. He is a D.P. recently arrived in the United States. We have investigated his record and can vouch for its veracity. He figured prominently in a show trial in Korosten, the Ukraine, late in 1937, of so-called railway wreckers, a trial which was widely reported in the Soviet press and abroad. He had been seized at the height of the panicky Yezhov era of Red Terror in the Great Purge, and found himself several months later in the Alexandrovsk Prison for Politicals, a huge plant near Irkutsk, Siberia.

When the psychopathic and dreaded Yezhov was deposed for his excesses by Stalin in 1938 and himself consigned to the execution squad, a considerable number of his victims were released and sent home, presumably for new trials. The writer, Didenko, was one of those fortunates. To this unusual circumstance we owe his survival and his eventual coming to the United States. And we are thus enabled to get a new insight into one of the most secret operations of the Soviet regime, a horror which tops all those previously disclosed and which shows that Stalin was Hitler's precursor in one more department of dehumanization.]

THE ONLY PLACE in the Alexandrovsk Prison Compound for Politicals where prisoners met was in the bathhouse. We looked forward to it as an extraordinary treat, for there would be about 100 men from various cells in each party. We were allowed about 15 or 20 minutes for bathing.

This was one of our happiest moments, as we had opportunities to get acquainted, to talk about any subject without the presence of guards. When we left the bathhouse, we had all the news. Moreover, the personnel in the establishment consisted exclusively of prisoners who had freedom of movement in the prison yards, and therefore could converse with many prisoners scattered in the various blocks.

In spite of the fact that this personnel was strictly forbidden to engage in conversation with ordinary prisoners, we managed to do so and to learn things.

We even conducted surreptitious correspondence with our acquaintances and friends through the attendants.

In the course of one of our routine trips to the bathhouse I heard that the prison administration was selecting qualified engineers, mainly specialists in railroading and mechanical construction, for exceptionally secret assignments. This meant an increased bread ration as well as a supplementary allotment of soup and dried fish. It was the kind of news which cheered many of us. To begin with, I saw an opportunity of working at my profession instead of stagnating in the cell. And then it meant extra food, so that I would not go hungry, which often happened. I also hoped that the work might be outside the confines of the prison area so that I might send a letter to my children to let them know I was still alive.

Soon enough the rumors were confirmed. I was called to the office of the Special Section where I was interviewed at length by a prison official and a military personage with the rank of colonel. It was the latter who questioned me most. He was interested in all the details of my past service and my knowledge in handling military transport and traffic. The interview was strictly formal, but most courteous. The colonel addressed me by my last name, to which I had long since become unaccustomed. During all the NKVD interrogations in the thirteen previous months I had been called bandit, enemy of the people, prostitute, fascist, capitalist lackey, Trotskyist, etc. No wonder it seemed strange to be spoken to in a Soviet prison in a decent tone. Not that the likable colonel made such a moving impression upon me, for I understood only too well that this was part of the NKVD game and I even began to suspect that there was something strange about it all.

When the session was over I was led to another cell, not even in the same block. There were only two other inmates in my new cell—a certain mining engineer by the name of Fedorchenko, who had been convicted in the famous Shakhta Trial, and an old family acquaintance, Igor Stepanenko, an instructor of the Moscow Institute of Railway Transport Engineering.

FROM MY colleagues, who were very happy at my joining them, I found out that my transfer to this block meant that I would be put to work in my profession.

"You've guessed right, my dear compatriot," Stepanenko, himself a Ukrainian, said to me in his deep voice. "They will take you and use you like a tool, but at what kind of work? And for how long?" Lowering his head, Fedorchenko chimed in, whispering: "For eternal penal servitude."

"You seem so glad that you are going to be outside of this accursed Stalinist prison, that you'll be working in the open spaces, but you don't realize that you have landed in Death Row."

"What do you mean, Colleague Stepanenko—I am in Death Row?"

"Looking at you, it is pleasant to meet for the first time the son of a good friend, after more than a decade in jails in spite of my absolute innocence before my people and my government. On the other hand, I want to cry, and cry again, because you are so young and in all likelihood you have a young wife and little ones who will never see their father again. I am talking this way not because it will crush your spirit; I am saying it so as to warn you and enable you to exploit every possibility to gain freedom, even if it involves extreme risk to your life. I think you understand what makes me talk this way."

When Stepanenko mentioned my children and my wife, I was numbed for a moment and could not speak. I sat down on the iron seat attached to the wall, and it took me quite a while to regain possession of myself.

"I beg you to tell me everything," I said to Stepanenko. "I don't understand it." He looked at me searchingly with his tired black eyes, shook his long grey hair and moved over close to me. He put his hands on my shoulder, and tears began to stream down his cheeks. He kissed me on the head and said:

"I'll tell you everything as if you were my own son. I'll tell you all I know about Death Row. I have been here seven years. During that time I have participated in and directed the construction of many military establishments, mainly in the Urals and in the Far East. I had a hand in the building of a great arms plant which is situated deep in the forests, near the city of Chita. About 20,000 political prisoners took part in this project.

"I did much building, aviation bases in the Far East and all kinds of military enterprises, some in the *taiga* [Siberian forests] where a great deal was put up. And all the work was done by people like you and me, from the chief engineer to the ditch digger. Leading scientists and outstanding technicians, all prisoners like yourself, were in on these projects.

"And now I see that they are drafting fresh reinforcements of technicians. So many of my colleagues have been destroyed in these last three years that now the prisons are being filled with new masses of victims who will be crowding Death Row."

"But why do you call it Death Row?" I asked. Stepanenko replied:

"And you haven't caught on yet? It's the name the prisoners themselves have given this block. After the completion of each war project, which is carried out mainly with the labor of political prisoners, certain columns of workers on the project, including some technical staffs, are exterminated, regardless of the numbers involved. The method of this extermination is simple.

"WHEN a project is finished the NKVD announces to the entire force that new underground construction will be undertaken in the neighborhood of the plant. For this purpose the working force sinks a new subterranean gallery of special construction in accordance with a prepared plan. When the gallery is almost finished, a special unit is assigned by the NKVD. All the hoisting apparatus is then removed from the gallery so that no one can get out. A specially trained brigade of the NKVD then fills the gallery with poison gas. In a few minutes all the trapped men are dead. When the job is done, the gallery is filled in with earth, the surface is leveled, trees are planted, and all traces disappear.

"By this method three objectives are attained: the speedy and easy destruction of superfluous men, the testing of poison gas for future chemical warfare, and, finally, the safeguarding of a military secret. I myself have witnessed several such operations.

"When we were finishing the military project near the city of Chita where I served as deputy to the chief engineer, I was entrusted by Colonel Kalashnikov of the NKVD, the director of the project, with orders to sink four underground galleries in the woods about one kilometer from the completed plant. I carried out the task in exact conformity with the plans given to me. According to my estimates, some 10,000 people were exterminated there.

"In charge of this mass terror was Alexander Gridin, NKVD colonel, who held the post of chief of security in Death Row. All such experiments, upon the completion of projects, were under his supervision. It was my unhappy lot to be assigned to the leveling of the ground over the fraternal graves, and to plant saplings instead of crosses over them.

"I had a similar experience in the *taiga* where I built large subterranean warehouses for explosives. There, too, I sank three shafts, for people like yourself. Some 5,000 of them were asphyxiated in them under the direction of the same Colonel Gridin.

"THE SYSTEM in these operations is to spare, upon completion of each project, only the leading specialists and scientists who cannot be replaced, and the most skilled technicians. These are to be used until their usefulness is exhausted. Those unfit for one reason or another are ordered exterminated.

"Take my last military project, for instance. My very good friend, an outstanding engineer, Alexander Petrovich Kukharov, with whom I served four years in Death Row, accidentally broke a leg on a job. Instead of putting him in the hospital, Colonel Gridin had him shot on the day after the accident. The entire engineering staff that has been working at secret military construction, regardless of the terms of their sentence, will never return to their homes and will never know freedom again.

"In this very prison compound, there is a big chemical laboratory in which outstanding chemists from Death Row are at work. They are experimenting in all kinds of scientific methods of perfecting gases and inventing lethal substances for the next war. The effect of these gases and poisons is tested on human beings, the so-called 'counter-revolutionists' and 'enemies of the people.'

"This block houses engineers who have had their share in Stalinist construction, but who are at present not overloaded with assignments, and are kept in reserve awaiting the next routine call to another project. This is my situation as well as that of our colleague, Fedorchenko. We are absolutely isolated here, not only from the rest of the world but from other inmates of the Alexandrovsk Prison.

"Take me, for instance, I was given a five-year sentence, but I have been serving seven years now in Death Row. I know that I will never return home and that I am losing strength every day. I am only awaiting that day, which is not very far off, when the Soviet regime under our 'Beloved *vozhd* [leader]— the genius of progressive mankind' will subject me to its next scientific test of asphyxiating weapons."

June 1949

Stalin Purges Jewish Writers

By Herschel Weinrauch

[*One of* Plain Talk's *journalistic "firsts" was this report on Stalin's extermination of Jewish intellectuals by Herschel Weinrauch, a recent refugee from Soviet Russia. A full decade before Harrison Salisbury published in* The New York Times *a roster of scores of names of Jewish writers, artists, and scientists who perished in the great purge, Weinrauch exposed the main facts of Stalin's earliest anti-Semitic crusade. The author, under the name of Winokur, was a well-known Yiddish writer in the Soviet Union, having published four novels between 1932 and 1939 in Moscow and Minsk. During World War II he served as a lieutenant in the Red Army, was wounded in action and decorated. His book in Yiddish,* Blood on the Sun, *was published in Brooklyn in 1950.*]

THE MYTH of Soviet advancement of national minorities has been exploded in the case of the suffering of the Ukrainians and other ethnic groups. But the truth about the Soviet maltreatment of the Jews has hardly been touched on. I could cite hundreds of cases of the arrest, torture, and liquidation of the finest leaders in Jewish letters, drama, and other fields of culture.

As one of the Soviet Jews who has succeeded in escaping from the Soviet inferno, I was an eyewitness to the facts which I am going to recite, facts which cannot be dismissed or denied.

I know well that many think that most of the Jews in the U.S.S.R. are Communists, and that life for them there is easier than for the others. This is a gross misapprehension and must be corrected. The world must learn the truth. For, on the contrary, it is the Jews who suffer most in the Soviet Union.

310

For the past 30 years, thousands of Jews, one-time Zionists and Socialists, have been sent to prisons, concentration camps of Siberia, the Far East, and Kamchatka, and through "trumped-up" trials, sentenced to death. One may be led to think that because the U.S.S.R. calls for the recognition of the State of Israel, the plight of the imprisoned Jews in Russia would be eased. That is far from the truth. The situation has not altered one iota: Jews still remain in jails and concentration camps, without any hope of ever getting out.

For the record, I shall here set down a score of cases of leading Jewish figures in the arts and sciences who have been purged in recent years.

ONE OF the outstanding poets in Russia was Izzie Charik, the father of Soviet poetry in Yiddish. In his early days he glorified the Soviet mode of life. In *Muds of Minsk,* his work most beloved by Jews and non-Jews alike, he describes the struggle for power in Russia. Another one of his popular poems, *Body and Soul,* was about a schoolteacher who sacrificed everything to help further the Revolution. His last book was *At a Strange Wedding.* This is the story of a Jewish minstrel—his life under the Czarist regime as contrasted with life under the Soviet system. This poet, Charik, the shining light of Yiddish literature in the U.S.S.R., an innocent and blameless man, was arrested in 1937 and tortured.

Another victim was Moishe Kulbak, a fine novelist, poet, and teacher, who came from Poland when it was a semi-fascist country. Hitlerism had begun to rear its head in Germany. The promise of Russia beckoned to many enslaved and homeless. Kulbak was eager to go to the land of his dreams. After a great deal of red tape, the Soviets permitted him to enter the country. He received a warm welcome in Minsk and his novels and poems were translated into many languages. One of his best works, *Zemelyanir,* was written there. It was the story of the life of a Jewish family before the Bolshevists came to power, and the psychological changes that took place in their home during the dictatorship. It was highly praised. Then suddenly, for no reason, Kulbak was arrested. It has been nearly 20 years since this talented writer was last seen or heard from.

The first and oldest Jewish proletarian poet in the U.S.S.R. was Chaim Gildin. By trade he was a shoemaker, but his calling was that of a poet—a poet who had his roots in the people, and who loved them with all his passionate soul. His songs were sung by Jews everywhere. A faithful follower of the Soviet regime, he was nevertheless arrested and no one knows what became of him.

Tsadik Dolgopolsky was an old Russian playwright and novelist. Author of dozens of novels and plays, his drama, *Noise of Machines,* was performed at the Minsk Government Theater, and received with enthusiasm. Then Dolgopolsky was secretly arrested, and no one dares ask the Soviets what has happened to him. Whether he died a natural death or whether he was put to death may never be known.

In Berlin there lived a young and talented writer, Suskind Lev. When Hitler came to power and Jews fled in all directions from Germany, he got to Russia. For a while his works were very popular. His book, *The Revolt of the Peasants,* met with great success. In 1936 this Jewish writer, who had escaped from a Nazi concentration camp, was accused by the Soviets of being a German spy. His fate was sealed.

One of the leading authorities and critics of Jewish literature was Moishe Litvakov, editor of the Moscow Yiddish newspaper, *The Truth.* His writings carried great weight, both in Russia and abroad. His best work is his two-volume *Restlessness.* At the age of 70, during the 1937–38 purge, he was arrested and subsequently died in a Soviet jail.

Yashe Bronstein, a young man still in his thirties, had already achieved general recognition for his literary style as a critic. A graduate of the Moscow Academy, he was popular as a lecturer and writer. His book, *Attack,* aroused wide interest. He, too, was imprisoned and tortured.

There was Selig Axelrod, the lyric poet who was also a famous chess player. His poems displayed a love of nature and of music. Politics was not his concern. His books were entitled *Songs* and *More Songs.* In 1940, at a meeting in Vilna, he protested against the Soviet proscription of Jewish schools and newspapers. Upon his return to Minsk he was arrested. He was jailed and shot by the NKVD.

Max Erich, whose life work was research into Jewish literature, was primarily concerned with the works of Sholem Aleichem, and his book on the great Jewish humorist had made a deep impression. Erich was professor at the Kiev University, and also lectured at Odessa, Minsk, and Moscow. Without any why or wherefore, he was liquidated by the Soviets.

Professor Milomet, lecturer on "Dialectical Materialism" at the University of Odessa, was the author of many scientific treatises. Notwithstanding the fact that he suffered from tuberculosis, this scholarly man has been imprisoned by the Soviets.

The great director of the Minsk Jewish Government Theater, who earned the high title of "People's Artist of the Soviet Republic," Mark Rafalsky, was suddenly dismissed from his post and declared an "enemy of the Soviet people." The GPU arrested him and he has not been heard from since.

The Yiddish newspaper *October* was published in Minsk. When the editor, C. Dunetz, was arrested he was replaced by a journalist, Osherowitz. The latter, too, was arrested and his place was filled by Bear, who was later sent to prison. Kabakov, an ordinary worker, then became editor. With his arrest, the entire newspaper plant was shut down.

Professor Lieberberg, director of the Kiev Jewish Institute, part of the Ukrainian Scientific Academy, later became president of Birobidjan, the autonomous Jewish Soviet Republic in Siberia. He was arrested by the Soviets and perished.

In Birobidjan there lived Yosel Fier, a machinist and Stakhanovite, who had come from Argentina. All the newspapers praised him for his devotion to the Soviet Union. Why was he arrested and shot? The Soviets never answered that question.

GEZERD was an organization to help Jews settle in Birobidjan. Its leaders, Rashkis, Deimenstein, Weinstein, and others, were arrested by the Soviets and the organization disbanded, although its counterparts in the United States and other foreign countries have continued to function as propaganda and fund-raising agencies.

These few and sketchy cases should serve to illustrate one of the least known aspects of the Soviet terror. Far from being free, Jewish life in Russia is being crushed by the Soviet regime.

February 1949

ODYSSEY OF A JEWISH PARTISAN

By JOSEF SIGELBAUM

[*On June 4, 1943*, The New York Times *carried a long dispatch from London announcing the suicide there of Szamul Zygielbojm, Jewish labor leader and member of the Polish National Council. It was a story which went around the world, even at the height of the war, because the suicide had left a moving letter which showed his act to be a last resort to shake world apathy in the face of the unprecedented mass slaughters of Jews. In it he charged that "the responsibility for the crime of murdering all the Jewish population in Poland falls in the first instance on the perpetrators, but indirectly also it weighs on the whole of humanity, the peoples and governments of the Allied States, which so far have made no effort towards concrete action for the purpose of curtailing this crime."*

Mr. Zygielbojm died in the belief that his whole family had been wiped out. He did not know that his son, the author of this exciting out'ine, had survived, and had joined first the Red partisans and then the Red Army to fight against the Nazis. Josef Sigelbaum (anglicized spelling) attained the rank of captain, was wounded twice, and was repeatedly decorated for bravery in action, having been awarded the Order of the Red Star, the Medal of Moscow, the Medal of a Partisan of the War for the Fatherland, 1st Class. In spite of a promising career in the Soviet service he found life unbearable under the Communist dictatorship and made his way to Poland, thence to Germany where he landed in a concentration camp. He finally reached a DP camp in the American zone. He arrived in the United States last December, and published a series of articles in the Jewish Daily Forward *on his experiences as a Red guerrilla.*]

313

I CLOSE MY EYES and I can see the entire terrible nightmare which was my life during the last seven years—and I can hardly believe that all of it is already part of the past; that I go on, living; and that I am in a free country; that the people around me are free people; that I can truly tell—tell without fear, without danger to my life—all that has happened to me during these blood-drenched seven years.

I was in Russia for almost six years. In September 1939 when Hitler struck, I was one of the horde of 600,000 Jewish refugees who fled from Poland eastward, in the direction of the Soviet Union, in the hope that there all our sufferings would end. When I first heard that the Russians had crossed the Polish border I naturally assumed that they were coming to help the Polish Army in the fight against Nazi Germany. What a shock it was to learn that both the Fascists and the Communists entered Poland as aggressors!

I reached Brest Litovsk, normally a small city, where a quarter of a million human beings were encamped. Soldiers and refugees were all over, wherever there was a bit of space to stretch or a corner to huddle in. Here I met two of my closest comrades in the Socialist movement, who had been schoolmates of mine, and were still under the impression of an astonishing scene they had witnessed.

On September 19, 1939, the day when the Germans had handed over the city to the Red Army, there was an impressive military parade. A reviewing stand had been erected in the main street of Brest Litovsk, and was decorated with red banners and swastikas. High Nazi officers stood side by side with high Soviet officers while first the German and then the Red formations passed in review. A military band played the *Hosrt Wessel* song first, then the *Internationale.* Photographs of the ceremony appeared in the German press.

The populace, particularly the Jewish onlookers, were dumbfounded by the spectacle. A few days later large-scale arrests of both inhabitants and refugees began. The NKVD struck first at those known to be Socialists. It was here, while I was still in town, that the Jewish leader, Henryk Ehrlich, whose wanton execution together with Victor Alter aroused worldwide protest, was arrested. Here I saw many of my comrades for the last time.

I MOVED EASTWARD and arrived at Gomel with a large transport of Polish refugees. The Soviet administration received us in a very friendly manner.

I found employment at a peat works, about 12 miles from Gomel, as a lathe operator. I did piece work aiming at the best quality, but soon found that it took me longer and my earnings were correspondingly less. I recall how the foreman of my group told me, smilingly: "We work here differently than in capitalist Poland."

The following morning I went to watch one of the Soviet lathe operators. I stood in front of his bench for almost two hours—and I could not help staring at

314

him in utter amazement. He turned out triple the amount of work I was doing. I checked the bearings which the operator was producing with lightning speed. About 70 percent of them were faulty—they simply fell through the holes in the wheels. When I showed it to the operator, he merely took a sharp hand-tool, made a few notches on the outside of the brass bearing, and forced it into the wheel. "Ready," he said, and laughed heartily.

"But in three more days the wheel will have to be repaired again," I said with astonishment.

"That is none of my business," he said with a smile, "in the meantime we'll make money. . . ."

Once, long before the war, I had read in a newspaper that Soviet locomotives had to be completely overhauled every month. I could understand the reason for it now.

I finally quit my job, and went back from White Russia to the occupied Polish regions. I was arrested in Lida in the course of the mass roundups of refugees. My wife and I spent three months in the prison. We were freed, but our new passports contained the stipulation that we were forbidden to live in larger cities, and within 60 miles of the border. Eventually I came to Baranovichi, where after many difficulties, I was granted permission to live and work.

All this took place during the first half of 1941. Then came Hitler's sudden attack on Russia, followed by terrible months in the ghetto of Baranovichi, where we felt the full force of German brutality.

JOINING THE UNDERGROUND resistance movement, I smuggled arms into the ghetto. We learned to use them in cellars and in specially constructed subterranean passages. Floggings, hangings, and shooting of Jews for the smallest offense were a daily occurrence.

My wife and child were betrayed, and slain by the Nazis. Already as a full-fledged guerrilla, I later caught up with the traitor to avenge their death.

This period of my life was spent with a band of partisans fighting the Nazis in the Pripet marshes of Polesye.

From there I was sent with another man across the front lines to establish contact with the Red Army. We were looking forward with joy to our reception. Instead, when we arrived on the Soviet side, we were seized as spies, and narrowly escaped being shot.

I was then sent to a military school at Moscow, where I was trained for sabotage and reconnaissance work. We were dispatched for a brief but difficult assignment amidst the snow-fields of Murmansk, Kandalaksha, and Petsamo. Then, for several months, we took part in the defense of Moscow.

IN OCTOBER 1942 I was one of ten Red Army officers parachuted by a Soviet airplane behind the German lines in Yugoslavia. All of us were graduates of the sabotage academy of the secret section of the NKVD. Our mission was to instruct the raw troops of the partisan chief, Josip Broz, better known to the world as Tito.

We were expected. Seven fires on the ground marked the spot. I jumped into the strangest, most intensive adventure of my war experience. A crowd of rough-hewn partisans greeted us enthusiastically. Among them I recognized Tito—I recognized him as one of the Yugoslavs who had attended our school in Moscow.

The same night a group of ten British officers were dropped at the same spot. All of us, Russians and Britons, were attached to the personal staff of Tito; I was one of those who shared a dugout with him during the first few weeks.

Thereafter we were deployed among different partisan divisions. Mine was stationed in the hills between Split and Sarajevo; a British officer, John Scott, was also attached to my division. My special assignment was to train the partisans in reconnaissance and sabotage activities; Scott taught them mass attack and strategy.

For nearly eight months I shared the life of a Red partisan. One of my first undertakings, at the head of a fine lot of courageous fighters who seemed contemptuous of death, was to ascertain the German positions on the Sarajevo-Zagreb railway. It was during this episode that we ran into a large group of Chetniks, at the grave of the legendary national hero Milosh, in the Jancharn hills. They greeted us with the cry, "Long live free Yugoslavia!" Among them was a stocky man with a thick, gray-streaked beard, wearing horn-rimmed glasses. Later I learned that it was the fabled General Mihailovich. Such bloodless meetings of partisans and Chetniks became rarer with every passing month.

Early in 1943 the Germans surrounded our territory. Tito was cornered and wounded in the hand in the course of the fighting. We understood later that he was rescued by a daring Soviet air mission which made a miraculous landing under the most difficult conditions.

I was in the thick of the great partisan offensive in the spring of 1943. My group captured a small town on the river Vrbas. In the abandoned German staff headquarters I picked up a copy of the Berlin paper, *Voelkischer Beobachter*. Casually I glanced through its pages. Suddenly my own family name caught my eye in a headline.

It was a cynically written report of the suicide of my father in London.

WHEN MY UNIT RETURNED to Moscow, I was assigned once more to guerrilla warfare ·behind the German lines. I spent the last two years of the conflict operating as a partisan in the vicinity of Pinsk, Baranovichi, and Brest Litovsk, and rose to the rank of captain in the Red Army. During reconnaissance raids we often crossed the Bug River and met Polish partisan bands. We also encountered and sometimes joined forces with Jewish partisans from Slonim and

Volkovysk, fraternizing with Jewish heroes who had distinguished themselves in battle against SS and Gestapo troops.

I visited scores of cities and towns and villages where the mass of Russia's Jews had once lived. It was impossible not to realize that although officially anti-Semitism is forbidden in Russia, nevertheless one feels it in daily life, in the factory, in the office, and, most of all, in prison.

Conversations with Russian Jews on the subject would almost invariably strike the note of praise for the Communist regime, although the speaker might have been suffering acutely. The reason for it became clear. It is generally believed that a third of the adult urban population serves the NKVD. Brother fears brother, a father fears his son. Each high official, each officer, has his aides in the NKVD, and these in turn are watched by other informers and operatives.

The powerful machine of the NKVD sees to it that no vital news from abroad penetrates the cage which is Russia. The youth of the country does not know any other life and has no conception of how workers, for instance, live in America.

I once saw a picture in a Soviet newspaper designed as propaganda against the United States. The picture showed a group of tramps. The legend underneath it read: "This is how American workers live."

I left for good the Soviet "land of promise" where a great career beckoned, to return to my native Poland. Here I met comrades who had fought in the ghettos, and lived to tell their tales of horror.

Columns of refugees streaming back from Russia to Poland looked like people from another world. Their experiences still form one of the great untold chapters of our times. These were survivors of the hordes which had been deported to do forced labor. They had died by the thousands at their tasks, in their bunks at night, of typhus and malaria. They had died on the roads, and no one cared.

Of the 600,000 Polish Jews who had escaped to Soviet Russia during the war, only 200,000 had come back by the end of 1946, according to the official figures published in Warsaw. The remaining 400,000 perished, not in gas chambers and crematoria, but in the forests of Siberia and the wastelands of Central Asia. They died building "socialism" on the Soviet pattern, creating "the happy life" according to Stalin.

May 1947

WHEN STALIN TOOK A WALK

By SERGEI MAXIMOV

[Sergei Maximov, a talented Russian writer who, at the age of 20, had a book published in Moscow, was seized during the great purge and served a five-year sentence in the vast Pechora penal labor camp. In 1941, while living in Smolensk, he was arrested by the invading Nazi forces and assigned to do prison labor in the interior of Germany. The United States Army set him free at the end of the war. In 1948, as a refugee, he reached New York. In this unembellished memoir, contributed to Plain Talk *in September 1949, Maximov crowned all of Solzhenitsyn's subsequent disclosures with a fitting finale to the nightmare of life under Communism where an iota of suspicion can lead to a death sentence.]*

THE RESIDENTS of Moscow were surprised, upon opening their newspapers on the morning of September 6, 1935, to see on the front pages of the *Pravda* and *Izvestia* a huge picture of Stalin surrounded by children and adults. The legend under the photograph read: "Comrade Stalin on a promenade in the Gorki Park of Culture and Rest." The text went on to tell briefly how Stalin, accompanied by his closest colleagues, paid a visit the morning of September 5 to the Moscow amusement park where he spent a whole hour inspecting the grounds and chatting with the visitors. . . .

IN THE SPRING of 1936 I was arrested in Moscow together with a group of fellow students and charged by the NKVD with anti-Soviet activities. I spent the first three months of my detention in a solitary cell of the Lubianka prison. I was then transferred to the Butirki prison where I was confined until the preliminary investigation ended early in 1937.

We then faced the Special Tribunal of the Moscow Municipal Court. The judicial proceedings were conducted behind closed doors. We were all sentenced to various terms of imprisonment. After the sentences were pronounced, we were transferred to the distribution jail, the former Butirki chapel which had been transformed into a three-story prison. From here all prisoners are shipped out to the various concentration camps. The cells were terribly overcrowded, and our group was split up. It was my lot to be assigned to cell No. 3, on the second floor. I was the 108th prisoner to be shoved into a cell the maximum capacity of which was 40 persons.

I became acquainted with many of my partners in misfortune. The first friend I made was a young man by the name of Arkady Tokman. He was a member of a professional swimming club. I learned from him that he had been sentenced as a political offender to a ten-year term, commuted from a death sentence, a common enough procedure under Soviet justice. The second prisoner with whom I became acquainted also turned out to be a professional swimmer. The third man I talked with was also a swimmer. And so was the fourth inmate! My amazement knew no bounds when my 32nd new acquaintance in the cell turned out to be . . . a swimmer! I had begun to wonder whether the prisoners were not playing a joke on me. How was it possible for the entire population of the cell to be made up of nobody but swimmers? Actually, there were exactly 32 swimmers who were members of a sports organization. Among the other prisoners were some football players, sharpshooters, and plain working people who had been rounded up for various reasons. It took some time before the hapless athletes confided to me their sad story.

EARLY on the morning of September 5, 1935, the all-star team of the Moscow swimming clubs, under the direction of the head instructor, Grobovsky, was practicing in the Gorki Park of Culture and Rest at a diving stand in the Moskva River, in the vicinity of the Neskuchny Garden. At the football field of the park two teams were also practicing—the team of the workers of the machine building factory, Red Proletaryi, against that of the Terekhgorka factory. The students of the second class of the Moscow Textile Institute were practicing at the rifle range.

It was seven o'clock in the morning. There was not a soul in the park except the members of the athletic organizations and about a dozen youngsters—children of the park employees who were playing in the children's playground. Not far from the football field, on the grass, his head resting on a massive camera, a Red Army soldier who had not quite sobered up from the evening's entertainment lay sleeping. The park was open to the public only from nine in the morning, but the athletic teams had permission to practice there beginning at six A.M.

At ten minutes to eight, emerging from quiet Kaluga Street, three closed limousines drove through the gates of the Neskuchny Garden, passing the gateman who stood dumbfounded. Upon descending to the Moskva River the three cars came to a stop in the mapled shade of a deserted lane. A small group of people climbed out: Stalin, Molotov, some three or four commissars, two women, and several unidentifiable civilians wearing nondescript and modest dress. The latter were obviously Stalin's guard. At a leisurely pace the party moved to the river bank in the direction of the diving stand. Stalin walked ahead. Leaning against the iron railing at the water's edge, the visitors watched the practicing swimmers.

"Stalin!"

The astounded athletes jumped out of the water and timidly climbed the bank en masse. Stalin asked the instructor to come up and when Grobovsky presented himself, Stalin casually questioned him about his origin, his family, how long he had been interested in sports, was he getting enough pay, was he satisfied with the progress of his team, and so on. Grobovsky, pale and confused, stuttered incoherently in reply in spite of his 50 years and his silver-gray head. Stalin genially clapped him on the shoulder after a three-minute chat, wished the team success, and started toward the center of the park accompanied by the whole group. The swimmers surged forward as if to follow, but two civilians stopped them and requested them to attend to their own affairs. After Stalin had passed out of view, the athletes proceeded noisily to discuss the extraordinary event. One of the youths reflectively remarked: "How come he's not afraid?" But there were some daring youths who, hiding behind trees, followed the distinguished guests in spite of the guard's order. Stalin reached the football field. "Stalin!!"

He behaved toward the players the way he had toward the swimmers. He hailed the captains of the teams and asked the same kind of questions. The bold swimmers who had come up to the football field were again warned by the guards not to follow the party so as not to interfere with Comrade Stalin's walk. It was here that the Red Army soldier suddenly awoke and was shocked into sobriety. He approached the party and asked one of the guards for permission to take a picture—he had only one exposure left in his camera. He received benign permission but was advised, because of his single exposure, to use his camera at the children's playground. The soldier was invited to follow the gathering of notables.

STALIN did not visit the rifle range, from the direction of which could be heard the sound of small-caliber rifles. Instead he went to the playground. However, the news that Stalin was taking a walk through the park had spread like wildfire. The practicing riflemen dropped their arms and rushed to the children's playground.

Here Stalin spent the most time. He sat down on a bench and chatted and joked with the youngsters. He even tossed a ball back and forth a couple of times to a seven-year-old girl. By this time the breathless Miss Glan, the director of the park, appeared, having been called by one of the employees. More and more spectators began to arrive—gardeners, watchmen, keepers, and sweepers. The Red Army soldier took the picture. Somebody suggested to the children that they pick flowers and present them to Stalin. The youngsters eagerly threw themselves upon a showy flower bed and in a flash picked a huge bouquet of nasturtiums and asters, and presented it to Stalin. He patted the head of the little girl who gave him the flowers and handed them to a member of his party. More people kept streaming to the scene. The swimmer Tokman heard the guards, who were pressing the crowd back, quietly and courteously urging the men: "Please, don't keep your hands in your pockets."

The three limousines now drove up from the direction of the Neskuchny Garden. The distinguished guests began to hustle, bidding goodbye to the crowd and taking their places in the cars. One of the civilians who tarried some distance behind suggested to the spectators that they shout a farewell greeting. And there was a loud roar: "Hooray for the great Stalin! Long live the great Stalin!" . . . The athletes and employees of the park stayed behind in little knots exchanging their impressions. And this is what led to their doom.

DURING the night of September 21 a special dragnet brought in 74 prisoners: 32 swimmers, 22 football players, 13 sharpshooters, 2 charwomen, 1 gardener, and 4 organizers of mass games. All the prisoners were charged under Article 58 of the Criminal Code, some as follows: 10 with anti-Soviet agitation, 11 with counterrevolutionary formations, 8 with planning an act of violence! The prisoners were forced to give absurd testimony; the examiners resorted to trickery, threats, and torture. The unfortunates were coerced into signing the transcripts of their examinations. A monstrous edifice was built up under the skilled hands of the NKVD agents out of some vague phrases dropped by a few of the athletes, such as, "How come he's not afraid?" or "Suppose somebody shot off a rifle?"

The instructor Grobovsky now became a "former officer of the White Army and the initiator of a terrorist plot of the Moscow athletic teams." Day and night, scores of examiners questioned the prisoners. Their dossiers swelled. The preliminary investigation alone lasted 13 months. And only toward the end of October 1936 were all the defendants brought before the Special Tribunal of the Moscow Municipal Court. The prisoners were denied the right to counsel.

It took seven days for the tribunal to hear the case. The verdicts were severe. Five were sentenced to be shot; more than half of the prisoners were given ten-year sentences with the loss of civil rights for five years after their release; the rest received different sentences ranging from two to eight years to be served in remote "corrective-labor camps of the NKVD." Early in 1937 the decison was handed down commuting the death sentences to four- to ten-year prison terms. All other sentences were sustained.

The instructor Grobovsky, whom Stalin had genially clapped on the shoulder in the Gorki Park of Culture and Rest, was shot.

September 1949

ORPHANS OF TYRANNY

By EUGENE LYONS

[*Aleksandr Solzhenitsyn in his* Gulag Archipelago *focused a universal spotlight on the horrendous chapter of World War II that Eugene Lyons cites in March 1948 in "Orphans of Tyranny." It deals with the suppressed provision of the Yalta agreement, exacted by Stalin from Churchill and Roosevelt, calling for the forced repatriation of some two million Russian prisoners in Germany at the end of the war. Two books recently published furnished harrowing accounts of what became one of the most massive crimes against humanity on record. Julius Epstein, an associate of the Hoover Institution at Stanford University, in* Operation Keelhaul, *pioneered in researching the history of the gory affair. He was followed, in 1975, by Nicholas Bethell, a British lord, whose work,* The Last Secret, *attributes most of the responsibility for the inquisitorial operation to his countrymen; above all, to Anthony Eden, the wartime head of the British Foreign Office.*]

. . . In November 1946 a Ukrainian Committee in Canada headed by Dr. B. Kushnir addressed an appeal to the United Nations to prevent the forcible repatriation of 300,000 displaced Ukrainians in Western Europe. The following January *The New York Times* published an appeal from non-returners (its authenticity vouched for by Alexander Kerensky and Prof. Michael Karpovich) urging the rights of political asylum for "hundreds of thousands of new refugees from the Soviet Union."

The two categories overlap; the refugees of *The Times* appeal include the Ukrainians. But the magnitude of the desertion cannot be doubted. Under the Yalta agreement the American and British forces were obligated to return the runaway Russians, by force if necessary. More than two million Soviet nationals were, in fact, turned over to Russia from camps in the non-Soviet zones; how many of these went willingly, how many had to be pressured or actually bayoneted into going, no one can say with certainty.

Did President Roosevelt and Prime Minister Churchill foresee that their lighthearted consent to Stalin's demand for forced repatriation of his citizens would amount to a death warrant for hordes of Russians opposed to the Soviet regime? One wonders whether ever before in modern history a statesman demanded and received the right to get millions of his own subjects sent home by force. One shudders at the spectacle of supposedly democratic leaders, with miles of speeches about four freedoms and human rights to their credit, agreeing to the crime.

THE STORY of the forced repatriations has never been told; it is so vast and so bloody that perhaps it never can be told.

One of the Russians who went home voluntarily, a Red Army captain who had fought with the Resistance in Belgium, regretted his step after he had been screened in the Soviet zone and sentenced to hard labor. In the Russian-language New York *Socialist Courier* (April 1946 issue) he described the brutality with which even voluntary repatriates were handled:

> How could they send me, loyal to their Party and government, who risked my life for them, to ten years in prison? We expected to be greeted with flowers and music, and they met us as if we were criminals. . . . All of us, without exception, were condemned. During interrogation we were beaten and threatened with shooting. Many, in fact, were shot. Every day we heard firing squads not far from our camp.

Soviet citizens caught in Europe by the German collapse recalled that prisoners of war returning from Finland, after the first Soviet-Finnish war, were all deported to labor colonies. They were aware of the Stalin decree No. 270 under which Russians falling into German hands alive were branded deserters and traitors. And now terrifying accounts of the abuse and punishments visited on returning citizens began to reach them from every direction.

The mystery is not that so many resisted repatriation but that so many accepted their lot in a fatalistic spirit. Vivid descriptions of the suicidal despair that overwhelmed Russians faced with repatriation have been given by witnesses of the macabre scenes in Dachau, Plattling, Weibling, and other assembly points. They tell how wounded, bleeding, scorched men and women who had not quite succeeded in killing themselves were dragged to waiting American or British trucks. A Russian, describing how American MPs herded 1,600 of his countrymen with clubs, rifles, and machine guns for delivery to the Soviets, ends his story with the ancient cry, "Father, forgive them, for they know not what they do."

A *Christian Science Monitor* dispatch from Frankfurt, dated September 10, 1945, tried to convey how distasteful Americans found the job of driving Russians home by force. Of 25 soldiers assigned to one such task, he reported, 21 turned up sick, obviously wishing to evade the onerous duty.

Under date of December 3, 1946, a Russian priest in touch with the situation wrote to friends in America:

> Displaced persons of Soviet citizenship . . . are oppressed by the continuing illegality of their situation, by the need to hide their real identities and pretend they are émigrés of 1920 or Poles or Baltic citizens. The inhuman Yalta agreement not having been revoked, they go on living in a harrowing atmosphere of uncertainty, dread and enervating rumors. . . .
>
> When it comes to repatriation, truly horrible scenes occurred. In Dachau, where there were no prisoners of war but just ordinary deportees, *Ostarbeiter*,

Americans ordered them handcuffed in order to turn them over more conveniently. The unfortunate men, driven to desperation, smashed window-panes with their heads and cut their throats with glass. They managed somehow to set fire to one of their barracks and threw themselves into the flames, having first soaked themselves in spilled gasoline. Ten of the men were burned to death. There were 275 cases of suicide or attempted suicide.

This is typical of dozens of other eye-witness reports. Whatever the legalities of forcible repatriation, Yalta or no Yalta, its piled-up horrors, its mountains of corpses, its droves of slave laborers in Siberia and the Soviet Arctic should weigh heavily on the conscience of the non-Soviet world. When the anesthesia of wartime insensibility will have worn off, Dachau and Plattling and the other Soviet assembly centers under Allied control will seem a shocking finale to the drama of a war for Four Freedoms.

OBVIOUSLY the 600,000 to 700,000 non-returners are only a tiny portion of the disaffected Soviet nationals who would have preferred not to go home. Their ranks are being swelled constantly by thousands of deserters from the Red Army occupation forces. They all believe that they are the quarry for a manhunt of unprecedented size and brutality.

I have before me the statement of a Red Army officer who was at one time engaged in that manhunt. He refers to procedures in 1945–46 which may have been amended, for better or worse, since then:

> Several NKVD members are assigned to the tracking of a single man, often for weeks on end. This group of hunted men is under no illusions as to the fate which awaits them. After their arrest, in spite of the extensive precautions which are taken to guard them on their journey to the Soviet zone, they attempt most desperate escapes.
>
> For instance, if 15 men escape, 10 or 11 are recovered and slain, but 3 or 4 escape and this is considered too much by the NKVD. For some time now this class of escapee is no longer transported to the U.S.S.R. After interrogation they are liquidated either in the basement of the Military Mission or the Embassy or at Camp Beauregard on the outskirts of Paris.
>
> Some of the more interesting prisoners, who have to be interrogated in Moscow, are shipped by plane. But we have received strict orders that if any of these offer resistance they are to be shot immediately if it can be done discreetly.

Informers as well as those who make the arrests, he attested, were at that time getting 3,000 to 5,000 francs per head as a bonus.

The story of one of the "desperate escapes" to which he alluded has been described to me by a woman who had the gruesome details directly from a survivor. N. X., as she calls him, joined a repatriation center voluntarily. Though he hated the Soviet regime, he was intensely homesick for his mother. It was in the Soviet camp behind barbed wire, hearing of what happened to others, that he changed his mind.

He succeeded in escaping. But soon the French police caught up with him and, on the pretext that he had no documents, he was turned over to the Russian military. They confined him in Camp Beauregard—the notorious camp outside Paris which was run until recently by the Soviet police on an extraterritorial basis. From Beauregard he was loaded, with 17 other men, into a sealed freight car for the journey eastward. They decided on a desperate scheme. With great exertion they broke a hole in the floor of the car and one by one slid down to the tracks below under the speeding train.

"A certain number were killed," the woman reports. "N. X. described to me the horrible tension of the moment when he slid down and pressed flat against the ground. He was drenched by hot blood and saw parts of a torn body on the nearest wheel. Those who waited their turn to escape heard the anguished cries of comrades who perished. But all of them preferred the nightmarish kind of escape to repatriation." . . .

March 1948

BOOK 6

FROM CHURCHILL
TO STALIN

MY THREE TALKS WITH CHURCHILL:

WHEN BRITAIN APPEASED STALIN

By GENERAL WLADYSLAW ANDERS

[*Poland was the acid test of the postwar relations between the Soviet power in the East and the United States as the protagonist of the West. From the Yalta Conference in February 1945, which marks the beginning of the 30-year Cold War, to the latter's current phase labeled détente, the basic issue between the two giant rivals has not been resolved. It is graphically presented in General Anders' "My Three Talks with Churchill," in the course of which the British leader vowed several times "You should trust Great Britain who will never abandon you—never." How Poland was abandoned is now a matter of general knowledge. The method was emulated at the great international Helsinki Conference in July 1975, where the diplomacy of détente continued the game initiated at Yalta.*]

I

UPON MY LANDING at Teheran, August 19, 1942, the British military authorities informed me that an aircraft would be ready at dawn to take me to Cairo, where I was to meet Prime Minister Winston Churchill.

My meeting with Mr. Churchill took place at the British Embassy in Cairo on August 22. Also present were General Sir Maitland Wilson, and Colonel Jacob of the British Army, who recorded the conversation.

Churchill opened the talks by saying that he had studied the documents I had submitted on the organization of the Polish force, and had turned them over to General Wilson. But, he added, he understood that I was not authorized to discuss those details. I agreed that this was so.

Churchill then went on to say that the view of the British authorities coincided with mine on the general shape of the organization of the Polish forces, but he thought it would be best to come to a final agreement on this with General Sikorski in London. It was originally intended, he said, to locate the Polish forces in North Persia, where the Tenth Army was being mustered as part of the command to which General Wilson had just been appointed.

Here I stressed that, in my opinion, there was some danger of the Germans breaking through in the Caucasus, but Churchill doubted this. He hoped the line of mountains and the Volga would both be held until the winter. Nevertheless, as my opinion was based on personal experience, he would act on the assumption that I was right.

I said I would be very glad to fight with my troops as part of General Wilson's army. Churchill promised to do all he could to get equipment sent to the Polish forces as soon as possible.

Then we talked for some time about the situation of the many Poles still in Russia, and of recruiting them for the Polish army, on which subject I handed the Prime Minister a memorandum. Churchill said he was as anxious as I to secure as many Poles as possible from Russia to reinforce the Polish army, but he must be the judge of the right moment for making an approach to Stalin. At that time the Russians were hard-pressed, and felt that their allies were being somewhat inactive. Soon, there might be a better opportunity to take up the matter with Stalin. Churchill also said it might be well to obtain President Roosevelt's cooperation in the matter.

I then took up the subject of the disappearance of large numbers of our best officers in Russia, and the urgent need of effecting the evacuation of Polish children, who were not expected to survive another winter. Churchill said he had given orders for the women and children to be released from Russia together with the troops. As for the officers, he thought it possible that the Russians were averse to releasing them for fear of the stories they might spread about their treatment.

I told Churchill I was very satisfied with the way our people had been cared for after leaving Russia, but, once again, I stressed how necessary it was to secure the release of the remainder. Stalin's attitude had been most illogical. He was refusing further recruiting because the Polish government had not placed its army on the Russian front—an army to which he had refused to give arms, contrary to his previous agreement—and whose rations he had limited for 26,000 men and which had been increased to 44,000 only after my personal representations of March 18. There was, I said, no justice or honor in Russia, and there was not a single man there whose word could be trusted.

Churchill pointed out to me that such language as I was using would be dangerous if spoken in public. No good, he said, could come of antagonizing the Russians. I replied that I fully realized this, and had, indeed, given strict orders to my people that nothing disparaging should be said about the Russians, particularly in the period preceding the evacuation.

Churchill then expressed the hope that I would place myself at the disposal of General Wilson, so that all necessary arrangements could be made. He said he was sure the men in the Polish army would give a good account of themselves. They had proved their worth in the United Kingdom, where one of their fighter squadrons was admitted to be the foremost in the Fighter Command.

Churchill closed the talk by saying that he believed Poland would emerge from the war a strong and happy country.

This, in brief, is the account of our conversation. It was satisfactory as far as it went, but it left me with the impression that, to avoid antagonizing Russia, sufficient pressure would not be put upon her for a solution of Polish problems.

II

[Two years later, in 1944, General Anders, in command of the 2nd Polish Army Corps in Italy, was in the van of the Allied advance on the Gothic Line when he received the announcement of an impending visit by Churchill to the Polish forces.]

ON AUGUST 26, at 10:55 A.M. Mr. Churchill, accompanied by General Sir Harold Alexander, arrived at our headquarters. The conversation is so interesting that I will perhaps be forgiven if I quote verbatim the record made at the time in Polish by Lieutenant Lubomirski. This text is, of course, translated back into English from the Polish:

After cordial greetings, Prime Minister Churchill, addressing General Anders, declared: "Do you remember, General, the last time we met and talked, in Cairo?"

Anders: "I do remember, of course."

Churchill: "You were right at that time." Then the Prime Minister offered his congratulations on the magnificent victories of the 2nd Corps and expressed his great appreciation of its deeds. After that he asked: "What is the state of your soldiers' morale in view of the events they witness at present?"

General Anders answered that the morale of the troops was excellent, that each soldier was perfectly aware that the first task and obligation was the destruction of Germany and the fight to achieve this aim. But they were most anxious, at the same time, about the future destiny of Poland and about all that was happening [the uprising] in Warsaw.

Churchill said that he, also, was fully aware of these facts, but when, with President Roosevelt, he had approached Stalin for assistance to the Warsaw fighters, they had received no answer at all to their first request and a negative reply to their second. Stalin justified his refusal by stating that General Sosnkowski was responsible for the uprising and that the men fighting in Warsaw were Sosnkowski's men. "We were not ready for any action in Warsaw, and now we are trying to do our best to give assistance from the air," Churchill added.

Anders: "For three years the Bolsheviks have continuously demanded the uprising. When moving across Poland they even intensified their propaganda on this point, proclaiming recently that they had reached the suburbs of Warsaw. But since the uprising started, that is, since August 1, they have become quite silent, and have made no move to grant any form of assistance whatever to the Home Army."

Churchill: "I know it only too well; the Americans declared themselves ready to organize flights from the United Kingdom to Warsaw (50 flights) landing on Soviet territory at Poltawa—shuttle service. Stalin was asked about it, but he refused even that."

Prime Minister Churchill also stressed that fact that the Russians were barely 30 kilometers (18 miles) from Warsaw, and there could be no obstacle in the way of their giving assistance, whereas the British must fly 780 miles from their bases in Italy.

Then Mr. Churchill mentioned that he did not think we were satisfied with his speech last winter.

Anders: "We had and still have a grudge against you, Mr. Prime Minister."

Churchill: "In concluding the treaty of alliance with Poland, Great Britain never guaranteed her frontiers. She pledged and undertook the obligations for the existence of Poland as a free, independent, sovereign and great state, in order that her citizens might live happily with the opportunity for their unfettered development, free from any alien interference. I can assure you, General, that we have not changed our point of view; Poland will not only exist but she must be a champion of Europe.

"You must trust us; we will keep our pledges. But you must not rigidly insist on the maintenance of your eastern boundaries. You will get territories in the west much better than the Polesie marshes. The Oder will be your frontier in the west, and as regards the littoral, there are many much better and wider prospects than any sort of corridor. All Germans, even women and children, will be removed to Germany from the territories which will be granted to Poland. There are people who pretend that there will be no room for evacuated Germans in a diminished Germany. But I assume that more than six million Germans have already perished, and still more will perish, and that there will be no trouble on this account."

Anders: "History tells us that some corrections of frontiers occur after each war. I understand that frontiers may be moved 10 kilometers to the west or 15 kilometers to the east. But the problem of frontiers should be definitely and exclusively dealt with at a peace conference, after the war has been completely finished. But we will never consent to the Bolsheviks, even during the war, taking as much territory as they wish. We will never consent to *faits accomplis*."

Churchill: "Obviously these matters can be settled at a peace conference." (Turning to the General and touching him) "You will be present at the conference. You must trust us that Great Britain entered this war in defense of the principles of your independence, and I can assure you that we will never desert you."

Anders: "Our soldiers have never for one moment lost faith in Great Britain.

They know that first of all Germany must be beaten and are ready to carry out any task toward this end. This can be confirmed by General Alexander, who knows well that all his orders have always been and will always be carried out. But we cannot trust Russia, knowing her too well, and we are convinced that all Stalin's announcements that he wants a free and strong Poland are lies and impostures. The Bolsheviks want our eastern provinces in order that they may ruin us more easily and enter more deeply into Europe, to make her Communist. The Russians entering Poland are arresting and deporting our wives and children to Russia as they did in 1939. They disarm the soldiers of our Home Army, shoot our officers, and imprison members of our Civil Administration, destroying all those who have been fighting the Germans without interruption since 1939. Our wives and children are in Warsaw, but we prefer that they should perish there rather than live under the Bolsheviks. We all prefer to die fighting rather than to live cringing."

Churchill (deeply moved): "You should trust Great Britain, who will never abandon you—never. I know the Germans and Russians are destroying your best elements, particularly the intellectuals. I deeply sympathize with you. But be confident, we will not desert you and ultimately Poland will be happy."

Anders: "Russia has been preparing for this war for 20 years; in 1939 she had 35,000 aircraft and 18,000 tanks, and immediately after the war she will resume this policy. But after the war, you will not keep six million men under arms and 70,000 aircraft in the air."

Churchill: "We have a 20-year treaty with Russia." (After a short pause) "It may be that this will not last. But I believe that the situation in Russia has changed, and the men who hold power at present will not keep it to the same degree after the end of the war. The present generals and others of high rank, their wives and children, will never tolerate a state of affairs in which, on returning home, they would have no say. They must come to power and take their part in government. It is their due, and they will certainly be against the regime at present ruling Soviet Russia. Hence, all your apprehensions are superfluous, especially as you must trust Great Britain and the United States who will never desert you.

"The time is past when Great Britain was only able to send to France three divisions, and was weaker than Poland from the military point of view. And it is necessary to realize that the potentialities of Great Britain and the United States are unlimited. At present we have a powerful army, which we did not have before, and soldiers who have undergone three and a half years' training. We used only two-fifths of our forces in invading Europe, scoring successes which far outweighed all Soviet contributions to the war. Stalin must be aware of that and understand that Stalingrad has ceased to be his monopoly, and that all that has happened in France was on a much bigger scale. We know well that in consequence of this war two great powers, Germany and Japan, will disappear. Russia will remain. And the United States and Great Britain will possess huge stores of aircraft, guns, and tanks. We wish Russia to be strong, but in friendly relation to us and to you. We also wish for a strong France, but she must be friendly with us."

Churchill, observing that the meeting was being photographed by Lieutenant Romanowski, said, "If Stalin sees this photograph of me calling on you and at this particular moment, General, he will be furious. But I give you my consent to publish this photograph, General. Let Stalin be angry.

"But I do insist that you send me one copy. Stalin dislikes you—he says you are a wicked man."

Anders, turning to the question of the Committee of Liberation, observed that Stalin had governments ready for all the countries he would like to put under Communist rule. Then he added, jokingly: "I am sure that he already has a man to take your place, Mr. Churchill."

Churchill (laughing): "The same as the Germans had one. But they did not have the chance." Then Mr. Churchill rose, and in taking leave of General Anders repeated once more his admiration for the splendid achievements and operations of the 2nd Army Corps and the magnificent spirit of the Polish soldiers. . . . "I am also full of admiration for the Armored Division fighting in France, which is also doing extremely well." Again he repeated: "I, and my friend President Roosevelt, who will again be elected President, will never abandon Poland. Put your trust in us."

Anders: "From the outbreak of the war in 1939 we have wished that Great Britain might be as strong as possible."

Churchill: "Perhaps after this war we shall no longer be as strong, but in any case we shall be more skillful than others." (Getting into his car) "General, tell your soldiers about the talk I have had with you—of course not all the details—but you understand that I am a politician, not a mischiefmaker."

Anders: "We are soldiers, and for this reason we are well able to distinguish between politics and truth."

Churchill (smiling): "Oh yes, I see you are also a good politician."

Anders: "We were taught this in Russia."

Mr. Churchill left at 11:35 A.M. I was fully aware of the difficult circumstances with which he had to deal during his visit to the Polish troops in Italy. The conversation reported above took place at the time when the Polish armed effort in this war was at its greatest since September 1939. On many occasions I had stated our aims in the war, and I thought my point of view must have been known to Mr. Churchill. For this reason his words, repeating and stressing the point that Great Britain and the United States would never desert Poland, and that the Poles should trust their Allies, carried special weight with me.

III

[*Eight days after the Yalta Conference, on February 20, 1945, General Anders was flown to London where he met again with Prime Minister Churchill.*]

THE NEXT day I was invited to a conference with Churchill. Sir Alexander Cadogan, Under-Secretary of State for Foreign Affairs, showed me into the room of the Prime Minister, who soon appeared. My aide and interpreter, Captain Lubomirski, remained in the anteroom, and the conversation took place in French, of a kind. I give it from the notes I made immediately afterwards.

Churchill: "You are not satisfied with the Yalta conference."

Myself: "It is not enough to say that I am dissatisfied. I consider that a great calamity has occurred. The Polish nation did not deserve to see matters settled the way they have been, and we who have fought on the Allied side had no reason to expect it. Poland was the first to shed her blood in this war, and sustained terrible losses. She was an ally of Great Britain from the very beginning and throughout the most crucial times. Abroad we made the greatest effort possible in the air, on land and sea, while at home we had a most important resistance movement against the Germans. Our soldiers fought for Poland, fought for the freedom of their country. What can we, their commanders, tell them now? Soviet Russia, until 1941 in close alliance with Germany, now takes half our territory, and in the rest of it she wants to establish her power. We know from experience what her intentions are."

Churchill (irascibly): "It is your own fault. For a long time I advised you to settle frontier matters with Soviet Russia and to surrender the territories east of the Curzon Line. Had you listened to me, the whole matter would now have been different. We have never guaranteed your eastern frontiers. We have enough troops today, and we do not need your help. You can take away your divisions. We shall do without them."

Myself: "This is not what you said during the last few years. We still want to fight for Poland, free and independent. Russia has no right to our territory, and she never questioned our possession of it. She broke all treaties and grabbed these territories on the strength of an agreement and an alliance with Hitler. There are no Russians in these territories. Apart from Poles there are only Ukrainians and White Ruthenians. No one asked them to which country they would like to belong. You understand that the elections held in 1939, under the pressure of Russian bayonets, were a sheer mockery."

Churchill then put forward arguments in favor of the Yalta settlement of the Polish problem. Several times he emphasized that Great Britain had never guaranteed the eastern Polish frontiers and he declared that the problem of the frontiers would be finally settled at the peace conference. He recalled his conversations with me in Italy on August 26, 1944, and spoke of Poland's receiving compensation in the west, as far as the Neisse and the Oder.

I then said that I was very much against a government based on the Lublin Committee, which was composed exclusively of Soviet citizens and of traitors directed from Moscow.

Sir Alexander Cadogan interrupted me at this point to say: "Then you would prefer that the Polish Government should be organized by Russia alone!"

"Certainly," I said. "That would not change things a jot. And at least the whole world would know that it was not a Polish Government. Public opinion in Poland and abroad would thus not be deceived."

Churchill ended the conversation by saying that Great Britain would only recognize a government composed of representatives of all political trends. The provisional government would only have the task of organizing elections. He said he would soon be making a speech on Polish matters in the House of Commons.

This conversation only increased my concern about Poland's future.

May 1949

An Interview with Stalin

By Erich Wollenberg

[*A rare and fresh insight into the enigmatic character of Stalin is afforded by this report of an interview with him in the crucial days preceding Hitler's rise to supreme power. Its significance, however, goes beyond its value as a contribution to history. It also lies in the conclusion drawn by the man who conducted the conversation with the Soviet dictator. He was Erich Wollenberg, once a leading figure in the German section of the Communist International, and the author of an authoritative book,* The Red Army. *The editor of* Plain Talk *came to know him in March 1950, in Munich, where he edited a weekly newspaper. His analysis of Stalin's dogmatic mentality and that of the politicians of the regime he had established, grounded in the "fatalistic belief in the inevitability of war," led Wollenberg to the conviction that so long as that regime exists, there will be "the danger that the Kremlin will plunge mankind into chaos and the abyss of the atomic world war."*]

In the middle of January 1933 I was summoned by Helena Stassova, who at that time combined the functions of president of the MOPR (International Red Relief) and Stalin's secretary for German questions, to come to the Central Committee of the Bolshevik Party. "Two o'clock sharp; not one minute later!" she admonished me.

I had just finished in rough draft, by order of the Comintern's international book publishing concern, the German translation of Stalin's speech on "The Fulfillment of the First Five Year Plan in Four and One-Half Years." Helena Stassova, who as the daughter of a highly cultured Czarist governor had been brought up a polyglot and spoke and wrote perfect German, had editorial and political control over all German translations of Stalin.

A few minutes before 2 o'clock, therefore, I entered the huge complex of buildings behind the "Kitai Wall," which housed the Central Committee. GPU officers and men were watching with sinister looks the street, the entrance, the steps, the corridors, and even the lift which brought me to the upper floor where the Politburo had its offices. It had been almost two years earlier—in March, 1931—that I had last been in the Central Committee, there to deposit my Bolshevik Party book before my return to Germany. At that time there had been no special police protection except for a few militiamen.

I immediately assumed that the gigantic mobilization of the GPU had become a daily arrangement since forced collectivization and famine had brought the whole country into a situation resembling civil war. I could not dream that the GPU had turned out to protect Stalin, who was at home.

"Herta," as Helena Stassova had been called twenty years earlier when she led the illegal apparatus of the KPD (German Communist Party) in Germany, received me with marked cordiality although she naturally knew that I had been disciplined by the Central Committee of the KPD and at its request summoned to Moscow by the Comintern because of my opposition. It was a way to rid KPD members of my influence.

We talked standing in the middle of the room. That was not accidental, as I soon realized: Stalin loves to appear before people suddenly and unannounced.

Herta asked me whether I found myself in any special difficulties with the translation. I was able to answer no. In reality, Stalin writes and speaks elementary and poverty-stricken Russian which any peasant can understand. Translation of his speeches and writings was esteemed a responsible party task and was twice as highly honored as the literary work of Tolstoy or Maxim Gorky. The reason why the other editors of the publishing house had withdrawn in my favor was that every error or even a relatively too strongly or weakly expressed nuance of Stalin's train of thought was immediately regarded as a deviation if not actually an ill-intentioned distortion, with the usual dangerous consequences for the translator.

The Comintern editors, as I told Herta, were deeply shocked because I had translated as "whip onward" the word *podkhlestivat* (literally: beat down with the knout). This refers to the following passage from Stalin's speech:

"Four and one-half years ago when we began our first Five Year Plan, was it necessary, in view of the backwardness of our country and the threatening danger of war [on the part of Japan. E.W.], to 'whip onward' the Russian people? I think it was! But now, after we have completed the first Five Year Plan in four and one-half years—is it still necessary to 'whip onward' the Russian people? I think it is no longer necessary!"

People in the publishing office had insisted that Stalin's statement that the

Russian people had been "whipped onward" would be water on the mill-wheels of the "social-fascist traitors." Even the word "spurred" was rejected as politically dangerous. However, precisely because of Stalin's announcement that it was no longer necessary to whip onward the Russian people, I had myself conceived a faint hope that the terrorist dictatorship, steadily more oppressive since the beginning of the first Five Year Plan, would now be somewhat relaxed. Therefore I believed that it was necessary to translate the word *podkhlestivat* as strongly as possible.

While Herta and I were discussing it, the door opposite me opened and Stalin entered the room. He gave me his hand in greeting and asked: "What's new in Germany?"

I HAD KNOWN Stalin since 1924, and during my seven years in Russia before 1931 had quite often met him at congresses, meetings, and conferences, and also privately—in Moscow and at his summer home at Sochi in the Caucasus. I had last spoken with him early in 1931. Stalin was visibly aged. The catastrophic situation in which the Soviet Union then found itself appeared to have shaken his self-confidence. He gave the impression of being tired, even somewhat ill.

I was glad to be able to explain to Stalin my point of view on the German situation. When Wilhelm Pieck had informed me in October 1932 that I was to go to Moscow at once by order of the Comintern to do editorial work in the international publishing house, I had at first refused. At last, however, I had permitted my close political friends to persuade me to answer the call, which was in reality a party order. My friends thought I could seize the opportunity in order to take advantage of my personal relations with Stalin and other Russian comrades in the party, government, and General Staff of the Red Army, to warn them of the weaknesses and errors of the entire policy of the Central Committee of the German Communist Party, and the threat of Hitler's imminent rise to power.

EARLY IN January I had spoken with the General Secretary of the Comintern, Pyatnitsky. After listening silently to my report he had explained: "You will understand that I cannot take you to Stalin behind the back of Fritz Heckert [KPD representative in the Comintern. E.W.]. Naturally I have nothing against your going to him on your own, but Stalin has such great Russian worries at present that he cannot concern himself with German questions."

Tukhachevsky, Gamarnik, and other leads of the Red Army had answered in the same vein. And so at last I had given up. Now Stalin stood before me and repeated the question. "Well, Comrade Wollenberg, what's new in Germany?" Knowing Stalin's liking for brevity and precision, I spoke more in key words than in coherent sentences.

"The German crisis"—I said in substance—"is approaching solution. Theoretically the question, Thaelmann or Hitler, is not yet decided. However, Papen's coup of July 20, 1932, against the the Braun-Severing government of Prussia demonstrated that the KPD under its present leadership cannot lead any defense of democratic institutions. The broad masses, among them even sections of our Communist workers, argue that Thaelmann has no chance, therefore Hitler must come to power. Our Communists add: 'Only for the moment! Later, when Hitler has played himself out, our turn will come!' That is a dangerous illusion. It is easier to stop Hitler's march to power than to oust him once he has built up his dictatorship. This spring [1933] we shall have to reckon with great social and political struggles. Unless the policy of the KPD is considerably activized toward the creation of the united front on the broadest basis, we are threatened with a victory of National Socialism in the fall or 1933 and the establishment of Fascist dictatorship."

STALIN had listened attentively without interrupting me, his head inclined a little to the left. His facial expression did not betray his thoughts. When I had finished my report the following dialogue took place.

Stalin: "I have other information. I have been told that a Hitler government is impossible in Germany."

Myself: "The opinion of the German Central Committee is naturally known to me. At the end of December, a few days before I left Berlin, I spoke at length with Teddy [Ernst Thaelmann]. He considers a further sharpening of the German crisis impossible, and looks for a gradual stabilization. Teddy is of the opinion that the bourgeoisie cannot dispense with the Center Party and especially with Bruening, and that within the next few weeks a stable new Bruening government will be formed."

Stalin: "I know that Teddy is no great light but this time he is not entirely wrong. The Reichswehr is against a Hitler government."

Myself: "The Reichswehr is not united. The young officers are largely in sympathy with National Socialism. The soldiers are against the Republic; they don't want to fight for Weimar."

Stalin: "And the generals?"

Myself: "There are two ways for Hitler to come to power. If Hindenburg makes him Chancellor or Vice Chancellor, the generals will range themselves in disciplined order behind him, as General Rundstedt aided the Papen coup on July 20 when so ordered by his Field Marshal. However, if Hitler comes to power through civil war, then the decision in the Reichswehr will be made not by the generals but by the younger officers, from the lieutenants to the commanders of battalions and regiments. Generals do not shoot."

Stalin: "You see German matters only from the internal point of view, and thereby come to false conclusions. In Germany—I speak of capitalist Weimar Germany, which is in no position to break the chains of Versailles—no government is possible against the will of London and Paris. London and Paris will never tolerate a Hitler regime in Germany."

BEFORE reporting this dialogue further I must refer to a conversation which I had in the fall of 1932 with Sokolnikov, at that time Soviet ambassador in London. Sokolnikov, a leading member of Bukharin's opposition group, had been summoned back to Moscow to report. On his way through Berlin he had got in touch with me and entreated me to leave Germany as quickly as possible because a Hitler regime was imminent. When I remarked that the Central Committee of the KPD considered a Hitler government impossible, Sokolnikov answered: "From my observations post in London I see a great deal which you cannot know. Believe me, London has already decided for a Hitler government!"

Naturally I could say nothing to Stalin about this conversation with Sokolnikov (who, by the way, never returned to London). So I answered his question in a general way.

Myself: "London is afraid of a Communist Germany and sees in National Socialism the lesser evil. Downing Street will not protest against the establishment of a Hitler government."

Stalin (very quickly and with a threatening undertone in his voice): "Who told you London is resigned to the thought of a Hitler government?"

Myself: "A change of attitude toward National Socialism has lately been evident in the English press. Hitler's declaration, 'A National Socialist Germany will be England's sword on the Continent,' has found a strong and positive echo in London, and especially in Conservative circles."

Stalin (a little tired and almost apathetic): "Perhaps you are right. Perhaps there will be a Hitler government in Germany."

Myself: "Hitler in power will mean that the imperialist war against the Soviet Union will come before the inter-imperialist war."

Stalin: "This war is unavoidable."

Myself: "The triumph of the Socialist revolution in Germany would make this war impossible."

Stalin regarded me for a moment as if he doubted my sanity. I had misunderstood him, as I realized only much later, and had thought only of the order of events, of the priority of the imperialist war against the Soviet Union in case of Hitler's victory. Stalin spoke quite generally of the second world war, which was axiomatic for him and whose outbreak would be accelerated precisely through a victorious socialist revolution in Germany. He regarded armed intervention by the Western powers as certain in that case. In view of the famine in the Soviet Union this must inevitably lead to catastrophe. On that account the Central Committee of the KPD had received from Moscow the strictest orders to refrain from anything which could have led to a socialist way out of the German crisis.

I do not know whether Stalin was aware that I had misunderstood him. At any rate, he broke off the conversation, visibly disgruntled, with the words: "All right, drop in on me when you have the opportunity, and we will discuss it further."

Helena Stassova wished me well in memory of our old acquaintance in illegal times. She tried to give the conversation a conciliatory turn. She told Stalin about the panic which my translation of *podkhlestivat* had loosed in the Comintern publishing office. Thereupon,

Stalin (smiling): "That is still too weakly translated. You can express it more brutally."

Myself: "The word *podkhlestivat* as you used it was the one in your whole speech which pleased me most."

Stalin threw me an astonished, distrustful glance, mumbled something unintelligible and with a brief goodbye left the room.

I DID NOT see Stalin again. Early in April the International Control Commission, on the motion of Fritz Heckert, representative of the German Central Committee, expelled me from the Comintern because of my criticism of KPD policy. Russian questions did not enter into the expulsion procedure. That was my good luck.

Heckert demanded that I be turned over to the GPU. Stalin prevented my arrest, and said to Pyatnitsky: "Naturally Wollenberg is right in his criticism of the German KPD Central Committee. But I thought he was a political person who knew that as a politician a man must not always tell the truth."

Those words reveal the whole Stalin, the whole Stalinist "socialism," built on lies and deception of the people; this peculiarly Russian-Asiatic form of modern totalitarian imperialism and fascism. In contradiction to the view of the Kremlin dictator, the essence of any democratic policy lies in free expression. And the attempt to deceive "only" others must inevitably lead to self-deception and hence to catastrophe through a policy based on illusions. Rosa Luxemburg was right ten times over when she said, "Nothing in politics is more dangerous than illusions!"

Stalin deceived himself when he believed, after the end of the first Five Year Plan, that his regime could hold on to power without "whipping onward" the Russian people. This "whipping onward," this regime of total terror which cannot be relaxed but only overthrown, is the logical result of Stalin's entire concept of the state, and of his policy. When Stalin, after his "great patriotic war," announced an epoch of democracy, internal pacification, and social adjustment, he was under the same illusion that he had cherished in 1933 at the end of his "great patriotic famine."

Fed on false information, Stalin made the mistake of believing that a Hitler government was impossible, and that even if it came to pass it would, as the "captive of the eastward-looking Reichswehr," be less dangerous than a government of "Western-oriented social fascists." And this mistake led to the fact that the Moscow-guided Central Committee of the KPD became the stirrup-holder for Hitler's dictatorship.

The most portentous of Stalin's errors, for the Russian people and all humankind, was his fatalistic belief in the inevitability of war. He never learned from history that war is always made by men, not by "conditions," which to be sure can favor it but cannot unloose it. Whoever, like Stalin or Hitler, believes in the inevitability of war, will be driven to a policy which will make war inevitable in the end. We saw it in the case of Hitler, who strove for war, and we see it in that of Stalin, who in his heart of hearts fears war.

The world picture of Stalin and his paladins is distorted by preconceived notions, petrified dogmas, and misinformation. From this hodgepodge of prejudices, dogmas, and misinformation the Kremlin politicians draw false political conclusions. Therein lies the key to Moscow's whole foreign policy. So long as Stalin and the Stalin regime exist, so long will exist the danger that the Kremlin will plunge mankind into chaos and the abyss of the atomic world war.

May 1950

A PRIMER FOR INNOCENTS

By MURRAY C. BERNAYS

[As a guidebook for American diplomats and politicians dealing with Soviet affairs, "A Primer for Innocents" by Colonel Murray C. Bernays is remarkable for its up-to-date contents. It adds depth to the light cast by the preceding memoir of General Anders and that of Alexander Kerensky which follows. Mr. Bernays, upon graduating from Harvard in 1915, achieved distinction early as a civil liberties lawyer. He was commissioned as an officer in World War II and became Chief of the Special Projects Branch of the Personnel Division, G-1, War Department General Staff, and was associated with setting up the Nuremberg trial of the Nazi war criminals. He was awarded the Legion of Merit and returned to the practice of law in New York.]

I HAVE HEARD friends say in all seriousness, though they admitted the nature of Soviet conduct, "We must be patient, because whatever the Soviets are doing today, their ultimate ideals are so noble!" I have heard others say that what the Soviets do is the same kind of thing we do ourselves; for example, that there is no more freedom of the press in the United States than there is in Russia, because our great newspapers are as much dominated by advertisers as *Pravda* is by the Politburo. It is even said that the Soviets have done better than we have. This is proved by the singularly irrelevant argument that the Soviets have given Russia civil liberties because they have promulgated a Constitution that says so, but that civil liberties have not been equally established everywhere, or perfectly established anywhere, in the United States under our own Constitution.

These are honest folk who say these things, and they say them in all sincerity. They have been persuaded into exaggerating beyond all reason our own shortcomings, but minimizing with fantastic wishfulness the evil that threatens us.

The most brilliant achievement of the Soviets has been in getting acceptance, by this kind of illogic, for the idea that they are only "another form" or "a different form" of democracy, and dissociating themselves in the public mind from "fascism."

Now there are different degrees of democracy, but there cannot be different forms of it. There is only one feature that distinguishes democracy from any other form of government, and that is the right of opposition. The presence or absence of this right is decisive.

Where citizens have the right to speak, write, organize, and vote in opposition to their Government; where they can contest its monetary exactions, or the seizure of their persons or property, and submit the issue to a vote or to decision by an independent judiciary, and can depend on it in either case that the Government will abide by the outcome; and where they can modify, or displace wholly, any given administration by the nonviolent method of adverse majority vote, under assurance of the right to "get out" the vote and to have it cast in secrecy—where these rights exist in fact, there is democracy. Where they are denied in fact, there is tyranny.

A tyrannical government is no less a tyranny because, as has been done by the Soviets, it has given a paper promise, unenforceable except by violence, that at some unspecifiable future time, and upon conditions which it alone will determine, it will grant its subjects the free institutions which are today denied them.

It may be granted to the Russophiles that the United States is a democracy deplorably imperfect; but it must not be granted them that Soviet Russia is any kind of democracy at all.

If we are to keep our thinking straight on this subject, we shall, accordingly, reject resolutely the poisonous fallacy that the Soviets are only "another form" or "a different form" of democracy; refuse to be diverted from the fact of Soviet conduct today by its promises for tomorrow, and test that conduct by its workings, not its pretensions; and never forget that tyranny comes to power by talking freedom but holds to power by destroying it.

The Two Meanings of "Revolution"

TYRANNY, being based on force, lives in fear and insecurity. The only remedy for these is ever more and ever-widening force. When the last dissident voice has been silenced at home, there will remain dissident voices to be silenced beyond the borders. Therefore it is that from violence at home to aggression abroad is tyranny's ineluctable destiny.

That was the way of the French Revolution and of Napoleon, for example, though theirs was a world of vast distances and primitive communications as compared with ours. The monarch having been overthrown, the bourgeoisie must go next to the guillotine. Resistance having been stamped out at home, the Directory was compelled by inner necessity to carry the fight abroad, because only by that means could the ever-elusive "security" be further pursued. But even conquests that attained for France its "natural" frontiers were not enough. There was then a France swollen, yet more exposed than ever. The "peril," being within the dictatorship itself, remained—the need for "security" continued unsatisfied—the whole continent was not buffer enough, therefore Napoleon must march destruction into Moscow.

Hitler walked the same road, and for the same reasons. Stalin is walking it now. His need for force, and ever-widening force, cannot be sated so long as there is still an outpost for him to march against. This compulsion is the greater in a world in which space, once a barrier, has become a lane of travel at supersonic speeds and a channel of instant communication.

We tell one another that because the destructions of the last war were so immense, and those of the next one promise to be so final, therefore we may count upon a breathing spell between them, and we rationalize our prayer in persuasive ways. The world, we say, is too exhausted to fight at once again. We console ourselves that the Soviets do not have the A-bomb yet, and it will be years before they do. Perhaps, indeed, there need be no next war at all, we reason. The fallacy of such thinking lies in the assumption that war is a product of rational decision, when in fact it is the by-product of irrational conduct.

The innocents are befuddled because they ignore the fact that a revolution can just as well be foul as fair. "Revolution is a word with a double meaning; sometimes it means a new orientation of the human mind, and sometimes the subversion of law and order," Ferrero writes in *The Reconstruction of Europe*. The American Revolution was of the first kind, Hitler's was of the second, and not many can be found any longer who confuse the two. If we will but apply the same test to the Soviet Revolution by which we judge the other two, we shall know in which category it belongs.

At the threshold of our nationhood we made the considered declaration that when a government even so much as evinces toward its people "'a design to reduce them under absolute Despotism, it is their right, it is their duty, to throw off such Government, and to provide new Guards for their future security." We continue to pride ourselves on our revolutionary origin. However, the meaning of our revolution seems to have become blurred to many Americans, and the Soviets have made use of this situation to parade under false colors, as the Directory and Napoleon did under the banners of "liberty, equality, and fraternity," and as Hitler did under the banner of "socialism." Thereby the Soviets have enlisted, in many minds, friendly tolerance, if not actual support, for a revolution whose every act in more than a quarter-century has been to establish at home, and extend abroad wherever it could, just the "absolute Despotism" we rose against—intensified and aggravated by modern technology.

The American Revolution opened, and keeps open, horizons of freedom. The Soviet Revolution shuts off men's eyes from those horizons. The doctrine of the Declaration of Independence still remains valid. But there is nothing in it that glorifies revolution for its own sake or for subversion's sake; and it is a perversion of the doctrine to turn it into a defense of Soviet designs to reduce free peoples "under absolute Despotism."

It is often said in extenuation of Soviet terrorism, "Their revolution is still young; we must give them a chance." Such a plea might be valid if the Soviets were being criticized for not having built enough miles of improved road, for example. It is an affront to intelligence to offer it as a reason for our still believing in the good faith of the Soviets' democratic professions, when after thirty years of absolute power they continue to govern with unexampled, calculated, and unrepentant oppression.

The Myth of Soviet "Sacrifices"

A BIT OF recent history—the record of the Soviet contributions to victory in World War II—needs to be set straight. It is pure fiction that Russia helped to defeat Japan. The Soviets used the victory that we had already assured as a means for getting a toehold in Korea and China.

The contributions the Soviets made to the victory over Hitler were made under the duress of German attack. There is little to the alleged analogy between the Soviets' entry into the European war and ours. The Soviets knowingly and deliberately precipitated Hitler's attack on Poland, by agreeing to safeguard Germany's rear. They were offered a clear choice in 1939 between supporting the Allied efforts to prevent the war and the German plan to force it. Not only did they choose to help bring on the war; they agreed to help the Nazis wage it. The United States, on the contrary, followed from the very first a policy which was bound eventually to get us into the war on the side of the Allies. When the Nazis invaded the Soviets they attacked a friend; when they declared war on us they were launching a "preventive war" against a known enemy. That was the reason, of course, why the party line for the American Russia Firsters from 1939 to 1941 was to oppose and discourage American help for Allies. The war was a "capitalist-imperialist" struggle according to their line, and they sang that the Yanks were not coming, until their totalitarian mother-by-adoption needed the Yanks to come to the rescue. Whoever, looking at the record, still thinks there is any likeness between the way we entered the war and the way the Soviets entered it, has simply closed his mind to fact and reason.

By no sane process, and upon no sane basis, can it be argued that anything which the Soviets did to help defeat the Nazis justifies the view that we shall now suffer the Soviets to do to the world what the Nazis tried to do. On that question the number of Nazis the Soviet Army destroyed, or the number of casualties it suffered, is as pertinent as the color of Ivan the Terrible's beard.

Our "Undemocratic Alliances"

A PRIME SOVIET technique for confusing the unwary is to play on their sense of guilt. The admonition that none of us is without sin is a wise and humane one, but never before has it been seriously argued that we are therefore constrained to give legal immunity to crime.

We are to be complacent, for instance, about the fact that the Soviets have condemned millions to slavery without trial, because in some sections of the United States it is not possible to get a fair trial for Negroes, and elsewhere there are miscarriages of justice for other and equally indefensible reasons. The difference between these miscarriages of justice and the utter denial of justice as a matter of governmental policy is brushed aside as quite unimportant.

One particular application of this technique deserves special mention. Many Americans object in good faith to our supporting the resistance of other countries against Soviet aggression, on the ground that these countries are themselves "undemocratic." That would be irrelevant in any event, because the reason for supporting China, for example, against Soviet aggression is not the merits of Chiang Kai-shek but the menace of the Soviets. Only the Russia Firster could keep a straight face while comparing the Soviets and China; but even accepting the comparison, let us remember that it was on like grounds of practical selection that we accepted the Soviets as an ally in the war against Nazi Germany. It is well enough to say "a plague on both their houses" when it really does not matter which comes out on top, but it is criminally frivolous to say that when it matters so greatly.

Guideposts Through the Confusion

To AVOID confusion in our policy toward Russia, so long as it remains a Soviet tyranny, the following guideposts should be set up:

1. We shall pay no attention to the Kremlin's professions of wanting peace, because its leaders have forfeited the right of choice between peace and war. They are committed to aggression as the *sine qua non* of their survival, and they will not give it up until confronted by a show of force abroad so overwhelming, that the danger of overthrow at home has become a lesser risk than that of defeat abroad. Whether or not the Soviets are to make that choice does not lie with them, however. Only the strength of the free world outside can compel them to make it.

2. We shall pay no attention to the excuses that the Soviets and their apol-

ogists offer for Soviet aggression. The excuse-in-chief, that the Soviets are motivated by "fear" of Western democracy, is undoubtedly true. But the picture is falsified by the inferences that are mistakenly drawn from that fact. Soviet fearfulness is a ground, not for less concern than we would otherwise have, but for the very highest degree of concern. Any criminologist will confirm the fact that the nervous felon is quicker to shoot, and shoots oftener on inadequate provocation, than the calm and collected felon. Moreover, the very fact that the Soviets are fear-ridden proves conclusively that there is nothing to be gained, and everything to be lost, by attempts at mollifying them. That alone explains why appeasement got nowhere with Hitler, and has gotten us nowhere with the Soviets. They that govern by terror have chained themselves to fear. To seek peace with them by mollification is the sure way to invite attack.

3. We shall give up any and all trust in the reassuring words, the pacific gestures, and, above all things, the overtures of "cooperation," that the Soviets may offer us when the occasion suits them. These are not likely to be in the future, any more than they have been in the past, anything except devices for entrapping us. It was thus that the Soviets beguiled us into surrendering the Balkans to them, allowing them to get their forces through the doors that we had so helpfully opened for them into China, assisting them to deploy their troops on the Continent, and setting them astride Korea.

4. We shall stop deceiving ourselves with the hope that time is working for us. Time would be our ally in normal circumstances, but it is the ally of revolution, and especially subversive revolution, when men and nations are ravaged, weary, and discouraged. It is in just such times that free men are sorely tempted to throw in their hand to the dictator when he puts on the face of benignity and promises them rescue from their dilemmas. The Soviets have heretofore understood this very well. The fact that they are now forcing the pace so dangerously is an impressive commentary on the explosive power of the fear that drives them. There comes a point, and we are perilously close to it already, when the dictator cannot retreat, or cannot be persuaded any longer that retreat is his lesser risk. When that point is reached, our only choice will be to surrender or fight.

5. We shall recognize, accordingly, that our only safety is to confront the Soviets with firmer spirit and greater strength than theirs, and act upon that recognition without delay.

We, who in less than two centuries have turned a wilderness into freedom's greatest strength and hope, need not apologize because we have not done more, or be afraid to try to do better. The problem of superior strength need not give us undue concern. Once we recognize the danger, we shall have the will and the organization to meet it.

There is no record anywhere of the so-called Communists winning victory by their own strength. Their reliance is always on democracy's confusions. They even boast of it. These confusions, operating in a vicious circle, are both cause and effect of the weakened faith, the debased values, and the divided will that are democracy's undoing. We can avoid these only if we remember, always, that in the same way that democracy lives by justice, tyranny lives by conquest. Nothing could be more fatal than to confuse the occasional truce the tyrant grants us with the peace that is our hope and prayer.

May 1948

IN DEFENSE OF MY COUNTRY

By ALEXANDER KERENSKY

[*A prophetic message to the West, warning against the advancing Soviet imperialism, came from Alexander Kerensky, premier of Russia during the short-lived democratic government in 1917, and was published in* Plain Talk *in April 1947 on the occasion of the 30th anniversary of the fall of the Romanov autocracy. Until his death in June 1940, for some 52 years as a political refugee, Kerensky struggled to enlighten European and American public opinion on the illusions fostered abroad by the Soviet rulers. Although the name of Kerensky has been invoked by many to describe a gullible leader who opens the door to dictatorship, his stature grew in the postwar era that witnessed the rise of even more gullible statesmen who had learned nothing from his bitter experience.*]

AS IS KNOWN, I supported Russia, my native land, with every fibre of my being during the war. I defended those Soviet demands which seemed to me historically just and strategically essential. Although I never let myself be hypnotized by the myth—so useful for Moscow's brilliantly calculated strategy —that Stalin "betrayed the Leninist proletarian world revolution," I continued to hope that the inexpressible sufferings, sacrifices and heroism of the army and the people of my martyred motherland in this horrible war would soften the dictator's heart; or that within the Kremlin men would arise who, in the name of the salvation of their native land, would put a speedy and final end to Bolshevist world plans.

Instead, in concert with the followers of various nationalities and of all countries, the victorious U.S.S.R. dedicated itself to imposing everywhere the dictatorship of the "one and only" Communist Party—to imposing, that is to say, a regime of political and social slavery.

That has now become the basic, imperative goal of Stalin's domestic and foreign policies. He has not violated the oath he took at Lenin's grave in January 1924—"We swear to you, Comrade Lenin, that we shall not spare our lives in order to strengthen and widen the union of toilers throughout the world, the Communist International."

Stalin's prediction that "the second wave of wars brought about a second wave of revolutions" has been realized in full. And finally it must be granted that he will not spare any lives, Party or non-Party, in promoting that overwhelming surge.

It is this policy which arouses throughout Europe and Asia, and here in America, irritation, indignation, and hostility *toward Russia,* the Russia that has paid so dearly for the common victory. The entire capital of sympathy, enthusiasm, and affection which Russia has earned through the blood and suffering of her people, is being frittered away to the last penny.

I see here, in the United States, how those feelings of hostility are deepening. When I returned here recently, after a year's absence, I was shocked by the profound change in popular sentiment toward my country. For the day is not distant when the people of Russia will have to pay—and pay heavily—*for a bill they had not contracted.* Foreigners may not know that the Communist "bill" is not Russia's "bill." The Soviet leaders learned during the war that neither the Russians nor any other people in the U.S.S.R. wanted to go into battle to the tune of the *Internationale.* They did not want to sacrifice their lives for world revolution. The Kremlin knows better than anyone else that faith in Communism has been shattered—shattered forever—in Russia more than anywhere else in the world.

RECALL THE YEAR 1941. . . . The fierce months of Hitlerite invasion. The relentless drive, unprecedented in Russian history, of enemy forces from all directions into the very heart of my country. The dismay of the commanding personnel. The passivity of the troops. The strange and suspicious mood of the population. The appeal for aid to the Church which had been so long and so bloodily persecuted. The patriotic call to "brothers and sisters" (no longer "comrades") for loyal defense of "the native soil and the heritage of our forbears." The disappearance from the pages of the press and the mouths of the propagandists of partisan and international slogans. The transformation of literature with "shock-brigade speed" to nationalistic and patriotic themes.

In short, at the outbreak of war everything that was Communist, everything that was of the Party, was hastily swept out of sight of the Russian peoples. They were called upon to make sacrifices on behalf of "the imperishable image of eternal Russia," with no remote hint of ulterior intentions.

Once during the darkest days of the war Stalin remarked to a certain foreign visitor, speaking with bitter irony about the Russian people: "They will not defend Stalin, they will not fight for Communism. But perhaps they may fight in defense of their native land."

"Perhaps." . . . In his cynicism he doubted even that! Apparently he saw clearly and in fright the spiritual gulf separating the people from the dictatorship. Apparently he conceded the possibility that the people might decide to seek domestic liberation from his totalitarian yoke through an external catastrophe.

It was Hitler himself who ended the chance of a defeat for the Soviet regime by his stupid and savage treatment of the peoples of the U.S.S.R.

Thus the "Second Patriotic War" (the first was in 1812 against Napoleon) temporarily created a close alliance between the people and the government. In order to safeguard for the future the dictatorship of the Communist Party, Stalin seemingly renounced his oath to Lenin and devoted his great organizational talent to the military forces. The troops and the people, giving their all in defense of their country, recognized him as their military leader—as if singling him out from the other denizens of the Kremlin.

The Russian people, deeply generous and patriotic, infuriated by the barbarities of the invaders, needed a miracle of faith. They chose to believe in his transformation from an international conspirator into a national patriot.

Meanwhile life—outside the army, in the rear, all over Russia—continued to be as dreadful as before the invasion, at times more dreadful. There was the same persistent animal fear of the NKVD; the same civil disfranchisement and suppression of thought; the same lawless, tyrannical administration; the same vast concentration camps teeming with millions of victims.

But the entire population had no doubt that the horrors would soon come to an end; that after the war everything would be different. Strange as it now seems, a great many—especially the ardent youth—saw in the new military-patriotic course confirmation of their faith that war and victory would bring about an internal liberation. This passionate expectation of a "change" after victory was the topic of conversation of all those who during the war traveled abroad—Soviet engineers, officers, sailors, students. Some were in a mood to *demand* that liberation, others actually believed that Stalin would bring the change about himself.

During the war I came in contact with Soviet Communist students in the American universities. I recall how one of them, arguing with me about the two revolutions in 1917, exclaimed, "Do you mean to say that we, the present Soviet youth, do not desire liberty?"

"Do you really want freedom, then?" I asked.

"Of course we do."

"In that case there is no real difference of opinion between us."

"No, there's a great deal of difference," he insisted.

"How so?"

"You seem to insist on the need for a revolution, but we think it isn't necessary. After the war, Stalin himself will grant us freedom."

BUT SUCH BELIEVERS in the coming liberation became fewer and fewer toward the end of the war. This is evidenced by an unparalleled fact in Russian history: The fact that hundreds of thousands of Soviet citizens, men and women, liberated in Germany from military prisons and slave labor, are *unwilling* to return to their victorious motherland.

What is more, Moscow knew in advance that such would be the case. That is why, at the Yalta conference, Stalin insisted that the representatives of the freedom-loving countries give him a privilege unheard of in civilized societies— *the right to repatriate his subjects by force!*

As the war ended these subjects were driven with bayonets and machine guns into trains which took them directly to Siberian concentration camps. They were escorted under heavy guard, like murderers, to ships from which many of them jumped overboard. They were hunted. Soviet agents conducted raids in European cities with the cooperation of the local democratic police to round up Soviet citizens hiding in panicky dread of going home! Has history any match for this macabre business?

The majority of these victims of the immoral Yalta agreement consisted of soldiers and officers, workers and peasants, engineers, physicians, teachers, nurses, students—a cross-section of the Soviet population. By this time the Russian camps in Europe have been emptied. But there are many tens of thousands of new refugees—outlawed and tortured Soviet people. Their life is a nightmare of penury and uncertainty. Yet they prefer to face poverty in lands where "it is possible to live without constant fear and to think and speak freely." Their main concern is "not to be betrayed to the Soviet authorities. . . ." These are their own words, quoted from their own letters.

It was not the optimistic student but these desperate victims of Yalta who proved right after the victory. Stalin promulgated no manifesto about any "change" or any new freedoms. He told the country curtly, like Nicholas II before him, "Forget your idle dreams" of freedom; everything shall be as it was before the war—and worse. Having exploited their generous faith to save Stalin's regime, he could again ignore and dash their hopes of a free life.

Let us turn to *The History of the USSR* published under Stalin's personal aegis, and open it to Volume I, page 316. There, in the account of the War of 1812, one can read:

The general upsurge of popular patriotism in Russia was the *decisive* factor in the triumph of the Russian Army. Frightened, not only by Napoleon but first of all by their own peasants and serfs, the Russian feudal lords appraised the victory as a triumph of the autocracy and serfdom. They asserted with satisfaction that the simple people had never displayed such loyalty as in 1812. Others went to the extreme of insisting that for the Russian the word liberty had no meaning; that obedience had become a habit with him.

The parallel today is terrifying in its exactness. For "peasants and serfs" read "collectivized peasants." For "feudal lords" read "Soviet bureaucrats." For "autocracy" read "totalitarian dictatorship." Yes, after the patriotic people played their *decisive* role they were deprived of their victory in the name of a Communism they loathe, precisely as the Czarist feudal masters had done in the name of their absolutism after the expulsion of Napoleon.

THE COMEDY IS FINISHED. Stalin has cast off Kutuzov's mask and returned to his pledge to spare no lives for the triumph of the Communist International. So that there may be no doubt in anyone's mind on this score, the U.S.S.R. and the rest of the world will soon be viewing his Communist apotheosis in the new Soviet film *The Pledge!*

As a matter of fact he began preparing himself for the second wave of revolutions while still wearing his patriotic Marshal's uniform. In 1943 he staged the celebrated "dissolution" of the Communist International. How he must have laughed at the enthusiastic applause of the "capitalists" and at the indignant protests of the old-fashioned proletarian "internationalists." The former saw in this voluntary disbanding of the International the final proof of his "statesman-like genius"; the latter saw in it conclusive evidence of his betrayal of the revolution.

Yet the reason for the "dissolution" was as clear as day. After Hitler's invasion of Russia, the existence of an official Comintern became for practical purposes unnecessary, even harmful, to the successful development of the Communist movement *outside* Russia. After playing their role as defeatist organizations during the life of the Moscow-Berlin Pact, the Communist Parties in all the nations of the anti-German coalition turned overnight into the vanguards of "resistance." They infiltrated all government and public institutions to an unprecedented extent. All the restrictions on the activities of "former" members of the "former" Comintern were removed. The capitalist governments themselves began to aid the Communists with arms and money in their work of organizing European workers, peasants, students, and intellectuals into Partisan groups of resistance, led in each country by local Communist centers.

And when at last "the triumph of democracy over international fascism" came, all these French, Italian, Czech, Balkan, and other members of the executive committee of the Comintern found themselves at the helms of governments! The "dissolution" of the Comintern, as Stalin shrewdly foresaw, paid off handsomely in "revolutionary" dividends.

Quite naturally, all these Bieruts, Titos, Togliattis, Thorezes, like himself, loathe the free-thinking human being. They share his deep belief in the right of a ruling minority to impose its will on the majority, unlimited by either human or divine laws. Wherever his so-called "'union of toilers" has triumphed, terror reigns on the pattern of the Soviet Union itself.

But if he were asked whether Russia knew about his preparations for a world revolution, whether the Russian people have collaborated with him in this conspiracy, the answer would have to be *No*.

Throughout the war Stalin hid from the people the true international objectives of the struggle as he conceived them. Those objectives which he advanced aloud and which *officially* coincided with the national interests of Russia: defense of the Soviet fatherland; restoration of the frontiers lost in the 1918 Brest-Litovsk Treaty, but with Poland and Finland excluded; security of these boundaries against invasion from any direction; the guarantee of a rightful place for the U.S.S.R. among the other great Powers commensurate with Russia's past, her vital interests and the present world equilibrium.

I was with the Soviet people and their government in defending this program, disregarding charges of "imperialism" and "Stalinism" hurled against me.

After the total destruction of the Axis Powers, the three surviving world powers, Britain, the U.S.A., and the U.S.S.R. became, in the words of former Secretary of State Hull, "the guardians of peace." In their hands remained the whole heritage of the fallen empires. It was inevitable that in the changed world, the aims of war, which had become the aims of victory, should also change. The "guardians" themselves changed. Britain, as Winston Churchill acknowledged, fell back to third place. Russia became the most potent nation on the Eurasian land mass. The United States, having come into the hierarchic position formerly occupied by the British Empire, became mistress of the seas and the skies.

THE UNPRECEDENTED economic, geopolitical, and strategic expansion of the United States is self-evident. It is equally self-evident that Russia, having regained her might, is again seeking outlets to warm-water seas and oceans. Germany and Japan, who made it necessary for the U.S.A. and the U.S.S.R. to be potential allies against potential common foes, have collapsed. For the first time, from Korea through the Dardanelles to Berlin, new vital interests of America may clash, and in some instances are already clashing, with the old primordial interests of Russia.

There is no more pressing problem in the world today, therefore, than that of Soviet-American relations. Without the reconciliation of the basic interests of these two Powers, there can be no durable peace; there can be no peace at all.

But such a reconciliation does not exist. It is not even being seriously sought. The relations between Moscow and Washington are becoming increasingly strained. Of the idylls of Teheran and Yalta nothing remains.

I do not believe, however, as so many abroad do, that Moscow's diplomats are always in the wrong; or that where Soviet and American interests collide right and justice are automatically on the American side. It would be easy to prove, for example, that on the issue of the Dardanelles the case presented by the Kremlin was stronger than that put forth by Washington. Yet it is especially on such issues—in which the Kremlin could have the support of the Russian people—that Washington and London are most adamant. Why?

It is not true that this is because the interests of these nations and Russia are "irreconcilable." They could be reconciled. That's not the point at all. The issue lies elsewhere. And this brings me to the central point: Stalin's eternal sin before the Russian people who, in saving their native land, also saved his regime in the Kremlin.

For many tortured years the people of Russia struggled in solitude for human rights and a decent life—behind an iron curtain of *indifference*. After all, it was only in Russia that Communism crushed all semblance of civil and political freedoms; only in Russia that hundreds of thousands, then millions, of peasants, workers, intellectuals, former "boorzhooies," priests, and Communists fallen from grace languished and perished in concentration camps; only in Russia that uncounted numbers of "enemies of the people" were being slaughtered.

As long as this was happening only in the "land of the Soviets," the outside world remained stolidly apathetic. Western democrats, with few exceptions, were silent about the horrors. Nay, they even sang the praises of the new "economic democracy" under "the most democratic constitution in the world." They sang hymns to the "genius" of the leaders of that chained and lacerated nation. They shut their ears against its groans. As for the ruthless cruelty, either they pretended not to notice or they placated their conscience with libels about the "barbarism" of the Russian masses.

Then Bolshevism with its NKVD and executioners broke into Europe. There, too, the whirlwind of violence swept through the land as it had done in Russia in the annihilation of our free peasantry during collectivization. The former members of the Comintern, now installed as rulers, undertook in the West to extirpate democracy by the methods of Lenin and Stalin. When all this that is loathsome and frightful began to transpire not in "savage Russia" but in cultured Europe, not only the "capitalists" but the farmers, the workers, the common people of all countries began to despise my country. . . . Even most of the liberals who in the past made excuses for the Soviet terror could no longer hold their pose of being superior to human suffering. The wall of indifference has collapsed.

And this great hatred, softened by distance, has reached also the shores of the United States.

For few here understood that Stalin has stolen the victory from the people, stepped up the terror, resumed his purges in the army, the government, the collective farms, the Communist Youth, schools, literature, even music. All this has been done specifically for the purpose of transforming the might of victorious Russia into a cradle of world revolution. And it is being done despite the intense abhorrence of the Russian people for Communism.

354

So long as the Western democracies remain callous to the tragedy of my country, the world will never find its way back to peace and progress.

The World's Greatest Myth about Russia

IN THE COURSE of a recent lecture tour I was repeatedly confronted by one of the biggest propaganda myths of our epoch. Since I addressed only college audiences, where a higher standard of historical accuracy might be expected, the persistence of the falsehood is specially remarkable.

If it were a *harmless* error we could afford to ignore it despite its size and absurdity. But it happens to be a *mischievous* error—one that confuses public opinion in all democratic countries—and therefore should be exploded once and for all.

I refer to the deep-rooted myth that the Bolsheviks under Lenin and Trotsky overthrew the Czarist regime. Men and women who should know better said to me at the lectures: "At least we must give the Bolsheviks credit for putting an end to the Romanoff despotism."

Whereupon I had to explain, for the thousandth time, that they did nothing of the sort. The regime the Bolsheviks overthrew by force and deceit was not the ancient monarchy but the brand-new democracy, the so-called Kerensky regime.

On March 12, 1917, when the first World War was still in full blaze and one month before America entered the struggle, Czarism collapsed. The great Russian Revolution began. The first and only democratic regime in the tragic history of my country came into being.

The Bolsheviks took no part in that crucial event. Lenin and Zinoviev were in Switzerland. Trotsky was in New York. Stalin (at that time a minor figure) was in Siberian exile. Virtually all the top leaders of the future Bolshevik dictatorship were similarly abroad, imprisoned or in distant banishment.

That upheaval, moreover, took them all by surprise. They did not believe that it could or would happen so soon. Lenin wrote to his friends from Zurich that his generation had no hope of seeing a revolution in Russia. His followers in Petrograd (now Leningrad) told me and my associates only a few hours before the explosion: "There are no signs of a revolution; we are entering a long period of Czarist reaction."

It was only after political amnesty had been extended by the democratic Provisional Government of a Russia freed from the yoke of monarchy that the leaders of Bolshevism began to congregate in the Russian capital. Lenin, Zinoviev, and others arrived one month after the downfall of the Romanoffs— in the notorious sealed train provided by the German Kaiser for their journey.

What kind of Russia did these amnestied Bolsheviks return to? We have Lenin's own testimony. "Russia is now the freest country in Europe, where there is no oppression of the masses," he declared publicly on reaching Petrograd. These words he repeated several days before the Bolshevik insurrection of November 7, 1917 which killed the democratic regime in the eighth month of its existence.

Lenin, the father of Bolshevism, thus openly acknowledged that his successful *putsch* was directed not against Czarism but against a free people's government. This simple truth has been buried under mountains of doubletalk. It must be dug up without delay. The myth that the Bolsheviks overthrew Czarism has been purposely spread in order to conceal their crime of having strangled the first Russian democracy.

The Communists everywhere are today trying to seize power by the same cynical device which Lenin used in 1917, namely by posing as a "defender of people's freedom and of democracy." The Bolsheviks knew full well how passionately the Russian people desired freedom. That is why they organized their blow against liberty under the banners of liberty.

"It is necessary to overthrow the Kerensky government," Lenin hammered away day after day, "in the interests of the present democratic revolution."

Only after his victory did he admit publicly that his freedom-loving slogans had been a deliberate deception. In preparing the *coup,* he declared, "the Bolsheviks firmly and decisively . . . favored the dictatorship of the proletariat."

At that time the world had had no experience whatever with modern totalitarian techniques. The Russian people therefore cannot be blamed too hard for falling into the Communist trap baited with democratic verbiage.

There is no such excuse for the millions of workers, farmers, and intellectuals in the democratic West who are offered the bait today. The frightful experience of my native land should serve them as a grim warning. They must refuse to be lured into slavery by the propaganda of the lie. And they can begin by rejecting the central myth that the Bolsheviks overthrew Czarism.

April 1947

SOLUTION FOR PALESTINE

By ISAAC DON LEVINE

[*Even at this late hour in the Middle East crisis, with its constant threat of a world war of unimaginable horrors, there is enough vital substance left in the Hoover-Lowdermilk proposed solution for the brewing Arab-Israeli conflict. As unfolded in* Plain Talk *in March and April 1948, when the Palestine partition plan voted by the United Nations was rejected by the Arabs, former President Herbert Hoover's project depended for its realization largely on American finances. Since then that aspect of the problem has lost its importance in view of the untold billions in oil revenues amassed by many Arab nations. However, statesmanship of the highest order is required to take over the political consummation of the grand design. Its author, Walter Clay Lowdermilk, former President of the American Geophysical Union, approached the critical issue with pure scientific detachment, as part of his blueprint for reclaiming and revitalizing the whole Middle East, as presented in his book* Palestine, Land of Promise. *In the face of an imminent conflagration of the first magnitude, Mr. Hoover's suggestion for a "serious investigation" of the project may still bear fruit after a lapse of some 27 years.*]

IT IS not yet too late to find a peaceful and constructive solution for the crisis in Palestine and in the United Nations over Palestine. The challenge posed by the report of the U.N. Palestine Commission—that the partition plan adopted last November could not be carried out without the assistance of an international armed force—calls for bold and far-visioned statesmanship.

It is a challenge which transcends the issue of dreaded full-scale civil war in the Holy Land after the scheduled British evacuation next summer. It is a challenge which goes beyond a defi to the authority of the United Nations, which has already been denigrated by big and small powers alike. It even involves more than the crucial question of sending American troops into an area of strife, entailing sacrifices which the American people are loath to assume. The paramount peril in the challenge lies in the invitation to Soviet Russia to help police and keep order in Palestine, for an international force could not be organized by the United Nations without the participation of Soviet troops. And that is bound to lead eventually to a major catastrophe for all concerned.

Before outlining the three preliminary steps that can and should be taken at this eleventh hour, when the Security Council finds itself with its back to the wall on the Palestine question, it is essential that we stop and consider the truly great and statesmanlike proposal advanced by ex-President Hoover [and here reproduced on pages 358-359] on November 9, 1945, in a statement to the Scripps-

Howard newspapers. It is a proposal which was made from a practical, engineering, and humanitarian standpoint, and not for political reasons, and it still points to a sane way out of the blind alley in which the mentors of the United Nations have maneuvered themselves.

1. Conditioned upon the implementation of Mr. Hoover's plan through the extension of ERP as suggested below, the United Nations should defer the execution of the partition plan until Decemebr 31, 1948. The Security Council may be forced to take some such action anyway, because the time is too short to improvise an effective international force and transport it to Palestine by mid-summer, even if a majority of the powers agreed on this course.

2. With a fund of $375 million, less than the sum that will have been expended on aid to Greece alone, the Hoover plan could be put into effect as part of the European Recovery Program which already includes relief to China. The expense of redeeming through irrigation the once-fertile Tigris-Euphrates valleys in underpopulated Iraq, whose government would surely welcome it as a boon, is estimated today at $175 million. To finance the settlement of 200,000 families by loaning to each of them $1,000 in housing and agricultural equipment on a long-term low-interest basis would amount to $200 million. Thus a total of $375 million would take care of the settlement of about one million Arab *fellahin* (peasants) from Greater Palestine in a veritable bonanza country under a brother-Arab rule. There would be no need for any compulsory transfer of the population as at least one-half of the wretched and usury-ridden Arab laborers of Palestine would stream down to the reclaimed Mesopotamian belt.

3. President Truman could cut the present Gordian knot of the Palestine crisis by calling upon Herbert Hoover to head a commission to work out the details of the plan and the form of the organization required to put it into operation. Pending this study, the Government of the United States should make representations before the Security Council which would assure the postponement of the partition plan as well as United Nations cooperation in the ultimate solution to the whole Palestine problem.

* * *

HERBERT HOOVER'S PLAN FOR PALESTINE

"THERE is a possible plan of settling the Palestine question and providing ample Jewish refuge. It is at least worth serious investigation, for it offers a constructive humanitarian solution.

"In ancient times the irrigation of the Tigris and Euphrates valleys supported probably ten million people in the kingdoms of Babylon and Nineveh. The deterioration and destruction of their irrigation works by the Mongol invasion centuries ago, and their neglect for ages, are responsible for the shrinkage of the population to about 3 million people in modern Iraq. Some 30 years ago Sir William Willcocks, an eminent British engineer, completed a study of the restoration of the old irrigation system. He estimated that about 2.8 million acres of the most fertile land in the world could be recovered at a cost of under $150 million.

"Some progress has been made under the Iraq government, but their lack of financial resources and the delays of the war have retarded the work greatly. Some years ago it was proposed that this area should be developed for settlement by Jewish refugees. This did not, however, satisfy the Jewish desire for a homeland.

"My own suggestion is that Iraq might be financed to complete this great land development on the consideration that it be made the scene of resettlement of the Arabs from Palestine. This would clear Palestine completely for a large Jewish emigration and colonization. A suggestion of transfer of the Arab people of Palestine was made by the British Labor Party in December 1944, but no adequate plan was proposed as to where or how they were to go.

"There is room for many more Arabs in such a development in Iraq than the total of Arabs in Palestine. The soil is more fertile. They would be among their own race, which is Arab-speaking and Mohammedan. The Arab population of Palestine would be the gainer from better lands in exchange for their present holdings. Iraq would be the gainer, for it badly needs agricultural population.

"Today millions of people are being moved from one land to another. If the lands were organized and homes provided, this particular movement could be made the model migration of history. It would be a solution by engineering instead of by conflict.

"I realize that the plan offers a challenge both to the statesmanship of the Great Powers as well as to the goodwill of all parties concerned. However, I submit it, and it does offer a method of settlement with both honor and wisdom."

*   *   *

"'BENEATH the banner of Politics, Reason sits howling over an intellectual chaos."

This line from James Stephens' *The Crock of Gold* would make a fitting epitaph for our age. It fits the crisis over Palestine to perfection.

Imagine a visitor from another planet beholding the Great Sanhedrin of all the civilized nations of the earth caught in a blind alley and confessing to helplessness in the face of the Palestinian problem. Imagine further that the interplanetary visitor, upon inquiry as to the cause of the impasse, learned that it was a question of settling a few million members of a homeless race. And then imagine that the visitor, an irrigation engineer, after looking over Palestine and adjacent Iraq, observed:

"What's the problem? Here you have the most fertile undeveloped agricultural zone on this entire planet, an area proven to be capable of sustaining some 35 million inhabitants. And at the present there are only about 5 million in it. There is room here for ten times the number ever likely to go to Palestine. I can't understand what's troubling you."

THE DOOM of the partition plan was foreshadowed since the day the United Nations Palestine Commission declared the need for an international armed force to set up separate Jewish and Arab states in the Holy Land. If it were not so tragic, the agitation to "save the United Nations in the Palestine crisis" might be regarded as sardonic. For only daydreamers and wishful thinkers could treat the U.N. as an effective instrument after it had shown itself incapable of even slowing up the rapid march toward an atomic war.

The stark truth is that the United States, and *not* the United Nations, is the key to the Palestine problem. Those who cling to the unworkable partition plan, crying that the fate of the U.N. is at stake, dig their heads, ostrichlike, deeper into the sands of futility.

What is needed is a moratorium on politics over Palestine. President Truman should call on Herbert Hoover to head a commission of scientists to formulate a nonpolitical engineering solution for the Palestine crisis, on the basis of the Hoover plan—to be financed under the ERP.

The framework of the Hoover plan for Palestine has been provided by two of the foremost irrigation experts in the world, Walter Clay Lowdermilk and F. Julius Fohs. The following article by Dr. Lowdermilk and the digest of a special memorandum by Mr. Fohs highlight the Hoover plan. Mr. Hoover himself, during his world food survey in 1946, carried away from the Middle East the conviction that the reclamation of that area is one of the simplest and least costly engineering projects in the world. But where are the forces of reason to prevail at this late hour in the political chaos which has enfolded the Palestine problem?

April 1948

THE UNTRIED APPROACH

By WALTER CLAY LOWDERMILK

THE SAYING "westward the course of Empire took its way" only hides the tragic fact that mankind has tended always to use up resources, devastate the forests and waste fertile fields. As soil erosion has been allowed to damage old lands, peoples have constantly moved to new ones.

But today there are no more continents to discover, to explore and to exploit. All lands except possibly some of Antarctica have been taken into possession. The frontier of new land, with only minor exceptions, is gone and gone forever. In its place, however, is a new frontier—the improvement and conservation of lands under use and the reclamation of damaged and misused lands. Here is a challenge to the United Nations as great as the challenge of war.

In a very real sense, civilization is on trial for its waste of the limited areas of good land that must supply food as the basis of peace within and among nations. If but a fraction of the amounts spent for war and destruction could be spent for reclamation, great numbers of "TVAs" could be established in strategic areas throughout the world where vast water resources flow unused and irrigable lands remain parched while peoples are discouraged and undernourished or actually starving.

As a result of society's failure to understand the basic importance of proper land use, the application of modern agricultural science and technology is not yet keeping pace with land depletion around the world. It is profoundly significant, therefore, that in Palestine, in a region depleted of forests and grasses and soils, where ruins of great works bespeak former populous and powerful peoples, but where now general decadence and poverty reign, Jewish agricultural settlements are reversing the long trend of wasteful land decline. On the seven per cent of the land, which is all that the Jews have thus far been permitted to redeem, the colonists have done the finest reclamation work of modern times. I am convinced, after studying the relation of peoples to their lands in twenty-six different countries, that these colonists have done something new under the sun; they are working out a lasting adjustment of a people to their land in which all people of the world should be interested.

By a balanced combination of scientific agriculture and industry, and a voluntary cooperative social system, they have managed to achieve a European standard of living in the midst of the backward, depressed subsistence economy of the Middle East. Their approach to the problem of industrializing subsistence agrarian economics promises a new day not only for Palestine and for the Middle East, but for the world at large. . . .

The valley of the Jordan River and the maritime plain of Palestine offer a combination and concentration of natural features that set the stage for one of the most unique and far-reaching reclamation projects on earth, comparable to the Tennessee Valley Authority of the United States in scope and function.

It was while making an airplane survey of Palestine in 1939 that I was struck by the possibility of a great power project based upon the extraordinary difference in altitudes between the deep rift of the Jordan Valley and the Mediterranean Sea only a few tens of miles away. Palestine's two chief economic needs are supplies of water for irrigated agriculture and power for industrial development. The JVA would supply both. It would divert the sweet waters of the Upper Jordan and its tributaries into a network of irrigation canals, while, in order to compensate the Dead Sea for the loss of these waters, it would introduce sea water from the Mediterranean, starting at a point near Haifa, and conduct it through a tunnel and open canals down the Jordan depression to the

Dead Sea. As this sea water dropped into the Jordan rift, there would be almost 1,200 feet of effective fall for the development of hydroelectric power.

The original sketch of the Jordan Valley Authority appeared in 1944 in my little book, *Palestine, Land of Promise.* The idea was not allowed to remain a mere sketch, nor—though the war was still raging—were the many practical problems involved in so important an engineering project, allowed to remain unanswered. While the book was still in manuscript form, I sent the first draft of the chapter on the JVA to Dr. Emanuel Neumann, and proposed the formation of a commission of experts to study the project, to engineer and to prepare a detailed scheme. With the aid of David Lilienthal, then head of the Tennessee Valley Authority, and with the expert advice of the late Colonel Theodore B. Parker, Chief Engineer of TVA, the necessary engineering studies for the projected JVA were outlined and technical personnel recommended for the work. A Commission on Palestine Surveys was set up under Dr. Neumann's direction to gather a body of experts, engage the necessary technicians, and organize the engineering investigations both in America and Palestine.

Like California, Palestine has more land suitable to irrigation than it has water for irrigation; hence no marginal lands need be considered in the JVA's plans. As in the case of California, too, Palestine's power and irrigation projects could adequately be protected from possible earthquake effects by use of standard techniques in designing. It is interesting to note that water use and costs per unit in Palestine to farmers would be comparable to conditions in California's Imperial and Central Valleys.

IN THE light of the crucial changes about to take place in Palestine's political and economic status as a result of the forthcoming termination of the British Mandate and inauguration of the plan adopted by the United Nations General Assembly last November, the Jordan Valley Authority is now of more timely significance than ever.

In view of the pressing need of providing in the immediate future for several hundred thousand to a million or more of dispossessed persons looking forward to settlement in Palestine, it is well to see which stages of the Jordan Valley project can be carried out in the Jewish State without waiting for cooperation from the Arab State. Stage I, for example, includes the construction of a medium power dam on the headwaters of the Jordan River and the development by wells and pumping of underground waters and spring waters in the coastal plain. This water would be pumped with electrical or diesel power, and is estimated to be sufficient to irrigate about 190,000 acres lying chiefly in the coastal plain. Almost all of that area is to be in the Jewish State, but a small fraction of it lies in the Arab State in northwestern Galilee, and could also be made to benefit from new irrigation waters. Stage I could be completed within one or two years depending on how rapidly the work is pushed and would cost about $25 million. The capital cost of providing water to these lands in Stage I is much lower than the average of capital costs of similar works in California.

Altogether, about 347,000 acres, approximately half of the 750,000 acres which are irrigable under the completed project, could be supplied with irrigation water in the Jewish State alone, without the cooperation of the Arab State.

Moreover, as reclamation projects make the desert blossom again, to the advantage of the workers of the Jewish State, Arab farmers and village folk across the line may well be expected to want to share in similar benefits. The expression of such desires on their part would be the signal for the United Nations to arrange for cooperation in installing all remaining stages of the project, to the greater benefit of the Arab and Jewish States.

The Jordan Valley Authority would not aid Palestine alone, or its Jews or Arabs alone. It would give an example to the backward Middle East, to stimulate other and greater valley projects in Iraq, Syria, and Egypt. Irrigation and power projects in the Tigris-Euphrates Valley would enable ancient Mesopotamia, now Iraq, to support twenty to thirty million people in decency, instead of four million now mostly in dire poverty, for Iraq is the greatest undeveloped bread-basket in the world. A Jordan Valley Authority would serve as a training ground for engineers and specialists in agriculture, grazing management, conservation and forestry, equipping them to carry out other projects that are possible in the Middle East. These might well restore this region to a condition worthy of its glorious past, to the benefit of Arab, Christian, and Jew.

There are few places in the world where mankind has a more favorable opportunity to adopt a constructive approach toward the problems of the common man, removing the basic causes of conflict and war by the creation of abundance for all. We can, through this approach, make the Middle East a blessed example rather than a breeding ground for strife.

April 1948

DEVELOPMENT OF IRAQ

[*A digest of a report made in February 1946 by F. Julius Fohs, noted American engineer.*]

THE IRRIGABLE lands of Iraq represent the greatest single undeveloped area in the Middle East. The Tigris-Euphrates-Shatt el Arab Delta, with proper additional irrigation works, can be made to produce much food, ample for home use and for export.

There are possibilities for hydroelectric power to be developed from mountain streams in northeastern Iraq and adjoining regions. Damming for this purpose would conserve much water for land reclamation. A highway was built during the war, connecting Beyrouth, Damascus to Rutba; also Haifa to Rutba, and thence from Rutba to Baghdad. The connecting link of the railway between Nusaybin and Baghdad was completed, thus giving direct rail communication from Palestine, Lebanon, and Syria to Iraq.

To carry out the program would probably require an expenditure of $175 million and a farm population of 6 million to work the irrigated lands of the areas. Total present population is about 3,750,000, mostly rural. About half the cost would be for agricultural works, taking into consideration canal-fed irrigation ditches. Wherever the sprinkler system is substituted for direct irrigation, the cost would be reduced and a one-third to one-half higher efficiency obtained —with less water consumed, and supporting a population at least one-third larger. . . .

The necessity of importing people to build up future Iraq is unquestioned. Immigration will greatly speed the land's development and in ten to twenty years accomplish more than Buckley proposed for fifty years. The leaven would eventually raise the standard of all. The agricultural possibilities of Iraq are such that it can support a farming population of at least 9 million, in addition to a nomad group of 250,000. Using the factor of 2.5 for industry and services, a population of 31.75 million is possible in the foreseeable future.

It is clear that Iraq offers the most promising field for agricultural development of any state of the Middle East, and the greatest unused fertile lands. Arabs from Palestine and other Middle East states could find in this development a much higher standard of living, and Iraq would greatly benefit from such immigration.

April 1948

BOOK 7

ON FREEDOM AND ITS ENEMIES

MORAL DECAY

By ISAAC DON LEVINE

[*The moral decay that was sapping the foundations of the free world and that offered a fertile soil for the bogus ideology of Marxism was a dominant concern of* Plain Talk *throughout its brief existence. Its pages were ever open to sound exposés of the illusions and panaceas dispensed by totalitarian healers and their adherents, just as they were open to constructive criticism and remedies of the ailing but yet free society. In this batch of essays the reader will find a wide range of topics adumbrated in the '40s that astonishingly fits the condition in the '70s of the sick human race.*]

HOW DID it come to pass that a major political figure, who had held the second highest post within the gift of the American people, could be put up for the Presidency through the machinations of the agents of a foreign power—a power which stands for the negation of the American creed?

It seems to us that this is the key question raised by the Henry A. Wallace candidacy. Yet in scanning the innumerable columns of comment upon his third-party movement we have found it conspicuously absent. To raise the question alone is to invite digging into the intellectual corruption and moral decay of our times. That the secret hand of the world's most oppressive despotism could manipulate the democratic mechanism of our free republic so as to advance a puppet candidate for the highest office in the nation goes to the root of the contemporary crisis.

Speaking Frankly

HOW DID it come to pass that a former Secretary of State, who had negotiated the peace treaty with Italy and whose book, *Speaking Frankly,* purports to share with the American people the confidences of diplomacy, chose to suppress a secret protocol annexed to that treaty?

We refer to the disclosure, made by Hanson W. Baldwin of *The New York Times,* that in the Italian treaty negotiated by Secretary Byrnes the United States had undertaken to deliver to the Soviet Government a sizable part of the Italian Navy. We scanned the pages of the best-selling *Speaking Frankly* in vain for any mention of this shocking transaction, although Mr. Byrnes himself exposed President Roosevelt's suppression, even from his intimate collaborators, of his deals with Stalin.

Or was Mr. Byrnes haunted by the ghost of Roosevelt's secret agreement at Teheran to surrender about "one-third of the Italian Fleet" to Stalin, an agreement kept secret even from the United States Navy Department? Or did the author of *Speaking Frankly* seek to protect President Truman, who announced to the country last year that he had released all the secret agreements of his predecessor? But the record of the Teheran pledge involving the Italian Navy remained under lock and key until January 16, 1948, and is still awaiting full and official publication.

How is one to characterize the conduct of Secretary Byrnes, President Truman, and President Roosevelt? How does it happen that the American people find themselves victims of such conduct on the part of their trusted servants? Nowhere is this question being pursued with any noticeable diligence.

What Price Disloyalty?

How DID it come to pass that a member of the national committee of what passes for a properly-constituted political party of voters in the United States— the Communist Party—was not required to be a citizen of the United States? And how did it happen that the recognized head of one of the strongest Communist-led unions in New York City was also a noncitizen?

In reporting the arrest of Alexander Bittelman for deportation to his native Russia and of Michael J. Obermeier to his native Germany as undesirable aliens, our press seems to have overlooked this important question. The Government of the French Republic faced it squarely some weeks ago when, at the risk of antagonizing the powerful Soviet Government, it acted upon the principle that a political party is a strictly home affair and that a labor union is an equally internal institution.

Yet here is an issue which those well-meaning leading churchmen and laymen who are concerned with the immaculate preservation of our civil rights will not face. If they would raise it, they may very well discover some of the basic reasons for the spiritual disintegration of our society. Civil liberties cannot be maintained by standards which honor conspirators as equal citizens.

Chinese Puzzle

How DID it come to pass that in non-Communist China, whose people had long been schooled in regarding the United States as their greatest friend, American prestige has been rapidly declining and the legend of American "imperialism" has been growing among the common people and the intellectuals?

The answer to this question, which is all too easily explained by blaming Chinese Communist propaganda, is in reality to be sought in Washington and throughout the rest of this country. When those who make our policy in the Far East are themselves infected with the virus of Communist propaganda, as parroted by Wallace, that the United States is a warmongering, imperialistic power; when our own spokesmen and officials transmit to China the Communist-slanted comments of Americans and propound in China views in consonance with Moscow's rather than America's interests; is it any wonder that the Chinese are turning against America? But how do such things happen? It would take a powerful searchlight to expose the origins of this puzzling phenomenon.

Double Bookkeeping

HOW DOES it come to pass that Eleanor Roosevelt, who as the First Lady of the Land has unrivalled opportunities to get at the facts, dispenses different truths with either hand? In her daily column, in disparagement of the Wallace candidacy, she affirms that secret police are the earmarks of a Fascist or Communist state and that Communists the world over sow chaos to defeat democracy; in her monthly page in *The Ladies Home Journal,* she offers such pearls as that the Soviets are anxious for peace and are not preparing an attack against us now, and that they have brought "advantages to them (the Russian people) in the past twenty-five years." . . .

THESE ARE but a very few specimens from a monthly sheaf of questions of worldwide range and variety. How did we come to such a pass? Is it merely an accident that the lie has been enthroned, that the double standard has become an accepted norm of public opinion, and that conspiracy has its place in the political life of a free people?

February 1948

369

Democracy and the Republic

By Edna Lonigan

Is it true that there is an inherent conflict between democracy and a republic?

Many who believe in the American form of government keep insisting we are a republic, not a democracy. Thus we are asked to abandon a shining symbol of what our country stands for to the enemies of that faith.,

The idea of democracy is too great an idea, it is too deeply embedded in our traditions, for us to surrender it so easily to those who would destroy freedom. We have little time left in which to seek the true meaning of democracy in America, and make it once again a symbol of hope for the world.

The framers of our Constitution gave us the most skilful and ingenious design for a republic which had ever been devised.

They were determined that the new nation should not suffer the fate of the Republics of Greece, Rome, and Italy. They looked for the source of the weakness in free society and found it just where Aristotle had found it: in a country governed by the people, ambitious demagogues always try to climb to power in time of crisis by playing on the fears of the citizens, and turning them into frightened mobs who follow the would-be leaders for a slogan or the promise of bread.

To prevent that clear danger, the leaders of the Convention devised a simple strategy—the dispersion of power. They divided governmental power into many smaller pieces and set up barriers so that no one could get hold of more than a single piece. The first barrier is that the states were made independent sovereign entities, equal to the central government. The Federal Government was *primus inter pares,* first among equals. It was given power to manage specific things, mostly connected with national defense; all other powers were reserved to the states forever.

The founders not only divided governmental power so that it flowed in separate Federal, state, and local channels, but they further divided the Federal power, by setting barriers between legislative, executive, and judicial arms. Power over the flow of taxes and spending was given wholly to the Congress, the body which was closest to the people who paid the taxes, and which could gain no power for itself by spending other people's money. The work of the courts was also made completely independent of the executive power.

This system of checks and balances meant that the new central government was strong in dealing with foreign nations, but could not turn its power against its own people. The executive had the army and the police power, but it could not use them to interfere with the citizens, the Congress, or the courts, because

Congress could withhold the executive's money, and the courts could protect the citizen from seizure.

It is not correct to say American democracy means '"government of the people" or "majority rule" unless those phrases are carefully qualified. Much confusion arises from the fact that the word "government" applies to two quite different meanings. It may refer to the whole political organization of the people of a nation, or merely to the executive apparatus (the state). We in America have a *political system* which is free, because we have a *governmental apparatus* which is limited, so that even the majority cannot use it to control the rest.

The correct statement is that in the American Republic the majority elects the officials but *the officers do not rule*. They administer duties carefully defined in the Constitution. We can change our officials, because they cannot get power enough, if they obey the Constitution, to control us.

We teach government courses to our young people as if these checks and balances were verbal abstractions. But the American colonists did not think of power as an abstraction. They thought of it, as those who try to escape from Soviet Russia think of it, as the power to seize and to destroy. Brooks Adams has told how colonial officials hanged men and women, whipped them or cut off their ears because they were Baptists or Quakers. The royal governors used power to wipe out the colonial legislatures and make the courts subservient.

The colonists knew power-seekers firsthand and they were thoroughly sick of them. They decided that *no one needed power over other men*, or was wise enough to use it well.

The design sense of the Greeks culminated in the Parthenon. The design sense of the Middle Ages culminated in the cathedrals. Eighteenth-century Americans built with intangibles. Their design sense left us the exquisitely balanced structure for the control of the police power, which we call the American Constitution. No one can destroy our Republic so long as our citizens understand that design and insist that public officials live and work within it.

WHAT THEN does democracy mean in America, why does it stand for something warm and vital, if it does not mean literal majority rule?

The answer is best given by a story. A prominent American official was speaking. "My grandfather came from England," he said. "He was a farmer. One day when his wheat was ripe for cutting, the squire came riding by to hounds and started across the fields with his party. My grandfather rushed out to protest but the squire paid no attention. When grandfather ran up to ask him to stop, the squire struck him across the face with a riding crop.

"Grandfather kept quiet with the greatest effort, and said to himself, 'I mustn't say anything, I must go to Ameriky. I mustn't say anything, I must go to Ameriky.' He took all his money and came over, and then sent for his family."

Millions have made the long journey from Europe to America to get away from just such conditions. The story is an epitome of the centuries of feudal restraint from which they sought to escape.

The philosophy invented by the growing classes to help them in their struggle was the philosophy of individualism. When Jefferson said that all men were created equal, he did not mean that they were of the same height, or had the same abilities. He meant that they ought to start equal, without any hereditary privileges or disabilities, such as had grown out of the feudal division of labor. They were neither lords nor serfs, but persons. Burns put it, "The rank is but the guinea's stamp. A man's a man for a' that."

American democracy has then a very real meaning. It meant and still means the absence of privilege, especially privilege for the few, obtained through law or government. Success won by personal ability or effort is good under our democracy, but any step by which individual advantages are converted into hereditary privileges or legal rights for a few is a violation of our democratic faith.

The founders knew that attempts would be made again and again to set up new privileged classes. They refused to create a nobility or a large army, or even a social organization of officers of the Revolutionary Army, like the Cincinnati, because they were mortally afraid of the rise of privileged groups.

They believed that governments should be changed every few years, and the "ins" turned out, because if any one group practiced the arts of government for any length of time, it would make a closed corporation of it. It was a matter of honor for army officers and civil servants to return promptly to civil life, like Cincinnatus. No American needed or wanted rank or title, office or authority. Citizenship was the highest honor.

Democracy in America comes from our rebellion against every form of privilege based on fixed or inherited rights, or rights derived from membership in a class, instead of on performance. That is our idea of equality. The republic of limited powers comes from our rebellion against the strong governmental apparatus of the kings. There is no conflict between our idea of democracy and our republic. On the contrary, strong resistance to the rise of privileged groups is the best protection against those who would destroy the Republic.

NOTHING in American democracy says that citizens have a right to govern anybody but themselves, or that a majority has the right to tell a minority what to do.

The idea that "democracy" means the control of some citizens by others, whenever the majority wishes, came out of the French Revolution. Lafayette tried to guide the French Revolution in the direction of liberty, like the American, but he failed, and the French devised a new concept of the republic, one in which the people wielded a central apparatus as strong as that of Louis XVI. With that apparatus, the majority could impose religious, political, economic, and educational restraints on the minority.

The French achieved results exactly opposite from ours. Their Republic was strong in imposing its controls on its own people, but weak against outside foes, because the nation was divided. The people were engaged in a constant struggle of factions to become the majority, so that they could get hold of the governmental apparatus, and impose their will on the rest.

Lafayette could not persuade the French to adopt the American idea of limited government because the French had had no experience with liberty. The English-speaking people knew liberty from centuries of practice. They had kept their kings in check, and managed their business without government interference. When they set up a republic on this continent, they knew all government must be kept in check, and they knew how to invent checks that worked.

The democracy that emerged from the French Revolution was immature. The people, not used to power, wanted to play with it. The English people, used to power, wanted to restrain it. They didn't want to rule anybody and they didn't want anybody to rule them.

Every country in Europe which had been trained in absolutism created its democracy in the image of absolutism. That was all they knew. Germany, Russia, Italy, attached popular government to the strong central apparatus with power to rule the people. It was just a question of time before the central apparatus was taken over by new "kings."

UNTIL recently Americans were vigorously opposed to the Continental idea of democracy. To us, as to Jefferson and Franklin, citizens were not governed by anybody. They governed themselves. We would have opposed as vigorously as did John Stuart Mill any suggestion that a majority of citizens had any right to control the rest. We put it into the Constitution, that the majority could not impose uniformity in religion. They could not restrain the power of the states. They could not take away the property of a minority except for government needs, under protection of the courts.

In the last few years, however, a great many Americans have been subtly won over to the Continental concept of democracy, with its strong central government operating in the name of the majority. Now we talk of special privileges for the "underprivileged." We urge Federal management of housing, medical care, schools and colleges, Federal contributions for school lunches, and Federal control of the franchise. We are already tolerant of Federal control of criminal and police work. We are more and more financing our mayors from Washington, and encouraging them to look to Washington for their policies. Yet we seem hardly aware that the Continental form of democracy will destroy both American democracy and the American Republic.

THERE ARE a thousand reasons why Americans should not exchange their freedom for the promises of demagogues. We mention only two.

The turn from American to Continental democracy is being voted by people who believe they are "minorities." But our Federal system was designed to *protect* minorities. Limited government was designed to prevent any majority persecuting anyone because he was a Baptist or a Quaker, or a Southern slaveholder, or an abolitionist. How are members of "minority groups" persuaded to support the trend to Continental democracy? How can capitalism preserve the rights of *minorities?* Of course, the members of "minority groups" are told that they will have more privileges if they accept the Continental way, but free men should not give up their birthrights for words.

The second objection to Continental democracy is that the majorities which vote it into power do not spring up naturally, but are organized by someone. From past history, from Greece and Rome, from Renaissance Italy and modern times, we can draw only one conclusion. The discontented masses who ask for the strong state are organized by those who want to be the new "kings." The liberty of Florence was destroyed by Lorenzo D'Medici; that of the First Republic in France by Napoleon I, the Second Republic by Napoleon III, the Third Republic by Laval. The Republic in Germany was taken over by Hitler, limited government in Italy by Mussolini, and the constitutional Republic in Russia by Lenin.

We have recently learned in this country how little the people, or even the officials, know of what is going on in Big Government. Government cannot be controlled by the citizens unless the central apparatus is restricted to very few functions, about which there is almost total agreement.

The Continental idea of democracy has now grown, under the stress of two world wars, to the point where it threatens to sweep over us and obliterate our freedom. Back of every appeal in this country for a change from American democracy to the strong central government with large spending powers and virtual self-direction, is the voice of the would-be "kings." Neither the majority nor the minority can gain by a change to Continental democracy. The only people who can gain are the new kings and their subservient elite.

OUR SYSTEM of government, with liberty for the people and restraint on the governmental apparatus, is the greatest step forward in the art of government ever devised by the mind of man. Our democracy with its emphasis on *equality of opportunity,* not identity of results, is the system which best releases the powers in the individual.

It is not easy for a rich nation to remain truly democratic. Like the people of the late Middle Ages, we have forgotten how our society should function. Crystallization has set in, and with it a measure of rigidity. That is why we have not recognized the inroads made by the strong and subtle power-seekers on the integrity of our Republic.

But if we are truly ready to preserve our democracy and our liberty, we can make the United States once again a beacon light for those who want men to be free everywhere in the world.

November 1948

THE PHILOSOPHY OF THE
PSEUDO-PROGRESSIVES

By LUDWIG VON MISES

[*Dr. Ludwig von Mises, with his* Socialism, *first published in 1922, and two other works,* Omnipotent Government *and* Bureaucracy, *issued by the Yale University Press in 1944, firmly established his reputation in the United States as a foremost critic of Marxism and all economic tota'itarianism. For more than 20 years a professor at the University of Vienna, and from 1934 to 1940 at the Graduate Institute of International Studies at Geneva, he came to the United States as one of the most distinguished opponents of Nazism. His major work,* Human Action, *published in 1949, has been hailed as an enduring contribution to the world literature on economics. Von Mises passed away in New York at the age of 92.*]

The Two Lines of Marxian Thought and Policies

IN ALL COUNTRIES which have not openly adopted a policy of outright and all-round socialization, the conduct of government affairs has been for many decades in the hands of statesmen and parties who style themselves "progressive" and scorn their opponents as "reactionaries." These progressives become sometimes (but not always) very angry if somebody calls them Marxians. In this protest they are right in so far as their tenets and policies are contrary to some of the Marxian doctrines and their application to political action. But they are wrong in so far as they unreservedly endorse the fundamental dogmas of the Marxian creed and act accordingly. While calling in question the ideas of Marx the champion of integral revolution, they subscribe to piecemeal revolution.

For there are in the writings of Marx two distinct sets of theorems incompatible with each other: the line of the integral revolution as upheld in earlier days by Kautsky and later by Lenin, and the "reformist" line of revolution by instalments as vindicated by Sombart in Germany and the Fabians in England.

Common to both lines is the unconditional damnation of capitalism and its political "superstructure," representative government. Capitalism is described as a ghastly system of exploitation. It heaps riches upon a constantly diminishing number of "expropriators" and condemns the masses to increasing misery, oppression, slavery, and degradation. But it is precisely this awkward system which "with the inexorability of a law of nature" finally brings about salvation

375

The coming of socialism is inevitable. It will appear as the result of the actions of the class-conscious proletarians. All machinations of the wicked "bourgeois" are doomed to failure.

But here the two lines diverge.

IN THE Communist Manifesto Marx and Engels designed a plan for the step-by-step transformation of capitalism into socialism. The proletarians should "win the battle of democracy" and thus raise themselves to the position of the ruling class. Then they should use their political supremacy to wrest, "by degrees," all capital from the bourgeoisie. Marx and Engels give rather detailed instructions for the various measures to be resorted to. It is unnecessary to quote in extenso their battle plan. Its diverse items are familiar to all Americans who have lived through the years of the New Deal and the Fair Deal. It is more important to remember that the fathers of Marxism themselves characterized the measures they recommended as "despotic inroads on the rights of property and the conditions of bourgeois production" and as "measures which appear economically insufficient and untenable, but which in the course of the movement outstrip themselves, necessitate further inroads upon the old social order, and are unavoidable as a means of entirely revolutionizing the mode of production."*

It is obvious that all the "reformers" of the last one hundred years were dedicated to the execution of the scheme drafted by the authors of the Communist Manifesto in 1848. In this sense Bismarck's *Sozialpolitik* as well as Roosevelt's New Deal have a fair claim to the epithet Marxian.

But on the other hand Marx also conceived a doctrine radically different from that expounded in the Manifesto and absolutely incompatible with it. According to this second doctrine "no social formation ever disappears before all the productive forces are developed for the development of which it is broad enough, and new higher methods of production never appear before the material conditions of their existence have been hatched out in the womb of the previous society." Full maturity of capitalism is the indispensable prerequisite for the appearance of socialism. There is but one road toward the realization of socialism, namely the progressive evolution of capitalism itself which, through the incurable contradictions of the capitalist mode of production, causes its own collapse. Independently of the wills of men this process "executes itself through the operation of the inherent laws of capitalist production."

The utmost concentration of capital by a small cluster of expropriators on the one hand and unendurable impoverishment of the exploited masses on the other hand are the factors that alone can give rise to the great revulsion which will sweep away capitalism. Only then will the patience of the wretched wage

* It is important to realize that the words "necessitate further inroads upon the old social order" are lacking in the original German text of the Manifesto as well as in the later authorized German editions. They were inserted in 1888 by Engels into the translation by Samuel Moore which was published with the subtitle: "Authorized English Translation, edited and annotated by Frederick Engels."

earners give way and with a sudden stroke they will in a violent revolution overthrow the "dictatorship" of the bourgeoisie grown old and decrepit.

From the point of view of this doctrine Marx distinguishes between the policies of the petty bourgeois and those of the class-conscious proletarians. The petty bourgeois in their ignorance put all their hopes upon reforms. They are eager to restrain, to regulate, and to improve capitalism. They do not see that all such endeavors are doomed to failure and make things worse, not better. For they delay the evolution of capitalism and thereby the coming of its maturity which alone can bring about the great debacle and thus deliver mankind from the evils of exploitation. But the proletarians, enlightened by the Marxian doctrine, do not indulge in these reveries. They do not embark upon idle schemes for an improvement of capitalism. They, on the contrary, recognize in every progress of capitalism, in every impairment of their own conditions and in every new recurrence of economic crisis, a progress toward the inescapable collapse of the capitalist mode of production. The essence of their policies is to organize and to discipline their forces, the militant battalions of the people, in order to be ready when the great day of the revolution dawns.

This rejection of petty-bourgeois policies refers also to traditional labor union tactics. The plans of the workers to raise, within the framework of capitalism, wage rates and their standards of living through unionization and through strikes are vain. For the inescapable tendency of capitalism, says Marx, is not to raise but to lower the average standard of wages. Consequently he advised the unions to change their policies entirely. "Instead of the *conservative* motto: *a fair day's wage for a fair day's work,* they ought to inscribe on their banner the *revolutionary* watchword: *Abolition of the wages system.*"

It is impossible to reconcile these two varieties of Marxian doctrines and of Marxian policies. They preclude one another. The authors of the Communist Manifesto in 1848 recommended precisely those policies which their later books and pamphlets branded as petty-bourgeois nonsense. Yet they never repudiated their scheme of 1848. They arranged new editions of the Manifesto. In the preface of the 1872 edition they declared that the principles for political action as outlined in 1848 need to be improved, as such practical measures must be always adjusted to changing historical conditions. But they did not, in this preface, stigmatize such reforms as the outcome of petty-bourgeois mentality. Thus the dualism of the two Marxian lines remained.

It was in perfect agreement with the intransigent revolutionary line that the German Social-Democrats in the eighties voted in the Reichstag against Bismarck's social security legislation and that their passionate opposition frustrated Bismarck's intention to socialize the German tobacco industry. It is no less consonant with this revolutionary line that the Stalinists and their henchmen describe the American New Deal and the Keynesian patent medicines as clever but idle contrivances designed to salvage and to preserve capitalism.

The present day antagonism between the Communists on the one hand and the Socialists, New Dealers, and Keynesians on the other hand is a controversy about the means to be resorted to for the attainment of a goal common to both of these factions, namely the establishment of all-round central planning and the entire elimination of the market economy. It is a feud between two factions both of which are right in referring to the teachings of Marx. And it is paradoxical indeed that in this controversy the *anti-Communists'* title to the appellation "Marxian" is vested in the document called the *Communist* Manifesto.

The Guide of the Progressives

IT IS IMPOSSIBLE to understand the mentality and the policy of the Progressives if one does not take into account the fact that the Communist Manifesto is for them both manual and holy writ, the only reliable source of information about mankind's future as well as the ultimate code of political conduct. The Communist Manifesto is the only piece of the writings of Marx which they have really perused. Apart from the Manifesto they know only a few sentences out of context and without any bearing on the problems of current policies. But from the Manifesto they have learned that the coming of socialism is inevitable and will transform the earth into a Garden of Eden. They call themselves progressives and their opponents reactionaries precisely because, fighting for the bliss that is bound to come, they are borne by the "wave of the future" while their adversaries are committed to the hopeless attempt to stop the wheel of Fate and History. What a comfort to know that one's own cause is destined to conquer!

Then the progressive professors, writers, politicians, and civil servants discover in the Manifesto a passage which especially flatters their vanity. They belong to that "small section of the ruling class," to that "portion of the bourgeois ideologists" who have gone over to the proletariat, "the class that holds the future in its hands." Thus they are members of that elite "who have raised themselves to the level of comprehending theoretically the historical movements as a whole."

Still more important is the fact that the Manifesto provides them with an armor which makes them proof against all criticisms leveled against their policies. The bourgeois describe these progressive policies as "economically insufficient and untenable" and think that they have thereby demonstrated their inadequacy. How wrong they are! In the eyes of the Progressives the excellence of these policies consists in the very fact that they are "economically insufficient and untenable." For exactly such policies are, as the Manifesto says, "unavoidable as a means of entirely revolutionizing the mode of production."

The Communist Manifesto serves as a guidebook not only to the personnel of the ever-swelling hosts of bureaucrats and pseudo-economists. It reveals to the "progressive" authors the very nature of the "bourgeois class culture." What a disgrace in this so-called bourgeois civilization! Fortunately the eyes of the self-styled "liberal" writers have been opened wide by Marx. The Manifesto tells them the truth about the unspeakable meanness and depravity of the bourgeoisie. Bourgeois marriage is "in fact a system of community of women." The bourgeois "sees in his wife a mere instrument of production." Our bourgeois, "not content with having the wives and daughters of their proletarians at their disposal, not to speak of common prostitutes, take the greatest pleasure in seducing each others' wives." In this vein innumerable plays and novels portray the conditions of the rotten society of decaying capitalism.

How different are conditions in the country whose proletarians, the vanguard of what the great Fabians, Sidney and Beatrice Webb, called the *New Civilization,* have already "liquidated" the exploiters! It may be granted that the Russian methods cannot be considered in *every* respect as a pattern to be adopted by the "liberals" of the West. It may also be true, that the Russians, properly irritated by the machinations of the Western capitalists who are unceasingly plotting for a violent overthrow of the Soviet regime, become angry and sometimes give vent to their indignation in unfriendly language. Yet the fact remains that in Russia the word of the Communist Manifesto has become flesh. While under capitalism "the workers have no country" and "have nothing to lose but their chains," Russia is the true fatherland of all proletarians of the entire world. In a purely technical and legal sense it may be wrong for an American or Canadian to hand over confidential state documents or the secret designs of new weapons to the Russian authorities. Form a higher point of view it may be understandable.

SUCH WAS the ideology that got hold of the men who in the last decades controlled the administration and determined the course of American affairs. It was against such a mentality that the economists had to fight in criticizing the New Deal. . . .

If one wants to repulse the onslaughts of the Communists and Socialists and to shield Western civilization from Sovietization, it is not enough to disclose the abortiveness and impropriety of the progressive policies allegedly aiming at improving the economic conditions of the masses. What is needed is a frontal attack upon the whole web of Marxian, Veblenian, and Keynesian fallacies. As long as the syllogisms of these pseudo-philosophies retain their undeserved prestige, the average intellectual will go on blaming capitalism for all the disastrous effects of anticapitalist schemes and devices.

There are people who think that economic history neglects what they call the "human angle." Now, the proper field of economic history is prices and production, money and credit, taxes and budgets, and other such phenomena. But all these things are the outcome of human volitions and actions, plans and ambitions. The topic of economic history is man with all his knowledge and ignorance, his truth and his errors, his virtues and his vices.

February 1950

THE MYTH-MAKERS

By LEOPOLD SCHWARZSCHILD

[*This essay came as a fitting sequel to the author's brilliant biography of* Karl Marx, The Red Prussian, *which reveals some astonishing facts about the father of Communism.*]

ONE HUNDRED YEARS AGO two German writers, who had made their headquarters in Brussels, sat down to collaborate on a pamphlet.

They were very young: Karl Marx, doctor of philosophy, was twenty-nine; Friedrich Engels, his "second fiddle," was twenty-five. A few years back both of them had been caught up in the swelling tide which went by the name of communism or socialism. But they had immediately thought up their own brand of socialism. This differed from the others because of certain rules for practical politics which it propounded—and still more because of its remarkable theoretical revelations.

As far as practical politics were concerned, Marx and Engels had decided that the cursed system of private property and private enterprise could not be abolished peacefully and legally, but only by means of armed revolution; and not by any kind of cooperation on the part of various levels of the population, but through one chosen class alone—the proletariat, the industrial workers.

But these practical postulates were as nothing compared to the discovery which the two young writers called the "science of socialism." This was essentially the assertion that mankind has no choice as to whether it wishes to preserve or dispense with any particular economic or political system. No, this decision rests solely with the superhuman power of economic fatalism. Certain iron laws, to which economics is subject, determine irresistibly and all-powerfully the whole course of human events. Certain iron economic laws had, three or four generations previously, given birth to the system of free enterprise. Certain iron economic laws now condemned it to death. The particular brand of socialism which the two young writers had invented was characterized above all by this amazing new "science" of the utterly inevitable collapse of capitalism.

Armed with this science, Marx and Engels had in 1845 founded a "Communist Party" in Brussels—the first party in the world to be called by this name. They had been able to drum up only seventeen members. Shortly thereafter the party, together with some similar groups in various countries, were welded into a "Communist League," which boasted about three hundred members. The League commissioned Marx and Engels to draw up a Communist "confession of faith." And this was the remarkable pamphlet which they produced in December 1847 and January 1848. They called it the "Communist Manifesto."

Here were twelve thousand words which were destined to shake the world! When they appeared in print they evoked no noticeable echo. That which we now call Marxism progressed very slowly. But this was its starting point. The two young writers grew old, and they went on writing. But all their subsequent works—including the famous *Capital*—were fundamentally only attempts to bolster up with belated proofs the unproved assertions and prophecies of the Manifesto. The substance of what they had to say had already been presented to the world. We are celebrating the centenary of the birth of Marxism. And in the normal course of events it is sufficiently clear after a trial period of a hundred years whether the basic assertions of any science have been confirmed or disproved.

But never did a science have such an abnormal career as Marxism—and a most curious example of this is the very document with which its career began. For this document prophesied the inevitable collapse of capitalism and the inevitable Communist revolution not for some uncertain point in the distant future. No, the deluge was expected any minute. At that moment the whole of Europe was awaiting the "bourgeois" democratic uprising which actually broke out in February 1848. But that, said the Manifesto, would be only a passing "prelude to the immediately following proletarian revolution."

IN SHORT, communism was to triumph around 1848. And do not forget that this refreshingly early date was not just a dream of run-of-the-mill politicians, but a strictly "scientific" discovery. For, according to one of Marx's iron laws, every economic system reaches a point where it can no longer digest any further technical developments, any new machines or processes. When a system has arrived at this stage of "maturity" it will no longer be advanced by the further expansion of the forces of production; it will be destroyed. Now Marx and Engels had discovered that in the most advanced countries capitalism had long since been devoured by the cancer of overmaturity. The gigantic new forces of production—particularly the steam engine—had "no more room" within the narrow confines of the obsolete system. For long enough they had been carrying on their work of destruction. The depression which had seized Europe in 1847 was not, as the ignorant believed, the usual periodic episode of purification, but the death-rattle of the system—its coma. And for these strictly scientific reasons the "immediately following proletarian revolution" was a certainty within the next few months.

Two years later these prognostications had burst like a soap-bubble. Although Marx himself, in the midst of the turmoil of 1848, had gone home to Germany to organize a frantic campaign, the democratic revolution had in no way been transformed into a revolution of "the proletariat." And the depression had not turned out to be the coma of capitalism; rather, it had been followed by a new boom. Any other science, introducing itself to the world with a prognosis which was so swiftly and drastically disproved, would have been forever burdened with at least a heavy mortgage of distrust. But this was the abnormality in the history of Marxism: it did not suffer through being refuted by reality.

Millions of people—hundreds of millions—were indoctrinated by the Communist Manifesto with the ABC of Marxism. How many of them ever awoke to the realization that the prophecies in this document represented a check which was due long ago and could not be cashed? That was hushed up. Instead, people were taught, and they believed, that the Manifesto had dedicated itself to the task of foretelling, amazingly early, events which only future generations would see. And the entire history of Marxism followed this pattern! Professional Marxists and amateur enthusiasts always refused to admit any error in their science. Whenever the facts of reality refused to bear out the Marxian prophecies, two things happened: the facts were glossed over, and the fulfillment was postponed to some future date.

Recently, when Stalin, in half a sentence of an interview, hinted at the possibility that Marx and Engels had not prophesied quite correctly, it amounted to a sensation. But even that vague remark referred to a single detail, and even this miniature heresy in the interest of an immediate end could only be permitted to the dictator. In the official Communist doctrine the revelations of 1847 are still as unchangingly valid as though nothing had happened in the meantime.

WHAT really happened was this: all the relevant facts throughout the whole course of the century turned out precisely the opposite of what Marx and Engels had foretold. Every article of their science turned to dust. Every one of their theories collapsed. And in order to understand this, it is not necessary to penetrate any alarming thicket of mysteries. It is, on the contrary, as simple as this "science" itself basically is. For to repeat: it consists of nothing else than the overall assertion that the collapse of capitalism and the victory of communism—no matter whether desirable or not—are completely inevitable for superhuman reasons. And all the allegedly iron laws with which Marx and Engels undertook to prove this inevitability are reduced, in fact, to two easily traceable subassertions.

There is, in the first place, the iron law that no system is able to digest unlimited forces of production; and that every system must collapse when—and cannot collapse before—"the forces of production have outgrown it." How has this iron law proved itself when applied to the system of free private enterprise? The steam engine which, according to Marx, was bound to unleash the cataclysm as early as 1848, balked at the job. But electricity, the oil-motor, and modern chemistry have done no better. In fact, the forces of production developed to a tropical profusion such as no one imagined in the wildest dream. In the most highly developed countries they rose to ten and twenty times the volume of 1847—and there was still room for all of them in the system which had supposedly so long been doomed.

And on the other hand, how about the one country, Russia, in which the free enterprise system was really destroyed in 1917? Evidently it was the most backward country—a country in which the capitalist system was by far the least mature, and which still afforded immense unexploited space for further forces of production. In Russia there was, according to the Marxian iron laws, not the remotest possibility of abolishing capitalism, for "no social order ever disappears before all the productive forces for which there is room in it have developed." In short, the iron law was doubly refuted; by that which did not happen, although it was predicted—and still more by that which, contrary to all predictions, did happen. The course of actual history may have been set in motion by any force; evidently it was not set in motion by those mysterious "forces of production" which in Marxian science figure as the sole irresistible superhuman motor of the whole of human destiny.

The second of the iron laws came in for still rougher treatment. The capitalist system, says the law, is also inevitably doomed because it makes people constantly poorer. It is doomed to produce nothing but increasing misery—except, naturally, for a small, ever-shrinking number of supercapitalists—and neither governments nor labor unions have ever been, or ever will be, able to halt the march of ever-increasing misery. With stiff-necked obstinacy the two scientists of socialism clung all their lives to the theory of ever-increasing misery, and they described to the last detail the course of the gruesome process: wages would continually drop, working hours would grow ever longer, the workshops would grow ever smaller and more unhealthy, the life-span of the workers ever shorter—and all this, naturally, would take its most revolting form in the most advanced capitalist countries.

"Even in America," Engels pontificated in later life, "the condition of the working class must gradually sink lower and lower." But it was precisely in the most capitalistically developed countries that wages rose, work hours became shorter, more model workshops were built; and not only did the workers fail to die at an increasingly early age, but for the first time in history the average life span rose. Not increasing misery, but increasing ease! From time to time there were setbacks of depressions. But the general trend was consistently upwards.

So every pillar of the Marxian science crumbled under the test of reality. Fifty years after the Manifesto appeared, the refutation of its assertions was so far advanced that some outstanding Marxists began to admit that their science was bankrupt. They spoke up and demanded that socialism again be purged of the Marxian adornments which had turned out to be fakes. Is it not enough, they said, that we, like every other political trend, consider our objective desirable? Why not abandon the extraordinary spice of "inevitability" with which Marx has so liberally seasoned the dish?

With this demand on the part of the so-called "revisionists," an internecine struggle broke out among the Socialists which raged for years, and particularly in Germany—for Germany, until 1917, was the Mecca of socialism; there was no other Socialist party anywhere in the world which could rank with that in Germany. And the "revisionists" were defeated in epic battles.

Probably there were but few in the inner circle of their comrades who did not more or less agree with them. But a prosperous party, like a prosperous firm, does not easily decide on daring changes. And obviously the inner circle of the party was convinced that the Marxian contribution to socialism had most certainly done its bit towards the success of the party. Most definitely the Marxian adornments had attracted a considerably larger audience than could have been mobilized without them. The mere fact that the "inevitability" of socialism was preached under the auspices of that infallible and idolized thing known as science had a magnetic effect on uncritical minds. Anyone who became a socialist could rest assured, thanks to Marx, that he was siding with no common, everyday, debatable opinions and claims, but was taking part in carrying out the superhuman will of history itself. He could rest assured that the devil—capitalism, and Paradise—socialism, were no longer superstitious or ecstatic fantasies, but the unassailable discoveries of the most thorough modern research. Why change anything? Let people go on believing in this science— and if it is a pseudo-science, then let them go on believing in the pseudo-science. Illusions, chimeras, legends, myths are no less effective than the truth. The Marxian science may be dead—who cares?—long live the myth of Marxian science! There was no need for any revision.

TODAY, a hundred years after the Manifesto, we know all too well what dynamite was this thing which was then brought into the world, and today we know the secret of this dynamite. It is not the Marxian science itself—a chimera —which has changed the face of the world, but the belief in the reality of this chimera. Even the reddest of the Red leaders derived none of their success from following the prescriptions of Marx's iron laws. When Lenin made his revolution in 1917, he exploited to the utmost, like every other revolutionary in history, the opportunity which presented itself, and paid not the slightest attention to the Marxian iron law which strictly forbade a revolution of that kind in that country. Still less use was made of Marxian science in the building-up of Soviet Russia after the revolution—and that for the simple reason that Marx had all his life busied himself exclusively with the destruction of capitalism, not with the building-up of socialism; exclusively with the negative, not with the positive side of the problems. Nevertheless, Lenin—and his followers after him—insisted on attaching the label of "Marxian science" to everything he did. Why? Precisely because the myth of this "science" had assumed such proportions in the minds of so many people, and provided him with such indispensable support.

There is no doubt that in our day this myth has become more virulent than ever, and has penetrated into countries which were formerly almost untouched by it—among them the U.S.A. The very existence and expansion of Soviet Russia fill the hollow myth with growing strength—for does not such existence and expansion prove that a superhuman "inevitability" must have been at work there? And there is another reason, too, in our day for the increasing virulence of the hollow myth—ignorance. In the early days fairly wide circles, especially in Europe, had at least read the Manifesto; they had a certain rudimentary knowledge of the content of the Marxian science. In our day this knowledge seems everywhere (even among the Communists) to have dwindled to practically nothing. The average man has vaguely heard that a genius named Marx correctly predicted the course of past and future events—and that is all. In the United States there are probably millions of people who are Marxists without even knowing it themselves; who firmly believe that some hidden superhuman causes make the collapse of the free enterprise system inevitable, and who do not suspect that this conviction comes from none other than Karl Marx, and that this very belief essentially, if unconsciously, makes them the tools of Moscow. Indeed, even if the Marxian science itself remained sterile, the cloud of myth which arose from it has made history, and threatens to go on making it.

BUT SOMETHING must be added to this. There exists not only the Marx who is manifest in his writings and who has generated by means of his printed works the fateful illusion of a glorious science. There is another Marx who has never appeared in print. It is the Marx of practical politics—the man whose principles and methods were characterized in all his battles by the most alarming immorality and unbridled lust for power. Every page of his life tells the story of his monomaniacal striving for sole authority in any circle, any group, any organization in which he was able to set foot; of the scorn and contempt with which he brushed away such childish inhibitions as "truth, morality and justice"; of the technique of petty intrigues, shameless slander, pitiless persecution which he used again and again against every one of his rivals, even against any possible rival in the future; in fact, against everyone who did not completely and unconditionally knuckle under to him.

And this is the second Marxian legacy which is making history. If his pseudo-science degenerated into pure window-dressing, although of a most magnetic kind, his methods in the field of practical politics produced the most drastic, most unexpected actualities. In the maxims and practices of Marx the politician, Lenin found some guidance which he could really follow. From this model there arose a second kind of Marxism. It manifests itself revoltingly in the one-party state of the Soviets; in the purges, the forced-labor camps, the intellectual monopoly, the cruelty, the broken agreements, the complete untrustworthiness—and in the cascade of monstrously false and unscrupulous accusations, slanders, and insults which are poured forth day after day against all and sundry.

This second kind of Marxism—which is the one real legacy—leads to the destruction of well-nigh all that we call civilization. It is stronger than ever and still in the ascendant. In the course of its first century it has been able to accomplish this destruction in only one part of the world, containing between 300 and 600 millions of the 2,200 million inhabitants of this globe. But it is not lacking in the frenzy and determination to complete the great work in its second century.

January 1948

SCREEN GUIDE FOR AMERICANS

By AYN RAND

[*Ayn Rand, a native of Petrograd and a refugee from Soviet despotism, achieved fame in the United States as a novelist glorifying the profit motive. As an ultra-conservative economist, she founded a cult of believers in uncontrolled free enterprise whose uncompromising position was to the Right of the school identified with the philosophy of Ludwig von Mises. In "Screen Guide for Americans," Miss Rand outlined "the most penetrating analysis of totalitarian propaganda we have yet seen"—as described by the editor of* Plain Talk, *who emphasized that the author wishes to acknowledge the assistance of the Editorial Board of the Motion Picture Alliance for the Preservation of American Ideals in drafting the final form of the guide. It was recommended as "a first-rate educational course in coping with the technique of Communist infiltration to radio magnates, producers of plays, newspaper owners, publishers of books and magazines, executives of news services, tycoons of advertising and public relations, endowers and directors of cultural foundations." The recommendation has not lost its force since the publication of this essay.*]

POLITICS IS NOT a separate field in itself. Political ideas do not come out of thin air. They are the result of the moral premises which men have accepted. Whatever people believe to be the good, right, and proper human actions—that will determine their political opinions. If men believe that every independent action is vicious, they will vote for every measure to control human beings and to suppress human freedom. If men believe that the American system is unjust, they will support those who wish to destroy it.

386

I

We are living in an age when politics is the most burning question in everybody's mind. The whole world is torn by a great political issue—Freedom or Slavery, which means Americanism or Totalitarianism. Half the world is in ruins after a war fought over political ideas. To pretend at such a time that political ideas are not important and that people pay no attention to them, is worse than irresponsible.

It is the avowed purpose of the Communists to insert propaganda into movies. Therefore, there are only two possible courses of action open to you, if you want to keep your pictures clean of subversive propaganda:

1. If you have no time or inclination to study political ideas—then do not hire Reds to work on your pictures.
2. If you wish to employ Reds, but intend to keep their politics out of your movies—then study political ideas and learn how to recognize propaganda when you see it.

But to hire Communists on the theory that "they won't put over any politics on me" and then remain ignorant and indifferent to the subject of politics, while the Reds are trained propaganda experts, is an attitude for which there can be no excuse.

II

Don't pretend that Americanism and the Free Enterprise System are two different things. They are inseparable, like body and soul. The basic principle of inalienable individual rights, which is Americanism, can be translated into practical reality only in the form of the economic system of Free Enterprise. That was the system established by the American Constitution, the system which made America the best and greatest country on earth. You may preach any other form of economics, if you wish. But if you do so, don't pretend that you are preaching Americanism.

Don't pretend that you are upholding the Free Enterprise System in some vague, general, undefined way, while preaching the specific ideas that oppose it and destroy it.

Don't attack individual rights, individual freedom, private action, private initiative, and private property. These things are essential parts of the Free Enterprise System, without which it cannot exist.

Don't preach the superiority of public ownership as such over private ownership. Don't preach or imply that all publicly owned projects are noble, humanitarian undertakings by grace of the mere fact that they are publicly owned—while preaching, at the same time, that private property or the defense of private property rights is the expression of some sort of vicious greed or antisocial selfishness or evil.

III

THERE IS an old fable about a pig who filled his belly with acorns, then started digging to undermine the roots of the oak from which the acorns came. Don't let's allow that pig to become our symbol.

Throughout American history, the best of American industrialists were men who embodied the highest virtues: productive genius, energy, initiative, independence, courage. Socially (if "social significance" interests you) they were among the greatest of all benefactors, because it is they who created the opportunities for achieving the unprecedented material wealth of the industrial age.

Yet all too often industrialists, bankers, and businessmen are presented on the screen as villains, crooks, chiselers, or exploiters. . . . It is true that there are vicious businessmen—just as there are vicious men in any other class or profession. But we have been practicing an outrageous kind of double standard: we do not attack individual representatives of any other group, class, or nation, in order not to imply an attack on the whole group; yet when we present individual businessmen as monsters, we claim that no reflection on the whole class of businessmen was intended.

IV

IN A free society—such as America—wealth is achieved through production, and through the voluntary exchange of one's goods or services. You cannot hold production as evil—nor can you hold as evil a man's right to keep the result of his own effort.

It is a basic American principle that each man is free to work for his own benefit and to go as far as his ability will carry him; and his property is his— whether he has made one dollar or one million dollars.

If the villain in your story happens to be rich—don't permit lines of dialogue suggesting that he is the typical representative of a whole social class, the symbol of all the rich. Keep it clear in your mind and in your script that his villainy is due to his own personal character—not to his wealth or class.

If you do not see the difference between wealth honestly produced and wealth looted—you are preaching the idea of Communism. You are implying that all property and all human labor should belong to the State. And you are inciting men to crime: If all wealth is evil, no matter how acquired, why should a man bother to earn it? He might as well seize it by robbery or expropriation.

It is the proper wish of every decent American to stand on his own feet, earn his own living, and be as good at it as he can—that is, get as rich as he can by honest exchange.

Stop insulting him and stop defaming his proper ambition. Stop giving him —and yourself—a guilt complex by spreading unthinkingly the slogans of Communism. Put an end to that pernicious modern hypocrisy: everybody wants to get rich and almost everybody feels that he must apologize for it.

V

IF YOU denounce the profit motive, what is it that you wish men to do? Work without reward, like slaves, for the benefit of the State?

An industrialist has to be interested in profit. In a free economy, he can make a profit only if he makes a good product which people are willing to buy. What do you want him to do? Should he sell his product at a loss? If so, how long is he to remain in business? And at whose expense? . . .

If what you mean, when you denounce it, is a desire to make money dishonestly or immorally—then say so. Make it clear that what you denounce is dishonesty, not money-making. Make it clear that you are denouncing evildoers, not capitalists. Don't toss out careless generalities which imply that there is no difference between the two. That is what the Communists want you to imply.

VI

AMERICA was made by the idea that personal achievement and personal success are each man's proper and moral goal.

There are many forms of success: spiritual, artistic, industrial, financial. All these forms, in any field of honest endeavor, are good, desirable, and admirable. Treat them as such.

Don't permit any disparagement or defamation of personal success. It is the Communists' intention to make people think that personal success is somehow achieved at the expense of others and that every successful man has hurt somebody by becoming successful.

It is the Communists' aim to discourage all personal effort and to drive men into a hopeless, dispirited, gray herd of robots who have lost all personal ambition, who are easy to rule, willing to obey, and willing to exist in selfless servitude to the State.

America is based on the ideal of man's dignity and self-respect. Dignity and self-respect are impossible without a sense of personal achievement. When you defame success, you defame human dignity.

VII

FAILURE, in itself, is not admirable. And while every man meets with failure somewhere in his life, the admirable thing is his courage in overcoming it—not the fact that he failed.

Failure is no disgrace—but it is certainly no brand of virtue or nobility, either. It is the Communists' intention to make men accept misery, depravity, and degradation as their natural lot in life. This is done by presenting every kind of failure as sympathetic, as a sign of goodness and virtue—while every kind of success is presented as a sign of evil. This implies that only the evil can succeed under our American system—while the good are to be found in the gutter.

Don't present all the poor as good and all the rich as evil. In judging a man's character, poverty is no disgrace—but it is no virtue either; wealth is no virtue —but it is certainly no disgrace.

VIII

TOO MANY of us, without thinking, have fallen for one of the worst slogans of the Communists—"the common man."

It is only in Europe—under social caste systems where men are divided into "aristocrats" and "commoners"—that one can talk about defending the "common man." What does the word "common" mean in America?

Under the American system, all men are equal before the law. Therefore, if anyone is classified as "common"—he can be called "common" only in regard to his personal qualities. It then means that he has no outstanding abilities, no outstanding virtues, no outstanding intelligence. Is that an object of glorification?

In the Communist doctrine, it is. Communism preaches the reign of mediocrity, the destruction of all individuality and all personal distinction, the turning of men into "masses," which means an undivided, undifferentiated, impersonal, average, common herd.

In the American doctrine, no man is common. Every man's personality is unique—and it is respected as such. He may have qualities which he shares with others; but his virtue is not gauged by how much he resembles others; it is gauged by his personal distinction, great or small.

In America, no man is scorned or penalized if his ability is small. But neither is he praised, extolled, and glorified for the smallness of his ability.

America is the land of the uncommon man. It is the land where man is free to develop his genius—and to get its just rewards. It is the land where each man tries to develop whatever quality he may possess and to rise to whatever degree he can, great or modest. It is not the land where one glories or is taught to glory in one's mediocrity.

No self-respecting man in America is or thinks of himself as "little," no matter how poor he may be. That, precisely, is the difference between an American working man and a European serf.

IX

THERE is a great difference between free cooperation and forced collectivism. It is the difference between the United States and Soviet Russia. But the Communists are very skillful at hiding the difference and selling you the second under the guise of the first. You might miss it. The audience won't.

Cooperation is the free association of men who work together by voluntary agreement, each deriving from it his own personal benefit.

Collectivism is the forced herding together of men into a group, with the individual having no choice about it, no personal motive, no personal reward, and subordinating himself blindly to the will of others.

Keep this distinction clearly in mind—in order to judge whether what you are asked to glorify is American cooperation or Soviet collectivism.

Don't preach that everybody should be and act alike.

Don't fall for such drivel as "I don't wanna be dif'rent—I wanna be just like ever'body else." You've heard this one in endless variations. If ever there was an un-American attitude, this is it. America is the country where every man wants to be different—and most men succeed at it.

If you preach that it is evil to be different—you teach every particular group of men to hate every other group, every minority, every person, for being different from them; thus you lay the foundations of race hatred.

Don't preach that all mass action is good, and all individual action is evil. It is true that there are vicious individuals; it is also true that there are vicious groups. Both must be judged by their specific actions—and not treated as an issue of "the one" against "the many," with the many always right and the one always wrong.

Remember that it is the Communists' aim to preach the supremacy, the superiority, the holy virtue of the group—as opposed to the individual. It is not America's aim.

X

THE COMMUNISTS' chief purpose is to destroy every form of independence—independent work, independent action, independent property, independent thought, an independent mind, or an independent man.

Conformity, alikeness, servility, submission, and obedience are necessary to establish a Communist slave-state. Don't help the Communists to teach man to acquire these attitudes.

Don't fall for the old Communist trick of thinking that an independent man or an individualist is one who crushes and exploits others—such as a dictator. An independent man is one who stands alone and respects the same right of others, who does not rule nor serve, who neither sacrifices himself nor others. A dictator—by definition—is the most complete collectivist of all, because he exists by ruling, crushing, and exploiting a huge collection of men.

Don't preach that everything done for others is good, while everything done for one's own sake is evil. This damns every form of personal joy and happiness.

Don't preach that everything "public-spirited" is good, while everything personal and private is evil.

Remember that America is the country of the pioneer, the non-conformist, the inventor, the originator, the innovator. Remember that all the great thinkers, artists, scientists were single, individual, independent men who stood alone, and discovered new directions of achievement—alone.

XI

A FAVORITE trick of the Communists is to insert into pictures casual lines of dialogue about some important, highly controversial political issue; to insert them as accidental small talk, without any connection to the scene, the plot, or the story.

Of all current questions, be most careful about your attitude toward Soviet Russia. You do not have to make pro-Soviet and anti-Soviet pictures, if you do not wish to take the stand. But if you claim that you wish to remain neutral, don't stick into pictures casual lines favorable to Soviet Russia. Look out for remarks that praise Russia directly or indirectly; or statements to the effect that anyone who is anti-Soviet is pro-Fascist; or references to fictitious Soviet achievements.

Don't suggest to the audience that the Russian people are free, secure, and happy, that life in Russia is just about the same as in any other country—while actually the Russian people live in constant terror under a bloody, monstrous dictatorship. Look out for speeches that support whatever is in the Soviet interests of the moment, whatever is part of the current Communist party line. Don't permit such dialogue as: "The free, peace-loving nations of the world—America, England, and Russia . . ." or, "Free elections, such as in Poland . . ." or, "American imperialists ought to get out of China. . . ."

XII

THE COMMUNIST PARTY line takes many turns and makes many changes to meet shifting conditions. But on one objective it has remained fixed: to undermine faith in and ultimately to destroy our American political institutions.

Don't discredit the Congress of the United States by presenting it as an ineffectual body, devoted to mere talk. If you do that—you imply that representative government is no good, and what we ought to have is a dictator.

Don't discredit our free elections. If you do that—you imply that elections should be abolished.

Don't discredit our courts by presenting them as corrupt. If you do that— you lead people to believe that they have no recourse except to violence, since peaceful justice cannot be obtained.

It is true that there have been vicious Congressmen and judges, and politicians who have stolen elections, just as there are vicious men in any profession.

But if you present them in a story, be sure to make it clear that you are criticizing particular men—not the system. The American system, as such, is the best ever devised in history. If some men do not live up to it, let us damn these men, not the system which they betray.

XIII

Now a word of warning about the question of free speech. The principle of free speech requires that we do not use police force to forbid the Communists the expression of their ideas—which means that we do not pass laws forbidding them to speak. But the principle of free speech does not require that we furnish the Communists with the means to preach their ideas, and does not imply that we owe them jobs and support to advocate our own destruction at our own expense. The Constitution guaranty of free speech reads: "Congress shall pass no laws. . . ." It does not require employers to be suckers.

. . . Freedom of speech does not imply that it is our duty to provide a knife for the murderer who wants to cut our throat.

November 1947

An Open Letter to Rockwell Kent

By Max Eastman

[Max Eastman, widely known author who edited, between 1913 and 1922, the revolutionary magazines, The Masses and The Liberator, spent the next couple of years in Soviet Russia where he formed a close friendship with Leon Trotsky. Upon his return to the United States he produced many works critical of Marxism and the Soviet dictatorship. One of these, Artists in Uniform, was a severe arraignment of Communist censorship and literary regimentation. In the message that he addressed to his erstwhile friend Rockwell Kent, President of the Artists' League of America, Eastman raised the issue that the Kremlin's treatment of Boris Pasternak and Aleksandr Solzhenitsyn—both Nobel Prize winners—dramatized before world public opinion. As roving editor of the Reader's Digest, Eastman continued to expose the ideological frauds of the Soviet system until his death early in 1969.]

DEAR ROCKWELL:

I learn from a Tass dispatch that your career as a pro-Communist artist and writer has brought you to Moscow, and to the extreme statement, in a speech in the Kremlin: "The American government is not my government."

I wonder if you realize that you are lending your prestige to a regime of contemptuous political dictation and gag-rule by bribery and terror in the field of arts and letters such as history never knew before. There is a humiliation in this that I find hard to reconcile with your boisterous and venture-loving character. I wish you would explain to me why so many free-thinking, free-speaking, free-traveling, free advertising, free *shouting* American artists and writers find it necessary to their comfort to defend the enslavement of men's minds and bodies to a tyrant. Are they sick, ignorant, or hypocritical? Is some demon in the *Zeitgeist,* some analyzed force in the historic environment, pushing you to this suicidal behavior? Are you seeking, under the pretext of radicalism, a place for yourselves in the top circles of a worldwide police regime you see advancing? Or are you really so poor in intelligence, so blind or lazy in the brain, that you *don't know* what it is you are defending?

I have thought of a way to tell you what it is. I am going to recite to you the names of those who have died in the cause of creative independence under the Soviet slave state. Their names ought to be inscribed somewhere, for they have not even a tombstone or a marker, or so much as a plot in a cemetery in all Russia, to remember their genius or mention who they were. They were either shot in the back of the neck and shoveled out with the refuse of the Lubianka prison, or shipped away to hard labor and starvation in a prison camp so remote and so well guarded that no news of them ever leaked out.

There are thirty names on my list.* I will mention one or two who still live, but for the most part this is a record not of suppression, but death. Even of murdered writers the list is far from complete; these are only the *eminent* writers; and of the other arts I have no record. But this will give you an idea of the regime in creative art that you and your friends of the National Council of the Arts and Sciences are defending.

I BEGIN with *Isaak Babyel,* whom I think the most richly endowed, both in intelligence and imagination, of all the writers of his epoch in Russia—the one man whose name might be linked with those of Chekhov and Gogol among the great storytellers of his nation. Believing in the integrity and independence of creative art, Babyel refused to produce made-to-order stories on command from some gangster-politician in charge of the propaganda office of the Russian Communist Party. His contribution to art was a noble silence adhered to inflexibly for over fifteen years. Even silence is crime in a totalitarian police state,

---

* It was compiled with the collaboration of Vera Alexandrova, an outstanding authority on modern Russian literature. So far as it can be at this distance, and without access to the police records, the list is a work of careful scholarship.

where when the dictator says three cheers the whole population must shout hurrah, and for that crime Babyel disappeared from the world.

Boris Pilnyak, perhaps the next most gifted, certainly the most famous. His novel, *The Naked Year,* was translated into all Western languages, and his visit to America after its publication was a triumphal tour. He was acclaimed by the Communists and their fellow-travelers as the supreme example of proletarian art. Ten years later he was arrested by the GPU, denounced as an "enemy of the people," and shot. If you want to conceive this vividly, imagine the FBI picking up Ernest Hemingway on the street, taking him in handcuffs to the federal penitentiary at Atlanta, shooting him in the cellar, and issuing four words to the press: "Enemy of the people." Not a word more.

. . . THERE IS a worse crime than individualism. That, after all, only causes a crack in the monolithic state. There is a crime which if widely spread would crumble it altogether, by getting people to believe in the dignity of man as such, whether he happened to be highly marked as an individual or not. This worse crime is humanism. It is perfectly obvious, isn't it, that while engaged in constructing a socialist society, while moving steadily by police order in the direction of the Brotherhood of Man, humanism can not be tolerated? In the name of humanism, writers might actually state that they don't believe in human slavery, they don't believe in execution without trial, they don't believe in the right of a uniformed gangster to drag people out of their beds at night, shoot them in a prison cellar, or ship them to a slave camp, without informing their families, their shuddering parents, their sobbing wives, their frightened children, why they have gone, where they have gone, or what possible single thing can be done to try to get them back. . . .

You may find it hard to believe, but there is actually a worse crime than individualism, or humanism, or even sincerity. This crime is so terrible from the standpoint of the state religion of dialectic materialism, so depraved and gruesomely obscene, that one hesitates even to call it by name: Idealism! *Dmitri Gorbov,* philosophic essayist and critic, author of a book with the intriguing title *The Search for Galatea,* disappeared in a purge under denunciation for the crime of revealing "sympathies with Idealism." I will quote you one sentence from his book which seems to have been the high point of his crime: "Art is not a mere repetition of reality . . . art has a reality of its own."

One more crime was discovered in the recent postwar purge, a crime that could be committed without saying a thing, the crime of being *nonpolitical.* That smokes out from his last refuge the artist or writer who wants to express a little of his true self.

They pounced on *Anna Akhmatova,* one of the two greatest lyric poets of this age in Russia. They denounced her for writing poems "empty of political content," and barred her from the magazine *Zvyezda,* which alone published her poems and upon which she depended for an income. And they did the same thing to *Mikhail Zoshchenko,* Russia's most popular humorist. He and Akhmatova were denounced simultaneously by a special resolution of the Executive Committee of the All-Russian Communist Party. . . .

This is the point of insane, power-drunk bigotry at which they have arrived in this postwar purge of the literary arts in the Soviet Union, a purge which is still continuing. They have attacked vaudeville actors and entertainers, declared that they too must have a "political content" in their acts. Even circus clowns must take part in the denunciation of the capitalist world and glorification of life under the divine rule of the Russian Communist Party. How much farther could you carry the dictatorship of ignorant political gangsters over the mind and spirit of man?

But they *have* carried it farther. They've thought up one crime that is worse than all the rest together—worse than individualism, humanism, sincerity, idealism, being nonpolitical, or even laughing in the wrong direction. I hardly know how to name it abstractly—except as human decency.

Ivan Katayev (not to be confused with Valentin Katayev) and *Nikolai Zarudin,* novelists of talent and popularity, disappeared for the crime of *trying to send money to their friends in the slave camps of Siberia.* . . .

CAN IT BE that the mere barrier of language, the fact that these are funny-sounding Russian names, prevents you from realizing what this *means* to actual people like you and me—what it means to their families, their friends, their surviving colleagues, what it means to the whole life and being of creative art? And it is supplemented, as you know, by rewarding those writers and artists who *will* toady to the powers with such fees and royalties as almost no other Soviet citizens receive. Do you honestly support such a system of control by massacre and corruption over the thoughts and feelings of men?

I keep trying to think of excuses for you. Is it perhaps just a zeal to be "radical," to be against the capitalist as of old, that constrains you to play the lackey to an infinitely more dreadful tyrant? Can't you see that freedom is on the defensive? Are you so desperately in need of Hope that you must chase the ghost of her dead body half across the world? Or is it Faith you are so avid of? Is it necessary to your inner comfort to believe, to adore, to bend your knees to a Lord and Master after all? Was all your obstreperousness and independence just bluff and adolescence?

I sincerely wish you would enlighten me.

April 1950

ON THOUGHT CONTROL

By GEORGE S. SCHUYLER

[*George Schuyler, the dean of black journalists in the United States, was deeply troubled, like Max Eastman, by the increasing trends towards intellectual regimentation in the Western world. On June 10, 1947, he delivered an address to the American Writers Association which, in abridged form, appeared in* Plain Talk *under the caption "On Thought Control."*]

WE WRITERS should not be lulled into complacency because we defeated the so-called Cain Plan for totalitarian control of the nation's thinking. There will be further attempts because the whole intellectual atmosphere of America has been poisoned by the miasma of planning and centralized control. In a nation where the idea of regimentation and paternalism has taken deep root, especially during the past twenty years, it will seem more and more incongruous that the writers should be free while others pace the treadmill.

It does not matter that other forms of regimentation and group control have failed here and elsewhere to prove themselves social panaceas.

It does not matter that the totalitarian state has everywhere developed inevitably into a slave state, and an incompetent state, when the gaze of millions of intellectuals is fixed on wishes and promises rather than on performances.

It does not matter that history proves beyond doubt that arts and letters have always become stereotyped and sterile when chained by artificial controls and forced into a political mold.

Those who are supposedly most capable of analytical thought and independent judgment, have become so indoctrinated by false teachings of the siren singers of perpetual security through "magic" formulas of government and institutional planning and regimentation that they are ready to fall like ripe fruit before the winds of propaganda.

This sinister propaganda which has been an increasingly prominent part of our educational processes in schools, newspapers, periodicals, and books for the past three generations has now reached the point of effectiveness where the oldtime doctrines of freedom, liberalism, independence, and individualism have actually become suspect and at best are given only lip service.

Totalitarian regimentation has become respectable and popular among the class which does most to shape thought and influence opinion in the modern world generally and in America in particular. It is now regarded as liberal and progressive, revolutionary rather than reactionary.

Ironically, those who have profited most, materially and culturally, from our free society seem to be the ones who are most intent upon destroying it. Is it not the literati, the artists, the professionals, and some of the upper bourgeoisie who supply the disproportionate percentage of fellow-travelers and crypto-Communists? In a literate society in which the written word wields such prepotent influence, is it not alarming that so many writers (and publishers) believe that the best interests of their society will be served by a *new* autocracy which makes that of yesteryear pale into insignificance?

If the view becomes general among writers that totalitarianism is the "wave of the future" bringing Utopia on its crest, and that the multiplication of bureaus, departments, and snooping agencies to bedevil the populace with added plans, panaceas, and taxes will lead to a better, freer life, then we who see the signs of the times will bear a terrible guilt if we have made no great effort to retard or halt the trend.

In sum, it is not enough for us to defeat efforts to control the freedom, production, and income of writers, important as that unquestionably is. We must, in addition, assume the much larger task of counteracting the influences and trends outlined above, and at the same time re-educating the intellectuals to a new appreciation of the desirability of freedom of thought and expression as essential to the preservation and improvement of the civilization which we all prefer.

February 1949

On *Gone with the Wind*

By Margaret Mitchell

[*In March 1947* Plain Talk *invited Margaret Mitchell, the author of* Gone with the Wind, *to write the story of her experiences in the smear campaign waged by the Communists against her immensely popular novel. She had adverted to the attacks upon her in correspondence with contributing editor Eugene Lyons. On April 1, 1947, Miss Mitchell (who was known in her community by her married name, Mrs. John Marsh) replied with the following letter. It was published in September 1949, after her death in August of that year. Her untimely death was a grievous blow to* Plain Talk, *as she was one of its earliest subscribers and sustaining friends. On July 8, 1949, she wrote to the editor: "I believe that many of the things pointed out by* Plain Talk *three years ago are now becoming increasingly clear to many people." In the same letter she flatly declared: "Both I and* Gone with the Wind *have been under fire by Communists and Left Wingers all over the world." This testimony bore out other evidence that Moscow was leading an international "thought control" campaign.]*

"I KNOW VERY WELL the value of my experiences with the Communists and fellow-travelers. I know the value is enhanced by the fact that I am not a public figure—I mean like Mrs. Roosevelt or Miss Dorothy Thompson or Mrs. Luce or Miss Gahagan—but only Mrs. Marsh who wrote a bestselling book and who continues to live the same quiet life she did before she wrote the book. I wish to write such an article myself and against that day I have been saving clippings for some years. If such an article is to be written at all, so that it will have any value in the present fight in which we are engaged, it must be written at length, with care, with documentation. It must explain the ABC's of the Communist plan to millions of people who do not understand such matters as, for instance, why the Communists attack the South and attempt to inflame the Negro press and public against the South. For instance, you and Mr. Lyons and I understand this Communist-Negro slant so well that there was no need for me to elaborate it in my letter to Mr. Lyons. The three of us are so fully aware of this that we can employ a sort of shorthand when discussing it. But there are millions of people who do not know what this is all about, and such an article would have to explain the situation step by step. . . .

"I want to write a full length article on this situation, and if I ever do it it will mean that I am going to sacrifice much of my peace and quiet, my security, perhaps my health and my good reputation, for I know very well the type of character-assassination these people deal in. . . . Your publication is for highly intelligent and well-informed people. I would want my experiences to reach the uninformed person. I believe you are unselfishly in the same fight I am in and that you want to accomplish the same things I want to accomplish— to see that our country is not overwhelmed by any type of Totalitarianism, from the Right or the Left. I believe you want people to know what goes on behind the various Fronts which appear so innocent. I believe you feel that the best way to accomplish this is to give the widest publicity possible. Believing this about you, I do not hesitate to tell you frankly that if I ever get around to writing this full and completely documented article I am going to get it published, if possible, in the magazine which will reach the most people. If I am willing to risk the things I value most in the world, then I want to inflict as much damage as possible on the other side."

September 1949

KARL MARX:
FATHER OF MODERN
ANTI-SEMITISM

By ZYGMUND DOBBS

[*Zygmund Dobbs, a resident of Detroit, pioneered with this essay in a field few dared to invade. A lifelong student of Communism, he was the owner of a singularly rich collection of literature on revolutionary Marxism. He was convinced that modern anti-Semitism had its origin in the socialist movement fostered by Marx.*]

AN ANTHOLOGY distributed by American Communists during the late twenties included this significant passage in its pages:

> We will not look for the secret of the Jew in his religion, but we will look for the secret of the religion in the real Jew.
> What is the secular basis of Judaism? Practical needs, egoism.
> What is the secular cult of the Jew? Huckstering. What is his secular God? Money.
> Very well. Emancipation from huckstering and from money and therefore from practical, real Judaism would be the self-emancipation of our epoch.

This anti-Semitic tirade was not a quotation from the drivel of some rabid Silver Shirter or Nazi, but came from the pen of Karl Marx, the political father of the Stalinist dictatorship. The article containing the foregoing lines bears the title: "On the Jewish Question."

Marx's bitterness against Jews stemmed from his personal resentment against his own Jewish ancestry. He had the fanatical intolerance of things Jewish which one finds so often in the proselyte.

Marx thus laid the groundwork for modern anti-Semitism by branding Judaism as a cloak for money-grabbing practices. He ignored the exhortations in the Talmud against usury and its moral elevation of scholar and teacher above the merchant.

THE PRESENT campaign of official anti-Semitism in Soviet Russia came as a shock to those who have been under the illusion that the Soviets are opposed to anti-Semitism. The liquidation of thousands of Russian Jews was always passed off as a purely political purge which had nothing to do with the Jewish question.

Even the killing by the NKVD of Ehrlich and Alter during the recent war was excused on the ground that the two Polish-Jewish Socialist leaders who had fled from Hitler may conceivably have been undercover agents of the Nazis.

With the establishment of the Jewish state of Israel as the cultural and political center toward which the Jews of the world could turn their eyes, the Soviet schemers were given a body blow. They could no longer claim that Communism represents the ultimate solution to the problems of the Jewish people.

The deteriorating internal situation in Russia and the discontent of the Russian masses today are responsible for the new Soviet policy of making scapegoats of the "rootless" Jews under the brand of "cosmopolites."

It will come as a surprise to many people that this is not a new Communist idea. It is in fact one hundred and five years old. The founder of modern anti-Semitism was Karl Marx, also the founder of modern Communist theory.

Hitler obviously plagiarized Marx when he taught his Brownshirts that the "Christian religion is in fact a Judaistic development." And no wonder, since Hitler boasted in his *Mein Kampf* that he had made an exhaustive study of German socialistic books in order to perfect his propaganda methods.

Let us listen to Marx on this topic:

> The Jew has emancipated himself in Jewish fashion, not only by taking to himself financial power, but by virtue of the fact that with and without his cooperation, money has become a world power, and the practical Jewish spirit has become the practical spirit of Christian nations. The Jews have emancipated themselves in so far as Christians have become Jews.

Marx thus defines the word "Jew" as being synonymous with anyone who is engaged in financial power manipulations, and all those who deal in usurious financial methods are, in effect, Jews. He adopts the primitive prejudice, harking back to Europe's Dark Ages, that to be a Jew is to be a usurer. Seventy-six years after Marx, Hitler picked up this cry and made the same lie the basis for killing millions of men, women, and children. Marx, the father of Communism in Russia, is also the spiritual ancestor of Hitlerism. Hitler condemned not only the Jews, but legions of others whom he placed in the "Jewish" category when they fought his tyranny on the basis of Christian principles.

The Jew-hating Marx included the New World in his fanatical opposition to the rising democracy when he charged:

> The practical domination of Judaism over the Christian world has reached such a point in North America that the preaching of the Gospel itself, the Christian ministry, has become an article of Commerce, and the bankrupt merchant takes to the Gospel, while the minister grown rich goes into business.

The present attack of Stalinism against the Jewish religion as an enemy of the Soviet state and as a tool of Wall Street interests is strangely reminiscent of the Nazi creed which spread the same blatant lie. Karl Marx's intolerance on the subject of the Jewish religion drove him to make a blanket charge ignoring the spiritual aspect of Judaism which gave birth to the religious morality of half the world's population. With the same pseudo-scientific air which marks all his writings, he stated:

What was the foundation of the Jewish religion? Practical needs, egoism. Consequently the monotheism of the Jew is in reality the polytheism of many needs. Practical needs or egoism are the principle of bourgeois society, and they appear openly as such as soon as bourgeois society gives birth to the political state. The God of practical needs and egoism is money.

Money is the jealous God of Israel, by the side of which no other god may exist. Money degrades all the gods of man and converts them into commodities. Money is the general and self-constituted value of all things. Consequently it has robbed the whole world—the world of mankind as well as Nature—of its peculiar value. Money is the being of man's work and existence alienated from himself, and this alien rules him and he prays to it.

The entire world remembers when Hitler and his murderous gang attacked the Jews as being devoid of a culture of their own, charging that Jewish intellectuals and artists were only intellectual usurers without any real substance. Marx goes Hitler one better. He sweeps all Jewish culture into the wastebasket, and throws in personal relationships as well:

What remains as the abstract part of Jewish religion, contempt for theory, for art, for history, for man as an end in himself, is the real conscious standpoint and virtue of the monied man. The generic relation itself—the relation of man to woman, etc., becomes an object of commerce. Woman is bartered.

Hitler's denunciation of modern democracy as a "Judaistic" bourgeois society and the current hounding of Zionist elements in Russia and the satellite countries as "cosmopolites" is merely a repetition of Marx's old analysis in which he declared:

. . . the Jew who exists as a secular member of bourgeois society is only the particular expression of the Judaism of bourgeois society.

Judaism has survived not in spite of, but by virtue of history.

Out of its own entrails, bourgeois society continually creates Jews.

Marx's definition of Jews included those who are born as such, plus all those who adopt the practice of capitalistic (bourgeois) enterprise. The Soviet propaganda apparatus has learned to be more subtle in its anti-Semitic campaigns. Like Marx, the Soviet overlords are willing to be more lenient than Hitler. They hold out the promise of individual survival if the Jews abandon their culture, heritage, and religion. The Russian Jews then become vague nonentities subservient to the state, mentally and spiritually. They are told to "embrace the state to be saved." The same hope was held out to the Jews by the Spanish Inquisition. The demand then was, "embrace the faith and be saved."

Karl Marx expressed it in this way:

As soon as society succeeds in abolishing the empirical essence of Judaism, the huckster and the conditions which produce him, the Jew will become impossible, because his consciousness will no longer have a corresponding object, because the subjective basis of Judaism, viz.: practical needs, will have been humanized, because the conflict of the individual sensual existence with the generic existence of the individual will have been abolished.

The aim of Marx then, and the policy of the Stalin machine now, is to liquidate all remnants of Jewish culture. The Kremlin seeks, by state-sanctioned murder, to intimidate the Jews in Russia and the satellite countries into conformity with the dominant rigid slave pattern.

Anticipating Hitler and Goebbels by three-quarters of a century, Marx tried to peddle as scientific fact such slanders as:

> The God of the Jews has secularized himself and become the universal God. Exchange is the Jew's real God.

And in another passage, Marx re-emphasizes this falsehood by stating:

> The chimerical nationality of the Jew is the nationality of the merchant, of the monied man generally.

WHAT DO the Communists have to say about this Marxist anti-Semitism today? At first mention of the subject they are confused and mutter something about the entire matter being a fabrication. Later, when apprised by "headquarters" that Marx actually did write this piece of bigotry, they change their tune. Then they reply, "well—you see this was an article written about Jews at that particular time, and it referred to a special condition." When pressed to explain under what conceivable condition could the entire Jewish community be placed under such an attack, the comrades hint at Marx's immaturity at that time, and that he had not as yet become a real Marxist.

Now the truth of the matter is that this very essay was considered by Lenin as an indication that Marx had matured and that the anti-Jewish tirade marked Marx's "transition from Idealism to materialism and from revolutionary democracy to communism."

After the Communists came into power in Russia, Lenin, the leader of the Soviet Revolution, pronounced Marx's article "On the Jewish Question" as among "the most noteworthy" writings of the master. This can be verified by a reference to Volume 18, page 47, of Lenin's Works issued by and for the American Communists through International Publishers in the authorized edition of 1926.

At that time the Communist International instructed its followers throughout the world to take an anti-Zionist position. Marx's essay condemning the Jews was printed in all major languages as historical justification for the anti-Zionist campaign. Later, for tactical reasons, Stalin decided to try luring large segments of Jews living outside of Russia into his orbit. The anthology containing Marx's anti-Semitic essay was secretly put on the "too hot" list, and available copies were bought from the bookshops, often at high prices, to eliminate the book from circulation.

The present Stalinist campaign against Jewish "cosmopolitanism" marks a return to the long-range program of Karl Marx to eliminate Judaism from society. It is a twin-brother to the relentless drive to wipe out Christianity. And both have the same aim of eradicating all religion and substituting for it the economic and political humbug of Marxism.

September 1949

WHY COMMUNISM IS REACTIONARY

By KARLHEINZ E. BOEHM

[*This paper was awarded the prize offered by* Plain Talk *in its essay contest for college students. The author, a student at Berea College in Kentucky, had seen service as an intelligence officer in the army during World War II, and discovered early that instead of a classless society the Soviet revolution brought a new ruling class into existence.*]

AT THE TIME Patrick Henry made his famous statement, "Give me Liberty, or give me Death," this country was laying the foundation of a way of life which has since become tradition. Freedom of the press, freedom of speech, freedom of religion, freedom from want, freedom from fear—all these have become so firmly incorporated into this tradition, that today most Americans take them for granted.

These liberties were not proclaimed into existence overnight, however, but they developed over a period of decades and centuries, during which people fought to establish for themselves rights and recognition as individuals.

In contrast to this, another people likewise struggled for centuries to improve their standards, their rights, and their liberties. Ironically, however, a group of these very people have succeeded in establishing a reactionary system of government which, in the name of improvement, has actually led that people back into a mode of living more characteristic of the feudal system of the Middle Ages than of a modern, progressive nation.

Today, the United States, alongside the rest of the non-Communist world, is locked in a struggle with Soviet Russia and her satellites, a struggle which involves basic principles and fundamental differences. The question arises, wherein exists the disparity between communism and democracy? Exactly what *is* communism?

Before considering the difference between the way of life, as fostered by the applications of the Stalinist-Communist doctrine, and the way of doing things in the non-Communist world, it would be well to examine first the basic principles of the Marxist doctrine. When this is followed by a survey of conditions in the Soviet Union today, one important fact will immediately become apparent to the reader, namely that there is a great difference between Marxist ideology and its deviated applications in present-day Russia. In fact, this difference is so great in certain points that historians are coming to the conclusion that this new "ism" of Russia might better be called "Stalinism" than plain "communism."

Karl Marx, in advocating his theories for the betterment of man, outlined a definite pattern for the evolution of society. According to his outline, a society must pass through the stages of capitalism before it can become communistic. A relatively high state of industrialization was an absolute must to Marx, who very much belittled the existence and status of the agrarian. Moreover, Marx excluded the agrarian's role from his theories. One of the main reasons for the failure of the Paris Commune in 1871 was the lack of support the Marxists received from the rural regions. Interestingly enough, the countries he considered most likely to succeed, and which he considered "nearly ripe" in gaining a communistic society were Germany, France, and England, while the country least likely to succeed was Russia. Strange, too, in the light of the above, is that Russia even today is still 60 percent agrarian.

Marx set forth five steps along the road over which society must travel in order to attain pure communism: (1) Overthrow of the existing government (by force, if necessary); (2) Establishment of the dictatorship of the proletariat; (3) Establishment of a classless society; (4) Dissolution of the State; and (5) Pure communism.

THESE, then, are points through which society must move in order to become communistic in an ideal form. At this time it would be well to note that Soviet Russia has *never* surpassed the second step. The government of Kerensky was overthrown during the November revolution of 1917, and shortly thereafter the establishment of the new government was announced as the formation of the first dictatorship of the proletariat. At no time, however, has the character of society in Soviet Russia even approached that of a classless one. It is often said in Russia that the only time at which all classes are equal is at the time of a purge. Another person expressed this by saying: "There is only one thing that makes the party functionary, the political commissar, the general, the doctor, and the plain worker of one and the same class—the fact that they all may, even without provocation, find themselves in a labor camp."

Few societies exist where there can be found greater differences among the classes than in Soviet Russia. "Classless society" implies, among other things, few, if any, variations in incomes, in order to insure no economic advantage to anyone, or to make the opportunities available to everyone. However, in a country of an alleged classless society, an ordinary soldier earns 17 rubles per month as compared with 1,700 rubles for a lieutenant and 2,400 rubles for a captain. A scientist may expect government prizes and bonuses up to 100,000 rubles. A common citizen may stand in line for months waiting to buy necessary items, while a political functionary may use special stores, where shelves are bending with selections of the best there is to buy. These, or similar stores, are also set aside for the other members of the elite—officers, doctors, scientists, and, on top of the Soviet hierarchy, high-ranking members of the party. This same matter of privileges is carried from pay through stores to vacations, medical care, schools, and every other walk of life.

. . . Every worker in Russia has a labor card or record which he must constantly carry with him. On it are made entries of all kinds, such as his production ability or percentage, his hours, his regularity (absence may be considered sabotage), etc. Without this card he can receive neither quarters from the local housing agency nor food—for his rations, like his pay, are governed by the amount of work he is able to perform in direct relation to the percentage of the required quota or norm; he is not entitled to any medical service or recreational facility without the card, nor can his children attend school without it. If he desires to change his work, he must appear before a series of boards, including a political committee, which decides if his transfer will be beneficial to the state. If he changes too often he may be accused of being "dissatisfied," a "deviationist," or a "saboteur," all of which spells trouble for the unfortunate.

. . . And then there is one of the darkest pictures of the "fatherland of all workers," the story of the concentration camps—in Russia referred to as "corrective labor camps," in which between 10 and 15 million people, mostly Russians themselves, are slaving under the most inhumane conditions.

December 1948

Mr. Sulzberger Speaks Out

By Arthur Hays Sulzberger

[*In this interview with representatives of the press in London in the summer of 1947, distributed by Reuter's, the publisher of* The New York Times, *Arthur Hays Sulzberger, offered a far-sighted, and sober analysis of the Soviet challenge to the free world. He voiced opinions that his heirs, now directing the editorial policy of the paper, might find unfit to print, although they apply to the issues of our day with greater force than ever.*]

I AM CONSCIOUS of the fact that free peoples are not the enemy of other free peoples, and the only potential enemies in the world are those who are ruled by dictatorships.

If these dictatorships, or any one of them, desire to impose an iron curtain and refuse to raise that curtain, I think we have to accept it and do business on our side of the curtain with these people who are, or desire to be, free.

I would not exchange ideas beyond that curtain, I would not exchange goods, I would not do business in any way, shape, form, or manner.

But I should let them constantly know that when they want to become adult and raise the curtain, we are willing to accept them into the group of free peoples that we have organized.

I do not mean by that that I have not got faith in the United Nations, or that I wish to see Russia excluded from the United Nations, because that would be wrong. I merely think it is high time that free people stopped being frustrated by Russia. . . .

I am concerned with the freedom of mankind. To explain what I mean by freedom, I would say that a country is free where its citizens have the right to oppose the government, to vote for another party than the one which is in power, where a man has freedom of speech, freedom of the press exists, and where, if a man gets into jail, he can invoke the right of habeas corpus.

I think it is necessary to emphasize these attributes because there are countries in the world today which use the words "freedom" and "liberty" but do not mean anything like that which I have described. . . .

In Secretary Marshall's Harvard speech he stated, "Governments, political parties, or groups which seek to perpetuate human misery in order to profit therefrom, politically or otherwise, will encounter the opposition of the United States." With this in mind I was not able to understand why Mr. Molotov was invited to the Paris meeting, but now that he has eliminated himself surely we must go on without him. . . .

I do not believe for a moment that taking the action I am suggesting would mean war with Russia. I see no reason why there should be war with Russia. I do not believe that Russia is ready to fight a war, or wants to fight. So long as she insists upon secrecy we must at least be prepared for the worst.

And the more she insists on playing a lone hand the more wise it becomes for us to pool our efforts at reconstruction.

I do not believe the United States can stay strong and can stay free if it permits the type of freedom that I have described to disappear in countries which have previously enjoyed it.

I believe that freedom is indivisible and that the destruction of it anywhere is an assault upon the free world.

August 1947

WHY IS A DARK HORSE?

By HENRY HAZLITT

[*Although Henry Hazlitt is internationally known for his prolific writings on economics and as a disciple and collaborator of Ludwig von Mises, he is also the author of several stimulating and original studies of the American constitutional system. A native of Philadelphia, Hazlitt started his distinguished career with the publication, at the age of 22, of a book entitled* Thinking as a Science. *He served as financial editor on several New York newspapers, as editor of* The Nation *in the early '30s, and as a member of the editorial staff of* The New York Times *from 1934 to 1946, after which he joined* Newsweek *as a columnist. Written in the election year of 1948, this article proposes reforms that are even more timely in our days, when improvement in American political life is more urgently needed than ever.*]

OUR CURRENT President is a man who was never elected to the office. He is the result of a biological accident, an act of nature, not a conscious or intended act of the people or of their representatives.

The institution of the Vice-Presidency is unsound, unnecessary, and irrational. Even Latin American countries that slavishly imitated our constitutional system in other respects refused to imitate this. If a President dies in mid-term, it is obviously far more sensible to have Congress choose his successor for the unexpired term than to have his place automatically filled by a man who was never

408

seriously expected to be President when he was nominated to the needless office of Vice-President.

I have discussed this subject at length, together with the general superiority of responsible cabinet government to our Presidential or multiple-agency system, in a book published in 1942 called *A New Constitution Now*. I need not elaborate upon it here. But it is important to remind ourselves that we are politically the most conservative people in the world, the most averse to any improvement in our institutions, however small, whether or not it requires a constitutional amendment. This is obvious when we consider the immediate questions raised by the primary and convention system under which our Presidents are now chosen.

The direct primary system was introduced long ago under the plausible argument that it gave more power to the people. But as Henry Jones Ford long ago pointed out in his book *Representative Government*: "Whatever assigns to the people power that they are unable to wield, in effect takes it away from them." Few stop to examine the enormous gap between the theory of primaries and the actual practice. One of the major defects of primaries as at present conducted is that they go directly counter to the basic principle that the office should seek the man, rather than the man the office. In practice the people who get the votes in primaries are the people who go after them. If their candidacy is not self-announced, they must at the very least connive in its promotion by their friends. Under such a system no man can be chosen for President unless he is in advance presumptuous enough to think that he deserves it.

The choice in the primaries is thus to a large extent determined by accident. It often seems to depend upon who does the most campaigning in a particular state. Accident also plays a role in other respects. Much depends upon political sentiment in the particular states in which the primaries are held first; for the results there have a certain bandwagon effect on other states. And all the states taken together that hold meaningful primaries are only a handful of the total.

Another weakness of the primary system is that unless one candidate gets a clear majority of all the votes cast, there is no way of telling the extent of the acceptability of that candidate to a majority of the voters of his party. A may get 30 percent of the total vote, B 25, C 20; and so on. But B or C may be acceptable to a large majority of all the voters of the party, while A might be violently opposed by the whole of the 70 percent who did not vote for him. It should be clear that the real task of picking a nominee is not that of finding which candidate is the first choice of the largest minority, but which one is acceptable to the largest majority.

An incidental defect of the primaries is that the merely personal rivalries they develop among the competing candidates driven by their merely personal ambitions may tend to create deep and sometimes irreparable divisions within the party itself. They therefore have an eventual tendency to split parties.

409

A final touch of absurdity is put into the proceedings in states in which the primaries are open to members of the opposing party. These then have the privilege of helping to nominate a candidate who is easy for their own party to beat, or a candidate who more nearly represents the principles of their party than the principles of his own.

LET US now go on to the party conventions. The whole system of party conventions is extra-constitutional. It was not contemplated by the founding fathers. The document they drafted says nothing about it. Yet the convention system has shown itself in practice to be just as resistant to change and improvement as if it were an integral part of the Constitution itself.

It is clear that the party convention, if we compare it with a parliament that chooses a prime minister, is an irresponsible body. It has a one-shot purpose—to select candidates and to draft a platform. And then it dissolves. It does not have to face realities by putting its vague principles and promises into detailed legislative form. It does not pledge *itself* to do anything. The pledges it makes are supposed to be carried out by members of the party in Congress, who have often had no say whatever in framing these pledges. The pledges are also imposed on the Presidential candidate, who also has often had no part in framing them. There is no way in which the delegates to the convention can be effectively held responsible to the people. And after the delegates have named their candidate, there is no way in which they can effectively hold him responsible to them. Unlike a continuing parliament, they cannot watch his later acts and pass upon them; they cannot keep him to their pledges; they cannot, if he disappoints or reverses their expectations, vote a lack of confidence in him. Once they have named him, they no longer exist as a body at all. They are not responsible to anybody, and nobody is responsible to them.

American political conventions have an elaborate ritual—a ritual of opening prayer, of election of chairman, of "keynote" speech, of platform drafting and adoption, of nominating speeches (which have their own inner ritual), of method of balloting, of final choice and "acclamation." All this is as precisely prescribed as the ritual of a secret cult or an Oriental religion.

But one item in particular in this ritual would repay a careful and objective study that it has never had. This is the method of voting on the nominee. The vote, as traditionally conducted, is public from the first ballot. An inevitable consequence of this is that one motive becomes dominant in the mind of each of the overwhelming majority of the delegates. He is concerned from the beginning, not with voting for his own personal choice for the nomination, but with trying to guess as early as possible who the winner is going to be. For the winner is the man who will have the power to distribute favors. His earliest supporters will have the strongest claim on such favors. The Johnnies-come-lately will be left in the cold; and those who opposed him till the deciding ballot run the risk of earning his enmity.

410

What are some of the consequences of this voting system? The gravest of them is that the President in office, no matter how unpopular he may personally be with the rank-and-file of the party, has the power to dictate his own renomination. The delegates of the party in power consist to a large extent of officeholders, whose tenure or renomination depends upon the Presidential incumbent's goodwill, while the rest cannot afford his animosity. If anyone within the party wishes to start a revolt against the President's renomination, he must be sure in advance that the revolt can succeed. He must be sure in advance that the majority secretly think as he does, or it is political suicide for him to try to start a revolt at all.

This situation exists only to a somewhat lesser extent in the party out of power. Therefore each delegate from the beginning tries to pick, not his own real choice, but the probable winner.

An incidental effect of the public ballot is sometimes a quite unnecessary stalemate resolved by the final nomination of a dark horse or a nonentity. In the prolonged deadlock between the supporters of Alfred E. Smith and those of William G. McAdoo in the Democratic convention of 1924, the nominee (John W. Davis) was not chosen until after 103 ballots. The balloting was carried over many weary days. It was a spectacle that, according to more than one historian, "tired the country" and "created a bitter split in the party." It underlined the lengths of absurdity to which the system can lead.

THE REMEDY for at least this part of our present system of choosing Presidential candidates is a comparatively simple one, if either party wished to adopt it. It is the simple device of taking a secret "informational" ballot, or series of ballots, preliminary to the final effective and officially binding ballot or ballots.

The reason for the secrecy of these early "informational" ballots would be substantially the same as the reason for the secrecy that at present protects the ballot of the ordinary voter. It would be to prevent an intimidated vote—to allow the delegate to express his real choice rather than his guess regarding the ultimate winner.

Each delegate on the first secret ballot could be asked to express his first choice. The result of the ballot would then reveal to each of the delegates themselves what the real collective preferences of the delegates were. If no one candidate got a majority of all first choices, then a second secret ballot could be taken in which each delegate could be asked to name both his first and second choice. In this second ballot the first choices would of course doubtless themselves alter somewhat as a result of the knowledge revealed to each delegate by the first ballot. But if even the second ballot did not show that any one candidate had either an absolute majority of first choices, or of first and second choice combines, then a third secret ballot could be taken in which each delegate could name his first, second, and third choices, and so on; until one candidate did appear as acceptable to a majority of all the delegates.

SUCH a voting method would determine the real choice of the majority of the delegates, and would do it in the quickest possible way. Such a method, also, would be least likely to result in the ultimate selection of a very dark horse or a nonentity.

Not until the secret informational ballot revealed such a majority choice would the public and really binding balloting begin. This public balloting would of course be necessary as the final step. We must remember that the party delegates, unlike the final voters, are not choosing simply for themselves, but as the representatives of all the members of their party. These have a right to know how their representatives voted in the determining ballot.

Those who object to the preliminary and purely informational ballots, however, on the ground of their secrecy, would logically have to object to *any* private exchange of opinions among the delegates before the official balloting began. For this informational balloting would be, in effect, merely a systematization of this private exchange of opinions—with the additional advantage that all the delegates would have the benefit of this knowledge and that their confidences would be automatically protected.

IT IS overwhelmingly probable, once the informational ballots were taken, that the convention's choice would be determined on the first effective or officially binding ballot, and certainly on the second or third. And that choice would far more often represent the true wishes of the party, and its strongest possible choice, than it has in the past.

A preliminary informational ballot of the kind I have described is, in fact, the only workable alternative to the traditional method of resolving a convention deadlock. That method has consisted of private conferences among the leaders to agree upon a compromise candidate—which is another name for a secret settlement in a smoke-filled room. A preliminary informational ballot, in short, would be the only rational alternative to a boss-ruled convention. For a very small reform in procedure it would bring a very large return.

Today, wherever Americans discuss the forthcoming Presidential election, they talk almost invariably in terms of personalities—of the comparative views, qualities, or defects of Dewey, Taft, Stassen, Vandenberg, Eisenhower, Martin, or Truman—but practically never about the method by which Presidents are chosen. It is in large part because our political methods are seldom discussed and never improved that American political life has fallen to its present level.

June 1948

LIBERTY TO DESTROY LIBERTY

By ISAAC DON LEVINE

MUST representative government commit suicide? This is the dilemma dogging liberty in our day.

When the American Revolution set in motion, with the rallying-cry of "Give me liberty or give me death!" a tidal wave of self-government all over the earth, the framers of the Republic fully apprehended the suicidal elements lurking in democracy.

For one hundred and forty years the builders and philosophers of the American experiment in human freedom repeatedly warned against the danger of liberty destroying itself. "Only under a democracy can a nation commit suicide," was the fear expressed in the calm years preceding the first World War even by Walter Weyl, one of the most militant apostles of "The New Democracy."

But from 1776 to 1917 the worldwide forward march of freedom swept everything before it. New areas of popular government were being opened in the darkest corners of all the continents. The revolutions which toppled the ancient dynasties of the Shah of Persia and of Sultan Abdul Hamid in Turkey in 1909, of the Manchus in China in 1911, and finally of the Czar of Russia in March 1917, represented the apotheosis of the impulse generated in faraway America in 1773 against monarchist and despotic rule.

The idea of the rights of man made steady progress and cut deeply into arbitrary government. This advance carried human welfare everywhere to ever greater heights and encompassed ever larger segments of the world's population. Then came the first modern assault on man. It was launched in the name of paternalism against individualism, in the name of the benevolent trustee against the fledgling freeman.

Thirty years ago liberty committed suicide for the first time in the modern world, setting in motion a universal counterrevolution which is now lapping at the shores of America. The democratic Provisional Government of Russia, yoked to a formidable Socialist machine, made a fetish of liberty by permitting its avowed enemies, led by Lenin and wearing the cloak of freedom, to operate with impunity. The tide of freedom which had originated in America was now put in reverse.

The Bolsheviks, who fathered totalitarianism, were self-admittedly organized as a conspiracy. Enjoying to the full all the civil liberties, they plunged the dagger into Russia's first representative government, seizing power by insurrection, dispersing the first freely elected Constituent Assembly, and setting up the first dictatorship of modern times. All this was done in the shadows of the great illusion of a new birth of freedom in the world.

Ever since then liberty has been on the defensive. The history of the past thirty years is a record of one democratic government after another, of one free nation after another, succumbing to the very forces which they nourished. They have gone to their death fraternizing with the power-seeking carriers of dictatorship masquerading as a new freedom.

The Communist, Nazi, Fascist, and other statist ideologies have with the aid of modern technology reforged all the weapons in the arsenals of the usurpers and tyrants of yore, and have added new ones. Plotting, intimidation, blackmail, frame-up, bribery, counterfeiting, forgery, mutiny, abduction, assassination, civil war, terror, taking hostages, torture, sabotage, falsification, infiltration, espionage, and propaganda; all of these and many more devices and means have been used to subvert human freedom.

The long train of subversive operations which have led many free peoples, from the Russia of 1917 to the Czechoslovakia of 1948, to commit suicide indicates the magnitude of the dilemma facing liberty in America today.

Yet the very existence of this dilemma is not recognized by many of our professional defenders of civil liberties. There is undoubtedly room for legitimate differences of opinion as to the remedy for the disease. But not to acknowledge the diagnosis is to suffer from the very blindness which has already struck down more than half of the free world.

When the American Civil Liberties Union, the suicide squad of deluded liberalism, came to the defense of Hitler's Bund in this country before the war, it hardly foresaw that several youthful Bundists schooled in Nazi ideology would return to this country on enemy submarines during the war. These beneficiaries of the Bill of Rights landed surreptitiously on Long Island and the Florida coast to commit acts of sabotage and treason.

The trials of these Bundists, most of whom were executed, revealed that they exploited our liberty to train in the art of assassinating liberty. Their undivided loyalty was not to their own country, but to their ideological sovereign—Hitler and his New Order.

Must we wait for another war to have Stalin's Communist vassals in this country—who even now proclaim their prime loyalty to his leadership by avowing that they would not bear arms in defense of this country against the Soviet Union—prove that the Communist Party is not a political party in the traditional sense, but a conspiracy of sworn enemies of liberty? Might it not be too late? Must we take the risk of having Stalin's saboteurs in our midst set off some portable atomic bombs to open the eyes of our myopic liberals?

A political party by its very nature is a national, domestic institution. A party which has external bonds linking it with a foreign state, is a fraud and not a party. But when such an organization is used as a decoy for espionage, treason, and mutiny, liberty must find a way to save herself.

414

A scientific and public autopsy on all the democratic corpses among the fallen nations of the world in the last thirty years would establish beyond question that the Communist Party everywhere is a deadly fifth column. Once this truth is recognized, the problem of meeting its challenge can be tackled by all believers in representative government. . . .

As a first step to the solution of the problem, the Federal Government might attempt to enforce the Voorhis Act which requires the registration of political organizations controlled by or affiliated with foreign governments. This law is on the books, but it has never been put into operation.

The world is in a state of emergency. Representative government is being hard-pressed on many fronts. The democratic process is being put to unprecedented tests. Surely there must be a line on which liberty can take a stand without committing hara-kiri and without dumping overboard the inalienable rights of man. To meet this ultimate challenge we must first of all identify the foe who has been reaping his sinister harvest to the tune of "Give me liberty to destroy liberty."

July 1948

APPENDIX

(The reader of the following three essays may find it of interest to learn something of the background and circumstances of their publication by consulting the concluding paragraph of the Introduction to this volume.)

DÉTENTE AND REALITY

(Published Summer 1974, Strategic Review, *Vol. II, No. 3, pp. 44–50)*

By ISAAC DON LEVINE

[*From President Franklin D. Roosevelt to President Richard Nixon, the United States has vigorously pursued a grand design for an era of peace premised on the cooperation of the Soviet government. U.S. hopes have repeatedly been dashed by the hostility of Soviet responses, but the basic design has not been abandoned. SALT I and the October War reveal how far the United States has gone and how costly its pursuit of peace can be. Presidents should forswear summit negotiation and meet there only to sign previously agreed documents. Disarmament should take place where belligerency reigns—in the Middle East and Southeast Asia. Oil wealth should be committed to the development of blighted lands. And cooperation in trade should be extended only to countries in which labor is not enslaved. The principles of freedom should be voiced vigorously in all forums. There can be no true détente except on the basis of common decency.*]

THE GRAND design for an era of peace sketched and promoted by Franklin D. Roosevelt and Harry Hopkins over forty years ago, and recently refurbished and pursued with renewed vigor under the label of détente by Richard M. Nixon and Henry Kissinger, is now undergoing its acid and final test.

President Nixon's histrionic *hadj* to Mao Tse-tung's red Mecca was carried out in the spirit and tradition of Roosevelt's pilgrimages to Soviet-occupied Teheran and to Yalta for his long-coveted meetings with Stalin. And although the framework of this latest model of a durable world peace has not yet been completed, it is already creaking at every joint.

It is scarcely necessary to recapitulate here the score of well-known occasions when the United States went far out to chase the *fata morgana* of an enduring settlement with the Kremlin. From November 16, 1933, when Roosevelt and Maxim Litvinov signed the accord which extended recognition to the Soviet dictatorship, to our own days, the air has been reverberating with the familiar tunes of the grand design.

And what did that design promise to the American people and to the rest of the Free World! Peace in our lifetime. Lucrative trade to the merchants. High profits to the financiers. Increased employment to industry and labor. Liberalization of the despotic system within the Soviet Union.

The Unity of Civilization

THE RATIONALE for seeking an understanding with the Communist outcasts was sounded by F.D.R. in his ground-breaking message of October 10, 1933, to the head of the Soviet government, proposing to put an end to the "present abnormal relations between the hundred and twenty-five million people of the United States and the hundred and sixty million people of Russia." Since then this keynote has been struck again and again by American policy-makers and replayed as a stirring novelty by President Nixon when he ushered in his Ping Pong diplomacy.

It is a theme which evokes the noble ideal of the brotherhood of man, and it is imbedded in at least four outstanding instruments of the grand design: the Roosevelt-Litvinov recognition agreement and the subsequent Consulate Treaty, the Atlantic Charter of August 14, 1941 subscribed to by the USSR, in the Declaration of the United Nations of January 1, 1942, and the Teheran Declaration of December 1, 1943. These pacts, to which the Soviet Government is a solemn party, contain pledges to uphold and practice the principles without which normal relations among civilized nations are impossible. The pledges included, under the aegis of a common dedication to peace and the enactment of measures of disarmament to ease "the crushing burden of armaments," assurances that "all men in all the lands may live out their lives in freedom from fear and want," permitting "all men to traverse the high seas and oceans without hindrance," securing "the elimination of tyranny and slavery, oppression and intolerance," and aiming "to preserve human rights and justice in their own land as well as in other lands." By living up to these contractual conditions, the freedom of emigration and the untrammelled flow of news and ideas among the people of all countries would be guaranteed. Reinforcing these undertakings is the covenant of the United Nations dedicated, among other things, to faith in "fundamental human rights."

While the world press and other organs of public opinion were debating the pros and cons of the looming crisis for the détente policy, *The New York Times,* in a dispatch from Moscow dated April 12, 1974, reported an incident which in itself posed no threat to world peace, but which nevertheless goes to the very heart of the problem of how to build an enduring understanding between the West and the Kremlin. The report read in part:

> Soviet policemen today grabbed and marched off a middle-aged Russian couple who tried to enter the American Embassy, then drove them away in an unmarked black sedan apparently for interrogation.

420

The noontime incident, witnessed by a handful of bystanders that included some American diplomats and their wives, was the latest in an apparent new effort by Soviet authorities to restrict access to the Embassy.

Yesterday, two Soviet nationals were taken into custody by policemen when they sought to enter the Embassy's consular section to discuss prospects for joining relatives in the United States.

Both were carrying written invitations from the Embassy, which has taken to issuing such letters to help Soviet visitors get past the policemen on duty outside.

The two were physically intercepted. . . . According to eyewitnesses, two policemen hustled them roughly off in the rain to a warming shack on a side street under the supervision of the senior police officer on duty.

Several diplomats who rushed out heard shouts and screams from inside the shack. They could not confirm whether the would-be visitors were beaten by the police, as was initially reported.

No serious student of Soviet affairs will doubt that the incident in Moscow occurred on orders from the highest authorities.

Did Washington issue a clear warning against any further violation of the elementary code of conduct among civilized governments which might involve a rupture of diplomatic relations between the two powers? Quite the contrary. Secretary Kissinger had spelled out his stand unmistakably during the tempestuous deportation of Nobel Prizewinner Aleksandr Solzhenitsyn which caused a worldwide revulsion. Mr. Kissinger then publicly conceded that the Kremlin action was a matter of internal Soviet politics. Without even a remote allusion to Moscow's various pledges in international pacts to observe "fundamental human rights," the Secretary of State virtually assured the Brezhnev junta that its domestic barbarities would "in no way [be] standing in the way of détente." President Nixon, a few days before the "ugly" Moscow incident, had urged German Chancellor Willy Brandt, in a meeting in Paris, to advise President Sadat of Egypt to "be a little nicer to the Russians."* Would it be so far from reality to suggest that the state of mind of the White House encouraged the Kremlin, because of adverse developments for the Soviets in the Middle East, to renew its old bullying tactics by intensifying its siege of the American Embassy in Moscow?

If Solzhenitsyn had compiled a volume recording the cases of affronts, scurrilities, injuries and other instances of uncivilized conduct inflicted upon the United States by the Soviet rulers during the past forty years—a volume which the State Department could easily fill with massive evidence—he would probably sum it all up in one of his characteristic comments as follows: "Dig up the precedents from the courts of Genghis Khan and Ivan the Terrible, and you will have the bones of the Communist doctrine of coexistence."

It is, however, to Aleksandr Solzhenitsyn and nuclear scientist Andrei Sakharov

* Jack Serkoff, The *Washington Post*, April 14, 1974, A-4.

that we owe a great debt for exposing the theory of Soviet diplomacy which the Kremlin has just demonstrated in Moscow in front of the American Embassy. Those two valorous Russian spokesmen were the first in our generation to raise their voices and warn the Western world that without observing fundamental human rights no lasting *modus vivendi* with the totalitarian regime is attainable. Responsible American and European statesmen took up their cry. Senator Edward M. Kennedy, in his conference with Leonid Brezhnev in the Kremlin on April 21, joined it when he obliquely raised the issue of "the free emigration of peoples," not as a high international obligation, but in the form of a plea for "magnanimous action" on the part of the Soviets that would promote the "condition needed for our own progress in controlling nuclear arms."

The record cited here should suffice to formulate the precondition of a workable relationship with the Soviet oligarchy which would command credibility in the courts of world opinion:

A decent mutual regard for all members of the family of nations, with the unswerving observation of solemn pledges guaranteeing unobstructed intercourse among citizens of all countries, are indispensable to an enduring structure of peace.

Precepts of Negotiation

ALL EXPERIENCE with expanding totalitarian powers, from Mussolini's Fascism, Hitler's National Socialism and Stalin's Communist imperialism, has shown that a workable accord with such a regime can be achieved only on the basis of superiority of force enjoyed by the Free World. To assure a viable peace this superiority must rest on a force in being, wielded with restraint, without resort to bullying, to exercises in violence, to threats, blackmail or other forms of extreme pressure. As all totalitarian rulers are deeply ridden with fear, usually rooted in the illegitimacy of their governments, it is not surprising that common to them all are bluster and aggression. The history of our times has demonstrated that equality is not a workable principle in dealing with a modern out-and-out dictatorship. Yielding an inch to such a power in the expectation of gaining favor with it or cementing a true friendship is a sure invitation to aggression, as little Finland learned in November 1939, when she yielded to Soviet pressure to withdraw her troops from the border zone. On November 30, the Soviet forces attacked Finland and bombed Helsinki, which led to Russia's expulsion from the League of Nations two weeks later.

To ignore this experience is to expose the very life of a free society to mortal danger. The United States took to that road in the course of the protracted SALT negotiations initiated in Helsinki and Vienna by the Nixon administration and then virtually stalemated for years until the spring of 1972 when President Nixon made his well-publicized journey to Moscow which resulted in the SALT Treaty and interim agreement. It is by now a matter of common knowledge that under these suddenly improvised pacts the President conceded to the Soviets a steep increase of land-based intercontinental ballistic missiles to the number of 1,618 as against 1,054 for the United States and an even more awesome advantage in submarine nuclear missiles. It was claimed in explanation of this concession that the U.S. superiority in numbers of MIRVed warheads offset the Soviet superiority in missiles; though our representatives knew that Soviet MIRVing would soon dispel this advantage. What has never been authoritatively divulged to the American people are the considerations of political expediency which led our diplomacy to make such a major concession to the Kremlin. It was widely proclaimed that the next round in the negotiations, SALT II, would lead to a substantial reduction of nuclear arms on both sides.

However, sober observers warned at the time that the great concession to the Soviets would boomerang and, instead of meeting Washington halfway in an accord for curbing offensive weapons, Moscow would take our sacrifice as a sign of weakness and seek further advantages. In March 1974, during Secretary Kissinger's mission to the Kremlin to pave the way for the President's projected trip to Moscow this summer, Brezhnev made his unyielding position clear. And the following month the Soviet Army was testing in Syria, under actual war conditions against Israel, its latest model missiles with multiple warheads, according to the *Beirut Al Moharrer*, which revealed that these missiles "could fire between three and seven warheads." And another paper, *Al Safir*, described the new weapons as "SAM 9s, among the most sophisticated surface-to-air missiles in the Soviet arsenal."

What does this mean to the security of the United States? It means a rapid escalation of the nuclear arms race brought about by a diplomatic game of short-sighted diplomacy. In the face of the blank wall behind which the Soviet leadership has taken its stand on the top critical issues involved in SALT II, it is not too late to redress some of our lost ground.

Would a return to the time-honored principle of conduct among heads of state, consonant with the status of the United States in the ranks of world powers, not be a salubrious riposte to Moscow's increasing appetite and intransigence? Such a breakthrough in reverse is now called for to restore this basic maxim:

To negotiate equitable agreements with totalitarian regimes, the President of the United States should forswear traveling to foreign capitals in quest of favors and should confine himself to meeting opposite contracting parties for the ceremonious signing of international pacts on neutral territory, such as Geneva or Vienna.

Curbing Arms Arsenals Now

THERE ARE no magic formulas for stopping the arms race. For nearly one hundred years the nations of the world have talked disarmament and, with the exception of a few brief pauses in limited areas, have succeeded only in accelerating the tempo of distribution and increasing the volume of weapons manufactured and marketed in every quarter of the globe. Now, with two super powers in the van of the arms race, the problem of coping with it has in theory at least been simplified. With goodwill on both sides and a sincere resolve to ease the crushing burden and peril of the vast stores of nuclear arms, a workable program for disarmament could be laid down. But it cannot be advanced by unilateral disarmament of the United States in the face of expanding Soviet military power.

In October 1973, during the Yom Kippur War in the Middle East, both the Israeli and Arab sides found themselves short of arms and frantically appealed to their respective protagonists for critically needed supplies. Washington is reported to have suggested to Moscow that both powers stop their shipments of weapons to the belligerents, a suggestion which was never pressed home. At that hour, the two super powers were engaged in a diplomatic game to gain a preferred position *vis-à-vis* its opponent at the strategic crossroads of the Old World's sea lanes. This rivalry reached a critical confrontation the night of October 24, when the Soviet Navy in the Mediterranean was on the point of landing marines to bolster the hardpressed Arab troops. President Nixon boldly declared a worldwide alert for all the United States armed forces. That history-making decision, which nipped in the bud the threat of Soviet landings, illustrates the point that dictatorship respects firmness and superiority on the part of an adversary.

But how much more would the United States have gained in its promotion of a "generation of peace" had it addressed at the same time a note to Moscow, backed by a move in the United Nations, along these lines:

To promote an immediate cease-fire in the Middle East, the United States and the Soviet Union propose to halt all shipments of arms, whether by sale or by grant, to the theater of war and to call on all nations to join in similar action or face expulsion from membership in the U.N.

Such a step would open the door to a genuine détente or to an exposure of the Soviet intentions. The people everywhere are looking for a leadership which would attack the blight of the modern merchants of death.

Instead of the old arms manufacturers who were branded before the masses as financial monsters sowing war with their lethal wares, we now have the phenomenon of governments serving as the main purveyors of death-dealing weapons. The Soviet Union and certain of its satellites, such as Czechoslovakia and East Germany, have pioneered in this spoliative and profiteering commerce, as Peking and Cairo have more than hinted. It would be sheer hypocrisy to overlook the fact that the United States, in the course of the Cold War foisted on it by Stalin and his heirs, was constrained to follow suit and develop into a Soviet rival in the world's arms markets.

But if disarmament in the nuclear age is to be inaugurated, why not begin modestly and realistically on the lower levels instead of reaching out for utopian heights to the tune of incantations on the theme of an era of peace? Why not make a start in the two major danger zones in the world today, the Middle East and Southeast Asia, by outlawing the arms trade in clearly defined areas? Or better still, why not declare a moratorium on the building of nuclear submarines which the Soviet Union, once primarily a land power, is now pushing at a frenetic pace? Such a move would add another plank in a workable platform for an authentic détente, namely:

Disarmament should begin with an unmistakable reduction in the accumulated weapons of mass destruction and with a ban on weapons trade in areas declared as active war zones or on the periphery of armed conflict.

Perspective on Oil

THE ARAB oil embargo of last winter has focused attention upon the disparate distribution of the oil reserves of the Old World as well as upon the need for a constructive international amelioration of that abnormal condition. It could be argued that it is manifestly unfair for a handful of tiny sheikhdoms at the gates of the Persian Gulf, with a total population of one million inhabitants, to find themselves in possession of a lion's share of the fuel upon which the entire civilized world depends.

These guardians of the oil deposits collect a toll of some $25 billion a year at current prices. When the very large production of Saudi Arabia, with its population of barely eight million, is combined with that of its smaller neighbors, a total approaching an impressive $50 billion in annual revenue is realized, according to official estimates. The incredible figure of $250 billion for the next five years has been cited by experts as due to pour into the coffers of the Persian Gulf sheikhdoms. When that vital energizer of modern industry was mined and supplied in normal trade at cost plus a reasonable profit, such concentration of ownership was not a world problem. But assertion by the owners of a right and intent to raise prices arbitrarily and without limit constitutes a serious threat to the whole fabric of trade and industry.

During the oil crisis, voices were raised calling for the forcible internationalization of the oil resources of the region in question. Although a few of these threats emanated from high political quarters, no responsible leadership in the United States or abroad seriously entertained the idea of such an adventure. It would surely lead to a world war, as the Soviet Union could not fail to come to the aid of Iraq, its virtual satellite, which in 1972 alone supplied four million tons of oil to Moscow. Moreover, such an adventure would provide the Kremlin with incendiary propaganda material of immense value against the Free World, showing itself in the role of an out-and-out aggressor.

The crisis, however, had its positive by-product. The Shah of Iran, who was in the forefront of the campaign by the oil exporters to raise their prices, took the constructive initiative of proposing the creation by the petroleum producers of a pool of money to help the underdeveloped poorer countries. "We have promised at least one billion dollars towards that end, and have committed three hundred and fifty million already to the World Bank and other agencies," Iran's Finance Minister, Jamshid Amouzgar, announced on April 12 on the eve of the special session of the General Assembly of the United Nations, convened to discuss the world crisis in raw materials.

The proposal, warmly welcomed by World Bank President Robert S. McNamara but which neither the underdeveloped nations nor the great oil-consuming countries have so far taken up for long-range planning, and to which the United States remained inexplicably cool, does contain the seed of a corrective cure for the muddled Arab oil situation. Promoted by Iran and backed by the United States, it could lead to the establishment, on the order of the Marshall Plan, of a constructive new agency affiliated with the United Nations, a fund dedicated to the long-term and low-interest financing of the fifty-odd underdeveloped countries in Africa and other continents. In view of the signs that the fantastic oil revenues threaten to smother their beneficiaries and to create worldwide financial havoc, it is not beyond practical statesmanship for the Arab oil producers to join the consuming nations in setting up an institution for the sound exploitation of the avalanche of their profits.

And if only 10 percent of the enormous surplus revenues expected in the next few years, say a fund of $5 billion, were set aside for the resettlement of one million refugees in reclaimed areas of neighboring Arab lands, the dream of Herbert C. Hoover who first advanced such a plan, could be realized. Hoover's far-sighted engineering study of this project is a matter of public record. It goes without saying that the Palestine refugees should not be coerced into such resettlements. In very recent years, Saudi Arabia has been attracting many dispossessed Palestinians to take up a new life in its booming communities. The torrential capital descending upon the Arab makes for developments at home which in turn create lucrative markets for labor. The hundreds of thousands of Palestinians in refugee camps could easily be absorbed by Saudi Arabia alone.

The almost unlimited oil wealth of a few Arab states could and should be put to work by nonviolent means, under the shield of the United Nations, for the redemption of the many blighted lands of the planet and for the advancement of world peace.

Free Labor the Key

IN FRAMING a workable foreign policy, the United States, because of the peculiar nature of its democracy, is particularly responsive to domestic public opinion in two areas, the business world and organized labor. Both are highly sensitive to the power of trade as a political weapon. From the beginning of the Soviet revolution, when Lenin offered major concessions to American capitalists and when unionized labor under Samuel Gompers fought the red dictatorship as a system of slavery, the two forces contended for influence over our relations with Moscow.

In the fifty-six years of its existence, the Soviet regime has never been able to beat the ace which the Free World, led by the United States, holds in its hands, namely, credit. To develop its chronically lagging economy, to bring its technology up to date, to realize its ambitious industrialization plans, the Soviet Union must have the credit facilities which our side commands. It is only with credit from the United States and other free industrial nations that Moscow can construct fertilizer plants to revive its retrogressing agriculture, to lay transcontinental pipelines for the exploitation of inaccessible fuel resources, and to build automotive factories needed for a modern economy.

The American business world has always had its entrepreneurs. There is no gainsaying the fact that over the years their influence has not been without effect in Washington. The myth of a vast Soviet market for American goods, nourished by a gullible press and uninformed politicians, would not die down even in the face of cold figures sufficient to freeze the most fervent traders. But the last grain deal consummated two years ago on this continent appears to have shocked the American people and taught them a memorable lesson. That Moscow could purchase a stupendous volume of wheat on this side of the Atlantic, facilitated by our credit and our diplomacy, on terms detrimental both to American producers and consumers, was a traumatic experience. The Congress of the United States heard from the aroused electorate. And the various business projects encouraged by the Nixon-Kissinger wooing of the Kremlin have struck snags in the legislative chambers that do not augur well for their realization.

Simultaneously, organized labor under George Meany has taken a stand for a policy toward Moscow which enhances America's impaired prestige in the world. In hailing Aleksandr Solzhenitsyn for his courageous exposé of the *Gulag* system—the great network of Soviet slave labor camps—the American Federation of Labor has to a considerable degree offset the impression created in the public eye by American businessmen looking for a quick dollar in the land of Communist imperialism. That is the mark under which new generations everywhere should identify the Soviet regime. To American labor, and none other, must go the recognition for picking up and displaying the standard of freedom in the very face of the totalitarian tyranny.

It is a snare and a delusion to believe that a workable policy for peace can be realized in the wake of trade relations with the Soviet autarchy; only in partnership with free labor organizations is there any prospect of effecting an eventual liberalization of the regimented Communist order.

Adhering to Common Decency

THERE ARE many other avenues, all short of war, open to the freedom-loving nations seeking an alternative policy for coexistence with the expanding Soviet power. There are many weaknesses in its armor which could be probed to the embarrassment of the Kremlin before the masses it has always courted. A couple of examples should suffice here. There is the Berlin Wall, a symbol of the Dark Ages, the dismantling of which the United States could urge from every forum. Why talk of the free flow of ideas and men when such a monstrosity stands in the heart of Europe!

In Asia, there are China's valid claims to vast territories annexed by Czarist Russia through corruption and intimidation, supplemented by the 600 thousand square miles of Outer Mongolia seized by the Soviet regime in the 1920s, continuing evidence of Muscovite imperialism. While the Kremlin belabors the United States unremittingly as an imperialist power, we never expose Russia's rapacity in Siberia and the Far East. Yet who can doubt that to do so would keep the Kremlin on the defensive and be in the interests of peace?

Thirty-six years ago, before Solzhenitsyn's message rang out around the globe, George Orwell foresaw the ultimate evolution of the Soviet state and dedicated himself to the promotion "of intellectual decency, which has been responsible for all true progress for centuries past, and without which the very continuance of civilized life is by no means certain." The road to a genuine détente in our relations with Russia can only be found by a Free World leadership convinced, in the words of Orwell, "that human society must be based on common decency."

Washington, May 1974

The Fruits of Teheran

(Published January 1945, American Affairs)

By Isaac Don Levine

The year that began under the promising sign of Teheran left behind it a crop of evil and bitter fruit. What did we think had been planted in that garden? The three gardeners said: "We leave here friends in fact, in spirit and in purpose." And what was the harvest like?

Teheran was to establish a second front and to coordinate military operations in the East and in the West against the common enemy in such ways as to finish the war in Europe before the end of the year. But the end of the war has been made to wait.

Teheran was to cement indestructibly the unity of the United Nations. Today that cement is pulverized and the discord in the Allied camp is the chief source of strength for the enemy.

Teheran was to lay the foundations of a lasting peace. Today the spectre of an approaching civil war waged by forces trained in the underground and led be men sworn to the cause of Communist revolution is haunting Europe from Greece to Holland and from Finland to Sicily.

Finally, Teheran was to confirm the promise of Secretary of State Cordell Hull, upon his return from Moscow, that "there will no longer be need for spheres of influence, for alliances, for balance of power." Today the entire half of Western Europe, roughly marked by a line from Stettin on the Baltic to Trieste on the Adriatic, an area comprising a prewar population of 90 million, has been staked out by Moscow for Soviet domination or complete sovietization.

Beginning of the Greek Tragedy

THE WHIRLWIND of recent events has ripped the veil off Teheran and exposed the fatal character of the main decisions taken there. These decisions were primarily concerned with the question of the second front or fronts. It was, on the surface, a military question, but we now see that it went to the roots of the fate of Europe.

The British had long favored the opening of a front in the Balkans, not only to safeguard their Mediterranean lifeline from traditional Russian encroachments but also to keep the southeastern flank of Europe from becoming a base for Soviet domination of Germany. To Stalin, a balkanized area of Europe, centering around the dismembered Austro-Hungarian Empire, offered the most fertile field for the extension of the new Soviet order with the aid of Slavic "national liberation" movements. Since 1939, when Britain and Germany bid for the Soviet hand, which then was won by Hitler, the grandiose aims entertained by Stalin in the strategic zone stretching from the Black Sea to the Adriatic had been no secret to Churchill.

The rivalry between Churchill and Stalin had developed long before Teheran. To both leaders it was obvious that there could be no permanent vacuum in the center of Europe once Germany had been crushed, and that he who dominated Germany would eventually dominate the Continent. The question of the second front thus became identified with the question; What kind of Europe shall it be?

Churchill's Council of Europe

EIGHT MONTHS before Teheran, in his world broadcast of March 21, 1943, Churchill projected his answer to that cardinal question. He suggested the setting up of a Council of Europe and a Council of Asia in harmony with the "high permanent interests of Britain, the United States and Russia." The Council of Europe was to be a "really effective League" of Western European unity as distinct from the Soviet Union, although the Council "must eventually embrace the whole of Europe."

Elaborating upon his proposed basis for world organization, Churchill declared in his address at Harvard University on September 6, 1943, that "nothing will work soundly or for long without the united effort of the British and American peoples. If we are together nothing is impossible. If we are divided all will fail."

To Stalin, these were ominous trends. Anglo-American unity spelled an inferior global position for the Soviet Union. Western European unity spelled a barrier against Communist infiltration. British hegemony over Germany spelled a mighty capitalist dyke against proletarian dictatorships. A healthy and restored continent brought about by a system under which, in the words of Churchill, "the glory of Europe will rise again," spelled the ultimate decline of Communist revolutionary doctrine and power.

The Hand of Stalin

STALIN BEGAN early to checkmate Churchill. He broke diplomatic relations with the Polish government with which he had recently concluded a solemn alliance, and set up an embryonic puppet regime for Poland. This was a warning that the Kremlin would build its own bridge to Germany across a vassal Polish state. He set up a Free Germany Committee as another counterbalance to Churchill's scheme of Western European unity. He wooed the government of Czechoslovakia, headed by Benes, away from the arms of London, and after a tug of war which lasted many months won over Czechoslovakia to the Soviet side and made Czechoslovakia the spearhead of a successful drive against any federation in Eastern or Southeastern Europe. Stalin remembered Bismarck's warning that to control Prague is to dominate the gateway to Europe.

At Teheran, the head-on collision between Churchill and Stalin came on the issue of the opening of another front in the Balkans. Stalin's strenuous objections to the proposed Allied invasion of the Balkans was altogether political and ideological in character, since the British had already proved their readiness to make territorial concessions to Soviet Russia from the Baltic to the Black Sea.

The President Persuaded

BUT STALIN was able to convince President Roosevelt, by citing the formal dissolution of the Communist International and the introductions of reforms permitting religious worship in Russia, that the Soviet policy had long since abandoned international Communism and world revolution. Stalin went out of the way to "prove" to the President that the purge of 1936–37 had been conducted by him against the Trotskyite internationalists. Ideologically, Mr. Roosevelt came already conditioned to accept Stalin's assurances at their face value. The Soviet experiment, in the eyes of the President, had been assuming more and more the aspect of a Russian home-made New Deal. Hence, it seemed to him that Churchill's fears were in reality grounded in British imperialism solely, as they were fears for a lifeline which was in no wise threatened by Stalin, whose concern was national reconstruction above all.

Mr. Roosevelt joined Stalin against the idea of a Balkan front. That moment was Churchill's diplomatic Waterloo. Right there and then Stalin achieved the isolation of the United States from her British ally. Churchill and the permanent policy makers in the Foreign Office realized that the Red Army would reach the Balkans first, enabling Stalin to build his own dominion between the Mediterranean and the southern frontiers of Germany. Churchill had to scrap his ideas of a Council of Europe and to yield to that British imperial school of thought which ever since the rise of Hitler had played with the grand scheme of a division of Europe into two spheres of influence.

The British Foreign Office had never accepted Churchill's scheme for European Federations, which was essentially a democratic solution. The permanent policy makers prided themselves upon their realism. They who had favored a deal with Hitler for the partitioning of Europe before the war now favored a similar deal with Stalin for the same reasons. France was knocked out. Germany would be out for a long time. The two remaining great powers on the frontiers of Europe must of necessity get together and divide the Old World into their respective spheres.

Oriental Trading

TEHERAN NOW deteriorated into an Oriental trading post. Stalin had the advantage of Mr. Roosevelt's break with Churchill. Stalin also had the advantage of geographic proximity which had enabled him to sink an anchorage in Czechoslovakia for his great design and to ride roughshod over Poland to achieve the ultimate encirclement of Germany. Churchill tried to save as much as he could for the direct protection of the British defenses in the Mediterranean, and was compelled in his haggling with Stalin to make sacrifices at the expense of Poland and in other zones in return for British retention of vital positions along the sea routes of the Empire.

Here then were the seeds of Teheran. Mr. Roosevelt appeased Stalin ideologically and Churchill appeased him with a division of spoils. Stalin emerged from Teheran enormously strengthened both in the field of Russian expansion and in that of world Communism.

The fruits of Teheran began to ripen in the late summer, after Eisenhower's armies had broken through France and Belgium, and seemed to be racing to

431

Berlin. From the Kremlin's point of view, an early rendezvous of the Soviet force with Anglo-American forces in Germany was most undesirable. For Stalin to meet Roosevelt and Churchill in Berlin, at a moment when the entire southeastern basin of Europe still remained outside of Soviet control, would have meant a showdown on the paramount question of Germany and would have forced Moscow to follow the lead of the United States and Great Britain on the organization of Europe.

Playing for Time

THE BIG THREE had an agreement for a tripartite occupation of Germany and for joint control of Berlin. But if the Red Army met the Anglo-American armies in the vicinity of the capital of the Reich, Stalin would face a European settlement drafted in the shadow of triumphant Western arms and be obliged to assist in laying the foundations of a Western European peace not at all in harmony with his designs. Stalin plainly needed time to exploit the gains of Teheran.

An early termination of the war in Europe would have redounded to the glory of the Western Allies and to their diplomatic prestige, checking the Soviet diplomatic offensive in its initial satges. Stalin's political strategy called, first, for Soviet control of the balkanized areas of Europe, and, second, for the balkanization of Germany as a base for the future sovietization of Western Europe. Both operations required time. Both were in danger of being defeated by a lightning-like conquest of Germany.

Just when Anglo-American forces were pounding at the demoralized western defenses of Germany and it looked as if a race for Berlin was on from the West and the East, Stalin withdrew his armies from the Western side. The plans of Teheran had provided for just such a nutcracker squeeze of Hitler's fortress. It was the height of summer when the Soviet forces reached the suburbs of Warsaw; the rivers were at their lowest and the dry plains of Poland marked the shortest route to Berlin on all the military maps. Stalin's horde rested on the Vistula, in the center of the eastern front, and then streamed in an unexpected direction, southward, striking towards Czechoslovakia, Rumania, Yugoslavia, Bulgaria, Hungary, and Austria.

The Ten Fateful Events

THERE FOLLOWED a succession of events which, in the course of a little more than three months, at first baffled and confused the Allied world and then well-nigh splintered the camp of the United Nations.

FIRST

Late in August came the capitulation of Rumania in the form of an armistice agreement signed by Soviet Marshal Malinovsky, to which the United States and

432

Great Britain gave their belated assent, and which embodied a permanent territorial settlement. The crucial point in this settlement, which figured as a somewhat muddled issue in the Presidential campaign, was the Soviet unilateral transfer of Transylvania from Hungary to Rumania. Although the United States did make that transfer subject to "confirmation" at the general peace conference, Great Britain appended no such reservations, for the reason that she had secretly recognized Rumania as within the Soviet sphere of influence. What did Transylvania represent in Stalin's postwar design? London knew it only too well. Transylvania is the strategic northern pillar of that great Southeastern European domain which Stalin had carved out for himself. The other pillar was Bohemia, which Stalin had secured after Teheran through a treaty of alliance with Czechoslovakia. He now had in the heart of Europe the two key bastions of his projected great dominion.

SECOND

The Bulgarian armistice provided the next major shock. The United States and Great Britain had been at war with Bulgaria. Soviet Russia had all along been at peace with Bulgaria. The Bulgars had sent emissaries to Cairo to negotiate an armistice. The Western Allies were playing here in reverse the role Russia had performed in the negotiations with Finland, which had remained at peace with America. The Western Allies drafted the terms of a Bulgarian armistice to which the Soviet Government was to become a cosignatory. Then something happened. The Soviet Government suddenly declared war on Bulgaria. The Kremlin had notified the British and American ambassadors in Moscow of this move—two hours before it was made public. The Cairo negotiations exploded. Stalin took over the sponsorship of the armistice. He dictated new terms which made Bulgaria formally an ally, but actually a ward, of the Soviet Union.

THIRD

The Churchill-Roosevelt meeting at Quebec last September was a hurried attempt on the part of London to check the Soviet flood towards the Mediterranean. With Bulgaria in Soviet hands, the great part of Salonika lay within the grasp of the Red Army. And Salonika dominated the Aegean Sea and the European defenses of Turkey, an ally and protege of Great Britain. Moreover, Yugoslavia and Greece were exposed to occupation by Stalin's forces. Indeed the Partisan leader Tito, who had been coddled by the British in the naive belief that he could be wooed away from Moscow's arms, suddenly began to display an "independence" which was downright shocking. He treated his chief of state, the London-sponsored Premier of Yugoslavia, Ivan Subasitch, with unconcealed disdain. Tito even hinted at setting up a Balkan federation allied to Soviet Russia and extending it to the Dardanelles in the East and Trieste in the West. Churchill rushed to Quebec to enlist Roosevelt's support and to arrange another meeting of the Big Three. He also endeavoured to bring about, with American aid, an early settlement of the Polish crisis so as to be in a stronger bargaining position in Balkan affairs when dealing with Stalin. In the end, Churchill proceeded to Moscow on his own, bringing the Polish Premier Mikolajczyk as the sacrificial goat to the altar of Stalin.

FOURTH

At the Moscow conference held in the middle of last October, Churchill was forced to gamble away the sovereignty of Poland in return for what looked at the moment like a *modus vivendi* on the Balkan issues. Greece was to remain in the British sphere of influence. Yugoslavia was to be administered under a joint policy of the two powers providing for a union of the Tito leadership with that of the Royal Yugoslav Government. Churchill purchased these concessions by his unqualified support of Stalin's designs upon Poland. These included not only the cession of the areas lying east of the famous Curzon Line and of the Galician areas, comprising the great city of Lwow and the only Polish oil fields, but, also the annexation by Soviet Russia of the industrial triangle of East Prussia centering around Koenigsberg. Poland was to receive as compensation Prussian zones stretching almost to Berlin, a gift which the Poles did not seek and did not wish to accept. The Poland thus projected by Stalin was to be headed by Premier Mikolajczyk, who was to include twelve ministers drawn from the Lublin puppet regime in a cabinet of sixteen, making it a Soviet vassal. Churchill is known to have stormed and raged at Premier Mikolajczyk in Moscow when the latter declared himself without authority to sign such a capitulation. Nevertheless, Churchill left Moscow in the belief that he and Anthony Eden would be able to deliver Poland to Stalin from London.

FIFTH

When the Polish government-in-exile, with the full backing of its underground leaders in the homeland, decided rather to be slaughtered in the open than to commit suicide in the dark, and defied Churchill, strange things began to happen in the Balkans. Marshal Tito took a plane to Soviet headquarters to plead for the fraternal aid of the Red Army. True, there had been an agreement between Stalin and Churchill for joint control of Yugoslavia. But how could the Kremlin turn a deaf ear to the pleas of the southern Slavs for help? The Red Army marched into Yugoslavia. Portraits of Stalin appeared everywhere in the liberated countries. In neighboring Macedonia and Greece and Albania the resistance forces suddenly emerged wearing badges of the hammer and sickle. In Trieste there were reported "popular" demonstrations for union with Yugoslavia. Marshal Tito had now undergone a complete metamorphosis and was speaking the brusque language of a Soviet commissar to his former protectors. A storm was brewing for Britain in the Mediterranean.

At the same time a new area of Soviet pressure developed in October on the other side of Britain's ally, Turkey. Moscow demanded from the Iran government of Saed the immediate granting of oil concessions in North Iran which had been under complete Soviet occupation since 1942. Although the Teheran declaration officially described Iran as an ally, Moscow caused the downfall of Saed's government when it had refused the demand for oil grants. The attempt of the United States to intervene in a friendly capacity in behalf of Iran led to Moscow's sharp denunciation of America's presence in Iran without consent, although its presence had been dictated by the need to help the Soviet war effort with millions of tons of vital supplies. Simultaneously there developed a "spontaneous" movement in adjoining Turkish Armenia for fusion with the Soviet Union, another warning to Turkey as well as to Britain of things to come.

The Red Army continued to penetrate Southeastern Europe while the Allied armies in the West were preparing for another direct assault upon Germany. The Warsaw front remained inactive. The main Soviet thrusts were directed at Hungary and later at Austria. Behind Stalin's victorious armies there appeared Free Hungary and Free Austria committees, precursors of Soviet puppet regimes. Halted at the gates of Budapest, the Red forces swung on towards Vienna, extending the new Soviet dominion in Central Europe.

To stem the spreading Soviet tide, the British decided to land troops in Greece, Salonika, and on the Dalmatian coast of Yugoslavia. Did not London have an accord with Moscow for a joint policy in Yugoslavia and had not the Soviet Government broken its pledge by sending troops there without consulting its partner? The landing of the British detachments on the Dalmatian shores was announced to the world in November as designed to help the partisans clear their country of the enemy. But Tito's men gave the advance British landing party a most unexpected reception. The British troops were disarmed and threatened with internment. Confronted with the problem of fighting his way into the country, the British commander asked London for instructions and received orders to withdraw. The disarmed British units were allowed to re-embark and sail away with the rest of the expedition from the shores of the land which they had helped to "liberate."

Marshal Tito now found his Premier Subasitch so tractable that the latter was soon on the way to Moscow, where he was received openly with great warmth. In Moscow, the Yugoslav Premier kept completely away from the

American and British embassies. London recognized that its former protege was now an interloper in Stalin's camp, but it was anxious for some face-saving formula. Churchill sent a personal message to Stalin requesting that any agreement reached in the Kremlin between Tito and Subasitch be withheld from publication until the return of Subasitch to London where it could be released simultaneously with Moscow in accordance with their understanding of joint policy. Two days later Moscow alone announced officially Marshal Stalin's approval of an accord between Tito and Subasitch, making Tito the Premier of a "democratic" Yugoslav federation and Subasitch one of its ministers. At this time Stalin also took occasion to make a startling public declaration to a delegation of pro-Soviet Poles. Beholding the framework of the grand edifice he was building with the help of the Slavs scattered from the Vistula to the shores of Trieste, Stalin proclaimed: "The alliance of the Slav peoples is not the tactics of a great sovereign Pan-Slavonia. It is the union of the various Slav nations. The Soviet Union stands guard over such a union."

TENTH

Now that the lines of the new Soviet empire in middle Europe over which Stalin had declared himself guardian appeared in clear outline, the strategic relationship of Greece to it became self-evident from a glance at the map. The "sphere of influence" which Stalin demands is a wide belt running from the Baltic, between Stettin and Riga southward, and tapering down to the Mediterranean in the form of Greece, which strategically dominates the ingress to both the Aegean and the Adriatic. In this situation, with Stalin's known impatience to secure his war booty before the general peace settlement, it was to be expected that Greece would become the first theater of open civil war in liberated Europe. Moscow kept officially aloof from the developments in Greece. As far as the world was concerned, the Greek resistance movement simply "took matters into its own hands." In his speech before Parliament Churchill suggested "a well-organized plot" on the part of the Communist-led ELAS "to march down to Athens and seize it by armed force." What would prevent a Communist-controlled Greece from repeating Tito's experiment for joining hands with the Soviet Union? So far as Churchill could see, there was no choice for Britain but to use force to prevent the rounding out of Stalin's great dominion through an eventual union with Greece in the heart of the Mediterranean.

Churchill's Terrifying Vision

THE FRUITS of Teheran are far from full ripening. But already the blackout of news has engulfed all countries "liberated" or occupied by the Soviet forces. From Finland and the Baltic nations to Rumania and Hungary, a great part of Europe has already been placed outside the pale of Western civilization. Already the coming balkanization of Germany as a base for its future "national liberation" by Moscow is indicated for those who can read the handwriting on the wall. Already the lines are formed across Western Europe for a full-scale civil war to follow the present conflict. And there is no indication that Stalin has forgotten or renounced Lenin's dictum to turn the imperialist war into a civil war. Of this impending cataclysm Churchill imparted a terrifying vision in these words on December 15th: "Another great war, especially an ideological war, fought as it would be not only on frontiers but in the heart of every land with weapons far more destructive than men have yet wielded, will spell doom perhaps for many centuries of such civilization as we have been able to erect since history began to be written."

Washington, December 31, 1944

YALTA AFTERMATH

(Published July 1945, American Affairs, pp. 163–169)

By Isaac Don Levine

THE ROAD to Berlin, where the Big Three are scheduled to meet soon, is by now a well-beaten track. It is the same road at the end of which Teheran was once written in the roseate colors of a new dawn. Its designer, Franklin Roosevelt, had conceived it as a short cut to enduring world peace. But that magic terminus has been retreating farther and farther the longer we have journeyed towards it.

Roosevelt pocketed the pride of this, the most powerful nation on earth, and went as far as Soviet-dominated Teheran in quest of unity with Moscow, which he deemed indispensable to a lasting peace. Upon his return, he announced that he had laid the basis for common action among the Great Powers. A year later he found it necessary to go one step further and to travel to Yalta, on Soviet territory, to seek that which presumably he had brought back from Teheran. And now his successor, President Truman, is about to take to the same mesmerizing road and go once more across Soviet lines, this time to Berlin, still in quest of that unity which twice before we thought we had achieved.

Roosevelt went to Yalta after a long train of unilateral acts on the part of Moscow had profoundly shaken the harmony proclaimed from Teheran.* Upon his return from Yalta, he told the Congress, the American people, and the world:

* See article on Teheran in *American Affairs* for January, 1945.

I think the Crimean conference was a successful effort by the three leading nations to find a common ground for peace. It spells—and it ought to spell—the end of the system of unilateral action. . . .

That was on March 1, 1945. The President hailed the agreement of the Big Three to call an international conference and to proceed with the earliest possible establishment of a world security organization. These decisions of Yalta spelled to Roosevelt "the beginnings of a permanent structure of peace." A little more than four months later that structure of peace was launched at San Francisco. It was dedicated to "respect for the principle of equal rights and self-determination of peoples" and to the abstention "from the threat or use of force against the territorial integrity" of any state.

Cloudy Dawn of Peace

YET THERE was a strange and inexplicable urgency in the message delivered by President Truman at the closing of the San Francisco Conference. "You have created a great instrument for peace," he proclaimed. Then he added this emphatic warning: "The world must now use it."

Use it against whom?

The ink on the charter of the United Nations was hardly dry and the new era of peaceful collaboration had not yet officially dawned when an ominous cloud appeared on the already troubled horizons of the battle-scarred Western World. At the very moment he was voicing his injunction, President Truman had in his possession the text of a series of unilateral demands presented by one member of the newly formed world organization, the Soviet Union, to its good neighbor, Turkey.

Thunder on the Left

THESE DEMANDS included the cession to the Soviet Union of the three Transcaucasian districts of Kars, Artvin, and Ardahan, which had belonged for about half a century to Czarist Russia, but which are completely devoid of Russian or Slavic inhabitants. Another demand called for territorial concessions on the part of Turkey to the Soviet satellites in the Balkans. And a third asked for bases along the Bosporus and the Dardanelles for their "common defense" by the Soviet Union and Turkey.

President Truman did not deem it propitious to tell the solemn assembly at San Francisco, consecrated to the settlement of international disputes by peaceful means, that Moscow backed up its demands upon Turkey with large movements of Red Army forces both in the direction of the Dardanelles and in Transcaucasia.

Consider the extraordinary character of the Soviet action. The Soviet Union has a treaty of alliance with Great Britain. Turkey also has a treaty of alliance with Great Britain. All three are bound by the pledges of mutual amity embodied in the San Francisco charter. Yet Stalin chose to take a unilateral step threatening an international crisis of the first magnitude and imperiling world peace by exerting pressure against Turkey, which is pressure against Britain's citadel protecting the Empire's life line to Asia from the Northeast. And it presages greater and further pressure against the entire Middle East as far down as Arabia.

President Truman fully realized the gravity of the situation. Behind his cryptic warning that the world must now use the instrument created at San Francisco there was both moral indignation and determination to invoke the provisions of the new international compact. If unilateral transgressors could not be curbed now, the world body to keep the peace would be doomed from its birth. The United States and Great Britain decided to take a firm stand against the threat to Turkey.

The road to Teheran, Yalta, and Berlin has from its very inception witnessed a race between President Roosevelt's pursuit of Soviet cooperation within the framework of a world organization and Stalin's unrelenting efforts to expand, through seizure and aggrandizement, the Soviet realm. While Roosevelt was busy building the peace of tomorrow, Stalin was preying upon his smaller and weaker neighbors in both Europe and Asia, from Finland to Iran.

The Race Between Peace and Power

THIS RACE is the pivot of history of our days. It is a race between direct action and devious policy. For President Roosevelt never directly challenged the unilateral performances of Moscow. Instead he pressed more and more for the creation of international machinery to checkmate such action. However, the more Roosevelt sought to pin Stalin down through the device of a world organization, the more hurried and frequent became Stalin's overt and covert acts of expansion. Through such procedure Stalin had carved out for himself a vast new domain in Europe while the atmosphere of the great democracies reverberated with the song of international cooperation. By the time the Yalta conference convened, even the blind could see that Soviet unilateral action was making a mockery of world cooperation. President Roosevelt had to go to Yalta. He went determined to win the race against Stalin—by bringing into being his world organization for peace.

Now it can be told that although the President of the United States and Prime Minister Churchill traveled to the distant Soviet Union, they were kept waiting for nearly twenty-four hours at Yalta by Stalin, who somehow could not manage to arrive in time from near-by Moscow to receive his guests. This was an unprecedented discourtesy to the President of the United States, whose rank, moreover, took precedence over that of Premier Stalin.

When Stalin reached Yalta, he announced to Roosevelt and Churchill that he would be unable to stay longer than a couple of days or so. It is hardly a secret at this date that Churchill was greatly incensed by this additional insult. So anxious was President Roosevelt, however, to bring home an accord on the projected San Francisco Conference that he merely laughed the matter off.

As the Crimea conference opened, it appeared that the hosts had taken exceptional care to keep the British and American delegations apart in the hours between sessions so as to prevent a free and full exchange of views between them. When the British representatives used some automobiles for an occasional drive, the Americans would be told that no motor cars were available for them, and *vice versa*.

"What price Soviet cooperation now?" was the plain writing on the chilly mat of welcome spread out by Stalin at Yalta. What did President Roosevelt bring with him? The stalemated Dumbarton Oaks draft of a world league to keep the peace. And what did Stalin hold in his hands? The unchallenged Bolshevization, behind a news blackout, of half a dozen "liberated" Central European countries where Allied military and diplomatic representatives were either barred or functioned as helpless observers.

Stalin knew only too well, through his superb network of agents abroad, that Roosevelt and Churchill had agreed they must at all costs secure his consent to an international conference for the establishment of a world organization. Here, indeed, was a golden opportunity for Stalin, who was dealing with the immediate settlement of boundaries and of destinies of nations. Roosevelt, on the other hand, was collecting pledges and promissory notes against the Great Future. In exchange for virtual Allied recognition of his unilateral acts since Teheran, Stalin would at most have to sign a membership card in an international society dedicated to noble conduct.

When Roosevelt first broached the idea of the San Francisco conference, Stalin did not bother to conceal his contempt. Voicing the view that only the big powers could keep the peace and deprecating the need for any public discussion of the subject, the Soviet leader remarked:

> Surely you don't expect Ecuador or Ethiopia to help you maintain world peace. But if you must have your conference and open debates to satisfy your public opinion, then it's another matter.

Black Sea Bargain

IN THIS setting and against this background it was inevitable that out of Yalta would come a high-sounding document serving as a cover for surrender to Stalin on all substantial issues.

The Soviet leader demanded and obtained the Allies' consent to allow the Red Army alone to take Berlin—an immense prize in prestige for Moscow. Stalin secured the extension of the Soviet area of occupation far and deep to the west in Germany, and regardless of the lines held by his forces at the cessation of hostilities.

Next Stalin exacted the recognition of his Polish puppet regime, thus winning his main objective, a broad highway from Eurasia to Germany, the heart of Europe. Roosevelt's abandonment of the legitimate Polish government in London, the first victim of Nazi aggression in the war, did not come off without a struggle within the American delegation. There were some high-ranking officers whose code did not permit them to cast a small but tested ally into the maw of a great though doubtful associate power. In return for the agreement to organize a new government of national unity around the core of his satellite Lublin Committee, Stalin joined in a pledge to hold free and unfettered elections in Poland. That he could well afford to grant, having had long experience with elections under a one-party system, without a free press, without freedom of assembly and speech, and under the vigilant supervision of a secret police. Such elections were known to pile up majorities closely approximating that well-advertised figure of 99.4 percent.

As a bonus, Stalin gave Churchill and Roosevelt some bones to throw to their troublesome public opinions back home. First, he joined them in assurances that German military power must be broken so that it could not rise again. Stalin knew too well that the military power of Germany depended upon German economy, and that there could be no real disagreement between Moscow and the Allies on that point. Second, he agreed to give by April 25 a year's notice for the renunciation of the Soviet mutual assistance pact with Japan, in accordance with the expiration date provided in that treaty. He was assured that in the United States the step would be hailed as almost tantamount to a declaration of war against Japan. It is indubitable, in view of the sensational victories scored by American arms against the Mikado's Empire, that Moscow would have automatically made that move. Does it not put the Soviet Government in a strong bargaining position in the Pacific?

Votes and Vetoes

WITH THESE preliminaries out of the way, Roosevelt discovered that courting and surrendering to Stalin did not bring him any nearer to victory on what was to him the crucial question of the conference. Although after Dumbarton Oaks Roosevelt had abandoned his dream of a world organization with teeth to keep the peace, he held out for endowing it with some powers to curb aggressors. But Stalin was still reluctant to fall into the "trap" which Roosevelt thought he had laid for the Kremlin fox. Stalin would not budge an inch in his insistence that the big powers on the proposed Security Council have the right to veto any action against them. Not to return home empty handed, Roosevelt had to yield to Stalin once more. The big powers reserved for themselves the right to veto both charges of aggression brought against them as well as any investigation of such charges.

When the authority of the proposed world organization had thus been whittled down to not much more than that of an improvised arbitration board, Stalin brought forth his chief demand. He asked for sixteen votes in the proposed world organization for each of the so-called sixteen republics making up the Soviet Union. The opposition to this proposal in the American delegation was so violent that President Roosevelt suggested that the United States should then receive forty-eight votes for all its component states.

The climax to the tug-of-war which developed on this issue at Yalta, and which was to have unforeseen and shattering consequences, has been kept an innermost secret even though the chief figure of the conference is no longer among the living and the war in Europe is over. Premier Stalin found an occasion, at the termination of a session, to chat with President Roosevelt when all the American delegates, with the exception of one, had left the room. The one was Alger Hiss, deputy director of the office of Special Political Affairs in the State Department.

With the aid of the Soviet interpreter, and in the absence of the official American interpreter, Stalin pressed President Roosevelt for consent to the Soviets having three votes at the world organization, one each for the Soviet Union, for the Ukraine, and the White Russian Republic. The President, in the presence of Mr. Hiss, finally yielded, with the proviso that the United States would also ask for three votes at San Francisco.

When the President, upon rejoining the American delegates a little later, broke to them the news of his private understanding with Stalin, the effect was shocking. There were some who remonstrated with the President, fearing the consequences at home. Wearily Roosevelt, who was then a very sick man already, replied:

> I know, I shouldn't have done it. But I was so tired when they got a hold of me. Besides, it won't make much difference.

President Roosevelt was enabled, however, to announce to the world the coming San Francisco conference to launch a world organization. "Our meeting here in the Crimea," read the joint statement of the Big Three, "has reaffirmed our common determination to maintain and strengthen in the peace to come that unity of purpose and of action which has made victory possible and certain for the United Nations in this war."

Yalta, like Teheran, was triumphantly hailed as the symbol of a new harmony with the Soviet Union.

What Yalta Yielded

THE AFTERMATH of Yalta came with overpowering swiftness. While most of the opinion makers in the United States were still celebrating the newest era of cooperation so eloquently promised by the Yalta Declaration, and even before

President Roosevelt had returned to Washington, a fresh chain of startling developments was unleashed from Moscow. The cook in the Kremlin, who had once been characterized by his master Lenin as capable of serving only peppery dishes, had prepared a series of surprises. During the six weeks which elapsed between the President's return from Yalta and his sudden death, these events followed with the precision of well-calculated blows.

FIRST

On February 27, as soon as Roosevelt stepped on the shores of his homeland, a disagreeable development occurred in "liberated" Rumania where the Red Army was exclusively in control. Deputy Commissar A. Y. Vishinsky, who had won his laurels in the Great Purge, unexpectedly arrived that day in Bucharest. The coalition government of General Radescu, a pro-Ally leader, was overthrown the following day. General Radescu found it necessary to flee for his life and seek shelter in the British diplomatic quarters. King Michael made an unsuccessful attempt to entrust the government to Prince Stirbey, who enjoyed Anglo-American confidence. Soon afterward, the Communist leader, Groza, was installed as the head of the new government—in a country where the Communist Party had numbered before the war 2,000 members. Mr. Vishinsky returned to Moscow.

Now the Yalta Declaration, barely two weeks old, had specifically stated in ringing phrases the "mutual agreement to concert during the temporary period of instability in liberated Europe . . . in assisting the peoples liberated from the domination of Nazi Germany . . . to solve by democratic means their pressing political and economic problems." The Yalta Declaration reiterated and reaffirmed the joint pledge of the Big Three to consult with each other in the interests of the peoples of liberated Europe and the "sacred obligation" to maintain and strengthen the peace to come.

SECOND

In March, Moscow denounced the Russo-Turkish Treaty of nonaggression, to the accompaniment of a campaign by the Soviet radio and press attacking the Turkish Government as pro-Fascist for remaining neutral during the war. Yet, Great Britain and the United States had for years nurtured Turkey's neutrality by supplying her with arms so as to enable her to withstand Nazi pressure. It was clear in Ankara, as well as in London and Washington, that the new Soviet attitude portended trouble on the issue of the control of the Dardanelles as well as in the matter of other Soviet claims.

This was hardly in accord with the month-old Yalta Declaration of the Big Three pledging "continuing and growing cooperation . . . among all the peaceloving nations" and mutual consultation with "other governments in Europe when matters of direct interest to them are under consideration."

President Roosevelt was confronted during the same month of March with a new grave crisis over the Polish problem which had seemingly been settled at Yalta a few weeks earlier. That settlement called for an inter-Allied commission consisting of Foreign Commissar Molotov, United States Ambassador W. Averell Harriman, and British Ambassador Sir Clarke Kerr to set up a Polish government of national unity from among "democratic leaders from within Poland and from abroad." The commission met in Moscow, but made no headway whatsoever. The Soviet representative again and again discarded every name of a Polish leader suggested by the Allied commissioners for the new government. Molotov interpreted the Yalta agreement as making it mandatory to recognize the Lublin puppet regime with the addition of some hand-picked Polish leaders from abroad.

Although the Soviet stand was justified in barring members of the London government-in-exile from the new government, according to the unfortunate wording of the Yalta Declaration, it could not possibly apply to the heroic chiefs of the Polish underground movement who certainly would qualify as "Democratic leaders within Poland." Stalin took measures to remove their candidacy as well.

While the inter-Allied commission was discussing various proposals, an invitation reached the heads of the underground forces in Poland on March 11 from Colonel of the Guards Pimenov to meet with the high command of the Red Army. Wrote Colonel Pimenov: "As an officer of the Red Army who had been entrusted with such a highly important mission, I guarantee to you on my word as an officer that . . . after your arrival at our quarters, you will be absolutely safe."

As a result of an exchange of messages establishing that the Soviet command was acting with the personal knowledge of Stalin, the leaders of the underground revealed themselves and made a date to meet on March 27 General Ivanov of the Soviet high command. On March 25, General Okulicki of the Polish underground radioed to his government in London:

> The Soviets have promised to make it possible for the Government Delegate and two representatives of each of the political parties to consult with you. For this purpose, they are to provide a plane on March 29. It may be that I, too, will be able to come. We have given the Soviets our guarantee that the consultations and the flight to you will be kept secret.

All the while the governments of the United States and of Great Britain were kept fully and promptly informed of these developments. There were those in Washington and London who hoped for an early and most satisfactory solution of the sore Polish dispute. But the fifteen underground leaders who proceeded to the headquarters of General Ivanov were lost without trace after March 28.

Rumors spread that they had been taken east in a motorcade. In Moscow, however, the tripartite commission dealing with the Polish problem heard or saw nothing of them. Churchill and Roosevelt were advised of their disappearance. To all inquiries from London and Washington, the Soviet Government turned a deaf ear and its representatives looked as bland as if they had never heard of the matter. On April 12, the day of President Roosevelt's death, the Moscow correspondent of the Communist *Daily Worker* in London, John Gibbons, categorically stated in a dispatch that it was "absolutely untrue that the Polish political and military leaders were in Moscow." Here was an international mystery of the first order.

(Weeks later, at San Francisco, Commissar Molotov casually announced at a dinner party for Foreign Secretary Eden and Secretary of State Stettinius that the Polish leaders were under arrest in Moscow and that the guilty ones would be punished. They were subsequently given a show trial and convicted of plotting a British-Polish-German attack against the Soviet Union.)

Having first eliminated by diplomatic means at Yalta the legitimate London government from the proposed new regime of national unity, Stalin now eliminated by other means nearly the entire surviving leadership within Poland. As Foreign Secretary Eden declared at San Francisco, "most of these men were just the type who should, in our view, have been consulted about the new national government in Poland, if such a government was to be truly representative of Polish democratic political life, in accordance with the Crimea decision."

FOURTH

On the very day the fifteen Polish leaders were surreptitiously abducted to Moscow in violation of the safe conduct granted by the Red Army, a bombshell exploded in the lap of President Roosevelt. The deal which he had made with Stalin at Yalta and which he had kept a deep secret, leaked out. It became known that the President had agreed to let the Soviet Union have three votes in the assembly of the world organization, reserving for the United States three votes also. The White House was forced to confirm the existence of this deal on March 29.

Not perhaps since the announcement of the Supreme Court packing proposal was the country so shocked and stirred. An army of newsmen descended upon Secretary of State Stettinius with a catechism of searing questions. Public opinion was aroused not so much over the strange Yalta bargain itself as over the unsavory handling of the matter. The faith of the smaller nations in the United States leadership at San Francisco was put to a severe test. On April 3 President Roosevelt announced that the United States would drop the plan to ask for itself three votes in the assembly of the United Nations. Although this eased the atmosphere considerably, the blow to the moral prestige of Roosevelt's leadership was painful.

At the same time, the Soviet Government presented sudden demands upon the United States and Great Britain that the puppet Lublin government be allowed to send a delegation to the San Francisco conference. This was equivalent to a demand that the Moscow-sponsored regime be recognized as the rightful government of Poland. But Washington and London rejected Moscow's proposal. Stalin was highly displeased, and he repeated his demand in more insistent terms. The scene of the gathering world-security meeting began to look more and more ominous.

SIXTH

The final blow came when the preparations for the San Francisco Conference were going on at a feverish pitch. President Roosevelt expected to open it in person within three weeks. The race against Soviet unilateral action which he had run at Teheran and at Yalta, the President was confident, would enter its final lap at the Golden Gate. There Stalin would at last be pinned down to a code of conduct prescribed by all the nations of the world.

And then Moscow announced its delegation to San Francisco. The list did not include Foreign Commissar Molotov or any representative equal in rank or standing to those of the other big powers. This was a flagrant insult, which the smaller nations and the colonial peoples of the world could not fail to read. Whether or not it was intended to wound the pride of President Roosevelt by showing the Soviet contempt for his Messianic scheme, there could be no question that it served notice that the Soviet delegates would pursue the same tactics of sabotage and nullification adopted by them in all the international conferences up to and including Dumbarton Oaks.

Such were the major events since Yalta, which in a short time had filled the cup to overflowing. On April 12, President Roosevelt died.

The Post-Crimean Clean-up

ROOSEVELT'S SUDDEN death was something which Stalin could not have anticipated. Moscow had learned from experience that the hunting is best after conferences such as those of Teheran and Yalta, when the democracies become intoxicated with their Pyrrhic victories. So general was the rejoicing in America after Yalta, that Stalin decided to capitalize on it without delay and to secure the maximum of advantages in his campaign of Soviet aggrandizement.

When President Truman took over, there followed a period of uncertainty in the Soviet attitude towards the United States. On the one hand, Stalin continued his policy of unilateral action. His setting up of a government in Austria, without consulting the Allies; the unleashing of a wave of terror in

Bulgaria preparatory to "free elections" which led to the flight of the pro-Allied peasant leader, Dr. G. Dimitrov, to the American legation where he is still finding sanctuary; the mock trial of the abducted Polish leaders in Moscow on charges of loyalty to their own country and government; Tito's seizure of Trieste and his attempt to force the city and the surrounding littoral into Sovietized Yugoslavia; the Kremlin's demand that the SHAEF (Supreme Headquarters of the Allied Expeditionary Forces) be dissolved before the Allied troops are permitted to enter Berlin; the steadfast refusal to admit Allied press representatives into nearly a dozen "liberated" countries and areas now occupied by the Red Army; the unilateral publication of the zones in Western Germany claimed by Moscow as set aside for Soviet occupation; the seizure of the Danish Island of Bornholm in the Baltic; the pressure on Iran, where the Soviet forces are in possession of the northern provinces; the deal with Czechoslovakia providing for the cession to the Soviet Union of Carpatho-Ruthenia; the annexation simultaneously of certain Hungarian districts by the Soviet Union; the transfer of large populations from the East to Western Prussia and of ancient Danubian settlements to the Russian steppes; the peremptory series of demands on Turkey; all of these, and many similar Soviet steps, were in clear defiance of the spirit and the letter of the Yalta Agreement.

Changing Winds in Washington

AT THE SAME time Stalin proved himself pliable enough to conciliate President Truman now and then. When the latter showed firmness, Stalin put on a show of yielding. He sent Molotov to the San Francisco Conference to appease Truman. And when Molotov arrived in Washington and made his first call on the new President, Stalin quickly learned that a new wind was blowing in the White House.

Commissar Molotov, after the formalities of the introduction, started off brusquely to talk of the help which the United States was expecting from Soviet Russia in the war against Japan. He even went as far as to raise the question of the price which America would be willing to pay for Moscow's aid in the Far East.

President Truman interrupted Commissar Molotov and plainly told him that the United States does not seek and does not want Soviet help in the Pacific struggle, and has shown herself able to take care of Japan alone if need be. Commissar Molotov, taken aback, launched into a long exposition of the subject. President Truman withdrew and left the Secretary of State to listen to Stalin's mouthpiece.

This act of Truman's had upset the preconceived ideas with which Molotov came from Moscow. The results were prompt to follow. At San Francisco, the Soviet delegation was far more amenable and cooperative than before Roosevelt's death.

Another incident also had its sobering effect upon the Kremlin and its emissaries. On April 24, an unscheduled extraordinary conference took place at the Pentagon Building where President Truman had gone to consult with the nation's top military leaders. There were reports, some of which appeared in reliable journals, that the President came to seek advice as to the Allied ability to back up with force our stand against unilateral Soviet action in Central Europe.

For a moment something approaching panic seized the pro-Soviet circles in Washington. There were even those who expected Truman to purge the administration of its Communist and Sovietist elements. But the latter quickly rallied. A campaign was inaugurated aiming to discredit Truman's leadership on the ground that he was not carrying out Roosevelt's policies.

More "Missions to Moscow"

THEN HARRY Hopkins and Joseph Davies went on their missions respectively to Moscow and London.. Contrary to the general belief, the initiative of this step did not stem from the White House. It came from our pro-Soviet group. Originally it was Mr. Joseph Davies who proposed himself to the President as the man for another mission to Moscow. Was it not necessary to restore that harmony, that idyllic cooperation, which the country believed had been achieved at Teheran and Yalta by President Roosevelt and which was now in danger of being ruptured?

Thus was the road to Berlin being paved. President Truman, however, disappointed Davies by sending Harry Hopkins to Moscow. To appease him, he sent Davies on a simultaneous mission to London.

In Moscow, Hopkins succeeded in putting back on the Roosevelt tracks the train of American foreign policy—at least, for the time being. Hopkins engineered, with the aid of Davies in London, our complete surrender on the Polish question by reversing the Anglo-American stand as to the proportions of Lublin and London Poles to be included in the new government under the provisions of Yalta. We now agreed to give Stalin's puppets four fifths of the posts in the proposed Polish government, and the key posts at that.

Then Hopkins arranged for another meeting of the Big Three, this time in Berlin, which has been made in Soviet Russia the symbol of Soviet unilateral victory over Germany. It was Marshal Zhukov who told the world from the Red Square in Moscow on June 25:

> The Soviet Union played the main, decisive part in the achievement of this historic victory over Germany. For three years the Red Army single-handedly fought the armed forces of Germany and her satellites.

Thus does the President of the United States once more take secondary rank in traveling to meet the Soviet Premier within the Soviet zone of occupation.

And this at a time when Stalin no longer has the excuse of having to conduct a war, while the United States is bearing the brunt of the fight against Russia's age-old enemy, Japan.

Where the Road Leads

AS PRESIDENT TRUMAN starts on the road to Berlin, will he and his advisors, after the experience of Teheran and Yalta, take the trouble to read what is Stalin's equivalent of "Mein Kampf"? That certain British statesmen might have saved humanity untold suffering had they studied "Mein Kampf' in time is now generally agreed. Stalin's lifetime creed is an open book to be found in his widely published writings. To any one familiar with his orthodox Bolshevist doctrines, there is no Russian riddle or enigma.

To the Western democracies, the supreme principle in international relations is the right of a nation, large or small, to self-determination. Not so to the Soviet State, which recognizes a higher right. Declares Stalin in his standard work, "Marxism and the National and Colonial Question":

> It should be borne in mind that besides the right of nations to self-determination there is also the right of the working class to consolidate its power, and to this latter right the right of self-determination is subordinate. There are occasions when the right of self-determination conflicts with the other, the higher right—the right of a working class that has assumed power to consolidate its power. In such cases—this must be said bluntly—the right to self-determination cannot and must not serve as an obstacle to the exercise by the working class of its right to dictatorship. The former must give way to the latter. That, for instance, was the case in 1920, when in order to defend the power of the working class we were obliged to march on Warsaw.

Between the democratic principle of self-determination and the pre-eminent right of the dictatorship of the proletariat, according to Stalin, there is no common ground. One must give way to the other. In the light of this fundamental Soviet canon, the road to Berlin promises to be a continuation of the road to Teheran and Yalta, with the same destination.

Washington, June 30, 1945

Index

(Boldface figures denote authors
or subjects of major articles.)

Johnstone, William C., 119
Joliot-Curie, Irène, 44

Service, John S., 104, 109, 112, 115, 116
Shaplen, Joseph, 199
Sheinberg, Arthur, 115
Sigelbaum, Josef, **313**
Sikorski, Gen. Wladyslaw, 295, 329
Silone, Ignazio, 88
Silvermaster, Nathan G., 206
Smedley, Agnes, 40
Smith, Gen. Walter B., 27f., 171
Smyth report, 65
Snow, Edgar, 15, 125
Sokolsky, George, on Acheson and Baruch, 67
Solzhenitsyn, Aleksandr, xi, 9, 43, 235, 318, 322, 393, 421, 427
Soong, T. V., 108f.
Southern Conference for Human Welfare, 71
Stalin, Joseph, xiii, 8, 9, 25, 29, 32, 39, 78, 84, 89, 91, 431, 449; attacks Korea, 34; at Teheran, Yalta, Potsdam, 44, 131; in China, 47; reacts to atomic bomb, 64, 74; in Panama Canal, **186**; and Negroes, **191**; and Katyn Forest, 295; Purges Jewish Writers, **310**; incident of brutality of, **318**; and Yalta repatriation agreement, **322**; betrays Poland at Yalta, **329**; Interview with, **336**; on Hitler, 339ff.; Kerensky on USSR and, **348**
Stassova, Helena, 336ff. *passim*
Stein, Gunther, 125
Stettinius, Edward R., Jr., 133, 445
Stewart, Maxwell, 125, 129
Stilwell, Gen. Joseph W., 40, 48, 103, 109, 110, 140, 164
Stimson, Henry L., 133, 146
Stolberg, Benjamin, 200
Stotski, Andrey, **240**
Strategic Review, xiv
Strauss, Adm. Lewis L., 70
Strong, Anna Louise, 125
Suez Canal, 82

DAT

HIGHSMITH 45-220